© 1987 Ignatius Press, San Francisco
All rights reserved
ISBN 0-89870-138-4 (PB)
ISBN 0-89870-137-6 (HB)
Library of Congress catalogue number 85-81511
Printed in the United States of America

THE COLLECTED WORKS OF
G. K. CHESTERTON

XXVIII

The Illustrated
London News

1908 - 1910

Edited by Lawrence J. Clipper

General Editors: George J. Marlin,
Richard P. Rabatin, and John L. Swan

IGNATIUS PRESS   SAN FRANCISCO

THE COLLECTED WORKS OF
G. K. CHESTERTON

XXVIII

*This new edition
of Chesterton's articles is
dedicated to Frank Petta,
lifelong Chestertonian, teacher,
inspirer of friends and
inspiration for this work.*

The dates used in this volume are from the American edition of the *Illustrated London News*, which normally appeared two weeks later than those of the English edition.

CONTENTS

1908

CONTENTS   9

1910

CONTENTS 13

1908

January 4, 1908

Christmas Thoughts on Vivisection

Last week, when I was in the middle of talking about vivisection, my own article was vivisected. It was cut in two while yet alive and quivering. But, just as the severed tail of the worm continues to writhe, so the end of my article is still writhing. This is it. In the ordinary way, it would be a great deal too near Christmas to discuss such nasty things; but, oddly enough, the very name of Christmas recalls it to me. For just about this time of the year one always sees in the newspapers the protests of certain humanitarians against what they call the "slaughter" of animals at Christmas. This will stand as a very good example of the sort of humanitarianism which I do not accept at all—the moral theses which, as I said before, I rule out at the start. I do not know whether an animal killed at Christmas has had a better or a worse time than it would have had if there had been no Christmas or no Christmas dinners. But I do know that the fighting and suffering brotherhood to which I belong and owe everything, Mankind, would have a much worse time if there were no such thing as Christmas or Christmas dinners. Whether the turkey which Scrooge gave to Bob Cratchit had experienced a lovelier or more melancholy career than that of less attractive turkeys is a subject upon which I cannot even conjecture. But that Scrooge was better for giving the turkey and Cratchit happier for getting it I know as two facts, as I know that I have two feet. What life and death may be to a turkey is not my business; but the soul of Scrooge and the body of Cratchit are my business. Nothing shall induce me to darken human homes, to destroy human festivities, to insult human gifts and human benefactions for the sake of some hypothetical knowledge which Nature curtained from our eyes. We men and women are all in the same boat, upon a stormy sea. We owe to each other a terrible and tragic loyalty. If we catch sharks for food, let them be killed most mercifully; let anyone who likes love the sharks, and pet the

17

sharks, and tie ribbons round their necks and give them sugar and teach them to dance. But if once a man suggests that a shark is to be valued against a sailor, or that the poor shark might be permitted to bite off a nigger's leg occasionally; then I would court-martial the man—he is a traitor to the ship.

And while I take this view of humanitarianism of the anti-Christmas kind, I wish to finish the sentence I broke off last week, and to finish it by saying that I am a strong anti-vivisectionist. That is, if there is any vivisection, I am against it. I am against the cutting-up of conscious dogs for the same reason that I am in favour of the eating of dead turkeys. The connection may not be obvious; but that is because of the strangely unhealthy condition of modern thought. I am against cruel vivisection as I am against a cruel anti-Christmas asceticism, because they both involve the upsetting of existing fellowships and the shocking of normal good feelings for the sake of something that is intellectual, fanciful, and remote. It is not a human thing, it is not a humane thing, when you see a poor woman staring hungrily at a bloater, to think, not of the obvious feelings of the woman, but of the unimaginable feelings of the deceased bloater. Similarly, it is not human, it is not humane, when you look at a dog to think about what theoretic discoveries you might possibly make if you were allowed to bore a hole in his head. Both the humanitarians' fancy about the feelings concealed inside the bloater, and the vivisectionists' fancy about the knowledge concealed inside the dog, are unhealthy fancies, because they upset a human sanity that is certain for the sake of something that is of necessity uncertain. The vivisectionist, for the sake of doing something that may or may not be useful, does something that certainly is horrible. The anti-Christmas humanitarian, in seeking to have a sympathy with a turkey which no man can have with a turkey, loses the sympathy he has already with the happiness of millions of the poor.

It is not uncommon nowadays for the insane extremes in reality to meet. Thus I have always felt that brutal Imperialism and Tolstoian nonresistance were not only not opposite, but were the same thing. They are the same contemptible thought that conquest cannot be resisted, looked at from the two standpoints of the conqueror and the conquered. Thus again teetotalism and the really degraded gin-selling and dram-drinking have exactly the same moral philosophy. They are both based on the idea that fermented liquor is not a drink, but a drug. But I am specially certain that the extreme of vegetarian humanity is, as I have said, akin to the extreme of scientific cruelty—they both permit a dubious speculation to interfere with their ordinary charity. The sound moral rule in such matters as vivisection always presents itself to me in this way. There is no ethical necessity more essential and vital than this: that casuistical exceptions, though admitted, should be admitted as exceptions. And it follows from this, I think, that, though we may do a horrid thing in a horrid situation, we must be quite certain that we actually and already are in that situation. Thus, all sane moralists admit that one may sometimes tell a lie; but no sane moralist would approve of telling a little boy to practice telling lies, in case he might one day have to tell a justifiable one. Thus, morality has often justified shooting a robber or a burglar. But it would not justify going into the village Sunday school and shooting all the little boys who looked as if they might grow up into burglars. The need may arise; but the need must have arisen. It seems to me quite clear that if you step across this limit you step off a precipice.

Now, whether torturing an animal is or is not an immoral thing, it is, at least, a dreadful thing. It belongs to the order of exceptional and even desperate acts. Except for some extraordinary reason I would not grievously hurt an animal; with an extraordinary reason I would grievously hurt him. If (for example) a mad elephant were pursuing me and my family, and I could only shoot him so that he would die in agony, he would have to die in agony. But the elephant would be there. I would not do it to a hypothetical elephant. Now, it always seems to me that this is the weak point in the ordinary vivisectionist argument, "Suppose your wife were dying." Vivisection is not done by a man whose wife is dying. If it were it might be lifted to the level of the moment, as would be lying or stealing bread, or any other ugly action. But this ugly action is done in cold blood, at leisure, by men who are not sure that it will be of any use to anybody—men of whom the most that can be said is that they may conceivably make the beginnings of some discovery which may perhaps save the life of someone else's wife in some remote future. That is too cold and distant to rob an act of its immediate horror. That is like training the child to tell lies for the sake of some great dilemma that may never come to him. You are doing a cruel thing, but not with enough passion to make it a kindly one.

So much for why I am an anti-vivisectionist; and I should like to say, in conclusion, that all other anti-vivisectionists of my acquaintance weaken their case infinitely by forming this attack on a scientific speciality in which the human heart is commonly on their side, with attacks upon universal human customs in which the human heart is not at all on their side. I have heard humanitarians, for instance, speak of vivisection and field sports as if they were the same kind of thing. The difference seems to me simple and enormous. In sport a man goes into a wood and mixes with the existing life of that wood, becomes a destroyer only in the simple and healthy sense in which all the creatures are destroyers; becomes for one moment to them what they are to him—another animal. In vivisection a man takes a simpler creature and subjects it to subtleties which no one but man could inflict on him, and for which man is therefore gravely and terribly responsible.

Meanwhile, it remains true that I shall eat a great deal of turkey this Christmas; and it is not in the least true (as the vegetarians say) that I shall do it because I do not realise what I am doing, or because I do what I know is wrong, or that I do it with shame or doubt or a fundamental unrest of conscience. In one sense I know quite well what I am doing; in another sense I know quite well that I know not what I do. Scrooge and the Cratchits and I are, as I have said, all in one boat; the turkey and I are, to say the most of it, ships that pass in the night, and greet each other in passing. I wish him well; but it is really practically impossible to discover whether I treat him well. I can avoid, and I do avoid with horror, all special and artificial tormenting of him, sticking pins in him for fun or sticking knives in him for scientific investigation. But whether by feeding him slowly and killing him quickly for the needs of my brethren, I have improved in his own solemn eyes his own strange and separate destiny, whether I have made him in the sight of God a slave or a martyr, or one whom the gods love and who die young—that is far more removed from my possibilities of knowledge than the most abstruse intricacies of mysticism or theology. A turkey is more occult and awful than all the angels and archangels. In so far as God has partly revealed to us an angelic world, he has partly told us what an angel means. But God has never told us what a turkey means. And if you go and stare at a live turkey for an hour or two, you will find by the end of it that the enigma has rather increased than diminished.

January 11, 1908

The Survival of Christmas

There are two methods of advertisement in the world. One is to advertise something by saying that it is succeeding. The other is to advertise a thing by saying that it is failing. You can advertise ordinary sermons by calling them the New Theology; or on the other hand one can advertise an ordinary flower by asserting (on your personal word of honour) that it is the Last Rose of Summer. The entrance of a thing into the world, or its departure from the world, are the great opportunities for praising it; that is why all healthy men and women have always felt that christenings and funerals were such fun. But in the area of strict advertisement the thing is equally true; you can push a thing by saying that it is coming on; but you can also push a thing by saying that it is going away. To take any two obvious examples: it is an advertisement to say "Positively Largest Circulation" of a newspaper. It is an advertisement also to say "Positively Last Appearance" of an actor. There is, however, a very important distinction between these two methods. If you are going to announce a thing as a failure, it must be a good thing. If you are going to attract attention to the last rose of summer, you must only do it when a long and historical human experience leads you to believe that mankind is really rather fond of roses. You must not play that game with soap, or any slight, faddish, secondary sort of thing. The sunset is poetical because the sun is popular. Even a slowly fading fire of wood or coal is a thing that can attract people to its last red embers; they will linger over it because real fire is in itself a fine thing. But if you have hot-water pipes in your house (which God forbid), do not, in a light and hospitable manner, ask your friends to come and put their fingers on the hot-water pipes and feel them gradually cooling. It is not the same thing. Fires are nice things, and when half-cold are still poetic; hot-water pipes are nasty things, and the sooner they cool the better. You must be quite certain of the real merit of a thing before you risk a declaration that it is dying. If a thing is weak, insist on its enormous success; it is your only chance. But if a thing is strong, insist that it is defeated.

By this simple principle we can find a really workable division between the two chief types of human institutions. Really healthy institutions are always supposed to be dying—like nations. Thoroughly diseased institutions are always praised as being in a state of brutal and invincible health—like empires. When an Englishman, whether Tory or Radical, wants to praise England he says that England is going to the dogs; that the sturdy English are gone. But when a British Imperialist—whether German, Austrian, Polish, Jewish, or American—wishes to praise the British Empire, he says that it is going ahead like a house on fire, and that nothing can stop its success. He says that because he does not really believe in the British Empire at all; he knows that the optimistic advertisement is the only tip in the case of a shaky piece of goods. But the English patriot, whether Tory or Radical, knows that there is a real sound article called England, and he tells people to snap it up before it has vanished, instead of telling them to buy it merely because it has a boom. This is only one example; but the principle is of universal application. People attached to things they do care about tend to fear for them. People attached to things they do not care about tend to brag about them. Lovers tend to be sad. Commercial travellers tend to be artificially and inhumanly cheerful.

I have been reminded of all this by the inevitable discussions in the current papers about whether the keeping of Christmas is destined to die out, whether Christmas itself will disappear. Of course, Christmas will not disappear. Christmas is one of those very strong things that can afford to boast of its own approaching disappearance. Santa Claus is an actor who can always have a "positively last appearance" with advantage to himself; because people really want him. Weak things must boast of being new, like so many new German philosophies. But strong things can boast of being old. Strong things can boast of being moribund. In the case of Christmas it is quite easy to put a simple test. All the great writers who have praised Christmas customs have praised them as antiquated customs. All the authors who have eulogised Father Christmas have eulogised him as a very elderly gentleman. Now, there is no man who believes in tradition more than I do. Tradition (it seems to me) is simply the democracy of the dead. But there is a certain kind of tradition which, while it is immensely valuable, is obviously, by reason of its own eternal renewal, not quite accurate. If tradition records that things have been growing more and more hot or cold or blue or triangular, then the longer the tradition has been going on the more clear it must be that it is not quite true. Supposing that your father and grandfather and great-grandfather and great-great-grandfather had all left it on record that the sun in the sky was growing smaller before their very eyes, then I think we should not believe it; not because we are any wiser than they, but because if that had been the exact truth there would not by this time be any sun at all. So that when we find our fathers perpetually saying age after age that religion is dying, that religious festivity is dying, that the hearty human customs are dying, I think we are justified in saying that they were mistaken, not in their praise, but in their despair. The truth was that religion, being really a good thing, could thrive as a continual failure; just as it would be quite worth a brewer's while to announce the last cask of real ale in England.

The Christmas celebrations will certainly remain, and will certainly survive any attempt by modern artists, idealists, or neopagans to substitute anything else for them. For the truth is that there is an alliance between religion and real fun, of which the modern thinkers have never got the key, and which they are quite unable to criticise or to destroy. All Socialist Utopias, all new Pagan Paradises, promised in this age to mankind have all one horrible fault. They are all dignified. All the men in William Morris are dignified. All the men even in H. G. Wells are dignified, when they are men at all. But being undignified is the essence of all real happiness, whether before God or man. Hilarity involves humility; nay, it involves humiliation. Anyone can prove for himself this spiritual principle before a month is out, by walking about in the actual cap that he really found in the cracker.[1] Religion is much nearer to riotous happiness than it is to the detached and temperate types of happiness in which gentlemen and philosophers find their peace. Religion and riot are very near, as the history of all religions proves. Riot means being a rotter; and religion means knowing you are a rotter. Somebody said, and it has often been quoted: "Be good and you will be happy; but you will not have a jolly time." The epigram is witty,

---

[1] At birthday or Christmas parties, small paper containers holding party hats and other prizes are "pulled", thus making a loud noise and revealing their contents.

but it is profoundly mistaken in its estimate of the truth of human nature. I should be inclined to say that the truth is exactly the reverse. Be good and you will have a jolly time; but you will not be happy. If you have a good heart you will always have some lightness of heart; you will always have the power of enjoying special human feasts, and positive human good news. But the heart which is there to be lightened will also be there to be hurt; and really if you only want to be happy, to be steadily and stupidly happy like the animals, it may be well worth your while not to have a heart at all. Fortunately, however, being happy is not so important as having a jolly time. Philosophers are happy; saints have a jolly time. The important thing in life is not to keep a steady system of pleasure and composure (which can be done quite well by hardening one's heart or thickening one's head), but to keep alive in oneself the immortal power of astonishment and laughter, and a kind of young reverence. This is why religion always insists on special days like Christmas, while philosophy always tends to despise them. Religion is interested not in whether a man is happy, but whether he is still alive, whether he can still react in a normal way to new things, whether he blinks in a blinding light or laughs when he is tickled. That is the best of Christmas, that it is a startling and disturbing happiness; it is an uncomfortable comfort. The Christmas customs destroy the human habits. And while customs are generally unselfish, habits are nearly always selfish. The object of the religious festival is, as I have said, to find out if a happy man is still alive. A man can smile when he is dead. Composure, resignation, and the most exquisite good manners are, so to speak, the strong points of corpses. There is only one way in which you can test his real vitality, and that is by a special festival. Explode crackers in his ear, and see if he jumps. Prick him with holly, and see if he feels it. If not, he is dead, or, as he would put it, is "living the higher life."

For in this matter, as in nearly all modern matters, we must continually remember the question I think I mentioned recently in connection with Francis Thompson and religious symbolism.

When we talk of things like Christmas we must remember what we have to compare them to. It is not a question between Christmas ceremonies and a free, pure life: it is a question between Christmas ceremonies and vulgar society ceremonies; between the exciting conventions of a pantomime and the dull conventions of a dinner-table. It is not Christmas against liberty. Though if it were I should still choose Christmas.

January 18, 1908
The Hysteria of Mobs

It is painful to notice that at the present time mobs are not properly admired. In this specially undemocratic age it is always assumed that large masses of men, especially of enthusiastic men, must somehow be wrong. One angry man is called strong, but four hundred angry men are (for some extraordinary reason) called weak. The modern newspapers have one word kept in type for any mob on any side: the word "hysterical." Tennyson, I am sorry to say, agreed with the newspapers on this and many other points. And when we wrote about France or the French Revolution he was not only unlike a great poet, he was unlike an educated man. It is not given to every man to sum up all the ignorances on a certain subject in a single line; but Tennyson did it when he alluded to the Revolution as "The mad hysterics of the Celt."[1]

I only quote this line for the sake of the interesting word "hysterics." I resist the temptation of pointing out that the people were not Celts (if there are any Celts), and that they were much

[1] More accurately: "The blind hysterics of the Celt", *In Memoriam*, cix, 16.

less mad than Tennyson. The real interest is the meaning of the word "hysterical"; and, being a scientific word, its meaning is not very clear. But I have seen it applied to both the most interesting modern mobs in the best modern daily papers. The mob that acclaimed the acquittal of Wood[2] was called "hysterical"; the professional mob which tried to wreck the Brown Dog[3] was called "hysterical."

This charge of hysteria against a mob is highly misleading. If it means that a mob is angry, extravagant, capable of awful acts for good or evil, then a mob is not hysteric, but heroic. But if it means a mob is weak and silly, that it has no basis, that it celebrates some irresponsible or morbid fancy, then it simply is not true.

Mobs have their faults, but at least they are perfectly reasonable. All the great mobs of history (as far as I remember) have been perfectly reasonable. To take but one example, I can never comprehend why all historians and romancers talk of the Gordon Riots as things without object or excuse. The Gordon Riots[4] had the perfectly reasonable object of preventing the pure, consistent, and intolerant policy of English Protestantism from being reversed; and they had the perfectly reasonable excuse that it was being reversed. Whatever my own convictions may be, I cannot see why Protestants should not have ordinary human

[2] Robert Wood was accused of killing a young prostitute in September 1907; his trial inflamed passions on both sides, but he was acquitted, leaving the identity of the murderer still a mystery.

[3] In the same year, in Chesterton's own neighborhood of Battersea, a conflict arose between anti-vivisectionists (including, in a precarious alliance, suffragettes and ordinary laborers) and medical students at the University of London over a statue erected to "an old brown dog", which, as the inscription said, had "endured Vivisection extending over more than Two Months and having been handed over from one Vivisector to another". Numerous meetings and riots had to be broken up by the police until finally the offending statue was removed.

[4] Anti-Catholic riots took place in London on June 2–7, 1780, which were instigated and led by Lord George Gordon. They began as demonstrations against the removal of civil restrictions for Catholics, but they resulted in riots of destruction and plunder.

rights, such as the right of festivity and the right of insurrection. For this reason, I have complete emotional sympathy with Guy Fawkes Day and with the Gordon Riots. But a riot is always reasonable even when it is not right. Imperialism is not right, but it is reasonable; and it was so with the riots on Mafeking night.[5] Socialism is not right, but it is reasonable; and it was so with the old riots in Trafalgar Square. Protestantism may not be right, but it is reasonable; and it was so with the Gordon Riots. It is when a thing is reasonable, but cannot get itself accepted or realised, that a ruinous violence breaks out. Men fight when they are furiously reasonable—when, so to speak, they are quite unreasonably reasonable. But no fight can arise out of mere unreason. One might fight about Mrs. Eddy, but not about Edward Lear.[6]

Now let me take these two modern instances of mobs; the mob about the Brown Dog and the mob congratulating Wood. They were both "hysterical" from the newspapers' point of view; I think they were both quite sensible from their own point of view. Touching the Brown Dog, I have remarked already in these columns that I am an anti-vivisectionist; but no one seems really to have troubled about the actual ethics underlying the students' outbreak. That such passions are a mere madness is absurd; that it is mere rowdiness is equally absurd. Mad people might smash anything; and rowdy people would smash every-thing. The idea behind the students' action was, I think, this quite rational idea, right or wrong—that a public street and a public monument were being used against a public decision and a public morality. The anti-vivisectionists may be right or wrong; but they are not Great Britain; but Battersea is Great Britain; at

[5] On the night of May 18, 1900, news reached London that Mafeking, a town in South Africa which had been beseiged by the Boers for 217 days, had been liberated by a relief column. This news resulted in jubilant celebrations through-out the British Isles.

[6] Edward Lear (1812–1888), an artist and author, invented the *Book of Nonsense* (1846) for the grandchildren of his patron, the Earl of Derby.

least, it is an unusually favourable sample of it. The mere fact that certain people are humanitarians and have a reasonable ideal ought not to permit them to erect brown dogs in the streets of Battersea, any more than it ought to permit them to prevent the driving of brown donkeys in the streets of Battersea. Public monuments ought to be erected by the public—not by a small minority, even when it is right. There are people who think it wrong to vivisect dogs. I am one of them. There are people who think it wrong to drive donkeys or eat rabbits. I am not one of them. But I think we should all complain if enormous statues were erected to commemorate the mere fact that some individuals had used animals for food or traction and that some other individuals disapproved of it. If an ordinary Christian coster-monger, walking innocently down the street, found himself face to face with a colossal equestrian statue (so to speak) of himself and his donkey, in which his donkey had an expression of saintly suffering, while he himself had a leer of hideous cruelty, and if a large and legible inscription underneath commemorated his vices and the donkey's virtues, then I do seriously think that that costermonger, as a citizen, would be justified in kicking up a row. He ought to be punished for any separate acts of cruelty to his donkey, but not to be pilloried before the British people merely for having a donkey.

Yet again, I know many people of the noblest moral nature who have really persuaded themselves that the eating of any kind of animal food is a cruel and obscene cannibalism. They meet me, they shake me by the hand, they ask me to give them lectures, but the fact remains that they must, from their own point of view, quite rightly regard me as wicked for eating a haddock at breakfast. I know this, and I accept it. But I must confess that I should be annoyed if I walked out one morning into Battersea Park and found a monument to the haddock. It would displease me if there were a statue of a haddock, in a pathetic and arresting attitude, with an inscription underneath saying—"This is the Martyred Haddock, Murdered to Make the Bestial Breakfast of G. K. Chesterton, who Lives in the Mansion

Just Over the Way." I do not say that I should knock the statue down, being averse to all forms of prolonged manual labour; but I do say that I should have a reasonable case against it. I should object to being made the object of a public rebuke when I had no reason to believe that it came from the public. I should insist that if I was to be insulted in the streets it should be in accordance with some opinion as wide and general as the streets. Now, if the monument commemorated a hundred haddocks off a hundred breakfast-tables (it sounds a rich sculptural scheme), and if, in consequence, a hundred haddock-eating men came down to protest with me, I should not think that that made the protest any less rational; rather more: I should think they were a mob, but quite reasonable. I should think they were all the more reasonable for being a mob.

Exactly the same applies, I think, to the mob which awaited the release of Wood: a mob which was also called hysterical. A mob may, indeed, be immoral; but a mob is hardly ever anti-moral. A mob is hardly ever morbid; for secrecy is the chief part of morbidity. The mob is like a child, not like a lunatic. Its moral ideas are few, but as far as they go they are innocent; killing tyrants, abolishing hunger. It is very rare, it is almost unknown, for any large mob to have ideas in themselves hysterical, fads, heresies, cranks, and ethical side-issues. It is extravagantly improbable that the huge mob waiting outside the legal building had any special sympathy with any of the hysterical elements in the individual case. The mob was not fond of loose aesthetics, or egomania, or semi-intellectual impudence. In other words, the mob was not fond of Mr. Wood. What the mob was fond of, and always has been fond of, was justice. The mob had a very well-founded feeling that getting men hanged has become a great deal too easy a job. The mob had, as it has everywhere, a profound distrust of the police. The mob knew (what the educated classes are not sufficiently educated to know) that the police are not impartial in any sense whatever: the police work for a conviction exactly as the prosecuting counsel works for it. And the mob, knowing all this, knew that it outraged eternal honour—as it does. But our age has grown so utterly out of sympathy with any idea of the people that no one will believe me when I say that a mob met for so manly and reasonable an aim.

A friend of mine who knows many of the students at University College assures me that many of them, many even of those who took part in the riot, dislike vivisection in practice, and even hold it unnecessary in theory. I do not know whether this is so; but I can quite believe it. Hating vivisection is not at all inconsistent with also hating anti-vivisectionists. In the same way the public that hailed the release of Wood consisted of people who would never have stood him for ten minutes as a secretary or a son-in-law. The protest was against two minorities. The humanitarians are felt to be even more unnatural than the tormentors. The detectives are felt, and felt rightly, to be even more base than the criminals.

January 25, 1908

Aristocrats as Mystagogues

I once heard a man call this age the age of demagogues. Of this I can only say, in the admirably sensible words of the angry coachman in "Pickwick," that "that remark's political, or what is much the same, it ain't true." So far from being the age of demagogues, this is really and specially the age of mystagogues. So far from this being a time in which things are praised because they are popular, the truth is that this is the first time, perhaps, in the whole history of the world in which things can be praised because they are unpopular. The demagogue succeeds because he makes himself understood, even if he is not worth understanding. But the mystagogue succeeds because he gets himself misunderstood; although, as a rule, he is not even worth mis-understanding. Gladstone was a demagogue: Disraeli a mys-tagogue. But ours is specially the time when a man can advertise his wares not as a universality, but as what the tradesmen call "a speciality." We all know this, for instance, about modern art. Michelangelo and Whistler were both fine artists; but one is obviously public, the other obviously private, or rather, not obvious at all. Michelangelo's frescoes are doubtless finer than the popular judgment, but they are plainly meant to strike the popular judgment. Whistler's pictures seem often meant to escape the popular judgment; they even seem meant to escape the pop-ular admiration. They are elusive, fugitive; they fly even from praise. Doubtless many artists in Michelangelo's day declared themselves to be great artists, although they were unsuccessful. But they did not declare themselves great artists because they were unsuccessful: that is the peculiarity of our own time, which has a positive bias against the populace.

Another case of the same kind of thing can be found in the latest conceptions of humour. By the wholesome tradition of mankind, a joke was a thing meant to amuse men; a joke which did not amuse them was a failure, just as a fire which did not warm them was a failure. But we have seen the process of secrecy and aristocracy introduced even into jokes. If a joke falls flat, a small school of aesthetes only ask us to notice the wild grace of its falling and its perfect flatness after its fall. The old idea that the joke was not good enough for the company has been superseded by the new aristocratic idea that the company was not worthy of the joke. They have introduced an almost insane individualism into that one form of intercourse which is specially and uproariously communal. They have made even levities into secrets. They have made laughter lonelier than tears.

There is a third thing to which the mystagogues have recently been applying the methods of a secret society: I mean manners. Men who sought to rebuke rudeness used to represent manners as reasonable and ordinary; now they seek to represent them as private and peculiar. Instead of saying to a man who blocks up a street or the fireplace, "You ought to know better than that," the moderns say, "You, of course, don't know better than that."

I have just been reading an amusing book by Lady Grove called "The Social Fetich," which is a positive riot of this new specialism and mystification. It is due to Lady Grove to say that she has some of the freer and more honourable qualities of the old Whig aristocracy, as well as their wonderful worldliness and their strange faith in the passing fashion of our politics. For instance, she speaks of Jingo Imperialism with a healthy English contempt; and she perceives stray and striking truths, and records them justly—as, for instance, the greater democracy of the Southern and Catholic countries of Europe. But in her dealings with social formulae here in England she is, it must frankly be said, a common mystagogue. She does not, like a decent demagogue, wish to make people understand; she wishes to make them painfully conscious of not understanding. Her favourite method is to terrify people from doing things that are quite harmless by telling them that if they do they are the kind of people who would do other things, equally harmless. If you ask after somebody's mother (or whatever it is), you are the kind of person who would have a pillow-case, or would not have a pillow-case. I forget which it is; and so, I dare say, does she. If you assume the ordinary dignity of a decent citizen and say that you don't see the harm of having a mother or a pillow-case, she would say that of course *you* wouldn't. This is what I call being a mystagogue. It is more vulgar than being a demagogue; because it is much easier.

The primary point I meant to emphasise is that this sort of aristocracy is essentially a new sort. All the old despots were demagogues; at least, they were demagogues whenever they were really trying to please or impress the demos. If they poured out beer for their vassals it was because both they and their vassals had a taste for beer. If (in some slightly different mood) they poured melted lead on their vassals, it was because both they and their vassals had a strong distaste for melted lead. But they did not make any mystery about either of the two substances.

They did not say, "You don't like melted lead? . . . Ah! no, of course, *you* wouldn't; you are probably the kind of person who would prefer beer. . . . It is no good asking you even to imagine the curious undercurrent of psychological pleasure felt by a refined person under the seeming shock of melted lead." Even tyrants when they tried to be popular, tried to give the people pleasure; they did not try to overawe the people by giving them something which they ought to regard as pleasure.

It was the same with the popular presentment of aristocracy. Aristocrats tried to impress humanity by the exhibition of qualities which humanity admires, such as courage, gaiety, or even mere splendour. The aristocracy might have more possession in these things, but the democracy had quite equal delight in them. It was much more sensible to offer yourself for admiration because you had drunk three bottles of port at a sitting, than to offer yourself for admiration (as Lady Grove does) because you think it right to say "port wine" while other people think it right to say "port." Whether Lady Grove's preference for port wine (I mean for the phrase port wine) is a piece of mere nonsense I do not know; but at least it is a very good example of the futility of such tests in the matter even of mere breeding. "Port wine" may happen to be the phrase used in certain good families; but numberless aristocrats say "port," and all barmaids say "port wine." The whole thing is rather more trivial than collecting tram-tickets; and I will not pursue Lady Grove's further distinctions. I pass over the interesting theory that I ought to say to Jones (even apparently if he is my dearest friend), "How is Mrs. Jones?" instead of "How is your wife?"; and I pass over an impassioned declamation about bedspreads (I think) which has failed to fire my blood.

The truth of the matter is really quite simple. An aristocracy is a secret society; and this is especially so when, as in the modern world, it is practically a plutocracy. The one idea of a secret society is to change the password. Lady Grove falls naturally into a pure perversity because she feels subconsciously that the people of England can be more effectively kept at a distance by a perpetual torrent of new tests than by the persistence of a few old ones. She knows that in the educated "middle-class" there is an idea that it is vulgar to say port wine; therefore she reverses the idea—she says that the man who would say "port" is a man who would say, "How is your wife?" She says it because she knows both these remarks to be quite obvious and reasonable.

The only thing to be done or said in reply, I suppose, would be to apply the same principle of bold mystification on our own part. I do not see why I should not write a book called "Etiquette in Fleet Street," and terrify everyone else out of that thoroughfare by mysterious allusions to the mistakes that they generally make. I might say: "This is the kind of man who would wear a green tie when he went into a tobacconist's," or "You don't see anything wrong in drinking a Benedictine on Thursday? . . . No, of course *you* wouldn't." I might asseverate with passionate disgust and disdain: "The man who is capable of writing sonnets as well as triolets is capable of climbing an omnibus while holding an umbrella." It seems a simple method; if ever I should master it perhaps I may govern England.

February 1, 1908

Gossip and Public Journalism

It seems a just and reasonable thing, a part of the cosmos, as reasonable as the rain and the sun and green leaves in summer, that the wrong people should have the wrong arguments. The really startling and supernatural thing, the thing that makes the soul stagger, is the fact that the right people have the wrong arguments. The people who really are right are always misrepresented; they are not misrepresented by their enemies, but by themselves. The people who really have an excellent case cannot be induced to state it. For instance, it happens from time to time that the police are really right. It does not happen often, of course, but it does happen; and, when it does, there is always some mistake about the mode of presenting the matter to the public. When the Government is right in principle, it takes a special and peculiar care to be wrong in detail. There have been many examples of this; but I suppose no example could possibly be stronger than that of certain prosecutions within living memory. If you read the public reports of most prosecutions in the ordinary newspapers, the whole thing seems to be pure nonsense. But then nearly everything, as reported in the ordinary newspapers, seems to be pure nonsense. The man who reports a criminal trial in a modern newspaper seems to have (as far as I can make out) only three quite clear and definite objects. First, in all cases, he desires to conceal the name of the crime. Second, in aristocratic cases he desires to conceal the name of the criminal. And third, in all cases political, religious, or in any way important he desires to conceal the whole course of the argument. I am quite sure myself that this mysterious method provokes much more indecent imagination than any indecency could provoke. I can quite understand not reporting a case at all; but I cannot see the value of reporting it at great length, but so as to mean nothing. I have read long police paragraphs at the end of which one literally could not tell whether it was a case of arson or forgery or stealing a horse.

One of the worst examples of this obscurity and illogicality in the legal proceedings or in the reports of them is furnished by such curious cases as those to which I have already alluded. If you read the newspapers, the tale is plain bosh; but, fortunately, I have penetrated far enough into the facts of the modern world never to believe the newspapers. I have heard men talking contemptuously of private gossip; and I have heard men talking proudly of the dignity of the Press. But I have come to the conclusion that if you never believe the Press and if you always believe private gossip (within reason) you will probably be right. Private gossip is so much more serious than the Press. Private gossip is so much more responsible than the Press. I say this literarily, not flippantly; for, indeed, the thing is perfectly clear. A man does not wear a mask when he tells you a story in a club; but a man does wear a mask when he tells you a story in the columns of the *Daily Post* or the *Morning Telegraph*. The man in the club may be drunk—he generally is—but he is sober enough to remember his own name. But the Special Correspondent is sober enough to forget his own name, or, at least, to conceal it. All that anybody ever really meant as the evil of gossip is much more characteristic of established journalism: the fact that gossip comes from nowhere in particular and from everywhere at once; that no name can be put to it as the name of an author, that you cannot run it to earth, but when you attempt to contradict it strange obstacles of entanglement and denial seem to cross your path. All this, which is so true of private scandal, is very much truer of public journalism. The frivolous chatter is now all in public journalism. The public responsibility is all in private conversation.

So it is specifically about criminal prosecutions. If I had gone by the newspapers I should have thought the whole thing not only unjust but unmeaning. But suppose I have come across some gossip; gossip is another name for democracy. Then I have heard something of the man against whom the charge is brought from people who have actually heard him speak. That is, I know something about him in the way that a strong, successful, and therefore small democracy knows something about one of its noisier and more annoying citizens. I know something about him, just as an Athenian citizen (who had no newspapers) knew something about Socrates. If the witty reader of this page (I should think there can be only one reader of this page, and I feel somehow that he must be witty)—if the witty reader of this page replies that Athenian citizens, if they knew about Socrates, did not at any rate know him well enough to leave him alone; if that sparkling person remarks that at least they were wrong to kill Socrates; then in that case I have only two remarks to make. First, that I do not say that ordinary knowledge, gathered from seeing men in the streets of your own little town, is infallible, but only that it is more infallible than high-class journalism. Second, that I am not by any means sure that they were wrong in killing Socrates. But that is another argument; we will have it another week.

The present subject (whenever I attempt to get to it I seem to get somewhere else) is that private assurances are generally much more reliable than public explanations; especially when (as generally happens nowadays) the public explanations are not intended to explain. These personal statements that I have heard assure me that whether or no the man is guilty of the crime which is charged to him, he is at least odd from the point of view of ordinary manners. I have known many such men, at any rate, marked by essential or spiritual bad manners, by brutal disregard for the age or sex of the people to whom they speak, and generally of an ugly disposition, not so much to argue with their equals as to shock those who are their inferiors in experience or their superiors in innocence. I say I have heard of such men. I do not of necessity believe the description; but I do understand it. The newspaper description I do not understand at all.

That a man should be tried in secret merely for attacking certain institutions affects me as merely meaningless. A man who attacks, say, the Christian religion in the modern world is not an unheard-of or extraordinary person. The extraordinary person is the person who defends the Christian religion; I (for example) am an extraordinary person—I mean in that respect. If a man violates verbal decency, let the Government prosecute him for violating verbal decency, of which all modern men approve, instead of prosecuting him for violating religious orthodoxy, of which nearly all modern men, except a few of my personal friends, strongly disapprove. Why should they dig up an old Act of Parliament which, taken literally, applies quite as much

to Mr. John Morley[1] or to Mr. Lecky,[2] when they might take
other ground, or, best of all, leave the matter to a public opinion
which can really distinguish between one class of cases and
another? One can only explain it by that mysterious and universal
law which leads persons in a position of authority to manage to
be wrong even when they happen to be right.

As I am myself one of those who do believe in orthodoxy, I
may be allowed, perhaps, to say that I am certain that orthodoxy
loses, at this moment, even in a worldly sense, every time it
uses these legal and official weapons. For the weapons are not
merely antiquated weapons; they are such very weak weapons.
We cannot give our enemy a gag; we only give him a grievance!
Cynically, these powers do us no good. Ideally, they do us harm.
It is as if two duellists had to fight with sharp swords, but one
was allowed to wear a shirt and not the other. The shirt would
be a privilege: but yet not a protection. It would not be enough
to give him the victory: but it would be just enough to make
his victory unpopular.

February 8, 1908

Suffragette Demonstrations

The incident of the Suffragettes who chained themselves with
iron chains to the railings of Downing Street is a good ironical
allegory of most modern martyrdom. It generally consists of a

---

[1] John Morley (1838–1923), an English statesman, a man of letters and a
freelance journalist whose various writings and political activity reflected his
agnostic, liberal and individualist positions.

[2] William Edward Hartpole Lecky (1838–1903), an Irish-born historian and
essayist of Scottish descent; he was a liberal in politics and supported Irish Church
disestablishment and the Irish Land Act of 1870.

man chaining himself up and then complaining that he is not free. Some say that such larks retard the cause of female suffrage, others say that such larks alone can advance it; as a matter of fact I do not believe that they have the smallest effect one way or the other.

The modern notion of impressing the public by a mere demonstration of unpopularity, by being thrown out of meetings or thrown into jail, is largely a mistake. It rests on a fallacy touching the true popular value of martyrdom. People look at human history and see that it has often happened that persecutions have not only advertised but even advanced a persecuted creed, and given to its validity the public and dreadful witness of dying men. The paradox was pictorially expressed in Christian art, in which saints were shown brandishing as weapons the very tools that had slain them. And because his martyrdom is thus a power to the martyr, modern people think that anyone who makes himself slightly uncomfortable in public will immediately be uproariously popular. This element of inadequate martyrdom is not true only of the Suffragettes; it is true of many movements I respect and some that I agree with. It was true, for instance, of the Passive Resisters, who had pieces of their furniture sold up. The assumption is that if you show your ordinary sincerity (or even your political ambition) by being a nuisance to yourself as well as to other people, you will have the strength of the great saints who passed through the fire. Anyone who can be hustled in a hall for five minutes, or put in a cell for five days, has achieved what was meant by martyrdom, and has a halo in the Christian art of the future. Miss Pankhurst will be represented holding a policeman in each hand—the instruments of her martyrdom. The Passive Resister will be shown symbolically carrying the teapot that was torn from him by tyrannical auctioneers.

But there is a fallacy in this analogy of martyrdom. The truth is that the special impressiveness which does come from being persecuted only happens in the case of extreme persecution. For the fact that the modern enthusiast will undergo some inconvenience for the creed he holds only proves that he does hold it, which no one ever doubted. No one doubts that the Non-conformist minister cares more for Nonconformity than he does for his teapot. No one doubts that Miss Pankhurst wants a vote more than she wants a quiet afternoon and an arm-chair. All our ordinary intellectual opinions are worth a bit of a row: I remember during the Boer War fighting an Imperialist clerk outside the Queen's Hall, and giving and receiving a black eye; but I did not think it one of the incidents that produce the psychological effect of the Roman amphitheatre or the stake at Smithfield.[1] For in that impression there is something more than the mere fact that a man is sincere enough to give his time or his comfort. Pagans were not impressed by the torture of Christians merely because it showed that they honestly held their opinion; they knew that millions of people honestly held all sorts of opinions. The point of such extreme martyrdom is much more subtle. It is that it gives an appearance of a man having something quite specially strong to back him up, of his drawing upon some power. And this can only be proved when all his physical contentment is destroyed; when all the current of his bodily being is reversed and turned to pain. If a man is seen to be roaring with laughter all the time that he was skinned alive, it would not be unreasonable to deduce that somewhere in the recesses of his mind he had thought of a rather good joke. Similarly, if men smiled and sang (as they did) while they were being boiled or torn in pieces, the spectators felt the presence of something more than mere mental honesty; they felt the presence of some new and unintelligible kind of pleasure, which, presumably, came from somewhere. It might be a strength of madness, or a lying spirit from Hell; but it was something quite positive and extraordinary; as positive as brandy and as extraordinary as conjuring. The Pagan said to himself: "If Christianity makes a man happy while his legs are being eaten by a lion, might it not make me happy while my legs are still attached to me and walking

---

[1] A reference to that area in London used as a place of execution, particularly the burning of Protestant martyrs during the reign of Queen Mary.

down the street?" The Secularists laboriously explain that martyrdoms do not prove a faith to be true, as if anybody was ever
such a fool as to suppose that they did. What they did prove,
or, rather, strongly suggest, was that something had entered
human psychology which was stronger than strong pain. If a
young girl, scourged and bleeding to death, saw nothing but a
crown descending on her from God, the first mental step was
not that her philosophy was correct, but that she was certainly
feeding on something. But this particular point of psychology
does not arise at all in the modern cases of mere public discomfort
or inconvenience. The causes of Miss Pankhurst's cheerfulness
require no mystical explanations. If she were being burned alive
as a witch, if she then looked up in unmixed rapture and saw a
ballot-box descending out of heaven, then I should say that the
incident, though not conclusive, was frightfully impressive. It
would not prove logically that she ought to have the vote, or
that anybody ought to have the vote. But it would prove this:
that there was, for some reason, a sacramental reality in the vote,
that the soul could take the vote and feed on it; that it was in
itself a positive and overpowering pleasure, capable of being
pitted against positive and overpowering pain.

I should advise modern agitators, therefore, to give up this
particular method: the method of making very big efforts to get
a very small punishment. It does not really go down at all; the
punishment is too small, and the efforts are too obvious. It has
not any of the effectiveness of the old savage martyrdom, because
it does not leave the victim absolutely alone with his cause, so
that his cause alone can support him. At the same time it has
about it that element of the pantomimic and the absurd, which
was the cruellest part of the slaying and the mocking of the real
prophets. St. Peter was crucified upside down as a huge inhuman
joke; but his human seriousness survived the inhuman joke,
because, in whatever posture, he had died for his faith. The
modern martyr of the Pankhurst type courts the absurdity without making the suffering strong enough to eclipse the absurdity.

She is like a St. Peter who should deliberately stand on his head for ten seconds and then expect to be canonised for it.

Or, again, the matter might be put in this way. Modern martyrdoms fail even as demonstrations, because they do not prove even that the martyrs are completely serious. I think, as a fact, that the modern martyrs generally are serious, perhaps a trifle too serious. But their martyrdom does not prove it; and the public does not always believe it. Undoubtedly, as a fact, Dr. Clifford is quite honourably indignant with what he considers to be clericalism; but he does not prove it by having his teapot sold; for a man might easily have his teapot sold as an actress has her diamonds stolen—as a personal advertisement. As a matter of fact, Miss Pankhurst is quite in earnest about votes for women. But she does not prove it by being chucked out of meetings. A person might be chucked out of meetings just as young men are chucked out of music-halls—for fun. But no man has himself eaten by a lion as a personal advertisement. No woman is broiled on a gridiron for fun. That is where the testimony of St. Perpetua and St. Faith comes in. Doubtless it is no fault of these enthusiasts that they are not subjected to the old and searching penalties; very likely they would pass through them as triumphantly as St. Agatha. I am simply advising them upon a point of policy, things being as they are. And I say that the average man is not impressed with their sacrifices simply because they are not and cannot be more decisive than the sacrifices which the average man himself would make for mere fun if he were drunk. Drunkards would interrupt meetings and take the consequences. And as for selling a teapot, it is an act, I imagine, in which any properly constituted drunkard would take a positive pleasure. The advertisement is not good enough; it does not tell. If I were really martyred for an opinion (which is more improbable than words can say), it would certainly only be for one or two of my most central and sacred opinions. I might, perhaps, be shot for England, but certainly not for the British Empire. I might conceivably die for political freedom, but I certainly wouldn't die for Free Trade. But as for kicking up the particular kind of shindy that the Suffragettes are kicking up, I would as soon do it for my shallowest opinion as for my deepest one. It never could be anything worse than an inconvenience; it never could be anything better than a spree. Hence the British public, and especially the working classes, regard the whole demonstration with fundamental indifference; for, while it is a demonstration that probably is adopted from the most fanatical motives, it is a demonstration which might be adopted from the most frivolous.

February 15, 1908

Charlatans and Quacks

One of the few really satisfactory things that have happened lately was the verdict in the matter of the *Lancet* and the gentleman whom it called a quack doctor. It will probably be a landmark; because of late the decision has so commonly gone in such cases in favour of the more formal or more wealthy classes or professions. This is not because the judge or jury have not desired to be fair and find for the worthier party; it is rather because in our society the wealthier or more established person somehow always looks the more worthy; certain things about him happen in our atmosphere to be symbols of merit. To take a crude example from other matters, cleanliness always suggests to us honour and self-respect; and undoubtedly it is a very desirable quality either in a rich man or a poor one. But cleanliness is only a virtue in poor man; in a rich man it is a pleasure. Yet many people will unconsciously decide in favour of the clean collar against the dirty collar, and sincerely believe that they are deciding after an elaborate synthesis in favour of the generally good man against the general blackguard. Somewhat similar is the instinctive feeling of many people against what is called a charlatan and in favour of what is thought to be an established reputation. In many cases the distinction really rests on a certain type of worldly success or its absence; but those who make the distinction are quite sincerely unconscious that it rests on this. In many cases, doubtless, a man gets on because he is clever; but in some cases (and those high up in the State) a man is only thought clever because he has got on.

The truth is there are two kinds of charlatan: the man who is called a charlatan, and the man who really is one. The first is the quack who cures you; the second is the highly qualified person who doesn't. As I know nothing about the case of medical science, I will take the parallel case of the study I do slightly understand—the study of literature. There is one kind of writer who beats a drum, wears spangles, stands on his head until he has collected a crowd, and then tells them something quite sincere and generally quite true. Then there is the other man, who observes all the rules, exhibits all the dignities and the decencies, and then says nothing at all in the most modest and gentlemanlike way. Mr. Bernard Shaw, for instance, is a case of the charlatan who has something to say—the cheapjack who has something to sell. He is the quack who can cure you. In the same way Doctor Emil Reich[1] is the charlatan who has something to say— he is the quack who can cure you. I shall probably not be permitted to give examples of the other kind of charlatan, who has nothing to say; of the solemn and responsible quack who cannot cure you. There are plenty of them among Dons and Cabinet Ministers.

To take but one matter, it is not, generally speaking, true that the solemn and established man even knows more than the man

[1] Emil Reich (1854–1910), a Hungarian-born historian who settled in England in 1893; he was a voluminous writer and lecturer at Oxford, Cambridge and London. His work, while full of provocative suggestions, was inaccurate in detail, and his tendency to omit essential facts discredited his conclusions.

called a quack. We should justly regard Mr. Arnold-Forster,[2] for instance, as an established and important figure in our politics and our English history. Yet Mr. Arnold-Forster (as I discovered to my astonishment in reading his book on Socialism) does not know that the French Revolution was strongly Individualist. Dr. Emil Reich is spoken of as if he were a fantastic and *flaneur* for ladies' tea-parties; but Dr. Emil Reich could tell Mr. Arnold-Forster not only what the French Revolution thought of Socialism, but probably the date of every discussion on the matter and the name of every isolated Socialist, and when they cut his head off. If Mr. Bernard Shaw were arguing with the average Chancellor of the Exchequer, it would be found most probably that Mr. Shaw knew not only more about economics, but more about the Exchequer. What people mean when they say that Mr. Shaw or Dr. Reich are quacks is simply that they do not observe all the preliminaries or approach the matter with the usual forms. This may be a fault of taste in them or a deficiency of a reasonable respect for civilisation. But it remains grossly unjust that they who do give their audiences pleasure and profit for their money should be called quacks and impostors by prosperous and solemn persons who have nothing to give. It is grossly unjust that the proof of a man being a humbug should be shifted from the question of whether he delivers the goods, to the quite secondary question of whether he advertises them too much. Surely the humbug is not the noisy fellow who forces his wares upon you, but the decorous, dignified, really respectable gentleman who takes the money for them and decamps.

The *Lancet* case of this was a small and simple one; but it establishes a sound principle. It establishes the principle that respectability shall be held to consist in doing what you profess to do, not in doing it in the exact way that you are told to do it. A man must not be held up to moral rebuke because he works outside certain professional formulae; to social, professional, or

[2] Hugh Oakeley Arnold-Forster (1855–1909), the author of numerous books, including *English Socialism of Today: Its Teaching and Its Aims Examined* (1908).

intellectual rebuke, of course, he is quite open. The qualified practitioners of medicine are quite entitled to make rules for any society they form. We will even do them the honour of comparing it to a trade union, though it is seldom so actual or indispensable a thing. Let us agree that doctors in council have a right to limit the methods of their number; but the strongest trade unionists would admit a limit to the punishment of black-legs. The Bricklayers' Union have a right to rebuke an isolated bricklayer, to send him to Coventry, to deprive him of all brick-laying advantages, to denounce him as a traitor to the bricklaying cause. But they would not think it right to print positively in so many words in the public Press that the bricks laid by this man were invariably dynamite bricks, intended to blow up the house. The Blessed Brotherhood of the Good Greengrocers would be right in casting out a recalcitrant greengrocer, but not in swearing that he systematically put arsenic in his brussels sprouts. Yet this is practically done when medical authorities apply to a man whose only real fault in their eyes is irregularity or disloyalty, terms which in the ordinary English language point to poison and swindling. Altogether, we are returning to a more reasonable view of unofficial discoveries and unofficial healing; and, indeed, our theory in this matter has required improvement as much as our practice. The really equitable doctrine of what we owe to doctors and what to old women in villages has yet to be stated.

The argument used by professional men of science that what they call quack remedies are superstitions is really an argument in a circle. It amounts to this, that the herbs used by an old woman are untrustworthy because she is superstitious; and she is superstitious because she believes in such herbs. Her method is bad because she is stupid; but the main proof of her stupidity is that she pursues her own method. To put it shortly, the doctor does not believe in the old woman upon the ultimate ground that she does not believe in the doctor. For the scientific man has a simple method of dealing with the mere thing called human evidence. He has only to say that it is ignorant evidence: as in one sense it must be until everyone in this country has a medical degree. I may have a considerable experience of a subject, but I cannot be so learned as a specialist or (I hope) as mad as a specialist. I may have worn a great many hats in my life, but I am not so learned as a hatter—or as mad as a hatter. Professional science is thus in a singularly strong position. It can go on day and night calling for evidence, and it can rule out the evidence of the mass of mankind. This method applied by modern science to old wives' cures or popular discoveries is also the method which it applies to the dreams or faiths which are the mark of mankind. Again it is a simple circular argument. The people of the East believe in miracles because they are ignorant. How do you know they are ignorant? Because they believe in miracles. Thomas Aquinas believed in Catholicism because he lived in a darkened age. Why was it a darkened age? It was darkened by Catholicism. The Highlanders believe in second sight because they are superstitious. Prove that they are superstitious? Well, for instance, they believe in second sight. Father Murphy believes in relics because he is a fool; he is certainly a fool, for he positively believes in relics. Jones tells me that he saw the ghost of his uncle last Tuesday. But, of course, you wouldn't believe a liar like that—a man brazen enough to say that he saw a ghost last Tuesday. In short, the elephant stands on the tortoise and the tortoise stands—on the elephant. By such mental processes it is possible to escape from the narrow methods of deductive logic.

February 22, 1908

Socialism and First Principles

Some correspondents have remonstrated with me touching the suggestion I made last week that there is often more humbug, in the strictest sense of the word, about the official and professional types to whom the world trusts than in those quacks and adventurers whom the world distrusts even while it enjoys them. I took the case of a man like Mr. Bernard Shaw, who largely advertises his goods, but who has some goods to advertise. And I compared him with the other and far more subtle and insidious type of professor—the grave official who in the most stately and delicate manner draws attention to the merits of goods that are not there. Mr. Shaw is the cheapjack greengrocer who does, after all his patter, hand me some brussels sprouts. When I have got them, I will then, with all solemnity, curse him for his disgusting Vegetarianism. But I will not say that he has given me nothing for my money.

But it so happens that an exact example of the contrast that I mean has just occurred in the first debate in Parliament. It is rather a curious and interesting case, and I really ask the reader to study it if he is at all concerned about the moral and intellectual future of our country. It is a perfect case of the two things: the able and essentially serious man who is considered absurd, and the really able man who has to be essentially absurd in order to be considered serious. No party question is raised in this Parliamentary incident; for as it happens, both the true and the false quack (I use the word without offence in both cases) were on the same side. They were both saying (as far as the debate and division went) the same thing. They would both be called Radicals. They were both Radicals repudiating Socialism; while expressing sympathy with social reform. They were both clever men, and both sincere men. But one was a free-lance talking sound philosophical sense: he was greeted with laughter as a mere lark. The other was a very capable official, talking the most wild and shapeless nonsense: he was considered at once impressive and important. He had the manner, though not the greens.

Here is the case. Mr. Kettle, an Irish Nationalist, made a speech in which he said that he liked everything about Socialism except its fundamental principle. This is an extraordinarily acute, forcible, and thoughtful remark. It would be impossible to put more clearly and curtly, in one epigram, the whole position of most

Irishmen (and most Roman Catholic Radicals, like Mr. Belloc) on the present quarrel of the rich and poor. It is not an easy position to sum up, but Mr. Kettle here summed it up with humour and precision. He meant, of course, that he liked the spirit and connotation of most popular Socialism; he liked its sincerity, its thirst for abstract fairness, its pity, its Christian anger. Of its occasional fierceness—being an Irishman—he had no great horror; with its war with landlords and the oppressive rich he naturally had historical sympathy. What he could not and would not accept was the Socialist first principle: the theory that the means of production ought all to belong to the State. He would not admit, as a point of abstract ethics, that one man ought not to own one field. He was just as much horrified as any Socialist at one man owning all the fields. But his first principle was that every man, if possible, should have absolute property; not that no man should have it: therefore he could not be a Socialist. All this important and interesting mental position he summed up in a few words. He put a book full of solid ethics and economics into a sentence—"I like everything about Socialism except the principle on which it rests." Very well. The remark was greeted with roars of derisive laughter. And a Radical paper headed the incident "An Irish Bull"!

Now for the solemn and official attack on Socialism. Dr. Macnamara is a man of distinguished mental force, for whom I have personal regard; and I here pause to implore him not to become a good Parliamentarian, not to catch the tone of the House, not to talk as our successful public men are all talking. In other words, I implore him not to hang up his head like his hat. I cannot believe that a man of his mentality really thought about what he was saying on this occasion; I believe he unconsciously caught at a certain note in the air; that he made himself into an echo. What he said (according to the reports) was in substance this. Some people wanted Socialism. But there was one slight objection to that—it wasn't coming along just yet. As a practical man, he must dismiss such chimerical impossibilities—or words exactly to that effect. This was cheered; and it undoubtedly represents the established view held by the House of Commons and perhaps by the British public, of what an attack on Socialism ought to be like. And knowing that, look at it!—consider it! It is not an attack on Socialism; it is not an objection to Socialism at all. It does not even hint whether Socialism, if it came, would be good or bad. It only says that it is not coming "just yet"; to which the Socialist would naturally reply "That depends on whether I can make it come or you can prevent it coming." If Socialism is a good thing, why should not men try to make it "come along" as soon as possible? If it is a bad thing it ought not to be denounced as an impossibility; it ought to be denounced as a possibility. Why is it "chimerical" to try to make something you want very much "come along," even if it can't come "just yet"? Why is it particularly "practical" to stare at a railway-train that has not reached the station, and then call it a Chimaera? What is a "practical man"; and why is it more practical to say that things won't come along just yet, than to try and make them come along?

In these two or three vague sentences can be found nearly all the weird fallacies that are wasting and eating away the intellect of England. There is the extraordinary talk about Socialism "coming along" all by itself, as if it were some sort of large animal. People believe (apparently) that a vast and ferocious elephant has just started from Peking, and is walking across Asia and Europe towards us; but it has hardly reached Russia, and is not coming along to us just yet. Apparently we can only await its advent in quaking stillness. And we are not even allowed, by way of passing the time, to ask whether we want an elephant, or whether, when we get him, he will be a white elephant. And if anyone points out that Socialism is not an elephant coming from Peking, but a business arrangement, which we may, or may not, make ourselves to suit ourselves, then he is called "unpractical." We who are Radicals often speak of the evils of a slavish and panic-stricken submission to the past. But I think there is one thing meaner; a slavish and panic-stricken submission to the future.

Then there is the everlasting nonsense about being a practical man. When will people see the simple fact that practicality is a question of means, not of ends? Whether your course is practical depends on what you want to do? If two men in London want to go to Glasgow, you may then say that one is more practical than the other; you may say (for example) that the man who in the course of his journey is found at Brighton is somewhat the less practical of the two. But it is not "unpractical" to go to Brighton if you like Brighton. It is not "unpractical" to go to Lapland if you like Lapland. There are unpractical methods. There is no such thing as an unpractical aim; though there may be such a thing as a wrong aim. There can be nothing "unpractical" about a serious ultimate desire; though there may be something wrong about it. It is not unpractical to want to be a tramp. It is unpractical, if you want to be a tramp, to buy a large house in Grosvenor Square.

Similarly, it is not unpractical in Socialists to seek to make their scheme "come along," even if it must take a long time in coming, if they really want it very much. The only question is whether we want it very much. That question the official speech did not even begin to discuss. That question Mr. Kettle did begin to discuss, and began at the right end. I only mentioned the contrast as typical of the strange war between the recognised official who talks nonsense and the derided outsider who talks sense. A member of the Ministry ties himself in a useless knot of words that lead nowhere, and is fully reported and duly praised. An Irish Member argues like an educated man, alludes to the only objection to Socialism in phrases that have the clearness of a logician and the virile reticence of a gentleman; and *he* is treated not only as a clown, but as an unconscious clown.

February 29, 1908

The Ethics of Fairy-Tales

Some solemn and superficial people (for nearly all very superficial people are solemn) have declared that the fairy-tales are
immoral; they base this upon some accidental circumstances or
regrettable incidents in the war between giants and boys, some
cases in which the latter indulged in unsympathetic deceptions
or even in practical jokes. The objection, however, is not only
false, but very much the reverse of the facts. The fairy-tales are
at root not only moral in the sense of being innocent, but moral
in the sense of being didactic, moral in the sense of being mor-
alising. It is all very well to talk of the freedom of fairyland, but
there was precious little freedom in fairyland by the best official
accounts. Mr. W. B. Yeats and other sensitive modern souls,
feeling that modern life is about as black a slavery as ever oppressed
mankind (they are right enough there), have specially described
elfland as a place of utter ease and abandonment—a place where
the soul can turn every way at will like the wind. Science
denounces the idea of a capricious God; but Mr. Yeats's school
suggests that in that world everyone is a capricious god. Mr.
Yeats himself has said a hundred times in that sad and splendid
literary style which makes him the first of all poets now writing
in English (I will not say of all English poets, for Irishmen are
familiar with the practice of physical assault), he has, I say, called
up a hundred times the picture of the terrible freedom of the
fairies, who typify the ultimate anarchy of art—

> Ride on the crest of the dishevelled wave
> And dance upon the mountains like a flame.

But, after all (it is a shocking thing to say), I doubt whether
Mr. Yeats really knows his way about fairyland. He is not simple
enough; he is not stupid enough. Though I say it who should
not, in good sound human stupidity I would knock Mr. Yeats
out any day. The fairies like me better than Mr. Yeats; they can

take me in more. And I have my doubts whether this feeling of the free, wild spirits on the crest of hill or wave is really the central and simple spirit of folk-lore. I think the poets have made a mistake: because the world of the fairy-tales is a brighter and more varied world than ours, they have fancied it less moral; really it is brighter and more varied because it is more moral. Suppose a man could be born in a modern prison. It is impossible, of course, because nothing human can happen in a modern prison, though it could sometimes in an ancient dungeon. A modern prison is always inhuman, even when it is not inhumane. But suppose a man were born in a modern prison, and grew accustomed to the deadly silence and the disgusting indifference; and suppose he were then suddenly turned loose upon the life and laughter of Fleet Street. He would, of course, think that the literary men in Fleet Street were a free and happy race; yet how sadly, how ironically, is this the reverse of the case! And so again these toiling serfs in Fleet Street, when they catch a glimpse of the fairies, think the fairies are utterly free. But fairies are like journalists in this and many other respects. Fairies and journalists have an apparent gaiety and a delusive beauty. Fairies and journalists seem to be lovely and lawless; they seem to be both of them too exquisite to descend to the ugliness of everyday duty. But it is an illusion created by the sudden sweetness of their presence. Journalists live under law; and so in fact does fairyland.

If you really read the fairy-tales, you will observe that one idea runs from one end of them to the other—the idea that peace and happiness can only exist on some condition. This idea, which is the core of ethics, is the core of the nursery-tales. The whole happiness of fairyland hangs upon a thread, upon one thread. Cinderella may have a dress woven on supernatural looms and blazing with unearthly brilliance; but she must be back when the clock strikes twelve. The king may invite fairies to the christening, but he must invite all the fairies, or frightful results will follow. Bluebeard's wife may open all doors but one. A promise is broken to a cat, and the whole world goes wrong. A promise is broken to a yellow dwarf, and the whole world goes wrong.

A girl may be the bride of the God of Love himself if she never tries to see him; she sees him, and he vanishes away. A girl is given a box on condition she does not open it; she opens it, and all the evils of this world rush out at her. A man and woman are put in a garden on condition that they do not eat one fruit: they eat it, and lose their joy in all the fruits of the earth.

This great idea, then, is the backbone of all folk-lore—the idea that all happiness hangs on one thin veto; all positive joy depends on one negative. Now, it is obvious that there are many philosophical and religious ideas akin to or symbolised by this; but it is not with them I wish to deal here. It is surely obvious that all ethics ought to be taught to this fairy-tale tune; that, if one does the thing forbidden, one imperils all the things provided. A man who breaks his promise to his wife ought to be reminded that, even if she is a cat, the case of the fairy-cat shows that such conduct may be incautious. A burglar just about to open someone else's safe should be playfully reminded that he is in the perilous posture of the beautiful Pandora: he is about to lift the forbidden lid and loosen evils unknown. The boy eating someone's apples in someone's apple-tree should be a reminder that he has come to a mystical moment of his life, when one apple may rob him of all others. This is the profound morality of fairy-tales; which, so far from being lawless, go to the root of all law. Instead of finding (like common books of ethics) a rationalistic basis for each Commandment, they find the great mystical basis for all Commandments. We are in this fairyland on sufferance; it is not for us to quarrel with the conditions under which we enjoy this wild vision of the world. The vetoes are indeed extraordinary, but then so are the concessions. The idea of property, the idea of someone else's apples, is a rum idea; but then the idea of there being any apples is a rum idea. It is strange and weird that I cannot with safety drink ten bottles of champagne; but then the champagne itself is strange and weird, if you come to that. If I have drunk of the fairies' drink it is but just I should drink by the fairies' rules. We may not see the direct logical connection between three beautiful silver spoons and a large ugly policeman; but then who in fairy-tales ever could see the direct logical connection between three bears and a giant, or between a rose and a roaring beast? But this general aspect is not my concern; and I have left myself hardly any space to say what is my concern.

The aim with which I originally introduced this discussion on fairies was that of discussing the Blasphemy case. The connection between the two ideas will at once leap to the mind. It is time we cleared our ideas a little on the matter of law and of liberty in expression. I am myself in favour of complete liberty of religion (as ordinarily understood; strictly, it would cover human sacrifice), but do not let us deceive ourselves into the supposition that either I or anybody else believes in complete liberty of speech. That a man should be prosecuted for blasphemy in modern England strikes me as iniquitous. But that a man should be prosecuted for obscenity of language strikes me and all ordinary men as a right and natural protection. Why is this? It is not because there is anything more intellectually indefensible, in the abstract, about one than about the other. Blasphemy is as bad as indecency, in so far that it must mean the giving of a cruel shock to inoffensive souls, the inhumane presentment of a terrible idea in the ugliest and most abrupt way. Indecency may be as good as blasphemy in the sense that it may be given from good motives. A man may think religious humbug so solidly entrenched that nothing but intellectual dynamite will do any good. But a man may also think a bad sex-convention is in the same security and must be given the same shock. The real distinction is that England is divided on religion and irreligion in a real sense in which it is not divided on the need for verbal decency in mixed society. The law may protect religion: the people would protect decency. Religion may be the law of England: decency is the law of the English. As in the fairy-tales, all that we may say and do hangs on something we may not say and do. But do not let us forget that we have a veto, and that others had more liberty on that point. If you and I walked to-morrow into the Middle Ages, we should find ourselves (in some ways) less free to discuss unbelief, but much freer to discuss sex.

In the Middle Ages, people were not divided on religion and irreligion. There was only one way of belief, if a man was to be saved. If he did not choose to believe in that way, the Holy Office took him in hand and saved his soul for him, although in doing so it had to destroy his body by fire. But the Middle Ages were not so united as we are on the need for verbal decency in mixed society. Not that mediaeval men were more shameless: they were simply shameless in the absolute sense, and your truly shameless person is one for whom the idea of the word shame has no existence. Only your shameful modern person understands shame. He is a man who cannot call a spade a spade. He calls it, with a blush, an implement for tilling the soil, and so the spade becomes forever unmentionable.

March 7, 1908

The Anomalies of English Politics

Somewhere about the beginning of the nineteenth century, we English came to the conclusion that we could not think. This seemed, for some reason, to please us very much. And indeed it would not have mattered seriously if we had not immediately begun to think about our own thoughtlessness. We had a theory that we had no theory. Now, this kind of thing will not do; because whatever advantages there really are in being vague involve the idea that one does not know that one is vague. The one advantage of a child is that he does not know that he is a child. Unconscious carelessness may sometimes mean genius; conscious carelessness never means anything but bad manners.

The English may or may not have won so long as they were unreasonable. But if you have ever known an unreasonable person (which seems humanly probable), you will know that the very soul and strength of an unreasonable person is that he thinks he is reasonable. He is insufferably proud of being reasonable. But when England became proud of being unreasonable, then England lost all the force that belongs to pure folly. England became a child conscious of childishness, a virgin conscious of innocence, a simple man conscious of his simplicity—in short, a portent and a peril.

When we began to think that it was better not to think, one of our thoughts was this: we said that an anomaly—that is, an illogical action not obviously harmful—did not matter. We even boasted that the British Constitution was full of contradiction and unreason. The most trenchant and typical intellects of the nineteenth century asserted again and again that illogicalities were in themselves quite harmless. "I would not lift my hand," said Lord Macaulay, in his prompt and picturesque way, "to destroy an anomaly which was not also a grievance." And ever since his time it has been assumed more and more in our Parliamentary system that it was in no sense against a thing that it was unreasonable. It was in no sense against a thing that it was nonsense. It is impossible to doubt that English politics is more and more disdainful of theory. It is impossible to doubt that our Parliament increasingly ignores sentiment. Yet there is an explanation of those facts which does not sound so comforting as the facts themselves. That explanation is pathetically plain.

The simple fact is that Parliament is the one institution that believes in this old English doctrine of doing things anyhow, because Parliament is the one institution which doesn't do the things at all. Parliament is disdainful of theory for the simple reason that Parliament is disdainful of practice. Parliament increasingly ignores sentiment, because Parliament increasingly ignores everything. It is not strange that people are still careless about illogicality in the place where they are increasingly careless even about efficiency. They endure the anomalies of the Con-

stitution with the same cheerful English good sense with which
they also endure the injustices of the Whitechapel Road.[1] The
intellectual objection to anomalies (or rules devoid of reason) is
that they accustom the human mind to what is untenable and
unfair. He who has got used to unreason is ready for unkindness.
It would not do the men in Battersea any material harm if they
had to touch their hats whenever they met a man from Chelsea.
But for all that it would make it much easier for the men of
Chelsea at some time or other to cut off the heads of the men
of Battersea. It would seem more natural that those who had
touched their hats should lose their heads, than if the two races
had always been theoretically equal. It does a woman no material
good that a man should take off his hat to her; but it has saved
women, as a whole, many well-deserved assaults with a walking-
stick. When you have accustomed men to what is mentally wrong,
you have half-accustomed them to what is morally wrong. Give
me fifty years of any anomaly I choose, and I will undertake to
carry through quite easily any injustice that I like.

But my position was that Parliament is only illogical because
it is unpractical. Take any other institution, take any really practical institution, and you will find that it does not tolerate anomaly for an instant. Parliament, being an unpractical body, permits
the Lower House to be really the Upper House. But no well-
managed villa or hotel would ever allow the under-housemaid
to be really the upper-housemaid. A house is a practical thing;
therefore it has to consider sentiment. It has to consider the
sentiments of the two housemaids. The British Constitution,
being an unpractical thing, can rejoice in the fact that the head
of the State is a nonentity and can be kept out of politics. But
no regiment could be run upon the avowed principle that the
Colonel was a nonentity. A regiment is a practical thing, and
has to consider sentiment—the sentiments of the regiment with-

[1] A district of Stepney in the East End of London which was the scene of the
notorious Whitechapel Murders in 1888 where at least five prostitutes were
mutilated by Jack the Ripper.

out a real Colonel, the sentiments of the Colonel without a real
colonelcy. The House of Lords, being a useless institution, can
submit with great good-humour to a rude form by which the
Lower House locks them out altogether until their representative
has knocked three times. But a grocer's shop is not a useless
institution. And I should by no means advise the lower functionaries of the grocer's shop to follow the Constitutional example by locking out the grocer. A grocer's shop is a practical
thing, and therefore one has to consider feelings—especially the
grocer's feelings. The plain truth is that no practical institution
in this world would submit to what are called the practical working anomalies of the British Constitution. Really practical institutions know too much of the human heart ever to play tricks
with the human reason. The two things lie too near together.
In no business seriously intended to succeed would it ever be
arranged as a minor concession that the manager who was to be
obeyed during the rest of the day should be symbolically kicked
by the office-boy every morning on condition that the boot did
not actually touch his person. It would not much hurt the manager, though it might needlessly entertain the office-boy. But it
would be unpractical because it would be illogical. Exactly as
anomaly infringes authority so it infringes equality. If the office-
boy were merely allowed to give his harmless and abstract kick
to another office-boy, it would make all the difference; if the
other office-boy were paid a million pounds a-week, he still
could never be the superior.

This intellectually lawless element in our Constitution has
recently been growing more and more dangerous; it has the
danger of every lawless thing, that at last it becomes mean. Men
are no longer careless of their irrational system because it enables
them to do the right thing. They are now very careful of their
irrational system because (when deeply studied and dexterously
applied) it enables them to do the wrong thing. A strong case
of this is the increasing use of the quite absurd and atrocious
fiction commonly called the blocking motion. Jones wants to
move something; Brown does not want to move anything. But

Brown can stop Jones from saying what he wants to say by the power and importance of the thing which he, Brown, does not want to say. This is indecent in its folly; it would not be endured for an instant in any meeting of ordinary Zulus. Yet, for the past twenty years at least, this imbecile expedient has been constantly employed by both political parties whenever the Government did not wish to say something. But if the Government of a great nation does not wish to say something, I think that Government should say so. It is beneath the dignity of a European people that it should be saved from saying so by a motion about pink umbrellas which even the proposer of it does not propose. The thing hurts our dignity, and nothing shall persuade me that it does not hurt our morals.

May I remark, as a minor provocation to the intellect, that one of the paragraphs in my article last week was not written by me. I may add that it was entirely my own fault, like most other things that happen to me. I merely mention it here in order to state that any person detecting the correct paragraph will be rewarded with thirty-seven obsolete tram-tickets, four yards of potato-peeling, and one burnt match. I have no more to add.

March 14, 1908

Public Confessions by Politicians

A curious incident happened the other day, illustrating a curious principle. Men can confess separately and privately or generally and publicly. But no ordinary men ought to be asked to confess separately and publicly. It is very hard for a private man to make a public admission. Jones, Brown, and Robinson can all say in church, with complete sincerity, that they are miserable sinners. They are. They know it. But it is quite another matter to ask

Jones to say all by himself (his fine tenor voice ringing in the rafters) that he is a miserable sinner, while Brown and Robinson sit grinning at him. This principle may seem a mere piece of selfishness and vanity; yet, in truth, it rests on a very fair basis. To say that Jones has put sand in the sugar without mentioning the fact that in the whole of that Empire or civilisation there is no sugar without sand, is an unfair way of stating the case of Jones. It is true, but it is, in the strictest sense, a lie. It is as if we heard a man accused of being short of one leg, and then only discovered long afterwards that the accuser was a centipede. There is a real sin in being as bad as your society; but it is not the same sin as that of being deliberately worse than your society. If Jones is convicted of a crime he has no claim to be excused of it; but he has a claim to a bare statement touching whether his crime is as common as being cross or as rare as boiling one's mother in oil.

The chief nuisance of this world is that in the case of such common crimes each person or party hurls them at the other. And the chief practical discovery of Christianity was that it would be much more sensible if each person would hurl them at himself. Most merely worldly wisdom, most merely party politics, consist simply in the pot calling the kettle black. Christianity suggested that the efficiency of the kitchen might be greatly improved if both the pot and the kettle called themselves black. The great part of practical politics consists in calling our enemies scoundrels, and while it may be true of our enemies (it generally is) the disadvantage is that it becomes more and more true of ourselves. But the moment we have dropped the pretence of virtue we can get to the fact of it. The moment we agree that we are all scoundrels we can begin to talk like honest men. I ask the reader to imagine, if only for a moment, how happy, how reposeful, how reasonable, and how much released from petty sorrows all our dignified politicians and stately statesmen would become if for one moment they were allowed to base their whole case upon the plain truth that they are all scoundrels. The doctrine of original sin is the most kindly and genial of all doctrines. I

wonder whether the reader has ever noticed when dining with
his numerous friends in the Cabinet or the House of Lords, that
peculiar and painful expression which marks the great modern
English statesman. It is a curious expression of face; it is at once
unnaturally absent-minded and unnaturally vigilant; it is
abstracted and yet hard and strung tight, like that of a man in
pain; it combines all the sadness of the brooder with all the
morbid alertness of the man of business. It is a difficult expression
to decipher properly; but I have deciphered it. I know what that
powerful and concentrated look on the face of a Cabinet Minister
really means. It means that he is longing to burst into tears and
tell the truth.

Now, some few days ago he almost did it; he almost did it
in the House of Commons. All men thirst to confess their crimes
more than tired beasts thirst for water; but they naturally object
to confessing them while other people, who have also committed
the same crimes, sit by and laugh at them. The one really strong
case for Christianity is that even those who condemn sins have
to confess them. It is a good principle for Pharisees that he who
is without sin should cast the first stone. But it is the good
principle for Christians that he who casts the first stone should
declare that he is not without sin. The criminal may or may not
plead guilty. But the judge should always plead guilty.

There are many instances of the historical matter that I mean;
but if anyone has not come across it, here is a case. When people
attempt to defend (more and more feebly as time goes on) that
great *coup-d'etat* of Henry VIII. which did the two disastrous
things of abolishing the monasteries and founding the British
aristocracy, they commonly fall back on one class of facts. They
quote letters in which Bishops and Abbots of the age spoke with
the utmost loathing of the corruptions in the monasteries. They
discredit the Church with these criticisms. They never credit the
Church with criticising itself. They forget that as human institutions go, the Church was not peculiar in having evils, but
peculiar in admitting them. We all remember the old story of
the Irish pilot who took a gentleman's yacht into port, declaring

that he knew every rock in the harbour. A few minutes afterwards the vessel crashed upon an enormous crag, and when the owner cried angrily to the pilot, "But I thought you knew every rock in the harbour!" the pilot replied with equal freshness and indignation, "And so I do; and this is one of them." When Christianity splits on the rock of original evil she has a right to say that the rock is not marked down on any chart except her own. The sins of Christians are a doctrine of Christianity. But it is by no means true that the sins of Imperialists are a doctrine of Imperialism, or that the sins of Socialists are a doctrine of Socialism, or that the sins of the Worshipful Company of Candlestick-Makers are a record dogma of that institution. We do not lack abuses in the strict sense of that word; what we sadly lack is abuse, in the popular sense of it. We have not enough people to abuse the abuses. We do not lack what corresponds to the corrupt monastery; we lack what corresponds to the courageous and denunciatory priest. It is not that we have not got enough scoundrels to curse, but that we have not got enough good men to curse them—to curse them with that violence and variety which we have a right to expect.

But I have wandered from my first intention, which was to illustrate this from a recent scene in Parliament. It is a strong case of the fact that reform is commonly impeded by the dramatic interchange of accusations, while it might be advanced by a general chorus of confessions. Once (to take an old case first), Mr. Dillon called Mr. Chamberlain a liar, because Mr. Chamberlain had called him a good judge of traitors. In that special interchange of epithets Mr. Dillon[1] showed himself a gentleman, while Mr. Chamberlain showed himself—well, we will say a master of modern procedure. But what a comfort it would be to everyone if we could all fall back on the simple statements that we are all liars and all traitors. All men are liars; and David

[1] John Dillon (1851–1927), an Irish politician and a leader in the Irish Nationalist movement; he was known for his vituperative language and was suspended from Parliament for insulting Joseph Chamberlain by calling him a lair.

had no need to apologise for the remark or attribute it to his own temperamental impetuosity.[2] But though we are all liars, we all love truth. We are all traitors; we have all betrayed our country, or our country would not be what it is. But though we have all betrayed it, we all love it.

A Parliamentary resolution was moved by Mr. Belloc[3] which was, in the most powerful sense, a non-party motion. It regretted that both parties made use of secret funds. If this had been an attack upon somebody the trumpets would have blown, the hosts been set in order, and we should have heard above the whole battle-field the old metallic clash of the kettle and the pot. But though Mr. Belloc's attack was daring, it was not an attack on somebody. It was an attack on everybody; therefore, it could be welcomed by everybody. Sir Henry Campbell-Bannerman would repudiate a charge brought by Mr. Balfour; Mr. Balfour would repudiate a charge brought by Sir Henry. But Mr. Balfour and Sir Henry, standing hand in hand, would confess anything. This beautiful image might really have been achieved by Mr. Belloc's soothing influence. In the ordinary way Mr. Belloc is not what you might call a soothing person, but here he really tried to be gentle in order to encourage coy sinners from the two Front Benches to come forth. Then happened a most extraordinary thing, whether by accident or design. It may have been coincidence; it may have been the Cabinet; it may have been the Devil. But Mr. Buckmaster[4] moved an Amendment to the effect that while everybody was very bad, Tariff Reformers were especially bad. I need hardly say that this smashed all hopes of a general confession.

[2] See Psalm 116: "I said in my haste, All men are liars."

[3] Belloc's resolution of February 19 did express the "regret" of the secrecy of the funds, regarding such secrecy as "a peril to its privileges and character". Belloc feared that the public might not know why particular candidates were chosen, and whether any government action was free of the influence exerted by donors to the parties.

[4] Stanley O. Buckmaster was a Liberal M.P. who, as Chesterton hints, stood on both sides of many questions; thus, while he said he was for female suffrage, he deplored their current leadership and the disorder the movement was causing.

March 21, 1908

Popular Jokes and Vulgarity

I believe firmly in the value of all vulgar notions, especially of vulgar jokes. When once you have got hold of a vulgar joke, you may be certain that you have got hold of a subtle and spiritual idea. The men who made the joke saw something deep which they could not express except by something silly and emphatic. They saw something delicate which they could only express by something indelicate. I remember that Mr. Max Beerbohm[1] (who has every merit except democracy) attempted to analyse the jokes at which the mob laughs. He divided them into three sections: jokes about bodily humiliation, jokes about things alien, such as foreigners, and jokes about bad cheese. Mr. Max Beerbohm thought he understood the first two forms; but I am not sure that he did. In order to understand vulgar humour it is not enough to be humorous; one must also be vulgar, as I am. And in the first case it is surely obvious that it is not merely at the fact of something being hurt that we laugh (as I trust we do) when a Prime Minister sits down on his hat. If that were so we should laugh whenever we saw a funeral. We do not laugh at the mere fact of something falling down; there is nothing humorous about leaves falling or the sun going down. When our house falls down we do not laugh. All the birds of the air might drop around us in a perpetual shower like a hailstorm without arousing a smile. If you really ask yourself why we laugh at a man sitting down suddenly in the street you will discover that the reason is not only recondite, but ultimately religious. All the jokes about men sitting down on their hats are really theological jokes; they are concerned with the Dual Nature of Man. They refer to the

[1] Sir Henry Maximilian (Max) Beerbohm (1872–1956), an author, cartoonist and dramatic critic; he was considered by many to be the best essayist, parodist and cartoonist of his age.

primary paradox that man is superior to all the things around him and yet is at their mercy.

Quite equally subtle and spiritual is the idea at the back of laughing at foreigners. It concerns the dark and delicate conception of a thing being like oneself and yet not like oneself. Nobody laughs at what is entirely foreign; nobody laughs at a palm-tree. But it is funny to see the familiar image of God disguised behind the black beard of a Frenchman or the black face of a Negro. There is nothing funny in the sounds that are wholly inhuman, the howling of wild beasts or of the wind. But if a man begins to talk like oneself, but all the syllables seem different, then if one is a man one feels inclined to laugh, though if one is a gentleman one resists the inclination.

Mr. Max Beerbohm, I remember, professed to understand the first two forms of popular wit, but said that the third quite stumped him. He could not see why there should be anything funny about bad cheese. I can tell him at once. He has missed the idea because it is subtle and philosophical, and he was looking for something ignorant and foolish. Bad cheese is funny because it is (like the foreigner or the man fallen on the pavement) the type of the transition or transgression across a great mystical boundary. Bad cheese symbolises the change from the inorganic to the organic. Bad cheese symbolises the startling prodigy of matter taking on vitality. It symbolises the origin of life itself. And it is only about such solemn matters as the origin of life that the democracy condescends to joke. Thus, for instance, the democracy jokes about marriage, because marriage is a part of mankind. But the democracy would never deign to joke about Free Love, because Free Love is a piece of priggishness.

As a matter of fact, it will be generally found that the popular joke is not true to the letter, but is true to the spirit. The vulgar joke is generally in the oddest way the truth and yet not the fact. For instance, it is not in the least true that mothers-in-law are as a class oppressive and intolerable; most of them are both devoted and useful. All the mothers-in-law I have ever had were admirable. Yet the legend of the comic papers is profoundly true. It draws attention to the fact that it is much harder to be a nice mother-in-law than to be nice in any other conceivable relation of life. The caricatures have drawn the worst mother-in-law a monster, by way of expressing the fact that the best mother-in-law is a problem. The same is true of the perpetual jokes in comic papers about shrewish wives and henpecked husbands. It is all a frantic exaggeration, but it is an exaggeration of a truth; whereas all the modern mouthings about oppressed woman are the exaggerations of a falsehood. If you read even the best of the intellectuals of to-day you will find them saying that in the mass of the democracy the woman is the chattel of her lord, like his bath or his bed. But if you read the comic literature of the democracy you will find that the lord hides under the bed to escape from the wrath of his chattel. This is not the fact, but it is much nearer the truth. Every man who is married knows quite well not only that he does not regard his wife as a chattel, but that no man can conceivably have done so. The joke stands for an ultimate truth, and that is a subtle truth. It is one not very easy to state correctly. It can, perhaps, be most correctly stated by saying that, even if the man is the head of the house, he knows he is the figure-head.

But the vulgar comic papers are so subtle and true that they are even prophetic. If you really want to know what is going to happen to the future of our democracy, do not read the modern sociological prophecies, do not read even Mr. Wells's Utopias for this purpose, though you should certainly read them if you are fond of good honesty and good English. If you want to know what will happen, study the pages of *Snaps* or *Patchy Bits* as if they were the dark tablets graven with the oracles of the gods. For, mean and gross as they are, in all seriousness, they contain what is entirely absent from all Utopias and all the sociological conjectures of our time: they contain some hint of the actual habits and manifest desires of the English people. If we are really to find out what the democracy will ultimately do with itself, we shall surely find it, not in the literature which studies the people, but in the literature which the people studies.

I can give two clear cases in which the common or Cockney joke was a much better prophecy than the careful observations of the most cultured observer. When England was agitated, previous to the last General Election, about the existence of Chinese labour, there was a distinct difference between the tone of the politicians and the tone of the populace. The politicians who disapproved of Chinese labour were most careful to explain that they did not in any sense disapprove of Chinese. According to them, it was a pure question of legal propriety, of whether certain clauses in the contract of indenture were not inconsistent with our constitutional traditions: according to them, the case would have been the same if the people had been Kaffirs or Englishmen. It all sounded wonderfully enlightened and lucid; and in comparison the popular joke looked, of course, very poor. For the popular joke against the Chinese labourers[2] was simply that they were Chinese; it was an objection to an alien type; the popular papers were full of gibes about pigtails and yellow faces. It seemed that the Liberal politicians were raising an intellectual objection to a doubtful document of State; while it seemed that the Radical populace were merely roaring with idiotic laughter at the sight of a Chinaman's clothes. But the popular instinct was justified by the Chinaman's vices.

But there is another case more pleasant and more up to date. The popular papers always persisted in representing the New Woman or the Suffragette as an ugly woman, fat, in spectacles, with bulging clothes, and generally falling off a bicycle. As a matter of plain external fact, there was not a word of truth in this. The leaders of the movement of female emancipation are not at all ugly; most of them are extraordinarily good-looking.

---

[2] Mine owners in the Transvaal, South Africa, had convinced the government to permit the importation of large numbers of Chinese laborers to work the mines; during off hours, they were to live in what were virtual concentration camps. The system scandalized Great Britain, offending particularly the labor movement. It was not until 1910 that the last of these "slaves" were sent back to China, but by then the system had become very controversial.

Nor are they at all indifferent to art or decorative costume; many of them are disgustingly attached to these things. Yet the popular instinct was right. For the popular instinct was that in this movement, rightly or wrongly, there was an element of indifference to female dignity, of a quite new willingness of women to be grotesque. These women did truly despise the pontifical quality of woman. And in our streets and around our Parliament we have seen the stately woman of art and culture turn into the comic woman of *Comic Bits*. And whether we think the exhibition justifiable or not, the prophecy of the comic papers is justified: the healthy and vulgar masses were conscious of a hidden enemy to their traditions who has now come out into the daylight, that the scriptures might be fulfilled. For the two things that a healthy person hates most between heaven and hell are a woman who is not dignified and a man who is.

March 28, 1908

Joan of Arc and Modern Materialism

A considerable time ago (at far too early an age, in fact) I read Voltaire's "La Pucelle," a savage sarcasm on the traditional purity of Joan of Arc, very dirty, and very funny. I had not thought of it again for years, but it came back into my mind this morning because I began to turn over the leaves of the new "Jeanne d'Arc," by that great and graceful writer, Anatole France. It is written in a tone of tender sympathy, and a sort of sad reverence; it never loses touch with a noble tact and courtesy, like that of a gentleman escorting a peasant girl through the modern crowd. It is invariably respectful to Joan, and even respectful to her religion. And being myself a furious admirer of Joan the Maid,

I have reflectively compared the two methods, and I come to the conclusion that I prefer Voltaire's.

When a man of Voltaire's school has to explode a saint or a great religious hero, he says that such a person is a common human fool, or a common human fraud. But when a man like Anatole France has to explode a saint, he explains a saint as somebody belonging to his particular fussy little literary set. Voltaire read human nature into Joan of Arc, though it was only the brutal part of human nature. At least it was not specially Voltaire's nature. But M. France read M. France's nature into Joan of Arc—all the cold kindness, all the homeless sentimentalism of the modern literary man. There is one book that it recalled to me with startling vividness, though I have not seen the matter mentioned anywhere; Renan's "Vie de Jesus." It has just the same general intention: that if you do not attack Christianity, you can at least patronise it. My own instinct, apart from my opinions, would be quite the other way. If I disbelieved in Christianity, I should be the loudest blasphemer in Hyde Park. Nothing ought to be too big for a brave man to attack; but there are some things too big for a man to patronise.

And I must say that the historical method seems to me excessively unreasonable. I have no knowledge of history, but I have as much knowledge of reason as Anatole France. And, if anything is irrational, it seems to me that the Renan-France way of dealing with miraculous stories is irrational. The Renan-France method is simply this: you explain supernatural stories that have some foundation simply by inventing natural stories that have no foundation. Suppose that you are confronted with the statement that Jack climbed up the beanstalk into the sky. It is perfectly philosophical to reply that you do not think that he did. It is (in my opinion) even more philosophical to reply that he may very probably have done so. But the Renan-France method is to write like this: "When we consider Jack's curious and even perilous heredity, which no doubt was derived from a female greengrocer and a profligate priest, we can easily understand how the ideas of heaven and a beanstalk came to be combined in his mind. Moreover, there is little doubt that he must have met some wandering conjurer from India, who told him about the tricks of the mango plant, and how it is sent up to the sky. We can imagine these two friends, the old man and the young, wandering in the woods together at evening, looking at the red and level clouds, as on that night when the old man pointed to a small beanstalk, and told his too imaginative companion that this also might be made to scale the heavens. And then, when we remember the quite exceptional psychology of Jack, when we remember how there was in him a union of the prosaic, the love of plain vegetables, with an almost irrelevant eagerness for the unattainable, for invisibility and the void, we shall no longer wonder that it was to him especially that was sent this sweet, though merely symbolic, dream of the tree uniting earth and heaven." That is the way that Renan and France write, only they do it better. But, really, a rationalist like myself becomes a little impatient and feels inclined to say, "But, hang it all, what do you know about the heredity of Jack or the psychology of Jack? You know nothing about Jack at all, except that some people say that he climbed up a beanstalk. Nobody would ever have thought of mentioning him if he hadn't. You must interpret him in terms of the beanstalk religion; you cannot merely interpret religion in terms of him. We have the materials of this story, and we can believe them or not. But we have not got the materials to make another story."

It is no exaggeration to say that this is the manner of M. Anatole France in dealing with Joan of Arc. Because her miracle is incredible to his somewhat old-fashioned materialism, he does not therefore dismiss it and her to fairyland with Jack and the Beanstalk. He tries to invent a real story, for which he can find no real evidence. He produces a scientific explanation which is quite destitute of any scientific proof. It is as if I (being entirely ignorant of botany and chemistry) said that the beanstalk grew to the sky because nitrogen and argon got into the subsidiary ducts of the corolla. To take the most obvious example, the principal character in M. France's story is a person who never

existed at all. All Joan's wisdom and energy, it seems, came from
a certain priest, of whom there is not the tiniest trace in all the
multitudinous records of her life. The only foundation I can find
for this fancy is the highly undemocratic idea that a peasant girl
could not possibly have any ideas of her own. It is very hard
for a freethinker to remain democratic. The writer seems altogether to forget what is meant by the moral atmosphere of a
community. To say that Joan must have learnt her vision of a
virgin overthrowing evil from *a* priest, is like saying that some
modern girl in London, pitying the poor, must have learnt it
from *a* Labour Member. She would learn it where the Labour
Member learnt it—in the whole state of our society.

But that is the modern method: the method of the reverent
sceptic. When you find a life entirely incredible and incomprehensible from the outside, you pretend that you understand the
inside. As Renan, the rationalist, could not make any sense out
of Christ's most public acts, he proceeded to make an ingenious
system out of His private thoughts. As Anatole France, on his
own intellectual principle, cannot believe in what Joan of Arc
did, he professes to be her dearest friend and to know exactly
what she meant. I cannot feel it to be a very rational manner of
writing history; and sooner or later we shall have to find some
more solid way of dealing with those spiritual phenomena with
which all history is as closely spotted and spangled as the sky is
with stars.

Joan of Arc is a wild and wonderful thing enough, but she is
much saner than most of her critics and biographers. We shall
not recover the commonsense of Joan until we have recovered
her mysticism. Our wars fail, because they begin with something
sensible and obvious—such as getting to Pretoria by Christmas.[1]
But her war succeeded—because it began with something wild

---

[1] A goal (it quickly became a public slogan) of the English military in the fall
of 1899, immediately after the outbreak of the Boer War. A series of humiliating
defeats under the leadership of Sir Redvers H. Buller quickly dispelled the anticipation and the slogan.

and perfect—the saints delivering France. She put her idealism in the right place, and her realism also in the right place: we moderns get both displaced. She put her dreams and her sentiment into her aims, where they ought to be; she put her practicality into her practice. In modern Imperial wars, the case is reversed. Our dreams, our aims are always, we insist, quite practical. It is our practice that is dreamy.

It is not for us to explain this flaming figure in terms of our tired and querulous culture. Rather we must try to explain ourselves by the blaze of such fixed stars. Those who called her a witch hot from hell were much more sensible than those who depict her as a silly sentimental maiden prompted by her parish priest. If I have to choose between the two schools of her scattered enemies, I could take my place with those subtle clerks who thought her divine mission devilish, rather than with those rustic aunts and uncles who thought it impossible.

April 4, 1908

New Religion and New Irreligion

Our generation professes to be scientific and particular about the things it says; but unfortunately it is never scientific and particular about the words in which it says them. It is difficult to believe that people who are obviously careless about language can really be very careful about anything else. If an astronomer is careless about words, one cannot help fancying that he may be careless about stars. If a botanist is vague about words, he may be vague about plants. The modern man, regarding himself as a second Adam, has undertaken to give all the creatures new names; and when we discover that he is silly about the names, the thought will cross our minds that he may be silly about the creatures. And never before, I should imagine, in the intellectual history of the world have words been used with so idiotic an indifference to their actual meaning. A word has no loyalty; it can be betrayed into any service or twisted to any treason. There has arisen an intolerable habit of using special and partisan terms with words like "true" or "nobler" put in front of them. I see in a Liberal daily paper such a sentence as this: "We are concerned with that higher and nobler Imperialism which devotes itself solely to the destiny of the poor at our own doors." I see in a Conservative daily paper something like this: "The so-called Liberals—who are, indeed, only demagogues—may ramp and roar; we appeal to that truer Liberalism which is expressed in submission to a patriotic discipline, in trust in a patriotic monarchy, and in defence of a patriotic House of Lords." Then recent religious teachers will cry out—"I am for that real Christianity which can do without help from a supernatural world, that truer Christianity which does not believe in God or any such symbolic dogma." In the same way the people who believe in Protection tell us that they are "the true Free Traders." And if the Parliamentary wheel takes another turn we shall no doubt hear the Free Traders saying that they, after all, are the "true" Protectionists. A true Free Trader is a man who believes in import duties; a true Christian is a man who does not believe in Christ.

Really, I do not see why I should not carry this principle to any length whatever. I cannot see why I should not call myself a true Mahometan because I believe in Christianity, or a true Confucian because I do not believe in Confucius, that fine but pharisaical agnostic. Or one might say (speaking of some trade dispute in the neighbourhood), "Jones was a greengrocer—he was a greengrocer in the purest and highest sense. He was that best type of greengrocer who sells boots for the benefit of humanity." Or if a house has been burgled by a man dressed up as a policeman, we might say, "And was he not indeed a policeman? May he not have had the policeman's essence, the care for mankind, the appeal to eternal law, more perfectly than any common constable on the beat? Is not every man, in a sense, a policeman? Is he not set as a silent watch over society, etc., etc." Or again, if the burglar had dressed up as a chimney-sweep, it might be said by someone who loved him, "And who could be more a chimney-sweep than he who devotes himself to eternal truth? What man has more right to call himself a chimney-sweep than he whose eyes have ever been fixed upon a vision of happiness beyond the world? In the sense, surely, we are all chimney-sweeps, etc., etc." It is all very earnest and emotional, and for all I know it may mean something. But I think that an ordinary poor person in the Battersea High Road would pay the tax to a man who said he was the tax-collector; but would certainly refuse it to the man who said he was the *true* tax-collector.

The fact is, that all this evasive use of words is unworthy of our human intellect. To concentrate political attention on the tortured population of England is not "sane Imperialism." It is sane anti-Imperialism; and more power to its elbow! To put a special trust in the tact of the Monarchy or in the commonsense of the House of Lords may or may not be rational, but it is not Liberal; it is not any kind of Liberalism, true or false. A man who desires to erect import duties at all the ports of his country is not "a true Free Trader," but a perfectly reasonable Protectionist. And a man who thinks that men can get on perfectly well with the secular emotions of kindness and aspiration is not "a true Christian," but a perfectly reasonable agnostic.

If we are to look for a new religion or a new irreligion, I think we might at least keep our eyes clear to look for it, our heads clear to understand what it means. If we are to dissect historic religion, we might at least clean our knives; if we are to look out for a new Star of Bethlehem, we might at least clean our telescopes. But in this matter words are our knives, words are our telescopes. And we have not made any effort to clean our words at all, to wash off them all the alien substances of habitual sophistry and sentimental misuse. The modern man who prides himself on looking the world in the face and seeing what it means does not look one single word in the face and see what that means. Those very men who most boldly reject the creeds are those who most meekly accept the words of which creeds are made.

Here is one case out of a hundred of the utterly thoughtless way in which "advanced" people use their phrases; they never think of their words as they use them, or look at them as they write them down. I quote this passage from an interesting interview with the Rev. R. J. Campbell in the current *Review of Reviews*. The interviewer is trying to persuade Mr. Campbell that he, Mr. Campbell, is a Christian. Mr. Campbell, on the other hand, maintains that he, Mr. Campbell, is a true Christian. The interviewer smells danger in this discussion, and goes swiftly on—

"Now I go to the next phrase: 'transcendent as Maker and Ruler of all things.' "

"I do not like that phrase," said Mr. Campbell.

"But," said I, "why?"

"It is an attempt to define the indefinable."

"That is exactly what they mean when they say it is transcendent, as it transcends or is beyond our limited capacity to define it."

"Yes, you can take it in that way," said Mr. Campbell.

"Of course I will take it in that way," I said, "and you would not object to 'the Maker and Ruler of all things.' Although you dislike the phrase, how would you phrase it?"

"As the Source of Life and the Author of the universal law of being."

Now, supposing (I admit the dangers of an interview) supposing that Mr. Campbell said this, what on earth did he mean by it? If it is wrong to "define the indefinable," why did he go on immediately to define it himself? If God must not be defined as a Maker, why should He be defined as a fountain, like the fountains in Trafalgar Square? If He may not be called "The Maker of the World," as Chaucer was called the "Maker" of "The Legend of Good Women," why should it be more philosophical to call Him the "Author" of the world, as Mr. Cutcliffe

Hyne[1] is called the author of "Captain Kettle"? If it is right to call God the author of a universal law, how can it be wrong to call Him a Ruler? "Author" is only the Latin for a maker. "Ruler" is only the English for the author of a rule. But the fact is that Mr. Campbell has excellent brains, but thinks it more advanced and modern not to use them, as indeed it is. He is guided in his choice of phrases by mere aimless sentimentalism; he likes the phrase "Source of Life," because it sounds harmless and journalistic; and he dislikes the phrase "Maker and Ruler," because he recalls a time of clearer and stronger thoughts. Of all the expressions of our current indifference to the meaning of the words, I think that the most irritating is this cool substitution of one kind of definition for another. We must not (it seems) define the absolute as a person, which is the highest thing we know, but we may define it as a fountain, or a lamp, or a wheel, or a tree, or a piece of clockwork, or anything we see lying about. We may define the *anima mundi* as long as we define it as inanimate. We may describe the life of the universe as long as we describe the life of the universe as dead. I cannot see why I have not as good a right to say that God is a Ruler as Mr. Campbell has to say that He is a River; neither of us has seen God at any time. But this fallacy of the inanimate symbol, so dear to Pantheists, is very common in modern literature, and greater men than Mr. Campbell have undoubtedly fallen into it.

April 11, 1908

The Licensing Bill and Big Business

In certain debating clubs and in certain newspaper columns one has to submit to the veto that forbids anyone to mention

---

[1] Charles John Cutliffe Wright Hyne (1865–1944), the author of a number of adventure stories, of which the most popular and most frequently reprinted was *The Adventures of Captain Kettle* (1898).

party politics. I am not at all surprised at the veto, but I am very much surprised at the reason given for it. For it is generally said that party politics are undesirable because they are so exciting: it seems that they stir men's passions to the point of apoplexy. Now, if I believed that, I should talk nothing but party politics all day long. If party politics really inflame men, they must be as noble as music. But I object to party politics, not because they are exceptionally exciting, but because they are exceptionally dull. As a point of pure religion, I deny that any man is a bore. How can such an earthquake as the image of God in dust (literally an earthquake, for it is a cloud of dust shaken up into a shocking miracle of life and taking on a terrible shape), how can such a prodigy ever be a bore? But of all the times when I have seen this dreadful creature Man almost (as for an instant) in danger of being dull, he has never seemed so near it as when he was making remarks about party politics. A man should now avoid the topic of Tories and Radicals, not for fear of making men howl, but for fear of making them yawn. Practical politics are now quite dull—nay, they are quite unpractical. The only things worth worrying about just at present are unpractical politics. In fact, if you hear a leading politician say that something is "outside the sphere of practical politics" you may be certain that that thing is not only actual, but rather urgent.

For this reason I will not be drawn into the particular kind of debate into which many correspondents have desired to draw me. I have received letters from many readers of this paper asking me to rally to this or that flag in the discussion of the present Licensing Bill, and reminding me of articles I have before written in this page on the subject of Beer. I have always been ready, and am still ready, to state my politics on this topic; and, if they are not party politics, it is not my fault. It is the fault of the two huge, lumbering, half-witted parties, like one-eyed elephants, which will not choose their policy with any reference to intelligible principles. I have an intelligible principle. I detest and would destroy all tyrannical minorities; therefore I have an equally hearty hatred for brewers and for teetotalers. I would not deny the normal rights of either. I greatly objected when some people in Manchester said that a Mayor was not a Mayor because he was a Brewer. I should equally object to anybody who said that a Mayor was not a Mayor because he was not a Teetotaler. But I do most indignantly object to the abnormal rights or powers of both; to the influence which they exercise merely through being rich, or fashionable, or fussy, or "in the know." I object strongly to the abnormal influence exercised by a few rich tee-totalers, Puritans, Quakers, and so on, over the policy of the Liberal party. And I object equally to the influence of a few rich men over the policy of the public-houses. The principle is exactly the same in both cases. I object to a few wealthy Puritans deciding that I shall drink ginger beer instead of Bass's beer. I object also to a few wealthy Peers deciding that I shall drink Bass's beer instead of Tompkins' beer, or my own beer. If a few oligarchs can pay chemists to make a chemical change in the substantial drink of our people, it is really indifferent to me whether they alter beer by making it non-alcoholic, or by making it poison-ously and detestably alcoholic. In neither case can I, walking into the ordinary bar, get the thing I should like.

Let us put one side of the matter first. There is no doubt that this problem is enormously complicated by the presence of that extreme sect which disapproves of the ordinary drinks of Chris-tian civilisation upon some mystical ground which I am not here concerned to follow. Any attack on the brewing monopoly as a monopoly has been heavily handicapped by the fact that there are some people who object on principle not only to the modern spectacle of a brewer, but to the ancient spectacle of brewing. If the teetotalers really want to know who have frustrated Li-censing Reform for the last forty years, it is not the House of Lords, or even the brewers; it is they themselves. They have given an impression that the war is not against a monopoly in a certain healthy substance, but against the substance itself. Any-one can see how this would have upset the attack on any monop-oly. There was once, I believe, a monopoly in silk. If its opponents had called silk wicked, there would still be a monopoly in silk.

When Parliament protested against the monopolies of Elizabeth, one member sarcastically asked if bread had not become a monopoly. Obviously, the Queen would have had a very good retort if she could have answered: "And why should you reproach me with limiting bread when half your friends wish to abolish bread?" So the brewers may rationally answer that the people who blame them for monopolising beer wish to abolish beer. A little while ago, there was a just and powerful protest against the monopolist power of the water companies. But that protest would not have been so just, and certainly not so powerful, if half the protestors had disapproved of the use of water. It would not have been easy to maintain that the children in the East End had not enough water to wash in, if one were also maintaining that it would be wicked to wash in it. It would not have been easy to blame a group of tyrants, first for holding back all the water, and then for giving it away. Yet this is practically the position in which the temperance party has placed itself by attempting to combine the war on an oligarchic privilege with the war on a democratic practice.

But having granted this side of the matter, the other side of it remains at least as heavy, if not rather heavier. If teetotalers have largely crippled the case for temperance legislation, it is even more true that brewers have practically ruined the case for beer. And the moral advantage in the comparison certainly lies with the teetotalers. They have sought to destroy beer because they know nothing about it, and sincerely believe it to be a flaming drink of devils. But brewers have destroyed beer because they know too much about it; they knew quite well that it was not a flaming drink of devils, but they have done their best to make it so. There may be people who like the least possible touch of prussic acid in their tea; there may be people who think that a plum-cake is better without any real plums in it, but dotted all over with certain artificial chemical plums invented by some Prussian doctor. There are people who think that chemical beer has all the taste of real beer. These are people who think that a gas-stove serves all the purposes of a Christian fireplace. There is no lack of funny people running about. But if you are talking about any actual ancient thing, like fire or ale, it is perfectly useless to refer the matter to men of science. It is especially useless if you ask them to test the things without telling them what they are to be tested for. Doubtless chemical beer is so combined as to avoid certain particular poisons which the doctors have just discovered, or to prevent certain particular diseases of which they are making a hobby just now. All I say is that it does not answer the manifold and almost mystical purposes of beer.

To recur to the other case, go to the man who likes gas-stoves (if such a man there be) and ask him what he thinks a fire is *for*. If he thinks that a fire is for the sake of heat, dismiss him with derision to his doom. He will have heat enough if his spiritual ruin is at all parallel to his intellectual. Every sound human institution has at least four different objects and different justifications. Man was never so silly as to sit down on a one-legged stool. All his supports are quadrupedal. A man's fireside, the open fire on his hearth, is delightful for all kinds of different reasons. It does, among other things, heat the room; but it also lights the room. It looks beautiful. You can roast chestnuts at it. You can see pictures in it. You can toast muffins at it. If you happen (as is no doubt the case) to be a Parsee, you can worship it. You can, with dexterity, light your pipe at it; you can tell ghost-stories round it, with Rembrandtesque effects. If a man gives me heat instead of a fire, I am no more satisfied than if he gave me little red pictures instead of a fire, because I can see them in the coals. I want a fire; not one of the uses of a fire. Exactly similar is the whole problem of artificial beer. If you are to have this thing in its original healthiness, you must have it as it is handed down by simple people in small communities; you must not have it as it is altered by every well-meaning chemist. We shall never have any real brewing until we have destroyed the brewers.

April 18, 1908

Shakspere and Zola

The difference between two great nations can be illustrated by
the coincidence that at this moment both France and England
are engaged in discussing the memorial of a literary man. France
is considering the celebration of the late Zola, England is considering that of the recently defunct Shakspere. There is some
national significance, it may be, in the time that has elapsed.
Some will find impatience and indelicacy in this early attack on
Zola or deification of him; but the nation which has sat still for
three hundred years after Shakspere's funeral may be considered,
perhaps, to have carried delicacy too far. But much deeper things
are involved than the mere matter of time. The point of the
contrast is that the French are discussing whether there shall be
any monument, while the English are discussing only what the
monument shall be. In other words, the French are discussing
a living question, while we are discussing a dead one. Or rather,
not a dead one, but a settled one, which is quite a different thing.
When a thing of the intellect is settled it is not dead: rather it is
immortal. The multiplication table is immortal, and so is the
fame of Shakspere. But the fame of Zola is not dead or not
immortal; it is at its crisis, it is in the balance; and may be found
wanting. The French, therefore, are quite right in considering
it a living question. It is still living as a question, because it is
not yet solved. But Shakspere is not a living question: he is a
living answer.

For my part, therefore, I think the French Zola controversy
much more practical and exciting than the English Shakspere
one. The admission of Zola to the Pantheon may be regarded
as defining Zola's position. But nobody could say that a statue
of Shakspere, even fifty feet high, on the top of St. Paul's Cathedral, could define Shakspere's position. It only defines our position towards Shakspere. It is he who is fixed; it is we who are
unstable. The nearest approach to an English parallel to the Zola

case would be furnished it if were proposed to put some savagely
controversial and largely repulsive author among the ashes of
the greatest English poets. Suppose, for instance, it were proposed to bury Mr. Rudyard Kipling in Westminster Abbey. I
should be against burying him in Westminster Abbey: first,
because he is still alive (and here I think even he himself might
admit the justice of my protest); and second, because I should
like to reserve that rapidly narrowing space for the great permanent examples, not for the interesting foreign interruptions,
of English literature. I would not have either Mr. Kipling or
Mr. George Moore in Westminster Abbey, though Mr. Kipling
has certainly caught even more cleverly than Mr. Moore the
lucid and cool cruelty of the French short story. I am very sure
that Geoffrey Chaucer and Joseph Addison get on very well
together in the Poets' Corner, despite the centuries that sunder
them. But I feel that Mr. George Moore would be much happier
in Père-la-Chaise,[1] with a riotous statue by Rodin on the top of
him; and Mr. Kipling much happier under some huge Asiatic
monument, carved with all the cruelties of the gods.

As to the affair of the English monument to Shakspere, every
people has its own mode of commemoration, and I think there
is a great deal to be said for ours. There is the French monumental
style, which consists in erecting very pompous statues, very well
done. There is the German monumental style, which consists in
erecting very pompous statues, badly done. And there is the
English monumental method, the great English way with statues, which consists in not erecting them at all. A statue may be
dignified; but the absence of a statue is always dignified. For my
part, I feel that there is something national, something whole-
somely symbolic, in the fact that there is no statue of Shakspere.
There is, of course, one in Leicester Square; but the very place

---

[1] This really refers to Père Lachaise, a great Parisian cemetery. Originally the
site of a religious settlement founded in 1626 by the Jesuits, it was later enlarged
by Père Lachaise, the confessor of Louis XIV. The grounds were turned into a
cemetery after the French Revolution.

where it stands shows that it was put up by a foreigner for foreigners. There is surely something modest and manly about not attempting to express our greatest poet in the plastic arts in which we do not excel. We honour Shakspere as the Jews honoured God—by not daring to make of him a graven image. Our sculpture, our statues, are good enough for bankers and philanthropists, who are our curse: not good enough for him, who is our benediction. Why should we celebrate the very art in which we triumph by the very art in which we fail?

England is most easily understood as the country of amateurs. It is especially the country of amateur soldiers (that is, of Volunteers), of amateur statesmen (that is, of aristocrats), and it is not unreasonable or out of keeping that it should be rather specially the country of a careless and lounging view of literature. Shakspere has no academic monument for the same reason that he had no academic education. He had small Latin and less Greek, and (in the same spirit) he has never been commemorated in Latin epitaphs or Greek marble. If there is nothing clear and fixed about the emblems of his fame, it is because there was nothing clear and fixed about the origins of it. Those great schools and Universities which watch a man in his youth may record him in his death; but Shakspere had no such unifying traditions. We can only say of him what we can say of Dickens. We can only say that he came from nowhere and that he went everywhere. For him a monument in any place is out of place. A cold statue in a certain square is unsuitable to him as it would be unsuitable to Dickens. If we put up a statue of Dickens in Portland Place to-morrow we should feel the stiffness as unnatural. We should fear that the statue might stroll about the street at night.

But in France the question of whether Zola shall go to the Pantheon when he is dead is quite as practical as the question whether he should go to prison when he was alive. It is the problem of whether the nation shall take one turn of thought or another. In raising a monument to Zola they do not raise merely a trophy, but a finger-post. The question is one which will have to be settled in most European countries; but like all such questions, it has come first to a head in France; because France is the battlefield of Christendom. That question is, of course, roughly this: whether in that ill-defined area of verbal license on certain dangerous topics it is an extenuation of indelicacy or an aggravation of it that the indelicacy was deliberate and solemn. Is indecency more indecent if it is grave, or more indecent if it is gay? For my part, I belong to an old school in this matter. When a book or play strikes me as a crime, I am not disarmed by being told that it is a serious crime. If a man has written something vile, I am not comforted by the explanation that he quite meant to do it. I know all the evils of flippancy; I do not like the man who laughs at the sight of virtue. But I prefer him to the man who weeps at the sight of virtue and complains bitterly of there being any such thing. I am not reassured, when ethics are as wild as cannibalism, by the fact that they are also as grave and sincere as suicide. And I think there is an obvious fallacy in the bitter contrasts drawn by some moderns between the aversion to Ibsen's "Ghosts" and the popularity of some such joke as "Dear Old Charlie." Surely there is nothing mysterious or unphilosophic in the popular preference. The joke of "Dear Old Charlie" is passed—because it is a joke. "Ghosts" are exorcised—because they are ghosts.

This is, of course, the whole question of Zola. I am grown up, and I do not worry myself much about Zola's immorality. The thing I cannot stand is his morality. If ever a man on this earth lived to embody the tremendous text, "But if the light in your body be darkness, how great is the darkness," it was certainly he. Great men like Ariosto, Rabelais, and Shakspere fall in foul places, flounder in violent but venial sin, sprawl for pages, exposing their gigantic weakness, are dirty, are indefensible; and then they struggle up again and can still speak with a convincing kindness and an unbroken honour of the best things in the world: Rabelais, of the instruction of ardent and austere youth; Ariosto, of holy chivalry; Shakspere, of the splendid stillness of mercy. But in Zola even the ideals are undesirable; Zola's mercy is colder than justice—nay, Zola's mercy is more bitter in the mouth than injustice. When Zola shows us an ideal training he does not take us, like Rabelais, into the happy fields of humanist learning. He takes us into the school of inhumanist learning, where there are neither books nor flowers, nor wine nor wisdom, but only deformities in glass bottles, and where the rule is taught from the exceptions. Zola's truth answers the exact description of the skeleton in the cupboard; that is, it is something of which a domestic custom forbids the discovery, but which is quite dead, even when it is discovered. Macaulay said that the Puritans hated bear-baiting, not because it gave pain to the bear, but because it gave pleasure to the spectators. Of such substance also was this Puritan who had lost his God.

April 25, 1908

The Fiercer Suffragettes

A certain lady has written me a stern letter about some remarks I made in this column, in which (as she holds) I dealt too flippantly with the fiercer kind of Suffragette. I am not much concerned with the sham fight which a foolish modernity has got up between the sexes. I am not interested in a duel between a knife and a fork. Nobody ever doubted that a knife and a fork were equal; but it may still be maintained that a fork makes a poor knife, and that a knife is not up to much considered as a fork. But as I detest flippancy more than anything, and as I like fanaticism more than most things, I am not indifferent to the charge of being flippant at the expense of splendid fanatics. But I do not think that these people are fanatics in the true sense, or that their enemies are flippant in the true sense. And yet if I set out to explain my reasons for this, I cannot deny that the explanation might be a long business; it deals with the deepest and most tangled roots of the soul. Nevertheless, to satisfy my correspondent, I will attempt to explain why the violence of the Suffragettes impresses me hardly more than the violence of a drunken man. But I postulate first the ordinary human idea of the equality and diversity of the sexes. If a knife and fork had souls, it would not be unreasonable to suppose that their souls would be of a slightly different shape, like their bodies.

The fundamental fact may perhaps be approached in this way. Some time ago a lady bicyclist effected an astonishing and almost heroic ride across some great stretch of Great Britain. Riding with much of the energy of a man, she bore pain with all the endurance of a woman; but at the end of her journey she was found sitting on a bank and crying because the blind in the cottage opposite was crooked. Now, that story is one which literally rends the heart. It is not only full of tragedy, but it has all the dignity of tragedy. It has the piercing pathos of the female thirst for beauty and order; and a man who has realised its significance will seldom smoke in the drawing-room, and always wipe his boots on the mat. This female love of cleanliness and an artistic purity is not a foppery or an affectation. Women care about small things even when they are tortured by the greatest things. They call upon beauty in their agony as the girl did in front of the cottage. That the blind was bent was more to her than whether all her own bones were bent. It has something to do with their ultimate function, with the fact that they are the priestesses of education and the guards of the ordered enclosure of the home. Therefore, when your wife tells you that she hates a certain waistcoat or cannot endure a certain wall-paper, you may be impatient, but you have no doubt about her being in earnest. You do not call her an aesthete; you call her a nuisance. That is, you recognise the nuisance as a reality: as something that comes out of the depth of the human emotions. You know that it is all a part of her pathetic feeling towards the world—

> Would we not shatter it to bits, and then
> Remould it nearer to the heart's desire?[1]

[1] See "The Rubáiyát" of Omar Khayyám, XCIX.

Now about the time when I was a boy, there arose and flourished a race of men who affected to have this feminine sensibility.
They called themselves artists; other people called them aesthetes, and many other names much less polite. But the essence
of their position was that they professed that the aesthetic motive
was with them primary and dominant, as is the moral motive,
or the mercantile motive, with most men. They professed that
debased Tudor architecture gave them a pain, an eye-ache as
definite as a tooth-ache, as sacred as a heart-ache. It was a graceful
social accomplishment to be slightly unwell at the sight of a
Kidderminster carpet.[2] Big, well-fed men swooned and stag-
gered when they saw the right picture in the wrong frame. Now
this exhibition of sensibility never impressed me for a moment;
and the point is that it would never have impressed me, however
fiercely it had been uttered or however far it had gone. If a
gentleman had sprung out of a house without a hat and run
screaming down the street, having caught sight of the linoleum
in the front hall, I should still have felt no pity for him. If a
man, on being shown an original Guido Reni,[3] had fallen down
on the floor and foamed at the mouth, my demeanour would
still have left me open to the charge of flippancy. It did not
impress me, because I knew it was an artificial excitement. The
women really felt; the men only imagined that it would be fun
to feel like the women. If anyone has any doubt that there was
this sex-imitation behind masculine aestheticism let him remember that the tricks and decorations of women were actually imitated. Men carried fans and elaborately arranged their curls. One
of the writers of the time painted his face. One of the painters
of the time wore a ribbon in his hair.

Let us, however, return to the fresh air. The only purpose of
my comparison is to explain this; that I was not pierced with

[2] Kidderminster is a market town northwest of London, chiefly celebrated
for its carpets.
[3] Guido Reni (1575–1642) was one of the foremost masters of the Bolognese
school of painting and one of the most admired artists of his day in Italy.

any pathos at the quiverings and contortions of the aesthetes, because I thought that at the bottom the whole thing was a self-conscious lark. It had no root, as had the tragic sensibility of the woman. The man was trying to exaggerate his desire for daintiness; the unhappy woman was trying to restrain hers. With her it was an elemental hunger; therefore, like all true love, it brought with it shame. With him it was an overcivilised fantasy; and therefore it brought with it that product of over-civilisation—shamelessness. For it is only in complex civilisation that decorum is ever disregarded: barbarians are always decorous.

The masculine violence of the Suffragettes affects me precisely in the same way as the feminine touchiness of aesthetes; that is, it does not affect me at all. As a sort of symbolic joke, an acted paradox, there may be something in it; but not as an exhibition of elementary human passion. The Suffragettes are intellectually sincere, as the aesthetes were intellectually sincere in their own way. The Suffragettes have an arguable case, as the aesthetes had an arguable case. But there the matter ends; I am no more moved by the fists and clubs of a mob consisting of ladies than I should by the tears of Mr. Postlethwaite in *Punch*. For I am quite certain of this: that, though in both cases the person may be really excited, in both cases the person is excited by doing something odd or alien, not by doing something native and characteristic. It is not emotion, which is unconscious, but sentiment, which is conscious. Mrs. Pankhurst is not a woman of passion: she is a woman of sentiment. I am quite certain that she is not acting as she would if (in any real private tragedy) she wished to impress her personality on another person. I am sure that if a man (because he was in love or because he was starving) *really* wanted to show his value, he would not tie a ribbon in his hair. And I am sure that if a woman, under any deep provocation, *really* wanted to remind the world of her importance, she would not go and fight a policeman. The moment she was really angry she would use her own weapons, which are the most terrible in the world; just as the moment an aesthetic man was really in love he would leave off dressing up as a woman. If, instead of a few women

boxing and wrestling for the Suffrage all the women nagged for
it, it would unquestionably be granted in a week. But they do
not nag for it, because they have more important things to nag
for, such as keeping the blinds straight.

For the truth is that, while we are all concerned about little
things, those little things sometimes stand for big things, and
sometimes they do not. If I may use an awkward phrase, we
must consider the importance of things vertically as well as horizontally; some small things go down to the depths, just as tiny
islets may be the peaks of enormous mountains under the sea.
It is a small thing to take off one's hat in the drawing-room; it
is an even smaller thing to vote. But these things are trivial or
tragic according as they stand for certain strong desires in men
and women. Wear your hat before a lady, and you have said
that she is not a lady; you have destroyed the whole structure
of civilisation on which she stands. Tell a man that he must not
vote, and he will probably be angry, even if he does not want
to. For you are telling him that he is not a man at all; you are
turning him out of the club, the coarse and brotherly association
which is necessary to males. To sum it up in one awful phrase,
you are chucking him out of the public-house. That, very rightly,
shocks his sensibility. But the sensibilities of the woman are quite
different, and demand quite different consideration. And no one
will ever begin to understand men and women till he understands
this fact: that every man must be a man, but every woman must
be a lady.

May 2, 1908

Ceremonial Regulations and Costumes

I once remarked in this column on the fact that the ceremonial
of priests was infinitely simpler and more straightforward than
the ceremonial of men of the world; and it is one of those gener-

alisations which are ratified at every turn of our lives. It is much more fantastic that a Judge should wear a wig than that a Bishop should wear a mitre; for, after all, a mitre is only a certain pattern of hat, though, perhaps, it is not the exact pattern which you or I would of our own free will order from the hatter's. But that a public official should have an official wig is really quite as ridiculous as that he should have an official cork-leg. There is something essentially and intrinsically foolish in the idea that he who is to impress the people with the dignity of law should wear a false head of hair. You might as well say that he who is to impress people with the dignity of law should wear a false nose or false whiskers. The convex curve of a mitre is not in itself more extraordinary than the concave curve of a top-hat; but a Judge's wig is in itself, and considered as an idea, more extraordinary than even the wildest top-hat that he could possibly wear in private life. But the really extraordinary thing about the Judge's wig is that (unlike the Bishop's mitre) it provokes no obvious public merriment; the most extraordinary thing about the wig is that it is not considered extraordinary.

In this case, the wig is only a symbol. I use the wig to typify all that mass of powerful fictions and stately and historical hypocrisies which surround the wigs of Judges or the wig of the Speaker in the House of Commons. The extraordinary thing about the House of Commons is that it is supposed to be the practical part of our polity; but it is really the ceremonial part. Burke said that in the true logic and design of the British Constitution the House of Commons was not a check on the people, but a check for the people. It has now come near to being a check on the people as Heralds' College[1] is a check on the people; that is, a check so antiquated and elaborate as not to be even a check. In the original

---

[1] The herald was an officer whose duty it was to proclaim war or peace and to carry challenges to battle, messages between sovereigns, etc. Contemporary heralds are court functionaries who mainly superintend state ceremonies such as coronations and installations, grant arms, trace genealogies and attend to matters of precedence.

idea of the thing the Crown or the Lords or some such institution ought to provide the proper element of pomp and mystery; the House of Commons ought to be the house of common sense. As it is, the House of Commons is the house of pomp and mystery; it is specially and definitely the domain of bewildering formalities and futile etiquette. No religious ritualism that ever was heard of among men ever came within a hundred miles of it. Those writers who have satirised religious vows and religious orders have often made game of the fact that a man entering a monastery lost his name and became Brother Antony or Brother Ignatius, when his name was Smith. But though monasteries deal only with the exceptional, the maddest monastery never produced a rule so silly as the rule that you must call a man West Birmingham when his name is Joseph Chamberlain. No monastic communism or impersonality ever produced such a thing as this; that men spoke in one Parliament of the Right Honourable Member for Derby, in the next Parliament of that other interesting person the Right Honourable Member for West Monmouth, and men were absolutely forbidden to say that both phrases meant Sir William Harcourt. No monkish scheme for humbling human pride or obliterating human personality ever humbled or obliterated them by so strange an enactment as that: that certain neighbourhoods which nobody had ever heard of should be the only lawful way of alluding to certain people whom everybody had heard of and everybody was talking about. Suppose we journalists were not allowed to allude to Mr. Bernard Shaw except by the name of a street in Dublin!

These ceremonial regulations in the House of Commons, however, though comic, may be innocuous; they may be harmless in so far as the quickening and thickening of a forest of mere formalities is not in itself a harm. But there are some of these House of Commons regulations which are, unless I am much mistaken, mischievous and mortally bad. One of these came into considerable prominence some days ago in the House; I mean the regulation by which (according to the Speaker) members are forbidden to offer any criticism of "His Majesty's Judges." In reply to the remarks of one member in particular, who had strongly complained of the conduct of a Judge in Ireland, as being unparalleled since the period of Judge Jeffreys,[2] the Speaker distinctly laid it down that it was a rule of the House of Commons that a Judge could not be criticised. Naturally I accept at once from so fair an authority the assurance that this is a rule of the House of Commons. I merely add that in that case I suppose the House of Commons can alter it; and the sooner they alter it the better.

Parliament is supposed to be the supreme authority in this country; and two of the estates are supposed to govern by debate or deliberation. Parliament can cut off a Judge's head without trial. But Parliament must not (as a sort of mild preliminary) inquire whether he is a good Judge. The House of Commons is supposed to exist in order to see that the English are governed with justice; but the House of Commons must not discuss whether the officers of justice care for justice or not. It sits in order to see that its laws are applied; but it must never say a word about any of the people who apply them. Conceive for an instant what the condition of affairs would be if such an intellectual principle were really and generally introduced into government. Parliament is responsible for the postal service; but Parliament must not discuss the conduct of any postmaster. Parliament must discuss vaccination, but it must not discuss any medical officer. It must discuss the Army, but it must not discuss soldiers. It must discuss the Navy, but it must not discuss sailors. Or to sum up the whole astonishing situation in its present astonishing formula, Parliament is commanded to discuss law, but forbidden to discuss lawyers.

When the Speaker forbade a member to criticise a Judge by

[2] The justice who conducted what has become known as the "Bloody Assizes" which were held to deal with the followers of the Duke of Monmouth in the wake of his attempt to overthrow James II as champion of the Protestant religion. Monmouth was executed and his followers subjected to Jeffrey's brutal, severe and unfair proceedings.

comparing him to Judge Jeffreys, it must surely have occurred to him that he was forbidding that member to criticise Judge Jeffreys. If the Bloody Assize were at this instant going on in Western England it would be impossible (according to the Speaker) for Parliament to whisper a word against it. If the only answer is that no modern Judges are just like Jeffreys, the obvious rejoinder is, "Neither is the King at all like James the Second; yet we do not propose to abandon all the constitutional limits which we erected against James the Second." The case against all uncriticised despotism is not that the despots must be bad, but that they may be bad. The whole historical object of the House of Commons is to assert that a man may be bad when he wears a crown; why then, in heaven's name, should it forbid the suggestion that a man may be bad when he wears a wig?

The question has been raised again, in connection with certain flogging sentences, in a way that brings the injustice of the matter into an almost comic prominence. Certain men having been tortured in prison for robbery with violence, a question was asked in the House of Commons. The Minister responsible replied, saying that the sentences in question had been passed by a particularly and admirably humane Judge, or words to that effect, and that therefore he saw no reason for further discussion. The reason for further discussion is obvious. If Judges must not be discussed in Parliament, why may they be singled out and described as specially humane? If they are all above public criticism, they might be above mere compliment and personal excuse. Why is one Member of Parliament free to call a Judge exceptionally humane, but another member not free to ask if he is exceptionally inhumane? If the legal profession produces fantastic flowers of clemency, why should there not be, among successful lawyers, rare types of cruelty? But in this case the Minister did not treat the Judges as being above all personal criticism. He indulged in a personal criticism of his own, and then appealed to that personal criticism, and to that alone, to stop the mouths of all other critics.

Of one of the Judges in these cases of robbery with violence, we can, at any rate, say that he was worthy of some special notice; he may or may not have been exceptionally humane, but he certainly was not exceptionally intelligent. For, in defending the flogging sentences, he uttered (according to the reports) this extraordinary sentiment: that some sentimentalists objected to the lash, but he, for his part, would wait until one of the objectors had himself been robbed with violence. Which, being rationally interpreted, appears to mean that in every criminal case the prosecution should decide the punishment. The woman in Whitechapel whose eye has just been blacked by "another lydy," is to ascend the bench, put on the Judge's wig (and probably the black cap as well) and settle exactly what is to be done with the human being from whose hand she still smarts. Nobody must object to any punishment unless he has himself been the object of the crime. I may find a man being boiled in oil for motoring too fast, but I must not interfere unless I have been killed by a motor. A lady may be flayed alive for transferring a return ticket, but I must not criticise the sentence unless I can say, with my hand on my heart, that I am a railway company, and have been defrauded. The thing sounds light-headed enough, stated thus; but such exactly is the logical meaning of the Judge's utterance. Such are many Judges' utterances. Such, in short, are the utterances which the supreme authority of Great Britain is forbidden to discuss above a whisper.

May 9, 1908

On the World Getting Smaller

Captain Fletcher Vane, it seems, in his article in the *Spectator* on the possible suppression of war, has done one decidedly good thing. He has attacked the theory of M. Bloch.[1] The theory of M. Bloch, the reader will remember, was that war will die of its own terrors; the race of armaments will produce engines so enormous and so anti-human that no one will dare to encounter them. Captain Fletcher Vane denies this on the ground of historical fact; he maintains that the growth through recent centuries of arms of precision has made no difference to the readiness or reluctance of men to fight. A line broke in the Middle Ages at about the same chronological and psychological instant at which it breaks now. Captain Vane is probably right in denying the Bloch hypothesis on that ground. But on any ground, it is as well that the Bloch hypothesis should be denied.

There are some things more important than peace, and one of them is the dignity of human nature. It is a humiliation of humanity that humanity should ever give up war solely through fear, especially through fear of the mere machines that humanity itself has made. We all see the absurdity of modern armaments. It is a grotesque end for the great European story that each of us should keep on stuffing pistols into his pockets until he falls down with the weight of them. But it is still worse that we should only be friends because we are too nervous to stand the noise of a pistol. Let the man stop the pistol by all means. But do not let the pistol stop the man. Civilised man has created a cruel machinery which he now, it may be, finds bad for his soul. Then let civilised man save his soul and abandon his machinery.

---

[1] Jean Bloch (1836–1901), an industrialist and writer who devoted his last years to universal peace. He published *The Technical and Economic Impossibilities of a War Between the Great Powers* (1899) and *The Future War* (1900). He also founded the International Museum of War and Peace in Lucerne, Switzerland.

But the Bloch theory does not really abandon the machinery at all. It hangs the machinery *in terrorem* over the head of all humanity to frighten them from going to war for any cause, just or unjust. Man is cowed into submission by his own clockwork. I would sooner be ruled by cats and dogs. They, at any rate, are our fellow-creatures, not merely our creatures. I would have any war, however long and horrible, sooner than such a horrible peace. I would run any risk rather than submit to such a spiritual indignity as that man dare not, for the most crying justice or the most urgent chivalry, turn one of his own handles. War is an absolute calamity; so be it. Then let man silence his guns; but, in the name of human honour, do not let his guns silence him.

Captain Vane, having rejected this theory on other and historical grounds, goes on to suggest several ways in which, as he feels, modern war might possibly terminate. One of them is a point often urged in these days. It is what is called the shrinkage of space. I have not Captain Vane's text before me (I am writing these words in Bruges, where his works are less known than they should be), but I quote a good summary of the idea from a daily paper: "No less powerful a factor is the shrinkage of the world, which is bringing about that intimacy and understanding among the peoples which make war less and less thinkable. Paris is nearer in time than Brighton was a century ago, and St. Petersburg and Constantinople are as near as Edinburgh."

But this creed also (common in our time) contains several mistakes. First of all, it is surely a mistake to suppose that wars arise merely from a barbaric ignorance. A man does not fight another man because he does not know him. Generally he fights him because he knows him uncommonly well. Many modern peace societies act on the supposition that if they bring a great many Germans to see Englishmen, or a great many Englishmen to travel in Germany, they will never want to fight each other. But this seems to assume that all ordinary Englishmen believe that Germans have tails. It assumes that an average German regards an average Englishman as a monster from the moon.

The moment the German has seen the Englishman, counted his arms and legs, ascertained that he has the normal number of eyes or ears, realised, in short, that he is human, he will then drop all dreams of hostility. But this is missing the whole point of the modern antagonism. It is a morbid and suicidal thing for two great nations to hate each other. But when they do hate each other it is not because their aims are different, but because their aims are alike. A Prussian would not dislike an American for being an American Indian. On the contrary the Prussian, if he disliked him at all, would dislike him for being too like a Prussian: for rivalling Prussian commerce, or Prussian education, or Prussian Imperialism. Modern hostility is a base thing, and arises, not out of a generous difference, but out of a sort of bitter and sneering similarity. It is because we are all copying each other that we are all cursing each other.

And secondly, I deny (in the moral sense) that space has shrunk at all. I deny that Paris is nearer to our imaginations than it was a century ago; I should say without hesitation that it is much farther off. It is much easier to go to America than it was, but it is not any easier to understand it when you have got there. It is rather more difficult. Dickens may have taken nearly a month to reach the great Republic, but he found it a Republic of English republicans, with some ordinary faults. Mr. H. G. Wells can get there in a few days, but he would be the first to admit that, as far as making head or tail of it is concerned, one might almost as well stop at home. He does not find, as Dickens did, an ordinary English democracy with the ordinary exaggeration of democracy and optimism in England. He finds a frightful hotch-potch (I was going to say hell-broth) of new races, of which no man can even guess the end. America is physically nearer, but morally much more distant. When Sir James Douglas sailed from Scotland to Spain with the heart of Bruce,[2] he probably sailed

[2] Sir James Douglas (1286–1330), supporter of Robert the Bruce (1274–1329) in the fight for Scottish independence, was bearing the heart of Bruce to the Holy Land for burial when he was surrounded by enemies and killed in Andalusia, Spain.

very slowly; but when he got to Spain he found a set of Christian knights just like himself, with whom he shook hands on the spot. Sir Thomas Lipton, in *Shamrock XI.*, would, no doubt, get from Scotland to Spain much quicker; but the British millionaire tea-merchant would not find a crowd of tea-merchants waiting for him eagerly on the shore of Spain. He would only find what he would call a superstitious peasantry. He would find people whom he could understand far less than Sir James Douglas understood the Spaniards of the Middle Ages. It takes a shorter time to reach the place—but a longer time to see it. Spain is physically nearer, but morally more distant.

The real truth of the matter is that there are now all over the world, at regular intervals, places where you can get a Scotch-and-soda. These places have come closer together. You can get a Scotch-and-soda under one particular palm-tree in the desert. There are trains to that palm-tree. You can get a Scotch-and-soda on one particular crag of the Himalayas. There are lifts up to that crag. There is, in other words, a very swift and smooth system of transit for coarse, rich people between all the places to which coarse, rich people want to go. The article I have quoted speaks significantly of Brighton and Paris. Brighton and Paris are now much nearer to each other. But a decent village in Picardy is not an inch nearer to Paris. And a decent village in Sussex is not an inch nearer to Brighton.

There is no more deadly delusion, none more full of quite practical peril, than this notion that trains and wires have created a real understanding between the nations. Do you think that Chinamen will love you because you can write a Chinese telegram? Chinamen (and very right they are) will not love you until you can write a Chinese love-letter. The world has not shrunk at all. It is not one iota more easy at this moment to understand the Cannibal Islands. It is only more easy to look at them and misunderstand them. The misunderstanding has actually grown greater, because we ourselves have abandoned many healthy and instinctive things which would have helped us to sympathise with the savages. On the same page on which I read of these hopes from the coalescing and combining of the planet, I found a Moslem service called dirty or disgusting because it involved the idea of blood. A few hundred years ago we should have realized that our own religion involved the idea of blood. But we have got further away from understanding their religion by ceasing to understand our own.

May 16, 1908

Food and Alcoholic Drinks round the World

Some have cast doubts on the fact which I mentioned last week: the fact that there is spread all over Europe one thin layer of luxury, of rather caddish luxury, which none of the countries understand at all, but which all the luxurious and wandering cads understand perfectly. But since last week I have discovered that my own remarks were quite true. While wandering about the city of Brussels I wandered into a very vulgar and expensive restaurant, in which certain eager waiters thrust into my hands a bill-of-fare and a wine-list, as Mr. Mantalini[1] would say, "all of the demdest beauty." I could understand the French part of the menu well enough; it was the English that was quite unintelligible. The principle of a French menu is rational enough. I always know what the names on a French menu mean, because they mean nothing. A good cook tries experiments, generally very successful experiments; and whenever he puts too much pepper into one dish or an unexpectedly exact amount of garlic with another, he gives it any name that comes into his head. He names it after a favourite author or a long-lost love or some

[1] Mr. Mantalini. See Dickens' *Nicholas Nickleby*.

heroic incident in the history of his country. If in the ordinary confusion of the kitchen the eggs get mixed up with the onions in quite a new way, he calls it "Eggs after the Fashion of the Troubadours of Francis the First"; or if the beef looks a little bit more blue, green, purple, or orange than usual, he calls it "Beef in the Style of the Last Charge at Marengo." All that I understand quite well; it has no more to do with its subject than the names of the London streets. But the English things on the list did puzzle me. Nearly all the English names on the list were the names of things to drink. Some of them, I suppose, were American; though I really doubt whether any sane American has ever heard of them. In any case they were eagerly pressed upon me because I was English, and I am quite certain that most of them would be a novelty, not to say an adventure, to any ordinary Englishman. I was particularly asked to partake of a thing called "Mother's Milk," which I understood to consist chiefly of gin. My attention was also drawn to a thing described in the list as an "Oyster of the Prairie"—which scarcely seems, at first sight, the place where one would look for oysters. Such trivialities as the famous English drinks named "John Collins" and "Captain Lee" I pass over as too well known to need remark. I note that there was in the list a drink called "A Maiden's Blush," and another drink (to me of even darker fascination) called simply "A Locomotive." Finally there was a beverage which bore the rather menacing name of "Leave It to Me." I did leave it to him, whoever he was; I did not feel the smallest disposition to dispute his claim.

The curious thing was that the moment the waiters in this wild place understood that I was English (as they did at the first note of my faultless French accent) they urged all these drinks upon me with the utmost enthusiasm. They seemed quite certain that "Mother's Milk" would be really as natural as mother's milk to me. Words could not express my bewilderment, especially when they had to be French words. Who was John Collins, that I should care for him? Who was Captain Lee? Was he any relation of General Lee? Was he possibly the same gentleman at

an earlier stage of his military career? Did the most splendid of
American soldiers, before leaving his mark on American history,
leave it in the mere indolence of youth upon American drinks?
Why should a decent Englishman be asked to drink Blushes of
Maidens, or to consume the Oysters of Prairie? And what is
there English about doing so? Is it my daily custom to pour out
a "John Collins" or a "Captain Lee" for my friends? When my
guest is leaving the house do I give him something which bears
the inhospitable title of "Leave It to Me"? Do I tell him that his
cab will soon be here, but he has time for a Prairie Oyster? If
he has to catch a train, do I tell him that he can just swallow a
Locomotive? I assured the waiters that I had never said any of
these things in my life, that I had never even heard of them. But
they were not convinced; the things were printed in English,
and they were quite sure that all Englishmen inhaled them like
the breath of their nostrils. They felt sure that a Collins or two
poured into my inside would immediately make me see the white
cliffs of Albion, and probably the birthplace of Shakspere. To
which I only answered, "Leave It to me." Now, it is quite clear
that Englishmen outside asylums never drink things called
"Maidens' Blushes" or "Mother's Milk." The only interesting
question is whether anybody does. The obvious immediate
answer is that Americans do; but even here I am in some doubt.
I do not fancy that ordinary Americans do. To begin with,
ordinary Americans do not go to Brussels any more than they
go to the moon, for the ordinary people of all modern countries
are poor. Also, even supposing that these "long drinks" are
rendered plausible or refreshing by the climate of America, there
is no reason why anyone should want them especially in the
climate of Belgium—which is (particularly at the present moment)
a somewhat cool and cloudy climate.

The long American drinks are, I suppose, designed largely in
order to combine the two rather inconsistent ideals of alcoholic
excitement and coolness. In this particular Belgian café on this
particular afternoon a man might possibly have desired to pay
for alcoholic excitement; but he could hardly have wished to pay

for coolness, for the streets outside were full of a fine hail. But, in truth, I am profoundly disinclined to believe that any self-respecting white man ever asks for such things, especially before foreigners. Who is that strong man who can force his lips to frame the words "Mother's Milk" without either laughing or rushing from the room? Who is he who can really ask for a "Maiden's Blush" without imitating the maiden? I may easily be wrong, for the whole of this strange world is unknown to me; but I have a personal theory about who it is who drinks these things. I believe nobody drinks them—I doubt whether anyone ever has drunk them. I have wild moments when I doubt whether they exist at all except on the printed list. But I am sure of this, that by far the greatest importance of them is their importance on the printed list; and I think that this gives us a glimpse of a matter gravely important to our civilisation.

We of the self-supporting middle-classes, working fairly hard and fairly intelligently for our living—we, in short, who are doctors, tailors, journalists, brigands, and so on—are in the habit, when we go into inns or other such places, of looking out for what we like. We know what we want, and we want what we want—we want it very much. But there are (believe me) very rich people who on entering an hotel want what they don't want. Just as our eyes are instantly turned to whether the place provides the things we require—the necessities—so their eyes are instantly turned to whether it provides the luxuries that neither they nor anyone else requires, but which are a symbol of the solid and solemn wealth and fashion of the place. You and I look to see whether the wine-list includes the thing we can drink, such as good plain Burgundy or beer. But these people look to see if the list contains all the latest things that nobody can drink; the latest mixture of Mother's Milk with Prairie Oysters; the last embrace between John Collins and Captain Lee. They judge a restaurant by whether it offers them these great undrinkable things to drink. They never dream of drinking them, but they would miss them from cartes-des-vins. This is the key of that extraordinary rich class in its dealings with food and entertainment. What they least desire is exactly what they most demand; it is the more *recherché* because they do not desire it. They do not want a prairie oyster; but it gives them great pleasure to think that they are sitting in a place where they could order a prairie-oyster—or, if necessary, order a prairie. They admire a place in proportion as it provides the things that they do not want. Apply this test to great numbers of the solid things supported by wealth in the modern world, and you will be amused to notice what a large number of them are thus explained. The rich pay a great deal for the things they look at; but they pay a good deal for the things they do not look at—the mere upholstering of their life. They do not notice that the shirt-front of a waiter is white; but they would notice it if it was green. Similarly, they do not read Captain Spiker's long article in the *Nineteenth Century* about the needs of our Navy, but yet somehow they would miss it if it were not there; somehow there would be a gap in their strange lives if there were no Captain Spiker and no *Nineteenth Century*. All that output of ingenuity and patience serves at least to stuff the cushions of a particular class. But they no more dream of reading Captain Spiker than they dream of drinking Captain Lee.

It is this class spread thinly over Europe through its taste for travel and luxurious curiosity which is the real danger of our time. They seem to be drawing nations nearer together, whereas in truth they are only drawing together the denationalised men of all nations. They have not brought the democracies any closer: they have only taught the plutocracies to lose even their patriotism. They have not done anything to give the French the good beer of England, or the English the light wine of France. They have only made it possible for a rich man in any European capital to be offered "a Locomotive," and to decline it with thanks.

May 23, 1908

Speechmaking at the Royal Academy Dinner

The general regret, or to speak more sincerely, the general anger, at the celebrated speeches at the Royal Academy Dinner[1] being suddenly stopped, has a foundation of solid justice. It is easy to find minor arguments for the abolition; that the speeches were often dull, that there were too many speeches, that people might in the meantime have been listening to the band or looking at the pictures. But all these trivialities are nothing in the face of the practical fact that the thing was an empty bathos, an anti-climax. No speeches could have been so dull as that abrupt and unnatural absence of speeches. If we went to the theatre to-morrow night, and, after a spirited overture from the band, the curtain remained down for the whole evening, it might be possible to urge many ingenious arguments in favour of the innovation. It might be said, with truth, that many plays are dull; that there are too many plays; that the audience might in the interval be reading Plato or playing dominoes; it might even be said that there was something exquisitely artistic, delicate, and in the manner of Maeterlinck about a play so mysterious that it could not be seen at all. The most classic plays were those in which the great events occurred behind the scenes. Perhaps the most classic play of all would be one in which all the events occurred behind the curtain. But these ingenious arguments would not make the slightest difference to our positive sensation that the thing was a disappointment and very dull. The Royal Academy Banquet was a great English ceremonial institution. If you do not like ceremonial institutions, abolish it, but do not abolish

[1] The speeches at the annual Royal Academy dinner made it one of the major social events of the season; the event was controversial, however, since only reporters for *The Times* were allowed in to record the speeches. When the King decided to abandon the speeechmaking, the event lost its luster and all the papers ceased to cover the story.

only the interesting part of it. If people were interested in Royal Academicians at all, they came there to hear them on their social and oratorical side. They came to hear the Royal Academicians speak, not to see them eat. They do not eat differently from anybody else. If they did, indeed, there might be some fun in it. If the artist's manner of dining had some of the distinctive qualities of his artistic style, it would certainly be more interesting than any speech. I have always wondered whether Sir Edward Poynter[2] invented his own name in order to suit his pictorial method, or chose his pictorial method in order to live up to his name; but certainly he is, as an artist, one who works with a fine and sharp point, very delicate, and a little hard. If there were anything pointed about his way of dining, if he ate with a one-pronged fork, it might be amusing. If Mr. Briton Rivière's[3] eating were modelled on a careful study of that of lions, it might be an exciting spectacle. If Sir Lawrence Alma-Tadema always flung his head far back and squeezed grapes down this throat, in the style of some Capuan reveller in one of his own pictures, then I admit that the Academy Banquet might do very well without the dull accessory of speeches. But this is not the case. All these gentlemen eat their dinners exactly like other gentlemen. But as they would all speak in different ways, but all eat in the same way, I cannot imagine why, for the purposes of a great national celebration, they should be allowed to eat, but forbidden to speak.

It is just, however, that the case for this alteration should be briefly considered, so far as it exists at all. The excuses actually offered by Sir Edward Poynter in his reluctant explanation I take the liberty of dismissing. He said that the Prince of Wales had reproached him with keeping people sitting after dinner when they might be going round the gallery; as if any man in his five

[2] Sir Edward Poynter (1836–1919), an English painter, director of the National Gallery, and from 1896 the President of the Royal Academy.

[3] Briton Rivière (1840–1920), an English artist most notable for his paintings of wild animals.

wits wanted to walk through ten rooms after a heavy dinner and study over a thousand pictures by a false light. The real impulse undoubtedly had its only origin in the allegation (possibly not entirely without reason) that the speeches were too numerous or too long. It must be remembered that, even if speeches were thus elaborate or futile, there are different sorts of elaboration and futility appropriate to different occasions. There is a sort of silliness endurable at a picnic which would be intolerable in a smoking-room; and vice versa. Similarly there is a dullness a man can stand after dinner, such as listening to dull speeches, and a dullness he does not feel in the least inclined to stand after dinner, such as looking at dull pictures. The proposal of picture-gazing was entirely outside the atmosphere, outside the solemn conviviality, native to such occasions. The President might almost as well have said that there was a Greek library upstairs or a tennis court at the end of the garden.

Let it be conceded, however, that on occasions of the kind now under discussion there is a tendency to spin out the list too long, to multiply needless speeches and to encourage intolerable speakers. There is certainly a leisure about some speakers which seems to recall the age of Methuselah. In those primeval times, when everyone lived to be two or three hundred years old, one would naturally expect that the term of speeches would be proportionally expanded. You would say of a Cabinet Minister moving the second reading of a great Bill, "The right honourable gentleman resumed his seat, having spoken for three months and a quarter." Or you would say, "By the operation of the twelve o'clock rule, the Leader of the Opposition had only three weeks in which to reply, but of these he made good use." Or at a public meeting, "The chairman, as the hour was growing late, was obliged to limit the speakers to ten days each, and frequently had to ring his bell." But in our shorter and sharper existence there are, it must be confessed, some who begin and continue their speeches with this air of antediluvian expansiveness. It is these, and rather by their manner even than by the amount of their matter, who create a real irritation in the audience. It is these whom the discontented seek to silence. Their tediousness is a matter of quality, not of quantity. They are tedious before they open their mouths—because they are quite self-confident. The second of the real excuses refers to the influence of that special patronage of the Academy which gives its specific claim to be called the Royal Academy. But surely Sir Edward Poynter did a very poor service to the Monarchy in suggesting that the abandonment of a social ritual came from that particular source. In our modern world the Monarchy is a social ritual; and if the Monarchy begins to abolish social rituals it will end by committing suicide. The whole point of a modern King is that if he is no longer master of the State he is still master of the revels. In other words, he will on due and proper occasion consent to bore and to be bored.

The real root of the whole change lies, I think, much deeper than prosy speeches or private influences. It is part of a process. My scientific friends will be pleased to learn that it is part of an evolution, and a jolly bad evolution too. Notice all the most typical changes which society has made to suit its latest conceptions of ease and convenience, and you will see in almost every case that they consist, not in abolishing luxury, but in abolishing all the manly or generous things that happened to be connected with luxury. For instance, everyone will tell you that dancing is on the decline. Dancing is on the decline because it was the one wholesome and honourable thing in the fashionable world. Evening dress has not declined, except in the sense that with some ladies it has fallen considerably lower. Stupid breastplates of starch have not declined. Silly little waistcoats which begin at a man's waist have not declined. There is no modification of the mad luxury of the dresses or the refreshments. There is no simplification of things. The only thing that is being dropped is dancing—because it is simple. The only reform of aristocracy consists in abolishing the one hearty and human thing which is also done by a peasant and a peasant girl. The luxurious class is only abandoning one luxury. And that is the one luxury that is really a poem as well as a pleasure. I could give many more

instances; one of them is, for example, that when our rich philanthropists forbid their guests any detail of gorgeous diet, it is
always wine, because that is the only part of their long, luxurious
dinners that has any connection with charity and chivalry. But
as strong an example as any will be found in the case we have
been considering here. When the Royal Academy of our day
wishes to abolish some part of its ceremony, it abolishes the
intelligent part. It would not simplify the merely sensual part
by the smallest item of concession. It would not leave out a
single entrée. It would not give up a salted almond. It would
not surrender a sardine. When it has to knock something out of
the programme, it knocks out all the best speeches of all the best
speakers in England. It preserves the dinner and destroys the
occasion. This is what many friends of mine call "the upward
curve of the modern soul."

May 30, 1908

Moral Education in a Secular World

It is a great pity that people cannot leave well alone. For instance,
I have always been in favour of Secular Education. The reason
is obvious: I believe in a religion: and a man who believes in a
religion disbelieves in bits of that religion. The pedantic way of
putting it is that if once a thing is organic and living it cannot
be divided without death. If you love the dog on the hearthrug,
you don't like parts of him on the hearthrug. The more you
want to find your wife in the dining-room the less (as a rule)
you want to find half your wife in the dining-room. Half a wife
is not better than no marriage; it is worse, because it is being a
widower instead of a bachelor. Therefore, anything that has in
it a centre of being and a circulation of strength cannot be cut

up. To teach children only the first elements of religion is like reading children only the first chapters of a detective story. It is cruelty to children. The last chapters of a detective story are necessary in order to make any sense of the first. And religion differs from philosophy exactly in this: that religion is a detective story, in the sense that its secret is not only satisfying, but also startling. To break into the middle of a thing like that and say it must stop at page five is exactly like breaking into the middle of a romance, or of a riddle, or of an anecdote, or of a practical joke. In all cases you are cutting the thing off at a point before you have come to the point of it. You are making the thing immortal before it really exists. You are justifying the thing just before it has justified itself.

Well, I know I cannot teach all my religion to all English children; I also know that in the present intellectual divisions it would be wicked to try. Therefore, I am content that none of my religion should be taught, except in so far as I am able to teach it myself in smoking-rooms, on the tops of omnibuses, in newspapers and public-houses. But as I say, people will not leave well alone. And instead of the thing called Secular Education, which anybody can understand, there comes along an extraordinary thing called Moral Instruction, which nobody could stand for a week. I have just received a long, elaborate, and very able document from the Moral Instruction League, describing what they conceive to be a complete system of sensible education in ethics; a scheme of ethics to which everyone assents and which can therefore be substituted for the moralities of all the creeds. It is supposed to represent the morality in which all men agree. And really, I do not think I ever read a document with which I disagreed so much. I do not mean at all that it is an exceptionally silly document; in many ways it is exceptionally capable. The only mistake in it is the mistake (as I freely admit), of almost all the enterprising educationalism of our day. That mistake is simply that all the people who think about education never seem to think about children. I solemnly assure the reader that I have read whole books about education written by intellectual people with great ingenuity; and I can only describe the effect on my mind by some kind of wild parallel. It felt as if I were reading a book called "How to Breed Horses," and it was all written like this: "Many people can enjoy the sweet voices of the horses singing at daybreak who nevertheless know little of the way they build their nests; and who (when they have tamed them) will often neglect to clean out their cages and be content merely with occasionally smoothing their feathers." One could only come to a sort of blear-eyed conclusion that the man was not talking about horses at all. Exactly in the same way many modern educational documents, including this one, strike me as not being either bad for children or good for children. They are not about children. The man who wrote them has obviously not the most glimmering idea of what a child is like. To take the most obvious point, they all talk as if the child stood still to be educated. They talk as if the government of your home were entirely concerned with what you should do with the children. A great deal of it is concerned with the desperate question of what the children will do with you. They talk of giving this or that final touch to the shape of the child's will, as if the child had no will of his own. They talk of forming the child's mind as if the child had not formed his own mind and did not know his own mind uncommonly well. A child is weaker than a man if it comes to a fight or to knowledge of the world; but there is nothing to show that the child is weaker in will or in desire. You come away from a modern educational work with the feeling that you have been putting together little pieces of different-coloured clay until you have made the image or statuette of a small child. You come away from having to do with a small child with the sense of having been wrestling with gigantic angels and gigantic devils, with the first eddy of evil as it enters the universe and the first cataract of innocence as it comes from God.

But these educationists can neither understand where children are better than we, nor where they are worse. I take one instance out of this universal panacea of the Moral Instruction League.

It says in this publication that moral education should consist less in the pointing out of moral evils or dangers than in the making attractive of the ideals of good. Now I only want to point out that this is a sentiment uttered without any sort of reference to children at all. The man who wrote it was a grown man, thinking only of grown men and of their peculiar conditions in our community. As a warning to the modern adult the phrase has its value. We, who are mature and wicked, have constantly to be reminded that beauty is beauty, that kindness is kindness, that courage is lovable, or that lilies are white. We have to run a huge machine of society, in which the biggest complexity has to be used to produce even the smallest result. We have to think so much about the exercises that bring courage, or the manure that grows lilies. It is natural, therefore, that in us there arises, and has always arisen, the danger of dreary and detailed ethics, of routine and humbug, of mere negative morality. It is right to say to a sad and civilised man: "Oh, think a little less about laws and a little more about life!" But there is no sense at all in saying this to children. Children have more life than we have; the only thing they lack is law. Children feel the whiteness of the lily with a graphic and passionate clearness which we cannot give them at all. The only thing we can give them is information—the information that if you break the lily in two it won't grow again. We need not teach them the good of admiring the lily; the only thing we can teach them is the evil of uprooting it. We need not teach them to admire courage; they do admire courage. We can only teach them that certain things, such as the disgusting process of being washed, are in the long run found to increase that quality. But the man who wrote these words had not really got children in his mind at all. He was not thinking of an age which keenly feels the beauty but does not know the peril of living. He was thinking of our own generation, which, in a dirty, pessimistic period, has blasphemously underrated the beauty of life and cravenly overrated its dangers. He was thinking of Schopenhauer; he was preaching against suicide to a person whose only possible death would come through his extravagant love of life. The child does not fall into pessimism; he falls into the pond.

There is another mistake made by these educationists which always appears in their documents, and which appears in this document of the Moral Instruction League. There are always constant allusions to the idea of progress, the idea of training people to be reformers, the idea of teaching them to teach something other than what they have learned—some new truth as it is called. This is insanely unsuitable for children. A child wants to know the fixed things, not the shifting ones. He enjoys the sea, not the tides. He enjoys beauty, not fashion. There is no particular point in telling him (at the age of five) to invent a new fashion in hats; if he learns to take his hat off in the drawing-room it is as much as can be expected of the poor little brute. He cannot decently be expected to learn to respect humanity (which is often a hard thing to do) and at the same moment to learn to improve it. Yet these programmes of ethical instruction are full of the recurrent idea of novelty, of innovation, of the search after truth. What has a child to do with the search after truth? The most you can ask from a child is that he should tell the truth he does know: not that he should look for the truth he does not. But in these books and pamphlets, page after page, in a hundred elusive ways, is struck this same note: that the child must be progressive, that he must conceive morality as reform, that he must look for beautiful modern changes—in short that he must teach his grandmother how to suck eggs. Now, I am far from denying that, in the contact between the child and the grandmother, both have a great deal to learn. On the whole, I think the child has more to give the grandmother. But it is the essence of a child that he should give what he has to give unconsciously: it is the essence of a grandmother (it sounds a rather awful substance), it is the essence of a grandmother that she should give it consciously, out of the clear cunning of years. In other words, I do object to the child teaching his grandmother. I do not object to the grandmother learning from the child.

June 6, 1908

Practical Politics and Temperance Reform

Our practical politics are the reverse of practical, and I think I
know the reason. Men will not realise that the only sensible
thing to be done with a sentimental question is to talk about it
sentimentally. It is practical to discuss a material question in a
materialist way. But it is quite as practical to discuss a spiritual
question in a spiritualist way. If you are talking about hunger,
you can only talk about whether, in a physical sense, hunger is
satisfied. But if you are talking about honour, you can only talk
about whether (in the wildest sense of the duellist) honour is
satisfied. But modern government will go in for settling sentimental questions without considering sentiment. For instance,
the question of drink is an entirely sentimental question. The
man who drinks wine or beer with his friends does it from a
good sentiment. The man who drinks absinthe or whisky by
himself does it from a detestable sentiment. But they are both
sentimentalists: they both wish to achieve a certain state of the
emotions. And the real mistake of the practical politician who
treats this question is simply that he tries to treat it practically.
You might as well try to treat sunsets practically.

Suppose the government took account of that privacy which
is demanded by all engaged couples when they are in love. The
government might reasonably take no account of it at all; and
perhaps this is the most wholesome way: let the lovers find their
privacy how and when they can, as they do at present. But
suppose the government said—"We have provided small stone
cubicles for engaged couples, all in a row and lighted by electric
light, and they can be obtained by the male and female each
applying for a ticket." Then I think it would be fair to say to
the State—"You have gone out of your way to satisfy a mere
emotion, and you have not satisfied it. Either give us the sort
of sentimental secrecy we like, or let us steal it—which we like

115

even better. Either satisfy our hearts—or don't trouble your heads."

Now, all drink is divided into two inspirations, conviviality and morbidity. But neither of them can be discussed on merely material lines. So that when people continue (as they are still doing) to ask me my opinion of the Licensing Bill, I have difficulty in giving what is called a practical answer. A friend of mine, who is a member of Parliament, threw a sudden but soothing light upon the matter. He says that there is no Licensing Bill. It does not exist. He says that a Bill in Parliament is not a unity at all, but a string of quite separate and inconsistent clauses with any of which a man might agree, while detesting and despising the one before and the one after. I may add that my friend voted for the Second Reading, and so should I if I were so unlucky as to have the chance. I say this lest anyone should accuse me of hedging.

But the truth is that all our government is a system of hedging: they put this clause in to please this section, that clause to please another. It is often difficult to get to the great principle involved. As far as I am concerned, the great principle is that the circumstances should encourage decent drinking and discourage indecent drinking. And which is which is a mere matter of sentiment.

Let me state one broad contradiction. Temperance Reform generally takes two forms—the limitation of the places of drinking and the limitation of the hours of drinking. I think the first quite useful and the second quite useless. Shutting up three public-houses and leaving the other two would, I think, be good for temperance; shutting up all five an hour earlier would be good for drunkenness, and for nothing else. The late Lord Salisbury said, with great humour, that he did not think that the many public-houses increased the desire of drink, for there were many bedrooms at Hatfield and he had not found that they increased the desire of slumber. But this, though funny, is a fallacy, as well that statesman knew. It happens that stopping in one place is essential to sleeping, even of sleeping too much. But stopping in one place is not essential to drinking too much. If

Lord Salisbury had been an eccentric sort of sleep-walker, and found it necessary to take a three-minutes nap in each room, then he would have found that his many bedrooms encouraged his habit of slumber.

Now, there are sound human causes which do make men drink too much by this perambulatory process. It is true that the disadvantage of the numberless public-houses (like most other truths in our time) is generally put on the wrong ground and defended for a wrong reason. People describe the ordinary English working-man as strung-up to pass three public-houses, wavering at the fourth, reeling at the fifth, staggering at the sixth, and falling helpless into the seventh. But really the working-man is not such a miserable creature as that. A man knows well enough whether he intends to drink or not. The real objection to the unnatural number of public-houses is that it divides the responsibility for the man's drunkenness. A man might start sober from the Battersea High Street and arrive at my house drunk enough to burn down London without ever having taken more than his decent share at any individual tavern.

Now, in all these matters, which the law can only control very clumsily, the most valuable force is social pressure—the opinion of a man's neighbours and equals. Let there be as far as possible a local inn, and let a man behave there like a decent man—or like an indecent one, if he chooses to lose his friends. But it *is* an evil that he should be served as a decent man in seventeen successive houses and turn up an indecent man at the end of it. It is an evil that the multiplication of the very things meant to make men sociable should tend to make them solitary. It is an evil that while with one tavern you have friendly drinking, with ten taverns you have secret drinking. And it is an evil very typical of our times, for the chief evil of our times is that the social collectivity has increased spiritual solitude. Never were bodies so much jostled; never were souls so much deserted.

I do not say that a man will never drink to excess with his friends; but here comes in exactly one of those ultimate emotional facts which mere practical politicians cannot discuss. There is a kind of degradation a man will let his male friends see; but there is a kind he will not let them see. A man may submit to be called a "common drunk," but not to be called a dipsomaniac. He may be known to drink brutally in public, but he will not be known (if I may use the phrase) he will not be known to drink secretly in public. He will consent to be called a drunkard, but not to be called a drinker. If you force, as far as possible, all drinking into recognised and central places, under the eyes of acquaintances and relations, you will certainly cut off a great deal of the poisonous part of modern alcoholism. And if you ask me why I am so certain about the matter, I answer—because it is a sentimental question.

But the other process of Temperance Reform, the limitation of the hours, is, I think, not only useless, but eminently calculated to defeat its own object. And here, again, it is no good discussing the thing with practical politicians: for it is not a question of the desires of practical politicians; it is a question of the desires of men. God knows what practical politicians drink—petrol, I should think. But men inclined for moderate drinking are definitely encouraged to immoderate drinking by the shortening of hours. Anyone can see this who will sit and think for a minute, not about statistics, but about souls. Do not think of human nature as if you were making a law: think of it as if you were writing a novel. Think how people really feel. If you do you will see that to limit by the clock the time for drinking alcohol is to make normal people think a great deal more about alcohol than they ought to. Remember, in heaven's name, that alcoholism is a nervous habit: and looking at the clock makes people nervous. A man who might have drunk one glass of beer without knowing it and gone away arguing with his friend, takes three glasses of beer because it is three hours before he can get another. I see it going on every Sunday in Battersea. I take the only adequate parallel. Reading coarse writers like Rabelais or Wycherley may be right or wrong. But what would be the psychological result if we could only read them from one to three? Simply that where we might have read them innocently we should read them with a vile self-consciousness.

June 13, 1908

Empire Day and England

In a remarkable newspaper which instructs the Empire I read the following piece of information about Empire Day.[1] It said that a certain man had sent a telegram to Mr. Asquith to tell him that the Liberal Mayor of some town had allowed flags to be flown on that day. The telegram concluded with the thoughtful words, "Thank God, some Liberals are Englishmen," and it was signed "A Briton." It was immediately followed in the newspaper by the information that a firm with several n's and z's in it were flying a flag in honour of the occasion. So that there really seems no reason why we should in any way limit our religious gratitude in this matter. We need not only thank God that some Liberals are Englishmen. We can also thank God that some Germans are Englishmen. There is something significant to me about the anonymous character of the signature "A Briton"; and I should not wonder if the hearty Teuton really sent the telegram. However this may be, I fancy that we shall find the name a sort of magic "open sesame" which will be of great use to us if we want to decide (and, after all, it is well worth while to decide) how far rational patriotic feeling does

[1] Empire Day is celebrated on May 24 (Queen Victoria's birthday). It was begun in 1902 as a celebration of victory in the Boer War, and a reminder of the responsibilities of the Empire's citizens. In 1958 it became "Commonwealth Day".

desire such an institution and how far it does not. Let us take it for granted, for the moment, that we are all in our five wits: that is to say, that we all love our country, and that we all feel that she can be endangered both by feeble submission and by futile swagger. Let us really ask what is the idea of Empire Day and what is the good of it.

Now one thing can be stated with absolute certainty. Any man who is surprised at an Englishman disliking Empire Day does not know what an Englishman is. If any gentleman on the *Daily Jingo* or elsewhere is sincerely astonished at the Prime Minister shrinking from the celebration, then that gentleman is either a foreign gentleman or one quite divorced from the actual tradition of England. His name is more likely to be Guggenheimer than Asquith. *The* typical English feeling, the psychological fact which foreigners feel about us, is our embarrassment, our shyness, in the presence of anything earnest and pompous. I do not say this is merely a merit; I do not think it is. I do not say that we should not be better for more flags and more formalities; I think we should. I have often defended ritual in these columns; but I do not expect all Englishmen suddenly to become Ritualists. It might do an Englishman good to learn ceremonial. It may do a boy good to learn algebra. But anyone who is astonished at boys avoiding algebra simply does not know anything about boys, and there is an end of him. Similarly, it might do an Englishman good to salute a flag. But if the *Daily Jingo* does not know that an Englishman feels a fool when he is saluting a flag, then the *Daily Jingo* does not know anything about England; and there is an end of the *Daily Jingo*. Before we talk at all about whether Empire Day is a good thing, we may register this truth: that anyone who takes for granted that it is a good thing *must* be un-English. This does not prove that it is a bad thing. There are many good things which I for one should like to see increased in England, but which have not been, for some time past at least, at all characteristic of it; Republicanism, for instance, and Catholicism, and the break-up of the Party system, and the habit of taking off one's hat in a shop where there are

women. All these I should like to see instinctive in England; but
I am not astonished when I find that they are not instinctive. I
do not jump out of my boots because the policeman at the corner
of the street is not a Republican. I do not challenge a man to a
duel because he has not taken off his hat in Marshall and Snel-
grove's shop. I think myself that all good in nationality comes
from the Catholic tradition of Europe, just as the essence of the
Union Jack is a system of the crosses of Catholic saints. But I
do not call every grocer who distrusts Catholic saints a traitor
to the Union Jack. I know those saints are unfamiliar and embarrassing to an ordinary Englishman. I know also that suddenly
saluting flags, and going into a sacred perspiration for an entirely
new date called Empire Day, is unfamiliar and embarrassing to
an ordinary Englishman. I know it because I am an ordinary
Englishman myself. And if there is any man who does not know
it, if there is any man who takes it for granted that Englishmen
will fling themselves into half-baked frenzies for a half-baked
festival, if there is anyone who is sincerely surprised and angry
at the instinct of Mr. Asquith, then he is either a quite extraordinary Englishman or an ordinary alien.

And now, having got rid of the patriots, we can get back to
the Englishmen. Granted that the thing is an innovation and a
surprise, is it a good innovation or a good surprise? For certainly
the English, with all their merits, do need something to surprise
them. That must depend firstly, I think, on how far the thing
really appeals to all that is best in England. The root thing about
our people (as compared with most of the peoples of Europe)
is, as I have said, a certain mysterious quality for which the
nearest word is embarrassment. It has been mistaken for pride,
but it is not pride; it has been mistaken for vulgarity, but it is
not that; it has been sometimes explained by saying that Englishmen are cold conquerors bestriding the earth, and sometimes
by saying that they are shuddering savages on the ultimate edge
of the world. None of these explanations has at all hit the truth;
though it is true, of course, that England has been modified by
her land system and is therefore somewhat aristocratic; though

it is true, of course, also that England has been modified by her insular position, and is therefore somewhat provincial. But the secret of the shyness is something shyer than that.

It arises ultimately from the profoundly poetical character of the English, that quality of mixed feelings and emotional hesitation which makes the cloudy pictures of Constable or the vague rhythms of Keats. Shakspere is not so much the greatest of great poets as the most poetical of great poets; he depends less on a structure of hard thought than Dante or Goethe. It is the same with Turner; even if you think Turner was not a painter, you must admit he was a poet. This poetic heat and haze in the feelings produces the strong English shyness. It also produces the strong English sense of humour. And these two things together, the English shyness and the English humour, will always be hard nuts to crack for anyone who wants to establish, with entire solemnity, and on the spur of the moment, a thing like "Empire Day."

Surely the main deduction is obvious. We are dealing with a people at the bottom romantic; on the top, reluctant and humorous. If we really want to have a national celebration we should take great care to graft it on solid and genuine things already sacred to Englishmen. We have destroyed most of the healthy old English celebrations, with their greasy-poles and jacks-in-the-green. But there are still some English things left, such as the English celebration of Christmas and some of the legends of the sea-fights. If we started with something familiar and sensible, like plum-pudding or Nelson, it is possible that we might still pump into the new festival the blood of our fathers. Instead of that the men on the Yellow Press (men who come from anywhere and say anything) suddenly tell us that we are to observe a crude Canadian ceremony, a ceremony that has nothing English about it for the excellent reason that it was not started by the English. It is hard enough to get the English (in ceremonial things) to express their own emotions. It is quite hopeless to ask them to express other people's. Of course, schools will take up such things, as they will take up any fads, and children, if told to do so, will salute the Union Jack, as they would salute the Skull and Crossbones. But if the Yellow Journalist supposes that the English people care a farthing about such jerry-built jubilees, he can hardly have discussed them with a cabman or a railway porter. The two essentials of any celebration are the two ideas of authority and popularity. There is no authority for this project; it came from some Imperial newspaper. There is no popular basis for it in the nation; it came from Canada. It has in it no patriotic memory; for how can one remember what has never happened before? It has in it no public hope; for how can one look forward to a thing which will make no difference, even if it ever happens again? Yet I for one should be sincerely glad if we could have a national celebration, remembering our real achievements, and reminding us of our real work in the world. Only, for any such national celebration I should suggest two conditions: First, that our national celebration should be invented by our nation, and not by another nation. And secondly, that it should be forced by the people on the newspaper proprietors, and not by the newspaper proprietors on the people.

June 20, 1908

On Modern Sabbatarianism

A considerable discussion has arisen about whether the Franco-British Exhibition[1] ought to be opened on Sunday, especially for the benefit of the foreign visitors. And the discussion has suddenly shown up a remarkable habit among us of the modern

---

[1] A very popular exhibition which opened at Shepherd's Bush, West London, on May 14.

English—a habit which is a great nuisance to us and to everybody else. I do not complain of Puritanism, though, as a matter of private taste and sport, I hit it whenever I see it. But certainly Puritans have a right to be Puritan, and a Puritan nation has a right to make Puritan laws. If England could say frankly: "Our Government is a strictly Puritan Government, and if you come to our country you must put up with our religion," then the answer would be unanswerable, and the French would have no sort of right to ask for a technical violation of a national Sabbath. They would have no more right to make us open an Exhibition on Sunday than you and I, if we went to Spain, should have a right to make all the Catholics eat meat on Friday, or, if we went to Persia, to make the Moslems drink wine every day. It is true that some travellers tend rather to suggest that Spaniards do eat meat on Friday and that the Moslems do drink wine every day. But even if the rule of the country has been popularly relaxed, it is quite natural that the Government should still regard it as the rule of the country. You cannot expect a Government to arrange an official wine-party if the Government is supposed to have the Mohammedan religion. You cannot expect a Government to give a State banquet consisting chiefly of cow if the Government is supposed to hold the Hindu religion. But the English Government will not say that it holds the Sabbatarian religion. Even the Sabbatarians will not say that they hold the Sabbatarian religion. Even the Sabbatarians abandon the Sabbath and begin to talk about convenient public holidays and the hygienic advantages of resting one day in the seven. I have read letter after letter from people obviously Puritan and expressed in this sort of style: "Whether or no we believe in the old Jewish Sabbath, we can at least resist the introduction of the Continental Sunday. We have no religious or theological motives, but we feel quite certain that great inconvenience and extra labour will arise from opening the Exhibition even for these few Sundays." To this I think our French guests might reasonably reply: "We are sorry that you have no religious or theological motives. If you had had a religious motive we would easily have excused you. If your motive is only your own civic convenience we cannot help feeling that it is a little inhospitable. If you believed in the old Jewish Sabbath, we would not insult it, any more than we would insult the Turkish Fast of Ramadan. But if you only practically dislike the Continental Sunday, we can find nothing to respect in your attitude. You might surely admit the Continental Sunday for the short time that you admit the Continental people. If it were a strictly religious custom we should give way to you. But if it be a purely social custom we really think that you might give way to us. We can understand a man not giving sacramental wine to his guests; but any other sort of wine we think he ought to give, even if it caused a trifle of trouble. A religion is a religion, a rule is a rule, and we can quite understand that one violation of it is awful. But really we cannot do very much harm to your social system by walking about the Exhibition for a week or two."

The truth is that (in this matter) the Sabbatarians are simply hypocrites. They are a new kind of hypocrite, if that is any comfort to them. Most of the old hypocrites pretended to be religious when they were really irreligious. These new hypocrites pretend to be irreligious when they are really religious. They discuss the worldly advantages of a weekly holiday with an indifference amounting to impiety. But all the time they hide in their hearts the horrid fact that they are quite pious. Tartuffe pretended to be following heavenly aims when he was really following earthly aims. But the modern Puritan pretends to be following earthly aims when all the time (sly fellow) he is following heavenly aims. He likes a certain sort of religion, and he proceeds to find earthly excuses for it. What the Sabbatarian really likes is the Jewish Sabbath and nothing more or less; it is consonant with his personal emotions about the universe and the nature of God, and he has a perfect right to have it. But he has no right to insist, by the aid of a few cheap sociological phrases, that everyone must have it because it is a social necessity. It is nothing of the kind. The very phrase "Continental Sunday" shows that it is nothing of the kind. That which is omitted by the whole great Continent to which we belong cannot be a necessity of any sort of civilisation or happiness. It cannot be true that without the English Sabbath all human beings become harried and overdriven slaves. There is less Sabbath in Italy or South Germany; but certainly there is more leisure. As a general tendency, in fact, there are more holidays. And so one can find the same men who rebuke Continental people for working on Sunday also rebuke them for not working on their own corresponding festivals. You will find the same people complain that the shopkeepers are inattentive who also complain that the shops are open. The same people who lament the absence of Sabbaths also lament the recurrence of Saints' Days.

Of course, their real motive (and a perfectly sensible motive) is that they believe in their own religion and do not believe in the foreigners' religion. But I only wish to point out what a wild and wonderful object such a person is on the earth; the man who has a supernatural sanction, and positively pretends that it is only a natural sanction. It is as if a real magician should set up as a professional conjurer. The sanctity of the Seventh Day is a part of a certain religious scheme, which may be the true religious scheme. It is nothing against the philosophical truth of a religious system that it has certain physical vetoes or material observances. All the highest and most philosophical religions—Catholicism, Buddhism, Confucianism, and the Greek Mysteries—had vetoes and observances of that kind. I have no space here to go into the theory which justifies such vetoes; but it is a perfectly intellectual theory. A Catholic can be an enlightened philosopher and still logically insist on eating fish. A Buddhist can be an enlightened philosopher, and still logically refuse to eat cow. And in the same way, and with quite equal justification, a Judaic Puritan might be an enlightened philosopher, and still feel strictly about keeping the Jewish Sabbath. But he declares that he does not feel strictly about the Jewish Sabbath, but only about the health of men in buttons.

We can only really grasp the situation by imagining that any other religion were trying to thrust any other taboo upon us, not as a taboo, but as an artificial and elaborate social fad. We have no right to force Hindus (as people say we did before the Mutiny) to touch the flesh of cow: if they avow their religion, they have a right to have it respected. But suppose there were an active and increasing political party, caballing in all coteries and permeating all opinions, whose whole object was, on one excuse or another, to keep out cows. They would choose sides only with this object. When the Country party came to the front, they would oppose it, theoretically because it was narrow, but really because you can keep cows in the country. When the Manchester School came forward they would back it up, theoretically because it was rational, but really because there are no cows in Manchester. They would answer Mr. Chamberlain's celebrated proposal[2] (in his Radical days) by moving with many artificial arguments one particular amendment: they would propose that every man should have three acres, but not a cow. The political proposals would include a Bill for the Encouragement of Cattle Disease. Their triumphant National Anthem would be the tune the old cow died of—the psalm of a sublime deliverance. And for all these various objections or proposals they would give, not the real reason, but some ingenious other reason; they would advance any explanation except the simple explanation that they loved and believed in the religion in which they were brought up. They would compile statistics in a Blue-book[3] about the number of old ladies who were frightened by cows. They would say that it was very cruel to cowherds to make them look after cows. They would say that cows were unreliable because a cow jumped over the moon; they would say anything. It may

[2] Joseph Chamberlain argued that large landowners (as a kind of "ransom" for the security which property enjoys in society) should grant small holdings to agricultural laborers; the specific proposal was made in a speech at Birmingham in June 1885, but Chamberlain continued to argue the proposal throughout the summer and fall. When the plan was proposed in Parliament in January 1886, the Salisbury Conservative government was brought down.

[3] A Parliamentary report or some other official government publication of folio size, often having blue covers.

be thought that this apologue is irrational and remote; it is, in truth, an exact description of what is going on at this moment in all branches of our social system and our civil life. We have neither the advantages of having a religion nor the advantages of not having a religion. We are neither united nor independent. All around us are old superstitions masquerading as modern fads.

June 27, 1908

The Indeterminate Sentence for Prisoners

Before matters go much further we ought to make up our mind about this question of the indeterminate sentence for prisoners. I may hasten to say, as furious partisans generally do say, that this is not a party question. There is nothing Conservative about abolishing the ancient right of a man to hear the full force and meaning of his sentence. There is nothing Liberal about not liberating a man until you choose. The accident that this proposal of criminal amendment comes from the party with which I am in personal agreement, will perhaps make it even more permissible for me personally to disagree.

When we are making any alteration we ought to remember that the whole question is the question of what or whom we trust. In the ultimate sense perhaps we trust nothing or nobody. One of the strongest arguments for the prophetic theory of the Old Testament can, perhaps, be found in that famous quotation which the great Lord Strafford[1] made on his way to the scaffold. The Hebrew Prophet, foreseeing the monarchies of Europe, said, "Put not your trust in princes," and then, foreseeing the Republic

---

[1] Thomas Wentworth, Earl of Strafford (1593–1641), an English statesman and chief advisor to Charles I, was impeached, imprisoned by the King's enemies and executed on Tower Hill.

of America, added, "nor in any child of man." There may be an absolute sense in which men, as men, are not to be trusted; but we may fairly leave this out of account, since none of us are at all likely to taunt the others with the fact. But one broad generalisation has been felt to be true from the foundations of human history. That is that men working up to the level of a fixed rule were likely to be less utterly loose and brutal than men working anarchically and anyhow. If you must put your trust in princes, it was better to put it in legal princes. If we must trust the children of men, the children had better be well brought up. It was generally a mistake to make princes lawless when it was their only business to give law. It was generally a mistake to make Judges irresponsible when a Judge only means a man who is responsible. In the same sense I think it doubtful if we are doing well in making a sentence indeterminate. For a sentence only means a thing that has been determined. Even to talk of an indeterminate sentence is like talking of an immeasurable measure. It is like talking of a shapeless shape or of an unlimited limitation. If a man tied up a horse in a field with an indeterminate rope it would mean that the horse might be drowned because it could reach the Pacific, or starved because it could not reach the grass.

But this is a matter full not only of practicality but of pain; we will dispense with any verbal philosophising. Most people know, I presume, what the indeterminate sentence means. It means that a Judge or jury will henceforth have the power of comdemning a man to be kept in prison until the authorities say that he can come out. But who are the authorities? Who are the people who are to say whether the man is fit to be free? I think we require a little more clearness and freedom of mind in this matter, and with your permission I will take that freedom. The men who are to report upon the prisoner (in the first and most important points) are men of a class and type which all sane civilisations have unanimously detested and despised. When silly German sophists tell you that the glory of the feudal knight was in killing, just ask them this question, "Was the hangman knighted?'' Obviously the knight was only glorious because he was nearly killed: The hangman who killed, without being kill-able, was not a hero. He was an outcast. If you had said to any gentleman in any age, "Do dine with me to-night; I will intro-duce you to the hangman," he would have been annoyed. If you had said to any decent man anywhere, "Join us to-night: I'm entertaining all the Torturers—as jolly a lot as ever you saw," I think he would remember a previous engagement. If you said to the first old gentleman you met in any century, "The Prison Jailer wants to marry your daughter," the course of true love would not at first run smooth.

It may be very unfair; I am not discussing that: there may be a cruel illogicality in the human tradition which says of tortures and punishments, "It is written indeed that these things come, but woe unto them by whom they come." It may be very unjust to order a man to be whipped, and then despise the man who whips him. I only say, with absolute confidence, that all mankind always has despised the man who whips him; and despised the man who imprisons him, who guards him, who spies upon him, or who (in short) for any purpose ties the hands of another man. A gentleman in any century would as soon have had the thief for a son-in-law as the jailer who guarded the thief. Now, it is these people, the prison authorities, whom all human societies have assumed to be more or less brutal, who have every psy-chological temptation to be brutal, who, by the very nature of the case, must be brutal, who have been selected by the new arrangement for the subtle task of being specially humane. The poor tired ruffians who regulate prisons have to decide a question almost too delicate for the psychology of George Meredith or the charity of St. Francis of Assisi. He who was rejected as a son-in-law has become a universal father-in-law—very much "in law." This is what I mean by saying that all such questions as this come back to a question of whom we are to trust. Why not trust juries to pass fair verdicts, with a general prevision of the sentence?—juries are generally to be trusted. Why not trust Judges to pass just sentences?—Judges are sometimes to be trusted. But whomever you specially trust, do not trust the class which has never been felt to be dignified at all, that has never had the high importance of Judges or the freedom of juries: do not trust the prison officials, the spies, the heavy sentries, the solemn torturers, the men whose trade has been everlastingly ugly and unpopular; the men to whose trade every tailor and greengrocer in the jury would feel himself degraded if he sank.

I do not doubt that there are many prison officials who are perfect saints. I do not doubt (if it comes to that) that there are many prisoners who are perfect saints. The point is that no man wishing his son to be brought up in exquisite justice or delicate mercy would send him to school in Portland Jail either as a convict or as a warder. The *chances* are in favour of hardening. And the whole original object of law, of statutes, of assizes, of open courts, of definite verdicts, of the *Habeas Corpus*, of the rules of evidence, was simply the idea that we must have public justice and not private justice. Or, at the worst, we will have public injustice. Even a legal quibble is better than a mere caprice. Lawyers have often cut off a man's head, as one bisects a triangle in Euclid, after mere mental ingenuity and lucidity. But there are things worse even than this. It is better to cut off the head of a man as one bisects a triangle, for some reason, than to cut off the head of a man as one knocks off the head of a thistle— for no reason. I would rather have our law as hard as Euclid than have it as quiet, as incalculable, and as secret as a stroll along a lane. Now, all these proposals to make law indeterminate are simply proposals to make it despotic—or, at least, to make somebody despotic. Someone is to decide, absolutely, by instinct, by inspiration, or by whim, that a certain man shall be kept in prison for a certain time. But with this difference, remember, dividing him from those high and ancient authorities in whose absolutism humanity has often put its trust. In the old monarchic systems, among the Eastern Sultans or the Greek tyrants or the Russian Tsars, the autocrat was exhibited; he was the most obvious man in the State; he was lifted on a throne and lit up by a crown of gold. Everyone knew at least what sort of a man he was. Often he had popularity: always he had publicity. Even when he was not a public servant he was at least a public monument. Their despot was specially in the sun. But the new despot will be specially in the darkness. He will be something more than a private detective—which is bad enough. He will be a private Lord Chief Justice. He will be a private King. The man who despotically decides whether some poor fellow is to rejoin his family or fall back into his cell will not be a great King giving laws under a tree. It will be some governor or inspector, some doctor or jailer, whose name no one knows. Mankind must make a stand against this new and occult absolutism. Even when great nations were proud of their despots, I privately should have been ashamed of them. I am not likely to be less ashamed of the despots now that they are ashamed of themselves.

July 4, 1908

Old and New Puritans

When anyone discusses Puritanism (as I did in a recent article) he always opens a wild and useless discussion about whether it is wise to be strict or wise to be lax. But there is no sense in discussing that; all men whose heads grow between their shoulders (and not under their arms or in the middle of their backs) can see that both strictness and laxity can be dangerous. The really interesting point is this: that there are two quite different kinds of strictness. We apply the word strict, narrow, bigoted, or intolerant, to two separate states of mind which are not only different but are really quite opposite. To put the point quite crudely, we call a man narrow when he is illogical; but we also call a man narrow when he is logical. If a man has a pure doctrine you call him a bigot. Yet if a man has a mere prejudice (or, if you like, a mere sentiment or instinct), you call him a bigot too.

But a man must have something. If he has not got doctrines, he must have prejudices.

But all such matters are made clearer by examples. Almost the whole difference between the old Puritanism and the new is exactly this difference between principle and prejudice. The old theological Puritan had principles. The new enlightened Puritan has only prejudices. Puritans of the earlier type rejected the things they really loved because they thought them wicked. Puritans of the new type reject all the things they happen to hate, and then simply call them wicked. But, as I say, it is best observed in examples. A Calvinist who in the seventeenth century refused (in spite of agonised human entreaties) to pray for the soul of a dead sinner, was a perfectly reasonable and honourable man. He refused to pray for the man for the clear and simple reason that (according to his philosophy) the man was already in Hell. Probably his refusal hurt him as much as it hurt any of the suppliants; but he had a rational cause for his refusal. It was true to say that his principles forbade him to say prayers for the dead. Now let me take a typical instance of modern Puritanism. The following letter appeared in an excellent periodical which is often identified, rightly or wrongly, with all modern Puritanism. I will quote every word of it; because every word is precious—

Sir,—I went to the "Orient in London" Pageant on Tuesday evening, taking two of my sons, and, with sorrow and dismay, left before the close, as a protest.

I was arranging to take our Sunday School scholars to the Exhibition, but can do nothing of the kind. I had not expected to see the children of Nonconformity acting as garlanded chorus girls, and short-skirted Misses "disporting on a coral beach"—as it is officially put—nor had I thought to hear Christian young women sing a chorus addressed to a heathen goddess. Let it be clear that the pageant is absolutely a theatrical play—indeed, it includes four melodramas, set to music, with scenery, wigs, pigments, obviously professional players, and lurid stage effects—such as a volcano in partial eruption.

To see a mock Livingstone striking a theatrical attitude, brandishing a cardboard cross on the top of a ladder—the curtain being re-lifted to acknowledge the plaudits of the thoughtless—was surely a matter of profound regret. I came away with a burdened heart, feeling that Nonconformity and the mission-field workers had suffered a grievous wrong at the hands of their leaders. I heard expressions of disapproval from other visitors.

Many things might be said about this extraordinary letter and the lady who wrote it. But one thing it is primarily necessary to notice about her. She has no principles. That is certain. She has only a set of strange and hazy associations which the mind cannot easily follow. It is an intelligible intellectual position that acting is wrong, that pageants are wrong, that art is wrong, that symbolism is wrong, that festive meetings of the sexes are wrong, that all earthly enjoyment is wrong. But she does not stand for any of these principles. She vaguely dislikes certain things and she calls her social fancies Christianity. The result is simply dark and mysterious. One cannot make out what are the particular things that are supposed to be particularly immoral. The lady says (with hissing emphasis) that the garlanded children of Nonconformity "disport on a coral beach." Would it have been a shade more respectable if it had been any other kind of beach? Would a sand beach or a shingle beach have been less provocative of the lower passions? Why is Livingstone more likely to corrupt our morals on the top of a ladder than in any other position?

But the intolerable climax, the infernal crown of all this sickening profligacy, was (as far as I can make out) the fact that there was a volcano in partial eruption. I confess it is all very mysterious to me. Would the incident have been more indecent or less if the volcano had been in complete eruption? I cannot make it out. I cannot, I confess, imagine what form of human lust could be inflamed by the spectacle of a volcano, however complete. Nor do I understand exactly what the lady wanted as an alternative to any of the things of which she complained. She does not say that she disapproves of any pageant representing the conversion of heathens to Christianity. She only says that she does not like to see Christian young women pretending to be heathens in such a pageant. Would she like them to be real heathens? Would she like a number of savages kept heathen for the purpose? The truth is that it is quite useless to search for any principle in the protests or lamentations of these people. They have no principles. They have forgotten the Puritan theology. They have not even got the Puritan ethics. They have nothing but a sort of loose Puritan taste. The new Puritans are vitally and fundamentally frivolous.

A little while ago I was invited to take part in a debate on Puritanism. I took part in it: and when I had done speaking the principal orator rose indignantly to his feet and said that I had been guilty, not only of irrelevancy, but of bad taste, in discussing the *religion* of the Puritans. That distinguished club did not care about the *religion* of the Puritans. I mildly interpellated that the religion was the only thing the Puritans cared about, and I was justly called to order. We were (it appeared) discussing Puritanism, not the religion of the Puritans.

It sounded to me like discussing Buddhism, not the religion of the Buddhists. It seemed like talking of Mohammedanism, not the Mohammedan religion, or of Catholicism, but not the Catholic religion. Plainly, Puritanism was a religious movement, and when the movement ceases to be religious the movement ceases to move. The old-fashioned Nonconformists are not merely more solid and more consistent; they are also much more intellectual, much more broad-minded, much more free, than their modern successors. If it is really immoral to go to a theatre, let people keep away from theatres. But do not let them go to theatres and then go out again, because of the obscene and shameless introduction of a ladder. If all pageants are pompous and vain, let people keep away from pageants. But do not let them go to pageants, and then bitterly complain that they have been made to blush by the open exhibition of cardboard. Do not let them talk as if they had been lured into a trap, when they discover that the heathens in a pageant are not real heathens.

A theatre may be (as the old Puritans unwaveringly maintained) an un-Christian thing. But if there is such a thing as a Christian theatre, it cannot be expected to rival the realism of the amphitheatre. Only pagan theatres introduced real foreigners, who were really killed. Christian theatres can only be expected to introduce stage foreigners, who are killed only on the stage. However the excellent Nonconformist lady whose letter I have quoted may wish to hear real heathen girls singing to a real heathen god, she must stifle her passion till she can go out as a missionary and hear them singing for herself. However she may wish to see a real missionary really martyred, she must not expect to see it within the cold conventions of the Christian stage. The necessary symbolism and illusion of theatricals is something that she must take or leave. The old Puritan had the logical courage to leave it. The modern Puritan has not the courage to do either one or the other.

July 11, 1908

Imprisonment in Prisons and Hospitals

There is one quite naked piece of nonsense which must be destroyed if modern society is to go on at all. That is the pretence of teaching things "scientifically" which are not in their own nature scientific. A man may learn to be a good prophet about the stars; he may learn, after long assiduity and self-culture, to be a false prophet about the weather. But no man would dare to predict his wife's temper, even falsely. It is not a scientific subject, it is impossible to imagine whether the wife would be more annoyed if he prophesied wrong or if he prophesied right. Let a man keep a weather-chart then, but not a wife-chart. A comet is not any bigger or any smaller because you know it is coming. A quarrel may be either bigger or smaller because you know it is coming. Monday cannot be more materially hot because you have carefully examined the chart. Monday may be much more spiritually hot because you have examined the lady. All this seems very alphabetical and even inane in its obviousness. Yet it is not obvious; and the fact that it is not obvious is already the problem, and will probably be the destruction of our society.

For instance, in recent discussions about the law and principle of imprisonment, one argument perpetually recurs. It is this: that a prison is the same as a hospital, and therefore that people in one should be treated with the same indeterminate consideration as people in the other. A man is kept in hospital until he is cured of disease. Therefore a man ought to be kept in prison until he is cured of crime. In other words, if you have a weather-chart, you may have a wife-chart. Now there is only one broad, philosophical objection to the parallel between a prison and a hospital, and that is simply that the two things are not at all alike. In case, however, this large and simple idea is not sufficiently evident at a glance, I am willing to explain and expand it. A critic once complained that I had not enough separate paragraphs on this page. I will now, in a belated manner, accept his advice. I will gratify him with a sort of gush and glut of separate paragraphs. For I will proceed, in answer to all such as shall absurdly maintain that prisons are hospitals, that prisoners should be kept indefinitely, like patients, or that crime can be cured along lines analogous to disease—I shall maintain my position, in answer to all these, in no less than fourteen distinct paragraphs. Which I hope will satisfy him.

First Reason why a Prison is not like a Hospital: Because the person to be cured in a hospital is called a patient. But a person to be cured in any moral matter must be called an agent. If he is to be cured of any physical ill, he had better be passive. But if he is to be cured of any moral ill, he must be active. Lust, cruelty, deliberate drunkenness, envy—"herein the patient must minister to himself." He must be, not a passive person, but a very violent and creative person if he is to come back to morality. In short, the essence of medical cure is that a man is a patient. But the essence of moral cure is that the patient must be an *impatient*. Nothing can be done unless he hates his own sin more than he loves his own pleasure. The distinction can be put simply in one sentence. A man can be cured of appendicitis while he is insensible. Can he be cured of theft while he is insensible?

Second Reason why a Prison is not like a Hospital: Because complete cure can be tested in the case of extremes in malady, but not in the case of extremes in morals. If your mother is physically dead in a hospital, you are bound of hear of it. Even hospital authorities will inform you of so casual a fact. But if your mother is morally dead in prison, you will not hear of it at all.

Third Reason: No spiteful kings, no sneaking judges have ever yet thought of using hospitals as private houses of ingenious conviction or official torture. Lions were let loose on ancient Christians in a prison. But microbes are not let loose on modern Christians in Charing Cross Hospital. At least, I hope not. The machinery of police has been used persistently for oppression; some say even that it was invented for it. But no one says that hospitals have existed in order to suppress opinion; prisons certainly have.

Fourth Reason: On the whole, people are better (physically) for going to hospitals when they are ill. It cannot be shown that they do better for going to prisons when they do ill.

Fifth Reason: Doctors are not, perhaps, always so noble as those tall, dark, manly young doctors of whom we read in novels. Still, most doctors are a very decent sort of men. Hospital nurses are not all such saintly representatives of Florence Nightingale as you would suppose from the threepenny novelette. Still, many of them are really ladies, and some of them are actually women. The suggestion of the novels is not entirely untrue. But no novel ever dared to suggest that the ordinary jailer was a Galahad, or that the ordinary female warder was a woman. The comparison is not complete or fair. There is much humbug about the officials of a hospital. But there is not even any humbug about the officials of a prison. There is not any disguise. Everyone pretends that hospital officials are the noblest people. Everyone admits that prison officials are the lowest.

Sixth Reason: A man is only taken to a hospital when his ordinary animal health has disappeared. He is taken to a prison when his ordinary animal health has, if anything, become too obvious.

Seventh Reason: The body is finite; but the soul is infinite. There are some things that are irrelevant to the subject of Smith having a broken leg. But there are no subjects that are irrelevant to Smith having a broken heart. Anyone can discover if his leg is mended or not. No one will discover, until the end of all time, whether his heart is mended or not. That question will have to wait until that great day when the world shall be ended—or mended.

Eighth Reason: For some cause or other, an invalid is thought rather elegant in Society, while (on the other hand) a convict is often coldly received.

Ninth Reason: Doctors are, as a rule, really interested in the science of surgery or physiology. Warders are not interested in the science of crime, for the very excellent reason that there is no science of crime. If you follow two young surgeons to their lunch, it is really very likely that you will hear them talking, purely out of preference, about picturesque problems of their own profession. Even as they cut off the leg of a fowl, they will recall the yet more trenchant manner in which they cut off the leg of a stock-broker; they will really follow the details and delicacies of some operation which will be splendid if Slasher does it. Dickens was quite right: the doctor does talk about his trade, because it is a real and interesting trade. The doctor does talk about the bodies of men. But Lord! how Dickens would have laughed if you had told him that the turnkey and the jailer talked about the souls of men! When one prison official takes lunch with another does he begin discussing the exquisite poise of moral indecision which may be remarked in the attitude of B 93? I wonder. Or rather, I don't.

Tenth Reason: A disease is a thing that tortures oneself: therefore, one rushes at least to medical aid. But a crime is a thing that generally tortures somebody else; therefore one rather rushes away from that legal aid so eagerly extended and offered. Men want to be cured of toothache, therefore they go to the dentist. It is sad to think how few of them ever want to be cured of criminality and therefore rush wildly to the magistrate.

Eleventh Reason: Arising (as they say in the House of Commons) out of the last question, it may be pointed out that the most desperate physical pain tends to get into medical control. But the most desperate moral insolence exactly tends to keep out of moral control. And the men who will be shut up for ever for thieving three times will be the men who have really been tempted to thieve. The big thieves will escape—because they are big thieves.

Twelfth Reason: The tradition of all civilised law has been to fix when a man can come out of prison, not to unfix it. I have a tenderness for the Habeas Corpus Act.

Thirteenth Reason: Any ordinary Englishman would loathe the proposal.

Fourteenth Reason: I loathe it. There are many more.

July 18, 1908

Literature for Boys

I wish the newspapers would condescend to be intelligible to so simple a mind as mine. As it is, I find Browning and Meredith, and even Mallarmé, much more easy to understand. The newspapers (especially the rather vulgar newspapers) have command of a kind of vast and vague language, which they wield so triumphantly that I never have the most shadowy idea of what they are talking about. I read a protest against some particular entertainment at a music-hall; and when I have read it, I feel that there may be human sacrifices on the stage for all I can understand. Or I read (as I did the other day) a protest against some degrading sort of literature sent to boys. Well, some literature sent to boys is so unmistakably degrading that any people whose profession it is to send it ought simply to be sent to penal servitude. I would no more hesitate about locking up the ruffians who put such things in children's hands than if they had put arsenic in children's milk. I know this sort of thing exists, and I naturally supposed that it was about this sort of thing that the newspaper was talking. And then in the newspaper article there followed this extraordinary sentence: "Such literature as this cannot in any sense elevate."

It stunned me, and left my mind a blank. It seemed an almost insane observation. One does not talk like that about things that are obviously and intentionally vile. One does not say that poisoned daggers cannot in any sense improve the health, or that burglars do not in any sense add to other people's property. Nobody says, "Such incidents as the Massacre of St. Bartholomew cannot in any sense increase the population of Paris." No one says, "Falling down four pair of stairs cannot in any sense elevate the body." Yet it comes natural to this extraordinary journalist, when talking about common, malignant pornography, to say mildly that it "cannot elevate" the boy.

It is not very easy to elevate a boy. Many of us, I imagine, have passed some hours in the company of boys without elevating them much or without being ourselves much elevated, however much we may have been amused. Still, we hardly regarded ourselves as creatures on a level with the crapulous trade of which I supposed the journalist to be talking. But perhaps the journalist was not talking about that trade at all. Perhaps the journalist was talking about the undesirability of boys reading "Othello," or "Treasure Island," or *The Illustrated London News*. With this kind of journalist you never know what he is talking about; some even affirm that he does not know himself.

It is the duty of the Press to expound; occasionally it is its duty to expose. Rarely, very rarely, it is its duty to suppress, though this is almost the only duty which it still performs with gusto. But it can only be right to do one of two things—either to expose a thing because it is bad, or to hide the thing because it is bad. It cannot be right to ruin the thing by shaky allusion and shifty argument, to seek to suggest that it is wicked without even stating what you hold wickedness to be. There is a case for telling the truth; there is a case for avoiding the scandal; but there is no possible defence for the man who tells the scandal, but does not tell the truth. I may think my next-door neighbour a criminal, who should be denounced and cast out—as a fact, by some odd coincidence, I do not—or I may think him a fellow-sinner whose faults should be veiled by charity. But I cannot be right to go about saying, "My neighbour, Mr. Jones, has done something of which, as a man of principle, I cannot approve," when the thing I do not approve is really only the colour of his front door. It cannot be fair to inflame evil curiosity and send fifty spies to his gates if I am not sure that the full knowledge of the facts would be final. But this, I am sorry to say, is the exact practice of a certain section of the modern Press. These writers take some painful and delicate matter—such as the limits of exposure in statuary or in dancing—and they talk of it for columns and columns with a sort of sombre allusiveness which is really nothing more or less than an infinite license of libel. An honest man (one would think) would either avoid the subject or tell the truth.

It cannot in itself be a particularly pleasant atmosphere; but at least one can be intellectually clean in it. I am not going to talk about the actual cases of the thing that are going on; everybody knows them. There is a discussion about Miss Maud Allan's[1] dancing, and another about some decorative figures said to be on a building off the Strand. The main point to be seized can be much better discussed by any older and more wholesome example. On the morning after Lady Godiva's ride through

[1] More accurately, Miss Maud Allan. She caused something of a sensation by dancing bare-legged in *The Vision of Salome*.

Coventry the two best Coventry papers dealt with the incident definitely but discreetly. The *Coventry Cataract* (The Radical organ, written with great talent) stated exactly what she had done, and firmly disapproved of it. The *Coventry Comme-Il-Faut Gazette* (a paper written by gentlemen for gentlemen) felt so shocked that it suppressed the whole incident; or merely said in the Court news, "Lady Godiva went out riding as usual at 11:30." But there was another paper in the town, well financed, energetic, go-ahead, abreast of the times—in short, hateful to God and to the enemies of God. And it wrote an article every day about Lady Godiva's conduct, without even telling anybody what it was; and in about a fortnight people thought that poor Lady Godiva had eaten all her children or sold herself to the Devil, or done something so huge and shocking that they lay awake at night trying to imagine what it was, to the plain improvement of their morality. The articles would begin like this—"We have no desire to dwell on the sickening scene of yesterday. We are no prudes: but there are things so atrocious, so unnatural, so remote from men, even in their blackest and foulest moments; so inconceivable even to imaginations depraved with every common crime, that the mere mention of them would seem not so much obscene as mysterious, and those who have read the deepest in the darkest books of hell would yet be bewildered for a moment, and fail to understand the full and frightful meaning of the fact."

And when the journalists wrote like this they thought themselves very brave for denouncing Godiva, and also very delicate and chivalrous for not saying what she had really done. I may add that this paper made a considerable success, that its journalists went on writing in the same style, until they felt that a new sensation was needed, when they started a fiscal campaign against Godiva's removal of the tax. Whereupon, I am glad to say that Earl Leofric hanged the editor and all his subordinates.

I am not going to discuss again here, as I have lately been doing elsewhere, the question of the moral effect of anonymous journalism. But I cannot help thinking that the anonymous atmosphere, so to speak, must have much to do with this extraordinary vagueness. The writer is told that he must express, not his own principles, but the principles of the paper. The only defect of the arrangement is that he probably knows what are his own principles, whereas he does not always know what are the principles of the paper: and sometimes they are not there to know. It is not very easy for a man to be firm, sharp, and clear-cut in expressing the opinions of a mass of readers whom he has never seen, or a crowd of shareholders whom he does not even want to see. Some people say, I know, that if articles were signed they would really be more cautious and non-committal than they now are. But these are like the people who say that men will drink less if you make taverns uncomfortable: they have forgotten how men really feel. If you make the tavern uncomfortable the man will drink more—in order to forget the tavern. In the same way, a man who writes an unsigned article will feel that he is doing the paper full justice by being merely vague and polite. But no man will ever feel that he is doing *himself* justice merely by being vague and polite. If sincerity does not make him say what he knows, ambition will make him do it. He would rather put his name at the end of something interesting and decisive than at the end of something dreary and inconsequent. It is not a question (as in the weary war of Socialists and Individualists) about whether "self-interest" is the spring. The point is that even self-interest makes a man write a nameless article vaguely and a signed article crisply and clearly. These modern sophists have forgotten all natural gestures; the gestures of singing or of the sword. And they have even forgotten what it feels like to sign one's own name.

July 25, 1908

Nameless Journalism and Modern Secrecy

It is impossible to touch the question of anonymous journalism without stirring a swarm, I will not say of the wasps, but of the honey-laden bees who follow my own excellent trade; and my attitude has been sufficiently attacked to make it desirable to defend it. First of all, it is only fair to say that there is a sense in which this is really (to use a phrase of which all sensible men are sick and tired) a practical question. Generally, the distinction between practical and theoretic is entirely unmeaning; every practical action has reference to a theory of conduct or aim, as every practical machine has reference to a theory of science. But there is one useful sense in which the word may possibly be used. When I speak here of a practical question, I mean a question that is not concerned only with unalterable conditions of human nature, but is greatly concerned with circumstances that are in their nature various or occasional. Thus it is a practical question whether I shall take my umbrella; it depends on whether it is raining. But it is a highly theoretic question whether I shall take somebody else's umbrella; it depends on my conception of the eternal needs and unalterable destiny of the human soul. Now I do not profess that my desire for signed articles and my dislike of unsigned is ethically so rigid or so universal as this. I have written four leading articles in my life which I was not allowed to sign, and I do not regard myself as stained with four crimes. Also, as a correspondent reminds me, I have, in my innocent novitiate, masked a possible moral beauty in namelessness, like the namelessness of the craftsmen who carved the great cathedrals. All this is quite true. Anonymous journalism might be something as generous as anonymous charity. But it is not. That is what I mean by calling it a practical or relative matter; unsigned writing might be a great good, but in our actual conditions it is the great evil. If you praise at this moment the modesty of the nameless toiler, you are not taking out your umbrella when it is raining; you are putting on your fur coat in the dog-days.

The danger at this particular moment is in the other direction. People talk about the boldness of the modern world; but the most interesting thing about the modern world is its strange and sinister shyness. An eerie element runs through it of deliberate quietude and discoloration. The old mark of a gentleman was to dress gallantly; the new is to dress unobtrusively. The old uniform of soldiers used to be blazoned with silver or scarlet, that they might be unmistakable; the new uniforms are coloured with dust and clay that they may be mistaken. This is the age of khaki; and khaki is unpoetical, not because it is violent, but because it is timid. Every man wishes to be invisible in his environment, like a chameleon. Every man tries to put the responsibility on to the system, or the circumstances, or the laws of economics. The editor when hunted into his private room would be only too glad to take the exact colour of the carpet or to be (like certain insects on a twig), indistinguishable from the arm-chair to which he clung. The Prime Minister when confronted with a deputation would be delighted if he could melt into the wallpaper of Downing Street. How happy Mr. Balfour would be if he could turn tricolour on a platform covered with Union Jacks, and then turn bright green on a lawn at a garden-party.

It is not surprising that the modern pressman should feel the same, and should be only too glad to call in his own surroundings to protect him, to hide behind the huge white shield of his newspaper. Many have noticed, for instance, that the Cabinet has been steadily growing in power of late and the House of Commons steadily declining. But few have noticed that this is because the House of Commons is an open society, while the Cabinet is a secret society. We are in the habit of boasting because our fathers did not allow any report of the debates. But we do not allow any report of the important debates. For the important debates, the debates which settle the issue and the division of parties, are conducted in the Cabinet; in the place where Mr.

Balfour can really argue with Mr. Chamberlain, not in the House
of Commons, where Mr. Balfour simply gives the word to Mr.
Balfour's majority. In the same way, it has been said more than
once, and with much truth, that the journalists of to-day occupy
the nearest position to the priests in religious ages. But in what
religious age was a man allowed to thunder from the pulpit with
a mask on his face?

This question of nameless journalism has therefore to be discussed with distinct reference to the special evil of our time. If
we were talking about an ideal or an abstract paradise, many
sentiments might be felt on the subject. It might be a beautiful
idea that the noble books in a library should all be as blameless
as the bricks in a wall. It might also (I think) be a beautiful idea
that all the bricks in a wall should be signed by the brick-maker,
like the books in a library. To be able to look at every brick and
read a short account of the gentleman to whom one was indebted
for it, with his name, native town, complexion, creed, favourite
moral sentiment, and so on, might render a walk between brick
walls much more entertaining. But we are not discussing the
bricks of the New Jerusalem; we are not discussing whether
personality or impersonality would be the more perfect if the
aims of both of them were perfect; if there were no motives
involved except a saintly self-effacement in work, or a generous
pride in it. We are discussing whether in this wicked world a
very powerful profession should be allowed to keep peculiarly
to itself some of the advantages of a secret society, and especially
whether it should be allowed to do so at a time of which the
typical heresy and weakness is to quiet the individual conscience
with a talk about the system and the social trend. We are talking
about whether we will encourage anonymous writing in an existing society in which we know it must often mean anonymous
combination, anonymous tyranny, or anonymous vengeance. In
short, we will leave on one side the question of whether, in the
perfect city, the man who makes a brick ought to write his name
on it. But we will say decisively that the man who *throws* a brick
ought to write his name on it; and (with complete respect for

those who use the current custom) those who feel no echo at all of our emotions we shall venture to call persons somewhat unduly emancipated from the prejudice of honour.

Nobody maintains that writing any anonymous article any-where is an improper action. If the true test is wanted it is the same test that exists in all matters of morals: the test of the motive. If I wish to know whether I am acting honourably in leaving an article unsigned, I can find out in a moment by asking myself the question: "What is the objection to signing it?" If the objection is, as often in the case of a leading article, that I should like to sign it, but am not allowed to, I may myself be free from blame. If it is that the article urges the Government to give ten thousand pounds to my mortal enemy, and I wish to conceal my kindness and to spare his delicacy, then I may, perhaps, be a very fine fellow. But articles are not often left unsigned for this reason. Not many anonymous journalists are fired solely by the motive of doing good by stealth. And if, when I examine my motive for remaining anonymous, I find it is what it gen-erally is, some idea of caution or self-protection, then there is only one thing I ought to do—to kick that caution instantly out of my soul as I would kick a temptation to treason. If I am withholding my signature by command or from custom, or because the matter is colourless or because the authorship is known, then my motive, at any rate, is comparatively innocent. But if (in any shape or form whatever) I am withholding my signature because I do not want people to know that I am the author—then I am in the most emphatic sense not fighting like a gentleman or a free man: I am a bravo in a mask; I am a slave with a dagger; I am a low flunkey with a cudgel who bludgeons his master's enemies in the dark. But if anonymity is a precaution it *must* be a base precaution. With a sort of innocent wickedness people explain that it would really be very troublesome if they were made to own their own names and answer for their own statements. One gentleman said that if a journalist signed his copy his opinions would always be discounted in the light of his daily life: he would be reminded of his constant presence in country-houses—or in public-houses perhaps. It never seemed to occur to this gentleman that a clergyman's teaching or a doctor's teaching is discounted by his life; nor is there any particular reason why journalism should be the only art entirely separated from life. Why should a drunken journalist preach teetotalism with any more security than a drunken vicar? Another gentleman said to me with great solemnity, "I must say I find the anonymity a great convenience." To which I replied with equal gravity, "I have no doubt you do."

August 1, 1908

American Slaves and Female Emancipation

About American politics people like myself can only conjecture; we cannot be certain even that we know what the whole thing is about. Still, my conjectures may interest Englishmen, and might positively amuse Americans. And I am moved to offer them by two accidental circumstances: first, that in the middle of my article last week there was a large photograph of the late Joel Chandler Harris (the author of the famous "Uncle Remus"), which reminded me that I had meant to write about him; the other is the uproarious nomination of Mr. Bryan as the Democratic candidate. The two things are not without kinship; for Chandler Harris may be said to be a survival of the old Southern civilisation which waged the great war, while Mr. Bryan represents the new form of the political tradition which still holds the Southern States. "Uncle Remus" is quite as important for one aspect as "Uncle Tom's Cabin" for the other.

This peculiar value of "Uncle Remus" necessitates a somewhat difficult explanation. Slavery, the owning of a man's body as one owns a tool, is to me intrinsically immoral; therefore, I suppose that at any stage of the old struggle I should have been in favour of emancipation, as indeed were many distinguished Southerners. But it is always interesting to trace the obscure weaknesses which trip up such just and obvious attitudes. Now there is about all ideas of emancipation or enlightenment, all preaching of freedom to the captive or giving sight to the blind, a certain recurring perplexity or peril. And it is this: that the emancipator generally means one who brings his own special type of emancipation. The man bringing light brings his own special patent electric-light, and puts out all the previous candles. When we set the poor man free, it nearly always means that we set him free to learn from us. It ought to mean sometimes that we set him free to teach us. But we should be rather startled if he tried it on.

There are many cases of this emancipation meaning a new livery and a new subordination. For instance, if the people of India were to rebel successfully tomorrow and set up a Republic ringed round with Radical newspapers, it would be called the defeat of England. But it would really be the complete victory of England and English methods after a struggle of two hundred years. It would be called the victory of the Indian; but it would really be the final disappearance of the Indian tradition from India. Whether the English King governs as an Eastern despot, or the Eastern people govern as Western democrats, it is alike in neglect of any such idea as that the original and genuine India has anything particular to teach. I do not know how much good there ever was in the dreamy and unworldly India; I only say that whatever there was is as much obliterated by an Indian Radical as by an English Tory.

An even stronger case is that of the modern fight about female claims. They call the outbreaks of the Suffragettes a triumph for woman. But they are not. They are a triumph for man—for the original male point of view. This is not a movement of Feminism, but a movement of Masculinism. It is the complete victory of man over woman; of male logic over female common-sense. From the beginning of the world, in every cavern, in every wigwam, at every tea-table, there have been two points of view waging an amicable but incessant war and making up between them the dangerous romance called marriage. There has been the view that abstract rights must be asserted, logic chopped to the last straw, the invisible canons of club or Parliament kept inviolate, intellectual fairness eaten for its own sake like a food, quibbles taken seriously and the rules of the game considered with a grave face—there has been, in short, the man's point of view. And there has been the other point of view—that fruit is the only test, that happiness and unhappiness are unanswerable, that the only wit that scores is mother wit, that the only rule that works is rule of thumb, that it does not matter a dump whether one has privilege so long as one has power; and above all that the serious good a man does is in the fish he catches or the field he ploughs, and that all other things he does, from Parliament to polo, are the games of a school-boy. That has been in the crushing majority of cases the point of view of the woman. There is a very strong case for it, and, though I am naturally in the other camp myself, I like to see the female flag flying. But the female flag has been hauled down. The Suffragettes have surrendered the fortress of their sex; they have come into our camp in complete surrender, admitting that we men have always been right and the women always wrong; that we were right on insisting on the abstractions of the pot-house and the Parliament, and that they were wrong in laughing at them. Just as an Eastern newspaper is a victory of Western methods, so the Feminist movement is a surrender to the masculine intelligence.

Now I have taken these two cases at random because they have in them the same predominant truth. People say, "Let women have what men have got"; but one might reply, "Rather let us ask what women have that men have not got." The Indian Nationalist says, "We will have what the English have." But he would be more of a Nationalist if he said, "We will have what the English will never have." There is, I repeat, in all idea of emancipation this more doubtful idea of emancipation always coming from outside, and taking no account of the good already flowing from the emancipated or unemancipated thing. And it was this answer that Chandler Harris, in a manner, raised in "Uncle Remus" in connection with the problem of the negro. The ordinary Abolitionist, the ordinary Northern idealist, preached generosity to the blacks, saying, "We will give the negro liberty; we will give the negro light; we will give the negro education." Chandler Harris in "Uncle Remus" gave an indirect, unexpected, yet strangely forcible answer. He did not say—"I will give the negro whips and chains if he is mutinous," or, "I will give him a better light and liberty if he is good." He said—"This is what the negro has *given me*. You talk of educating the slave; this is how the slave educated me. He taught me the primal culture of humanity, the ancient and elvish wisdom without which all other learning is priggishness, the tales which from the beginning our Mother Earth has told to all her children at night. The negro has given something to the South and I will give it to the North."

Curiously enough, the slave, Uncle Remus, in revealing the root of humanity, revealed also the root of democracy. As always happens with evil things, the arguments of slavery are worse than slavery itself. And for slavery (an institution undoubtedly on the increase in the modern world) one of the principal arguments is this: that the original life of the earth is a life of conscious aristocracy. "Uncle Remus" struck a heavier blow at this defence of slavery than "Uncle Tom" struck at all the others. For the Uncle Remus stories reveal, what all real folklore reveals, that this cool superiority of one section of life over another has never been known among men, and probably never known among birds, beasts, or fishes. You may well say that scientific men discovered the Struggle for Life. They did indeed discover it. It had never been known until they came. It had never existed until they discovered it. It is certain that no man ever felt as if he were a man struggling for life in a pitiless universe. It is highly probable (I should say) that no bird or beast ever felt like that. Certainly the beasts do not behave as if they took that view. The birds do not sing as if they held that philosophy. But the best argument of all is from the really primitive and powerful legends of humanity. Whenever we can get at so much as the echo of what negroes or Red Indians really feel, we find that they feel original equality. Men think primarily of men as equal. Nay, they think primarily of animals as equal: there are the tales of Uncle Remus to prove it. All the modern phrases about the cruel castes in nature can be most effectually answered in one vigorous and contemptuous syllable, "Brer!" It is a syllable well adapted for an expression of scorn at public meetings, like the "Grrrr!" at the beginning of Browning's poem.[1] But the word "Brer" (which I need hardly say means Brother, and is the title of all animals in "Uncle Remus"), is a solid symbol of the attitude of mind with which all real primitive thought begins. It begins with Brother Fox and Brother Rabbit. It is no answer to say that the Fox tries to eat the Rabbit, and the Rabbit succeeds in cheating the Fox. That is sin; that is vice, violence, bullying, swindling; but it is not inequality. They start as equal, because they start as brothers. They start as brothers, but brothers occasionally quarrel. The first brothers on earth quarrelled and left a living legend of murder, but not in any sense a legend of aristocracy. Abel, even when he was dead, was quite equal to Cain.

August 8, 1908

Local Pride and Pageants

Some little time ago, when I was sitting in a small tavern not far from the river, the door of the place swung open behind me, and there came striding in one of the Kings of the Saxon Hep-

---

[1] See the opening of "Soliloquy of the Spanish Cloister".

tarchy. He was a big, blonde, handsome man, with something of that sleepy swagger which has in all ages been the innocent affectation of the German blood. His tunic was belted and clasped with big barbaric jewels; he had a clumsy, iron-hilted sword; he was cross-gartered up to the knee. And, by a custom which royalty has since, most unfortunately, abandoned, he wore his crown on his head, even when he went into a public-house.

This potentate sat down opposite me, and ordered a pot of beer, for beer is probably one of the few things that are still found surviving out of the Heptarchy. I fell into respectful conversation with him, and he told me he was the King of Wessex, and mentioned his very ugly name. I tried to remember the facts about that prince, but found them a little foggy in my mind. I said to him delicately: "Excuse my asking so personal a question, but, with the exception of your military reputation, I am disgracefully ill-informed about the rest of your career. Let me see, now—pray forgive my curiosity—but were you ever baptised?" The question seemed in some mysterious way to offend him. He said that he had been baptised, like other people; but it was (I understood him to say) "a long while ago," and "he did not remember the ceremony." I said of course it was a long while ago, as it must have been somewhere in the ninth century; but I thought that, even amid the numerous social functions of a King of Wessex, he might remember the occasion when, if ever, he embraced Christianity. By this time he had emptied his pewter pot and I reverently requested permission to have it refilled, a course of action which alone, I believe, averted a serious misunderstanding between that noble barbarian and myself. He explained, somewhat gloomily, that he didn't care much about centuries, but that they were rehearsing for the pageant and had got him to be King of Wessex. Then circumstances began to arrange themselves in my mind, and by the time that a little more beer had disappeared on both sides of the table, I fell into a comparatively friendly conversation with him, for he was hearty and sensible and companionable and a man, and, in short, much

more like a fighting Saxon King than any of the pompous versions of King Alfred in most statues and poems and plays.

And I came away from the conversation with the feeling that
these pageants of which the English grow so fond are open to
a certain criticism; that they have a defect which prevents them
from being the really national things they might otherwise be.
Of this defect my friend the King of Wessex was a large and
magnificent example. A local pageant ought to be a festival of
real local patriotism, which is one of the finest things in the
world. It ought to be concerned with the real pride of real people
in their town. Therefore, it ought never to consist of mere dead
history; but, as far as possible, of living traditions. Legends
should be honoured, if the legends are really current; lies should
be honoured, if the lies are really told. Old wives' tales should
be represented, if the old wives really tell them. But mere historical coincidences of place and person, the mere fact that such-
and-such a man did stand for a moment in such-and-such a
spot—these we do not require in a popular pageant. Suppose
they have a pageant in Pimlico—I hope they will. Then let Pimlico lift up in its pride anything that it is really proud of, if it be
only the parish pump or the public-house sign. Let Pimlico
parade whatever Pimlico delights to honour, whether it is its
best donkey, its blackest chimney-sweep, or even its member
of Parliament. That is all dignified and reasonable. But it is not
reasonable to send somebody to read up dry history until he
discovers that William Wallace[1] stopped three minutes at Pimlico
on his way to execution, or that on the spot now occupied by
the Pimlico Police-court Caractacus[2] made a speech to the blue
and bellowing Britons. There is no patriotism in the thought

---

[1] Sir William Wallace (1270–1305), a great national hero of Scotland who led
the Scottish resistance against Edward I; after early successes, he was eventually
taken prisoner, condemned as a traitor and hanged and quartered.

[2] Caractatus was a British king (died 54 A.D.) who warred gallantly against
the Romans until he was eventually defeated in battle and taken captive to Rome.

that some alien and uninteresting person stood on the soil of
Pimlico before Pimlico existed. The parish has no living legend
of the thing. Whatever be the cause of that faint poetic melancholy that does seem to hover over Pimlico, it cannot be referred
to any regrets at the fate of William Wallace. However blue the
modern Britons may look and feel in that district, it has no
connection with the blueness of the ancient Britons. There is no
true Pimlico sentiment in celebrating names which can be discovered in the British Museum Library, but cannot be discovered
in Pimlico. If Pimlico has any real memories, I care not of what,
of prizefighters or dandies, or gentlemen deservedly hanged, let
her celebrate these traditions. If she has none, let her celebrate
what is happening to her now, that at least she may have some
traditions in the future.

There are such living local tales and figures; there are even
many of them. For instance there is a real memory of Dr. Johnson
in Fleet Street; probably there has never been a time since his
death when people did not connect his name in conversation
with the place—and point out the taverns and coffee-houses in
which he is alleged to have sat. And the two things are spiritually
akin to each other: if there was always something of Fleet Street
about Dr. Johnson, there is still a great deal of Dr. Johnson about
Fleet Street, with its genuine but irregular work, its long talks
in taverns, its tone of comradeship, its touch of cynicism, its
coarseness in certain externals. There is an example of a true
historical tradition. But it must not be supposed that we can
only establish such connection with periods as recent as Johnson's. There are living local stories which seem to have been
handed on continuously, yet which are older than William Wallace, or as old as the Heptarchy. The obvious instance is the
story of Lady Godiva in Coventry, where the thing has always
been a point of local patriotism, as well as a joke. Another case
is the memory of Alfred in that noble Berkshire valley where
the White Horse has been picked clean of grass continuously for
a thousand years.

There ought not to be any figure in a popular procession who might not be received with spontaneous cheers. If the thing is recent let it be recent, if it is ancient let it be ancient; but let it always be intelligible. Sometimes a thing is well known because it is very new; sometimes it is well known because it is very old. Let it be Mr. Chamberlain's unmistakable costume, or Godiva's unmistakable uncostume—but let it be something that the real people can perceive and applaud. What people are likely to applaud a pre-historic King of Wessex, or Mercia, or Northumbria? A little while ago there was an excellent pageant in Chelsea, containing, among its more popular figures, the great Lord Chesterfield and Sir Richard Steele. How many people actually living in Chelsea, I wonder, ever even knew that Lord Chesterfield or Sir Richard Steele had set foot in the place? It would probably have been a better piece of pure local patriotism if they had relied on more recent memories—on the names and figures of men many of whose neighbours and friends and enemies must be still living in Chelsea. Did they have a triumphal car of Thomas Carlyle accidentally burning the first manuscript of "The French Revolution"? They might have represented Rossetti, followed by a long and foolish file of the wild animals he kept in his back-garden. What a large number of young artists would have jumped at the chance of dressing up as Whistler, impenetrably disguised behind a white lock and a monocle. Since there has been a pageant in Chelsea, I suppose there will soon be one in my own romantic Battersea. For this kind of witchcraft is not stopped by running water. In such a case, I know what they will try to do. They will try to maintain that, because Bolingbroke House stood in Battersea, therefore all Battersea people are throbbing with reminiscent enthusiasm about the celebrated and unreliable Lord Bolingbroke. There is a statement that Pope wrote his "Essay on Man" in Bolingbroke House, Battersea. They will attempt to represent that to all Battersea workmen Pope's "Essay on Man" is a sort of Bible and daily guide; and for all I know (God help us), they will conclude by asking the whole crowd to sing that long and highly illogical poem in chorus. For my part, if it comes to that I shall protest. I shall make the monstrous demand that the Battersea Pageant shall be about things that have been heard of in Battersea. And if we have no old genuine traditions, we will have recent genuine traditions: for we are a living city. I should be prepared to enthrone John Burns[3] as a god; others among us would be prepared to burn him as a guy. We would have Mr. Birrell making up his Education Bill, and the little boys asking him the time. But two things we would have at least for any public festival, first, cheaper prices; and second, a healthy atmosphere of popular derision, such as that which glorifies Godiva.

August 15, 1908

Americans in Sport and Jingoism

The general stream of exciting events at the Stadium,[1] as well as some that were unfortunate as well as exciting, indicates many interesting things about national differences of instinct and opinion. The modern promoters of peace are always trying to discover the points on which nations agree. They will never really achieve peace until they discover and define the points on which they disagree. There are national peculiarities which will always be preserved, and which, for the variety and interest of our earth, always ought to be preserved. International bitterness, international bloodshed, does not come from recognising these differences. It comes from not recognizing them.

[3] John Burns (1858–1943), a labor leader and socialist, was the first member of the working classes to enter the British Cabinet (1905).

[1] The opening day of the Olympics at the Stadium in West London was on July 13; the United Kingdom stood first with thirty-eight total wins; the U.S.A. was second with twenty-two.

For instance, in consequence of certain events in the races at the Stadium, we have begun to hear all round us a murmur not unheard on other historical occasions: "The Americans are not sportsmen." Now, if we leave the matter there, we shall do a gross injustice to a great people. Probably, if an American were asked for his principal complaint, it would be to the effect that the English are not sportsmen. Unfortunately, the word "sportsman" means something entirely different in the American language. Of all barriers between two nations, the worst is having the same language—and meaning something different by it. An English major and a French commandant are much more like each other than an English colonel and an American colonel. In spite of such difficulties, however, I will make a respectful guess.

The only sense I can make, even hypothetically, out of America is this—I offer it as a mere conjecture—America is a serious parody. America is an exaggeration not more comic, but more solemn, than its original. We are all acquainted with the ordinary notion of a caricature, in which certain features are treated more largely, but more lightly. Thus, let us say, a King is given an outrageously large crown, and he becomes a pantomime King. But we must try and imagine the reversal of this process: we must conceive, not something heavy taken lightly, but something originally light taken heavily and hugely. It is not that the King becomes a comic character by the enlargement of his crown; it is actually that Punch becomes a serious character by the further elongation of his nose. Ordinary people treat their institutions as jokes. American people treat jokes as institutions. Englishmen make a picture absurd by expanding it into a hoarding. America makes a sketch eternal by expanding it into a fresco. All the things that are in this country casual, fantastic, fugitive, amusing, are in that country strenuous, patriotic, Puritanical, essential. They have sometimes boasted that they work harder and are more business-like than we: but this boast falls far short of the situation. They have taken our idlenesses and turned them into occupations. They have taken our relaxations and refused to relax an inch over them. They have taken our very jokes successfully—

and seriously. There are many cases of this; but it can be seen at a glance in the case of American sport.

I have noticed the thing for some time in English and American literature. In England Mr. Bernard Shaw is an influence; in America he is a school. His followers in that country solemnly put on a paradoxical manner, and might with equal solemnity put on a red beard. Similarly there were decadents in England, France and Germany. But the essence and even the virtue of a decadent is that he does at least know that decadence is (both in the literal and in the popular sense of the phrase) all rot. The English decadents, feeling life to be as light as dust and wind, at least took it as lightly. The true pessimist had even a kind of airy contempt for his own pessimism, and disdain of his disdain of things. Open an American magazine, and you will find Mr. Edgar Saltus,[2] the American decadent, entirely serious and entirely happy. You will see a monument and a prodigy; you will see the Strenuous Decadent. He devotes himself to the trade in dust and ashes with the same beaming and bustling cheerfulness with which he would have devoted himself to the trade in pork or white goods. All the epigrams are punctually delivered; all the cynical maxims about marriage are gravely recited; above all, the whole drivelling philosophy is definitely, honestly, and seriously believed. There are many other instances. Poor Nietzsche had much of the irritation of the invalid in his philosophy; but he had some of the laughter and light irony of the literary European in his manner of expressing it: he could to some extent feel the fighting folly of his own exaggerations. But no gleam of irony or self-criticism has ever crossed the black and cavernous brain of the American Nietzsche, a sublime donkey who actually writes under the name of "Ragnor Redbeard."

It is exactly the same with American sport: and this principle applies to and explains events which might otherwise be unfairly

[2] The author of a number of books on love, such as *Historia Amoris, A History of Love, Ancient and Modern* (1906), and *Imperial Purple* (1892), as well as *The Anatomy of Negation* (1886).

and unfriendlily explained. We English have always talked very gravely about sport; we have pretended that it was the root of our national virtues; we have associated it vaguely with extremely vague theories of racial superiority and evolutionary success. But all this gravity about the game is with us only a part of the game. About a game, as about a drama, there must be enough consistency to create a brief illusion.

But the American in sport is like those wild cowboys of the West who fired their revolvers at a villain in a melodrama; he is like Don Quixote when he drew his sword and dismembered the marionettes. Spain might produce Don Quixote, but Spain made game of him. We in England make sport prominent, we make it pervasive; but we do not in our souls make it important. To the American sportsman the thing is like patriotism or theology. We say as a half-laughing boast that the Battle of Waterloo was won on a cricket-field. But we cannot understand the American who really feels on a cricket-field as if he were at the Battle of Waterloo. He is not necessarily courteous; he is not always scrupulous. We must look in him not for the light vices of vain or sensual loungers, but for the solid vices of statesmen and fanatics, for the sins of men inflamed by patriotism or religion. He cannot shake hands after the fight. He feels towards his conqueror as a man towards the invader who has robbed him of his country, or the atheist who has robbed him of his God.

Thus, if the American athlete breaks a rule or does something that seems brutal or cunning in order to win, then the best and most representative Americans would certainly condemn him. But they would not condemn him, and we must not expect them to condemn him, exactly as we should all condemn him. We should condemn him not only as a cad but as a fool; as a man who in his desire for victory surrenders that general applause which alone makes victory pleasant. We are almost as much mystified as we are angry with the man who cheats in a mere game. What can be the fun of being a winner if one is not admired for one's way of winning? What is the pleasure of gaining glory if one loses honour? The game is not worth the candle when the candle burns down your castle and your coat-of-arms. But the Americans would not condemn their unscrupulous compatriot in this light and contemptuous way. They would not condemn him as a selfish fool who lost the fun of playing for the sake of winning. They would condemn him as one condemns dignified but desperate men for yielding in great moments to the powers of darkness; as one condemns Clive for forging, or Henri Quatre for denying his creed,[3] or Bruce for killing Comyn, or Hastings for hanging Nuncomar, or Nelson for letting his official actions be swayed by Lady Hamilton. One may condemn such men, one may shoot them, but one does not misunderstand them. The American is a bad sportsman because he is a good Jingo. The phrases quoted, even in the newspapers, from the American murmur and comment in the Stadium prove this contention completely. One American phrase constantly recurred: "Our boys were in to win." Which means: "This is sport to you, but death to us—death or immortality." For them the game is really worth the candle—because the game is not really a game. The real problem, I admit, remains with us. How are we to deal with this gigantic daughter who, in her youthful innocence, supposes that we mean what we say? We said that football was the foundation of English ethics and philosophy; but we never imagined that anybody would believe us. We said that commerce was a proof of Christian energy and sobriety; but it never crossed our minds that such a thing could be credited by anybody on earth. We said that the Jewish Sabbath was sacred, and in Puritan England people were damned for running about on Sunday. But in Puritan America they were killed for running about on Sunday. We pretended, for a passing fashion, that the chief glory of Britain was the British Empire. As a matter of fact, of course,

---

[3] Henry Quatre (IV) of France (1553–1610), raised as a Calvinist, was forced to become a Catholic after the St. Bartholomew's Day Massacre of 1572. Three years later, he escaped from his Catholic guardians and renounced his forced conversion. He finally became a willing member of the Church of Rome in 1593.

a patriot has far less pride in the British Empire than in the British climate. To a man who loves the English country, that the sun never sets on the Empire is far less important than that the sun never shines too much on the island. But the Americans, overhearing our interlude, began to take Imperialism seriously. What is to be done with such a people?

August 22, 1908

On Punishing the Rich

I believe that some ancient writers did maintain that the populace was always right. I know that most modern writers (especially revolutionary writers) maintain that the populace is always wrong. Yet the real and reasonable limits of popular wisdom and popular folly are not particularly hard to state. The mob generally has justice, but the mob generally has not got truth. The mob will generally be right in its view of the facts—if they are facts. Unfortunately, they are frequently not facts, but news from the newspapers. The practical distinction can be made plain enough. The people who think that puppies ought not to be made into pork-pies are the overwhelming majority of the people of England. The people who know for a fact whether puppies are made into pork-pies are of necessity a small minority of scientific experts. The people who want a race to be run fairly are merely the democracy of Englishmen; the people who know whether a race is being run unfairly are an aristocracy of swindlers. That prisoners should not be tortured in modern prisons is as certain and obvious as trial by jury—before Mr. Herbert Gladstone's proposal. I should have said as certain and obvious as the Habeas Corpus Act. But whether prisoners are tortured in modern prisons is as secret as the Inquisition.

Some great mystics maintained that the two great orders of angels were distinguished by their special dedication to knowledge or to love. The Cherubim loved and the Seraphim knew; or it may have been the other way round—I cannot remember. But certainly what was thus said of Seraphim and Cherubim may truly be said of aristocracy and democracy. Democracy loves—but it does not know. Aristocracy knows—but it does not care. If you want the facts, it is much better to go to the governing class. But if you want ideals, it is immeasurably better to go to the mob. The bulk of a people always has a fairly sane and honourable philosophy. It is its science, its accumulation of accurate phenomena, which is commonly in fault. For philosophy is a democratic thing, depending only on man's reason; while science is almost necessarily oligarchical, since it depends on man's opportunities. A man can philosophise about fleas in a cheap lodging; but he cannot biologise about fleas without an expensive microscope. Thus the democracy is commonly quite right in its cosmic or ethical view of fleas, while often mistaken about the configuration of their anatomy or the number of their legs. The faddists who would encourage the flea at the expense of humanity are a minority: that is, they are an oligarchy. Not one man in twenty really thinks anything so ridiculous as that it is wrong to drink wine. That is a matter of principle. But not one man in twenty really knows whether he is drinking wine. For that is a matter of the tact and technical compromise of the trade. Not one man in twenty, not one man in two hundred, really thinks that the glories and privileges of a great nation ought to be open to commercial barter. That peerages ought not to be bought and sold is universally admitted by all ordinary citizens. That peerages are bought and sold is often admitted only to the peers.

These two things, the invariable sufficiency of the popular instinct and the almost invariable insufficiency of the popular information, are very vividly presented in a great public trial that has recently come to its conclusion. The acquittal of Mr.

Robert Sievier[1] from the charge of blackmailing Mr. Joel is, when taken in connection with all its prejudices of the populace and all its ovations of the street, a curious instance of this curious combination of a sound sense of the abstract in morality, combined with a considerable amount of cheerful ignorance of the concrete. That Robert Sievier should be the national hero really suggests the nation's justice. But it also suggests its innocence. Many people must have rejoiced at Mr. Sievier's victory, and even felt a certain affection for him as a public figure, who would not have had the *Winning Post* in their houses. But, indeed, here again the average instinct was very accurate.

The strongest reason why one man should not go to jail is that he is the kind of man who tends to get there. The strongest reason why another man should be smashed in a law-court is that he is the kind of man who tends to be victorious in a law-court. We have begun to realise that we must leave the mere hunting of the evil-doers, for whom the law is a natural enemy, and begin to sharpen some public weapons against those evil-doers for whom the law is a natural protection. To have overthrown the wealthy, subtle, and cautious financier in a law-court is to have fought the monster on its native heath. It is to have choked the wolf in his lair and knifed the eagle on the edge of the precipice; to have trapped the Red Indian in the forest, and broken the clans in the pass of Killiecrankie. In the ordinary way the one set is sending the other to jail as monotonously as cats are eating birds. It is a reversal that amounts to a revolution that the bird should conquer: especially if he is a bird who seems specially doomed to be a jail-bird. Nor does a man of the one type nowadays tend jail-wards because he is bad: but because the traps of law seem to be only set for that particular jolly, brazen, free-living sort of man. I remember an eminent philanthropist who said to me with the utmost simplicity that he had rescued from their infamous existence two men, one of whom

---

[1] Sievier was arrested for blackmail in June and acquitted in July.

was a burglar and the other "the greatest treater in the town." He actually thought that taking another man's spoons and giving another man beer were acts of pretty much the same colour and quality. He classed together (when both were done by a poor man) the crime of theft and the virtue of hospitality. The notion that was really at the back of his mind and which is true as far as it goes, was that both the habit of burglary and the habit of hospitality were things likely to prevent a man "getting on," and even to assist in his "going under." Neither habit could lead to Park Lane. Both habits might lead to Clerkenwell Prison. In short, he saw the kind of man whom the law generally crushes; whom in this case, fortunately, the law had almost unexpectedly redeemed.

It may be hoped that this event is of good augury, and indicates a turn of the tide in such affairs. It may be hoped that we shall attempt to strengthen the legal machinery in the future more against the man who may become stronger than the law rather than against the man who is obviously weaker. We have been too much in the habit of pointing to a man with a ragged coat and a black patch over his eye with a bad hat or a new beard and saying, "There is a thief." But the man's rags are really a proof that he is not a thief—that is, not a successful thief. We have too often argued, "This man is poor; therefore he will steal." But it would be quite as reasonable to argue, "This man is rich; therefore he has stolen." In neither case is the logic quite conclusive.

Suppose a decent villager in a simple age is about to barter with a stranger; suppose he is prepared to give a horse and receive a measure of corn. Simple as the process is, there is one process even more child-like—that is, for the stranger to knock him down and take both. But there is also the other kind of robber who robs not by making the process plainer but by making it more complicated. Instead of stunning the villager with a club, he stuns him with a calculation. Instead of taking the horse and the corn and leaving nothing, this primeval financier takes the horse and the corn and then says with breathless and blinding rapidity, "I take these things and give you their equivalent in other materials with a handsome margin; I give you seventy-nine and a half trouser-buttons, two copies of the third edition of 'East Lynne,' two hundred and thirteen haricot beans, a ton of Hampshire soil, a little dog, the waste-paper baskets of fifteen solicitors' offices, a piece of cheese, a thimble, a copy of the *Spectator*, a half-bottle of sparkling cider, a cat, a nail, a stick, a boot, a bun—and I think that is a handsome offer." Throwing all these things down in a confused heap, the primaeval financier leaps upon the horse, shoulders the sack of corn, and leaves the villager in an agony of mental arithmetic. In forty years, perhaps, he suspects injustice.

August 29, 1908

Listening to Modernist Arguments

The actual proposals of the people who call themselves advanced are harmless enough. It is their arguments for the proposals which prove that the proposals are harmful. It can be maintained that Socialism would not upset the family; but it is maintained that Socialism would upset the family, and ought to be thanked for doing so. It is tenable that women having votes would not alter the intercourse of the sexes; but it is distinctly declared that it would alter the intercourse of the sexes, and a good job too. If a man offers me a medicine, it may be good or bad; but if he offers me a medicine along with á pamphlet in favour of suicide, then I am suspicious of the medicine, even if, like many successful medicines, it consists only of some kind of coloured water. If a man tells me that a certain road is safe for cyclists, but at the same time stuffs into my hand a long roll of lint, a bottle of embrocation, and a number of surgical appliances, I cannot very easily disconnect the two ideas. So, if a man proposes a small change, but is full of the language and allusions connected with a large change, it is difficult for us to think of the small change when we have once thought of the large one. Suppose a man says, "There ought to be a tunnel from St. Paul's Station to Farringdon Street," none of us feel any particular disposition to object. But suppose a man says, "There ought to be a tunnel from St. Paul's to Farringdon Street. For, after all, St. Paul's Cathedral is not an edifice in the most elevated style of architecture. It was abruptly erected by the vandal Christopher Wren in the corrupt and filthy reign of Charles II. Its only apparent dignity is due to its elevated and effective site, and that site will be used to even better effect when a nobler building has replaced it. Therefore, it may be said with certainty that a tunnel to Farringdon Street," etc. If this were said, a somewhat moderate degree of subtlety would be required to discover that, if the tunnel were constructed, the Cathedral would fall down.

Again and again I have found this a sound tip or test in the justice of any matter: wait until the people who like it have argued in favour of it; if they can once be induced with open hearts and mouths to say what is good in the thing, you are pretty certain to discover whatever is bad in it. For instance, the negotiations just before the Boer War were really a network of mystery and hypocrisy on both sides; therefore, I waited to make up my mind until I heard the moral arguments. And I decided; because I found that the moral arguments on our side were immoral arguments. Doubtless the Dutch had numberless examples among their individual citizens of rapacity, of double dealing, of secret cruelty or sudden injustice. Still their talk was of the truth of treaties, of the sacredness of national boundary, of the simple pride of Republican institutions, of the colossal courage of the weak. That is the talk of a people who are wronged. Doubtless there were among the English fighting in that field (certainly there were, for I knew them) men who lived and died only for a chivalrous fancy, of redressing wrongs, or even more manly principle of professional honour. Still our talk was of the need of expansion, of the hopelessness of the weak resisting the strong, of everything being inevitable, of everything being better in the long run. That is the talk of a people who are doing a wrong. Such a people is condemned not by its crimes; it is condemned by its justification. It was only when I had read the defences of the thing that I saw that it was indefensible.

In other words, the whole trouble is this: that a very small, innocent proposal often has tied on to its tail a whole huge and guilty philosophy. What people do is often not the supreme question, even if they blow up cities or lay waste continents. What people do is often of far less importance than why they do it. This strikes me especially in the case of the modern discussion about the position of woman. There was a moment when I might have been strongly in favour of female suffrage, if I had not happened to see some of the arguments for it. The moment I saw those arguments I realised that the people who used them were not right about women or wrong about women; they were not even talking about women at all. For instance, I have just read an enthusiastic essay by a lady suffragist which says (to put it shortly, which she is far from doing) that man has always been a faultless being in the eyes of his women-folk, but that under the influence of the modern movement his women are beginning to find him out. What does it all mean? I never met a woman who had not found out the man long before he was her husband. I never met a wife who did not know all the weaknesses of her husband and count on them as calmly as she counted on sunrise or the spring. I never met the woman who regarded the man as incapable of moral error. Did you?

Here again the argument would be almost unassailable if it were put in the right way; but these people will put it by preference in the wrong way; and that makes me think that they are wrong. If a man said this: "Women are trained too much to consider the sensual comforts of men; this arrangement is bad for the men and for the women," then that position would have a strong prima-facie truth, and would be well worth arguing. But if a man says, "Hitherto the man has been an infallible pope, whom the woman may not criticise," then really he might just as well say that the man has killed a wife every night, like Bluebeard. Ever since we have any human records, women have done almost nothing else but criticise the weaknesses of men. Everybody who has ever met a schoolgirl of sixteen knows that she is consumed with a criticism of the weaknesses of men. So far from blindly worshipping men after they are married to them, girls generally sneer at men even before they are introduced to them. It *is* true that Jane is taught to take John's breakfast seriously. It is simply not true that Jane is taught to take John and his sacred virtue seriously. You have only got to look at Jane to see that.

Now let any man or woman who knows such simple things, who has been married or who has even seen people who are married, read with as much gravity as possible the following passage, which actually occurs in a book recently published in the interests of what is called Feminism—

> The man who goes a-wooing is well compared with a hunter, and while in the past he was bold enough, or secure enough in superiority, to attack his prey openly, he is now content to act the part of a cat, which pretends innocence until the poor bird comes within reach. Then the velvet paw reveals the relentless claws, and the scowl of the bully replaces the smile of the wooer when the captive is securely bound. . . . If ever a lover goes through the farce of pretending to kneel to her, she ought to give him a hint with the toe of her boot that she knows a mean, deceitful fool by his actions, and knows he will be a bully as soon as he has a chance. . . . Men did not know themselves as long as women were without education and freedom; but now the little male tyrant is in daily dread of finding all his petty meannesses held up to public contempt by a lady novelist, and the blustering bully dreads the dramatic description which makes him an object of ridicule. How many callous men have shuddered at the thought of marriage after reading the works of modern female reformers.

This sort of stuff is really being solemnly and solidly written. It knows nothing either about men or about women; it might as well be talking about the long historical quarrel between camels and kangaroos. What lover ever does kneel to the woman he loves? What woman would ever dream of kicking him, even if he did? What wife ever required a lady novelist to explain to her her husband's deficiencies? What husband ever cared a button about what lady novelists said of his deficiencies? What does it all mean? Life is a real thing; it really matters whether you marry a good husband or a bad husband. And just as it is certainly to a woman's advantage to have a kind husband, it is certainly to a man's advantage to have a clever wife. What man ever does keep his wife in darkness and inferiority? Why should he? It is much jollier to have an intelligent wife than a stupid wife, considering the great amount of time that one has to pass in her company. I have met wives who were kept stupid because their husbands were stupid. But I have never met a wife who was kept stupid because her husband was clever. Where is this humble, dog-like, submissive wife? I have never seen her. Doubtless, she does exist, as an exception. There are men who have no fear of their wives. There are men who have no noses. There are men who have no legs, like Mr. Miserrimus Dexter. But taking men as they are, I really think that the man who has tamed a wife is more exceptional than the man who has tamed a tiger or a chimpanzee; and also much more unpleasant. The normal man is much more afraid of his wife than his wife is afraid of him. The woman's fear of the man is only like the modern aristocracy's fear of the democracy. If the majority chose to be violent they might be terrible; but we know that they will not. So if a gentleman hit a lady he would knock her down; but we know that he will not. The majority is only superior because it has a power that it will never use. The gentleman can only conquer the lady by ceasing to be a gentleman. The populace is utterly helpless up to the instant when it rebels with brickbats. The male sex is utterly helpless up to the instant when it rebels with pokers.

September 5, 1908

Modern and Medieval Monsters

Most people saw in the newspapers last week this paragraph, or something parallel to it—

"LEPRECHAUN" CAUGHT.

> Great excitement has been caused in Mullingar, in the west of Ireland, by the report that the supposed "Leprechaun," which several children stated they had seen at Killough, near Delvin, during the past two months, was captured. Two policemen found a creature of dwarfish proportions in a wood near the town, and brought the little man to Mullingar Workhouse, where he is now an inmate. He eats greedily, but all attempts to interview him have failed, his only reply being a peculiar sound between a growl and a squeal. The inmates regard him with interest mixed with awe.

This seems like the beginning of an important era of research; it seems as if the world of experiments had at last touched the world of reality. It is as if one read, "Great excitement has been caused in Rotten Row, in the west of London, by the fact that the centaur, previously seen by several colonels and young ladies, has at last been stopped in his lawless gallop." Or it is as if one saw in a newspaper: "Slight perturbation has been caused at the west end of Margate by the capture of a mermaid," or "A daring fowler, climbing the crags of the Black Mountains for a nest of eagles, found, somewhat unexpectedly, that it was a nest of angels." It is wonderful to have the calm admission in cold print of such links between the human world and other worlds. It is interesting to know that they took the Leprechaun to a work-house. It settles, and settles with a very sound instinct, the claim of humanity in such sublime curiosities. If a centaur were really found in Rotten Row, would they take him to a workhouse or to a stable? If a mermaid were really fished up at Margate, would they take her to a workhouse or to an aquarium? If people caught an angel unawares, would they put the angel in a workhouse? Or in an aviary?

The idea of the Missing Link was not at all new with Darwin; it was not invented merely by those vague but imaginative minor poets to whom we owe most of our ideas about evolution. Men had always played about with the idea of a possible link between human and bestial life, and the very existence—or, if you will, the very nonexistence—of the centaur or the mermaid proves it. All the mythologies had dreamed of a half-human monster. The only objection to the centaur and the mermaid was that they could not be found. In every other respect their merits were of the most solid sort. So it is with the Darwinian ideal of a link between man and the brutes. There is no objection to it except that there is no evidence for it. The only objection to the Missing Link is that he is apparently fabulous, like the centaur and the mermaid, and all the other images under which man has imagined a bridge between himself and brutality. In short, the only objection to the Missing Link is that he is missing.

But there is also another very elementary difference. The Greeks and the Mediaevals invented monstrosities. But they treated them as monstrosities—that is, they treated them as exceptions. They did not deduce any law from such lawless things as the centaur or the merman, the griffin or the hippogriff. But modern people did try to make a law out of the Missing Link. They made him a law-giver, though they were hunting for him like a criminal. They built on the foundation of him before he was found. They made this unknown monster, the mixture of the man and ape, the founder of society and the accepted father of mankind. The ancients had a fancy that there was a mongrel of horse and man, a mongrel of fish and man. But they did not make it the father of anything; they did not ask the mad mongrel to breed. The ancients did not draw up a system of ethics based upon the centaur, showing how man in a civilised society must take care of his hands, but must not wholly forget his hooves. They never reminded woman that, although she had the golden hair of a goddess, she had the tail of a fish. But the moderns did talk to man as if he were the Missing Link; they did remind him that he must allow for apish imbecility and bestial tricks. The moderns did tell the woman that she was half a brute, for all her beauty; you can find the thing said again and again in Schopenhauer and other prophets of the modern spirit. That is the real difference between the two monsters. The Missing Link is still missing and so is the merman. On the top of all this we have the Leprechaun, apparently an actual monster at present in the charge of the police. It is unnecessary to say that numbers of learned people have proved again and again that it could not exist. It is equally unnecessary to say that numbers of unlearned people—children, mothers of children, workers, common people who grow corn or catch fish—had seen them existing. Almost every other simple type of our working population had seen a Leprechaun. A fisherman had seen a Leprechaun. A farmer had seen a Leprechaun. Even a postman had probably seen one. But there was one simple son of the people whose path had never before been crossed by the prodigy. Never until then had a policeman seen a Leprechaun. It was only a question of whether the monster should take the policeman away with him into Elfland (where such a policeman as he would certainly have been fettered by the fatal love of the fairy queen), or whether the policeman should take away the monster to the police-station. The forces of this earth prevailed; the constable captured the elf, instead of the elf capturing the constable. The officer took him to the workhouse, and opened a new epoch in the study of tradition and folklore.

What will the modern world do if it finds (as very likely it will) that the wildest fables have had a basis in fact; that there are creatures of the border land, that there are oddities on the fringe of fixed laws, that there are things so unnatural as easily to be called preternatural? I do not know what the modern world will do about these things; I only know what I hope. I hope the modern world will be as sane about these things as the mediaeval world was about them. Because I believe that an ogre can have two heads, that is no reason why I should lose the only head that I have. Because the mediaeval man thought that some man had the head of a dog, that was no reason why he himself should

have the head of a donkey. The mediaeval man was never essentially weak or stupid about any of his beliefs, however unfounded
they were. He did not lack judgment; he only lacked the opportunities of judgment. He had superstitions; but he was not superstitious about them. He was wrong about Africa; but then, to
do him justice, he did not care whether he was right. He had
got that particular thing which some modern people call "the
love of truth," but which is really simply the power of taking
one's own mistakes seriously. He thought that ordinary men
were a serious matter; as they are. He thought that extraordinary
men were a fantastic fairy-tale; and he thought (very rightly)
that the fairy-tale was all the more fantastic if it was true. He
did not let dog-faced men affect his conception of mankind; he
regarded them as a joke, the best as a practical joke. But in our
time, I am sorry to say, we have seen some signs of the possibility
that such aberrations or monstrosities as spiritual science may
discover will be taken as real tests of, or keys to, the human lot.
For instance, the psychological phenomenon called "dual personality" is certainly a thing so extraordinary that any old-fashioned rationalist or agnostic would simply have called it a miracle
and disbelieved it. But nowadays those who do believe it will
not treat it as a miracle—that is, as an exception. They try to
make deductions from it, theories about identity and metem-
psychosis and psychical evolution, and God knows what. If it
is true that one particular body has two souls, it is a joke, as if
it had two noses. It must not be permitted to upset the actualities
of our human happiness. If someone says, "Jones blew his nose,"
and Jones is of so peculiar a formation that one may with logical
propriety ask, "Which nose?" that is no reason why the ordinary
formula should lose its ordinary human utility. This is, I think,
one of the most real dangers that lie in front of the civilisation
that has just discovered the Leprechaun. We are going to find
all the gods and fairies all over again, all the spiritual hybrids
and all the jests of eternity. But we are not going to find them,
as the pagans found them, in our youth, in an atmosphere in
which gods can be jested with or giants slapped on the back.

We are going to find them, in the old age of our society, in a mood dangerously morbid, in a spirit only too ready to take the exception instead of the rule. If we find creatures that are half human, we may only too possibly make them an excuse for being half-human ourselves. I should not be very painfully concerned about the Leprechaun if people had thrown stones at him as a bad fairy, or given him milk and fire as a good one. But there is something menacing about taking away a monster in order to study him. There is something sinister about putting a Leprechaun in the workhouse. The only solid comfort is that he certainly will not work.

September 12, 1908

History and Tradition

One often wonders what the world of the future will really think of our present epoch. It is all very well to say that they will find plenty of documents and an enormous amount of printed matter. Our newspaper language is obvious because it is printed in large letters. The names over our shops are obvious because they are printed in large letters. They are not obvious in any other sense. We think them simple because we know what they mean. But they are not by any means things of which one can say generally that it is easy to know what they mean. Take the first case that comes to hand. Suppose the traveller from New Zealand saw over a big London building the words "Child's Bank," I suppose he would think it meant a child's money-box. We read it quite simply and swiftly in another sense; but then, so did the ancient Egyptains read simply and swiftly the huge hieroglyphics that we can hardly decipher. When they saw a moon, six suns, a human hand, a lotus, and five birds standing on one leg, they immediately burst out laughing, because it was a joke. But our descendants, even if they know our language, may well have almost as much trouble with us as we have with Egypt. The opportunities for a natural error are so infinite; as in the case of Child's Bank.

I remember when I was a little boy (I was a poetical and unpleasant little boy) I always read the words "Job-Master" over some neighbouring door, as if the first word were the Job of the Old Testament. I also remember that over a shop of hatters or hosiers in Kensington were written the words "Hope Brothers." I supposed this to be an inspiring address to mankind, urging them not to fall into an impotent pessimism. I have since found that the thing has another and less invigorating meaning; and I am even able to appreciate the irony of the fact that over another establishment of an analogous kind is written "Hope, Limited." Try the experiment for yourself with almost any words on which your eye happens to fall. At the moment when I am writing (with fevered brow) this article, the words on which my eye falls first are "Typewriting Office," written backwards on a windowpane. That reminds me of an example. I once wrote a rather silly book about twelve historic figures whom I chose to consider symbolic—St. Francis of Assisi, Charles II., Tolstoy, and so on. As a book must have a name I called the thing "Twelve Types." I afterwards discovered that it had some sale as a book about technical printing; I found it myself in a library for working printers. I hope the poor brutes didn't read it.

It is essential, I say, to reflect on the multitudinous mistakes which antiquarian and historical students will be able to make about the minutiae and the mere coincidences of our times. The mistakes will be at once too numberless and too small to correct. The accidental survival of one document will distort and confuse the meaning of another. Suppose we merely write the words "Charing Cross," and then suppose the only other literary relic which seems to throw any light on it is something about women who go out charing, and about how they are often cross. That will be enough to plant an immortal error, of which the tangled tree shall grow fruit for centuries. How easily could an account of sham fight be taken by the casual historian as an account of real fight! How easily could a phrase like "We marched on Brighton," be understood in the same sense as the equally grammatical phrase, "We marched on Bovril"![1] The more one thinks about it the more clear it is that the whole history of the future will be wrong; that is, it will be wrong if it is merely scientific. It will be wrong if it goes merely by facts; it will be wrong if it goes by dates, documents, names, and legal demonstrations. It will be utterly wrong, in short, if once we lose the element of tradition. History will be wholly false unless it is helped by legend.

I say history will entirely misreport us if we lose tradition. But we must not lose it. It is, in fact, a considerable comfort to reflect that we certainly shall not. The only real question is whether we shall hand on a pure tradition or a corrupt one. This point is, indeed, too little remembered in most matters. For instance, those people who praise popular education are right enough in their real underlying idea. But they are always talking about the poor being educated as an alternative to the poor being ignorant. Whatever the poor are, they will never be ignorant. It is absurd to talk as if Tommy in Battersea, if he grows up without schooling, would grow up as a simple savage, running naked in the forests. He would be educated even if he was never schooled. He would grow up a complex, highly civilised, and rather cynical person, for the simple reason that he would grow up in a complex, highly civilised, and rather cynical society. The objection to leaving him untaught is not that he would not learn things; it is that he would learn all the wrong things. The school is of some value because it is just desperately possible that there he may learn the right things. Hence there is no such thing as

---

[1] The statement we "marched on Bovril" is a variation of the idea that an army "marches on its stomach". Bovril is a hot beef stock; thus, we "marched on Bovril" does not have the same meaning as we "marched on Brighton" although the grammatical structure is identical.

education; there is only the right education. And the right education aims not so much at making him complex as at keeping
him straightforward. He will not grow up an anarchist anyhow.
He will know about the police anyhow: the only question is
whether he shall know it from the *Police News*. In any case he
will find out that there are laws: the only question is whether
he shall hear them explained or only see them broken and avenged.
Life will teach him all about government; but only education
can teach him about good government. The gutter-boy will
certainly be civilised. Only education can prevent him being
over-civilised.

Not only does a schoolmaster not exist to teach mere facts,
but he exists to prevent people from learning mere facts, to insist
on their learning what the facts mean; to insist, that is, on their
learning the ideas. The schoolchildren will teach themselves that
there is such a thing as an electric tram. But they must be taught
that there is such a thing as electricity. Uninstructed infants will
find out very soon, and probably in the most graphic manner,
that there is such a place as a police-court. But they will need
to be taught that, in spite of all appearances to the contrary, it
is primarily supposed to be a court of justice. They can see a
policeman for themselves; but they require assistance in the intellectual effort of explaining a policeman. These human relations,
of which the idea is so simple, become in practice horribly twisted
and misleading in any highly civilised State. The very relation
of schoolmaster and pupil itself is capable of most curious entanglements in modern times. I read in the newspaper that a son
of the Kaiser, a German Prince whose name I forget (let us call
him Prince Alaric), has been permitted to pass an examination
for some degree in some science (let us say, in Comparative
Conchology); whereupon the student who had been passed by
the examiners immediately conferred on the examiners a lot of
magnificent medals, titles, and decorations—let us say the Order
of the Golden Battleaxe, the Knight Commandership of the
Nine-headed Eagle, the Third Hammer of the Holy Order of
the Worship of Thor—in fact, all the most sacred prizes of Prot-

estant Germany. Now this interchange seems to me to confuse a little the relations of teacher and pupil. The essence of the idea of conferring a degree is that the more important person gives dignity to the less important. The thing becomes absurd if the very person who confers honour is anxiously looking for honour from the person on whom he confers it. Suppose the aristocratic undergraduate says to the Don, "I will make you a K.C.B.[2] if you will make me an M.A."; then I think the true spirit of examinations is in some peril. Suppose the schoolboy can say to the schoolmaster, "If you don't flog me I will knight you," I cannot help thinking that the scene would be slightly funny, whichever ceremony took place about it. The plain relations of giver and receiver, of master and disciple, or of judge and pleader are gravely altered, not by being abolished, not by being improved, not by being set in order on a new basis, but simply by being hopelessly tangled and confounded. I admire equality, and I have considerable sympathy with anarchy. If the Prince, as a student, were free to put the Professor on a bonfire, or the Professor, as a citizen, free to put the Prince's head on a pike, I could understand the emotions involved. But that each should bow to the other and each bribe the other, that both should be servile and neither humble—that, I think, is not only a complication, but a complication of diseases.

September 19, 1908

Incompatibility in Marriage

I have always heard from my childhood that in America it is possible to get a divorce for incompatibility of temper. In my childhood I always thought it was a joke; but I thought it even

---

[2] Perhaps an allusion to Knight Commander of the (Order of the) Bath (KCB).

more of a joke when I discovered that it was true. If married people are to be divorced for incompatibility of temper, I cannot imagine why all married people are not divorced. Any man and any woman must have incompatible tempers; it is the definition of sex. It is the whole point of being married. Nay, it is the whole fun even of being engaged. You do not fall in love with a compatible person. You do not love somebody exactly like yourself. I am prepared to bet that no two people were ever betrothed for a week without discovering that they suffered from incompatibility of temper. As long as a marriage is founded on a good solid incompatibility, that marriage has a fair chance of continuing to be a happy marriage, and even a romance. Someone said, "As long as lovers can quarrel they are still lovers." Whoever said it had, at least, more wisdom and knowledge of human nature than some of the legislators of America.

My eye has just fallen upon a popular newspaper in which is recorded an extraordinary and typical case. The newspaper publishes a portrait of a rich American gentleman, calling himself a Socialist poet. Some months ago, he went off from his wife with his female affinity; and some days ago, hit his female affinity in the face. The paper also reproduces the face of the female affinity, not, of course, with the aim of excusing the blow. His name is Ferdinand Earle. The affinity's name is Kuttner. Into the other details of this interesting story we may enter in a moment; I wish, first of all, to register the extraordinary fact that "incompatibility of temper" is really, in that remote civilisation, talked about quite seriously. Mr. Ferdinand Earle seems to have given a sort of dinner-party to celebrate his separation from his wife, at which his wife was present. I know it sounds mad, but it is not my fault. They are like that. On this extraordinary occasion the genial fellow seems to have made an after-dinner speech, in the course of which he said the following words, which I would not have missed reading for a pound—

> My first wife and I were extremely happy, and our happiness was increased when we came to live at Monroe by the birth of our son. But soon something began to arise between us—call it what

> you will: incompatibility of temper, conflict of ideas. We did not explain, but I, who am an artist, and have the artistic temperament, sailed for Europe. On the voyage I met a young woman, who, I found, was, like myself, a Socialist. We quickly realised that our marriage was foreordained before our births.

It is impossible to parody that passage. The only way in which one can satirise it is simply to recapitulate it. Two people, a man and a woman, enter into a relation which, whatever be the right rules for regulating it, is, at any rate, a reality: a thing to which Nature attaches terrible results and responsibilites—literally a matter of life and death. They are happy together; but after a certain time a certain something seems to arise. Mr. Ferdinand Earle says that I may call it what I will; so, with his permission, I will call it ordinary bad temper, such as makes me dislike profoundly the necessity of getting out of bed or the necessity of writing this article. This mere human boredom and irritation, which ought to be taken for granted in any healthy marriage, strikes both the people speechless. Neither of them explains. One of them says he is an artist, and runs away. He gets on board some boat or other, on which he finds a woman who agrees with him on a point of political economy. In some extraordinary way this agreement about economics produces a highly mystical and partly Calvinistic conviction about theology. Mr. Earle and the economic lady "quickly realised" that they had been married before they were born.

Now, if we take this view of marriage and divorce as fairly typical of the tone of social philosophy, easily to be found in such English or American circles as call themselves emancipated, we can, I think, proceed to some further considerations which, with the reader's permission, may be ranged in definite notes. There is no truth in particular in Mr. Ferdinand Earle, so far as I can see, and yet no less than three or four truths may possibly be got out of it.

First Note. Let it be remembered that this question of incompatibility of temper has nothing at all to do with the sacramental or supernatural view of marriage, in which I happen to believe.

It is not a question here of making marriage a contract that cannot be loosed. It is a question of making marriage much looser than any other contract is allowed to be. You cannot get rid of your business partner because you do not like the tone of his voice. You cannot break the articles of an apprentice because you do not like the shape of his nose. There must be a solid reason for the rupture even of slight agreements. If I promise to pay you £10 on the 21st of November, I cannot content myself merely with saying that something, call it what you will, has gravely altered my point of view. You may make the marriage contract dissoluble at any definable moment, as after certain cruelties or after a certain time. I may happen to hold that the wife and husband should be bound closer to each other than any two other beings. That is another matter. But this philosophy proposes that the wife of a man should be less bound to him than his executor or his articled clerk.

Second Note. One is almost tempted to think that an intellectual set means a set which has less intellect than anybody else. Artistic colonies, advanced clubs, emancipated groups are constantly separating themselves from the common life. I used to dislike them because they were too intellectual, setting intellect above happiness and manhood; but I am strongly tempted to believe that they are not only not cleverer, but are actually stupider than other people. They take refuge in these modernist cliques, just as a cripple in warlike ages might have taken refuge in a monastery. They are seeking not a world of freedom, but a world of fastidiousness: a world where in their own special manner they can be as silly as they please. Such free-thinkers turn their backs on Mrs. Grundy, not from a desire that criticism should be free, but from a desire that they themselves should be free from criticism. These self-emancipators say that ordinary talk and thought is too tame and timid for them. The truth is that ordinary talk—the talk of a club or a camp fire—is much too free and daring for them. It does not allow for their airy and delicate artistic convictions. No man in a smoking-room, no man in a boat, would be allowed to talk such nonsense as Mr.

Earle talked. A man with brains says that he and a woman are in love with each other; he does not say that they are predestined to be married. A wise man marries a woman because she is pretty, or perhaps only funny or perhaps good. Only a fool marries a woman because she is a Socialist. The thoughts of ordinary men are too strong and too logical for these lovers of illusion and phraseology. They break the law, not because they are stronger than the law, but because the law is too strong for them.

Third Note. This free affinity business is another manifestation of a thing which has always existed—the real and genuine oppression of women. I am not one of those who think that we oppress women by making them wear skirts or by not boring them with ballot-papers. But there is a way in which we constantly are cruel to women; that is, by asking so much of them, demanding a desperately high standard of self-adaptation; turning them into a sort of heroic hypocrites. It is amusing to see that in this New World, as in the Old, the woman is made to grin and bear it. She has to accommodate herself to this masculine fad, just as if it were botany or drink. She has to pretend that "free love" doesn't matter, as she did when it was called profligacy. The first Mrs. Earle was present at the banquet, and pretended to like it; and among all those prigs there was not one near enough to humanity to laugh or cry at the sight of her.

September 26, 1908

Old Forms and Ceremonies

We constantly hear nowadays the statement that old forms and ceremonies must go under in the interests of humanity; but for my part I wish, strictly in the interests of humanity, that many old forms and ceremonies should be fulfilled quite literally. If gentlemen who go to Court are alone allowed to wear swords, it would not be a bad thing if gentlemen who go to Court were expected to know how to use them. One is tempted sometimes to think that it would be a good thing if baptism really meant having a bath, or if being a knight really meant being a horseman. The truth is that if you and I wanted to expose the modern aristocracy, we could hardly do it with more smashing effect than by insisting upon the exact formalities of the ancient aristocracy. We could easily call in the letter of the past to destroy the whole conservative spirit of the present. It is said that an old Teutonic King was chosen with the ritual of being lifted on a shield by the nobles. Let us insist upon that ritual. Let us refuse to accept any King or any aristocracy who cannot perform it. It would have a most important effect, for there are many nobles now who could not lift anything, and there are many Teutonic Kings whom it would be decidedly difficult to lift. Suppose, instead of abolishing orders of knighthood, we were to reinstate orders of knighthood. Suppose we were to insist that Sir Thomas Lipton should win glory in tournament or war. Many people wish to smash the modern men of rank by abolishing their privileges. But we should frighten them much more if we merely insisted on their privileges. Propose to abolish the House of Lords because it is an aristocracy, and the Peers will smile placidly and say that threatened men live long. But ask them really to behave like aristocrats, and they will fly from you, screaming.

The advantage of a fixed form is not at all understood by people in our times. The advantage of a fixed form is that it really varies—that is, by its very fixity, it measures the various moods in which we approach it. Getting up in the morning is a fixed form; if it were not a fixed form, I, for one, would never do it. No getting up for me—*nisi me compelleret ecclesiae auctoritas.*[1] But it is exactly because I have to get up every morning that I

[1] This may be translated as, "Unless the authority of the Church should compel me."

notice that one day is bright blue, another brown and foggy, another cold, clear, and silvery, and my mood varies accordingly. On the bright blue day my spirits go slightly down; there seems something pitiless about perfect weather. On the clear cool day, my spirits are normal. In the fog, my spirits go up; it feels like the end of the world, or better still, a detective story. But I should not appreciate any of these differences if I had not a fixed common duty to perform on each of such days; if it were not that under the blue dome of summer or the yellow umbrella of the fog, I have to go through the same disgusting rites of washing and getting dressed. It is the same with the advantages of keeping up a fixed ceremonial through the ages. The fixed formality stands as a permanent critic of the changing society. Thus, if we continue one form from childhood, such as keeping a diary, or a birthday, this is the only thing that enables us to realise change.

I once read a history of China (I need hardly say that I was paid to read it) and in this work there was an account of the Twenty-Four Types of Filial Piety. Of twenty-three of them I can now give no account. But one of them has stuck in my memory; he was an elderly statesman and Prime Minister of the Empire, or something of that description. And on his fiftieth birthday he dressed up as a child of four and danced gaily in front of his aged parents in order to soothe them with the illusion that they were still quite young. It would certainly be interesting if Mr. Balfour or Mr. Asquith would dress up as four-year-olds and dance before their gratified parents; but, upon the whole, I think this is carrying the principle of reminiscence and ritual unification a little too far, and requires at least a power of Oriental gravity which may not be completely at our command. But the principle involved is sound enough. Happy is he who not only knows the causes of things, but who has not lost touch with their beginnings. Happy is he who still loves something that he loved in the nursery: he has not been broken in two by time; he is not two men, but one, and has saved not only his soul but his life. I can count a fair list of things I have always desired and still desire—sword-blades, the coloured angels of religious art, a kind of cake called jumbles, Grimm's "Fairy Tales" and a shilling paint-box. Some of these things I confess thankfully that I now have (though jumbles have died with a decaying civilisation), but I am more thankful still that the desire in these cases remains. For this is a great gift from God, to have things and still to desire them. But there are other things that I cannot now desire, such as the *Boy's Own Paper*, and sweets, and the approbation of certain schoolmasters, which would now make me feel certain that I was wrong. But I am here wandering from the point, as all the very aged do when they begin to talk about their infancy.

What I originally meant to emphasise was this; that a fixed ceremony, so far from being a dead thing, will often wake men up in periods when they are otherwise dead. And this, which is true of our personal lives, is even more true of the life of a nation or a society. What we call the dead past is very often the only thing that has life enough to revivify the dead present. And I seriously think that we should all wake up to the evil and absurdity of our own age if we were all obliged to perform some ceremony copied point by point from the Dark Ages. I came across an interesting example of this kind of thing the other day, of all places in the world, in a parish magazine. I read my parish magazine; it is an effort of local patriotism in which I believe I stand alone.

In this periodical (which ought surely to be unimpeachable) I read this very interesting fact: that in former times there was a rule that the leaders and chief inhabitants of the parish of Battersea should meet in the middle of Chelsea Bridge the leaders and chief inhabitants of the parish of St. George's, Hanover Square. I know little or nothing of the history of either of these districts. I do not even know the origin and meaning of their names. On that of Battersea I have often speculated, with that delightful old Greek and mediaeval speculation, the only kind of speculation that is really free: speculation entirely without knowledge. Perhaps Battersea really means The Sea of Batter;

it may have been the vivid phrase of some satirist for the rich solidity of the river Thames. Or it might be named after the noble cannonading of the great naval wars, and have originally been Battery Sea. Or again perhaps it was Bather's Sea; so called when we Battersea people had that enthusiasm for washing ourselves which we have since unanimously abandoned. Or it may have some allusion to cricket-bats, which quaint old instruments can still be seen in Battersea Park; or it may be connected with "bateau," the French word for a boat; for there are still some boats on the Thames, though the Moderate Party considers such a state of things highly unnatural.

A similar historic darkness, as far as I am concerned, veils all the details of St. George's, Hanover Square. I suppose that St. George is our own original St. George, who killed the Dragon and afterwards married the grand lady. In many of the marriages of grand ladies, however, which take place in this parish, the preliminary ceremony of the gentleman killing a dragon is often omitted. I am against all this dropping of the full formalities. The title "Hanover Square" also has an unchivalrous sound about it; it seems to have more to do with King George than St. George. Nevertheless, I am humble and agnostic about all these historical speculations. I know so little about the matter that some one of the silly suggestions I have made about the origin of Battersea may be exactly the one which is favoured by the very latest school of historical and topographical learning. I am so ignorant that I may even be right. I do know vaguely, however, from varied reading, that about the time of which I speak, Battersea was a sort of small fashionable resort not far from the city. What St. George's, Hanover Square, was in those days I cannot imagine; very likely it was a slum. Now it is exactly here that the strict fulfilment of very ancient ceremonies would do a great deal of good. The rich and the poor, being forced to meet as officials, would be forced to meet also as men. One century, North Brompton is poor and South Brompton rich; the next century, North is rich and South poor. It would be a good thing if one custom could survive all fashions.

October 3, 1908

A Uniform Creed for Humanity

For some week or two past, all the papers that I like have been talking almost entirely about Tolstoy. This did not make me like them any the less; it is very right that this great European figure should be properly studied and honoured upon the festival of his old age. He has had it in him to win real literary glory; he has it in him now to despise the glory that he has won. He now goes about telling everybody not to read the novels that alone have made his name. There is something magnificent about that. It requires a great man, in first instance, to write a masterpiece. But it requires a very great man to repent of a masterpiece as though it were a sin. Most of those who have discussed Tolstoy on the occasion of this anniversary have complained of this condemnation; they have lamented the fact that a great novelist should seek to expunge his own great novels in accordance with some pedantic doctrine of his old age. But, upon the whole, I think Tolstoy is, in this matter, not only great, but right. We all owe him much, considered as a great artist; but we all owe him even more as the great opponent of art—of art in the sense of art for art's sake. Tolstoy is never more admirable than when he is declaring that art ought not to be the mysterious amusement of a clique, but the obvious self-expression of men: art is a language, and not a secret language. It is a part of his greatness, therefore, to feel that what he has to say is more important than how well he once succeeded in saying it; and I for one quite agree with him that his novels (which are all right) are far less important than his philosophy, which is all wrong. He has this really great quality, that his faith is greater than himself; he shall decrease, but it shall increase. He represents a whole school of thought and a whole tone of feeling in Europe; something that was prophesied by the Quakers and fumbled about by Shelley. He has really achieved something which he is quite magnani-

189

mous enough to like; Tolstoyanism is more important than Tolstoy.

The emotion to which Tolstoy has again and again given a really fine expression is an emotion of pity for the plain affairs of men. He pities the masses of men for the things that they really endure—the tedium and the trivial cruelty. But it is just here, unfortunately, that his great mistake comes in; the mistake which renders practically useless the philosophy of Tolstoy and the whole of his humanitarian school. Tolstoy is not content with pitying humanity for its pains: such as poverty and prisons. He also pities humanity for its pleasures, such as music and patriotism. He weeps at the thought of hatred; but in "The Kreutzer Sonata" he weeps almost as much at the thought of love. He and all the humanitarians pity the joys of men.

Of these humanitarians it is hard to say otherwise than that they hate humanity. They are compassionate to it doubtless, as one may be compassionate to the most revolting animal. But their dislike of it appears to be general and fundamental. Suppose I happened to be acquainted with a discontented elephant who said, "I pity all my fellow-elephants because they are so big and heavy; I hate this idea of having a long, flexible nose; I feel ashamed of myself for having such large tusks; I think it is a great shame that our children are always elephants too; I wish I had five legs or three, but four is such an awkward number; I think it most unfair that elephants should be worried with large, flapping ears, and large, reflective intellects"—if an elephant went on talking like this, there would come a point when we should say, "My good creature, what you dislike is being an elephant. You do not hate tusks or trunks or fatness or four legs. You hate elephanthood—or elephantishness, or elephantitude, or elephantiasis, or whatever be the abstract name." So if a man says, "I love humanity, and I pity it. I pity it because it is bewitched with the sickening superstitions of poetry and romantic love; I pity it for being burdened with the family and the foolish worries of fatherhood; I hate to think that human affections are chained to certain sites and sacred places; I detest the fantastic notion of a nation and a flag; I weep when I think that so much of mankind is engaged in external ceremonies; I wish men would not sing war-songs; I wish girls would not play with dolls":—in this process, as in the other, there comes a point in which one says to the man who is speaking, "What you dislike is being a man. You are at least next door to hating humanity, for you pity humanity because it is human."

These people are always telling us to make a larger morality and a more universal creed that shall take in all sorts and conditions of men. But the truth is that they themselves are the chief obstacle and exception to such a universal agreement. There really are some things upon which humanity is practically agreed, but unfortunately these are exactly the things with which the humanitarians do not agree. In short, there is sympathy between all men, with the exception of these apostles of sympathy. For instance, all men, savage and civilised, feel that they are in some spiritual way different from the beasts. When Europeans kill a man they do it with a ceremonial which would be absurd in killing a beast. When South Sea Islanders eat a man they do it with a ceremonial quite absent from their ordinary meals. Both peoples feel that the act, however traditional or necessary, is still possibly wicked and certainly dreadful. But the only men who do not feel this special sanctity of humanity are the humanitarians. They are the very people who tell us that it is cannibalism to eat a veal cutlet. So there goes one plank of the platform on which all men might stand together. Again, it is practically common to all men to owe life and death to some special tribe or city; to all men except Tolstoyans. It is practically common to all men to have a special horror of the charge of physical cowardice and to desire to disprove it in action—it is common to all men, that is, except Tolstoyans. It is practically common to all men to express religious or domestic feelings by external formalities, such as war-dances or funeral dirges—to all men except Tolstoyans. All men like music; but Tolstoy doesn't. All men like lovers and love-stories; but Tolstoy doesn't. All men like glory and feats of arms; but Tolstoy doesn't. In the face of this is may still be said, in a sense, that Tolstoy loves humanity. But it can certainly be said, in quite as true a sense, that Tolstoy hates humanity with a deep and sincere hatred.

One is reminded of the same difficulty by the talk about Moral Instruction and the Moral Instruction Congress.[1] We must have a philosophy fit for grown-up people before we can simplify it so as to make it fit for children. Men say indignantly that we ought not to be worrying about creeds: we ought to be worrying about education. They might as well say that we must not worry about cats, because we ought to be worrying about kittens. A kitten only means the first stage of a cat. Education only means the first stage of some creed, some view of life. It has been justly objected against purely Catholic teaching in England that it must be the mere teaching of a sect. It has been justly objected against mere Bible teaching that that is also (properly understood) the mere teaching of a sect. But it may be objected against Moral Instruction that it is really the teaching of the smallest sect of all. The particular sort of professors engaged on Moral Instruction are further off from the atmosphere of the populace than the Salvation Army, and immeasurably further off than the Roman Catholic priests. It is no answer to say that the actual things stated by the Moral Instructionists are mostly in themselves harmless. All the things which cause the strongest religious irritation are in themselves harmless. No Catholic can have an intrinsic objection to the Bible; for it is a part of the Church. No Protestant can have an intrinsic objection to the "Hail Mary," for it is a part of the Bible. Protestants who object to a crucifix do not deny a crucifixion. It is in the emphasis upon things that people differ passionately. And so, while I may agree with twenty truisms running in a Moral Instruction pamphlet, I can still think the whole pamphlet immoral.

---

[1] The International Moral Education Congress met at the University of London September 25–29; a major topic was the "various means of giving ethical training with or without religious instruction".

October 10, 1908

The History of Religions

The proceedings of the Congress at Oxford for discussing the History of Religions seem to have been highly fascinating. Whatever folklore and mythology may be, they are not dull; and it is the fault of the students if they are pedantic. They contain in abundance the two most popular and poignant elements: the comic and the terrible. The very names of sections and subjects of lectures sound like poetry: "Bird and Pillar Worship"—"The Sky Father and the Earth Mother"—"Tree Worship"—"Taboo"; and so on. I can never hear of one of these savage or idolatrous faiths without wishing that I belonged to it. When I read of savages worshipping an odd-looking stone, I think what sensible fellows they must be. When I am told of a chieftain who believes he is descended from a shark, I wish sincerely that I could share his delusion. As a matter of intellect and conviction I believe in one religion; but, as a matter of fancy and sympathy I can believe in any number. Charles Lamb said he could read any books, not counting books that were not books—such as works of history, science, philosophy, and politics. So I say that I can feel a sympathy with any religion that is a religion; I don't count the Higher Pantheism or the New Theology or the Newest Theosophy or the Christianity of Tolstoy. I mean really jolly religions, where you do something—bang on a gong or attempt to worship a bear. The study of this sort of religious history is really exciting and amusing; and it is a good sign that some of the most interesting matters discussed at Oxford were discussed in a direct and human sort of way. It is always pleasant to see the name of Mr. Marett, of Exeter,[1] who spoke on "Taboo"; he is one example of a learned man who talks of man's primitive conditions like a

---

[1] Robert Ranulph Marett (1866–1943), an anthropologist, was the author of such books as *The Threshold of Religion* (1900), *Is Taboo a Negative Magic?* (1907) and *Anthropology* (1911).

man, and not only like a Don. Nevertheless, it must be confessed that these Congresses of creeds and theories suffer from certain primary disadvantages (disadvantages in the logical idea of the thing) which were even more manifest in such things as the Parliament of Religions which was held some years ago at Chicago.

The root difficulty of the Parliament of Religions was this: that it was offered as a place where creeds could agree; whereas its real interest would have been that of a place where they could disagree. Creeds must disagree: it is the whole fun of the thing. If I think the universe is triangular, and you think it is square, there cannot be room for two universes. We may argue politely, we may argue humanely, we may argue with great mutual benefit; but, obviously, we must argue. Modern toleration is really a tyranny. It is a tyranny because it is a silence. To say that I must not deny my opponent's faith is to say I must not discuss it; I may not say that Buddhism is false, and that is all I want to say about Buddhism. It is the only interesting thing that anybody can want to say about Buddhism—either that it is false or that it is true. But in these modern assemblies, supposed to be tolerant and scientific, there is spread a general and tacit agreement that there shall be no violent assertion or negation of faith; and this is not only hypocritical, but unbusinesslike, for it is not getting to the point. In short, the awkwardness of a real congress of creeds is merely this: that if two absolute creeds meet, they will probably fight; and if they do not fight, there is really not much value in their having met. It is absurd to have a discussion on Comparative Religions if you don't compare them. And if the representatives of two energetic Eastern philosophies do begin to compare them, there is, of course, always the possibility that this delicate scientific analysis may be conducted with long curved knives.

Then there is another difficulty, or accidental disadvantage, which besets these attempts to bring all the faiths of our planet face to face. It is that it so often happens (for some mysterious reason) that the representatives who meet each other are exactly the people who are not representative. They are generally eccentrics, or even heretics, in their own land. The ambassador is always an exile. In the presidential address on "The Religions of India and Iran," Professor Rhys Davids "referred incidentally to the work of a Parsee ecclesiastic of Bombay, and said it was a sign of the times that we had a Parsee ecclesiastic, banished from his own country, publishing a book in Leipsic in the German language." It may be a sign of the times, but I do not think it is a nice one. I know no harm of the Parsee ecclesiastic, and I do not even know who banished him. But if he was banished by his own people, I should certainly prefer to learn about the Parsee religion from some Parsee whom other Parsees could stand. And even if he was banished by some alien power, I do not think it makes for clearing things up or for greater lucidity and mutual understanding, that he should be writing about the deepest matters in a language in which he does not think in a town which he cannot understand. It is hard enough anyhow, I should imagine, for an Englishman like myself to understand the real mind of a Parsee; but I resolutely decline to investigate his real mind if it is mixed up with an Indian's notions of what will go down at Leipsic. This is a real difficulty, not by any means confined to this question; the difficulty that those who seek to unite creeds or nations are not generally those who have the creeds and nations in sufficient strength behind them. Russia is not behind Tolstoy, nor France behind Mr. Pressensé,[2] or England behind Mr. Stead.[3] So it may be questioned whether those who come to us in the name of vast and unknown religions, from Burma or Tibet via Leipsic, are quite plenipotentiary. Some of these envoys have not been so much sent forth as chucked out.

[2] Francis de Pressensé (1853–1914), an important journalist and socialist of the period; he was very active in the defense of Dreyfus.

[3] William Thomas Stead (1849–1912) became, in 1885, the editor of the *Pall Mall Gazette*, until then a sedate chronicle and review of the day's events. It suddenly became the initiator of all kinds of new programs and movements, political and social, besides astonishing people by its dash and unconventionality.

In speaking of this difficulty also I am, of course, thinking rather of the large emotional aims of the Parliament of Religions than of the more scientific objects of the International Congress for the History of Religions. But even to the recent business at Oxford these two criticisms do to some extent apply. You will never get the thoroughly typical man of any land or creed to talk at Congresses or give evidence on scientific commissions. You will never get the Irish peasant who really is Catholicism or the Dutch farmer who really is Protestantism, into this atmosphere of analysis at all. These men are too representative to fit into a representative system.

And lastly, of course, there is always cropping up in connection with such occasions what I may call the fallacy of the open mind. An open mind is really a mark of foolishness, like an open mouth. Mouths and minds were made to shut; they were made to open only in order to shut. In direct connection with this question of mythology and human belief the point may roughly be put thus: An extraordinary idea has arisen that the best critic of religious institutions is the man who talks coldly about Religion. Nobody supposes that the best critic of music is the man who talks coldly about music. Within reasonable bounds, the more excited the musician is about music, the more he is likely to be right about it. Nobody thinks a man a correct judge of poetry because he looks down on poems. But there is an idea that a man is a correct judge of religion because he looks down on religions. Now, folklore and primitive faiths, and all such things are of the nature of music and poetry in this respect— that the actual language and symbols they employ require not only an understanding, they require what the Bible very finely calls an understanding heart. You must be a little moved in your emotions even to understand them at all; you must have a heart in order to make head or tail of them. Consequently, whenever I hear on these occasions that beliefs are being discussed scientifically and calmly, I know that they are being discussed wrong. Even a false religion is too genuine a thing to be discussed calmly. That the distinguished gentlemen at Oxford spoke placidly and with precision about ghosts or totems, witches or taboos, does not impress me at all in favour of the justice of their conclusions. I should be much more impressed if Mr. Marett shuddered from head to foot on the platform when he mentioned a taboo. I should feel nearer to accuracy if Professor Rhys Davids, while lecturing on Indian religions, went into a raging ecstasy on the platform and then tumbled down in a Buddhist trance. I should be more enlightened if Miss Jane Harrison, of Newnham College, instead of solemnly lecturing on "Bird and Pillar Worship," had stood up stiff like a pillar or fluttered about like a bird. It was interesting, no doubt, to hear Sir John Rhys deliver a lecture on Welsh traditions; but it would have been even more interesting to see him fulfil some Welsh traditions—suddenly produce a harp and smite its chords or fling himself into some goat-like mountain-dance. I say it would be more amusing, but it would also be more convincing. For then we should know that those who were studying fables and faiths had at least some conception of what goes to make a credible faith or even a credible fable; we should know for the first time that the professors in a literal sense really knew what they were talking about.

October 17, 1908

Practical Politicians

The English statesman has often offered old-age pensions to the English nation. The nation has generally answered by offering an old-age pension—to the statesman. The thing had passed into a sort of ruinous joke, expressive of wild senility, the same that some attributed to Gladstone's last Irish enthusiasm—the old man shall dream dreams. There is this degree of truth in such sentiments that the aristocratic politician who governs this country is one of the few men who cannot be superannuated. There are fairly practical tests by which one can prove that a man is too old to catch fish or to break stones, or even to slide down bannisters. But there is no way of proving that a man is too old to rule Empires—or to ruin them. Cashiers are too old at forty, but Chancellors of the Exchequer are not (as far as I know) too old at a hundred and forty. In commerce, men are often considered untrustworthy even in that vigorous middle age which is really a second manhood. But in politics they are thought trustworthy in their second childhood.

But if our politicians are pensioned off I insist that the style of it shall be graceful and humane—like Belial. Our aged statesmen must not be sent to the hideous and heartless routine of the modern workhouse. They must be gently led away by the hand to mellow and clustering almshouses, where they may sit on simple benches under silent elms (or poplars), and where a sunset that never leaves off may turn the red-tiled roofs to gold. I like to think of them as rustics in such a retreat. I like to imagine Mr. Balfour hanging over a gate with a long churchwarden pipe, and touching his hat to a squire specially provided for him. I should like to see Mr. Asquith (called in those circles Gaffer Asquith) hobbling up the street in a smock-frock and a stiff black chimney-pot hat. I can imagine Mr. Haldane singing an interminable song in a quavering voice, and feebly beating on the table with a pewter-pot. I can fancy Mr. Austen Chamberlain pointing a trembling crutch at the streets of Westminster, and falsely asserting that he remembers when it was all fields. For I assume that, in such a condition, politicians would lose all their separate characters, and fall into the common character of the aged peasant; would drink and grumble and tell tall stories just as if they had been good men all their lives. These are dreams, yet they have this touch of reality about them: that, when we are thinking about social schemes and methods of dealing with the democracy, it is a good thing to call up the image of one actual man whom we have seen or read about rather than a confused abstraction of the populace. The evil of our attitude to the masses is simply that we do think of them in masses. If Mr. Asquith, let us say, is going to do something by law and coercion to the Commons of this realm, it is better and clearer to think of him as doing it to Mr. Lyttelton than as doing it to England.

A great trouble in modern political discussions is that the very things which we consider quite clear and practical when we are talking about our private affairs are considered somewhat vague and sentimental if we apply them to public affairs. Practical politicians are always cracking jokes about the absurdity of the religious people who want to have in their schools the "atmosphere" of one creed. But these politicians all take care to send their own sons to schools where there is a much narrower thing— the atmosphere of one class. The truth is, of course, that every man, in dealing with his own affairs and in the enjoyment of his own wits, knows that atmosphere is the most practical thing in the world—perhaps the only practical thing in the world. The difference between heaven and hell is only a difference of atmosphere. Only a moral sense of smell enables one to guess whether young Smith in the Lancers will go with great heroes to glory or go with dog-fanciers to the dogs. Those principles of idealism and moral sensibility which sound so vague and pompous in a public speech or a leading article are, nevertheless, the only principles on which anyone ever chooses a butler, or a boarding house, or a schoolmaster, or a cook, or a clerk, or even a favourite horse.

Modern politicians are always trying to be practical; consequently, they never get to the point at all. For the core of life is not practical; the heart of a man desires beatitude, which is a spiritual state. A tailor does not want to be practical: he wants to be happy. A tinker does not want to be treated practically: he wants to be treated well. If once you have seen the life of our English poor even for an instant from the inside you will know that the things which are called sentimental or secondary by politicians are exactly the things which are primary and palpable. For instance, it is a far more really practical question in what *tone of voice* officials speak to the poor than even what they say to them. A solid social worker like Mr. Rowntree would consider this question very trivial; but he would soon find out what it meant if all his friends suddenly began to bellow at him like bulls. This matter of the accent and pitch of the voice is a perfect example of the thing that I mean, the thing that sounds so slight and sentimental, but which is really so strong and determining a thing. The voice is not written down in an official report or copied in any affidavit; but it makes all the difference in the matter of a housemaid getting a situation or a man getting a wife. Properly speaking, we ought to have phonographs in our Law Courts, to express the exact note of the voices in every quarrel, for there is a way of saying "Good-morning" which palliates a blow with a poker. Or the witnesses might imitate voices, like ventriloquists. Little Tommy, (who understands the nature of an oath) might render, with horrible contortions, the gruff tones of Uncle George. The housemaid, with gaiety and eagerness, might give a shrill imitation of the voice of Aunt Susan. It would greatly add to the entertainment of a Court of Law.

So remote is this truth from the tone of our times that one has to put it thus preposterously. But it is quite certain that we shall never really improve the condition of our people until we talk in terms of these atmospheric and emotional things which make up so much of the real happiness of life. The word politics and the word politeness have the same root. But at this moment it is much more practical to give the poor politeness than to give them politics. The politicians and the political newspapers tell the poor man day after day that he is a citizen and a free man. But a very small piece of ordinary politeness will make him feel that he is one. Many doctors, many municipal officials, for instance, commonly wear their hats in the parlours of the poor. For the sake of democracy it is far more important to knock the doctor's hat off than to knock twopence off the Income-tax. Whatever else is done or undone in our politics we must knock the parochial official's hat off. The further and more delicate question of whether we shall knock his head off, I leave to the discretion of democracy in its hour of triumph.

Tone, atmosphere, manners, are the most solid and real things in public as in private life; and we must particularly remember this in all speculations and proposals touching the Poor-law. I recollect, on the only occasion on which I was ever on a jury, I turned my eyes idly towards an enclosure which I supposed to be the dock, wondering vaguely whether I should see the Criminal Type which I had read about in very illogical little books by scientists. Generally speaking, I do not believe in the Criminal Type; I do not believe that there need be anything odd about the shape of the ear or the size of the thumb of a man who murders his grandmother. Suddenly there appeared in this box the Criminal Type itself: brutal, half-witted, with a jaw like a boar's jowl, a moustache like boar's bristles, a thick neck, with a stoop as if the creature fought with his head; eyes close together, ears far apart. But I was still more surprised when they offered this animal a little book to kiss. In fact, the enclosure was not the dock, but the witness-box: and the witness—was the Master of a London workhouse.

October 24, 1908

The Idea of Separation and Sense of Separateness

The news that some Europeans have been wrecked on a desert island[1] is gratifying, in so far as it shows that there are still some desert islands for us to be wrecked on. Moreover, it is also

---

[1] This may refer to the long-missing steamer *Aeon*, whose passengers were reported shipwrecked on Christmas Island; they were rescued in October, but word had gotten back to Australia some time before this.

interesting because these, the latest facts, actually support the oldest stories. For instance, superior critics have often sniffed at the labours of Robinson Crusoe, specifically upon the ground that he depended so much upon stores from the sunken wreck. But these actual people shipwrecked a few weeks ago depended entirely upon them; and yet the critics might not have cared for the billet. A few years ago, when physical science was still taken seriously, a very clever boys' book was written, called "Perseverance Island." It was written in order to show how "Robinson Crusoe" ought to have been written. In this story, the wrecked man gained practically nothing from the wreck. He made everything out of the brute materials of the island. He was, I think, allowed the advantage of some broken barrels washed up from the wreck with a few metal hoops round them. It would have been rather hard on the poor man to force him to make a copper-mine or a tin-mine. After all, the process of making everything that one wants cannot be carried too far in this world. We have all saved something from the ship. At the very least, there was something that Crusoe could not make on the island; there was something Crusoe was forced to steal from the wreck; I mean Crusoe. That precious bale, in any case, he brought ashore; that special cargo called "R. C.," at least, did not originate in the island. It was a free import, and not a native manufacture. Crusoe might be driven to make his own trousers on the island. But he was not driven to make his own legs on the island; if that had been his first technical job he might have approached it with a hesitation not unconnected with despair. Even the pessimist when he thinks, if he ever does, must realise that he has something to be thankful for: he owes something to the world, as Crusoe did to the ship. You may regard the universe as a wreck: but at least you have saved something from the wreck.

As a matter of fact, of course, it is quite unfair to compare "Robinson Crusoe" with such boys' books as "Perseverance Island," or even "The Swiss Family Robinson," not only because it is much greater literature, but because it is literature with an entirely different aim. To lump it with the others because they

all occurred on a desert island is no better than lumping "Wuth-
ering Heights" with "Northanger Abbey" because both concern
an old country house, or bracketting "Salem Chapel" with "Notre
Dame de Paris" because they are both about a church. "Robinson
Crusoe" is not a story of adventure; rather it is story of the
absence of adventure—that is, in the first and best part of it.
Twice Crusoe runs away to sea in disobedience, and twice escapes
with wreck or other peril; the third time we feel that he is set
apart for some strange judgment by God. And the strange judgment is the great central and poetical idea of "Robinson Crusoe."
It is a visitation not of danger, but of a dreadful security. The
salvage of Crusoe's goods, the comparative comfort of his life,
the natural riches of his island, his human relations with many
of the animals—all this is an exquisitely artistic setting for the
awful idea of a man whom God has cast out from among men.
A mere scurry of adventures would have left Crusoe no time
for thinking; and the whole object of the book is to make Crusoe
think. It is true that, later in the story, Defoe entangles him with
Indians and Spaniards; and for that very reason I think the story
loses the naked nobility of its original idea. It is absurd to compare a book like this with ordinary jolly stories about schooners
and palm-trees, cutlasses and scalps. It was not an adventurous
life, but an unadventurous life that was the doom and curse of
Crusoe.

But this, perhaps, is wandering from the subject—if there is
a subject. Let us try to get back to the desert island, and the
moral to be drawn from all the happy Australians and their
adventure. The first and most important point is this: that when
one reads of these forty-five people tipped out into an empty
island in the Pacific, one's first and instantaneous flash of feeling
is one of envy. Afterwards one remembers that there would
doubtless be inconveniences, that the sun is hot, that awnings
give you no shelter until you have put them up; that biscuits
and tinned meat might begin to taste monotonous, and that the
most adventurous person, having got on to the island, would
before very long begin to turn his thoughts to the problem of

getting off again. But the fact remains that before all these reflections the soul of man has said like the snap of a gun, "How jolly!" I think this instinct in humanity is somewhat interesting; it may be worth while to analyse this secret desire (seething under the top-hats of so many City clerks and country clergymen), this desire to be wrecked on an island.

The feeling partly arises from an idea which is at the root of all the arts—the idea of separation. Romance seeks to divide certain people from the lump of humanity, as the statue is divided from the lump of marble. We read a good novel not in order to know more people, but in order to know fewer. Instead of the humming swarm of human beings, relatives, customers, servants, postmen, afternoon callers, tradesmen, strangers who tell us the time, strangers who remark on the weather, beggars, waiters, and telegraph-boys—instead of this bewildering human swarm which passes us every day, fiction asks us to follow one figure (say the postman) consistently through his ecstasies and agonies. That is what makes one so impatient with that type of pessimistic rebel who is always complaining of the narrowness of his life, and demanding a larger sphere. Life is too large for us as it is: we have all too many things to attend to. All true romance is an attempt to simplify it, to cut it down to plainer and more pictorial proportions. What dullness there is in our life arises mostly from its rapidity: people pass us too quickly to show us their interesting side. By the end of the week we have talked to a hundred bores; whereas, if we had stuck to one of them, we might have found ourselves talking to a new friend, or a humourist, or a murderer, or a man who had seen a ghost.

I do not believe that there are any ordinary people. That is, I do not believe that there are any people whose lives are really humdrum or whose characters are really colourless. But the trouble is that one can so quickly see them all in a lump, like a land surveyor, and it would take so long to see them one by one as they really are, like a great novelist. Looking out of the window, I see a very steep little street, with a row of prim little houses breaking their necks downhill in the most decorous single file. If I were landlord of that street, or agent for that street, or policeman at the corner of that street, or visiting philanthropist making myself objectionable down that street, I could easily take it all in at a glance, sum it all up, and say, "Houses at £40 a year." But suppose I could be father confessor to that street, how awful and altered it would look! Each house would be sundered from its neighbour as by an earthquake, and would stand alone in a wilderness of the soul. I should know that in this house a man was going mad with drink, that in that a man had kept single for a woman, that in the next a woman was on the edge of abysses, that in the next a woman was living an unknown life which might in more devout ages have been gilded in hagiographies and made the fountain of miracles. People talk much of the quarrel between science and religion; but the deepest difference is that the individual is so much bigger than the average, that the inside of life is much larger than the outside.

Often when riding with three or four strangers on the top of an omnibus I have felt a wild impulse to throw the driver off his seat, to seize his whip, to drive the omnibus far out into the country, and tip them all out into a field, and say, "We may never meet again in this world; come, let us understand each other." I do not affirm that the experiment would succeed, but I think the impulse to do it is at the root of all the tradition of the poetry of wrecks and islands.

October 31, 1908

Arguing with Erudition

How far am I justified in arguing with a person much more learned than myself ? Or if you dislike this egoism, how far are you justified in arguing with a person more learned than yourself—supposing that such a person could exist? At what point may I come to the conclusion that a man who has certainly read more books than I, has, nevertheless, read them wrong? The problem must often cross the path of ordinary men who are sagacious rather than learned; for very few of us are learned, whereas all of us are frightfully sagacious. Can I call an eminent ornithologist an owl, when he assures me that his bodily structure renders this untenable? Can I call a distinguished biologist a donkey, when he is quite certain that my classification is incorrect.

As a first guide in this matter, I should like to offer one suggestion. I think that you and I are quite justified in disagreeing with doctors, however extraordinary in their erudition, if they violate ordinary reason in their line of argument. If they cannot even reason upon their facts, I think we are justified in doubting even their facts. Suppose a man says to me, "I know more than you do about the Tragic Drama of Athens." I reply: "Yes, you do know more than I; you could not well know less." But, suppose he goes on to instruct me, and says: "You see Euripides left ten plays, and Sophocles left four plays; and that makes seventeen plays." Then I think I am justified in breaking in and saying: "You are a horribly learned man, no doubt; but, as you obviously can't count, I don't see why I should feel certain that you can do anything else." Suppose a man says: "You know nothing about Danish churches: let me tell you that every Danish church is balanced on the tip of its spire." I then reply: "I know nothing about Danish churches, except that they aren't like that." The intellectual principle is a very simple one; and yet it will, I think, be found to be of interest, and even of utility, in the life of to-day.

There is a very good example which I find in turning over a daily paper. Some people got up a public argument between an elderly clergyman and a young student of Haeckel about the reconciliation of Genesis and geology, a subject that seems, somehow, more remote than the first stratum of geology or the First Book of Genesis. In the controversy itself my interest is somewhat feeble. I have no superstitious belief in Genesis, and much less belief in geology, which changes its own mind so much oftener. I do not approach the occasion with any bias in favour of the Christian champion; for that kind of Bible-worshipper and that kind of Bible-smasher seem to me merely varieties of the same Puritanical idolater. The only really interesting thing in the matter is this. The old clergyman quoted Haeckel: in these arguments the clergymen always do appeal to the authority of science, while the atheists always appeal to the authority of Scripture. He quoted Haeckel as having said that the Hebrew legend of Creation was certainly much higher and nobler than the Babylonian legend from which he believed it had sprung. And to this the young Haeckelite answered (according to the newspaper report): "As an Evolutionist, I should expect the later legend to be the higher and nobler one." I was not present at this discussion; if I had been I should at this precise point have leapt up with a loud yell. For I rebel against the man of learning when he suddenly, and in public, refuses to think.

I know nothing about the mythological question at issue. As I never had an Ancient Babylonian nurse, I do not know any Ancient Babylonian fairy-tales. If the Haeckelite had told me that the Babylonian Creation was a million times better than the Hebrew, if he had told me that the Babylonian Creation included the discovery of Radium, a prophecy of the French Revolution, the score of a complete opera better than Beethoven, and an eloquent Babylonian poster demanding Votes for Women, I should not have been able to contradict him. I have never read the Babylonian fable, so it may contain all these things. But I have read the English alphabet; I know the meaning of ordinary English words; and I find this sentence of the young scientist more incomprehensible than any Babylonian brick. I understand the word "evolution," I understand the word "expect," and the word "later," and I think that I understand the words "high" and "noble." Evolution means a general theory that the varieties which are so vivid in this world of ours were produced slowly under the pressure of some necessity without or some power within; that necks grow shorter or noses longer in accordance with some need which could only operate gradually. In the history of this business (if it ever happened) there were, of course, many ups and downs; but it depends on your philosophy of things in general what you call an up and what you call a down. Our thumbs are improved, our tails have been mislaid; the balance of good is a matter of opinion; a firm and fighting opinion it may be, but still an opinion that can be questioned. Now, what can the whole of this theory have to do with the question whether of two versions of a story the first or second is the better version? Evolution itself does not even affirm that it has been upon the whole an improvement. But even supposing that it did, what man in his senses would ever apply evolution so as to mean that any one thing that comes after another must be an improvement on it?

"As an Evolutionist I should expect the later legend to be the better." Simply imagine for an instant the same principle being applied to anything else. Imagine someone saying, "As an Evolutionist, I should expect that the hats fashionable in 1807 would be more artistic than the hats fashionable in 1707." Imagine someone saying, "As an Evolutionist, I should expect the Derby winner for 1890 to be a better horse than the Derby winner for 1870." Suppose someone said, "Evolution leads me to expect that the last edition of a book will be the best edition, or the last illustrations to a book the best illustrations." Suppose a man said: "The last baby born, of course, will be the most elegant and moral baby." We should send such people to Hanwell.[1] We know that even in the Modern West, which, on the whole, pants and toils for progress, better things are constantly followed by worse ones. We know that the hat of George IV. was not an improvement upon the hat of Charles I. We know that the tragedy of "Cato" was not an improvement upon the tragedy of "Othello." We know that Bentley's version of Milton is considerably inferior to Milton's version of Milton. We know that

[1] A mental asylum in Middlesex.

if the authors of the Revised Version knew more about Hebrew, the authors of the Authorised Version knew much more about English. We know that even good poets, when they alter their verses, generally spoil them. We know that the world is full of debased legends and half-destroyed traditions. And yet, it seems, an Evolutionist is bound to expect that every legend, in every place in every age, goes on getting better and better. We know things are often retrograde, even in the Modern West, where progress is popular. But we must (as "Evolutionists") assume that things were always progressive in the Ancient East, where people positively hated progress. This, I say, is the point at which I rebel against great reputations in learning and science. So long as learned men use their authority, I submit to it with the most exquisite meekness. But when learned men begin to use their reason, then I generally discover that they haven't got any. If a biologist contradicts me, I respectfully submit; he undoubtedly knows more than I do. But if a biologist condescends so far as to argue with me, I generally find that I have the best of the argument. Now, I am so constituted that I can accept authority, but I cannot and will not accept bad reasons. Even prejudice is saner than sophistry. If a first-class Hebrew historian says to me, "The sons of Solomon were wiser than their father," I accept it as a fact, knowing that he is wiser than I. But if he says "Sons always must be wiser than their fathers," then I gently and silently come to the conclusion that he himself is hardly an authority on wisdom.

November 7, 1908

Taking Reason by the Right End

I am glad to see that an English translation has been issued of one of the very few first-rate detective stories that have been written in the last ten or twenty years; I mean "The Yellow

Room," by Gustave Leroux. It recalls the days when really great men condescended to write detective stories; great men like Edgar Allan Poe or Wilkie Collins. I do not mean that the book is great in that sense; but it is at least great in this sense—that it contains an important intellectual principle. Nothing would induce me to tell the reader anything about the solution of the riddle. The man who tells the truth about a detective story is simply a wicked man, as wicked as the man who deliberately breaks a child's soap-bubble—and he is more wicked than Nero. To give away a secret when it should be kept is the worst of human crimes; and Dante was never more right than when he made the lowest circle in Hell the Circle of the Traitors. It is to destroy one human pleasure so that it can never be recovered, as if one had jerked the elbow of Roberts[1] when he was doing an unprecedented stroke in billiards, or smashed the skull of Milton the moment before he wrote "Lycidas." I will not destroy the pleasures of those who read detective stories; for the simple and selfish reason that I am one of them myself.

But there is no betrayal in saying this: that the triumphant detective in the book bases all his case upon what he calls "taking reason by the right end." The phrase, indeed, is full of the finest sanity of the French. What he means, if I understand him, is this: that this world is full of truths, half-truths, probabilities, and possibilities of various orders of validity and pointing in various directions. But there are some facts which are certain in a quite special way; and if other facts contradict them, then we must inquire into the other facts; but we must not waste our time inquiring into the one fact which is certain. In the tale there is a room absolutely sealed and absolutely bare. From the inside of it are heard the sounds of a struggle, pistol shots, screams; the door is broken down, and the body of a girl is found bleeding on the floor. There are footprints, bloody-hand marks, a cap, a

[1] John Roberts, an outstanding billiard player, was engaged in a triumphant series of billiard matches during 1908 which often involved his conceding large numbers of points to his rivals.

club, left behind. All the other investigators naturally begin by
asking how the murderer managed to escape. The triumphant
investigator does not pursue this speculation at all. He begins
with the two things that he knows for certain, that the room
was sealed hermetically, and that the room was empty. That is
all I will tell you about this interesting novel; it is not enough
to tell the story, but it is just enough to tell the moral.

This is the essential idea, that all good argument consists in
beginning with the indisputable thing and then disputing everything else in the light of it. It is of great working value in many
modern discussions, if its general principle is understood. First
of all, of course, one must leave out the element of the supernatural or the element of the insane. The element of the supernatural in practical affairs has always been regarded (even by
those who most strongly believed in it) as exceptional. If a miracle is not exceptional, it is not even miraculous. Nobody was
ever taught by any sane creed to count upon or expect anything
but the natural. To put the point briefly, we are commanded to
put our faith in miracles, but not to put our trust in them. The
other alternative of mania or some mental breakdown must also
be allowed for. If we have been seriously assured that there are
no snakes in Iceland and in spite of that we see snakes in Iceland,
it is always reasonable to ask ourselves if our past life has pointed
towards "D.T." But supposing that those two abnormalities,
the mystery that is above humanity and the madness that is below
it, are fairly and honestly out of the question, then the right line
of argument certainly is that seeing is believing and that the
things we have experienced are true in quite another and more
pungent sense than the things into which we can merely be
argued. If I am sitting opposite my aunt in Croydon, a telegram
may come from her in Highgate, a newspaper may announce
that she is taking part in a Highgate Pageant, an expert may
prove that it was impossible for her to have reached Croydon
in the time, a statistician may say that he has counted all the
aunts in Highgate, and there is not one missing; but all these
facts are facts of a secondary degree of evidence. They have the

expert, but I have the aunt. Unless my aunt is a devil, or I am a lunatic, I have possession of the primary fact in the discussion.

I have already said that this very plain principle of thought is useful in connection with many current problems. Take, for example, the problem of the Unemployed. It is very common to meet a prosperous gentleman who will point to a seedy and half-starved loafer in the street, and say: "This unemployment business is all bosh: I offered that man work the other day, and he wouldn't take it." Now, this may possibly be true; but it is always used in order to disprove the idea that the man is miserable. But to disprove that is simply to disprove the one thing that is proved. You have only to look at the man to say that, for some reason, by somebody's fault, or nobody's fault, he has not eaten enough to be a man, or even to be an animal. That he refused work is a curious circumstance, to be reconciled, if possible, with the palpable fact that he wants money. He may have refused it because he is half-witted, or because fatigue has killed all power of choice, or because wrong has moved him to an irrational anger, or because he is a saint, or because he is a maniac, or because he is terrorised by a secret society, or because he has a peculiar religion which forbids him to work on Wednesday. But whatever the explanation is, it is not that he is jolly and full of meat and drink; because you can see that he isn't. His impotence may have this cause or that cause, or the other; but his impotence is no defence of the existing system of wealth and poverty. To use the modern cant, it does not destroy the problem of the unemployed; it only adds to it the problem of the unemployable. But our main point here is this: that people ought to begin by the thing that they can see. It may take you twenty years to find out whether a man is honest. But it does not take you two seconds to find out that he is thin. The ordinary rich man's argument is that because the tramp is dishonest, he must somehow be secretly fat. That is the great fallacy. Believe me (I speak as an expert), it is impossible to be fat in secret.

I have noticed another instance at the opposite end of the economic scale. Mr. Rockefeller, the notorious millionaire, has recently been writing an account of himself. He says that the great American business man is not in the matter for money, but for something else—triumph or some rubbish. As a matter of fact, I should think much better of Rockefeller and his like if they were in it for money. To desire money is much nobler than to desire success. Desiring money may mean desiring to return to your country, or marry the woman you love, or ransom your father from brigands. It may mean something human and respectable. But desiring success must mean something inhuman and detestable. It must mean that you take an abstract pleasure in the unbrotherly act of distancing and disgracing other men. I think no better of Mr. Rockefeller because he does not collect dollars, but collects scalps. But this, though a true comment, is not the obvious comment. The essential is that, while we know nothing of Rockefeller's soul, we do know something of Rockefeller's income. He has, by huge efforts, obtained huge wealth. That prime fact may be explained, but it cannot be explained away.

November 14, 1908

The Proper Idea of Property

Nothing is more pathetic than the degeneration in the meaning of words. In the eighteenth century an "enthusiast" came to mean a common lunatic; and, though the word has somewhat revived since then, it is still very far from rising to its original meaning of a man full of God. In ancient Greek an aesthete means a man who feels things; in modern English an aesthete means a man whom one cannot imagine feeling anything, except a horse-whip. The chief trouble of life is that words get so *dirty* as they walk along the miry roads of this world. Why cannot I call myself a Free Thinker? I think quite freely. I have never been burned alive for my opinions; I have never been tortured for my opinions; only from time to time have I even been sacked for my opinions. I am, I honestly think, a free thinker. That is, I am not quite sure that I am a thinker, but I am quite sure that I am a free one. The reason is that a Free Thinker does not mean a man who thinks freely; a Free Thinker means a man who is not allowed to think that miracles happen. Surely (I feel inclined to cry pathetically), surely you will allow me to call myself a free thinker! I assure you that my thought has been free to the verge of looseness. Surely you will allow me to call myself an agnostic, when you call to mind the enormous and unusual number of things about which I know nothing. But it cannot be done, and the explanation of it is that these words have been dipped in dark waters and dyed in deep colours which are to me the waters of bitterness and the blended hues of an infernal heraldry. Words fall and are betrayed quite accidentally. Culture now means something quite little and vulgar, though agriculture still means something innocent and heroic. The word "citizen" has been one of our words of eternal crystal for nearly three thousand years; yet, after recent arguments in education and politics, it will be very difficult to use the word "citizen" without thinking of Dr. Clifford.[1] That admirable old man (for whom I have perfectly serious esteem) has among his many strengths just this intellectual weakness—that he always signs himself as a citizen at the very moment when he is entirely an anarchist. It is exactly when Dr. Clifford has made up his mind (very rightly, I often think) to support his religion against his citizenship—it is always then that he elaborately explains that this is a case of citizenship and not of religion. All that talk of not caring for creeds has simply become one fixed, very formal, and slightly hypocritical

---

[1] John Clifford (1836–1923), a Baptist leader and ardent evangelical who believed that religion was concerned with the whole of life. He was a voluminous writer, had great sympathy for the masses and opposed state aid for denominational schools.

creed. Unsectarianism is simply a sect—and a small sect. But if
these people were in a minority of five, if they were totally cut
off from the whole life of citizens and citizenship in their own
town, they would still call themselves the citizens.

But I think there is one case of a word ruined which is worst
of all. I mean the horrible modern meaning of the word "property." "Property" means (as to its original meaning) the fact
that something is *proper* to somebody. Property is propriety.
Now, it is obvious that in modern England and America property is gross impropriety; in fact, it is shocking indecency. That
one man should have four millions a year is something worse
than an injustice: it is a sort of filthy joke. In short, as the proverb
says, it is adding insult to injury; and insult is a thing much
worse than injury. Nations never rebel against injury: they only
rebel against insult. But the point is that the idea of property (if
there is any idea) is an idea of that which is proper to a man;
and the grotesque position of the modern millonaire might give
some shock of shame and laughter to a chimpanzee. It is proper
for one man to sleep securely in one bed. It is highly improper
(in the most ordinary sense) that he should be wandering about
all night in his pyjamas trying to sleep in two-hundred-and-
fifteen beds at once. It is proper that one head should have one
hat; but the cosmopolitan financier, when in the later stages of
his career he owns ten country seats, is exactly as comic and
contemptible a figure as when, in the earlier stages of his career,
he wore ten hats, one on top of the other.

The proper idea of property is almost universal among men,
women, and children—especially children. A child is not always
what you might call a pattern in ethical practice. But a child is
almost always a final oracle in ethical theory. What the child
thinks is substantially this: "I know that there ought to be equality and justice and fair sharing among fellows in the same commonwealth (or nursery); but I also want to have something that
is *of me*, marked with my name, soaked in my personality, something that I can compare with the possessions of others, even if
all are of the same value. By all means let Tommy have a marble

of the same size and value as mine. But let mine be red while his is blue; and, above all, let mine be *mine*. I may roll it about or not roll it about; I may carry it in my pocket, or give it to a beggar, or sit looking at it during the whole of my leisure. I must not go actually so far as to swallow it, because the Everlasting has, unfortunately, set His canon 'gainst self-slaughter. But, short of big crimes, such as being a self-murderer or a millionaire, I can do what I like with it. It can become in my hands something that it could never have been otherwise. I will sit down on the nursery floor and think what one might do with a marble."

That healthy conception of property is vivid to every baby. But that healthy conception of property is, apparently, almost entirely unknown to all the grown-up people who govern or would like to govern our modern politics. Yet here is a paragraph out of the best Socialist paper I know (in fact one of the best papers I know at this time), the *New Age*—

> Incidentally Mr. Asquith supplied an epigrammatic solution of the difficulties which appear to keep Messrs. Belloc and Chesterton from embracing the Socialist creed. "To be happy, a man must own," they cried; and Messrs. Shaw and Wells assured them in vain that they were mistaken. Now we have Mr. Asquith disposing of Young's phrase in a sentence which deserves to be printed in letters of gold: "The magic of property," he said, "is not possession, but security."

Now, Mr. Asquith's epigram, so far from "solving the difficulties" which I have about Socialism, only adds to them another difficulty, the problem of why the Premier and his fiercest opponents should agree in saying the one thing which is certainly untrue. The magic of property emphatically is *not* security, and emphatically *is* possession. It is as if you were to say, "The magic of a baby to its mother is that it contradicts the idea of a decrease in population," or "The magic of a lady's portrait treasured by a lover is that it will assist him to identify her body at an inquest." The truth is that people have the first idea without the other idea even crossing their minds. It is emphatically not the same to a schoolboy that he is always secure of being able to borrow a pocket-knife, as that he has a pocket-knife of his own.

If the magic of property is merely security, the people who ought to feel the magic of property most are the convicts in Portland Jail. There are no other Englishmen whose meals and beds are so secure. Yet I have never heard that the convict kisses his plank-bed with tears of pride; I have never heard that he rolls the skilly[2] on his tongue like a man retasting his father's fine old port. And it is not in the least true to say that this is merely because the physical arrangements are mean. The magic of property can be felt about the foulest hovels, but it could not be felt about modern prisons even if they were palaces. If the warder brought round champagne and oysters, if the beds were of gold and satin, there would be quite as little of the magic of property in a prison as there is now. The simple fact is that there is in property not only an idea of security, but also an idea of self-respect.

November 21, 1908

Anarchy and Revolution

I said some time ago in these columns that speeches seemed to me to be much improved by interruptions. But things are getting a little too stiff at present, when the interruptions commonly occupy much more time and space than the speeches. Under the Suffragette and other similar excitements, it begins to be really desirable that we should come to some general conclusion about

[2] A thin gruel or oatmeal soup. By extension, this word has come to mean something of little value.

the principle of riot and regulation. Now, I think there is one general principle which may fairly and emphatically be laid down. There is no excuse for any disorder which is not rebellion. It is permissible in extreme cases to smash the State; it is never permissible merely to make it work badly. I should almost be inclined to put the matter in this form: that active resistance is sometimes right, but passive resistance is always wrong. If I am so strongly convinced that the inhabitants of the Battersea flats have to pay too much income tax that I think myself justified in the sight of Heaven and humanity in joining a rifle club with a view to shooting all the authorities and replacing them by others, then I think that I might be a highly respectable person. But if I made it a general principle for the remainder of my life to subject them to small annoyances, I should be wrong. Suppose that, whenever I wrote to the officials, I made them pay twopence extra for the stamp. Suppose, whenever the official called on me, I worked a dexterous substitution by which he went away with an inferior hat and umbrella. Suppose I always kept him waiting twenty minutes when I could have come to him in ten. Suppose I kept a freshly-painted wall for him to lean up against, and a frail and insecure chair for him to sit down upon. Then I think I should have an insufficient conception of the State's dignity, and not a very satisfactory regard for my own.

The difference between rebellion and anarchy is that rebellion, by its nature, achieves a purpose; and, having achieved that purpose, returns to the normal rhythm of law and order. Rebellion is as abnormal as an emetic or an amputation, and it is sometimes as wholesome. But it is only wholesome if it is an abnormality which is intended promptly and decisively to restore the normal. I may thank a doctor for cutting off my leg if I am in deadly peril of poison; but I shall not thank any gentleman who continually chips larger or smaller pieces off my leg accordingly as he thinks that I am not looking quite the thing. I may thank a doctor for making me sick, but not for occupying himself through a long and busy life in making all my food more or less sickening. So rebellion, because it is crucial, must be responsible. It must be thinking not only of the disease, not only of the brief and desperate remedy, but also of that healthy condition which it desires to render permanent; and which, when once effected, it will respect as a fixed thing. In other words, we may restate our original proposition thus: To be responsible for a rebellion is to be responsible for a new Government. Anyone who is in revolt ought to be mainly thinking of that condition of affairs against which he would not be in revolt. But I will have nothing to do with this notion of a nibbling anarchy; the perpetual doing of small, indefensible things.

A gentleman ought either to welcome a man to his house or to kick him out of it; he has no business systematically to make him uncomfortable as long as he is there. In the same way, human society (to whom we stand in primary and natural relations) is either our mother or our wicked and usurping stepmother; she cannot be merely an objectionable acquaintance to be teased with vulgar, practical jokes. Our duty to human government is either to make it work swiftly or to stop it working. There cannot be any special value in its working hugger-mugger and anyhow. Anarchy is defensible as the only atmosphere in which a new Government can be created; but anarchy will be very dreary as the permanent and continuous atmosphere in which an old Government shall live.

Unfortunately, there can be little doubt that this notion of a mild, but perpetual mutiny has become very widely recognised as a weapon for those who believe themselves rightly or wrongly oppressed. Not to gag an enemy with rope, but to gag him with noise; not to suppress opinion by edict, but to suppress it by confusion; not to cut off the King's head, but to attempt by howling to make him lose it—these expedients are being more and more used. I do not say that there are not peculiar occasions upon which they may be the best expedients. But I object to the general recognition of the method myself, and I object to it for two very strong reasons. First, because it prevents order; and second, because it prevents revolution. As long as you can tell people that it is enough to carry banners, they will never again carry guns. And that will be a horrible pity.

As it is, the future of England opens before me as a vista of useless riots and no revolution. Every one will attempt to carry his own tiny reform by bluff and bullying, by threatening a civil war which will never happen. It is as if the correspondence between two paralytics should entirely consist of threats of horse-whipping. I, for instance, happen to think that the craze for Sunday closing is an oppressive and unmeaning fad, mingled of the dregs of Calvinism and the thick fat mud of plutocracy. I cannot picture any cause in my mind for honouring the day of rest by closing all the resting-places, or for celebrating a Church feast by forbidding feasting. But suppose that, in the future, I wish to resist this ridiculous law, I shall not do so by decent constitutional means, nor by honest revolutionary means. I shall neither write nor fight. I shall sit down outside a public-house every Sunday morning and keep on ringing the bell. I shall be a noble sight.

Therefore I think that the English are about to effect the last and worst of their compromises, a compromise of mere chaos. They are going not to alter the law, but to keep the law in so soft and futile a state that chance judges can manipulate it from above and chance mobs can manipulate it from below. Every reform which is effected by a feeble disorder will be open to the same feeble disorder in its turn. Miss Pankhurst will continue to shove her head through the window of Parliament and shout "Votes for Women!" until, out of mere dreary good-nature, people give her her vote and her seat in the House of Commons. She will rise from that seat to speak (and she speaks extremely well), and exactly at that moment somebody else will thrust his head through the window of Parliament, and by shouting "Votes for Rabbits!" (or whatever you like) will render her excellent speech entirely inaudible. There is no end to the process; not even by giving votes to rabbits. It does not come to a head as real revolution does. It does not give us first real war and then

real peace, as the genuine revolution does. The people who manage these things have neither the courage to fight nor the strength
to sit still. We belong to our nation until the awful moment
when we decide to split it with civil war; and then we ought to
belong to a perfectly peaceful nation which does not yet exist.

November 28, 1908

On Celebrating Birthdays

Years ago, when Mr. Bernard Shaw wrote on drama in the
Saturday Review, he was only prevented from saying of every
play that it was the worst in the world by the desire to say that
at any rate it was better than Shakespeare. The high-water mark
of his extraordinary hatred was reached, I remember, when
somebody (with singular innocence) asked him to contribute to
the celebration of a Shakespeare anniversary. He said—"I no
longer celebrate my own birthday, and I do not see why I should
celebrate his." And I remember that when I read the words—
years ago, when I was very young—I leapt up in my seat (since
I was more agile in those days), and cried out—"Now I understand why he does not appreciate Shakespeare. It is because he
does not appreciate birthdays." The fun of the thing was that in
all these articles Mr. Bernard Shaw was always exhibiting Shakespeare as an abject and snivelling pessimist, a person with nothing
to say except "Vanitas vanitatum"; whilst Bernard Shaw, Bunyan, and other people were harsh, but heroic optimists, who
exalted in the austere ecstasy of life. Mr. Shaw was always quoting, in various accents, of an unvarying contempt, the pessimistic
speech of Macbeth which contains the phrase "Out, out, brief
candle." Mr. Bernard Shaw explained emphatically that he had
never felt like that. The comparatively simple explanation

occurred to me that Mr. Bernard Shaw had never sold himself to the devil or murdered an old gentleman in bed. In fairness to a dramatist, one might read "Out, brief candle," as having some connection with "Out, damned spot." In any case, Shakespeare was very plausibly presented by Shaw as a mere sullen sentimentalist, weeping over his own weakness and hanging the world with black in anticipation of his own funeral. It was all very ingenious, and you can quote a great deal in support of it. But, all the same, I am pretty certain that Shakespeare celebrated his birthday—and celebrated it with the utmost regularity. That is to say, I am sure there was strict punctuality about the time when the festival should begin, though there may, perhaps, have been some degree of vagueness or irregularity about the time when it should end.

There are some modern optimists who announce that the universe is magnificent or that life is worth living, as if they had just discovered some ingenious and unexpected circumstance which the world had never heard of before. But, if people had not regarded this human life of ours as wonderful and worthy, they would never have celebrated their birthdays at all. If you give Mr. Jones a box of cigars on his birthday the act cannot be consistent with the statement that you wish he had never been born. If you give Mr. Smith a dozen of sherry it cannot mean in theory that you wish him dead, whatever effect it may have in practice. Birthdays are a glorification of the idea of life, and it exactly hits the weak point in the Shaw type of optimism (or vitalism, which would be a better word) that it does not instinctively side with such religious celebrations of life. Mr. Shaw is ready to praise the Life-force, but he is not willing to keep his birthday, which would be the best of all ways to praise it. And the reason is that the modern people will do anything whatever for their religion except play the fool for it. They will be martyred, but they will not be chaffed. Mr. Shaw is quite clearly aware that it is a very good thing for him and for everyone else that he is alive. But to be told so in the symbolic form of brown-paper parcels containing slippers or cigarettes makes him feel a fool; which is exactly what he ought to feel. On many high occasions of life it is the only alternative to being one. A birthday does not come merely to remind a man that he has been born. It comes that he may be born again. And if a man is born again he must be as clumsy and as comic as a baby. I can therefore say with sincerity that I approve of funny ways, and even of foolish ways, of celebrating one's birthday. But of all the funny ways of celebrating your birthday I think the funniest is that which our constitutional practice inflicts upon the King. Because it is his birthday, he has to give other people presents. The presents he gives are such odd presents, and the people he gives them to are such odd people. The English monarch gets up, I suppose, in a state of natural gaiety to think that he is still continuing his popular and successful existence; perhaps he remembers his childhood or his youth and expansive instinct that he would like to do something to brighten and decorate the day. He might do all kinds of things—hold a tournament, or have a huge banquet, or go to church, or revisit some scenes of his boyhood, but he is supposed to say to himself, "How can I express this leap of festivity? I think that if I do something nice to Arthur Isidore James Jupp, who is head of a firm of wine-merchants, it will give me some artistic satisfaction. Or if I lift up suddenly before the English people the figure of James Delacy Bootle, who is the head of a firm of jam and chocolate manufacturers in the town of Tonbridge—that would be a fine thing. Then there is John Thornton Huggeridge, who is a prominent haberdasher in Manchester; he naturally occurs to my mind at emotional moments such as these. So I will make them all Knights or Baronets, and regard the proceedings as a sort of delirious banquet expressing the joy of life." Of course, the King does not really say anything of the sort; and I really think that he is rather hardly treated, and has rather a poor holiday. Because the politicians who happen at the moment to be managing or mismanaging his kingdom have come to a number of private arrangements with all kinds of entirely insignificant rich men, the King is obliged to celebrate his own birth by carrying out other people's more or less despicable bargains. Really I think it would be better, as well as cheaper, to go in for republican simplicity than to have gold trappings and then drag them in the mire.

The absence of Peers from the Birthday List is an important innovation; but it affects rather the political than the social power of aristocracy. The truth is that aristocracy has, in our time, fallen into such an entirely meaningless welter that it is impossible to judge it either by its own principles or by any other. All our talk is vitiated by the attempt to make a thing separate and not separate at the same time. If it is impossible to have your cake and eat it, it is even more impossible to cut off your leg and have it. For instance, what really makes the Irish angry with the English attitude is not that we hate the Irish, nor even that we try to absorb them: it is that we try to do the two things at the same time. We try to include them because they are English and also to despise them because they are Irish. When the Ogre had eaten the Princess, he no longer disliked her, since she became part of himself. It would be a very unreasonable Ogre who should expect the Princess to remain intact in his inside solely in order to be hated. The Irish people might conceivably have come into our civilisation if we had simply told them to be British and to boast of Shakespeare. But no people can consent to remain separate solely in order to be the foil to the self-flattery of another people. But there are other instances of this attempt to have it both ways For instance, some excellent Jews suffer from a sad fallacy: they think it glorious to be a Jew, and yet they think it insulting to be called one. But of all these floundering examples of falling between two stools, there is none more absurd than the present notion of a nobleman. He is superior to us: he is not to think so; we are not to say so; and yet the superiority must remain as an institution of the State. He may be oppressive, but he must not be proud. He is to be decorated with a sort of feudal crown, and emblazoned with some heraldic star, but we must not notice these things: we may only notice that he is very fond of cows or of crossing-sweepers.

Children in the same class often play at being Lords and Ladies; but there is a funnier game than that. That is when the Lords and Ladies insist on playing with us at being children in the same class.

December 5, 1908

On Studying Other Nations

It is not often that we have the picture of a people, and when we do it is generally so perfect that we do not believe in the people, even if we admire the picture. Most descriptions of other nations are so simple and sweeping that they cannot be true. If a traveller says—"The Swedes have convinced me that they are all truthful," it is not difficult to make the deduction that some of the Swedes must be pretty stiff liars. Distrust the description of every nation when it can be easily described. If a people can really be covered by an adjective, you may be certain that it is the wrong adjective. Each of the nations that you and I are likely to know well has in herself a contradiction which is quite coherent in practice, but which centuries of controversy could hardly reconcile in theory. Thus, for instance, the English (the people whom many of us must have met) have in their political condition a very queer paradox indeed. The English are patiently law-abiding; only there is no law for them to abide by. No other nation could understand as we do the enormous contradiction of our country, with its dignified obedience and its outrageous decrees. With us it is the ordinary people who are grave and dignified; it is the judges who are wild and fantastic. But the case is the same with any other country that we know well. Thus, of all peoples, the French are the most stingy in spending their money and the most profligate in spending their blood.

Thus, the Irish have a much more fiery enthusiasm than we, and yet have a much colder chastity. Thus, the Scotch are much more Puritanical—and much less pure.

But of all peoples that have puzzled me in this sense, the most striking case is that of the Russian. In most English novels, Russia is so simple that it is simply impossible. Russia is all in shades of grey, from the stern tyrant to the sad serf. But this is elementary nonsense; this is impossible; nations are not monochrome. There was never any society in which the slave did not steal some glory, if it were only the glory of being grotesque. Even the black slaves of America have been able to start a tradition which is rich in strong colour and caricature. At New Orleans there were niggers who were slaves; but at Margate there are still free white men who pretend to be niggers. Every system, even when it is unjust, has some balance of benevolent nonsense to balance its wicked wisdom. There is no slavery without a saturnalia. Therefore I have long darkly declined to believe in the popular picture of Russian life as rendered for the English. So great a part of humanity cannot all be so gloomy; even if the Russian peasants are as much oppressed, they cannot be so much depressed as all that. And the other day I picked up a book which for the first time made the Russian people leap up alive in front of me: I mean; Mr. Maurice Baring's "Russian Sketches and Travels." Mr. Baring does not profess to be political. As far as he is concerned, the Russians may be abominably oppressed. So are the people in Battersea abominably oppressed; but that does not prevent them from being funny or well worth writing a book about. Mr. Baring has been the first to strike the note of the gaiety of Russia; and it is all the more effective because he does it, not romantically but realistically. He simply describes what the plain Russian people do; and it soon becomes apparent that the things they do most commonly are to laugh and sing like other ordinary sinners in this vale of tears. Our Manchester and London world has lost romance so completely that perhaps romance can only be brought back by realism. Perhaps before we discuss whether there are such things as fairies it may be necessary to assert solemnly that there are such things as farmers.

But the trouble with all English estimates of foreign countries is a very curious trouble. Generally, we are not right enough even to be wrong. I mean that we cannot even get on to the wrong side of the question in France, Germany, or Italy, because we do not really see the question at all. For instance, a number of really notable and responsible Frenchmen believed that Dreyfus was innocent; the men who govern England certainly took that view, and the men who govern France seem by this time to have accepted it. But turn back merely for a moment and open one of the books which were widely popular in England in the hour of the Dreyfus affair. I opened one of them idly a little while ago. My eye fell upon a furious tirade about the splendid men supporting Dreyfus and the abject men opposing him; and I say, without any sort of doubt or qualification, that the whole of that tirade would have seemed as nonsensical to a French friend of Dreyfus as to one of his French enemies. The passage in this quite solid and celebrated book ran somewhat thus: "We need not compare lovers of truth like Zola, Picquart, Reinach, Jaurés, Gohier, with such obscene creatures as Cavaignac, Du Paty de Clam, Mercier, Jules Lemaître, Colonel Henry, Déroulède, and Major Esterhazy." I do not think that this is at all unfair to the list. To a Frenchman it would simply sound like raving gibberish.

The Frenchman on the side of Dreyfus would find the list just as bewildering as the Frenchman against Dreyfus. He would feel about it very much as I should feel if, being a Home Ruler (as I am), I were to find in a French paper some such Home Rule sentiments as these: "Figure to yourselves, Messieurs, that of the one side there were men of State, of the most honest, of the most sagacious, such men as Jabez Balfour, John Morley, O'Donovan Rossa, Sir John Barker, Thomas Hardy, Mr. Schnadhorst, Mr. Labouchere, James McNeill Whistler, and the Phoenix Park murderers; and that of the other side there are miscreants and *canaille*, such as Professor Dicey, Mr. Harry Marks, Mr. George Wyndham, William Whiteley, Queen Victoria, the poet Swinburne, Sir Thomas Lipton and the infamous Archbishop Benson." It would make no sort of difference on which side of the Home Rule argument the Englishman happened to be. From neither point of view, from no point of view, could he make head or tail of such a list of names. Yet that list is far less absurd than the corresponding French list that I have quoted; there is no juxtaposition in it that is quite so insane as the association of Reinach with Picquart or Du Paty with Déroulède. And this list is by no means a bad example of the ordinary English method in dealing with the phenomena of foreign politics.

Now, the question is: How far can this kind of monstrous error be avoided? It can only be avoided by one of two things, either by close study of a foreign literature and constant travel in a foreign country (which are things difficult for many people), or else by the most general habit of writing books like Mr. Baring's. Such books would give one scrap of living experience from which all the rest could be deduced. If, let us say, a Russian writer really described the way an English politician saluted a lady on entering a room, then his readers might deduce with certainty, in spite of any rumours, that that politician had not caused any lady to be flogged at the cart-tail in public. Just in the same way if any English writer on France could convey any distant echo of the *voice* of Paul Déroulède at a public meeting, the English would deduce for themselves that Paul Déroulède at any rate was not a Jesuitical knave, and had no part in a paltry conspiracy to ruin a harmless private man. So, perhaps, if more books like Mr. Baring's could be written about Russia, we might begin to see things instead of names, and to understand whatever we studied in the light of what we had realised. We might be able to do what is most difficult of all—to be able to apply epithets or descriptions in different senses or in different degrees. Terms, for instance, are sometimes extreme and positive, and sometimes almost negative, and yet true. It may be true to say of some Russian that he is a Socialist or a Conservative; and we may still want to know whether it is in the sense in which one may use "Protestant" of Mr. Balfour, or in the sense in which one only uses it of Mr. Kensit.[1] How are we to know? I can only answer mystically: "Give me a few more good books about streets and boats and crowded carriages, and I will undertake to guess."

December 12, 1908

The Nature of Human Conscience

There is a certain kind of modern book which must, if possible, be destroyed. It ought to be blown to pieces with the dynamite of some great satirist like Swift or Dickens. As it is, it must be patiently hacked into pieces even by some plodding person like myself. I will do it, as George Washington said, with my little hatchet; though it might take a long time to do it properly. The kind of book I mean is the pseudo-scientific book. And by this I do not mean that the man who writes it is a conscious quack or that he knows nothing; I mean that he proves nothing; he simply gives you all his cocksure, and yet shaky, modern opinions and calls it science. Books are coming out with so-called scientific conclusions—books in which there is actually no scientific argument at all. They simply affirm all the notions that happen to be fashionable in loose "intellectual" clubs, and call them the conclusions of research. But I am no more awed by the flying fashions among prigs than I am by the flying fashions

[1] J. A. Kensit was the leader of extremist Protestants who had recently spoken before the Protestant Truth Society, warning against the further "aggressions" of the Roman Catholic Church, and vowing himself to defend the Protestant religion against priestcraft—Roman or Anglican.

among snobs. Snobs say they have the right kind of hat; prigs say they have the right kind of head. But in both cases I should like some evidence beyond their own habit of staring at themselves in the glass. Suppose I were to write about the current fashions in dress something like this: "Our ignorant and superstitious ancestors had straight hat-brims; but the advance of reason and equality has taught us to have curly hat-brims; in early times shirt-fronts are triangular, but science has shown that they ought to be round; barbaric peoples had loose trousers, but enlightened and humane peoples have tight trousers," and so on, and so on. You would naturally rebel at this simple style of argument. You would say—"But, hang it all, give us some facts. Prove that the new fashions are more enlightened. Prove that men think better in the new hats. Prove that men run faster in the new trousers."

I have just read a book which has been widely recommended, which is introduced to the public by Dr. Saleeby, and which is, I understand, written by a Swiss scientist of great distinction. It is called "Sexual Ethics," by Professor Forel.[1] I began to read the book, therefore, with respect. I finished reading it with stupefaction. The Swiss Professor is obviously an honest man, though too Puritanical to my taste, and I am told that he does really know an enormous lot about insects. But as for the conception of proving a case, as for any notion that a "new" opinion needs proof, and that it is not enough, when you knock down great institutions, to say that you don't like them—it is clear that no such conceptions have ever crossed his mind. Science says that man has no conscience. Science says that man and woman must have the same political powers. Science says that sterile unions are morally free and without rule. Science says that it is wrong to drink fermented liquor. And all this with a splendid

---

[1] August Henri Forel (1848–1931), a Swiss psychologist and professor of psychiatry at Zurich. He wrote on such subjects as the anatomy of the brain and nerves, the psychology of ants, and sex hygiene. The book referred to here is his *Sexual Ethics*.

indifference to the two facts—first, that "Science" does not say these things at all, for numbers of great scientists say exactly the opposite; and second, that if Science did say these things, a person reading a book of rationalistic ethics might be permitted to ask why. Professor Forel may have mountains of evidence which he has no space to exhibit. We will give him the benefit of that doubt, and pass on to points where any thinking man is capable of judging him.

Where this sort of scientific writer is seen in all his glory is in his first abstract arguments about the nature of morality. He is immense; he is at once simple and monstrous, like a whale. He always has one dim principle or prejudice: to prove that there is nothing separate or sacred about the moral sense. Professor Forel holds this prejudice with all possible decorum and propriety. He always trots out three arguments to prove it; like three old broken-kneed elephants. Professor Forel duly trots them out. They are supposed to show that there is no such thing positively existing as the conscience; and they might just as easily be used to show that there are no such things as wings or whiskers, or toes or teeth, or boots or books, or Swiss Professors.

The first argument is that man has no conscience because some men are quite mad, and therefore not particularly conscientious. The second argument is that man has no conscience because some men are more conscientious than others. And the third is that man has no conscience because conscientious men in different countries and quite different circumstances often do very different things. Professor Forel applies these arguments eloquently to the question of human consciences; and I really cannot see why I should not apply them to the question of human noses. Man has no nose because now and then a man has no nose—I believe that Sir William Davenant, the poet, had none. Man has no nose because some noses are longer than others or can smell better than others. Man has no nose because not only are noses of different shapes, but (oh, piercing sword of scepticism!) some men use their noses and find the smell of incense nice, while some use their noses and find it nasty. Science therefore declares that man is normally noseless; and will take this for granted for the next four or five hundred pages, and will treat all the alleged noses of history as the quaint legends of a credulous age.

I do not mention these views because they are original, but exactly because they are not. They are only dangerous in Professor Forel's book because they can be found in a thousand books of our epoch. This writer solemnly asserts that Kant's idea of an ultimate conscience is a fable because Mahomedans think it wrong to drink wine, while English officers think it right. Really he might just as well say that the instinct of self-preservation is a fable because some people avoid brandy in order to live long, and some people drink brandy in order to save their lives. Does Professor Forel believe that Kant, or anybody else, thought that our conscience gave us direct commands about the details of diet or social etiquette? Did Kant maintain that, when we had reached a certain stage of dinner, a supernatural voice whispered in our ear "Asparagus"; or that the marriage between almonds and raisins was a marriage that was made in heaven? Surely it is plain enough that all these social duties are deduced from primary moral duties—and may be deduced wrong. Conscience does not suggest "asparagus," but it does suggest amiability, and it is thought by some to be an amiable act to accept asparagus when it is offered to you. Conscience does not respect fish and sherry; but it does respect any innocent ritual that will make men feel alike. Conscience does not tell you not to drink your hock after your port. But it does tell you not to commit suicide; and your mere naturalistic reason tells you that the first act may easily approximate to the second.

Christians encourage wine as something which will benefit men. Teetotallers discourage wine as something that will destroy men. Their conscientious conclusions are different, but their consciences are just the same. Teetotallers say that wine is bad because they think it moral to say what they think. Christians will not say that wine is bad because they think it immoral to say what they don't think. And a triangle is a three-sided figure. And a dog is a four-legged animal. And Queen Anne is dead.

We have, indeed, come back to alphabetical truths. But Professor Forel has not yet even come to them. He goes on laboriously repeating that there cannot be a fixed moral sense, because some people drink wine and some people don't. I cannot imagine how it was that he forgot to mention that France and England cannot have the same moral sense, because Frenchmen drive cabs on the right side of the road and Englishmen on the left.

December 19, 1908

The Bottom Dog and the Superman

Why is it that certain eccentric ideas all run together? One would think that it was the whole fun of an eccentric idea to run alone, or, as the poet said, to swarm by itself. Why, for instance, should most vegetarians be also teetotallers? Obviously one indisputable thing that can be said for wine is that it is made entirely from vegetables. Even more obviously the one thing that can be said for vegetables is that they can be made into wine. Whatever are the crimes of the carnivorous animals, they are all solid and convinced teetotallers. We have heard of an ox in a tea-cup; but nobody has yet heard of an elephant in a liqueur-glass. Tigers have not been trampled into any horrible wine. Bacchus trod his grapes, but he never tried jumping on his leopards. On strictly logical principles it seems obvious that vegetarians ought to urge alcohol as one of the few really inspiring arguments for vege-tarianism. The crushed body of a bird or a beetle cannot be made to live a second and celestial life, as does the crushed body of the golden or the purple grape. These aesthetic calculations do not happen to concern me one way or the other. For I believe that, within the four corners of reason, the more careless a man is about his body the better. The only thing worse than the act

of carefully avoiding alcohol is the act of carefully obtaining it.
Upon Temperance Legislation, as discussed by prosperous politicians in the House of Lords and the House of Commons, my
final feeling is best summarised in four lines of a Buccaneer's
song by Mr. Masefield—

> Oh, there's many sorry fellows as go in
>   silken suits,
> And there's a mort of wicked knaves as
>   lives in good reputes,
> So I'm for drinking honest, and for dying
>   in my boots
> Like an old, bold mate of Henry Morgan's.

But this question is irrelevant, though agreeable. I used it only
to illustrate the fact that certain creeds and crazes always go
together politically, even when they do not in any way go together
logically. I might have given many other instances of the same
unmeaning association between quite separate or quite antago-
nistic ideas. For instance, why are those who are Revolutionists
as such generally opposed to Militarism as such? What is the
good of a revolution if it is not a military revolution? How can
it be ignoble to learn fighting if it is noble to teach the people
to fight? Or, again, why do those modern people who praise
women always abuse domesticity and the kitchen, which are
obviously what women have made them? Why do they urge the
female's claims to new powers by describing perpetually how
narrow and stupid she is with all her existing powers? Obviously,
in mere reason, women who wish to scale the seventh heaven
of a vote (the possession of which has already made men seem
almost like seraphs) ought to praise all their past domestic
achievements and represent the female fireside as an earthly paradise, evidently introductory to that heaven. Why should *they*
be concerned to explain that they have misgoverned one city
and therefore should be made rulers over ten cities?
Someone sent me this morning an angry little red paper called
the *Oxford Socialist* (or some such name), which had the note

which is most obviously lost in nearly all our newspapers; I mean the note of sincerity. Such young writers are separated from almost all prominent politicians by this distinctive and even dreadful mark—that they would fulfil their programme if they could. There is no doubt that if these young Socialists ever came into power, something would happen; even if it were something silly. As things are, no Government is admitted into power in England at all, except upon a positive understanding that nothing shall happen. Therefore, though I am not a Socialist, my sympathy with the Socialists against the hypocritical hilarity of this endless cricket match is quite too strong to be expressed. I like the Oxford Socialists and their funny little scarlet paper. I read through all such revolutionary literature with a quite steady sympathy, until I run bang into some other quite irrelevant fad; and then I stop. One ought to be denouncing something: not everything. It is simple enough to understand why a man believes in Socialism; but it is a real problem why he believes in Socialism and also in Buddhism and Breathing Exercises and Nietzsche and Art Nouveau, and plays all about the quarrels of very wealthy married people. None of these appeal to my intellect as having anything to do with the idea of the State owning all the means of production. But the case is really much worse than this. The Socialist instinctively accepts not only fads that have nothing to do with each other, but fads which directly contradict each other. For instance, looking through the *Oxford Socialist*, I find frequent allusions to that preposterous pre-natal bore, the Superman. If such a creature ever should come, we shall certainly be too tired of him even to laugh at him. That, however, is not my immediate point. I can respect a German professor who expects the Superman, just as I can respect an old woman in Essex who expects the Messiah, according to the prophecies of Mr. Baxter.[1] The

[1] Possibly an allusion to the writings of Richard Baxter (1615–1691), a Nonconformist minister, who wrote *Saint's Everlasting Rest* and his autobiographical *Reliquiae Baxterianae* (1696), neither of which is unusually laden with predictions or prophecies of the sort mentioned here.

two expectant persons seem to me much on the same level of philosophy and education. But, at least, the old lady who expects the Messiah next month is herself a Shaker,[2] or a Christadelphian,[3] or an Agapemonite,[4] or some such thing; and her expectation is quite consistent with her own theory of the universe.

Now when that pathetic and poisoned Puritan whose name was Nietzsche started his idea of a Superman, it was quite consistent with his idea of the universe. His notion was insane, but it was not unreasonable. His notion was this: that, just as a brutal and bewildering anarchy of animals had somehow brought man forth—a superior to the ape—so a brutal and bewildering anarchy of men might bring forth some inconceivable being who should be better still. An Anarchist like Nietzsche has a right to talk of "the Superman" without knowing what it means, just as I have a right to talk about the Winner of next year's Derby without knowing what horse will win it. In a chaotic struggle, the Superman simply means whatever creature finds itself on top of man. The creature may have five legs. He may have nine heads or none. You may, if you like, imagine some unthinkable huge hybrid evolved out of biological chaos; and you can call such a creature by a grand, unmeaning name. This, I suppose, is what Nietzsche did. He said: "Throw all creatures, nice and nasty, eye of newt and toe of frog, hand of ape and wing of angel, into the cauldron of anarchy; and whatever monster comes to the top like scum, I will call the Superman." This is a contemptible position, but not an incomprehensible one.

But for a Socialist to talk about the Superman is incomprehensible as well as contemptible. He has no need to use such foggy and shapeless phrases, because he is supposed to be cre-

---

[2] A sect started in Manchester in 1747 who practiced celebacy and communal living. They were so named for their strange behavior.

[3] A sect founded about 1848 which believed in "conditional immortality" and Christ's eventual return to reign on this earth.

[4] A sect also called Starkyites, for one of their leaders, Samuel Starky. They founded an agapemone, or Abode of Love, which embodied their interest in communal living, but they were forced to disband by the authorities.

ating something by conscious human efforts, and presumably knows what it is that he is creating. The Socialist can aim at producing any kind of man he likes: the Good Man, or the Acrobatic and Reversible Man, or the Very Refined Man or the Perfectly Spherical Fat Man. I do not know what kind of man the Socialists want, but I thought they did. Why, if they do, should they deliberately make themselves out mistier and more muddle-headed than they are? Whatever their faults, they are fighting as brave men fight, for a neglected or conquered ideal. Why should they use the pitiful phrase in which poor Nietzsche expressed his hazy intention of waiting till the end of the fight to praise the victor? What intellectual connection can there be between the savage chivalry of fighting for the Bottom Dog and the far-off prophetic snobbishness of prostrating oneself to the Superman? Why should this acrid ferment of the pity for poverty go along in the same books and pamphlets with this last night-mare of the worship of success? One can only answer—because of that mysterious modern tendency by which all follies tend to be bound up in one bundle—to be cast (let us hope) into the fire.

December 26, 1908

Carrie Nation and Teetotalism

I was inflamed with joy when I heard of the arrival on our shores of Mrs. Carrie Nation, the enthusiastic American lady who breaks other people's bottles with a large axe. My exultation, however, was dashed down again to the earth by the declaration which she made almost immediately on landing, that she had not brought her axe with her. What can be the fun of Mrs. Carrie Nation without her axe I cannot imagine; it is as if Kubelik said he had not brought his violin. On the present occasion Mrs. Carrie

Nation writes: "The only axe I have brought is the Bible." This is a painful instance of the error of changing one's weapons under the mistaken notion that the pen is mightier than the axe. I am sure that this distinguished lady managed the axe more neatly and gracefully than this; I feel certain that she could decapitate a champagne-bottle or bisect a pint of Beaune with a more elegant precision than she shows in the management of epigram. This expression, "The only axe I have brought is the Bible," is unfortunately open to three objections. To mention the smallest and mildest first, it happens, for some intangible aesthetic reason, to sound silly. It is as if a man said, "The only macintosh I wear is 'The Pirates of Penzance' "; "The only toothpick I carry is 'Paradise Lost.' " But I leave this elusive artistic matter, as perhaps not interesting to Mrs. Carrie Nation.

[Of your great mercy permit me here a passionate parenthesis. How in heaven or earth do Americans get their names? Does each American make up his own surname for himself ? Are there such things as parents in America? Or are the people with extraordinary names inspired from their cradle to be extraordinary? How comes it that an idealistic crank has such a name as Nation? Was there really an old Mr. Nation who was not cranky or idealistic? Who would believe us in England if we bore such appropriate titles? Who would be convinced by such convincing surnames? Suppose Mr. Joseph Chamberlain were called Mr. Joseph Empire? Suppose Mr. Belloc sent in his card as Mr. Europe. How do these things happen? Of what nature is this people? Pardon me; I resume my argument. The paroxysm of inquiry has passed.]

Disregarding the above, which is all between brackets, I pass on to the second and more solid objection to this perfect and flower-like phrase, which cannot be too often repeated, and which, therefore, I repeat: "The only axe I have brought is the Bible." The second objection which an Englishman might timidly offer is that a Bible is not quite so much of a novelty or marvel in England as an iconoclastic chopper. Many of us have seen Bibles, not apparently brought from America. In fact, our national vanity has invented a legend to the effect that the Americans originally got the Bible from us. This conviction, erroneous, no doubt, is deeply implanted in the mind of the British public. If Mrs. Carrie Nation wants to bring a fresh American product to purify and exalt us, she ought to have brought the Book of Mormon. Perhaps she has; in such cases one never knows. But she has not brought the one thing that I really wanted to see—the actual wood and steel axe with which a white Christian woman, not certified as insane, committed common theft and pillage from distrust of the medical quality of the beverages of her neighbours. That axe would be a relic really worth keeping, in the history of human unreason—like the tall soldiers of Frederick William or the consular horse of Heliogabalus.

But the third objection to this remarkable phrase ("The only axe I have brought is the Bible") is, unfortunately, the most solid and decisive of all. If Mrs. Carrie Nation's idea is to wither up the tradition of wine, she is by no means wise in bringing the Bible for that purpose: she had better have brought her chopper. After all, if she throws her axe at a publican he may very probably be killed; but if she throws her Bible at a publican there is always the danger that he may pick it up and begin to read it. It is not very likely, I admit; but he might. The book might happen to open at the page where Our Lord is so dissatisfied with water that He definitely turns it into wine; or at the page where St. Paul recommends wine to Timothy; or at the page which declares that this drink makes glad the heart of man; or at that which uses the inspiration of the vine as a violent metaphor for the immortal energy of God. I say it with the reverence which belongs to mere serious religious consistency when I say that Mrs. Nation might really almost as well bring us "Pickwick" as a purely teetotal book as bring us the Bible. No, Mrs. Nation, the axe was better. There is no answer to the axe; except another axe. But while I regret that Mrs. Nation has come to us and left the axe behind, while I should have been quite contented if the axe had come to us and left her behind, I think that she may have her uses. One of her uses ought certainly to be that of serving intellectually as an Awful Example to certain other people. The old *intransigeant* teetotalers, of whom she may be a survival, used, I believe, to exhibit a drunkard on their platforms as an example of the ghastly results of drinking wine. It cannot be wrong for us to exhibit Mrs. Carrie Nation as an example of the awful results of not drinking it. But her real exemplary utility has a rather wider scope. The true value of Mrs. Nation and her appearance at this moment lies in the fact that it teaches us something of the true nature of hysterical enthusiasms as distinct from heroic enthusiasm. This is a point worth clearing up, and worth pointing out at all times; but especially worth clearing up in our present social crisis or dissolution; and especially worth pointing out, not only to Mrs. Carrie Nation, but to many of her own sex who think themselves perhaps more enlightened. She is the parody of the progressive woman. She is the Comic Suffragette. I mean the person compared with whom even Suffragettes look serious.

In one respect at least, there is more sense in the head of the axe than in the heads of our indignant ladies. The head of the axe does actually destroy the bottle. It is no good crying over spilt port; and the toper will never drink again the whisky that is past. But the aim of the suffragette is not so much to tear up a Ministerial statement when made as to prevent, as long as possible, the Minister from making it. The Suffragettes do not want to hear their enemies' speeches; that is an absolute and final proof that they are not really fighting, but only fooling. The moment one becomes keen or serious on any controversial matter one listens keenly, however much one may reply violently.

Enthusiasts and logicians make notes; drunkards and Suffragettes only make noises: that is because they are both fundamentally frivolous, being only out for excitement. Take but one ludicrous example from last Saturday's orgie. When Mr. Lloyd George had hardly said a few sentences some women set up as a sort of chant this thoughtful and appropriate phrase: "Deeds, not words! Deeds, not words!" What can it conceivably have been supposed to mean? What "deeds" did these romantic ladies expect a gentleman to perform on a platform at the Albert Hall? Did they expect him to produce ballot-boxes, previously concealed about his person, and scatter them among the audience? Did they want him to worship Miss Pankhurst in pantomine, or stab Mrs. Humphry Ward on a sacrificial altar? Do they think the vote is something solid and eatable? I sometimes fancy that they do. The only "deed" Mr. Lloyd George had come to do, the only "deed" he could do, was to announce the Government policy; and that they wouldn't let him do. If they had made a row *after* he had spoken, then their action, whether right or no, would have been at least revolutionary. As it was, the thing was not even a riot; it was a noise. It might as well have been cows. I think there is a real doubt about the theory of female suffrage, but this is a blunder in the practice. Women obviously have political power; I think it is doubtful whether they ought to parade their political power. But surely there can be no doubt that they ought not to parade their political weakness.

1909

January 2, 1909

Dickens as Socialist

I feel impelled to write something somewhere about a book I have just read—a book which has moved me by its intelligence, its extravagance, its great sincerity, and its enormous errors. It is called "Charles Dickens: the Apostle of the People," and it is written by Mr. Edwin Pugh.[1] I like Mr. Edwin Pugh for this reason, that while he and I disagree upon twenty things, when we agree we are alone in our agreement. No one else, as far as I know, agrees with us. When Mr. Pugh is wrong (as when he says that Napoleon was head of an oligarchy), he is wrong with thousands of other people. But when he is right, he is right exactly where hardly anyone else is right; as where he suggests that "all Carlyle's sneers about 'the Sea-Green Incorruptible' are rather clumsy raillery," which do not disturb the fact that Robespierre really was a highly honourable man. Carlyle might call Robespierre a Sea-Green Incorruptible. He might with equal truth have called any average English Prime Minister "a Rosy-Pink Incorruptible." But in both cases one may be permitted to think the moral character rather more important than the facial complexion. But perhaps you think that these extracts have an air of some irrelevancy. Perhaps you think that the problem of whether Napoleon was oligarchical or the problem of whether Robespierre was green has not got much to do with the subject of Charles Dickens. That is where you make a mistake.

Mr. Pugh begins his account of Dickens with some preliminary statement about Robespierre, Napoleon, and revolutionary history. It was when I discovered that first fact that I decided to go on reading the book. A man who thinks about Marat in order to discuss Micawber must have done some decent thinking for himself. Mr. Pugh sets out to expound that Dickens was first

[1] Edwin Pugh was the author of *Charles Dickens: The Apostle of the People*, which was published by The New Age Press in 1908.

what is called a Democrat, and second was (or would have been) what is called a Socialist. I imagine that so intelligent a writer cannot require to be told that the two things have nothing to do with each other. Democracy is the reference of public problems to the people. Socialism is the ownership by Government of all national capital; as Mr. Balfour said with admirable limpidity, "This is Socialism and nothing else is Socialism." It is obvious that there might be a Democracy which always decided against Socialism. There are such Democracies. It is obvious that there might be a close and corrupt oligarchy owning all national capital. There soon will be such oligarchies. A Democrat necessarily faces many difficulties; but he need not accept the difficulties of the Collectivist State. The Socialist takes up heavy burdens, but there is no reason at all why he should take up the huge burden of being a Democrat. I fancy that the Socialistic State would work most swiftly and smoothly if it were managed by a very small class; and I am quite certain that all the intellectual Socialists that I have met have in their hearts agreed with me. That explains the strong rally of the English aristocracy to Socialism.

But we are not talking about Socialism so much as about Dickens; a much more enduring thing. Now when Mr. Pugh says that Dickens was the apostle of the people, I agree with him. When he says that Dickens poured a proper contempt upon the pretensions of the "gentleman," I agree with him. When he says that the poor are far more ceremonious and courteous than the rich, I agree with him with a leap of love and amazement, astonished that in these days anyone should have found out so obvious a fact. But when he says that all this proves Dickens to have been a Socialist, or even a potential Socialist, I am compelled to draw his attention to one of the most solid and startling facts about Dickens. It is true that Dickens did defy every despot and abuse every abuse. But, as it happens, some of the despots that he defied most frantically were official despots, State and Municipal despots. As it happens, some of the abuses which he abused most vehemently were abuses that arose from too much power being given to the central government. I have none of Mr. Grad-grind's belief in the abstract advantages of private enterprise. But Mr. Bumble was not a product of private enterprise. Mr. Bumble was a product of Socialism—of that amount of Socialism then permitted in the State. Mr. Tite Barnacle was not a representative of wild commercial competition. Mr. Tite Barnacle was a rep-resentative of Socialism—of the heavy official inevitable in any bureaucracy. I believe there are some people who say that they want Socialism, but do not want bureaucracy. Such persons I leave in simple despair. How any calculating creature can think that we can extend the number of Government offices without extending the number of Government officials and the preva-lence of the official mind, I cannot even conjecture. Some people look forward to a splendid transformation of the general human soul. That is a good argument for accepting Socialism—and, when one comes to think of it, an even better reason for doing without it.

But, in any case, the plain fact about Dickens's works remains. Dickens did, as Mr. Pugh generally suggests, really come out into the open in order to defy all types of tyrant. And of the tyrants he attacked, a good half were individualistic tyrants, appointed by money and anarchy, and a good half were Social-istic tyrants, appointed by the central sagacity of the State. Now the Socialist does show how a man will not become publicly rich, like Gradgrind. But he does not show how a man will not become privately rich, like Tite Barnacle. He does ensure that such a fool as Bounderby will not be a merchant prince. But how and where does he show that such a fool as Bumble will not be a beadle?

But the Pugh theory of Dickens as a Socialist, which he may or may not have been, is really not by any means so extraordinary as the Pugh theory of Dickens as a Democrat—which he certainly was. For after reading all Mr. Pugh's vigorous eulogies of the democracy of Dickens, the doubt left in my mind is a different one. I am fully convinced that Dickens was a Democrat; my only doubt is whether Mr. Pugh is one. If Democracy rests upon any comradeshp and community of instincts with the mass of the people, Mr. Pugh is rather anti-Democratic than otherwise. For instance (it is horrible even to have to write down the words), he does not really like "Pickwick." He complains of its "flippant, light-hearted disregard of vital issues," and "the blatant objectivity of its treatment." Now, it seems odd enough at first sight that anyone who dislikes "Pickwick" should trouble to like Dickens. There are hundreds of refined, sympathetic, well-balanced novels in the world; there is only one "Pickwick." But it seems stranger still that a person who finds the port and brandy of "Pickwick" too coarse for his stomach should at the same time offer himself, as well as his hero, as a representative of the masses.

The truth is, of course, that the blatant objectivity of Mr. Stiggins's nose and Tony Weller's waistcoat is one of the general and healthy tastes of humanity, which, if Mr. Pugh had it, might really link him with the people. As it is, Mr. Pugh, being an imaginative and compassionate man, can sympathise with the sorrows of the poor. But Walter Pater could do that. Mr. Arthur Symons could do that. Any aesthete, however secluded, any aristocrat, however fastidious, must, if he has any poetry in him at all, feel that there is something awful in the death of a coal-heaver and something pitiful in the tears of a scullery-maid. There is no doubt that we are all brothers in grief; but we shall never again be brothers in life and fact till we are once more brothers in fun and farce. Human equality will not only be created by cabmen coming to appreciate Rossetti, human equality will come when Mr. Pugh (after long vigils and mystic initiations) is at least able to appreciate what he calls somewhere the bestial monstrosities of Old English caricature.

As to the question about Socialism, surely it is very simple; and it is exactly because fastidious moderns, like Mr. Pugh, will not make themselves simple enough that they cannot understand it. What Dickens disliked was not individualism, or commercialism, or hereditary rule, or free competition: it was tyranny. He was not confined to defending the Commons against the

Lords, or the State against the capitalists, or the working classes
against the Trusts, or even the poor against the rich: he was
defending the powerless against the powerful. The man in power
might be an Individualist merchant or a Socialist official: it was
Dickens's business to remind him that he was a man, and, therefore, might be a wicked one.

January 9, 1909

The Wrong Books at Christmas

I have very little doubt myself that, somehow or other, an inspiring and compelling creed will return to our country, because
religion is really a need, like fires in winter: where there is no
vision, the people perish, and perish of cold. The nation that has
no gods at all not only dies, but what is more, is bored to death.
But if ever a faith is firmly founded again, it will be at least
interesting to notice those few things that have bridged the gulf,
that stood firm when faith was lost, and were still standing when
it was found again. Of these really interesting things one, in all
probability, will be the English celebration of Christmas. Father
Christmas was with us when the fairies departed; and please God
he will still be with us when the gods return.

Of course, it is covered up, like every other living thing, with
a sort of moss of convention and the unmeaning use of words.
I take an example which has just caught my eye. On the literary
advertisement page of a weekly paper to which I am strongly
attached, I see written in very large letters, "Books Suitable for
Christmas Presents." As I glance down the catalogue appended,
the first title which captures my eye is our old friend "Sexual
Ethics, by Professor A. Forel; with an Introduction by Doctor

Saleeby,"[1] about which I made some well-meaning but emphatic criticism in this column some weeks ago. As I think I made sufficiently clear, I consider Professor A. Forel's book an unreasonable book, and in parts an absurd book. But I really do not think it so frightfully funny that it is specially suitable to be read aloud amid roars of happy Christmas laughter by the family when gathered round the Yule log. It would not have occurred to me, even if I had admired the Forel philosophy, to describe a book called "Sexual Ethics" as falling under the special head of "Books Suitable for Christmas Presents." Nor does another book, admirable for all I know, but bearing the title of "Our Criminal Fellow-Citizens," strike me as being a sympathetic substitute for crackers or mince-pies. I can even imagine that the suitable Christmas book which is here mentioned under the title of "The Scientific Basis of Socialism"[2] might pall upon a children's party before the end of Christmas Eve, and might even be deserted in favour of honey-pots or charades. I am not making an unfair selection from this list of breezy and convivial books; they are all like that in one way or another. There is a book on Tolstoy; but surely nobody could possibly want to hear about Tolstoy on Christmas Day; I would as soon hear about Mrs. Eddy. There is a book by Mr. Belfort Bax; but I am sure that that able and distinguished gentleman would be highly disgusted if anyone ventured to tell him that he was suitable for Christmas. There is a book on Mr. Bernard Shaw. There is a book by Mr. Bernard Shaw. But Mr. Shaw does not like Father Christmas at all; and I am sure that, with all Mr. Shaw's admirable qualities, Father Christmas does not like him.

I confess that I took these chance headings with the mere feeling that Christmas did not fit in very well with these books; but when I come to think of the matter seriously, I think it can be safely said that what is wrong with all those books is that

[1] See December 12, 1908, footnote 1.

[2] Henry M. Bernard's *The Scientific Basis of Socialism: Two Essays in Evolution* was published in 1908.

they do not fit in with Christmas. There is nothing really wrong with those books except that they do not fit in with Christmas. There is nothing really wrong with the whole modern world except that it does not fit in with Christmas. The modern world will have to fit in with Christmas or die. Those who will not rejoice in the end of the year must be condemned to lament it. We must accept the New Year as a new fact; we must be born again. No kind of culture or literary experience can save him who entirely refuses this cold bath of winter ecstasy. No poetry can be appreciated by him who cannot appreciate the mottoes in the crackers. No log-rolling can rescue him who will not roll the Yule log. Christmas is like death and child-birth—a test of our simple virtue; and there is no other such test left in this land to-day.

But, for the sake of such frivolous criticism as seems appropriate to the occasion, let me simply take as examples those advertisements in order. Let us consider, for the benefit of those who like such books as I have named, why Christmas seems to have nothing to do with them. And let us consider, for the benefit of those who like Christmas, why Christmas seems to be ludicrously soiled by the mere mention of such books. The reason is really very simple: it is that on every one of these points the philosophy of the books is inferior to the philosophy of Christmas.

Take, for instance, our friend Forel and his "Sexual Ethics." Now, what is wrong with Forel's sexual ethics is quite simply this: that they are not tall enough to reach up to the mistletoe. The two first facts which a healthy boy or girl feels about sex are these: first that it is beautiful and then that it is dangerous. While all the philosophical Forels go floundering about in a world of words, saying that this is wrong if it disturbs your digestion, or that that is right if it does not disturb your great-grandchild, all plain, pleasure-loving people have an absolutely clean instinct in the matter. Mankind declares this with one deafening voice: that sex may be ecstatic so long as it is also restricted. It is not necessary even that the restriction should be reasonable; it is necessary that it should restrict. That is the beginning of all purity; and purity is the beginning of all passion. In other words, the creation of conditions for love, or even for flirting, is the first common-sense of Society. In other words, there is more serious philosophy in the sprig of mistletoe than in the whole of "Sexual Ethics."

Take again the next topic I mentioned, the jolly Christmas book called "Our Criminal Fellow-Citizens." What is it that really makes almost any upstanding human being, with his heart in the right place and supplying blood to his brain—what is that makes such a man instinctively despise and deride the whole science of criminology? On consideration, I incline to think that it is not merely the obvious stupidity of criminologists. It is not only because they say that Robespierre was hard and fierce because he had a retreating skull, while Charles Peace[3] was hard and fierce because he had a projecting one. It is something ultimately crazy in the whole criminologist position; and it cannot be better expressed than by saying that one cannot feel like that at Christmas. All Christmas feasts, all Christmas freaks, are founded on human equality: at least, upon what is now called equality of opportunity. Nobody is inordinately proud of having got a golden-haired doll out of a branpie, for everyone feels that it might have gone to another. No one is despised for failing to snatch the best raisins at snap-dragon,[4] because all the children are fundamentally frightened of the blue fire. And that is a much truer picture of our general condition towards crime and innocence than anything that I can hope to read in the book called "Our Criminal Fellow-Citizens." At this moment men (like myself) who know perfectly well that they might under temptation commit murder or forgery, are talking polysyllabic nonsense about the odd shape which a man's head must be before he thinks of murder, and the strange spatulate fingers a man

---

[3] Charles Peace (1832–1879), an English criminal and murderer.

[4] Snapdragon is a game in which the players snatch raisins or chestnuts, etc., from burning brandy and quickly eat them.

must have before he can manage to forge. But one feels this rubbish less at Christmas, because it is full of charity.

I could extend the same test to all the other cases I have mentioned if I had space to do it. What is wrong with the "Scientific Basis of Socialism" is simply that it is a scientific basis. The real basis of life is not scientific; the strongest basis of life is sentimental. People are not economically obliged to live. Anybody can die for nothing. People romantically desire to live—especially at Christmas. And, when all is said and done, the great case against those great men, Shaw and Tolstoy, is that when men desire most to live they desire least to read them.

January 16, 1909
Christmas Pantomimes

The only thing that is endurable about the ending of Christmas is that the pantomimes commonly come after it. And around the subject of pantomimes there rages an interesting quarrel very symbolic of the whole modern situation in many matters. For the theatrical public is separated on this subject into several easily distinguishable schools. Leaving out of account the entirely frivolous people, such as those who will not go to theatres at all because they think them wicked, or those who do go to theatres because they expect them to be wicked—leaving the essential levity of the Puritan and the sensualist on one side, those who discuss pantomimes can be roughly arranged under the following heads.

First: The Old Playgoers, who say that they wish we had the old-fashioned pantomime. These are subject to the simple objection which attaches to the mere *laudator temporis acti* in every connection and on every question. Which old pantomime does he want? Does he want the old pantomime of ancient Athens or only the old pantomime of Mr. Vincent Crummles?[1] That is the essential fallacy of a mere sentimental conservatism. The present cannot be compared with the past; the present can only be compared with a million separate and quite different pasts. I can understand a man saying that he would like to have lived in the seventeenth century; I can understand (indeed I can understand much better) his saying that he would like to have lived in the twelfth. But I am quite certain that a man who would have enjoyed the twelfth century would not have enjoyed the seventeenth; therefore I cannot understand his meaning when he merely says that he regrets the past. I can understand a man sighing for the good old times of George III, or for the good old times of Richard Coeur-de-Lion; but I cannot get the same picture in my mind. Therefore I do not know what a man means when he regrets the good old times. And in a smaller way something of the same inevitable fallacy belongs to that sentimental reminiscence which is so common among playgoers. The old style in things like pantomime covers so large a number of very different things. It may mean (I hope it does) the old harlequinade, the true substance and body of a pantomime, a real Christmas banquet, by the one noble test—that you can get ill over it. For I have been literally ill with laughing over a clown, a policeman, and a baker's shop. Or it may mean the Planché fantasias,[2] which were full of much real poetry and wit; or it may mean things in the style of the Nellie Farren burlesques, with sound English vulgarity and big brazen puns. Or it may mean something that first became fashionable ten years ago, and is hardly distinguishable from a musical comedy. You never know with the man who professes to be praising things merely as old things: they may be quite new things. Most of our first aristocratic houses, for instance, are extremely recent.

[1] The owner/manager of a touring theatrical company in Dickens' *Nicholas Nickleby*.
[2] James Robinson Planché (1796–1880), an English playwright and antiquarian who wrote numerous burlesques and extravaganzas.

Second: You have the man who does not like pantomimes at all—a foul deformity in the sight of gods and men. Unfortunately this class includes most of the modern dramatic critics. Still more unfortunately, it includes almost all the able and honest dramatic critics. There was, I suppose, a real period of coarse flippancy and crude mercantile hypocrisy in the English stage which necessitated the rise of and rebuke of men rootedly and bitterly serious— like Mr. Bernard Shaw and Mr. Max Beerbohm. Such Puritan spirits often do the work of God, if mainly in the spreading of doubt, which is the spreading of devastation. But such spirits are out of place at a pantomime, for a pantomime is founded upon faith. It is indecent that Mr. Bernard Shaw should be allowed at a pantomime. For the only true definition of indecency, as distinct from immorality, is an incurable misunderstanding between two things equally honest—say, an old Methodist woman and a statue of Aphrodite. I, for instance, happen to have no ear for music, and if ever, by accident or compulsion, I find myself at an opera, I have the wholesome experience of feeling half-witted; it is disgraceful that all that deafening glory should break about my wooden head. But a modern dramatic critic, of the best type, has no more business at a pantomime than I have at a concert. I cannot explain the clown to him any more than he can explain the sonata to me. But I at least am wise enough to envy, whereas he is often actually stupid enough to scorn.

Third: There are the people who want to replace what they call vulgar pantomimes by what they call "pretty children's plays." They point out with great justice that much of the fun of recent pantomimes has not referred to children at all—that children cannot care about topical songs with twenty verses dealing with such ordinary nursery topics as "Tariff Reform, Female Suffrage, King Leopold of Belgium, or Sir Thomas Lipton's yacht." This is true; it may be taken as certain that the recent pantomime has not been made for children. Its occasional impropriety is a proof of that, for no man would be so indecent as to be deliberately indecent for children. Let it be granted, then, that the conventional pantomime of some years ago, which still largely holds the field, was not suited or even intended for children. But it is still permissible to add that the delicate and fanciful fairy-play now so much admired and demanded is not suited or even intended for children either. The pantomime is too vulgar for infancy and the fairy-play is too refined. Both are really created by grown-up people to satisfy their own aesthetic needs; only the old pantomime was invented to suit their need for frivolity, suggestiveness, and rowdy allusions, while the poetic play is invented to suit their need for mystery and grace and distant dreams. In both cases the thing has the one essential mark of adult and even senile institutions: the element of strong stimulation.

The comic beauty of the principal boy in tights, and the tragic beauty of the fairy queen in Burne-Jones draperies, have alike to be piquant, stabbing—even abnormal. But exactly the one thing that need not, and ought not, to be given to children is stimulants. Children do not require to see loveliness in that piercing and concentrated form in which it appears either in slightly amorous or slightly mystical art: a form sometimes permissible for us, in order to prick or sting us into remembering, amid our fusses and fatigues, that there is superlative beauty in the universe—

> Lord, Thy most pointed pleasure take,
> And stab my spirit broad awake.

But a much blunter pleasure will suffice for a little boy: being nearer to divine innocence, he is content to be poked in the waistcoat with the clown's poker or with Mr. Punch's stick. What a child loves above all things is lucidity: a clear and culminating story, coloured and positive shapes. The child likes Red Riding Hood to have a red riding hood, and Blue Beard to have a beard unmistakably blue. It will not do to introduce any art colours into this sort of picture. Do not let there creep into the scarlet cloak and hood a delicate tinge of terra-cotta or of copper-brown because you think that it would tone well with the green woodland scene; do not let Blue Beard have a peacock-blue beard, fading away into mysterious greens or olives, like a background by Whistler. Or do all these things if you like, but say you are pleasing yourself; do not say you are pleasing the children.

Fourth: there are the people who agree with me, a very fine and thoughtful body of men, whom I have not yet had the pleasure of meeting. They are disposed to remark that it is a highly singular circumstance that the one part of a pantomime which was thoroughly suited to the vigorous psychology of the very young is the one part that has been cut down or cut out of it by both the schools of modern pantomime.

I mean the Harlequinade. We miss that noblest of human spectacles—a policeman being made into sausages, a sight which combines the three healthiest of human elements—the chivalrous rebellion against oppressive power; the mystical irony of the human body, which is a comic animal; and that looking for poetry in plain things of parlour and kitchen which is the epic of domesticity.

January 23, 1909

Truth in the Newspapers

It is by this time practically quite impossible to get the truth out of any newspapers, even the honest newspapers. I mean the kind of truth that a man can feel an intelligent curiosity about—moral truth, truth that is disputed, truth that is in action and really affecting things. Doubtless, the daily paper reports certain events in their simple actuality; but those events will generally be found to be the events that end an affair, not the events that produce it. One can find the fact that a man is hanged, but not the truth about his trial; one can believe the journalist when he says that war has broken out, but not when he says that war was inevitable. The *Daily Express* will tell me truthfully that the Tsar is dead. But it cannot tell me truthfully whether he is really still alive; whether his own personality is active and predominant in Russia. When my morning paper tells me that Messina is now in ruins I do not doubt that this is the truth. But it is the first truth it ever told me about Messina.

Everything in journalism smells of the obituary notice. People talk about the haste and headlong precipitancy of journalism; but I have always been struck by the systematic slowness with which journalism contrives to keep behind the times. No complete biography of a man is ever offered until he has left all his work in the world decades behind him, and tumbled in sheer senility into his grave. He has no "life" until he has ceased to live. He has no "works" until he can work no longer. A man like Mr. Bernard Shaw (to take an example) has thrilled and filled crowds of thinking and thoughtless people with his destructive and constructive theories, and is now, at a ripe age, sitting on a recognised and unassailable critical throne. Yet if he appears for an instant in a daily paper, he always appears as a juvenile and impertinent guttersnipe, saying smart things that no one can understand. Some day (may the day be far distant) he will die; and then we shall have a cataract of newspaper columns, telling an astonished public for the first time that he was a great sociologist, an original philosopher, and one of the pillars of the nineteenth century. About the real struggles of the modern world the newspapers are practically silent—until the struggles are over. Then they become matter for classical allusion along with Magna Charta, the death of Socrates, and Dickens's comic characters. In this manner Darwin began to be accepted by journalists just about the time when he had begun to be deserted by men of science. And so, no doubt, Mr. Bernard Shaw will suddenly become a classic when he has ceased to be an influence. In any case there is a curious incapacity in the newspaper method for conveying living truth, the truth that is still going on. It deals in catastrophes—that is, in conclusions. The reporter is always late for the tragedy of Hamlet, and comes in as the curtain goes down, with hardly anything but corpses on the stage.

I take one current case. I read in my daily paper that the famous Father John of Cronstadt is dead. I call him famous, but in my daily paper he was never anything like so famous while he was alive. Still, I had heard of him: I did know that he was some sort of popular Russian mystic, who had great influence with the Russian peasantry. Now suppose, for the sake of argument, that I wanted to find out the real truth about Father John of Cronstadt. It is an improbable supposition, I admit. I am not a Russian, and my efforts are quite sufficiently engaged in trying to find out the truth about the policeman and the public-house at the corner of my own street. Still, my very remoteness makes me impartial; I have no local bias: Father John may have been a complete Christ or an avowed cannibal for all I know about him. But suppose that a publisher has told me to write about Father John; and suppose my conscience has told me to write what is true. How far can I find out what is true? and especially how far can I find it out from the newspapers?

My daily paper (which, I need hardly say, is the best and noblest of all daily papers) has two descriptions of this mysterious priest. One is in a leading article and the other is in a special report, with a picture of the individual involved. And the interesting thing is this, that while there is no actual verbal contradiction, nobody would ever suppose, without the name, that the two descriptions referred to the same man. According to the leading article, Father John was a person detestable because of his perpetual prostrations before Imperial despotism and his perpetual contempt and oppression shown to all popular movements and all humane ideals. According to the personal sketch in the same paper, Father John was a man detested by the proud and powerful because of his perpetual denunciation of their tyranny and luxury and his perpetual championing of the poor. On one page of the paper I read: "That the Russian people should desire any change, any improvement in the absolute despotism of Tsar and Holy Synod seemed to him not merely incredible, but impious." On the next page I read: "His passionate denunciations of the luxury of the rich and his demand for justice for the poor brought upon him the hatred of the rulers of the city and the enthusiastic approval of the bourgeoisie. His style of oratory offended the ecclesiastical dignitaries, and he devoted himself more and more to the visitation of the sick and dying . . . the pilgrimages became a nuisance and the civic authorities endeavoured to put a stop to them, but without avail." There are the two accounts, both breathing sincerity. Perhaps one of them is a partisan lie; perhaps both of them are. But they are (if I know anything of literary expression) both *honest* lies; that is, lies with some serious emotion, some *story* at the back of them. But what is the story? What is the real essence of the business; and how can a well-educated and entirely ignorant Englishman find it out?

Then the leader-writer in this admirable paper mystifies me even more by saying something to this effect: that Father John of Cronstadt had hounded on his followers to torture and pillage the Jews; had exulted almost to the point of rubbing his hands, apparently in the blood and tears of Siberia and the ruthless judicial massacres of the Russian reaction; but that the worst and most wicked of all his actions was the denunciation of Tolstoy, who is (according to the leader-writer) revered as a saint in Russia, and throughout Europe as the noblest figure of our time. I have not the text by me; but I am sure I do not misinterpret the sense. And the sense is such as to give me some distress as well as some amusement. It is rather painful to hear that abusing Tolstoy is the crown and climax of all these crimes—worse than pillaging Jews, or encouraging State massacres, or exulting in prison tortures. I feel this keenly, for I have abused Tolstoy myself, and hope to continue to do so at every available opportunity. Yet I certainly never pillaged a Jew and I have only occasionally experienced any attempt on his part to pillage me. I have never encouraged any tortures but have, on the contrary, tried to discourage them even in those dim, barbaric haunts where they still remain—such as our English prisons. I never encouraged the Tsar to organise massacre—in fact I never encouraged the Tsar at all; thus the fact of his continued existence must be explained otherwise. All these acts—robbing Jews, approving tortures, and encouraging tyrants—seem to me to be very wicked acts. But abusing Tolstoy seems to me a very virtuous act, and yet this incomprehensible leader-writer puts it as the ultimate and intolerable crown of the offences of Father John, worse than his alleged cruelties or his alleged servilities. It is as if a man said—"Jones picked pockets and poisoned his grandmother, and, what was worse still, distinctly disliked the influence of Bernard Shaw"; or, "Not content with forging banknotes and murdering babies, Mr. Robinson used his influence against that of Professor Haeckel." How is one to get the truth out of people who in perfect honesty find it natural to talk in this way?

There is only one distinction which it occurs to me to suggest as a guide. Literature, especially good literature like Tolstoy's, is much more reliable than Government reports or journalistic facts. And good literature like Tolstoy's is quite as convincing when you think it wrong as when you think it right. I have never been inside a Russian prison; but I have been inside a Tolstoy novel. And, spiritually speaking, I have sometimes thought that I should prefer the prison.

January 30, 1909

Good and Bad Sentimentalists

If I were a despot (I mean an ancient, healthy, capricious despot, not a miserable, modern official trembling in the middle of all the telephones of Europe) I should be strongly inclined not to

suppress certain beliefs, but to suppress certain words. I do not
mean terms of abuse; those I might even encourage. I mean
certain phrases which are used as terms of abuse, but also convey
the impression of having some precise ethical or scientific meaning, when, as a fact, they have practically no meaning at all. I
would allow my Prime Minister to call the Leader of the Opposition a traitor. For that is a precise term with a fixed moral
meaning, and the other man might bring an action or a big stick.
But I would not allow the Prime Minister to call him a Pro-
Boer; because that is a phrase meanly selected for its doubtfulness
and double meaning; it might imply anything from pitying a
Dutch widow to living on Kruger's bank-notes. Similarly I would
permit my Court Prophet to tell my Court Priest that he was
telling blasphemous lies. But I could not permit him to tell the
priest that he was enunciating out-worn dogmas; for that is
trying to discredit a man without really saying anything intelligible about him. I should allow the people to call my Commander-in-chief a murderer, but not to call him a "militarist."
I should permit (nay, encourage) a journalist to be called silly,
but not to be called paradoxical. After a few years of my severe
but beneficent reign words that have wholly lost any working
meaning might almost have withered out of the land, and the
English race might have begun to think once more.

But since, by some queer turn of luck, I am not an ancient
despot, I can only make a note of the words that I would have
obliterated, as a sportsman without a gun might mark the birds
he might have shot. One of the worst is the word "sentimentalist," as used in connection with crime or punishment or the
treatment of animals. I saw it used twice within the last half-
hour, by one journalist in connection with the French view of
capital punishment, and by another in connection with my own
view of the Indeterminate Sentence.[1] The word as used in this

[1] There were numerous objections, particularly from Belloc, who was then
an MP, about that part of the Prevention of Crime Bill which empowered the
courts to "sentence habitual criminals to detention until sufficient assurance was
given that they would revert to an honest life". The Bill was passed nevertheless.

connection seems to have hardly any intellectual content or significance at all. There are three senses in which I can understand
a man of intelligence finding it convenient to use the word "sentimentalist." Very loosely it might mean simply an hysterical
person, whose minor emotions made his actual demeanour unreliable or undignified—one who gushed or shed facile and maudlin tears. This certainly does not apply to those humanitarians
who have, rightly or wrongly, opposed various pains and penalties. In mere historic fact most of the men who have fought
for reprieves and reforms of punishment have been hard-headed
and even harsh-minded men, men like Voltaire and Bentham
and Mr. Bernard Shaw. And while I have many friends among
such humanitarians, and while I honour them all, I must confess
that their chief defect strikes me as being, not sentimentality,
but a certain arid scientific frigidity. The only thing wrong with
humanitarianism is that it is often just a little inhuman. But the
hard-headed humanitarians are at least ten times stronger men
and stronger thinkers than the sort of people who sneer at them
as "sentimentalists." These latter are simply men who happen
to have hard hearts and soft heads.

The second sense in which I can conceive some use in the
phrase "sentimentalist" is more or less like this. It can only apply
to small affairs, and it is, I think, the true use of the term. A
sentimentalist is a man to whom the pure prettiness of certain
emotions (especially the slighter forms of sexual love) is so agreeable that he indulges them, not when they are overmastering
and real, but when they are weak enough to be contemplated
rather than experienced. He plays with the lion's cubs, but he
has never seen the lion. He sees himself in all sorts of half-serious
parts. He flirts with fifty women because he wants to be fifty
men. He sulks. Just as flirting is a profanation of holy love, so
sulking is a profanation of holy hatred. In all cases his spiritual
crime is this—that he takes things which God meant to be rare
and noble necessities and turns them into perpetual luxuries.
Now, here again it is clear (indeed, it is much clearer) that the
anti-flogging or anti-hanging humanitarians do not fall within

the definition. Obviously this kind of sentimentalist can have nothing whatever to do with the campaigns or causes such as those under discussion. No one will say that Mr. Collinson writes about the cat-of-nine-tails because he likes looking at pretty things. No one will say that Mr. Salt[2] investigates slaughter-houses because he is an aesthete only at home amid luxury and art. Obviously, in so far as the humanitarians face these things and speak about them, they are brave men, and even harder men than their enemies.

But there is a third purpose for which I can imagine a man finding the word "sentimentalist" of some use. It might imply this: a certain readiness to be influenced entirely by associations and emotional habits and indistinct memories upon occasions which call for clear analysis and the separation of thought down to its roots. Thus, if a man were a Free Trader only because there had been a bust of Cobden in the home of his happy childhood, he might be called a sentimentalist. Or if he were an Imperialist because he had seen a map all painted red, he might be called a sentimentalist; or if he were a Protestant only because he disliked candles and incense—or if he were a Catholic only because he liked them.

But if "sentimentalist" means a man who thinks by mere association, then we can have no doubt of where to apply the term. The worst sentimentalists, beyond question, are those very people who accuse their enemies of sentimentalism. For the word "sentimentalist" (as they use it) is a mere association, and a stupid one at that. They have heard somewhere that people who object to hurting anything in any shape or degree are called "sentimentalists." Therefore, if you object to a wasp being crushed, they will call you a "sentimentalist"; and if you object to a baby being boiled alive, they will call you a "sentimentalist" also. They use the phrase because the phrase exists, and therefore saves

[2] Henry S. Salt, a member of the Fabian Society and founder of the Humanitarian League (1891), was a frequent spokesman against vivisection and cruelty to animals.

them the pain of personal thinking. Quite without question it is the anti-humanitarians who are sentimentalists: if sentimentalism means a preference for fixed words over living ideas. I take the case that comes nearest. In one paper the word "sentimentalist" is applied to those (among whom I am happy enough to count myself) who object to Mr. Herbert Gladstone's extraordinary Bill or Act. I forget which it is, so unreal have all Parliamentary politics become. The Bill (or Act) provides that a man can be kept in prison until the authorities have a fancy for calling him cured. The journalist also applies the word "faddist" to a person opposing such a proposal. He might just as well use the word "forger" or the word "chimpanzee"; they are just as much terms of reproach; and they have quite as little to do with the question. Obviously, if anybody is a faddist, Mr. Herbert Gladstone is a faddist. He proposes to upset the Habeas Corpus Act and the whole legal system of Western Europe because of the fad of a few physicians who think that they might succeed in experimental psychology. But the journalist had heard that it was sensible to be harsh to prisoners and "sentimentalist" or "faddist" to be kind to them. And if he had heard a proposal to skin them alive in Oxford Circus, he would still have called any objection "sentimentalist" or "faddist."

February 6, 1909

Hangmen and Capital Punishment

We have so many questions in the modern world which are really difficult to answer; I wish the modern people would leave off asking questions which are quite easy to answer, or, rather, which are not even worth answering. Latter-day scepticism is fond of calling itself progressive; but scepticism is really reactionary in the only intelligent sense which that term can bear. Scepticism goes back; it attempts to unsettle what has already been settled. Instead of trying to break up new fields with its plough, it simply tries to break up the plough. And the worst symptom is this habit of our philosophers of asking nursery questions, questions that most of us in our babyhood either found answered or found unanswerable. Sophistry has gone so far as to unlearn the alphabet and reverse the clock. Many of the queries solemnly propounded in our most portentous books and magazines are queries which a schoolboy would answer with instantaneous and irritating smartness, and which a healthy child would not even admit to be queries at all.

I take such cases as come to hand. I read two articles this morning in two very able and distinguished periodicals which were devoted to this general consideration: "How extraordinary it is that the hangman is regarded with horror, while the soldier and the judge are not regarded with horror." The schoolboy would burst his Eton collar in his eagerness to answer so obvious a difficulty. He would say at once that a hangman is not so fine as a soldier, because he is not so brave. A hangman is merely a destroyer; a soldier is not. A soldier, at the best, is a martyr; at the worst, he is a good gambler. If the public executioner were obliged to have a personal conflict on the scaffold with the criminal, upon the issue of which depended which of the two were hanged, then general public sentiment would admire the hangman, just as general public sentiment admires the soldier.

All this is a very tiresome truism; but that is my point. I cannot understand anyone asking a question that has so obvious an answer. The writer, if I remember correctly, goes on to attempt a solution by talking about clinging memories of barbaric creeds and the slow advance through history of the humanitarian sentiment. But the thing has nothing to do with the advance of anything or the memory of anything. There never was a time in recorded history when soldiers were not liked, while hangmen, jailers, and torturers were regarded with marked coldness. There is no record of any civilisation in which the hangman was a desirable *parti* for the daughters of the aristocracy. There never was a Victoria Cross merely for killing people. There never was a civic crown *ob cives interfectos*.[1]

This does not appear particularly surprising to anyone whose heart is in the right place or whose head is screwed on correctly. It is not hard to see that the human soul has always recognised three degrees of moral value in the matter of killing. Highest is the martyr, who is killed without killing; second is the soldier, who is killed and kills; third is the executioner, who kills with no peril at all of being killed in return. He is disliked. It may be unjust, but I do not understand anyone thinking it unnatural.

Equally infantile and innocent is the answer in the matter of the Judge. Obviously the reason that a Judge is not hated as much as a hangman is a simple one. It never falls within the direct professional duty of a hangman to prevent a man being hanged; it does sometimes fall within the duty of a Judge. The Judge is at least supposed to do something else besides killing; he is supposed sometimes to prevent people from being killed.

But I only take these cases as cases of the curious needlessness of most current questions. We have a really complex and crucial problem before us; we need not perplex it with other questions which we could answer for ourselves by thinking for three minutes. The problem of capital punishment is really painful and important; we need not perplex it further by asking why a man who charges the guns, sword, in hand, is more fascinating than one who strangles a man whose hands are tied. We need not delay ourselves with an inquiry about why an official who kills a prisoner in complete silence is not so popular as an official whose business it must often be to compose quarrels, to clear up mysteries, to give people back their lost property and their prodigal sons, to give them advice which is often sensible, and compromises which are often fair. Let us get rid of the unnecessary questions. When we have done that, we shall come to the inevitable one.

[1] This may be translated as "for executing citizens".

This inevitable question has come to a climax in France; the question if, when, and upon what provocation the State should inflict upon one man the agony of being killed or upon another the ignominy of killing him. On this, as on all questions, the modern world has stiffened into an aimless Chinese unconsciousness and routine. I do not know which party is the more dusty and dehumanised, the humanitarians who forbade capital punishment, or their opponents who (as far as I can make out) seem actually to enjoy it. But though all Western Europe has grown very cumbrous and clumsy in this matter, the advantage is still to a great extent with France. In that country they do still seem to understand that killing a man is killing a man—even when they like doing it.

There still lingers in this country the absurd talk about the French juries being "sentimental" because they commonly treat crimes of passion with a special consideration. As a matter of fact, the French jurors do this not because they are sentimental, but because they are sensible. To treat a faithful lover who has madly struck his mistress, or a faithful husband who has avenged his hearth, differently from a professional poisoner or a hired assassin is not "sentimental"; it is perfectly ordinary common sense. It rests not only on the instinct of justice without which all laws would be mere omnipotent brigandage, but also on the coldest and coarsest calculations of police expediency.

A man who has poisoned three people for money is very likely indeed to go on and poison more people for more money. Both his methods and his aims are (to employ the sacred word) scientific. And being scientific they are, as my scientific friends are so fond of pointing out, in their nature progressive. There is always more poison; there are always more people; there is always more money. But there are not always more passions of a lifetime or more and more unfaithful wives. The insane fidelity of the lover and the husband may be a barbaric thing; but the very barbaric fidelity is a proof that the same extraordinary man will not very soon find himself in the same extraordinary situation.

In short, the *crime passionnel* is in its nature the crime of a crisis, and not the crime of a routine.

Now, the men about whose deaths the Parisian populace (always fond of an ugly emphasis) made their great demonstration recently were specifically criminals of routine. They were not men who had killed a man: they were killers. They were creatures with whom no life was safe. My own temperament being totally English, I am not fond of this French love of rubbing it in. But I fully recognise that the executions which the French people indecently glorified were among the few executions which any decent man could decently endure.

For my part, I would have no executions except by the mob; or, at least, by the people acting quite exceptionally. I would make capital punishment impossible except by act of attainder. Then there would be some chance of a few of our real oppressors getting hanged.

February 13, 1909

The Tottenham Massacres

If anything could startle the modern mind into simplicity upon any subject, and especially on the subject of crime and punishment, it might, I think, be the affair of the two Russians who left a trail of blood through the astonished suburb of Tottenham. Here we have something which might have happened in any ancient village of Europe or Asia: the primary conditions of the problem which everyone forgets, humanitarian and anti-humanitarian alike. For the trouble with us is not that we look at the question too harshly, nor that we look at it too humanely: it is that we do not look at it. We have no more notion of why we punish prisoners than of why we let them off. In certain energetic but rude societies—such as that of the Middle Ages, and that of California until very recently—men were hanged for stealing. It is a thing to be improved as quickly as possible; but it is a thing to be understood before it is improved. But with us an ordinary humanitarian means a man who does not realise that it is a nuisance to be robbed. And an ordinary judge means a man who does not realise that it is even more of a nuisance to be hanged. With us a judge is a drudge; his impartiality is mere indifference. We have long lost sight of the actual fundamental human situation which makes a savage crime possible or a cruel punishment conceivable. That fundamental human situation did leap into existence at Tottenham. Here were two men, confident in their strength, skill, and weapons, who undertook not only to defeat Society, but to destroy Society, or as much of it as they could. And here were ordinary citizens, aided by comparatively few even of the official police, who vigorously expressed the refusal of Society to be destroyed if it could help it. The thing was a reality; both sides ran risks for the realisation of the idea. The criminals would rather be killed than caught; and the ordinary respectable citizens would rather be killed than not catch them.

If you want to compare this perennial and primary situation with something quite elaborate and lifeless, compare it with the journalistic fuss that is being made about the escapade of Miss Charlesworth.[1] There is nothing whatever that is human or obvious in that pursuit. That one particular dashing and over-dressed young lady should happen to outrun the constable is a very different affair from one in which the fugitives shot the constable. The economic complexity of our society, the license of credit, the license of usury, the enormous number of people whom the advance of civilisation has enabled to owe money to other people, may, for all I know, require as one of its unpleasant

---

[1] Violet Charlesworth was a young woman who disappeared after committing a series of frauds in London; she then simulated her death in an automobile accident, but she was soon apprehended in Scotland.

necessities all this journalistic spying and humiliating hide-and-seek. A poet of whom I wish I could remember the name has written the two beautiful lines—

> It's human nature, p'r'aps; but oh!
> Oh! isn't human nature low?

In the same way, I may admit that the interentanglement of modern civilisation makes it seem natural for a man to dog a woman and her distressed family across England and push his head into the railway carriage in which her sister is crying. But I can only conclude, in accordance with several dim and personal premonitions to the same effect, that modern civilisation is a somewhat caddish affair. But the point at the moment is that there is no primary public feeling behind the pursuit. Nobody feels *angry* with Miss Charlesworth, except two or three people who feel very angry indeed. The whole thing is a game, a vulgar game indeed, but a magnanimous and English game in so far as this, that millions of the populace would probably rejoice if Miss Charlesworth ultimately eluded both the journalists and the creditors. There is no public passion of justice; there is no emotional root of punishment in such an affair. But those who, pursuing the Tottenham brigands, saw a boy of ten double up and scream and fall dead with a bullet in him—they were back on the old human basis of punishment, right or wrong; they would not have rejoiced if the murderers had escaped. I do not say that we ought to act on the undisciplined passions of popular revenge; though I would infinitely rather act on them than on the equally undisciplined and far less generous and honourable passions of popular curiosity and detective persecution. I would rather have Englishmen butchered as traitors or burnt as heretics than merely hunted accorded to sporting rules for the benefit of the sporting papers. But it is not necessary to say that this instantaneous and popular reaction against crime is always sufficiently merciful or even sufficiently just. It is not necessary to claim that human judgments are trustworthy. It is enough to say that they are human judgments; in the sense that they are instinctive, ethical, and completely sincere. And it is enough to say the judgments in nearly all our Law Courts are inhuman judgments; not in the sense that they are cruel, but in the sense that they are cold, crushing, accidental, and meaningless. But in Tottenham one could see the situation in its simplest form. The whole thing had the smell of some massacre in a small and ancient pagan city. One of the ruffians sought to take his own life on the field of defeat, exactly like a pagan. The other shot himself in a cottage he had stormed, terrorised, and barricaded. But the pungency of the whole position is this: that so corrupt and indirect have all our legal systems become that we feel far more comfortable about such a death on the battlefield than about any deaths on the scaffold. Here is a fact which judges all our judges; here is an awful situation which brings in a verdict against all the verdicts of law. We feel far more sure that the Russian in Tottenham died deservedly by his own hand than we do that any convicted murderer is deservedly hanged by the hands of others. But, indeed, he did not die without a public vote. He was condemned by his peers.

Considered merely as a romantic interruption of modern life, the event was, of course, amazing. It was simply a headlong series of short stories for the magazines. A milkman is mildly driving his cart along a mild and modern street; he is struck as by blasting magic, and two adventurers whirl away in his milk-cart. An ordinary elderly gentleman gets into an ordinary sub-urban tram-car; six or seven people get in, five or six people get out, in the ordinary way: two other people remain in the ordinary way. Then suddenly two more people get in, and he discovers that nothing but the violent virtues of a wolf may save him in a hail of bullets and a hell of inhuman fear. That elderly man in the tram-car is to me the most sublime and symbolic of human figures. When the ruffians first leapt on the car and held their loaded revolvers to the conductor's head, the elderly gentleman did nothing. He is not to be blamed if he was afraid, but it is much more likely that he was profoundly astonished, as if a hippopotamus had been shown into his dressing-room. But later in the run (as we read from the accounts) he seems to have made up his mind and "attempted to seize" one of the robbers.

Seriously, I think that splendid; I think he ought to have a statue. We have statues to all sorts of stupid old elderly gentlemen who, having been brought up in the Army, from a distant hill directed or misdirected military operations which they understood or were supposed to understand. We have statues of silly elderly gentlemen who, having been bred to politics, conducted or misconducted political campaigns. We have nothing so sensible as a statue to an elderly gentleman who could attempt something that could never be expected of him—an elderly gentleman who could so far forget the environment of Tottenham and so abruptly alter the habits of a lifetime as to "attempt to seize" two armed bandits on a tram-car. The delay before his desperate revolt makes it all the finer. He is a symbol of the patient modern man at last taking his fate in his own hands. He is typically and supremely the Man in the Street, when he shall at last remember that, though the street is strict and formidable, there is not only a street but also a man in it.

I admit that many of the crimes which are punished can hardly be so simple as this Tottenham crime. But some of the crimes that are not punished are almost as simple. There are secure and smiling millionaires to-day whose track across America or England is as much a trail of broken hearts and looted houses as that trail across Tottenham was a trail of bullets and blood. There are Yankee Trust magnates and British Peers of the Realm who have captured a monopoly or an illegal privilege with exactly the same cool and anarchist impudence with which those men captured the tram-car. My only hope is a dim impression that the elderly gentleman in the car is slowly waking up, and will soon "attempt to seize" somebody.

February 20, 1909

Modern Thinking about Marriage

I read the other day in some philosophical magazine or other that some Professor whose name I forget (why not say Posh?) was the most conscientious and thorough investigator of ethical origins; and that Posh had come to the conclusion that the old doctrine of a definite thing called the conscience could not be maintained. If I were to say that I had swum to an island where I learnt that there is no such thing as swimming, you would think it a rather odd remark. If I told you that I had read a book which conclusively proved to me that I could not read, your lips might murmur faintly the word "paradox." If I were to say that I had seen a diagram which distinctly proved me to be blind, it is barely possible that you would not believe me. Yet I wonder how many mild but intelligent modern mortals would have read or have read that phrase in the philosophical magazine, and not seen anything absurd in the idea of a man conscientiously discovering that he has no conscience.

This is the most irritating of all the modern illogicalities. I mean the habit of beginning with something of which we are doubtful and expounding (or even denying) in the light of it that of which we are certain. Superficially and to start with, it is obvious that the world around us may be almost anything; it may be anarchy or Providence or inevitable progress, or mere natural routine; there is something to be said for its being Hell. The thing of which we are certain is ourselves, and the existence or non-existence in us of such things as a moral sense or the art of swimming. That is the first situation; the origin of all religion and all irreligion. But these extraordinary Professors ask me to begin with evolution and all sorts of things that may never even have occurred; and in the light of them discuss whether my own experiences have occurred. They light up the certain with explanations from the disputed. Now I am not passionately anxious to be explained; and I resolutely refuse to be explained away.

Drive me away, if I am sufficiently submissive. Carry me away, if I am sufficiently portable. But do not imagine that you can explain me away and that I shall accept the explanation in a gentlemanly spirit; do not suppose that you can either browbeat or persuade me out of my mystic and primordial certainty that I am that I am. The point is very obvious; and yet the missing of it is responsible for a forest of the mistakes that are growing round us on every side and in every question. Generalisations absorb and employ details, but they cannot abolish them. General knowledge may prove that your experience is general, or it may prove that it is not general; but it cannot prove that it is not genuine. And yet in almost every one of the practical points in dispute in our society, people are being worried and poisoned and misled by this quite infantile fallacy.

Take the most obvious case: take marriage and the relation of the sexes. There is a vast deal to be discussed about what sexual relation is best, or about whether most existing relations are successful. But the ultra-advanced women whose works I read talk as if married people did not know whether they were happy or not until they had gone to certain lectures. According to them, a woman must rush out of her house in order to find out whether the inside of her house is pretty. Now, the married state, whether the best possible relation or no, is at least a real relation. The people who are placed in it know much more about it than they know about anybody else, and generally much more about it than anybody else knows about them. The Family is much more of a fact even than the State. The State can, of course, destroy the Family if it likes, as the English Government destroyed the Highland Clan. But the English Government was not such a fool as to try and explain to the Highland Clan what the Clan really felt about itself. But the tone of feminist talk is all upon this irrational line; the person you know best on earth is to be explained to you by people whom you know very slightly, and by historical or prehistorical facts that you do not know at all.

In a Socialist paper the other day there was a letter from a highly intelligent lady something to this effect: that such and such a problem-play must have awakened many wives and husbands to the falsity and meanness of the way that the ordinary wife wheedles her husband out of money. Now, every human being who is healthily married knows of what process this is a description, and that every human being knows that it is a false description. The wife grabs at the money because it is her duty to grab at money; we live, rightly or wrongly, in a society of divided duties, and it is as much her honour to be, within reason, avaricious as it is her husband's honour to be, within reason, extravagant. And she does it, by what is called wheedling, for two reasons; first, because it often happens that she has some affection for her permanent ally on this earth; and second, because, even if she had not, it is impossible to conduct existence in a perpetual state of seriousness. That, by the way, is one of the things which modern critics of marriage especially forget, owing to their absurd habit of trying to compress a lifetime of marriage into one stage-play. One of the conditions of marriage is a constant change in the temperature of levity and gravity. A man who is quite certain that his wife is a good woman is also quite certain that she wants money seriously, and will very probably ask for it amusingly. Then some Low Dutch dramatist, who has never seen her in her life, is supposed to convince him that she is only "wheedling." He is to take an acted play so seriously as to believe, in spite of knowledge, that his own real life has been an acted play.

A strange echo of the same fallacy I find in a magazine article by the distinguished French astronomer, Camille Flammarion, who holds that all the planets are inhabited, as they may be for all I know or care. I have no bias against his theory; if every star were crowded with giants twenty feet high it would not affect by a hair any of my habits or beliefs. But I notice here what I so constantly notice about the popular expositions of men of science. M. Flammarion is a great astronomer, and undoubtedly knows every speck in the Milky Way better than I know the shape of the moon. Therefore, if M. Flammarion simply *told me* that the planets were inhabited I should at once believe him. But when he proves it to me, I disbelieve him entirely. When he gives his arguments for his conviction I can only look at them and say that they are very weak arguments indeed. They begin with the usual business about its being no longer possible to regard our earth as the centre of the universe because it is an outlying and suburban star. Even this is a confusion; for a thing might be morally central without being physically central. A man's brain is not in his stomach, but is a small thing stowed away in an extremity. And it is irrelevant to the argument, because a thing that is not central may yet be exceptional. The earth-life might easily be a unique variation without being either supreme or miraculous. That one planet out of twenty should be inhabited is no more startling favouritism than that one animal out of twenty should be Civilised Man, or that one civilised man out of twenty should be Napoleon.

But it is not that which rivetted my eye, but this: "This analogy led to the conclusion that the similitude of the conformation of these worlds must extend to their role in the universe. If Venus were not inhabited, the earth would not be so either." If I could prove to the astronomer that there were no people on Venus, I feel sure that he would gravely draw the deduction that there are no people on the earth.

February 27, 1909

Female Suffrage and Responsibility

There are moments when I feel inclined to propose, in the matter of Female Suffrage, a simple and amicable compromise. Upon the whole, I think we might agree to give votes to all women except those who are especially asking for them. Let all females have the Suffrage except Suffragettes; and then, one almost feels, all would be well. The dream is merely symbolic, but it is symbolic of much. For the New Women wholly misunderstand the attitude of the average man on this matter. The New Woman says, indignantly: "Yes, you think women are slavish and hysterical." I reply: "Not in the least. I think New Women are slavish and hysterical; I think ordinary women are responsible and vigorous." The Suffragette says, with a withering smile: "For you a woman is weak, imitative, and dependent." I reply: "Far from it. A Suffragette is weak, imitative, and dependent. She repeats stale catch-words, and lives on infectious emotions. A woman is particularly original and unpedantic; a woman almost always thinks for herself." The point is not that woman is foolish; but that she can, if she likes, put herself in a particular position in which she looks foolish, just as a man does when he tries to hold the baby. The mere physical fact of the voice is a sufficient illustration. In a very large hall the average woman's voice sounds weak and shrill. But that is not an objection to the voice, but to the hall. In a drawing-room her voice is not only pretty, but powerful: it can have not only all the harmony of harps, but all the thunders of heaven.

I have long entertained this obscure conviction that the advanced Feminists were more "feminine" in the weak sense than anyone else; but the other day I came across a startling confirmation of it. A Miss Beatrice Tina wrote a letter to a paper in answer to some queries by a Fabian Socialist whose surname I have the honour to share. This gentleman had asked the Suffragettes to tell him what immediate legislative good they expected to get from the Suffrage; or, in other words, if they had votes what they would chiefly vote for. To this Miss Beatrice Tina made the extraordinary reply: "Mr. Chesterton is not quite sympathetic enough to be told things beforehand." Really——! You talk about the Early Victorian woman! If Miss Tina, immediately after writing down those words, had turned away her head, wept into a cambric pocket-handkerchief, fainted, and been revived with smelling-salts, and then confided her woes to a confidante in white muslin, she would have been following up the remark

in the most appropriate way. Our politics are far gone in degradation, but it is still thought necessary to keep up the pretence
of courage and candour, of letting the enemy know our principles
and policy. Imagine Mr. Balfour asking the intentions of the
Government, and imagine Mr. Asquith saying, "The Leader of
the Opposition has not that true sympathy with my plans which
I look for in a confidant." Suppose Mr. Bryan challenges Mr.
Taft for his policy; imagine Mr. Taft answering, "I cannot trust
Mr. Bryan to be tender and sympathetic enough to be told things
beforehand." That utterance proves either that women are generally, or that Miss Tina is specially, incapable of understanding
the very idea of public life. She does not even know that it is
public.

Among the real injustices that have been done to women is
the foolish and clumsy statement that a woman cannot keep a
secret. A woman can keep a secret well enough if she thinks it
worth keeping; or, what comes to much the same thing, if it is
her own secret. If she does not take great care to keep a secret
of the Freemasons or the Bona Dea[1] or the Eleusinian Mysteries,[2]
if she does not keep a secret of the Foreign Office or a secret of
the Stock Exchange, it is because she does not think such secrets
of any particular importance; and she may be right. But the
secrets that are of importance, the secrets of the soul, the unex-
pressed desire, the half-matured conviction, the heart broken
and mended, the head with the mad spot in it—a woman very
seldom plays the traitor about these. So far from not understanding a secret, women are, in a sense, a sort of secret society.
And this is exactly where Miss Beatrice Tina shows that she is
quite fitted for the old-fashioned role of hostess and housekeeper,
but entirely unfitted for that of voter and citizen. She proves it
when she says those almost tearful words that I have quoted:

---

[1] An exclusive and secret women's cult in classical Rome. It was illegal for
men to observe or participate in the rituals of this cult.

[2] Religious ceremonies held in honor of Demeter or Ceres at Eleusis in ancient
Greece. The secrecy which was attached to their performance explains the name.

"Mr. Chesterton is not quite sympathetic enough to be told things beforehand."

For this secretive method is quite suitable for social diplomacy. In love-making, in match-making, in choosing a set, in bringing the right people together, in keeping the wrong people apart, in all that gigantic and complex machinery of daily life over which women have had almost complete control—in this it is quite permissible to mask certain purposes or await certain developments. If Miss Tina were a mother trying to advance her sons, it would be quite natural that she should not explain all her schemes to everybody. If Miss Tina were in the earlier stages of a love-affair, it would be quite proper that she should say, "Mr. Chesterton is not quite sympathetic enough to be told things beforehand." But in politics this remark is treason. In politics this spirit is poison. It is against the whole conception of citizenship to have a political aim which you dare not avow to your fellow-citizens. Healthy human Governments in all ages have always hated and have often crushed such secret societies merely because they were secret, because they would not avow their public aims to the republic. Thus the Templars were trodden down; thus the Jesuits became unpopular; thus half the nations of the earth are fighting with Freemasons. The one thing odious to democratic politics is the thing called "tact"— which in public affairs always means conspiracy, and generally bribery. In every age there are bad men who indulge in this political reticence and obliquity of aim. In corrupt and plutocratic times like our own, there are even crowds of them. But no man of them, however dirty or dishonoured, has ever been as brazen as to avow that he hid his true policy up his sleeve. But to a woman it is quite natural: it is what sleeves are meant for. It is a part of her dignity— nay, her virtue—to keep her heart up her sleeve, and not to wear it on her sleeve. Miss Tina asks for sympathy before she sketches her political programme. This is indeed to be what the Victorians called "a womanly woman."

The real question touching the political power of the sexes has not been discussed at all. The only real case against Female

Suffrage may be right or wrong; but nobody has proved it wrong, because nobody has as yet even lucidly maintained it to be right. If the whole of life is law, there cannot be the slightest doubt that both sexes ought to make the law. But perhaps all life is not law; perhaps there is another equally large department, which for the sake of a word we call "tact." Now tact is anarchy. Social understandings imply the absence of coercive force. Women are all anarchists just as saints are all anarchists. That is, they do not see the need of rules when they are dealing with realities. They will not force a man when it is easier to persuade him. They will not be cruel by justice when it is better to be kind by jobbery.

There is a great deal to be said for this feminine opportunism. But one thing is fixed and essential. If we are to have an anarchic class, it must be a protected class. If one set of people are to do exactly what they like, they must do it in one definite department and not in the legal or legislative department. If legal coercion is everything, let women legally coerce. If social ingenuity and liberty is worth preserving separate, let a sex be kept apart to preserve it. But in either case we can complain of the Miss Tina type, who demands political responsibility, but brings into it exactly that looseness and laughing secrecy which is fit only for social intrigue. She wishes to be a candidate, but not to be heckled. She wishes to be a Cabinet Minister without any Question Time. She wishes to employ at once the vulgar repartee of a demagogue and the stunning silence of a hostess. This is not equality, but privilege.

March 6, 1909

Censoring the Newspapers

The question of what should and what should not be printed in the public press is one that suffers, like many other questions to-day, from the fact that before we reach the real arguments on both sides we have to wade through rivers of unreal arguments. Mr. Charles Marson,[1] that very interesting person, once declared that if you wanted to get old English songs out of a yokel, you must proceed along a certain line. You must sit up all night with him, supply him unremittingly with cider, and let him work backwards through all the songs he has ever heard. He will begin with this year's music-hall songs. He will go on to last year's. He will recapitulate all the vulgarities of his maturity and early manhood; he will give you the whole of "Villikins and his Dinah" and "Pop Goes the Weasel." Then when he is almost bankrupt, but still brave and unbroken, he will fall back on his childhood, and you will hear some of the old music of Merry England before it went into captivity. However this may be, it presents a remarkable analogy to the condition of the average mind on other matters. Ask an ordinary Englishman his view on Imperialism, and he will tell you first what he has read in the *Daily Mail* that morning. Mention a few truths about that newspaper and he will drop all defence of it, and tell you what some positive person in the public-house says. Put it to him that man, even in a public-house, is liable to err, and he will tell you that that is just what his wife always says, and he will begin to consider the whole matter quite fairly from a new standpoint. Press him a little further, and he will positively admit that he had a mother, and even that he learned something from her. And if you dig into him for another hour or so, it is quite likely that you may even discover his own opinion: the genuine personal opinion of the ordinary Englishman. And when you do discover it, it is almost always right.

Thus we may say that the whole case against democracy and for democracy is commonly stated wrong. It is not that the conclusion of a common man is worthless; the serious conclusion of a sane man is very valuable—if you can get it. The trouble is not that the ordinary sensible man is uninstructed. The trouble

[1] Charles L. Marson (1858–1914), a folklorist and author of *Folk Songs from Somerset* (1904) and *Glastonbury* (1909).

is that he is instructed—instructed out of his senses. The man
calls himself Agnostic who would naturally have called himself
ignorant; but ignorance is higher. The average man, even the
modern man, has a great deal to teach us. But the nuisance is
that he won't teach it; he will only repeat what he has been
taught. We have almost to torture him till he says what he does
think, just as men once tortured a heretic till he said what he
didn't think. We have to dig up the modern man as if he were
Palaeolithic man.

This question of the propriety of publishing certain forms of
news, a subject which several judges have spoken on of late, is
a good instance of what I mean. On the one hand, the puritan
idealists use phrases like "revelations that cannot edify" or "facts
that cannot elevate," as if it were the business of a newspaper
only to mention heroic actions and only to report pleasing news.
A journalist is a realist, a reporter of what has been. He is no
more pugilistic because he reports a prize-fight than he is murderous because he reports a murder. At all costs we must get
rid of this idea that the revealer of facts is defiled by any of the
facts that he has to reveal; it is hard enough to reveal facts in
any case, without the addition of this obscene sneer. The magistrate who investigates corrupt practices at elections is not accused
of sowing corruption. The auditor who discovers foul play in
the books of a firm is not accused of wallowing in foulness. We
must first of all establish the principle that we do not want a
newspaper to give us a vision of the world made perfect; we
want a church for that. We do not want a newspaper to give us
good news; we want a gospel for that. We want a newspaper
to give us true news, not elevating news or improving news.
And whichever ideal is the higher, mine is the harder. Ask an
ordinary editor to elevate and ennoble his readers, and he will
tell you, with a heat of sincerity, that he is trying to do it all the
time. Ask him to tell the exact truth, and he will have you thrown
out of the office.

A paper, then, is primarily a record of reality; it may quite
rightly draw the line somewhere, but it must have an exact and

exceptional reason for doing so. Of an article an editor may say that it is not good enough. But of news he must be forced to say seriously that it is too bad. It may be conceded then that the puritans talk nonsense; but it is equally true that the anti-puritans talk nonsense; and I know even more about the anti-puritans than about the puritans. It is absurd to expect journalists to mention no facts except those that purify. But, on the other hand, it is an even worse cant to pretend that all facts do purify. If cannibals boil a bishop's wife in a big pot it is a fact, but not a fact that can give spiritual exaltation to anyone concerned, except, perhaps, to the curates in the diocese. It does not really give any pleasure to the cannibals; they do it merely as a piece of painful etiquette. I was talking lately to one of the two or three men in England who really understand savages. And he told me that eating human flesh is a bore to barbarians, just as getting into dress-clothes is a bore to us. He also told me that the men have a very strong objection to the women eating human flesh, and that the women (particularly the elder women) are very severe on the same side. It is regarded as some people regard women smoking. It is thought a little fast.

There are things going on all around us in modern civilisation which are, lucidly considered, quite as revolting as cannibalism. It is the business of journalism to report them (within reason), but it is not the business of anybody to pretend that they are beautiful because they are true. For instance, the most serious sociologists, the most stately professors of eugenics, calmly propose that, "for the good of the race," people should be forcibly married to each other by the police. Eugenics seems to me quite as barbarous as cannibalism. If we have a right to mate and breed men and women like beasts, I cannot see why we should not cook and eat them like beasts. If a citizen may not settle what is to happen to his live body, why should he be allowed to be fastidious about what happens to his dead body? In short, eugenics is obviously an indecent thing. I should not for that reason forbid all reports of its philosophical discussions. But neither should I pretend for a moment that when published they were in the least likely to do anyone any kind of good. Lectures on eugenics are occurrences, like burglaries and bigamies; that is all that journalism, as such, has to do with them.

This problem of decorum—which has been raised about a hundred things, from Miss Maud Allan[2] to the divorce reports— will never be settled until these two cants are completely destroyed. On the one hand, we must get rid of all the language covered by the phrase "It cannot elevate." A dancing lady, like a jumping frog, is not bound to elevate anything except herself. On the other hand, we must get rid of the equally inhuman humbug which merely says, "The human body is beautiful." That is an absurd argument. You might as well say, "The Crown Jewels are beautiful," and use that as a reason for leaving them unprotected. The obvious distinction is that the human body is beautiful, but all the sentiments surrounding it are not beautiful. And this is what the ordinary man thinks—if he would only say so. No man on an omnibus wants to believe moonshine because it is beautiful. No man on an omnibus wants his young daughters to read filth because it is fact. That most tales should be told because they are true, but a few suppressed although they are true, is the real attitude of the sage and the average man. All my life I have heard that when the rabble rises we shall have lust and anarchy; but I sometimes fancy that when the rabble rises we shall for the first time have reason and restraint.

March 13, 1909

The South American Republics: A Defense

There is a current idea that a man should not pronounce about what he does not understand, an idea which, if consistently carried out, would be a restriction upon the freedom of the Press

2 See July 18, 1908, footnote 1.

little better than a Censorship. But, indeed, we all do admit certain exceptions to this apparently triumphant truism. One exception, for instance, is that universally admitted by judges and juries. It is wrong to condemn a man before one has heard his defence; but it is quite permissible to acquit him before one has heard his defence, though, if he has prepared a fine speech, he may be quite disgusted at his own acquittal. If I am accused of burglariously entering a pantry to steal Oswego Biscuits, it will be quite enough for the jury that the case is not made out against me, that the arguments of the prosecution are inadequate. They will dismiss the charge if the only arguments for it are, let us say, that I have a large appetite, or that my next-door neighbour has a pantry. They will not allow me to go on to that eloquent defence in which I shall prove (on the testimony of my weeping mother) that I do not like Oswego Biscuits, and also demonstrate (on the authority of anthropometrists, land surveyors, circumnavigators, etc.) that it would have been impossible for me to introduce myself through the small pantry window. In the same way, many controversial questions can be decided by a kind of default; there are cases in which we have heard only one side of the question, and are sure that that, at any rate, is wrong. Generally speaking, I form all my own political and moral principles in this way. I read the worst that can be said against patriotism, and then I realise how human it is. I read the best that can be said for Imperialism, and then I know how inhuman it is.

But these topics are dangerous and domestic; let us take some object which is placid and remote. Take South America. I do not mean to maintain that South America itself is particularly placid; but, at any rate, it is remote, so we may be placid about it. You may call me a Pro-Boer; but it has not, in all probability, crossed your mind to regard me as a Pro-Guatemalan. I may have received munificent cheques from Kruger, no doubt I did; but I get nothing from the President of Terra-del-Fuego; probably he has nothing to give me; more probably still, he is dead. There can be no particular partisanship among Englishmen in their view of South America; none, at any rate, along the usual lines of English political parties. But, as it happens, this case of the South American civilisation is a good example of the principle to which I have alluded above: the principle by which we hear a criminal lawyer prove a man's guilt—and at once believe in his innocence.

I never spoke to a South American in my life, or to anyone who liked South Americans. On the other hand I have heard torrents of talk and read wastes of journalism, as well as books of travel and philosophy all tending to the conclusion that a South American Republic is something between a shambles and a lunatic asylum. Finally, I have been reading a great many remarks by a gentleman named P. W. Crichfield, who has written a whole book on the matter called "The Rise and Progress of the South American Republics" (Fisher Unwin). It is sufficient to say of the book that it might more properly have been called "The Fall and Retrogression of the South American Republics." He says "that the barbarians of Haiti, Santo Domingo, Central America, Venezuela, Columbia, Ecuador, and Bolivia are out-rages on the civilisation and progress of the human race; that they are utterly devoid of internal elements of regeneration; that the only hope for betterment lies in the influence of exterior civilisation; that the Monroe Doctrine has stood as a wall of fire for a century between savagery and the possibility of outside help; that this state of affairs is a disgrace to the world; that it is incumbent on civilisation to wipe out this black spot on the face of the earth." He says this and a great deal more to the same effect; and the more I read what he says the more there grows in my mind, slowly and obscurely indeed, but steadily, the impression that a South American Republic must be, upon the whole, a very decent and jolly sort of place. In such a case I adopt a rough system of tests somewhat as follows: the reader, even if he does not agree with me in this case, may possibly find the method worth trying in other cases. By hypothesis I know nothing of the matter except what Mr. Crichfield tells me. I have listened to no one but the accuser. I have heard nothing but the accusation. I judge by the following four tests: (1) the Personality and Spirit of the Accuser, (2) the Apparent (or even Avowed) Motive of the Accuser, (3) the Nature of the Accusation, (4) Historical Analogy. Let us apply these one after another to Mr. Crichfield's crusade against Latin America.

(1) The personality of Mr. Crichfield is that of a certain type of American rhetorician who finds justice very difficult, but idealism very easy. His spirit is that of one who profoundly dislikes the very idea of democracy. Even in exalting the North American he wonders "whether this thing called Democracy is not a relative failure and in grave danger of becoming an absolute failure even among ourselves." His philosophy is that "the March of Progress must go on," which means, of course, that if any rich and powerful people want to go anywhere at any given moment they must go there—a doctrine much disseminated among motorists. And his style of writing is like this: "I see the United States of the future great and glorious beyond dreams of splendour. I see its citizens, by the hundreds of millions, free and happy as the winds of the mountains. I see it purifying itself as with fire, establishing justice and righting wrongs, and turning the searchlight of progress into the dark places. I see it ploughing up the anarchy and barbarism of Latin America as though they were poisonous weeds in a garden; and in their stead, like flowers, education and prosperity bloom." If the United States of the future is going to "purify itself as with fire," I suggest that it begin by purifying itself from that particular way of talking. This is the spirit of the thing, and I know it well; it is in Park Lane as well as in Fifth Avenue. Lazily despising the poor, lazily despising the foreigner, patriotic in the insolence of peace, and vulgar even in its visions—I know it very well. That is the first test; this is the accuser.

(2) The motive is easily stated. It is stated quite frankly by the author himself in this form, that the United States needs more territory. This ought, I think, to be quite sufficient. I may go up to a man in the street and say, "Your diamond breast-pin is a disgrace to civilisation: it is a corrupt breast-pin, a decaying

breast-pin," etc. But if I end up by saying, "Besides, I want a diamond breast-pin," I think you will know quite enough.

(3) Of the nature of the accusation. The accusation commonly brought against the South American Republics is that they are always fighting. And the Northern Americans always talk of this fight as a toy fight. But it is absurd to accuse the Latin Americans of perpetually risking their lives, and then talk of them as tremulous and decadent play-actors. A somewhat similar confusion occurs in connection with the French duel. Englishmen are always denouncing the French duel; but they can never make up their minds which of two inconsistent charges to bring. They cannot decide whether the French duel is wrong because people are hurt in it or wrong because people are not. They jeer at the duel as bloody and also as bloodless. None of the wars of the little Republics have been toy wars. The only wars that really deserve to be called toy wars are not those waged by little peoples who can suffer, but those waged by large peoples who are safe. The smaller a war is, as a rule, the more tragic it is, like the war of Montagu and Capulet. The larger a war is the more comic it is—like the war of Roosevelt and Lieutenant Hobson.[1]

(4) Historical analogies. —The charge brought against the South American Republics is that they are exactly like the Greek cities at the noblest time of Greece, or the Italian cities at the highest midsummer of the Middle Ages. That is, they are democratic, military, and prone to revolutions. There is much in history to indicate, and there is nothing in Mr. Crichfield's book to deny, that we might well look now for Dante in Paraguay or for Socrates in Nicaragua.

---

[1] The Spanish-American War, in which both men distinguished themselves. Hobson was a young naval officer who won the Congressional Medal of Honor for a feat in which he and seven volunteers sank the collier *Merrimac* in Santiago harbor.

March 20, 1909

The Office of the Censor

The most absurd incident in the whole of English history has just happened. There have been acts of tyranny more insolent, though not many of them; but there was never an act so ludicrous; there was never an act that so much humiliated the oppressor as well as the oppressed. The Censor of Plays has solemnly written to the manager of that excellent entertainment, "The Follies," in the following immortal and marmoreal words, that no skit upon "An Englishman's Home"[1] will be passed by the Lord Chamberlain. When I read this, of course, my first impression was that the Censor had suddenly perceived, with a roar of laughter, how silly his own position had always been, and had resolved to end it with one quick pantomimic outrage, which nobody would be likely to stand. He feels that the best way of abolishing his own grotesque and painful position is to use his own authority against itself. Thus, one fancies, a good Republican might deliberately be a bad King. And so, Mr. Redford, in the fire of his crusade against the Censorship, has resolved to do something more wild and witty than anything that has come from Mr. Bernard Shaw. Dramatists can only satirise the thing in theory; Mr. Redford can parody it in practice. And this time, at any rate, he has done so. He need have no jealousy of the admirable theatrical humourist to whom he sent his letter. He has not only robbed Mr. Pelissier[2] of the title of his play, but of the very name of his theatre. Henceforth, the rational Englishman will feel that the two institutions may very well exchange names. Mr. Pelissier is a real and valuable public critic, a healthy *castigator ridendo*,[3] a vigilant intelligence which pounces on pre-

[1] A play written by Major Guy du Maurier which was first published in 1909.

[2] Harry Gabriel Pelissier (1874–1913), an English composer and entertainer, was the creator of the Pelissier Follies, an extremely popular revue with music, humor and topical commentary.

[3] This may be translated as "one who admonishes by ridicule".

posterous attitudes and poisonous affectations. Mr. Pelissier is the Censor, a real *censor morum*,[4] a guardian of good sense and decency. No sensible Englishman will henceforth think it unreasonable if his theatre is called "The Censorship." And certainly no one who knows the history of the Censorship will think it unreasonable if that office is called henceforward "The Follies."

The mere fact as stated is sufficient to produce a mere shock of laughter in anybody. But the ordinary reader may not at once perceive all the successive and stratified idiocies of the situation; and this is no common folly to be dismissed before we have got the full and varied enjoyment out of it. I don't suppose anything so silly was ever done in the world before. Let us profit by the rich, extravagant age in which we live; and let me draw your attention to the inanity within inanity, like box within box in a Chinese puzzle, which can be found in those simple words, that no skit upon "An Englishman's Home" will be passed by the Lord Chamberlain.

In the first place, the thing represents a new stride in impudent autocracy which might make Peter the Great jump out of his boots. Many tyrannical Governments have said that certain jokes were not to be made at all. But very few have ever gone so far as to say that certain public topics were not to be joked about at all. Many have suppressed a certain casual levity because it happened to be insulting; but few have forbidden every kind of careless levity beforehand whether it was insulting or not. The Censor is surrounding one twopenny little amateur play with a protection which is not given to kings or princes, popes or saints. If some citizen made an ingenious Greek pun on the name of Nero, by which he made it the opposite of "hero," it is possible that Nero might be grieved, and might express his sorrows in boiling pitch or tigers. But even Nero would not lay it down universally that no pun, complimentary or other, should be made on his name. Frederick the Great might be slightly offended if he went to see a comedy in which he appeared humorously as

---

[4] This may be translated as "a censor of behavior."

stealing gin, or being horsewhipped by a bagman. But Frederick the Great would not be offended at the mere possibility of taking some humorous position in some kind of comedy. The Pope might object to an irreverent joke about him, but he would never dream of saying that all jokes about him must be irreverent. I must say that I regard with a very rigid dislike this new proposal of intellectual persecution; that we should not be repressed for certain statements, but restrained altogether from certain subjects. It is not enough that we may not call a millionaire a donkey. We must not even mention donkeys, for fear they should remind us of millionaires. It is not merely that the law will forbid us to say that the Cretans are liars; the law will forbid us to mention the island of Crete. We are not merely forbidden to say that the Scotch cannot understand a joke. We are forbidden even to make any joke for the Scotch to understand.

That seems the logical sequel of the first principle of this affair; the protection of one particular play from *any* skit, fierce or friendly, patriotic or anti-patriotic, which may be made upon it. We now advance cautiously to the second stage of the illogical. Emperors and pontiffs, we have said, do not surround even their public dignity with this sweeping and prospective defence. But this is not a public thing at all. It is one particular play, written by one particular private man on his own responsibility, possibly for fun, very possibly for money. That the Government should specially guard it against criticism makes the Government absurd and the play absurd, just as an edict forbidding anyone to reply to this article I am now writing would make the Government absurd and me absurd. "An Englishman's Home" has no sort of authority, direct or indirect, from Englishmen. It is not a proclamation of the King, it is not an Act of Parliament, it has not been voted on; it is no more national than any type-writer's advertisement or any tailor's shop. Therefore (and this is the second and very serious count in the indictment), we accuse the Censor of having lowered his office rather than exalted it. Most people denounce the pride of an oppressive ruler; but we have to complain of his squalid and repugnant humility, his readiness to make himself and his Sovereign ridiculous for the sake of any chance melodrama or advertisement of mustard of which the poster happens to catch his eye.

We now touch the third stratum of stupidity. Supposing that the State could rationally forbid a whole subject, instead of certain comments on it (which is absurd), and supposing that the State could with dignity draw this unusual ring of fire round an accidental private speculation (which is absurd also), it yet remains to be asked what particular small piece of private enterprise it has selected thus unnaturally to protect. Had they done it for Shakespeare it would be laughable. But they have done for Major Du Maurier what nobody ever dreamed of doing for Shakespeare; and really one can do nothing beyond laughing, unless one dies of laughter. By way of adding the last touch of ineptitude, the Censor has decided to protect from skits a play that is itself a skit. He has resolved that the forces of the King shall not only fight absurdly, but shall be fighting for something absurd. For "An Englishman's Home," valuable, I have no doubt, as a slight and suggestive fantasy, cannot possibly be regarded as anything else, even by a mind so mystical as that of the Censor of Plays. It is sufficiently degrading to the public service that it should interfere to suppress a joke; but that it should interfere to defend one joke from another joke is really as ignominious as if the Archbishop of Canterbury had supported Mr. Dan Leno[5] against Mr. Herbert Campbell. As a satire it is possible that the play called "An Englishman's Home" may do some good; but so noisy and avowedly exaggerative a satire is a most improper object of public sanctification and silence.

Fourthly, the Censor has introduced another element of weakmindedness into his action. He has suppressed not merely a joke, but a good joke—a joke of exactly that sincere and breezy sort that is required in this discussion. The sketch which Mr. Pelissier had intended to produce seems (by the newspaper account) to

[5] Dan Leno (1860–1904), an English music-hall star and master of Cockney humor.

be a much better play than "An Englishman's Home," and in many ways much nearer to the point. In mere humour the idea is good. A German army invades an English villa, and finds that the ladies and gentlemen living there already are Germans. This might be made a tag for trivial jingoism; so might "An Englishman's Home." But, of the two, Mr. Pelissier's is the more acute criticism of the special evils of England; for all the special English evils are the creeping and invisible evils—not the invader that enters by the gate, but the parasite that crawls in through a crack in the wall. The evil is not that we are not ruled and armed to repel aliens; the evil is that so many of the people who rule and arm us are aliens themselves. Our peril is not attack, either from Germans or Follies; it is decay, that internal weakness which tolerates the cosmopolitan banker—and the Censor of Plays.

March 27, 1909

Shakespeare and the Bacon Cypher

I have just been reading with great interest a book which appeared some considerable time ago: "The Shakespeare Problem Re-Stated," by Mr. G. G. Greenwood. It was published by John Lane, and contains a cautious but convinced plea for the Baconian theory. I cannot say that it has done anything towards converting me on the point, but the appearance of so scholarly and responsible a writer as Mr. Greenwood in support of that thesis is certainly a matter very different from the mere floundering hobbies of a few half-educated Americans. Hitherto the ordinary public (to which I am proud to belong) has regarded the Bacon-Shakespeare theory as a fad; and the ordinary public has been right, as it often is. The Bacon-Shakespeare theory would still

be a fad, even if it should turn out to be true. It would have had
a certain lop-sided and unwholesome character, which is only
covered by that word. It may be hard to define a fad, as it is
hard to define a cad; and sensible people do not define them—
they avoid them. One mark by which popular instinct detects
a fad is this: unnatural *seriousness* about a small matter. If Bacon
did write Shakespeare, it is not worth all that fuss. Of two
disputants on such a subject I should tend to trust the one who
seemed to care least about it.

But there is a second and stronger mark of a real fad, and it
is this: the tendency to concentrate on a *topic* rather than a *truth*.
The faddist will use many and mad arguments; he will advance
many and mad conclusions; but they will all be about his subject,
his problem, his period. Suppose a man comes to me and says—
"The letters of the alphabet are the initials of the first twenty-
six Kings of England, counting Harold." I investigate his proof,
and find that it is rather too ingenious to be satisfactory: things
have to be twisted and dove-tailed with such desperate neatness
to fit it. I find (for instance) that you have to call Harold 'Arold,
so that he may begin with A. I find that William the Conqueror
begins with B, if you call him Billy. I find that if Rufus is freely
translated "Carrots" he can be made to begin with C; and so
on. I lose faith in this method; I occupy myself with other matters; I do not meet the man for a year. When I do meet him he
says, "Are you aware that the letters of the alphabet are the
initials of the twenty-six sacred mountains of mankind—Atlas,
Bunker's Hill, Calvary, Denmark Hill, etc?" Or he says, "The
alphabet follows the initials of the chief possessions of the British
Empire—Australia, Birmingham, Canada, Dakota (which is ours
in blood and tongue), Ecuador (which we ought to have), France
(which we once conquered), Germany (which we shall conquer
soon), etc., etc., etc." If the man went on like this, I should
open my eyes, and a light would slowly dawn on my mind. I
should say, "Oh, I see; you are mad on the alphabet." Any one
extraordinary discovery about the alphabet might possibly be
true; but it is impossible that five should be true; and it is not

likely that the man who found the four false ones would find the one true one. The popular instinct, in short, smells insanity and error wherever there is an attitude towards some matter which evidently expects the sensational and the marvellous. And it is impossible to deny that there has been such an attitude towards the Baconian problem. It might conceivably be true that a cryptogram was concealed in the works of Shakespeare announcing another authorship. Such a thing is enormously improbable *a priori*; as improbable as that there is a Huxley cryptogram in "Vanity Fair," and that authorship by Matthew Arnold is somewhere coyly confessed in "Our Mutual Friend." More improbable; because to anyone who has the sense of literary individuality, Bacon and Shakespeare were more unlike each other than Dickens and Matthew Arnold. But though it would be an astounding fact; it might be a fact. There might be a Bacon-Shakespeare cryptogram. But there have been about five. And when there are five, the ordinary man begins to ask, "Why should there be any at all? These people are simply mad on finding Bacon cryptograms somehow."

A third mark of the fad is its infinite expansiveness. Imperialism, for instance, is a fad. Faddism has no sense of the shape and natural limits of its own original idea; its tendency is to eat up the whole universe. Thus you will always find that millennarians and expounders of Revelation, when they think that one phrase in St. John refers to Napoleon, always become wilder and wilder in their inverted Bonapartism. They read the whole Bible by that text; till at last it seems as if the Hebrew prophets had been reprehensibly negligent of Hebrew and other human affairs in their morbid concentration on the career of a Corsican officer of artillery. So those who begin by suspecting a conspiracy among their enemies generally end by suspecting also a conspiracy among their friends. It is quite plain that this mark of mania attaches to the Bacon-Shakespeare fad. Many Baconians are not content to maintain that Bacon wrote Shakespeare; they maintain that he also wrote the works of Spenser, Peele, Greene, Marlowe, Lyly, and the rest. I once met a man who added to this modest list the works of Cervantes and Montaigne, which Bacon cunningly translated into exquisite Spanish and French. In short, the brilliancy of the Elizabethan era is a mistake; there was only one brilliant man, and he was even more industrious than brilliant. Also, I once read a Baconian book which said that Lord Verulam was a legitimate son of Queen Elizabeth and heir to the throne of England. If any one fails to smell the air of Bedlam after that, I fear he must already be too much inured to that atmosphere.

I should say, therefore, that it would require a very considerable force of proof to shunt off the mind the accumulated impression that the thing belongs to the world of cheap creeds and crazes. Nor has Mr. Greenwood, with all his learning and ability, succeeded in shunting it off mine. For one thing, Mr. Greenwood, whom I know to be a very good Radical, is forced to adopt a line of logic which I can only, with all respect for him, call snobbish. He has to prove that no person so ignorant and obscure as the Stratford player could have risen to Shakespeare's heights of philosophy or worldly wisdom. He actually begins by explaining that Stratford was very dirty in Shakespeare's time; that it was not a meet nurse for a poetic child; that there were muck-heaps all along the street. An extraordinary argument; as if any boy ever born would have enjoyed the sky and the birds less because of muck-heaps. Shakespeare might perfectly well have made up the "Midsummer Night's Dream" sitting on top of a muck-heap. Again, he has gravely to explain that Shakespeare's mother was not really a charming lady, but was often engaged in "the homeliest of rustic employments." As if it mattered whether she was a lady; or as if a lady might not indulge in rustic employments! Poor Mr. Greenwood's doctrine drives him on further and further, against what I am sure are his real democratic instincts. He has to try and prove that there never were really any geniuses who arose out of ignorance and poverty. In short, he desires, on the most exclusive social grounds, to transfer Shakespeare's glory to Lord Verulam, just as, for all I know, some future critics may desire to transfer

Burns's glory to Lord Eldon.[1] He declares that no genius could possibly have picked up all that Shakespeare picked up about law and literature. On that I would take a very plain position. I say that not only could a genius have picked it up, but a man who was not a genius could have picked it up if he knocked about in loose literary society. I myself, for instance, know enough to talk fairly convincingly upon twenty subjects that I have never studied in any academy: the theology of the schoolmen or the economics of the Socialists, the poetry of Heine or the theory of Rousseau. But I am not a genius; I am a journalist. So was Shakespeare a journalist, as well as a genius: he was a Fleet Street sort of man. And when the Baconians say, "How could he have known this or that detail in law or hunting?" I answer that it is exactly one or two details of horse-racing or gunnery that I do know. I forget where I heard them; and so did Shakespeare.

April 3, 1909

Aliens in Our Midst

I have received a letter, the sincerity of which has arrested me, and which concerns a subject that ought to be cleared up. The correspondent (who is very young, but certainly none the less likely to be right for that) says this rather heroic thing—"I take

[1] John Scott, first Earl of Eldon (1751–1838), an English lawyer and politician and Lord Chancellor from 1801 to 1827. Unlike Burns, he was a strong opponent of reform and religious liberty. Chesterton is apparently thinking of how these two men, living in the same era (Burns died in 1796), were so vastly different in their views.

everyone seriously at first, and I am continually making a fool of myself." The moment I read those words I knew what I had to do with; the kind of boy that I was myself, who might be a rhetorician or a prig, but was not a hypocrite; as Thackeray finely said of Pendennis, "not a truth-avoiding man." This gentleman is in a dreadful state because he thinks that I hate foreigners. The sentence over which he weeps occurred in the "Note Book" of two weeks ago, and runs—"The evil is that so many of the people who rule and arm us are aliens themselves." To this my unhappy correspondent adds—"I have read and reread these words till I am black in the face," which seems to me to be carrying the love of alien races too far. He then goes on to ask me if I want everybody to be Anglo-Saxon? I want nobody to be Anglo-Saxon. By a great stroke of good luck nobody is. But the real ethics about a nation and aliens is one on which I should be quite willing to explain myself.

A certain amount of accidental "nationalisation," a certain number of Englishmen settling down in Italy or Norwegians getting rooted in England, is a part of the ordinary probabilities of life: a hundred adventures of travel, of marriage, or of political exile may produce it. Therefore (though I personally cannot imagine myself happy for life except in England), I should never dream of thinking worse of any one particular man because his name ended in "stein." There would always, in the normal case, be few of such people, and most emphatically they ought to be treated as honourable guests. But it is a totally different matter when we come to another class of people. It is a totally different matter when we come to the members of a strong and definite group which has its ambassadors in every country, and which cares for no country. I can put my kind of objection to aliens most briefly by saying that I do not object to aliens. I only object to cosmopolitans. I do not object to a man who through some extraordinary accident has left his country; but I do object to the man who, by the whole tone and habit of his life, has had no country to leave. Even to him I do not object personally; but I object to his holding great power in my own country. The question is, therefore, not so much "Are there foreigners in England?" but "Are there cosmopolitans in England, cosmopolitans who act in complete indifference to England, and all other countries?" I can best illustrate what I mean by a very rough parallel. Most human experience goes to show that the more a family is really a family the better it is—that is, the more it really consists of father, mother, and children. The best stepmother is a problem; the noblest mother-in-law may be a nuisance. And when we come to outsiders, paying guests, poor relations, permanent governesses, and so on, it is not untrue to say that most of them are a difficulty, though they may also be a benefit. Nevertheless, nobody would be so stupid and spiteful as to go round recommending everybody to turn out every friend or dependant who happened to be living with the family, because the cause in each case would be individual and probably creditable. In this house the alien would be there as a debt of honour, in that house as a real object of affection, in that other as a convenience rising out of some peculiar complication. We should still say that the normal family was father, mother and children; but we should expect there to be a certain number of people, for particular reasons, "nationalised" into the family. But suppose there was a secret society for providing poor relations. Suppose there was an office in Cheapside for scattering favourite aunts. Suppose there was a Stepmothers' Trade Union, and all the stepmothers entering all the homes went there with a common doctrine and a common demand. Suppose that the intruder into the family had to face the accusation, not that she did not belong to the family, but that she did belong to something else, which might come in contact with the family. Suppose, in short, the presence of the third person at dinner was not one of many accidents, but part of one design. I think in that case we should rebel against the invasion of the family; I think we should go and smash that office in Cheapside.

Now this is how the question stands, so far as I am concerned, with regard to the alien in England: I do not object to Handel being in England or to Max Müller[1] being in England, or to a French cook being in England, or to a Japanese wrestler being in England. All these are normal abnormalities, such as are likely to happen out of some personal speciality or some economic need. There ought to be one or two Italians in England, as there ought to be one or two Italian anemones at Kew Gardens. There ought to be some Americans in London, as there ought to be some American bisons at the Zoo. We ought to be proud of Dr. Emil Reich, as of some glorious foreign lion in a cage. We ought to cherish Mr. Hilaire Belloc, like some tender little flower opening timidly under Northern skies. In these cases the blood is a mere chance, and forms a very fortunate chance. But suppose there were six Emil Reichs (which is indeed an awful thought), and suppose one was planked in every European capital promoting the Reich interests against all others; then I think, we should consider that league too impressive to be reassuring. Suppose there were an international commercial house called "Belloc Brothers" which was powerful in Paris, New York, Berlin, and London, and played one game with four nations; then, I think, we might be impatient with the tender flower, and even tread it under foot. Now this is actually and certainly the case with some of the great cosmopolitan commercial interests. A family with the same name will be in five separate countries at once, the uncle in one, the nephew in another, the second-cousin in a third. This has nothing to do with the normal problem of the foreigner. These men are not aliens relatively, like a Spanish sailor wrecked on the Cornish coast, or an Irish peasant forced to seek the American Republic. These men are aliens absolutely; they are intrinsically alien; they are alien wherever they are. I do not object to their nationality, but to their absence of nationality.

[1] Friedrich Max Müller (1823–1900), a philologist and orientalist, born in Germany, but an emigré to England, where he became a professor of modern languages at Oxford, and eventually a naturalized British subject.

Of course, any generalisation of this kind is liable to be wrong in individual cases; there are cats who hate their kittens, and there may be cosmopolitan financiers who love their countries, whichever they are. But if we want a working test in the matter, a method of sifting the really undesirable from the really desirable alien, I think it can be found in the two or three methods I have suggested. The two great tests are whether we are talking of an individual or of a class; and, secondly, whether that class is a very powerful class. Dante Gabriel Rossetti was by extraction an Italian, and doubtless there are many other Italians in England—organ-grinders, waiters, ice-cream men, etc.—who are mostly much nicer men than Rossetti. Still, we cannot say, with any colourable truth, "Rossetti and the ice-cream men dragged us into a war for Italian independence." But we can say at least with colourable truth, "Mr. So-and-So and the South African Jews dragged us into a war for the destruction of Boer independence." The problem is not so much that a certain sort of alien becomes a part of my commonwealth, but that he almost immediately becomes an important part of it. He buys a newspaper, buys—I beg your pardon, I mean obtains—a seat in Parliament, and then stands up as a great English champion, to turn away from our shores those wretched people of his own race who make from necessity the voyage that he has made from greed. But there is one other test I should suggest, merely emotional, but all the safer for that. I do not object to these men being foreigners. I object to their not being foreigners. The exile ought to be a little sad. A good Italian in England will always have a hunger for the South; a good Englishman in Italy will always wish that he could see the hedges. He may be solidly happy, but there will be a streak of pathos in him. But I examined the face of a financier in a motor-car till the police moved me on; and I could see no hint of this sorrow.

April 10, 1909

The Modern Arms Race

Everyone is talking just now about machines of death made out of steel or iron. People whisper in a panic-stricken way that Germany is building ironclads of the size of small islands; and one can almost fancy that the sun is darkened at noon with flying ships, like a flight of iron birds. I have my doubts about both the moral and the military value of this sort of imagination. Machinery is only armour, and armour is only clothes; and a very superficial study of some suburban dandies will suffice to show that it is no good to have clothes if you do not know how to put them on. We do not offer exquisite trousers to a man who has no legs. Neither do we offer difficult machinery to men who have no heads, nor dangerous machinery to men who have no hearts. An obvious historical parallel suggests itself. Armour-plating is no new thing; ironclads are very old and romantic objects. Only in the old time the individual was an ironclad. They plated the man instead of the ship; but they calculated it carefully, so as to repel the shafts and bullets of the enemy. And this making of helmets and breast-plates was a very subtle and exacting trade; the armourer was both an artist and a man of science. A great deal depended on him; men were often killed, like Dundee[1] at Killiecrankie, only because one hole was found in their harness. No doubt there was a certain amount of international competition, and the advisers of a nation said: "Remember that you have to meet the steel coats of Milan," or "Remember that your enemies have admirable blades from Damascus." Still, these fears were kept within the four corners of dignity. I abso-

[1] John Graham of Claverhouse, first Viscount Dundee (1649–1689), raised an army to fight for James II. Dundee was shot and killed in battle at the Pass of Killiecrankie. Chesterton may be alluding to the fact that a hole was found in his armor, but apparently it was manufactured by a carpenter to improve the warlike appearance of the armor.

lutely refuse to believe that any English gentleman at the time of Crecy ever shrieked at the top of his voice: "Nine more new visors for the Knights of Acquitaine!" or "Seven more Barbary horses seen in Gascony!" or "French Government still buying Florentine gauntlets!" And, if we attempt to analyse the difference, I think we shall simply find it to lie in a sense of honour. Such an English gentleman would have thought it cowardly to attach so much importance as all that to a difference of armaments. He would, as a reasonable person, inform himself about the weapons of his enemy; and if he heard that his enemy had a curtal-axe which was rather a neat thing, he would probably go and buy one. But he would not talk as if he could be conquered by the axe, and not by the enemy. He would not talk as if there were a shower and hail of curtal-axes darkening the sun. He would not say that the German axes were growing larger and larger by a huge, incurable law of the cosmos. In the last resort, his own manhood would count for something; and that would despise an open fear of defeat as much as defeat itself. For, after all, the only possible shame of defeat is that it may have befallen us through fear. But we seem eager to confess the fear before we need confess the defeat.

That is the obvious difference between the mediaeval Englishman and the modern. He talked of contending against a German knight, not against a German lance. Nor would he have been scared if you had told him that German lances were growing longer and longer, and that whereas ten years ago a German lance was forty feet long, it was now two hundred and forty feet long, and would soon be a mile long. He would deny that this was any reason for his really being afraid of the German knight—a degree of degradation which he would, indeed, have refused altogether to discuss. He would have denied it for two very forcible reasons, both of which are in their turn well worth consideration at the present time.

He would have denied it, first, because his common-sense would have told him that the mere elongation of lances, at enormous expense and without any reference to the swift accidents of battle, was a piece of clumsiness and stupidity in the mere art of war. It would be much more worth while to teach a large number of healthy men to manage a short lance than to teach a few acrobats to manage partially a long lance that could not really be managed. And while a lengthy spear might be likely to strike an enemy first, it would be much worse than useless if it did not strike him at all; as he would simply sit smiling with a spiked mace in his hand until the monotonous lengths of timber had gone by him. Now, the average citizen is not an expert either upon lances or battle-ships. He cannot know much about the subject; but he can (I think) know a good deal about the expert. The good citizen possesses a sense of smell, given to him by God, like that of the dog; he has, in a mystical way, a nose for nonsense. And he smells something wrong when people go on talking blindly about bigger and bigger ships, though he may know nothing about naval war; just as he would smell something wrong if people went on talking about longer and longer lances, though he might know nothing about the technique of tilting. Common-sense tells a man that indefinite development in one direction must in practice over-reach itself: that wearing ninety overcoats cannot be the way to cure a cold, that drinking ninety pots of beer is by no means a protection against thirst. If you perceive your enemy plunging on blindly in a particular direction, the real thing to do, if you have any spirit and invention, is to calculate the weakness in his course and advance yourself in some other direction. You ought to take advantage of his infatuation, not to imitate it; you ought to surprise his plan of campaign, not copy it laboriously. If he is building very big ships, the best thing you could do would probably be to build small ones; ships lighter, quicker, and more capable of navigating rivers. If he has gone quite dotty on long lances, the chances are that you will win the battle with daggers. But there is another reason besides this more flexible experimentalism in war which would, I think, have prevented this fine old English gentleman from going in for a mere blind race in the length of spear-shafts. He would have known that if lances really grew longer and longer past all reason, there would certainly come a point when Europe would step in and stop it. Europe was a great deal too keen on the common sport of chivalry to let it be wiped out by cut-throat competition. They would have had sumptuary laws to cut short a gentleman's lance as they had them to cut short his plumes or his expenditure. But these could only have been enforced by a general argreement of Christendom. And in those old, barbaric, superstitious, dim, dark, and damned ages, there would have been a general agreement of Christendom. It might have been an agreement full of artificial feudalism, it might have been ratified by ecclesiastical mysteries, but it could have been obtained. It is all nonsense to say that we Europeans could not have an agreement about disarmament. We could have it right enough if we were Europeans. We could have it well enough if we loved our civilisation as much as we hate each other. People cannot love Europe, because Europe is either a map or else a mythical lady who was carried off by a bull. But men could love Christendom, because it was an idea.

Therefore with all the heartiness proper to one who is wholly ignorant of the subject, I throw down my two private doubts, which are almost strong enough to be called suggestions. First, I gravely doubt whether our hurried emulation in arms is not a great deal too much a mere breathless and crazy copying. If the other schoolboy throws big snowballs, it is the mere instinct of hurry to throw bigger ones; but it might be much better strategy to keep one's head, to throw a smaller snowball and to throw it straight. In short, I disbelieve in this modern war exactly because it is always talked of as a war of guns and ships, and never as a war of men. And secondly, I doubt whether this competition of longer spears or larger ships need go on at all, if once the nations could find something positive upon which to combine. Of course they cannot combine on mere peace; peace is a negation, like darkness. Is there any affection or institution or creed on which we can combine?—that is increasingly the question. It is our dreadful condition that we agree too much on all the things in which we ought to vary—arms, methods, and the arts of war. And we differ hopelessly on all the things on which we ought to agree—motives, reasons, and beliefs. In the things of life and love we are separated; in the things of death and blood we imitate each other. In a healthy existence the inmost thing should be secure, but the outer gestures energetic and varied. But with modern Europe it is the limbs that are heavy and the heart that has unrest.

April 17, 1909

Miracles and Scientific Method

Discussions about the value of evidence are almost always amusing. Quite recently some Professor of Psychology has been saying that the witnesses in the courts vary so much in their power of perceiving and remembering, that they ought to be examined by an expert as to how far they can be trusted to tell the truth, even supposing that they want to. Suppose (for the sake of argument) that a grocer has seen an auctioneer murdering a chartered accountant. Hitherto the use of the scientific man in the court of justice has been confined to the first and unsophisticated physical facts. The doctor was called in to say, first, that the accountant was certainly dead; and second, with more gravity and hesitation, that the fracture of the skull was such as might have been caused by an auctioneer's hammer. But all this only amounted to a necessary corroboration of the really important evidence—the evidence of the grocer who had actually looked on, with mingled horror and social respect, at the struggle between these two more intellectual professions. No one ever suggested that any doctor should examine the grocer; but that is exactly what is proposed now. A doctor is to overhaul the unhappy épicier, to judge by the expression of his eyes, by his recollections of his infancy, by the readiness with which he jumps when a gun goes off, by his hair, hereditary diseases, cerebral formation, and so on, whether he is likely to know when an accountant is being murdered in front of him.

The contempt which most intellectual people already feel for the elephantine interventions of physical science in the world could hardly have a better justification than this case. The trouble with nearly all these scientific theorists is quite simple: it is that they have cultivated the art of learning while they have entirely neglected the art of thinking. They find out the most varied and fascinating facts, but they always lose that thread of reason on which alone facts can be strong: their rotten string is always breaking, and their precious beads being lost. This notion of the expert giving evidence on the value of evidence is a very strong example. The only possible reason for distrusting the evidence of the grocer is the simple fact that it is human to err: that a thousand unknown circumstances in the grocer's education, physique, or bias may cause him to swerve slightly from his actual experience even when he seeks sincerely to recall it. In fact, we only doubt the fact told by the man because he is a man. The fact, when it has passed through a human mind, is always slightly altered. But the psychological expert is also a man; he also has a peculiar physique and mental bias; therefore, when the fact has passed through his mind also, it will be altered yet more. To see anything through human report is to see it through a slightly tinted glass; but to see it through a professional report upon a human report is to see it through two coloured glasses, one green and the other red—that is, in practice, not to see it at all. It is hard enough to find out the truth at its first remove, but, if we are to have Mr. Smith's superficial impression of the facts, confused with Dr. Brown's even more superficial impression of Mr. Smith, the whole thing will be a mere chaos of prejudice and caprice. The only possible answer to the contention I am now making can be found in the assertion that scientific men are not really men at all, are not subject to any weaknesses of habit, fatigue, impatience, or vanity, such as have to be allowed for in other witnesses. In short, scientific men are gods and other men men. Whenever I see this idea courageously asserted instead of tacitly assumed, I shall give myself great pleasure in dealing with it. But till then I shall certainly oppose the proposal to put up one man to tell the real truth about another, on the ground that no men ever tell the truth.

I am a little interested in this question of evidence myself, because two gentlemen whom I warmly respect have quarrelled with me on the point—Mr. Wilfrid Ward[1] in the *Dublin Review*, and Dr. Warschauer in a sermon printed in the *Christian World Pulpit*. The origin of the disagreement is this, that I wrote in some book a defence of miracles, in which I said, "The open, obvious, and democratic thing is to accept the evidence of an old apple-woman when she bears testimony to a miracle, as we accept it when she bears testimony to a murder." Dr. Warschauer (I am sure, with no unfair intention) leaves out the second part of the sentence, and proceeds to make game of my absurdity in saying that the evidence of the ignorant should be accepted. But the second part of the sentence is very important—in fact, it is unanswerable. Neither Dr. Warschauer nor anyone else has made the smallest attempt to answer it. When all has been said about ignorance, we do permit an old apple-woman to give evidence on a murder. We do allow the ignorant to testify in the most tremendous issues of fact. Nor is this done only in democratic countries; the validity of the ordinary man's oath about occurrences is an idea that is common to all societies, despotic and republican, civilised and savage. If Dr. Warschauer really denies the apple-woman's evidence because she is ignorant, then Dr. Warschauer is more undemocratic than any Tsar that ever shot students or any Sultan that ever decapitated slaves.

Surely, however, the distinction is so large and simple that it seems odd that my critics should have missed it. I never said

[1] Wilfrid Ward, the son of William George Ward (biographer of Newman) and a Catholic apologist himself; his article referred to here is titled "Mr. Chesterton among the Prophets".

that an old apple-woman was to be implicitly credited when she *explained* a miracle; any more than she is allowed to give judgment on jurisprudence and criminology in the case of a murder. As a matter of fact, a good and saintly apple-woman is very likely to know more of the only source of miracles than Dr. Warschauer or I. Nor will I deny that I have sometimes wished that the average administration of laws were as useful and humorous as the itinerant selling of apples. But these doubts were no part of my doctrine; and I did not for a moment lay them down. What I laid down was that a miracle is an incident, true or false, like a murder: and that all that we want in a witness to an incident is that the witness should be honest and in possession of his five senses. One does not need any learning to say that a man was killed or that a man was raised from the dead. One does not need to be an astronomer to say that a star fell from heaven; or a botanist to say that a fig tree withered; or a chemist to say that one had seen water turned to wine; or a surgeon to say that one has seen wounds in the hands of St. Francis. On such points an ordinary man is either a liar or he is a madman, or he is telling the truth; there is no possibility of being an expert witness. And it *is* undemocratic to refuse popular evidence on such points. It is like refusing to believe that anyone but a judge in wig and gown could really have been a witness to a burglary.

And this is the really important peculiarity of the new scientific proposal: that, like nearly all new scientific proposals, it is a proposal to crush the people. We are to examine the witness— that is, the ordinary citizen. No one suggests that we should examine the Judge as to his private life, his politics, and, above all, his enormous income. No one demands that we should allow for the bias and habit of the lawyer; no one asks whether men do not get dusty from living in gowns, or woolly from living in wigs, as much as efts get slimy from living in ponds or fish get wet from living in the sea. Mr. H. G. Wells has most sensibly protested against criminals being overhauled with thermometers and microscopes and "the silly callipers of witless anthropology." But now it is not even the criminal who is to be thus insulted. It is the witness—that is to say, the only man in the whole court who is doing a plain public service for nothing. The witness is, normally speaking, the only reliable man in court. The barristers are unreliable, avowedly and honestly unreliable: it is their duty to be unreliable. The prisoner is unreliable, with even more excuse. The prosecutor is unreliable, with the same excuse. The Judge is unreliable, as all human history proves, which is a mere tissue of the partialities, pious frauds, Government persecutions and hack butcheries of the hired Judge on the bench. The jury, though vastly more reliable than the Judge, is somewhat weakened, and, infatuated by the official atmosphere, may take itself too seriously and become a clique or club for the occasion. The one person who is conceivably trying to tell the truth is the ordinary man in the street who saw the murder in the street. Therefore, science has pounced upon him. All the diseases that devour States it easily passes by—the rapacity and ambition of magistrates, the leathern cruelty of lawyers, the corruption of experts, and the rust of routine. It is only the healthy man whom science cannot comprehend.

April 24, 1909

Regulations against Foreigners

We have seen lately a number of unusual combinations among rather extraordinary people; the principle of the strike or mutiny has extended to areas in which it was not expected. The students of Ruskin College have gone on strike about something or other. The postmen went on strike in Paris; and as I am a person with a large correspondence and an indolent temperament, I wish sincerely that they would go on strike in London. The French strikers, as so frequently happens with that light, charming, unstable, and visionary nation, got what they wanted. Whether the young men at Ruskin Hall will get what they want I am unable to conjecture, being somewhat in the dark as to what they do want. It seems to be something about the proposed removal of the Principal and the suppression of his subject, which is sociology. Now it is certainly a just and humane act to rescue any human beings from having sociology taught to them; but, on the other hand, it is certainly not equitable to allow an honourable and satisfactory official to suffer because, with blameless intention and being, as the theologians say, in "a state of invincible ignorance," he has taught people sociology. Being confused, therefore, about the bearings of this case, I can only pass on to a more transparent and picturesque example of combination.

The best league or mutiny I know of just now is that of the British barbers. "The Amalgamated Society of British Hairdressers" has sent forth from its central office in the Swan and Sugar Loaf, Fetter Lane, a document addressed to all the citizens of these islands, warning them "in all seriousness to pause and think before again patronising a foreign barber." I never mind pausing and thinking in any time or place; it is my favourite outdoor sport. As a rule, however, I prefer to pause and think while patronising a foreign barber, or rather—to describe the social relations more correctly—while he is patronising me. The manifesto proceeds to say, still more sternly, that these alien barbers "fill official positions in the various Anarchist clubs in London, but they have ingratiated themselves into the esteem of the British public by their dishonest servility, so frequently mistaken for politeness." I never realised before that Anarchists were remarkable for excessive servility, nor, for the matter of that, barbers either. Some people are of opinion that the hairdresser's conversational analysis of the top of their heads is one which cannot, even by the most simple Briton, be mistaken for politeness. But for my part, I have always had a high respect for barbers upon this point. Theirs is the most virile and veracious of trades. They are the only shopmen who take a high professional line, and claim the candour and discretion of the physician, the lawyer, and the priest. Milliners, I am told, assure ladies that they look charming when their appearance is enough to cause a riot; florists tie on buttonholes with an air of admiration and even sentiment; booksellers show a copy of "Ponderbury on Higher Trigonometry" in a confidential way to a total stranger as if he alone could appreciate it. But barbers exist to tell men of their baldness, as priests to tell them of their sins. They insist upon reality in their relations to their clients; they are truth-tellers, the hairdressers; they are a stern, rugged, heroic race.

If it is true, however, that we have among our barbers a new breed of morbidly polite Anarchists, the situation is no doubt serious. When we consider how utterly the man being shaved is at the mercy of the shaver, how a turn of the wrist would sever the jugular, we should desire that the operator, however harsh and realistic in speech, should be moral in intention; let him as it were, speak razors but use none. If this is to be the new Anarchist *coup d'état*, it certainly has about it something much more artistic than dynamite. It is an old-fashioned idea by now that at a special signal explosions should occur all over London. It was an idea in "The Dynamiter," I think, that at a signal the system of drainage should be broken up. But this notion has in its very silence and suddenness something more sweeping about it; that as the clock strikes ten every barber shall swiftly cut the throat of every British citizen sitting in the barber's chair. There could not well be a massacre more vast, faultless, instantaneous, and infallibly successful. Having done this, I suppose, the wicked German barbers would shoot out of their shops, form up in the street with all the dreadful beauty and discipline of a conscript army, and march through London, sabring our helpless population with their exquisitely sharpened and quite invincible razors. At least, I think this description of a German invasion is about as probable and as dignified as most of those which we read now in the patriotic newspapers. There is one passage in the journal from which I take my information on the barbers which not only fascinates, but also mystifies. The item of news ends thus: "A *Daily News* representative called yesterday on the secretary of the society, Mr. Ernest Ringler, a hairdresser in High Holborn." "We haven't exaggerated a bit the state of affairs," he said. "At least fifty per cent. of the barbers in the County of London are foreigners, and these mostly German. As soon as our society can collect sufficient funds we intend having a striking heraldic emblem made, with which every member may decorate his shop window. Then the public will be able to ascertain whether they are patronising a respectable barber or not." Mr. Ernest Ringler seems to have a somewhat inadequate idea of the difficulties of our spiritual pilgrimage. Alas, if it were possible to invent some "striking heraldic emblem" which should invariably indicate the presence of a respectable man, life would be somewhat simpler than it is. What the "striking heraldic emblem" of the higher hairdressing may be I do not know, and I somewhat tremble to conjecture.

I assure all my beloved barbers, with tears in my eyes, that we cannot keep out the real enemies, either of their trade or mine, merely by heraldic emblems, and but little by legal regulations. The small man can always enter by the small hole: the man who will crawl can always crawl through; the man who will change his name can always change his country. Our only chance is in preserving a certain spirit, which acts against parasites as the health of the body against microbes. If some gaining power among us are not English, at least let us be English; that is, humorous, sane, tolerant, and contemptuous of pessimists. If forces increasing on this earth are not European, at least let us be European—that is, chivalrous, open-hearted, fond of our free souls, Christian. Let not the barbarian or the Oriental have conquered our hearts before he has conquered our cities. But this is at the present moment the worst danger of all—far worse than all the war scares of the Press. The worst element in the German panic is that it is such a very German panic. The English journalists who cry out against Germany are filled to the brim with the very faults that are particularly German, the weaknesses which balance the industry and amiability of that great people; they are full of pedantry, of suburban pessimism, of a fantastic faith in figures and maps, of an ignorance of men and a denial of God. The chief evil of the Yellow Peril is that it is so very yellow. The Chinese panic is really like a panic among Chinamen. The articles and romances written about the Yellow Danger are full of the worst vices of the East; the vision of men as mere clouds of locusts; the triumph that is decked with cruelty; the war that ends in racial massacre; the silent admission that the gods are evil. It is not by this spirit that we of the West shall save ourselves or survive; if we are to win it will be as in all our legends, by a stubborn sanity and ancient instinct of honour, which counts courage so much higher than victory, that all its heroes have been defeated heroes from King Arthur to Joan of Arc, and which has defended our passes in the perilous hour by something half uttered in the horn of Roland and the lion of Thermopylae.

May 1, 1909
The Death of Swinburne

The first sensations with which one salutes the death of Swinburne are sensations of resurrection. The boy in each one of us leaps up and does honour to the pagan pyre, remembering *veteris vestigia flammae*.[1] In one of his prose works Swinburne said a very splendid thing, worthy especially to be remembered now. "I cannot imagine what should tempt any man to criticism except

[1] This may be translated as "traces of the ancient flame".

the whole pleasure of praising." I will not pretend that Swinburne showed a dull adherence to his own dictum; or that the passages in which he called the characters of George Eliot "ragdolls" or discussed the thickness of the skulls of Clough's admirers, were entirely explicable upon the motive of praise. It remains true that he has filled pages of prose with really passionate eulogy; and that perhaps no poet ever wrote so many good poems in praise of other men. From the high, buoyant outburst to Whitman—

> Send but over a song to us,
> Heart of all hearts that are free.

down to the deep agnostic wail to the dead Landor—

> But thou, if anything endure,
>   If hope there be,
> O spirit that man's life left pure,
>   Man's death set free.

> Not with disdain of days that were,
>   Look earthward now.

There are twenty or thirty fine poems of Swinburne celebrating the varied glories of varied men, from the marsh-lights of Baudelaire to the thunderbolts of Victor Hugo. Swinburne, whatever other faults he may have had, could truly claim the noble pleasure of praising. He did express the excellence of other writers; and when that is admitted, I may be permitted to wonder, with real doubt and admiration, how on earth he managed to do it. I have not the faintest doubt that praise is the noblest thing in the world. Indeed, it is obviously the highest function in man, since it is the one function that he can properly employ towards God. Unquestionably, praise is admirable, praise is sacred; indeed, the only objection to it is that it is almost impossible. I am sitting with this blank sheet of paper in front of me, struggling with that awful obstruction: the noble impossibility of praising.

What does one say to the sunrise, on the rare occasions when one meets it? What answer can be made to the unanswerable

height of great buildings, or the inimitable posture of some child,
or the unexpected smell of the sea? Or the poetry of Swinburne?
The noble pleasure of praising is too noble for me; I feel for the
first time an impediment in my speech. Anyone can be funny
when he is miserable, or even angry; anyone can say good things
about motor accidents or the income tax. But I cannot say good
things about good things; how is it done? I am trying to praise
the Swinburne of my boyhood; but what can I say—

> Thou art more than the Gods who number the days of our
>   temporal breath,
> For these give labour and slumber; but thou, Proserpina, death.

What can one do but say the syllables and then say, explosively,
"How good!" For my part, at any rate—

> Till God shall loosen over land and sea
> The thunder of the trumpets of the night—

I shall be equally unable to express my admiration for God's
universe and for Swinburne's English.

Moreover, this is a very technical joy—a patriotic pleasure in
what the great man has done for the edge and temper of our
ancient sword, the English tongue. There are only about eight
lines in all his eight volumes with which I agree in sentiment
and I have no time to make a list of them just now. One of them
is this fine line about death—

> Where God has bound for a token the darkness that maketh
> afraid.

But this is a good opportunity for expressing the hope that
someone will now deal adequately, in a technical sense, with the
great Swinburne style. Some parodists supposed that it was all
a matter of alliteration; others, even worse, thought it was mere
smooth, undulating verse, full of long, languorous words. Now
the sharpest point of the Swinburne style is that it is full of short
words—of short words that are like short swords—

> Waste water washes, and tall ships founder, and deep death
>   waits.

Nor is it by any means true that his work is marked by smoothness, in the sense of the avoidance of obstacles. If I told you
offhand that a man had rhymed "Arisbe" to "kiss be" and "statue"
to "at you," you would think it grotesque, and merely wonder
whether it was Browning or the "Bab Ballads." Yet Swinburne's
river carries us over those rocks quite easily in the verse of which
I quote half—

> That met you of old by the statue
>   With a look shot out sharp after thieves
> From the eyes of the garden god at you
>   Across the fig-leaves.

If people want either to praise or parody Swinburne they must
get over this notion of his smoothness: this is not smoothness;
it is style.

In a political and philosophical sense I fear Swinburne must
be admitted to have ended in a certain failure; like a strong river
losing itself to the sand. He is the great English example of the
unfortunate error of the revolutionists: that they would not confess a creed. Against the old and quite cynical oppressors of
Europe, the revolutionists were really fighting for justice. But
they would not admit it. They pretended, by the tongues of
Byron and Swinburne, that they were fighting for license—that
is, for anything or nothing; and the world, being inexperienced
in the perversity of artists, took them at their word and smashed
them. When all is said it is really unreasonable to complain that
the priests did not immediately burst into tears and confess all
their vices to a man who said to Dolores, "Come down and
redeem us from virtue."

I do not mean that the early Swinburne was vicious in his
poetry; on the contrary, I think he was virtuous, since simplicity
and honest anger and youthful faith are certainly virtues. But I
do say that his own decay and the decay of the whole republican
movement were due to the fact that he would call his virtues

vices and turn them into a poem, instead of calling his virtues
virtues and turning them into a creed. Some people call a creed
a dead thing; the truth is that a creed is not only a living thing,
it is the only thing that can live. It was exactly because revolutionists like Swinburne would not have a perpetual creed that
they did not have a perpetual revolution; it was because Swinburne would not fix his faith that he fell away afterwards into
accidental and vulgar jingoism; and, indeed, narrowly escaped
being made Poet Laureate.

But this is no occasion to dwell on the decay of that great
revolutionary tradition which he will always splendidly represent. It is rather a time for remembering the roots of his life, his
many real friendships, and especially that lifelong friendship which
leaves Mr. Watts-Dunton[2] almost as tragic a fact as his dead
friend. It happens that friendship is one of the few things that
Swinburne never blasphemed, even in poetry. And at the end
of the first book of "Poems and Ballads" there are lines which
are all the more effective after a hundred pages of pessimism (I
may remark that, like a true journalist, I quote all the verse in
this article from memory)—

> Though the seasons of man full of losses
>   Make empty the years full of youth,
> If but one thing be constant in crosses,
>   Change lays not her hand upon truth.
> Hopes die; and their tombs are for token
>   That the grief as the joy of them ends
> Ere time that breaks all men has broken
>   The faith between friends.

---

[2] Walter Theodore Watts-Dunton (1832–1914), a critic, novelist and poet. He
was a steady friend to D. G. Rossetti during his declining years, and when, in
1879, A. C. Swinburne's reckless life was making his health hopeless, Watts-
Dunton took him into his home in Putney. Watts-Dunton managed Swinburne's
affairs, and swept the macabre elements out of his life and writing. The two
lived together until Swinburne's death in 1909.

Though the many lights dwindle to one light,
  There is help if the heaven has one;
Though the skies be discrowned of the sunlight,
  And the earth dispossessed of the sun,
They have moonlight and sleep for repayment,
  When, refreshed as a bride and set free,
With stars and sea-winds in her raiment,
  Night sinks on the sea.

May 8, 1909

Rhapsody on a Pig

A dream of my pure and aspiring boyhood has been realised in the following paragraph, which I quote exactly as it stands—

> A complaint by the Epping Rural District Council against a spinster keeping a pig in her house has evoked the following reply: "I received your letter, and felt very much cut up, as I am laying in the pig's room. I have not been able to stand up or get on my legs; when I can, I will get him in his own room, that was built for him. As to getting him off the premises, I shall do no such thing, as he is no nuisance to anyone. We have had to be in the pig's room now for three years. I am not going to get rid of my pet. We must all live together. I will move him as soon as God gives me strength to do so."

The Rev. T. C. Spurgin observed: "The lady will require a good deal of strength to move her pet, which weighs forty stone."

It appears to me that the Rev. T. C. Spurgin ought, as a matter of chivalry, to assist the lady to move the pig, if it is indeed too heavy for her strength; no gentleman should permit a lady, who is already very much cut up, to lift forty stone of still animated and recalcitrant pork; he should himself escort the animal downstairs. It is an unusual situation, I admit. In the normal life of humanity the gentleman gives his arm to the lady, and not to the pig; and it is the pig who is very much cut up. But the

situation seems to be exceptional in every way. It is all very well
for the lady to say that the pig is no nuisance to anyone: as it
seems that she has established herself in the pig's private suite
of apartments, the question rather is whether she is a nuisance
to the pig. But indeed I do not think that this poor woman's fad
is an inch more fantastic than many such oddities indulged in
by rich and reputable people; and, as I say, I have from my
boyhood entertained the dream. I never could imagine why pigs
should not be kept as pets. To begin with, pigs are very beautiful
animals. Those who think otherwise are those who do not look
at anything with their own eyes, but only through other people's
eyeglasses. The actual lines of a pig (I mean of a really fat pig)
are among the loveliest and most luxuriant in nature; the pig has
the same great curves, swift and yet heavy, which we see in
rushing water or in rolling cloud. Compared to him, the horse,
for instance, is a bony, angular, and abrupt animal. I remember
that Mr. H. G. Wells, in arguing for the relativity of things (a
subject over which even the Greek philosophers went to sleep
until Christianity woke them up), pointed out that, while a horse
is commonly beautiful if seen in profile, he is excessively ugly
if seen from the top of a dog-cart, having a long, lean neck, and
a body like a fiddle. Now, there is no point of view from which
a really corpulent pig is not full of sumptuous and satisfying
curves. You can look down on a pig from the top of the most
unnaturally lofty dog-cart; you can (if not pressed for time) allow
the pig to draw the dog-cart; and I suppose a dog-cart has as
much to do with pigs as it has with dogs. You can examine the
pig from the top of an omnibus, from the top of the Monument,
from a balloon, or an air-ship; and as long as he is visible he will
be beautiful. In short, he has that fuller, subtler, and more universal kind of shapeliness which the unthinking (gazing at pigs
and distinguished journalists) mistake for a mere absence of shape.
For fatness itself is a valuable quality. While it creates admiration
in the onlookers, it creates modesty in the possessor. If there is
anything on which I differ from the monastic institutions of the
past, it is that they sometimes sought to achieve humility by

means of emaciation. It may be that the thin monks were holy, but I am sure it was the fat monks who were humble. Falstaff said that to be fat is not to be hated; but it certainly is to be laughed at, and that is a more wholesome experience for the soul of man.

I do not urge that it is effective upon the soul of a pig, who, indeed, seems somewhat indifferent to public opinion on this point. Nor do I mean that mere fatness is the only beauty of the pig. The beauty of the best pigs lies in a certain sleepy perfection of contour which links them especially to the smooth strength of our south English land in which they live. There are two other things in which one can see this perfect and piggish quality: one is in the silent and smooth swell of the Sussex downs, so enormous and yet so innocent. The other is in the sleek, strong limbs of those beech-trees that grow so thick in their valleys. These three holy symbols, the pig, the beech-tree, and the chalk down, stand for ever as expressing the one thing that England as England has to say—that power is not inconsistent with kindness. Tears of regret come into my eyes when I remember that three lions or leopards, or whatever they are, sprawl in a fantastic, foreign way across the arms of England. We ought to have three pigs passant, gardiant, or on gules. It breaks my heart to think that four commonplace lions are couched around the base of the Nelson Column. There ought to be four colossal Hampshire hogs to keep watch over so national a spot. Perhaps some of our sculptors will attack the conception; perhaps the lady's pig, which weighs forty stone and seems to be something of a domestic problem, might begin to earn its living as an artist's model.

Again, we do not know what fascinating variations might happen in the pig if once the pig were a pet. The dog has been domesticated—that is, destroyed. Nobody now in London can form the faintest idea of what a dog would look like. You know a Dachshund in the street; you know a St. Bernard in the street. But if you saw a Dog in the street you would run from him screaming. For hundreds, if not thousands, of years no one has looked at the horrible hairy original thing called Dog. Why, then, should we be hopeless about the substantial and satisfying thing called Pig? Types of Pig may also be differentiated; delicate shades of Pig may also be produced. A monstrous pig as big as a pony may perambulate the streets like a St. Bernard without attracting attention. An elegant and unnaturally attentuated pig may have all the appearance of a greyhound. There may be little, frisky, fighting pigs like Irish or Scotch terriers; there may be little pathetic pigs like King Charles spaniels. Artificial breeding might reproduce the awful original pig, tusks and all, the terror of the forests—something bigger, more mysterious, and more bloody than the bloodhound. Those interested in hair-dressing might amuse themselves by arranging the bristles like those of a poodle. Those fascinated by the Celtic mystery of the Western Highlands might see if they could train the bristles to be a veil or curtain for the eye, like those of a Skye terrier; that sensitive and invisible Celtic spirit. With elaborate training one might have a sheep-pig instead of a sheep-dog, a lap-pig instead of a lap-dog.

What is it that makes you look so incredulous? Why do you still feel slightly superior to the poor lady who would not be parted from her pig? Why do you not at once take the hog to your heart? Reason suggests his evident beauty. Evolution suggests his probable improvement. Is it, perhaps, some instinct, some tradition . . . ? Well, apply that to women, children, animals, and we will argue again.

May 15, 1909

Nonsense and Sense

I feel vaguely impelled to apologise for my article last week, which was, as far as I remember, an incoherent rhapsody about a pig. The truth is that I had been occupied all day in writing a theological article for a heavy and correct Quarterly; and as people object (why I cannot imagine) to theology and animal spirits being mixed up, one has to take those two essential elements turn and turn about. The serious magazines, without having any convictions to speak of, are just sufficiently stern or bigoted to forbid irreverence. The frivolous magazines are even more stern and bigoted; for they forbid reverence. They actually veto the instinctive mention of mighty and holy things. Thus the sincere journalist is kept constantly in a state of roaring inaction: having been forced to make his theology dry he plunges with ardour into pure folly; and then, having elaborately and seriously played the fool, he plunges with a far more boyish ardour into the pleasures of theology. But the swing of the pendulum is sometimes rather wild and dizzy, like my article about the pig. Yet I did mean to say something under the parable of the pig, something which, I think, I can now say better without the aid of that animal.

My meaning is this: that a good man ought to love nonsense; but he ought also to see nonsense—that is, to see that it is not sense. Our very pleasure in pure fancies should consist partly in the certainty that they are not facts. Nothing is more perilous and unmanly in modern thought than the way in which people will be led a dance by some dexterous and quite irresponsible suggestion, some theory in which even the theorist does not believe, some intellectual levity which is not honest enough even to be called a lunacy. They hear some flying notion—as that Cromwell wrote Milton, or that Christianity was stolen from the Aztecs; they receive it first laughingly, then fancifully, then speculatively, then seriously, then idolatrously even to slaying;

324

and yet all the time with nothing to go on but the fourth-hand version of a few entertaining coincidences. Exactly that sort of neat and fantastic solution which would make a glorious detective story is employed to make an utterly preposterous book of history or criticism.

No, I do not think it is wrong to play with these nonsensical hypotheses; I have had great fun out of fitting them together. One of my friends maintains that Tacitus never lived and that his works are a forgery of the sixteenth century; another explains the whole life of St. Paul in terms of an unabated hatred for Christianity. I am not against playing the fool with these fancies, but I am against letting them play the fool with me. To take one case at random, one could certainly make a huge theory, upheld by many coincidences, that men's surnames have constantly suited them. It really is a remarkable thing to reflect how many frightfully fine men have had frightfully fine names. How could we have rounded off our sentences without such words as "Hannibal" and "Napoleon," or "Attila" and "Charlemagne." But there are more startling cases. There is one great artist whose art was ultimately sacred and seraphic, yet in its labour and technique peculiarly strenuous and military; if one looked at his work only one would think of a harsh angel, an angel in armour. How comes it that this man actually bore the name of the Archangel Michael—Michelangelo? How comes it that a contemporary and more gracious artist happened to be christened after a more gracious archangel—Raphael?

Or take another case. If you or I had to invent out of our own heads a really shattering and shining name, a name fit for some flaming hero defying the stars, a name on horseback and high in the saddle—could we think of any so chivalrous or so challenging as Shakespeare? The very word is like Lancelot at his last tournament with a touch of the divine impotence of Don Quixote. In fact, I know only one surname that is really finer than Shakespeare, and that is Brakespear,[1] the only English Pope.

---

[1] Nicholas Brakespear became Pope Adrian IV (1154–1159).

A pleasing lyric in prose might be built up about the two of them; the one Englishman who rose to the highest of all official places, and the other who rose to the highest of all unofficial. Much eloquence and irony (if I had time to write them) might be uttered about the contrast between the English Pope, so humble and silent in his splendid publicity, and the English poet, so hearty and swaggering in his obscurity and neglect. It is at least certain that there was only one Englishman on the highest platform of priests, and only one on the highest platform of poets; and it is certain that each of their names is the only exact rhyme to the other one.

That is what you might call a coincidence; but the coincidence goes further. The actual meaning of the two names is appropriate to the two men in their two positions. If there was one thing more than another that the Renaissance did it was to shake the spear, to brandish the lance even more than to use it, to value the lance more for its flapping pennon than its point. If there was one thing, on the other hand, that a Pope in the twelfth century had to do, it was to break the spear—to bend the thick necks of the throned fighters who could not otherwise have conceived anything so fine as fighting. William Shakespeare is really very like the exultant monster in the old Testament, who laughs at the shaking of the spear. But Nicholas Brakespear stood in the Dark Ages for a simpler and more searching reminder, of Him who snappeth the spear in twain and takes off the wheel of the chariot.

The above is an impromptu instance of what I call playing with an idea; but the question is, what does one think of the idea? I will tell you what I think of it; I think it is complete bosh. I am almost certain that Raphael and Michelangelo are a coincidence. I am almost certain that Shakespeare and Brakespear are an accidental rhyme. I will carry the fancy as far as I choose; but if it tries to carry me as far as it chooses, I will remind it of several things. I will point out to it that in plain fact the names of literary men are often quite arrestingly unsuitable. Newman was by no means a worshipper of novelty; and one of the most

energetic and intelligent atheists of my acquaintance is saddled
with the surname of Priest.

Or take a classic example. Can anyone read the cold and cutting work of Swift without feeling that his surname should have
been Steele? Can anyone read the impetuous stuff of Steele without feeling that his surname should have been Swift? We should
really feel much happier if we could talk of the brilliant blunders
of Dick Swift, and the cool saturnine strength of Jonathan Steele.
In other words, my speculation about surnames is just large
enough to fill a magazine article, but is not large enough to fill
even a moderate-sized brain. It is this power of recovery after
extravagance that I urgently recommend. Indulge in all the most
decadent or futile fantasies, as long as you can curb the indulgence, like that of alcohol. Ride on the nightmare, if you prefer
such horse-flesh; only do not let the nightmare ride on you. Find
the mare's nest, which rocks on the tallest and darkest trees, and
steal the addled eggs: but do not make your breakfast off them
every morning for ever. Learn to be nonsensical, and then to be
sensible again; to create strange things and still to be independent
of them. Learn to suggest a thing, to urge it, to prove it, and
still to disbelieve it. For the very few things that are really worth
believing are not worth proving.

May 22, 1909

The Proper Support of Poets

It may seem somewhat late to remark on the grave moral which
was drawn by Mr. William Watson in the *Times* from the sad
story of John Davidson. But in such a matter, I think, delay is
even an advantage; partly because Mr. Watson's words were
words which may well sink in and be seriously ruminated, but

more especially because a decent lapse of time makes it more possible, with all delicacy, to discuss the matter from other points of view besides that of the dead poet or his friends. For Mr. Watson's appeal was not merely a fine tribute to a fine fellow-poet, a sort of prose "Adonais"; it was also a public and even practical suggestion which should be considered from a general and national standpoint. Mr. Watson attributed the disaster of John Davidson to lack of economic support, and substantially proposed that such support should be given in some form by the public, or even possibly by the State. That question is worth considering, even apart from the moving tragedy which gave it birth.

Like most questions in modern England, it is greatly clouded by the cant on both sides; by the people who want the poet to live on ecstasy and a biscuit, and the people who want the poet fed on champagne and turtle at the expense of grosser men. On the one hand, the pretensions of poets to override common morals or common-sense are nauseous; against them I am a pure Philistine, a Philistine out of the back numbers of *Punch*; as I listen to such things I can feel the mutton-chop whiskers growing on my face. But I think there is one particular kind of Philistinism which is quite as offensive on the other side. Thus, when the *Spectator* answers Mr. Watson by saying that most probably if poets got pensions they would be lazy and not write, I venture, in the case of a society like ours and a paper like the *Spectator*, to call the remark "cheek." The society in which we live and of which the *Spectator* is so solid and placid a prop, may be said, without exaggeration, to be based on the idea that men with much money can be trusted to work well. That is the whole defence, and the only defence, of our oligarchy, of the vast salaries and the vast estates. We are warned that if one miserable poet gets three hundred a year he will cease singing. In that case the governors who get thousands a year ought to cease governing. The orators ought to cease orating; the financiers ought to cease financing; the great bankers must be thinking only of dividends and never of economics; the great landlords must be thinking only of the rent and never of the land. This theory of the soporific power of money, true or false, is utterly subversive of the whole system of England; that venerable object, the stake in the country, becomes a deadly and even derisive object, like the stake driven through a suicide. This revolutionary spirit in the *Spectator* alarms me. I cannot promise to go all lengths with so explosive an organ of opinion, if it really proposes, without warning or compensation, upon the pure principle that money is a dangerous drug, to strip all young aristocrats of their allowances or all Dukes of their private parks. I do not believe that wealth is so utterly silencing and paralysing as all that, and I cannot but think that the *Spectator's* democratic fury rather carries it away.

On consideration, however, perhaps there is no ground for alarm. The writer on this paper, along with many other worthy modern Englishmen, seems to have generally adopted the view that money is only dangerous when it is given in small sums for work which is definitely good; whereas it is quite harmless if given in large sums for work which, whether good or bad, is never defined at all. A fixed income would be perilous for poor John Davidson, as it might make him cease to express himself; which, by the way, will appear an extraordinarily improbable suggestion to anybody who knew John Davidson. Yet the public could definitely judge whether it was getting its money's worth out of him. But a fixed income of twenty times the amount is not supposed to be perilous to say, a popular Duke, though what he does for it may be a secret between himself and his Maker. In the same way you will find solemn old gentlemen shaking their heads at the idea of Payment of Members as something cynical and mercenary. It does not seem to occur to them that we already have Payment of Members—Payment of Members on a most gorgeous and even greedy scale. Only it is payment of a few members, the members of the Government, most of whom are generally rich already. Evidently that is the principle; money is only dangerous to the people who are in need of it. Money should be given wildly, but never given judiciously. It is bad for poets, but good for patrons; it is good for Premiers, but bad for Parliaments. Perhaps it is some notion analogous to Gray's observations about knowledge.[1] A little money is a dangerous thing; drink deep or touch not the Pactolean spring. At least this is all the sense I can make out of the thing.

As against this sort of opponent my sympathies are all with Mr. Watson. If we really were a nation of hard workers, each toiling for bread, one might be content to have the poets so; one might comfort oneself among navvies who worked in order to live—or even among American millionaires who only live in order to work. But when our Constitution is one labyrinth of jobs and sinecures it is highly ridiculous to throw idleness in the teeth of the only trade in which idleness is of some use to the public. A poet who has done nothing in particular in the garden all the morning may really in some sense have been earning his pension as Poet Laureate. But a Government clerk doing nothing in his office all the morning is not laying up stores of patriotic inspiration.

But there is another consideration which Mr. Watson has surely overlooked, as did also, I think, the distinguished man whom he laments. It is tenable that there is a sort of implied obligation in a people to sustain, in no illiberal spirit, the poets who express the people. But surely there is also an implied obligation in the poets that they *shall* express the people. The contract is rightly kept vague and elastic: we will not dictate the poetry, nor should the poet dictate the pension. But the contract, though unwritten, is fundamental. Because I cannot express my feelings when I am in love with a woman, I owe gratitude and help to Robert Burns, who can express them for me. But because I pay Burns for expressing his love for a woman (which I feel, but cannot express), it does not follow that I need pay him if he expresses his love

---

[1] The observation is really by Alexander Pope (see *An Essay on Criticism*, II, 214–215), where the spring is "Pierian", named after the spring on Olympus. "Pactolean" comes from Pactolus, a river in Asia Minor, famous for the gold in its sands, supposedly there because Midas once bathed in it.

for a she-rhinoceros, a sentiment which I do not feel, and do
not even wish to feel. I admire the sky spangled with stars, but
I cannot praise it: Shelley can do it for me. But if Shelley takes
to praising the skin spotted with small-pox, then I have to tell
him, gently but firmly, that I not only cannot praise, but do not
admire. The breach between the people and the poets has been
bad for both: the people have gone without inspiration and the
poets without applause. But the error was in the poets as well
as the people, and certainly it was not absent from John Davidson. He chose, in his last stages, to praise inhuman and monstrous things, tyranny and chaos, which the heart of mankind
hates for ever—things in the highest and most serious sense
incredible. It is partly that which chokes the channel between
man and the modern poets. The real poet is the man who says
what men cannot say—but not what men cannot believe.

May 29, 1909

Whitewashing the Philanthropists

Philanthropy, as far as I can see, is rapidly becoming the recognisable mark of a wicked man. We have often sneered at the
superstition and cowardice of the mediaeval barons who thought
that giving lands to the Church would wipe out the memory of
their raids or robberies; but modern capitalists seem to have
exactly the same notion; with this not unimportant addition, that
in the case of the capitalists the memory of the robberies is really
wiped out. This, after all, seems to be the chief difference between
the monks who took land and gave pardons and the charity
organisers who take money and give praise: the difference is that
the monks wrote down in their books and chronicles, "Received
three hundred acres from a bad baron"; whereas the modern

experts and editors record the three hundred acres and call him a good baron. Of late, however, I am happy to say, some candid voices have been heard about the corruption and cruelty of the men who are the pillars of public benevolence; and if such voices have been raised, you may be sure that they have been severely rebuked. A gentleman, whom I take the opportunity to thank, has sent me, along with an interesting letter, the following extraordinary passage from an American leading article: "As often as we make a virtuous attempt to regard that arduous golfer, Mr. John D. Rockefeller, as an undesirable citizen of the big northern republic, he does something so superbly humane that one must feel impelled to come down hastily from the seat of the scornful and censorious. The incredible octopus, punctured by a thousand fountain-pens, has just authorised the New York Association for improving the Condition of the Poor to open Junior Sea Breeze, the summer hospital for babies at Sixty-fourth Street and the East River. For the last three summers Mr. Rockefeller has maintained this hospital for children entirely at his own expense. He has donated the land used, and, in addition, has spent between 20,000 and 25,000 dollars on the camp. Now, in all seriousness, we ask, what are you going to do with a man who comes to the help of the City-pale babies in this practical fashion and keeps the Recording Angel blotting out portions of his record with tears?"

For my part, I should reply that the Recording Angel must be a person of extraordinary and ungovernable sensibility if he is moved to tears by an old gentleman whose income is some thousands a day setting aside to feed his own fame and vanity some of the thousands which he could not possibly use to feed himself. Mr. Rockefeller must, in the nature of things, be drawing somewhat near to an examination in which I understand that he believes—an examination considerably more searching than that of the American law-courts; and if he had fifteen hundred years in front of him instead of fifteen, he could not even begin to eat, drink, and enjoy all his own money. If I kill an elephant, and the elephant nearly kills me, so that I have only ten minutes to live, even if elephant is my favourite dish I do not think myself monstrously magnanimous if, after partaking heartily of the end of his trunk, I observe, with my dying breath, that I do not propose to eat the rest. If I discover a mountainous continent at the age of ninety-nine (which does not seem very likely) I cannot think myself a hero because I allow some younger people to leap up the crags and dance upon the mountain-crests, and am content myself with a comfortable arm-chair and a view of the scenery. Rockefeller cannot be said to *give* his wealth to other people; one can only say that he leaves it for other people. In order to give one must first have; and the multi-millionaire does not truly possess his margin-millions: he cannot touch them, enjoy them, or even imagine them. Rockefeller decides not to absorb the whole of his own wealth just as he decides, with the same generous self-abnegation, not to drink up the sea or use up all the heat of the sun.

Of course, it may be at once conceded that in the case of ordinary charitable donors, of otherwise worthy or colourless characters, there is no need at all to enter into this matter of motives. If I die worth millions (which again is only a hypothesis) and leave a huge legacy of pots of beer to all the people in workhouses—for that is the form of charity I should choose—then my motives might be considered to be my own affair. Granted that I had done good to other people's bodies (which Sir Victor Horsley,[1] I fear, will hardly admit), it might be left to a higher tribunal whether I had done good to my own soul. But in the case of Rockefeller the motive is relevant, because his philanthropy, is, as we have seen, offered as a defence or expiation of his alleged commercial methods. If we are to set that philanthropy as a virtue over against his vices, then we have a right to ask if it is really virtuous. The question is about his morality; the question is whether he got his millions by tyranny

[1] Sir Victor Horsley (1857–1916), a surgeon, professor of surgery and a keen supporter of National sick insurance. As a candidate for Parliament, he was especially vocal in favor of the temperance movement.

or fraud; whereas if I died worth millions, it would be quite self-evident that I could only have got them by mistake.

I confess that I object to this particular style in which the millionaire is whitewashed, or, to speak more vividly, is silver-washed. In the case of Mr. Rockefeller it would, perhaps, be yet more correct to say that he is anointed with oil. But whatever metaphor we choose for this covering-up of his real features there are very strong moral and practical objections to the process. People complain of the whitewashing of historical characters, but that does not matter very much, simply because they are historical characters. Nero is dead, like that other and less intelligent sovereign, Queen Anne. I do not mind people whitewashing King John any more than I mind them whitewashing an ugly old picture. But the relief or indifference which might possibly attend the whitewashing of King John Plantagenet does not by any means apply to the whitewashing of King John D. Rockefeller. To be whitewashed alive is a terrible fate, like being buried alive. You go forth a frightful spectre among your fellows; all decent people fly from you screaming—as, indeed, I am given to understand, they do from John D. Rockefeller. God forbid that we should say that there is no angel's tear of such monstrous and supernatural bigness that it could wipe out his errors; I can imagine nothing much short of Niagara that could wipe out my own. But when a man is dying rich because he has deliberately ruined numberless babies whom he has never seen, I am not impressed with the fact that he has taken a handful of money, as useless to him as pebbles, and thrown it to a few other babies whom he has never seen. I feel this to be a dangerous moral precedent for myself. Translated into terms of my own income, it means that if I gave one beggar one glass of wine out of twelve dozen of good claret that little red wave would wash away all my sins. I cannot believe this.

It is sometimes alleged in defence of commercial anarchy, such as that of America, that it comes from, and in turn creates, the free play of personality. It seems to me to act in exactly the contrary way: you cannot see an American in the American forest of finance any more than you can see a Londoner in a London fog. If Mr. Rockefeller were in any fixed and recognisable place in a civilised state; if he were in the pulpit or in the dock, if he were on the throne or on the gallows, one might really know him as an individual. But as his functions have no limits and no outline, he is not, properly speaking, a person at all—he is not even a thing: he is a series of unpleasant occurrences. He has not really won fame, but only a kind of gigantic obscurity; not light, but rather darkness visible. These gigantic mushrooms are not trees, even though they overtop them; they have no roots; and when they are plucked away there will be nothing left but a stain.

June 5, 1909

The Death of George Meredith

The death of George Meredith is the real end of the Nineteenth Century, not that empty date that came at the close of 1899. The last bond is broken between us and the pride and peace of the Victorian age. Our fathers are all dead. We are suddenly orphans: we all feel strangely and sadly young. A cold, enormous dawn opens in front of us; we have to go on to tasks which our fathers, fine as they were, did not know, and our first sensation is this of cold and undefended youth. Swinburne was the penultimate, Meredith is the ultimate end.

It is not a phrase to call him the last of the Victorians: he really is the last. No doubt this final phrase has been used about each of the great Victorians one after another from Matthew Arnold and Browning to Swinburne and Meredith. No doubt the public has grown a little tired of the positively last appearance of the Nineteenth Century. But the end of George Meredith really is the end of that great epoch. No great man now alive has its peculiar powers or its peculiar limits. Like all great epochs, like all great things, it is not easy to define. We can see it, touch it, smell it, eat it; but we cannot state it. It was a time when faith was firm without being definite. It was a time when we saw the necessity of reform without once seeing the possibility of revolution. It was a sort of exquisite interlude in the intellectual disputes: a beautiful, accidental truce in the eternal war of mankind. Things could mix in a mellow atmosphere. Its great men were so religious that they could do without a religion. They were so hopefully and happily Republican that they could do without a Republic. They are all dead and deified; and it is well with them. But we cannot get back into that well-poised pantheism and liberalism. We cannot be content to be merely broad: for us the dilemma sharpens and the ways divide.

Of the men left alive there are many who can be admired beyond expression; but none who can be admired in this way. The name of that powerful writer, Mr. Thomas Hardy, was often mentioned in company with that of Meredith; but the coupling of the two names is a philosophical and chronological mistake. Mr. Hardy is wholly of our own generation, which is a very unpleasant thing to be. He is shrill and not mellow. He does not worship the unknown God: he knows the God (or thinks he knows the God), and dislikes him. He is not a pantheist: he is a pandiabolist. The great agnostics of the Victorian age said there was no purpose in Nature. Mr. Hardy is a mystic; he says there is an evil purpose. All this is as far as possible from the plentitude and rational optimism of Meredith. And when we have disposed of Mr. Hardy, what other name is there that can even pretend to recall the heroic Victorian age? The Roman curse lies upon Meredith like a blessing: "Ultimus suorum moriatur"—he has died the last of his own.

The greatness of George Meredith exhibits the same paradox or difficulty as the greatness of Browning; the fact that simplicity was the centre, while the utmost luxuriance and complexity was the expression. He was as human as Shakespeare, and also as affected as Shakespeare. It may generally be remarked (I do not know the cause of it) that the men who have an odd or mad point of view express it in plain or bold language. The men who have a genial and everyday point of view express it in ornate and complicated language. Swinburne and Thomas Hardy talk almost in words of one syllable; but the philosophical upshot can be expressed in the most famous of all words of one syllable—damn. Their words are common words; but their view (thank God) is not a common view. They denounce in the style of a spelling-book; while people like Meredith are unpopular through the very richness of their popular sympathies. Men like Browning or like Francis Thompson praise God in such a way sometimes that God alone could possibly understand the praise. But they mean all men to understand it: they wish every beast and fish and flying thing to take part in the applauding chorus of the Cosmos. On the other hand, those who have bad news to tell are much more explicit, and the poets whose object it is to depress the people take care that they do it. I will not write any more about those poets, because I do not profess to be impartial or even to be good-tempered on the subject. To my thinking, the oppression of the people is a terrible sin; but the depression of the people is a far worse one.

But the glory of George Meredith is that he combined subtlety with primal energy: he criticised life without losing his appetite for it. In him alone, being a man of the world did not mean being a man disgusted with the world. As a rule, there is no difference between the critic and ascetic except that the ascetic sorrows with a hope and the critic without a hope. But George Meredith loved straightness even when he praised it crookedly: he adored innocence even when he analysed it tortuously: he cared only for unconsciousness, even when he was unduly conscious of it. He was never so good as he was about virgins and schoolboys. In one curious poem, containing many fine lines, he actually rebukes people for being quaint or eccentric, and rebukes them quaintly and eccentrically. He says of Nature, the great earth-mother, whom he worshipped—

> . . . She by one sure sign can read,
> Have they but held her laws and nature dear;
> They mouth no sentence of inverted wit.
> More prizes she her beasts than this high breed
> Wry in the shape she wastes her milk to rear.

That is the mark of the truly great man: that he sees the common man afar off, and worships him. The great man tries to be ordinary, and becomes extraordinary in the process. But the small man tries to be mysterious, and becomes lucid in an awful sense—for we can all see through him.

June 12, 1909

Modern Jargon

We all feel that the only entirely inferior thing is to be superior; and various forms of cheap superiority are the most irritating facts of our modern life. One impudent piece of pedantry I have noticed as very much on the increase—it is the habit of arbitrarily changing the ends of abstract words (which are bad enough already) so as to make them sound more learned. I heard a young man, with thin, pale hair, speak some time ago at some Ethical Society; and words cannot convey the degree to which he drooped his eyelids whenever he said "Christianism," instead of Christianity. I was tempted to get up and tell him that what was the matter with him was Tomfoolerism, called by some Tomfoolerity, and that I felt an impulsion to bash his physiognomics out of all semblity of humanitude. I saw a magazine the other day in which Ethics had turned into Ethology. Now, the word Ethics is already a nuisance to God and man; but its permanent defence and its occasional necessity is that it stands for conduct considered statically as a science, whereas morality (or moralitude) stands for conduct considered actively as a choice. One can discuss ethics. One cannot discuss morality: one can only violate it.

The reasonable difference between ethics and morality is like the difference between geology and throwing stones or between jurisprudence and outrunning the constable. But if Ethics is the right word, as I always supposed it was, for the science of conduct, the dispassionate study of the *ethos*, in that case what the deuce is Ethology? In practice, I fear, it simply means that somebody or other, who was already too priggish to talk about morality, is by this time too priggish even to talk about ethics. The three phrases probably represent merely three stages in sniffing superiority and the perversion of all primary moral instincts. If a woman's husband has been silly enough to take more wine than is good for him, morality would lead her to send him to bed. Ethics would lead her to send him to Coventry.[1] And ethology would probably lead her to send him to a penal settlement for inebriates. If a man's wife throws a teapot at him (as happened recently in the aristocratic neighbourhood in which I live) morality would lead him to go out of the house for an hour or so and give her nerves a chance. Ethics would probably induce him to go out of the town and write to her from a Garden City that their temperaments were incompatible. What ethology would make him do I hardly dare to think.

However this may be, there seems to be a curiously bloodless and polysyllabic style now adopted for the discussion of the most direct and intimate matters. The human home, for example, which whether it be comfortable or uncomfortable is, after all, the only place in which humanity has ever lived, people discuss as if it were the nest of some extraordinary bird, or the cell of

---

[1] It is said that the citizens of Coventry once had such a great dislike of soldiers that a woman caught speaking to one was instantly ostracized. Hence, when a soldier was sent to Coventry, he was cut off from all social intercourse.

some occult insect which science had only just discovered. The combination of man and woman may be, and indeed is, a dangerous chemical combination; frequently resulting in an explosion; but the explosion is one to which we might have got pretty well used by this time. And if we are really to debate these matters with much effect, I suggest that we avoid these new polysyllables as much as possible; and if a word has already a long tail, at least that we leave it the long tail that our fathers gave it. I fancy it will be good for our intellects and certainly (as far as I am concerned) for our tempers. If we have to discuss the most familiar and fundamental human problems all over again, let us at least take advantage of their antiquity in the fact that the vocabulary of them is fairly popular and clear. Let us realise that marriage is not monogamy but marriage; that fighting is not natural selection but fighting; that wine is not alcoholic stimulation, but wine; that work is not the creation of capital, but work, a very unpleasant thing. It seems that we have a great upheaval and revision in front of us. The discussion will certainly be long, but at least the words might be short.

The most awful example of this silly and heartless pedantry that I have seen of late is in a recent issue of the *Review of Reviews*, which contains some extracts from a novel by a Mme. or Mlle. de Pratz. The editor calls it "The Love Ideals of a Suffragette"; but I do not wish for a moment to make the editor responsible for the foolish pomposities of the lady whom he quotes, even when he seems to quote her with approval. Mr. Stead is a man for whom I have always had, and have still, the heartiest admiration; I know that nothing but the most generous sentiments has set him on the extreme Suffragette platform. Feminism is against chivalry; but chivalry will always be rather in favour of feminism. And in all such things Mr. Stead's only fault, the only spot on a splendid fighting career, has been that he has been too easily led away with words. In the relation of the sexes, I think he has always been misled by the ridiculous word "comradeship." The very fact that the emancipated women use the word "comradeship" about love and marriage shows that they do not know what comradeship means. Comradeship means the club; it means a certain cool and casual association which is mostly masculine and which is always pluralist. If marriage were comradeship, it would have to be polygamy. Even then the comradeship would not be easy to work. But I do not mean here to quarrel with Mr. Stead, but only with his latest feminist philosopher. The word "prig" is but a faint adumbration of Miss Claire de Pratz's[2] heroine. The definition of a prig, I suppose, is this: one who has pride in the possession of his brain rather than joy in the use of it. And the difference is exactly this, that a very small brain is enough to be proud of, even when it is not big enough either to enjoy with recklessness or to use with effect. And there is this further fact, that people with large intellects know the limits of intellect; while to people of small intellects, intellect seems unlimited and therefore divine. For instance, any man who has really the intelligence to be a philosopher about philosophy will also have the intelligence to be a lover about love, or a housekeeper about housekeeping. As a citizen, I am by hypothesis an adviser of the nation, even if my advice is only a cross on a ballot-paper. In public life I must use my pure, impartial, theoretic capacity. In private life, of course, I make a home for myself in accordance with that enormous part of me and anybody else which is not intellect—the affections, the sense of fun, and the sense of honour. That is what we all do, but that is not what Miss de Pratz's heroine did. Being asked in marriage by an absolutely honourable and intelligent man who loved her and with whom she was in love, she replied in these interesting and (to me) quite precious words: "It will interfere with my work, dear, because it will interfere with my soul and brain. Believe me, I am not yet fully developed as a thinking entity. I am unable to separate my mental from my emotional self . . . I thought myself more developed as a thinker . . . I feel that if I once yield to it I shall not be able to keep my emotional soul

[2] Claire de Pratz was the author of *Eve Norris* (1907), *Elizabeth Devaney* (1909) and *The Education of Jacqueline* (1910).

within bounds. . . . If I become your wife I shall be Mme. André Nortier—no longer Elizabeth Davenay. And therein lies the terrible and great difference."

I wish to conclude with this quotation, as an illustration of my protest against all this pedantic beating about the bush; because I really think that much comment would spoil it. "Believe me," she cries, evidently expecting incredulity, "I am not yet fully developed as a thinking entity." I hasten to assure her that I can believe that, at any rate, with the utmost ease. She goes on to say: "I am unable to separate my mental from my emotional self." I never heard of anybody who was able to do so; certainly Plato was not, nor Dante, nor Shakespeare, nor Goethe; and I should think anyone who could do it would immediately turn into a very unpleasant person. Or perhaps he would split and turn into two very unpleasant persons. I do not presume to conjecture. But if Elizabeth Davenay was on the road to such a development, perhaps we may all be content with the reflection that Mr. André Nortier had rather a gratifying escape.

June 19, 1909

The Need for a Real Revolution

Our world to-day is full of fanciful substitutes for civil war; everybody is trying to invent ways of fighting without fighting. There is Passive Resistance, of course—the method of loading your embarrassed ruler with pieces of your furniture that he does not want, instead of nice portable coins. There is boycotting, which is done in Ireland by Nationalist peasants to Unionist agents, and in England by Primrose League ladies to Radical greengrocers. There is chaining yourself up to railings, which seems to me dull. If the ladies could chain Mr. Asquith up to the railings, I could see the fun of it, and let us hope that he could also. But their loading themselves with chains seems to me altogether too meek a confession of the servile and dependent state of woman. Then there is the strike, of course, and the lock-out, and the idea of overawing by numbers, and the militant patience of people who ask, quite respectfully, for money at one's front door, but will not go away. All these are a sort of half-fighting; they use the human body as a barricade, though not as a bombshell.

But the most amusing and original kind of half-war I have come across of late is that which Mr. Y. Brann, a Kentish farmer, is waging against the Kent County Council. The situation is thus summarised in a daily paper—

> The County Council insist on having a trench kept open in a large garden adjoining the main road to Rochester, and the owners of the garden, whose cause is championed by Mr. Brann, protest against the interference. For the last few days a number of men sent by the Council have been engaged in digging the trench, but they have been met by an equal number of Mr. Brann's farm-hands, who have shovelled back the earth into the pit as fast as the attacking party dug it out. The net result of the contest is, of course, that the position is exactly the same as it was when the battle began.

It must be an amusing scene if conducted on both sides with that queer, ingrained good-humour and queer, ingrained indifference which marks the English rustic. Mr. Brann himself is full of military fervour and moral conviction, but he also is, apparently, not without good-humour.

"You see there is not much damage done yet," said Mr. Brann, a typical English farmer of Falstaffian build and humour. "All the same, we have had rare sport here lately, and just the kind of sport I like. I have enjoyed it immensely," he commented with a hearty laugh.

He was standing at the door of the house rubbing his hands vigorously in anticipation of more sport. "You know," he went on, "we open fire again to-morrow. I have been told the Council

contingent will be stronger than usual, and that they'll have a
fire-engine with them. Why I don't know, but let 'em all come.
I have also an engine on my farm, and if necessary I'll have it
out too. The more men they send the better, for the fight will
then be soon over. I can bring fifty men, fifty carts, and fifty
horses into the field at five minutes' notice—a complete army,
infantry, cavalry, and artillery—that's more than the Council
can do. Ah, we are going to have a glorious time!"

As to who is in the right in this quarrel I cannot tell, and am
for the moment cynically indifferent: there is something romantic in Mr. Brann, in so far as he is fighting for friendship and in
another's quarrel. But what interests me is the new and highly
exasperating mode of war, in which one has perpetually to dig
a hole and perpetually see someone else fill it up. Psychologically
the thing sounds so maddening that I should think it would soon
be followed by simpler and more historic methods of protest.
Still, if the thing succeeds in Kent it might be tried in many
places and in many ways. Instead of the Big Navy party and the
Little Navy party conflicting in Parliament, let them conflict in
the dockyard. Let the war party be kept busy in building a
Dreadnought, while the peace party are equally and happily industrious in taking it to pieces again. Let us start making the Channel
Tunnel, while a happy band of Opposition enthusiasts make
holes in it as fast as it is built.

The South African War might have been avoided, and the two
sides peacefully and permanently employed—the Rand party in
pulling up the gold out of the mines, and the anti-Rand party
in emptying it back again. In matters of agricultural or pastoral
activity it would, perhaps, be rather more difficult fully to realise
the idea. The conscientious opponent of agrarian society might
indeed walk behind the ploughman carefully filling up the fur-
row. But it would be rather fatiguing work to walk behind the
reaper trying to tie all the corn on to its stalks again. The idea
of putting the wool back on to the sheep after shearing must
also, I think, be regretfully abandoned.

I am sorry Mr. Brann employs the modern Imperialistic boast

of possessing vast resources and innumerable carts and men; this seems to me unworthy of a gallant man of Kent. He ought rather to speak in the spirit of Henry V. and all real warriors—

> We few, we happy few, we band of brothers,
> For who this day shall shovel mud with me
> Shall be my brother; be he ne'er so vile,
> This day shall gentle his condition.

Moreover, a too great disproportion in the forces would destroy that balance of the *status quo* in which lies all the calm and beauty of the idea. As long as the two forces are equal in numbers and energy, they can toil and sweat with the soothing and refreshing certainty that they are leaving everything exactly as it was before. But if Mr. Brann puts too much faith in his horses and his chariots he will destroy his own conservative intention. If the fillers-up become much more numerous than the diggers-out, the level will disappear, and the estate of Mr. Brann's friend will be disfigured with a gigantic mound rapidly rising into the proportions of a mountain. I can imagine no better example of how necessary are equality and fair play to the very existence of romance.

This method, which may be called the method of Peaceful Frustration, has something poetical and promising about it; but I fear that its difficulties are to be found in the limits of human nature. Passive Resistance carried past a certain point is very likely to produce active resistance; I once saw the poster of a Nonconformist paper which bore this simple and unconscious irony: "Passive Resistance; Auctioneer Mobbed at Wandsworth." In the same way, this indirect destruction is, surely, very likely to inflame the soul towards direct destruction. I know that if I wanted to make a hole in the earth and saw another man perpetually filling it up, it would decidedly divert my imagination towards making a hole in the man and seeing whether he could fill that up. To see the stately homes or the holy places we have built pulled down by profane hands would in all cases be a call to battle. But to see them pulled down even while we were building them would be something past all toleration; and would result, I should think, not so much in battle as in massacre. If the Puritans had started to knock down St. Paul's Cathedral before Wren had knocked it up there would, I think, have been a civil war of the most uncivil description.

So, on the whole, I am in favour of simpler and more old-fashioned methods; and if there are in our Commonwealth cruelties and hypocrisies in which the soul of man cannot rest, I suggest that we have one real revolution and get it over.

June 26, 1909

Art as Private Property

The great Holbein portrait is now at last finally saved, or finally lost; I forget which. Anyhow, the papers may possibly leave off talking about it, which is the great thing. It appears to have been a prodigiously important and sacred national possession; but nobody ever talked about it before, and now nobody will ever talk about it again. We were all terribly fond of it, but we are a stern, reticent race, and most of us were sufficiently stoical even to give the impression that we had never heard of it in our lives. Now that it has been saved (if it has been saved) we shall pull our feelings together again and go on as if it did not exist. Hitherto it had been in the possession of a particular English gentleman, who graciously showed it to the English people. For a moment there was the frightful danger that it might come into the hands of an American millionaire who would not even show it to the American people. But this, as I understand, has been averted; I hear that the picture is saved; but I do not know whether the English people will save anything by it. It is in the National Gallery, and they can go and see it. But it is quite as fresh and foreign a picture to many of them as it could be to Americans. It is as new and alien to most Englishmen as it could be to American Indians.

This possession of pictures and such things by a few rich men in such costly accumulation and plenty seems to me to make a great deal of difference to the merely national appeal. England is individualist to excess; England is not England, but a cluster of feudal principalities. People talk of going back to the Heptarchy; we have never properly come out of it. The pictures, etc., in possession of the feudal princes are not possessed by England; they are only possessed in England. When we talk of France having a fine church or of Italy having a fine picture, we really mean something solid and national by the words. There is a law in France by which all fine public buildings belong to the soil and State of France. There is a law in Italy forbidding people to sell to foreigners those pictures which are the eternal glory of the Italian genius. But there is in England not only no such law, but no such public sentiment. The Duke of Norfolk's Holbein no more belonged to England than the Duke of Norfolk's umbrella. There might very possibly be an American millionaire of so mystical a type of servility that he would be willing to pay £70,000 for the Duke of Norfolk's umbrella. In that case, as a purely business question, I should recommend the Duke to close with the offer. And I should think it rather unreasonable if the English papers placarded London with posters saying, "Duke's Umbrella in Danger—Can We Save Duke's Umbrella?— Umbrella Almost Gone!—Eleventh-Hour Rescue of Ducal Umbrella!" I should begin to examine myself for emotions which would not be there. I should begin to remind myself that, until the newspaper boom began, I had not even been aware that the Duke had an umbrella. There would be a slight element of unreality, not to say humbug, in describing me as so particularly attached to the umbrella. It may be a very nice one; but so far it has been the Duke's, and not mine. I had never heard of it until the moment when the American gentleman was mysteriously moved to ask for it. That is often the fate of the great private picture in this country. It is hidden, like the family curse. It is never found till it is just going to be lost.

That is one real English problem about such things. We have as good a National Gallery as anybody. But nobody has so many Unnational Galleries as we have. Nowhere else in the civilised world are works of art of the most gigantic scope and importance so easily thought of as the possessions of some private man. I believe strongly in the sentiment of private property; and have often defended it in these columns. But there is a common sense and a humour in the sense of property; if it loses these it must perish. I should feel very nervous if I owned the original Venus of Milo; it would be like owning the moon. But I believe that an English oligarch—a Portland or a Sutherland—would think owning the Venus of Milo quite natural, all in the day's work or absence of work. I should not like to own Stonehenge; I should dream about it. But I fancy that an English Duke would indicate Stonehenge as gracefully and unobtrusively as a rockery in his garden. He would show the Elgin Marbles as if they were his family portraits, and the Pyramids as if they were his family tombs. This sort of thing is absurd; this is not a sense of private property, but rather the absence of all sense of what could possibly be the nature of private property. To own one of the great Raphaels is as nonsensical as to own Westminster Abbey.

The increasing triumph of those Collectivists who deny every claim of property is due to nothing so much as this unnatural quality in the property owned in our present wealthy communities. The Socialists do not understand very well what property is; but the anti-Socialists do not understand it at all. They will tell you that owning a farm is exactly like owning a railway— as if a man could love three hundred miles of lean metal-rods. When those who have property do not know what it is, it is not odd that it should be misunderstood by that unhappy multitude that has never had it at all. But of all the cases of such oblivion, there is none stronger than that which arises in these cases of what are called national treasures of art. They are often art, because great artists have wrought them; they are apparently treasures, since they fetch a great deal of money. The one thing they never have been is national. There are certain central masterpieces which cannot in their nature be private property, and which are not allowed to be public property. Our wealthy class will be chiefly tested by whether it perceives these things—and gets rid of them. A man may privately own that which is unique and is the object of a private affection. But he must not own that which is unique and the object of a public affection. If I choose to have red and yellow tulips growing alternately round the top of my house that, I think, is my affair. But if I possess the only black tulip in the world, then I do seriously think that I ought to present it to Kew Gardens. I trust that when the temptation comes my strength will be sufficient.

Of course, if it be answered that this particular case of the Holbein picture, or the majority of such cases, does not rise to such unique and public value, I do not know that I disagree. I admit that, with the assistance of Shakespeare's Cliff, the Nelson Column, the Tomb of Chaucer, and the Turners in the National Gallery, I might have managed at last to dry my tears for the loss of a picture that I never saw. But if it was small enough for the Duke to own, I think it was small enough for the Duke to sell. On that principle, it was his own affair every way. Perhaps Mr. Colnaghi[1] saved the Duke's life at an early age. Anyhow, this is a wild world, and I think the part inhabited by merchants and dealers is the wildest part of it. Not in the maddest religion that ever raved can there be anything quite so crazy as this business of the sale of pictures. There are two painted canvases, an original and a copy, which are so exquisitely alike that about two men in the world can tell the difference with a microscope; and they are often wrong. And yet stout, bald-headed men with watchchains, who would not like to be called poets, pay the worth of a townfull of houses for one of them, and will hardly give a bottle of champagne for the other. The poet, they say, pursues clouds; but he does not give a million for one cloud and sixpence for another, when he can hardly tell which is which.

[1] The Colnaghi family were art dealers and owners of an art gallery.

July 3, 1909

Modern and Ancient Pageants

The only objection to the excellent series of Pageants that has adorned England of late is that they are made too expensive. The mass of the common people cannot afford to see the Pageant; so they are obliged to put up with the inferior function of acting in it. I myself got in with the rabble in this way. It was to the Church Pageant; and I was much impressed with certain illuminations which such an experience makes possible. A Pageant exhibits all the fun of a Fancy Dress Ball, with this great difference; that its motive is reverent instead of irreverent. In the one case a man dresses up as his great-grandfather in order to make game of his great-grandfather; in the other case, in order to do him honour. What the great-grandfather himself would think of either of them we fortunately have not to conjecture. The alteration is important and satisfactory. All natural men regard their ancestors as dignified because they are dead; it was a great pity and folly that we had fallen into the habit of regarding the Middle Ages as a mere second-hand shop for comic costumes. Mediaeval costume and heraldry had been meant as the very manifestation of courage and publicity and a decent pride. Colours were worn that they might be conspicuous across a battlefield; an animal was rampant on a helmet that he might stand up evident against the sky. The mediaeval time has been talked of too much as if it were full of twilight and secrecies. It was a time of avowal and of what many modern people call vulgarity. A man's dress was that of his family or his trade or his religion; and these are exactly the three things which we now think it bad taste to discuss. Imagine a modern man being dressed in green and orange because he was a Robinson. Or imagine him dressed in blue and gold because he was an auctioneer. Or imagine him dressed in purple and silver because he was an agnostic. He is now dressed only in the ridiculous disguise of a gentleman; which tells one nothing at all, not even whether he is one. If ever he dresses up as a cavalier or a monk it is only as a joke—very often as a disreputable and craven joke, a joke in a mask. That vivid and heraldic costume which was meant to show everybody who a man was is now chiefly worn by people at Covent Garden masquerades who wish to conceal who they are. The clerk dresses up as a monk in order to be absurd. If the monk dressed up as a clerk in order to be absurd I could understand it; though the escapade might disturb his monastic superiors. A man in a sensible gown and hood might possibly put on a top-hat and a pair of trousers in order to cover himself with derision, in some extravagance of mystical humility. But that a man who calmly shows himself to the startled sky every morning in a top-hat and trousers should think it comic to put on a simple and dignified robe and hood is a situation which almost splits the brain. Things like the Church Pageant may do something towards snubbing this silly and derisive view of the past. Hitherto the young stockbroker, when he wanted to make a fool of himself, dressed up as Cardinal Wolsey. It may now begin to dawn on him that he ought rather to make a wise man of himself before attempting the impersonation.

Nevertheless, the truth which the Pageant has to tell the British public is rather more special and curious than one might at first assume. It is easy enough to say in the rough that modern dress is dingy, and that the dress of our fathers was more bright and picturesque. But that is not really the point. At Fulham Palace one can compare the huge crowd of people acting in the Pageant with the huge crowd of people looking at it. There is a startling difference, but it is not a mere difference between gaiety and gloom. There is many a respectable young woman in the audience who has on her own hat more colours than the whole Pageant put together. There are belts of brown and black in the Pageant itself: the Puritans round the scaffold of Laud, or the black-robed doctors of the eighteenth century. There are patches of purple and yellow in the audience: the more select young ladies and the less select young gentlemen. It is not that our age has no appetite for the gay or the gaudy—it is a very hedonistic age. It is not that past ages—even the rich symbolic Middle Ages—did not feel any sense of safety in what is sombre or restrained. A friar in a brown coat is much more severe than an 'Arry in a brown bowler. Why is it that he is also much more pleasant?

I think the whole difference is this; that the first man is brown with a reason and the second without a reason. If a hundred monks wore one brown habit it was because they felt that their toil and brotherhood were well expressed in being clad in the course, dark colour of the earth. I do not say that they said so, or even clearly thought so; but their artistic instinct went straight when they chose the mud-colour for laborious brethren or the flame-colour for the first princes of the Church. But when 'Arry puts on a brown bowler he does not either with his consciousness or his sub-consciousness (that rich soil) feel that he is crowning his brows with the brown earth, clasping round his temples a strange crown of clay. He does not wear a dust-coloured hat as a form of strewing dust upon his head. He wears a dust-coloured hat because the nobility and gentry who are his models discourage him from wearing a crimson hat or a golden hat or a peacock-green hat. He is not thinking of the brownness of brown. It is not to him a symbol of the roots, of realism, or of autochthonous humility; on the contrary, he thinks it looks rather "classy."

The modern trouble is not that the people do not see splendid colours or striking effects. The trouble is that they see too much of them and see them divorced from all reason. It is a misfortune of modern language that the word "insignificant" is vaguely associated with the words "small" or "slight." But a thing is insignificant when we do not know what it signifies. An African elephant lying dead in Ludgate Circus would be insignificant. That is, one could not recognise it as the sign or message of anything. One could not regard it as an allegory or a love-token. One could not even call it a hint. In the same way the solar system is insignificant. Unless you have some special religious theory of what it means, it is merely big and silly, like the elephant in Ludgate Circus. And similarly, modern life, with its vastness, its energy, its elaboration, its wealth, is, in the exact sense, insignificant. Nobody knows what we mean; we do not know ourselves. Nobody could explain intelligently why a coat is black, why a waistcoat is white, why asparagus is eaten with the fingers, or why Hammersmith omnibuses are painted red. The mediaevals had a much stronger idea of crowding all possible significance into things. If they had consented to waste red paint on a large and ugly Hammersmith omnibus it would have been in order to suggest that there was some sort of gory magnanimity about Hammersmith. A heraldic lion is no more like a real lion than a chimney-pot hat is like a chimney-pot. But the lion was meant to be a lion. And the chimney-pot hat was not meant to be like a chimney-pot or like anything else. The resemblance only struck certain philosophers (probably gutter-boys) afterwards. The top-hat was not intended as a high uncastellated tower; it was not intended at all. This is the real baseness of modernity. This is, for example, the only real vulgarity of advertisements. It is not that the colours on the posters are bad. It is that they are much too good for the meaningless work which they serve. When at last people see—as at the Pageant—crosses and dragons, leopards and lilies, there is scarcely one of the things that they now see as a symbol which they have not already seen as a trade-mark. If the great "Assumption of the Virgin" were painted in front of them they might remember Blank's Blue.[1] If the Emperor of China were buried before them, the yellow robes might remind them of Dash's Mustard. We have not the task of preaching colour and gaiety to a people that has never had it, to Puritans who have neither seen nor appreciated it. We have a harder task. We have to teach those to appreciate it who have always seen it.

---

[1] Probably the laundry product commonly called "bluing" which is used to keep linens white. "Blank's" and "Dash's" are made-up names.

July 10, 1909

Wisdom in Comic Songs

It is sometimes said that our age is too fond of amusement: but
there are further facts to be remembered. One of them is this:
that it so often happens that the amusing entertainments are the
only places where the serious truth is told. If it were really a
question between hearing a statesman talk sense and hearing a
clown talk nonsense I think I should sometimes, perhaps often—
say once in thirty times—wish to hear the statesman. But it is
not that: it is a question between hearing the statesman talk
nonsense that I am not allowed to laugh at and the clown talk
nonsense that I am allowed to laugh at. I would rather hear Mr.
Gus Elen than listen to a paper read before the Charity Organisation Society, not merely because Mr. Elen is more amusing
than the Charity Organisation Society, but because I am sure
that he knows more about the English poor. He has more Charity, though less Organisation. He is less of an official, but more
of an expert. I would rather read a comic paper than a grave,
prosperous Imperial paper Big with Our British Destiny: because
the truth sometimes gets into the comic paper by accident. And
I am very sure that the fantastic picture of the Press, put before
the footlights for the frivolous, in the play called "The Earth,"[1]
spoke of some real things that were never mentioned in the whole
of the Press Conference.

The fact is that we have reached so high and rarefied a condition of humbug that the most serious things we have left are
the comic things. Some of the most serious are the comic songs.
When (a little while ago) the popular singer exclaimed, "You
can depend on Young Australia," he uttered a pedantic political

---

[1] A play by James Bernard Fagan which was first produced in 1909. The plot
involves the machinations of a vulgar newspaper magnate who blackmails an
MP in order to have a bill withdrawn from consideration.

theory which is probably untrue. But when he said, "Bill Bailey, won't you please come home?" he uttered a real *cri de coeur* which resounds from many homes, rich and poor, and which is really tragic as well as really comic. The Return of Bill Bailey was as human and eternal as the Return of Ulysses. And it was certainly much more human and eternal than the mere speculation about Australia; because in that the right process was reversed. Heroes, like Ulysses, are adventurous and exciting because they are trying to get home. Imperialists, ne'er-do-wells, filibusters, etc., are dull and uninteresting because they are trying to get away from home. Centripetal people are jolly. Centrifugal people are a bore.

It is the same, of course, with innumerable cases; but I have not kept up my attendance at the Halls, and the comic songs I remember are old ones. Old or new, however, they illustrate the same point: that in our society the wise are talking folly, and only the fools, the avowed and professional fools, are occasionally talking wisdom. Take any question you like to mention; take capital punishment. Personally, I am against hanging, though I admit that it would be enormously improved if it were public hanging. But none of the arguments on either side of that question ever give the main fact as it appears to the great masses of the people. The defenders of Capital Punishment talk as if every execution were an awful and separate act of justice. The opponents of Capital Punishment talk as if every execution were a special and fiendish violation of mercy. Both assume that the spirit of the thing will at least be dreadful and exact.

While I endeavour to detach and define this unreal element on both sides of the question, there floats across my mind a bar of beautiful old melody, of which the words (I think) were these—

> When we come to Newgate Street,
> Jest to give the kids a treat,
> We showed 'em where their uncle 'e was 'ung.

I will not deny that here is something of the ecstasy and exaggeration of the artist. Probably it is not true that any poor people regard the gallows in the family with quite so much cheerful simplicity as that. But it is absolutely true that poor people regard the penal system, which is now everywhere hung over their heads, as an enormous and irrational calamity, like the calamities of Nature. They know that in practice only poor men do get hanged: that is because we have left off killing people for treason and heresy and all the sins of gentlemen. They know that the poor men who get hanged are not the worst poor men, but simply the poor men who happen to have thrown chisels or drawn knives, or used pokers, or had the best of it in a kicking match. Therefore the poor, very rightly, regard hanging as the sort of thing that might happen to anybody—provided he is poor. Therefore the phrase in the comic song is not so much of an exaggeration. One can really almost imagine an obscure family saying, "This is where Uncle Joseph was hung," just as they might point out a pool and say, "This is where Uncle Joseph was drowned," or indicate a cliff, saying, "This is where Uncle Joseph was dashed to pieces," or even point to a battlefield, saying, "This is where Uncle Joseph was shot." The thing is on the nerve of the truth; the poor do feel punishment as a mere flying fatality. They talk of being in prison as being "in trouble." And the real case against capital punishment in our time is simply that—that the mass of men do not feel it as a law, but as an accident. I am sure we must be hanging on the wrong principle, at any rate, for mankind can discover no principle when we hang.

Instances are numberless. I have only space for another. It is the modern squabble between the elder and the younger generation, especially in the case of women—the thing which was called in my youth Revolt of the Daughters. I am not going to discuss the female question any more in this column; but I may remark one fact about both sides in it. They are both colossally serious. To hear young women talk one would think that there was no such thing as a frivolous girl. To hear the old women talk you would think that there was no such thing as a vulgar and funny old woman. Every girl is as grave as Joan of Arc; and every mother as solemn as the Mother of the Gracchi. It is when

my mind is stretched to the sternest acceptation of these things
that a small and distant tune begins to run in my head, a tune
from the remote days of my boyhood, and which shapes itself
into some such sentences as these—

> Think of me, old Mother Scrubbs,
> A-joining these 'ere totty-clubs.
> Fancy me deserting the pubs
> At my time of life!

That washes and purifies me like a great wind. That recalls the
great fact which we have all forgotten; that one can grow, as
one grows older, at once more comic and more sensitive to
comicality. One of the few gifts that can really increase with old
age is a sense of humour. That is the whole fun of belonging to
an ancient civilisation, like our own great civilisation of Europe.
In my vision I see Europa still sitting on her mighty bull, the
enormous and mystic mother, from whom we come, who has
given us everything from the Iliad to the French Revolution.
And from her awful lips I seem to hear the words—

> Fancy me deserting the Pubs
> At My time of life!

July 17, 1909

The English as Hypocrites

I was reading the other day in a newspaper the detailed report
of the examination of an accused man in the witness-box; a thing
that would have horrified our legal fathers. I do not say that I
am for or against this innovation; but there is in it the sign of a
certain weakness in our national character which is curious and
worth careful study.

When foreigners say that we English are hypocrites, they do us an unmerited injustice. They also pay us a quite unmerited compliment. Really to be a hypocrite must require a horrible strength of character. An ordinary man such as you or I generally fails at last because he has not enough energy to be a man. But the hypocrite must have enough energy to be two men. It is said that a liar should have a good memory. But a hypocrite must not only have a good memory of the past, but a consistent and creative vision of the future; his unreal self must be so far real to him. The perfect hypocrite should be a trinity of artistic talent. He must be a novelist like Dickens to create a false character. He must be an actor like Garrick to act it. And he must be a business man like Carnegie to profit by it. Such a genius would not be easy to find in any country; but I think it can fairly be said that it would be exceptionally difficult to find him in England.

What is it, then, that people have meant when they called us hypocrites? They must have meant something; even slanders always mean something; and even misunderstandings can be understood. For instance, it is untrue that the Scotsman cannot see a joke. But it is true that the Scotsman *will* not see a joke until he is quite sure which way the joke is going to turn. That sort of childish and barbaric caution really goes with the good qualities of the Scots. It is untrue that Irishmen make more bulls[1] in the House of Commons than Englishmen. But it is true that an eager Irishman will make a bull and go on gaily; while a respectable Englishman, when he has made a bull, feels inclined to apply for the Chiltern Hundreds[2] and hang himself from his bedpost. It is untrue that Germans are mere ninepins stuck up in a row by the Kaiser or the Colonel. But it is true that the

[1] To "make a bull" is to make a blunder, particularly a contradiction in terms.

[2] A hundred is a division of a shire, and the Children Hundreds are located in Buckinghamshire. To apply for the "stewardship" of the Chiltern Hundreds was to apply for a totally meaningless position, but it did allow one to resign from Parliament, since one could not be an MP and hold a paying nonpolitical office such as this one.

genuine German has a positive pleasure in obeying the law; while the true Irishman enjoys resisting the law, and the true English-man enjoys evading it. Thus there is always some sense at the bottom of international prejudices; and there is some sense at the bottom of that singular legend which connects our partic-ularly clumsy, kindly, and uncritical race with the idea of hypoc-risy.

The truth at the back of it, I think, is something like this. We are pre-eminently the people who always want to have our cake and eat it. We explain pathetically that we are illogical; in return, it is politely pointed out to us that we are always illogical in our own favour. In short, about even our happy impulsiveness there is something a little mean; perhaps all the meaner because we seek to disguise it from ourselves. But it is not hypocrisy, but rather a clash of inconsistent affections, with a touch of timidity to keep it undecided. Thus a cricketer might combine increasing laziness with care for his athletic reputation. Or a retired states-man might combine a pride in dignified silence with a perpetual itch to interfere. He wishes to have it both ways. Such a man is not strictly a hypocrite; but he is in great danger of becoming a moral poltroon. Before I take the examples from the twentieth century, let me take an example from the eighteenth. I mean that very English institution, the Press Gang. We were swaying backwards and forwards in a desperate and dizzy wrestle with a giant, the French Revolution or Napoléon, its child. We were justified in doing hard things, still more in using hard words. And some of the hardest things we said were against conscrip-tion; against the ruthlessness with which the Republic and the Emperor tore the peasant from the plough and sent him to bleed on the Spanish mountains or the Russian plains. In our popular songs we boasted that our Navy and Army were a host of vic-torious volunteers—

> Then cheer up my lads, 'tis to Glory we steer,
> To add something fresh to this wonderful year;
> To Honour we call you, not press you like slaves,
> For who are so free as the sons of the waves?

But, as a matter of fact, when a son of the waves was just going back to his wife and family, he was frequently knocked on the head with a bludgeon and carted on board a ship again. Nelson's men were forced conscripts as well as Napoleon's. But Napoleon's conscription was official; ours was unofficial. It was done, but it was not supposed to be done. England wished to have at once the convenience of forced service and the fame of free service. This is one of the cases where our mental inconsistency comes uncomfortably near to meanness.

Now, I am very much afraid that another instance of it must be found in this new law which allows the criminal to go into the witness-box while solemnly asserting that it does not force him to do so. Just as there is a general French view of armies and a general English view also; so there are quite distinct a French and an English sentiment about criminal law. In both cases the custom of the one country appears not only mysterious but cruel to the other. In England we have always disliked conscription; it has seemed to us sinister and sanguinary that every man should be a soldier. But to the countries of conscription it seems sinister and sanguinary that any man should be a soldier and nothing else. In France every civilian is a soldier; but practically every soldier is a civilian. So it is with our differences about criminal procedure. The idea at the back of the French system is that the law is a horrible scientific instrument, an intellectual rack or thumbscrew, a shocking necessity for tearing the truth out of people who are really conspiring against their kind. Its object is to find the truth, the actual and ultimate truth, and the sooner that unpleasant business is over and men can go back to Burgundy and dominoes, the better. Therefore the French Court attacks first the chief authority, the best-informed man, the true expert witness in the case—the criminal. It bullies and bothers and entraps him till he tells the truth, which nobody else can tell, and there is an end of it. The idea at the back of the English system of law is that the whole thing is a sort of royal or national sport like stag-hunting or fox-hunting. No doubt it is believed, and believed truly, that the general effect of this institution is to keep down crime. So it is believed, and believed truly, that the general effect of fox-hunting is to keep down foxes. It is the effect, but hardly the motive. The spirit of our law is that the prisoner must be protected by the rules of the game; if he can be caught and killed in accordance with those rules, no one has the slightest pity for him. The person whom we badger and pursue is the witness, the man who is merely helping human society; but such happens to be the rule of the game.

Now, whichever is right, the new rule about witnesses is wrong. If we are going to force the prisoner to go into the witness-box and be badgered, we ought to say that we are forcing him, and do the dirty and indispensable work openly, as the French Judges do. If we profess to protect him from questions he does not wish to answer, then we certainly ought to protect him from the worst and most damning question of all—"Dare you go into the witness-box?" As it is, we do force him to answer questions in the witness-box, as much as Dreyfus was forced to answer questions in the dock; we elaborately give him a liberty which he dares not exercise. I fear it is very like the Press Gang. It may or may not be fated that we must be snobs; but I think we might resist the tendency to be sneaks.

July 24, 1909

The Poetry of Everyday Life

Those two interesting gentlemen who combined to make up the personality of "D. S. Windell" deserve more attention than they could receive at their trial, or are likely to receive in their cells. Despite the pathetic appeals made by Mr. Herbert Gladstone and Mr. John M. Robertson, in their recent abolition of the Habeas

Corpus Act, I cannot bring myself to believe that warders are tender and wily psychologists who lie in wait for faint signs of improvement in a human soul. In other words, I know, as everybody else does, that terms of scientific imprisonment are not given to improve people, but to keep them out of the way. Therefore the souls of Mr. Robert and Mr. King[1] are likely to be neglected; and considerably less effort will be made to cure their faults than might have been made by their friends and families if they had remained outside. On this subject it is as well that we should talk no claptrap. A speaker in Parliament implied that he had no more pity for a particular criminal than for a tiger. That is a conceivable position, though quite anti-Christian. Let him lock up a tiger behind bars, but do not let him pretend that he is waiting to see when it will evolve into a domestic cat.

Let us return, however, to those beautiful objects, the souls of Mr. Robert and his partner. They are of great significance in our time; because, unlike most crimes, their crime marks not only a moral, but an intellectual revolt. Both men made pleas founded on certain modern thoughts and emotions, of which we have heard very much in modern plays, novels, and newspapers. Robert appealed to the pure sense of adventure; he suggested that he had acted by the same impulse which moves a certain type of man, politician, or pirate, to raid an Empire or seize an island in the Pacific. He was an adventurer in the noble as well as in the mean sense. He claimed, in effect, to be the true Imperialist, the kind of man who has made our England what she is. Like many who make the same claim, he seems to have been of Oriental extraction, and to have been by nature nomadic and impatient of all rooted responsibilities. When a little gutterboy, who is really hungry, steals an apple and admits that he has been reading penny dreadfuls, those unlucky forms of literature are always sternly denounced by the magistrate and keenly

[1] Both had perpetrated a fraud against the London and South-Western Bank (Ltd.) by cashing banknotes that had been stolen.

persecuted in the Press. When Robert, who was not hungry, stole an enormous sum of money and openly appealed to the romance of the modern adventurer, we ought, in order to be consistent, to put it to the account of the more educated works which have in our time flaunted before the imagination of the middle classes filibustering and the poetry of mad finance. The magistrates ought to talk sternly about Mr. Rudyard Kipling and Mr. Cutcliffe Hyne. If a penny dreadful leads to stealing a penny apple, a six-shilling dreadful is just as likely to lead to stealing considerably more than six shillings.

Mr. King stands as the opposite type, the type that is represented by our unadventurous plays and novels; all the grey novels about grey slums, all the drab novels about drab suburbs, all the modern attempt to make art out of the mere fact of monotony. If books of the Kipling school are the penny dreadfuls of the first type of criminal, books of the Gissing school are the penny dreadfuls of the other type. For this man complained simply that he could no longer tolerate the mere grinding dullness of his duties; that to stand shovelling out vast sums and drawing a mean salary had been too much, not merely for his conscience, but for his nerves. Something in his soul had snapped. We have had both these types in all modern books, and have been very fond of them: it must now be seen how we like them in real life.

These are, at least, the two types that we have to fear; the adventurer of commerce, who will be content with nothing except adventures, and the drudge of commerce, who may suddenly rebel against his drudgery. What is the cure for both; or is there any cure for either? The approximate cure exists, but it has been neglected so long that people call it a paradox. A friend of mine has made game of me in a recent book for saying that lamp-posts are poetical; that common things, the boots I wear or the chair I sit on, if they once are understood, can satisfy the most gigantic imagination. I can only adhere with stubborn simplicity to my position. The boots I wear are, I will not say beautiful upon the mountains, but, at least, highly symbolic in the street, being the boots of one that bringeth good news. The chair I sit on is really romantic—nay, it is heroic, for it is eternally in danger. The lamp-posts are poetical; not merely from accidental, but from essential causes. It is not merely the softening, sentimental associations that belong to lamp-posts, the beautiful fact that aristocrats were hanged from them, or that intoxicated old gentlemen embrace them: the lamp-post really has the whole poetry of man, for no other creature can lift a flame so high and guard it so well. You may think all this irrelevant to the case of Mr. King and Mr. Robert. That is just where you make a mistake. This doctrine of the visible divinity in daily or domestic objects, this doctrine of the household gods, so old that it seems new, is the only answer to the otherwise crushing arguments of Mr. King and Mr. Robert. Our modern mistake has been, not that we encouraged the adventurous poetry that inflamed the soul of Mr. Robert, but that we have neglected altogether that religious and domestic poetry which might have lightened and sweetened the task of Mr. King. From the beginning there have two kinds of poetry; the poetry of looking out of the window, and the poetry of looking in at the window. There was the song of the hunter going forth at morning, when the wilderness was so much lovelier than the hut. And there was the song of the hunter coming home at evening, when the hut was so much livelier than the wilderness or the world. The first is expressed quite feverishly in modern literature; there is a mad itch for travel. We talk of the English as if they were the Gypsies. We talk of the Empire as if it were a vagabond caravan; as if the sun never set on it because the sun never knew where to find it. Our literature has done enough, and more than enough, for adventure and the adventurers; it has filled the soul of the Oriental Mr. Robert to the brim. But it has done nothing at all for the needs of Mr. King. It has done nothing for Piety, for the sacredness of simple tasks and evident obligations. There is nothing in recent literature to make anyone feel that sweeping a room is fine, as in George Herbert, or that upon every pot in Jerusalem shall be written "Holy unto the Lord." Only a strong imagination, perhaps, could have felt Mr. King's work in a bank as poetical. Undoubtedly, it was poetical. Had his fancy been forcible enough he might, in the act of shoveling out three golden sovereigns, have thought how one might mean a holiday in high mountains, and another an engagement-ring, and another the rescue of a poor man from oppressive rent. Mr. King might have handed out money with magnanimous gestures, as if his hands were full of flowers or wheat or great goblets of wine. He might have felt that he was giving men stars and sunsets, gardens and good children. But that he should feel all this (though it is strictly true) is a too severe demand on his imagination as an individual. Nothing reminded him of that. The bank did not look at all like that. And the books that he read at home could not help him; because modern books have abandoned the idea that there is any poetry in duty. It is useless now to say that desks are dreary and trains ugly: you have created a society in which millions must sit at desks and travel in trains. You must either produce a literature and a ritual which can regard desks and trains as symbolic like ploughs and ships, or you must be prepared for the emergence of a new artistic class who will blow up trains and desks with dynamite.

July 31, 1909

Pessimism about England

I see that Lord Curzon has been making a speech at my old school, and, since my absence from town did not allow me to hear it, I think I have at least the right to criticise it. There should be in these matters a division of labour, or, if you will, a division of pleasure. Some should have the rapture of hearing these speeches, and others the calmer joy of contradicting what they have not heard. As far as I can make out, Lord Curzon has joined the ranks of those who are at last repudiating Mr. Rudyard Kipling. So many people are repudiating Mr. Rudyard Kipling that I really feel that I ought to rush to his rescue. His last poem in the *Morning Post* was certainly a very bad poem; but we have all written bad poems. At least, I know that I would rather read Mr. Kipling's last poem even twice, nay, positively three times, than endure so much as one glimpse of the first five words of many poems that I wrote in my youth. The question, of course, is not merely literary. The point raised by the recent critics of Mr. Kipling, the point hinted at, I think, by Lord Curzon in his speech at St. Paul's School, was the alleged pessimism of Mr. Kipling; the suddenness and shrillness of his wail over the certain decline of England. Lord Curzon, as far as I know, did not mention Mr. Kipling's name, but I cannot doubt that he was in part denouncing Mr. Kipling's pessimism. He said that there was too much of the spirit of decrying ourselves abroad in the land at the moment. At the same time, one of the oldest and boldest champions of Kipling, the distinguished Fabian who signs himself "Hubert" in the *Manchester Sunday Chronicle*, has also turned upon his master and rent him. In fact, Mr. Rudyard Kipling, having been kicked by Radicals for cracking us up, is now to be kicked by his fellow-Imperialists for running us down.

Now I have no instinctive, no emotional objection to any Imperialist poet being kicked. But I think he ought to be kicked on correct philosophical principles, and for the right reason. It is not wrong either to crack your country up or to run it down, if you do either from a clean and patriotic motive. There is a place for both exercises. In poetry it is best to crack England up. In politics it is nine times out of ten best to run her down; for then she may begin to behave herself. But the real objection to much of Mr. Kipling's work has nothing to do with either one or the other. The weakness in his work is pride, which may be optimistic or pessimistic, but is always weak. Tamburlaine, in Marlowe, is optimistic and arrogant; Timon of Athens is pessimistic and arrogant. Schopenhauer was a conceited pessi-

mist. Mrs. Eddy is a conceited optimist. The question is not
whether a man feels well or ill: it is whether he feels superior.
A man may quite reasonably regard himself as a jolly good
fellow. He may at the same time quite consistently regard himself
as a miserable sinner. The evil comes in when he thinks himself
too good a fellow for fellowship. The evil comes in when he
thinks himself so very miserable a sinner that his misery is more
important than his sin. The good man is welcome whether at
the moment he is sad or glad; but what is utterly intolerable is
the Best Man—the man who is consciously better than others.
Perhaps that is why the young man at weddings is called "the
Best Man," because he is secure, supercilious, and solitary like
Satan. The bridegroom, on the other hand, is the Good Man,
because he is divinely distracted, and full of holy fear. I do not
vouch for the historical truth of this derivation. I have heard
others. Some people will tell you that the best man is so called
because he was the best warrior of the tribe in the times when
women were married by capture. But you will pay no attention
to that sort of bosh, I hope. Women never were married by
capture. They always pretended they were; as they do now.

The other day I came across a pamphlet of that peculiar sect
which tries to prove that the Anglo-Saxons, whoever they are,
are the Lost Ten Tribes, whoever they were. They must have
got very thoroughly lost in Palestine to turn up in the German
Ocean; it is rather as if a baby got lost in Battersea Park and was
found at the police-station in Hong-Kong. But when I read this
strange document I suddenly realised what is really the matter
with Mr. Rudyard Kipling. He is not an Imperialist; he is an
Anglo-Israelite. His error is not that he blesses Englishmen or
curses them, but that he blesses and curses them as the Chosen
Race, instead of blessing or cursing them as a Christian nation
in the comity of Christian nations. The argument in my little
Anglo-Israelite pamphlet was simple and pathetic. It was that
Israel was promised an empire and that England had an empire;
therefore, England was Israel. That anybody else had ever had
an empire did not seem to cross the writer's mind. Nor does it

ever seem to cross Mr. Kipling's. These two earnest Ango-Israelites never seem to remember that we should never have inherited the notion of an Empire except from that Christian continent from which they cut themselves off. They never reflect that Imperialism can hardly be a purely Anglo-Saxon thing, since it is not even a purely Anglo-Saxon word.

The truth is, of course, that the notion of an Empire has come to the English at last in a highly battered condition, having been tossed about from one nation to another ever since the fall of Rome. Except the Swiss I can hardly think of any nation so dull or sensible as not to have had an Empire at some time. Even the nations that are only just big enough to be called nations (like Belgium and Holland) are quite big enough to have colonies and dependencies and Empire-builders and mine-owners and Levantine financiers, and all that makes a people great.

If I went in for the problem of the Lost Ten Tribes, I should say that the Ten Tribes were England, France, Germany, Austria, Italy, Spain, Portugal, Russia, Greece, and Sweden. That is what one might call being lost on a large scale. But however it was exactly that the tribes got mislaid, my purpose is served in pointing out that Anglo-Israelite insanity which is the root error of Kipling and Kiplingism. It is not that the Jingo poet praises England too much. One cannot praise England too much, any more than one can praise a buttercup too much. But if I praise one buttercup while burning all other buttercups as weeds, then that is idolatry. The Kiplingite praises his country, not with too much ardour, but with an implied denial of the existence of other countries in the same quality and degree. He is right to praise his country because it is his own; but he is wrong to praise it as if it were the only country that could be praised. Patriotism should be a passion—like first love, or a woman's pride in a baby; that is, it should be special and fastidious in the particular case, but quite vulgar and universal in the general character. Kiplingite Imperialism tries to make it the passion of a man who should fall in love with the moon. It seeks to make English patriotism a sublime monstrosity among other patriotisms, something that no one has ever felt before. That attempt to create new passions in which our brethren have no part is the beginning of all madness and of all decay. It is well to be alone sometimes, with love or with religion. But there is a degree of evil insolence which is not even content to be lonely if it thinks that other men can be lonely also. It would like to be isolated in isolation.

August 7, 1909

Slander in the Allusive Way

There are three ways in which a statement, especially a disputable statement, can be placed before mankind. The first is to assert it by avowed authority; this is done by deities, the priests of deities, oracles, minor poets, parents and guardians, and men who have "a message to their age." The second way is to prove it by reason; this was done by the mediaeval schoolmen, and by some of the early and comparatively forgotten men of science. It is now quite abandoned. The third method is this: when you have neither the courage to assert a thing nor the capacity to prove it, you allude to it in a light and airy style, as if somebody else had asserted and proved it already. Thus the first method is to say, "Pigs do fly in heaven; I have had a vision of heaven, and you have not." The second method is to say, "Come down to my little place in Essex, and I will show you pigs flying about like finches and building nests in the elms." Both these positions require a certain valour to sustain them, and are now, therefore, generally dropped. The third method, which is usually adopted, is to say, "Professor Gubbins belongs to the old school of scientific criticism, and cannot but strike us as limited in this age of wireless telegraphy and aerial swine"; or "Doubtless we should be as much surprised at the deeds of our descendants as would an Ancient Briton at a motor-car or a flying pig, or any such common sight of our streets." In short, this third method consists in referring to the very thing that is in dispute as if it were now beyond dispute. This is known as the Restrained or Gentlemanly method; it is used by company promoters, by professors of hair-dressing and the other progressive arts, and especially by journalists like myself.

There is one infamous use of the allusive method against which a protest must be made. It consists in gliding gracefully over a subject as if we all knew about it and it was very horrid; whereas, in fact, most of us know nothing about it, and the few who do know may be finding it very nice. Thus, if one wrote: "On the private life of the Mayor of Dulcam we will not dwell"; or, "Of the moral state of East Dudsey little need be said," these would be extreme examples of this wanton and baseless style of slander. But there are real cases almost as unreasonable; I came across one a few minutes ago.

In the *Review of Reviews* for this month there is a very angry account of the Church Pageant, of which I once wrote in this place. I do not know whether Mr. Stead wrote it himself; as I have a very warm regard for Mr. Stead, I hope not. The writer complains that the High Churchmen have represented the monasteries as popular with the poor and the agents of Thomas Cromwell as brutal. As the people who represent this are not the High Churchmen, but merely all the good historians of our time, the organisers of the Pageant are not likely to be much moved by the complaint. There was not one touch in the scene of convent pillage which could not be as clearly justified from a Whig and Protestant history like Green's[1] as from Lingard[2] or

[1] John R. Green (1837–1883), the author of *A Short History of the English People* (1874), which he expanded into *A History of the English People* (1877–1880).
[2] John Lingard (1771–1851) was an English historian. He wrote *The Antiquities of the Anglo-Saxon Church* (1806) and *History of England to 1688* (1819–1830).

from Creighton.[3] But it is not of this that I wish to speak; it is of a singular and sinister example of what I have called the unfair allusive method. The writer says—

> The first part of the Pageant that dealt with the earlier history of the Church was not open to any other criticism than that it was extremely dull. It was perhaps inevitable that Thomas à Becket should have been posed as a Saint—that is one of the pious fictions that must be accepted, even by those who knew the manner of man he was.

Now what would Mr. Stead think of me if I used that vague and lurid phrase about any of the Puritan heroes? Suppose I said, "John Bunyan is always paraded as a pious and moral figure; and we must keep quiet even when we know the truth about his moral character." And when I had sown this *suggestio falsi*[4] broadcast among ill-informed people, suppose it turned out that I meant no more than that Bunyan was excitable. Now nobody can possibly say anything worse of St. Thomas of Canterbury than that he was excitable and politically troublesome. Many of us think that he was troublesome largely because he was right; but that is a fair matter for dispute. But all of us think—it is a matter quite beyond dispute—that there was nothing in Becket's character that prevented him from being a good man and a saint. It is not denied, it cannot be denied, that he was charitable to the poor and widely beloved by them, continent and self-restrained in his bodily life, passionately sincere in his social and religious convictions, and courageous enough to confront death in defence of them. If these things together do not make up a good man, the words have no working meaning, and yet, by using the Allusive or Gentlemanly method, how smoothly and swiftly it can be suggested that his name covers the most monstrous iniquities! The truth is that we are very unfortunate in

[3] Mandell Creighton (1843–1901), professor of Ecclesiastical History at Cambridge, Bishop of Peterborough, then of London. He was author of *History of the Papacy during the Reformation Period* (five volumes, 1882–1894).

[4] This may be translated as "a suggestion of that which is false".

our popular history; because it is not only fixed and pedantic, but it is the pedantry of exploded partisanship. An historical character stands before us not as he was, and not even as most people thought him, but as he appeared to some particular section of his friends or enemies that (through some historical accident) happened to say the last word about him. Thomas à Becket is a very strong instance. He was adored during his lifetime, and steadily for four hundred years afterwards, by the great populace of England. He was then denied and desecrated by one particular despot, for the quite clearly expressed reason that he had resisted despotism. The good Radical in the *Review of Reviews* is not expressing a Radical view of Becket, or even a modern view of Becket. He is simply expressing King Henry the Eighth's view of Becket, the violently monarchical view imposed by a Prince who wished to make the monarchy absolute master of souls as well as bodies. This autocratic condemnation of the saint happened to be the last public thing said or done about him; and therefore the innocent Radical on the *Review of Reviews* swallows it down like so much milk.

One sees everywhere the same repetition of old watchwords which mean nothing to those who repeat them. In the same article the writer says: "Only once in its later history did the Church of England stand for liberty, and the scene representing the Trial of the Seven Bishops[5] was one of the most spirited in the Pageant." Now, if one said that the Seven Bishops stood for the British Constitution or for Parliamentary Government that would be reasonable enough; but it is stretching a word very far to say that they stood for liberty. But I have a dark and mystical, but most deep-rooted conviction which I must only whisper in your ear: I have a rooted belief that the man in the *Review of Reviews* had quite forgotten what the Seven Bishops did stand

---

[5] The Trial of the Seven Bishops took place in June of 1688. The seven bishops were tried for seditious libel after having refused to read publicly the Declaration of Indulgence of James II which suspended the laws against Roman Catholics and dissenters; they were eventually acquitted.

for. Now let us suppose the affair of the Seven Bishops repeated exactly with other actors; it would be something like this. All Congregationalists as such are under penal laws; any Congregationalist minister in England can be hanged, drawn, and quartered. King Edward VII. becomes Congregationalist and asks the Anglican Bishops to read out a paper, of doubtful Constitutional force, offering to free Congregationalists from dungeon and gibbet, to give them civil rights, and to give the same to Unitarians and Ethical Societies, which are also under a ban. The Bishops, who are all practically despotists, passionately profess that they will obey the King in anything political, but that their religion commands them to go on persecuting Conregationalists and forbids them to propose toleration. Perhaps the King might be violating the Constitution and the Bishops accidentally defending it; but would not "liberty" be a rather strange word for what the Bishops were defending?

August 14, 1909

Being True to Oneself

Why is it nowadays considered a horrible insult to accuse a philosopher of holding his own philosophy? The people who call themselves modern thinkers are an extraordinary race. A modern thinker not only will not state his own opinion in clear, straightforward English, but he is hideously affronted if you do it for him. It is, apparently, wrong to classify a man, even apart from whether you condemn him. Yet surely there is no evident disgrace in belonging to any class; the only disgrace (as the exquisite poetic insight of the populace declares) consists in being "no class." Thus people will say just now, "This coalheaver

loved his mother; was he not more truly a gentleman than, etc."
To which the obvious answer is, "No; he was something more
important than a gentleman, but he was not a gentleman, any
more than he was a Marquis or a Master of Arts or a member
of the Privy Council. A gentleman is a particular kind of man,
who does not always love his mother and who frequently detests
his elder brother and his father." But this irrational mixture of
meaning, which is irritating in the case of classes, becomes absolutely maddening in the matter of political or moral convictions.
We are always hearing of Protectionists who are true Free Traders, of Monarchists who are true Republicans, of Little Eng-
landers who are true Imperialists, of pessimists who are true
optimists, of heathens who are true Christians. Suppose I commit myself to the statement that Oliver Cromwell, being an
Independent, was not a Churchman, someone is sure to say, "Is
the title of Churchman to be intolerantly denied to one of the
wisest and bravest of men?" If I venture to observe that Herbert
Spencer was very much opposed to Socialism, somebody will
certainly cry out, "Has not a man who toiled for the triumph
of knowledge as good a right to be called a Socialist as any, etc."
Or if I say somewhere that modern Germany is not a republic,
there will come a chorus of its admirers crying out, "And why
is the word republic to the all-producing mother-root of the
heroic Northern nations refused?" Or if I should innocently
allude to the general impression that Switzerland is not an island,
there will come a clamour of high-minded protests. "Not an
island! The land of aspiration and liberty! The house and tomb
of William Tell! Who is this insolent Fleet Street hack who denies
the name of island to one of the most, etc." That is the kind of
thing. I assure you it happens to me every day.

The other day I had cause to comment somewhere on an
interesting utterance by Mrs. Besant, in which that able and
earnest lady explained (not, I think, for the first time) her view
that although a state of greater economic equality should be
effected, it could not, or should not, be effected by the actual
poor who suffer from our present one. The change, she sug-

gested, should be made in the interests of the poor, but by the efforts of the comfortable; the latter, she explained, have better hearts and better brains, more leisure and more love. I simply noted down the manifest fact that this view of Mrs. Besant's (which is a perfectly rational one) is identical with the old argument against democracy, that the needy or desperate tend to be morally inferior. To say this was, of course, almost to repeat Mrs. Besant's own words. Yet what a whirlwind of lamentation and protest did I discover that I had loosened! I was told with tearful indignation that Mrs. Besant was high-minded, spiritual, sympathetic, pure, wise, and loving, and therefore (apparently) could not possibly have meant what she certainly said. An anonymous person in Bath wrote long letters to the newspapers to explain what sublime things the distinguished Theosophist had written about self-sacrifice. Another gentleman (his name, I am gratified to say, was Boger) sent me a postcard protesting against my imputing unrighteousness to an honest woman. What on earth can one do with people like that? What was the use of saying again and again that I had only described the honest woman's opinion as being what it evidently was? How explain to the bewildered Boger that I never imputed unrighteousness to anybody, that I only imputed anti-democracy to an avowed anti-democrat? In what words could one point out that an anti-democrat is not a goblin—that to accuse a lady of being anti-democratic is not to accuse her of having horns or the wings of a bat; that a great many people are anti-democratic; probably most people, or else we should have a democracy? No; they were all off on the wild dance of words without meaning of which I spoke at the beginning of this article. Mrs. Besant not a democrat, when she is so eloquent and idealistic! Switzerland not an island when it is full of such splendid mountains!

As I say, these things are always coming my way. I once wrote in an American paper, apropos of Christian Science, something to this effect—that I did not doubt the Science, but only the Christianity. I did not doubt that in practice mental cures were possible; but I could not see that in theory there was anything in common between Mrs. Eddy's philosophy and any of the Christian fundamentals. I thought this, and still think it, a reasonable and polite position. If a man brought me a cure which he called Jewish Science, and I found that it consisted entirely of pork and polytheism, I should, without throwing any doubts on the cure, express surprise that he had called it Jewish. If a thing called Moslem Science was based on denying the unity of God, or if a thing called Buddhist Science was based on the denial of Reincarnation, I should not denounce the medicines, but I should think they had very queer names. Now Christian Science is certainly based on the two ideas that there is no real flesh and no real pain. And Christianity is certainly based on the idea that the highest reality in the universe assumed flesh and endured pain. Such a distinction is surely not an impertinent one to offer. But when I offered it I received a flood of letters and newspaper cuttings from Christian Scientists, who seemed, in some unthinkable way, to think they were insulted. They seemed to suppose, because I had said that they were not Christians, that I thought they were burglars, perjurers, bigamists, black-mailers, assassins, cannibals, and fraudulent trustees. They sent me long lists of the cures that I had never disputed, and long refutations of the slanders that I had never heard of, far less endorsed. I had never denounced their practices; I had not even denounced their theory. I had stated their theory, almost exactly as they stated it themselves, and then pointed out that it was obviously inconsistent with another theory, which I happen to hold. So by this time I have begun to allow for the latitude and longitude of the sacred island of Switzerland to get past that seagirt crag as quickly as possible. There is little good in wasting one's time in that world of mental carelessness and confusion; and yet I have wasted the last hour or so in writing about it in this place. Something—a war or a revolution, or (most probable of all) a religious persecution on a large scale—will force us all to take the trouble of knowing what we mean. We shall realise one fine morning that the words "democrat" or "Jew," or "gentleman" or "Christian" are words just like "hat" and "dog," and "post" and "pork." They describe certain separate objects; they are not words like "snark" or "boojum," to be used merely as vague Society compliments.

August 21, 1909

Succeeding in Journalism

All journalists, I suppose, are asked by all sorts of people how to succeed in journalism; even those who have not succeeded. Moreover, even if the success be genuine of its kind, it by no means follows that the successful man is the man who knows most about it. It is one thing to do something, and quite another to know how it is done. But for such a distinction authors and critics would both perish miserably. There is no advice to be given to young journalists except the ordinary advice which is to be given to human beings. That is, not to get drunk, but to prefer even drunkenness to drinking. Not to be insolent, but to prefer insolence to servility. To write in a legible hand, and to make notes of everything which one cannot remember. These principles apply to a journalist, but, as they also apply to any tolerably efficient tinker or tailor, or bank clerk, or even burglar, they do not meet the particular demand which is so often made on us.

There is only one piece of advice that is generally given by all advisers on this subject: the advice to write with reference to the tone of the paper for which the contribution is meant. To study *Tit-Bits* when one writes for *Tit-Bits*, to steep oneself in the *Athenaeum* when one pants for participation in that fervid enterprise—that is the one piece of positive counsel which is always given to the young journalist. And even that is wrong. Many a man has succeeded simply because he wrote all the wrong articles for the wrong papers. If his remarks had appeared in the right place they would have appeared ordinary. But as they always appeared in the wrong place they seemed quite brilliant. My own effect, such as it is, is entirely due to this simple process. I began by reviewing books, about painting, and sculpture. Into these I introduced disquisitions on theology or folklore, disquisitions which would have seemed quite ordinary in the *Hibbert Journal*, but which attracted attention when abruptly introduced apropos of Etruscan Pottery, or "The Treatment of Poplars by Corot." Very often, while the journalist is doing his best to imitate the tone of the paper, the editor (torn with despair) is trying in vain to find someone who will alter the tone of the paper. A man might actually succeed in journalism by writing articles exactly appropriate to all the journals, and then putting them all into the wrong envelopes. Just when people were beginning to feel the *Spectator* a little dull, it might be redeemed by an article originally intended for *Pick-me-up*. Or again, some solid householder who had begun to feel that *Pink Peeps* was going rather too far might be reclaimed to his allegiance by an earnest essay which was written for the *Pragmatist*. I do not advise the young journalist to rely too recklessly upon this tip of the wrong envelopes. But I really think that it is about as safe as the opposite maxim that is so universally preached to him.

There are, however, occasions when one must fall back on the simpler view that what is suitable for one paper is not suitable for another. For instance, a gentleman has just written me a long letter, full of the frankest evidences of intellectual energy and honesty. He is so kind as to say that he knows that I am busy, that he will not expect a personal reply, but will be gratified if I refer to his objections in any public print. Now, as this admirable correspondent discussed in his letter almost everything there is, from the Trinity to tram-cars, he ought to understand that, even if I did deal with him in journalism, I could not do it all in one paper. Some parts of my answer would be proper to the *Church Times*, others to the *Clarion*. Some of my feelings I might express in the *Whitehall Review*; other feelings only in the *Billingsgate Bloater*, or whatever be the organ of that district. My friend and enemy must make up his mind to find me turning up all over the place: he might find fragments of my reply in the *Tailor and Cutter*, and other portions of it in the *Licensed Victuallers' Gazette*. What is left over I may possibly put in the magazines devoted to history and philosophy. There is only one part of my correspondent's remarks which I deem to be very appropriate to this paper, and that is the part which refers to the attitude taken up by myself and others in regard to certain problems of international protest and international diplomacy. The writer wishes to prove (I quote his words) "that the vast majority of Freethinkers of all classes are as democratic as you are and a lot more effectively." He proceeds: "For instance, I was on Sunday afternoon in Trafalgar Square, there to assist in protesting against the visit to this country of the Tsar—the most loathsome, anti-social tyrant on this earth, whose boots this Liberal Government cheerfully licks." He goes on to say that he saw no Anglican or Catholic divines protesting, but only Freethinkers like Hyndman[1] and Quelch. And he asks me what I think of that, as I call myself a democrat and a hater of tyranny.

Well, I also will ask a question. What would he think of six Zulus who recklessly defied the power of the Emperor of China? And what would he think of one Zulu who was slightly indifferent to the Chinese question and inclined to concentrate on the Zulu question? How much would he admire a group of Esquimaux who, with wild courage, refused to obey the King of Siam? To what degree would his blood kindle when he heard of some tribe in central Australia saying what it liked about the Lama of Tibet?

Is there, after all, anything so extraordinarily heroic about denouncing the Sovereign of a foreign country that it should be held up as the high-water mark of the magnificent audacity of free-thought? If I were a Russian I have very little doubt that I

[1] Henry M. Hyndman (1842–1921), a British marxist and socialist, was the founder of the Social Democratic Federation.

should be a revolutionary Russian. But as I am an Englishman, I find myself fully occupied in being a revolutionary Englishman. To denounce English abuses in England seems to me more appropriate than to denounce Russian abuses in England. It is certainly more dangerous.

A man must settle such questions by a sense of proportion: that sense which sounds so vague, but which is, in fact, so vivid and unmistakable. There are differences of degree which are as emphatic as a difference in kind. For instance, if a landlady told a lodger that she objected to cats and dogs, but did not mind a bird, she would still have a right to complain if she found the room occupied by an ostrich. In such cases proportion is highly practical. By proportion alone we must judge whether England runs most risk of neglecting the moral needs of other nations, or of dangerously neglecting her own moral needs. Among which are to be counted the need for modesty and self-knowledge. For my part, I think we have indulged far too much in safe foreign enthusiasms. Righteous indignation can be carried too far, like charity. But it is not here a question of carrying either too far. It is a question of indulging them as pleasures, without paying anything for them. A man should at last pay for his charity with his money. A man should at last pay for his anger with his blood. At least, there should be a reasonable risk that he will have to give if he is compassionate, and fight if he is angry. There is only one country in the world where a man may always pay this price for his passions, and that is his own. The others he may well let alone.

August 28, 1909

The Centenary of Tennyson

I have been glancing over two or three of the appreciations of
Tennyson appropriate to his centenary, and have been struck
with a curious tone of coldness towards him in almost all quarters. Now this is really a very peculiar thing. For it is a case of
coldness to quite brilliant and unquestionable literary merit.
Whether Tennyson was a great poet I shall not discuss. I understand that one has to wait about eight hundred years before
discussing that; and my only complaint against the printers of
this paper is that they will not wait even for much shorter periods. But that Tennyson was a poet is as solid and certain as that
Roberts is a billiard-player. That Tennyson was an astonishingly
good poet is as solid and certain as that Roberts is an astonishingly good billiard-player. Even in these matters of art there are
some things analogous to matters of fact. It is no good disputing
about tastes—partly because some tastes are beyond dispute. If
anyone tells me that—

> There is fallen a splendid tear
> From the passion-flower at the gate;[1]

or that—

> Tears from the depth of some divine despair[2]

is not fine poetry, I am quite prepared to treat him as I would
one who said that grass was not green or that I was not corpulent.
And by all common chances Tennyson ought to be preserved
as a pleasure—a sensuous pleasure if you like, but certainly a
genuine one. There is no more reason for dropping Tennyson
than for dropping Virgil. We do not mind Virgil's view of

---

[1] See Tennyson's *Maud*, I, xxii, 59.
[2] See Tennyson's *The Princess*, iv, 40.

Augustus, nor need we mind Tennyson's view of Queen Victoria. Beauty is unanswerable, in a poem as much as in a woman. There were Victorian writers whose art is not perfectly appreciable apart from their enthusiasm. Kingsley's "Yeast" is a fine book, but not quite so fine a book as it seemed when one's own social passions were still yeasty. Browning and Coventry Patmore are justly admired, but they are most admired where they are most agreed with. But "St. Agnes' Eve," is an unimpeachably beautiful poem, whether one believes in St. Agnes or detests her. One would think that a man who had thus left indubitably good verse would receive natural and steady gratitude, like a man who left indubitably good wine to his nephew, or indubitably good pictures to the National Portrait Gallery. Nevertheless, as I have said, the tone of all the papers, modernist or old-fashioned, has been mainly frigid. What is the meaning of this?

I will ask permission to answer this question by abruptly and even brutally changing the subject. My remarks must, first of all, seem irrelevant even to effrontery; they shall prove their relevance later on. In turning the page of one of the papers containing such a light and unsympathetic treatment of Tennyson, my eyes catch the following sentence: "By the light of modern science and thought, we are in a position to see that each normal human being in some way repeats historically the life of the human race." This is a very typical modern assertion; that is, it is an assertion for which there is not and never has been a single spot or speck of proof. We know precious little about what the life of the human race has been; and none of our scientific conjectures about it bear the remotest resemblance to the actual growth of a child. According to this theory, a baby begins by chipping flints and rubbing sticks together to find fire. One so often sees babies doing this. About the age of five the child, before the delighted eyes of his parents, founds a village community. By the time he is eleven it has become a small city state, the replica of ancient Athens. Encouraged by this, the boy proceeds, and before he is fourteen has founded the Roman

Empire. But now his parents have a serious set-back. Having watched him so far, not only with pleasure, but with a very natural surprise, they must strengthen themselves to endure the spectacle of decay. They have now to watch their child going through the decline of the Western Empire and the Dark Ages. They see the invasion of the Huns and that of the Norsemen chasing each other across his expressive face. He seems a little happier after he has "repeated" the Battle of Chalons and the unsuccessful Siege of Paris; and by the time he comes to the twelfth century, his boyish face is as bright as it was of old when he was "repeating" Pericles or Camillus.[3] I have no space to follow this remarkable demonstration of how history repeats itself in the youth; how he grows dismal at twenty-three to represent the end of Mediaevalism, brightens because the Renaissance is coming, darkens again with the disputes of the later Reformation, broadens placidly through the thirties as the rational eighteenth century, till at last, about forty-three, he gives a great yell and begins to burn the house down, as a symbol of the French Revolution. Such (we shall all agree) is the ordinary development of a boy.

Now, seriously, does anyone believe a word of such bosh? Does anyone think that a child will repeat the periods of human history? Does anyone ever allow for a daughter in the Stone Age, or excuse a son because he is in the fourth century B.C. Yet the writer who lays down this splendid and staggering lie calmly says that "by the light of modern science and thought we are in a position to *see*" that it is true. "Seeing" is a strong word to use of our conviction that icebergs are in the north, or that the earth goes round the sun. Yet anybody can use it of any casual or crazy biological fancy seen in some newspaper or suggested in some debating club. This is the rooted weakness of our time. Science, which means exactitude, has become the mother of inexactitude.

---

[3] Marcus Furius Camillus (447–365 B.C.) was a Roman patrician, censor and successful general.

This is the failure of the epoch, and this explains the partial failure of Tennyson. He was par excellence the poet of popular science—that is, of all such cloudy and ill-considered assertions as the above. He was the perfectly educated man of classics and the half-educated man of science. No one did more to encourage the colossal blunder that the survival of the fittest means the survival of the best. One might as well say that the survival of the fittest means the survival of the fattest. Tennyson's position has grown shaky because it rested not on any clear dogmas old or new, but on two or three temporary, we might say desperate, compromises of his own day. He grasped at Evolution, not because it was definite, but because it was indefinite; not because it was daring, but because it was safe. It gave him the hope that man might one day be an angel, and England a free democracy; but it soothed him with the assurance that neither of these alarming things would happen just yet. Virgil used his verbal felicities to describe the eternal idea of the Roman Imperium. Tennyson used his verbal felicities for the accidental equilibrium of the British Constitution. "To spare the humble and war down the proud," is a permanent idea for the policing of this planet. But that freedom should "slowly broaden down from precedent to precedent" merely happens to be the policy of the English upper class; it has no vital sanction; it might be much better to broaden quickly. One can write great poetry about a truth or even about a falsehood, but hardly about a legal fiction. The misanthropic idea, as in Byron, is not a truth, but it is one of the immortal lies. As long as humanity exists, humanity can be hated. Wherever one shall gather by himself, Byron is in the midst of him. It is a common and recurrent mood to regard man as a hopeless Yahoo. But it is not a natural mood to regard man as a hopeful Yahoo, as the Evolutionists did, as a creature changing before one's eyes from bestial to beautiful, a creature whose tail has just dropped off while he is staring at a far-off divine event. This particular compromise between contempt and hope was an accident of Tennyson's time, and, like his liberal Conservatism, will probably never be found again. His weakness was not being old-fashioned or new-fashioned, but being fashionable. His feet were set on things transitory and untenable, compromises and compacts of silence. Yet he was so perfect a poet that I fancy he will still be able to stand, even upon such clouds.

September 4, 1909

Scepticism about Tradition

It seems that they have just dug up near Peshawar a casket containing bones of the great Buddha. A tradition as old as the sixth century recorded the burial-place, but tradition was for some time considered by European historians as the positive enemy of history. They said that fables had their origin among the ignorant, which, put into plain words, means that if everybody in a village says that the Squire is drowned in the horsepond, he must be somewhere else. But if the nineteenth century was the time of the destruction of legends, the twentieth century bids fair to be the time of the return of legends. It will be much more exciting to find out that half fairy-tales are history even than to find out that history is half fairy-tales. A little while ago they dug up the Labyrinth of King Minos in Crete; the good old maze of the Minotaur and Theseus and Ariadne. It was like hearing that people had dug up the roots of the great Beanstalk. It was like being told that learned men had at last found the sepulchre of Cinderella. Suppose the elegant château of the family of Barbazure[1] were investigated, and a selection of female skeletons really found there? Suppose the castle of the Carabas

_____

[1] Literally: blue beard. The castle of Bluebeard, who in Charles Perrault's tale killed a number of his wives.

family[2] were thoroughly quarried, and we exposed the skeleton of a cat with remarkable cerebral developments and a pair of old leather boots. This would certainly be great fun, but I do not very fiercely or fixedly expect this. The real mistake has been mixing up a fable with a legend; or a fairy-tale with a tradition. They are two totally different things. A fable is a thing that men make up because it is not true; a legend is a thing that men vaguely cling to because it is true. A tradition is always vague and dim, because it is the truth. A fairy-tale is always exact and clear, because it is fictitious. There are hundreds of tales of King Arthur or of Robin Hood; and you may mix them up as wildly as you will, because the men probably did exist at some time, and lived vague and varied human lives. But if you tell the tale of Puss in Boots to a child, you will soon discover that there is only one tale that you are allowed to tell. Fable is fiction which cannot be too sharp and clear; legend is memory which can hardly be too mixed and mellow. Now that science is at last beginning to attach decent importance to the mere memory of mankind, we shall not necessarily find the site of Bois Dormant or be troubled with the personal society of Rumpelstiltskin. But I shall be very much surprised if Tell does not return in triumph into Switzerland and Arthur into England.

Besides such unquestionable cases as the Labyrinth of King Minos, there is a singular stir of anti-scepticism in archaeology all around us. One gentleman believes he has found at Glastonbury the stone cup that was the Arthurian Grail. Others have found—in Anglesey, I think—female bones and ornaments that confirm the peasant legend of some thousand years. There seems sufficiently little doubt in this new instance of the bones of Buddha. The professors are beginning gravely to admit that a whole population may at least give some hazy indication of the history of their own valley. They are beginning dubiously to concede that a man unacquainted with anthropology may nevertheless give a kind of hint about the situation of his own family vault.

[2] The castle appears in Perrault's tale of *Puss in Boots*.

It is at least a great improvement on the attitude of the Early Victorian folklorists, who seemed to suppose that popular conversation and reminiscence all over the earth must consist almost entirely of mendacity. I think they must have been confused by the double sense of the Latin "trado"; they regarded tradition as a huge form of treason. Modern people sometimes complain of what they call an old-fashioned habit of assuming that children will always tell lies to their parents. Such an assumption would be bad; but not any worse than the scientific assumption that parents have always told lies to their children.

There are two kinds of tradition; and two kinds of mistake made about it. The first may be called the careless or secular tradition, like that of the Cretan Labyrinth; the second the careful or religious tradition, like that of the bones of Buddha. In the first case the author merely tells his son generally about the past glories of the country; and the actual relic in stone or brass is valuable only as a confirmation. Still, it is a confirmation. On that point the sceptic has committed a great deal of clumsy jocosity. He has jeered uproariously at the peasants who recite a tall story about William Tell, and then point to his bow as a proof. But the mistake is much worse in the case of the problem of such relics as those of Buddha. In the face of all reason the sceptics say that such relics are probably deceptive and unreal, because their adorers are superstitious. But even if they are superstitious, that is all the more reason for supposing that their relics are not unreal. The sceptics talk as if, to a Buddhist monk, one bone would be as good as another. But it is exactly because one bone is not as good as another that he troubles to have relics at all. "Are these bones really the bones of Buddha?" may be an interesting question to a scientist, but it is a practical question to a Buddhist. In such a case the devotee will be as realistic as possible; nay, he will be as sceptical as possible. The more he is fanatical, the less he will be credulous. There is, therefore, not the smallest difficulty in supposing that the actual bones of Buddha would be verified, set apart, and protected with as much scientific care as can be applied to anything in this world; more care than goes to the keeping of a first folio of Shakespeare or a stuffed Great Auk in a museum, or a palimpsest or a trade secret or an unparalleled meteoric stone. We do not doubt that a chip of red pottery in the British Museum is really Etruscan. We do not doubt that an old tooth examined by the Royal Society is truly that of a mastodon. We do not doubt it because, shapeless and trifling as it is to us, we know that great hierarchies of civilised men are passionately eager and careful to know that it is really an Etruscan chip or really a mastodon. But if a Buddhist or a monk of the Dark Ages were to see these things, he would roar with sceptical laughter, "Do you ask me to believe," the monk would say, "that anyone took the trouble to bring that useless bit of red stone all the way from Italy, when it is not miraculous? Why, of course, the thing is a fake! What was there to prevent your professor picking up any piece of a flower-pot in his back garden and calling that Etruscan?" An Indian or a Goth might quite sincerely and rationally speak like this; because he would not understand the abstract passion of modern science, and so could not believe that people were so careful with their specimens. So also we in the industrial civilisation do not understand the abstract passions of supernatural religion, and cannot believe that people have been so careful with their relics. We talk about the very things that must have been protected against fraud, like the Crown Jewels, as if they were things that had been kicked about from one dustbin to another. This is the second and worse of the two great blunders about tradition. The first is that when a man tells the tale of the maze of Minos, we actually think him a fool because he points to the maze itself in front of him. The second is that, because three million men would have died in torments to find the real bones of Buddha, we deduce that they have probably put up with the bones of somebody else. It must be understood that I do not pin myself to the particular example; I know nothing of these particular bones. But it is often convenient to take a remote example in discussing a principle which applies much nearer home.

September 11, 1909

Taboos and Prohibitions

There was a time when a man would sail to strange islands or climb up into the hamlets hidden in high mountains, in order to find quaint old customs or strange superstitions still surviving. But this (I am glad to say) is rapidly becoming unnecessary. For nowadays it is not the old customs that are quaint, but the new customs. Superstitions are not surviving out of the past, but arriving out of the future. I do not need to sail to strange islands, for my own island is becoming quite strange enough for me. I am relieved with heartfelt joy of my previous duty of ascending steep precipices, for the ordinary ways of modern society are quite steep enough for anybody. The fads of the cultured grow every day more pleasingly identical with the habits of the barbarian. Why seek out a shaggy tribe of horsemen in Siberia who live only on mares' milk? Why, the nearest American millionaire very likely does the same. Why go to Ultima Thule to find real Highlanders living only on oatmeal and whisky? Be content with the first Earl and Countess among your friends: you will very likely find that the Countess is idealistic and lives on oatmeal, while the Earl, as a natural consequence, lives on whisky. Why seek in some huge yet secret desert of Arabia for that strange sect that holds wine in abhorrence? The next Bishop I meet may be an open and shameless teetotaler, giving scandal to the weak. The mountain (if I may so describe myself) need not go to Mahomet. Mahomet has come to the mountain; I am always meeting him at dinner. Why break through jungles to find black men who eat their meat raw, when the doctors may be telling us next year that white men ought to eat it raw? Why describe the dances of lightly clad Hottentots, when similar things are becoming so fashionable in the most exalted circles? And why search for the Missing Link, living on nuts and roots, when, by all accounts, the Superman (who is expected shortly) will do just the same. I abandon my project of emulating Captain Cook. By

389

THE ILLUSTRATED LONDON NEWS

merely sitting in an arm-chair and watching one's fellow-creatures progress, one may have all the exact sensations of a man travelling among savages.

For my part, I believe that this is how people really began to be savages. They progressed clean out of their clothes. They did so because they had already progressed clean out of their wits. They got some fad about food, and forgot how to cook it; they got some fad against houses, and forgot how to build them. They began to believe in doctors rather than in the wholesome tradition of the whole tribe. Over-civilisation and barbarism are within an inch of each other. And a mark of both is the power of medicine-men. But here, perhaps, an objection may be offered to this view. It may be said that with us these weird habits and abstentions are individual; whereas it is the mark of the barbarous tribe that they are always collective and coercive. It may be said that a man in the Siberian tribe drinking anything but mares' milk might be torn in pieces by six horses; and it might be urged, perhaps, that this seldom happens in London society. It may be said that the Countess eats oatmeal only as a private and partly insane person, but that the House of Lords does not officially eat oatmeal, it does not decree oatmeal as a part of its constitution. The tribe violently enforcing fantastic limitations; that (it may be said) is the real sign of savagery. Well, we are coming to that, too.

I invite the reader's attention to the following extract from an excellent English paper quoting from a well-known American one—

The war against the cigarette in the United States has been going one for some time past, but few people in this country realise the extent to which the American anti-cigarettists have impressed their views on public policy. The last Sunday edition of the *New York Times* to reach us contains some interesting facts relative to the matter—

"Eight States, speaking through their Legislators and their Governors, have said that the cigarette must go. In Tacoma they are even arresting smokers on the streets. Nobody has been able to buy a cigarette in Minnesota since midnight a week ago. More than a million were sold in Minneapolis alone the day before the law went into effect. Then the statute came down with a crash."

But what is the use of a statute's coming down with a crash on cigarettes that are no longer there?

"Ought sailors to smoke cigarettes?" is a question suggested by some further remarks of our contemporary—

"Strangely enough [it declares] the British Government keeps cigarettes aboard its war-ships to sell to its sailors, though the fact has been pretty well demonstrated that the excessive use of cigarettes is not conducive to good shooting or clear thinking. Here in this country we are a little more advanced. Like England, we sell cigarettes to our sailors, but we are apparently getting ready to stop it. The anti-cigarette specialists have long cried out against what they consider to be an act of Government criminality, and now the navy itself is beginning to swing into line."

Now, that is all pure barbarism; the unmistakable blind howl of the pack. Men must have wholly lost that instinct for individuality which is the crown of civilisation, that thing which we call freedom, if they can thus loosen all the tribal terrors against a thing like a cigarette. It is a mere wild taboo, imposed hypnotically by a few medicine-men. The physical danger of cigarette-smoking bears not the slightest proportion to such enormous and absurd spectacles of public panic. One might as well arrest people for walking about in the rain, a thing of which many a man has died. Possibly they will do that; perhaps we shall hear shortly that ten States of the Union have said through their Legislatures and their Governors that the rain must go. But what is a cigarette, what is it well known to be by every man who has ever seen one and whose mind is not influenced by the medicine-men? What are its effects as we actually know them? A cigarette is a thing which the overwhelming majority of our smoking acquaintances consume frequently, but in such a manner as to make it absolutely impossible to observe in them any effect of it at all. A fairly large minority consume it so that one may roughly form the opinion that they would be better in health if they smoked less, just as one forms the opinion that they would be better if they took a shade more exercise or ate a shade less meat. A mere dot on the map of this minority is a very small minority of people who are so constituted that they should not smoke at all; and a smaller dot marking a yet tinier minority who actually induce illness by smoking. Those are about the proportions of peril in the thing. It is about as dangerous as sitting in the sun, not so dangerous as sitting in a draught. It is about as questionable as drinking coffee, not quite so questionable as eating pork. If a policeman can take away my cigarette, there cannot be the slightest rational objection, on a warm day, to his taking away my overcoat. In wet weather he might change my boots for me violently in the street, or suddenly garrott me with a muffler. The thing is a typical mild human indulgence, enjoyed by most people and over-enjoyed by a few people, a thing like scent or sweetmeats. Realise that reality which we all know it to be, and then measure that mad abyss of disproportion, on the other side of which are the eight States holding up their streets with policemen and treating every man who is carrying a cigarette as if he were carrying a bomb. Thus all our cranks of culture are leading us back (or onward) into barbarism. For the essence of barbarism is idolatry; that is the worship of something other than the best reason and justice of the Universe. Idolatry is committed, not merely by setting up false gods, but also by setting up false devils; by making men afraid of war or alcohol, or economic law, when they should be afraid of spiritual corruption and cowardice. The Moslems say, "There is no God but God." The English Moslems, the abstainers, have to learn and remember also that there is no Satan but Satan.

September 18, 1909

On Moving Theatre Productions

Mr. Max Beerbohm once maintained that playgoers should go to the theatre as communicants go to church, in the early morning. He said it would favour the earnestness and actuality of the drama. He expressed the opinion (I forget in what exact words) that we should be ashamed to endure the vulgarities and maudlin falsities of most plays if we saw them in the cool morning air, while the dew was still upon the grass. I have no doubt he was right from his own point of view. I have no objection to earnest modern dramas being acted early in the morning, for I am a late riser myself, and they would all be over by the time I got up. I can picture the Early Bird of the *Saturday Review* catching the Worm of the Problem Play. But personally I do not like worms. I might get up early to catch a train or to see the sun rise, or even to take in the milk; but not for the intoxicating pleasure of seeing a sophisticated husband and wife getting on each other's nerves for five acts. I will not let the sun go down upon my wrath; and I do not wish the sun to rise on my depression.

But Mr. Maurice Maeterlinck, another exponent of earnest drama, has started an even more strenuous notion. We have all heard of such a thing as a travelling theatrical company, but Mr. Maeterlinck makes his company travel in a new style. It is not only the actors who have to keep on the move, but the audience too. Instead of the performers pursuing and persuading the public, the public has to be continually trotting after the performers. The following is the account which the newspapers give of the experiment—

> "Macbeth" was played last night, under strikingly novel conditions, at the venerable Abbey of Saint Wandrille, at Cauderbec-en-Caux, now the residence of the dramatic author, M. Maurice Maeterlinck, all ordinary scenic accessories being discarded. The tragedy was lived rather than acted in the spacious halls, stairs, corridors, and grounds of the abbey, which lent themselves mar-

vellously to the realisation of the tragic incidents in the play, the
monastery being built about the same period as the castle at Inver-
ness where Shakespeare's scenes are laid. The witches danced in
the moonlight round real cauldrons in the park, and the spectators,
who were limited to fifty, followed the actors from point to point
and from room to room as the tragedy was unfolded, the effects
being weirdly realistic. The role of Macbeth was played by M.
Severin Mars, that of Lady Macbeth by Mme. Maeterlinck. A
special translation of the play was made by M. Maeterlinck for
this unique occasion.

After reading that paragraph one sees a sort of vision of all
the theatrical audiences in one's experience, all the massive dowagers and all the red-faced old gentlemen in all the stalls of the
London theatres. I like to think of them being kept on the run,
panting up the stairs and padding along the corridors lest they
should be too late for the death of Duncan. To get the full athletic
value out of the idea, the scenes ought to be so arranged that
the changes covered the widest stretch of country, like a gigantic
game of Puss-in-the-Corner. The Blasted Heath having been
vividly presented in an attic, it would be hurriedly announced
that Macbeth's Castle was situated on the tennis-lawn, and the
stampede would begin. Many dowagers would doubtless be
trodden underfoot, and the effect would indeed, as the newspaper says, be weirdly realistic. At the end of the time all the
spectators would be as exhausted as the actors, and some of them
as dead as Macbeth.

Yet, the idea, though a little alarming, has its philosophical
value. It has this peculiar and important effect at least: that it is
the only thing that puts any sense into the ordinary way of talking
about the survival of the fittest. When people talk as if evolution
meant the victory of nobler and loftier creatures, we can at once
answer, "Only if the struggle is arranged by Mr. Maeterlinck
in his house at Caudebec." It is only *this* kind of struggle for life
that has any upward tendency. In the same paper which reports
Mr. Maeterlinck's experiment I see a report of an address to the
British Association at Winnipeg. The report is headed in the

paper "Towards the Superman. All but the Highest Types to Die Out." When will people leave off talking like this? A celebrated lawyer is said to have dismissed the evidence of an exalted official of Heralds' College by saying that the silly old man didn't even understand his own silly old trade. One is tempted to say of some of the modern evolutionists that the dismal old buffers do not even understand their own dismal old theory.

The theory of the survival of the fittest simply means this: that if there is nothing but dirt, those will survive who will eat dirt. It says nothing about the "height" of dirt-eating people; it does not even indicate that the dirt-eaters will improve the physical universe, let alone the human commonwealth. To hear these people talk you would think that nature conducted a competitive examination in the works of Ruskin; or put all the animals into a Sunday school where they got marks for politeness and clean collars. The truth at the back of all the confusion is quite simple. The truth is that the evolutionary theory, if true, is totally useless for human affairs. It is enormous, but irrelevant. Like the solar system, it is a colossal trifle. Though the earth is going round we must not be giddy. Similarly, even if we are beasts, we must not be beastly. All these attempts to apply the parallel of physical evolution to our ethical progress end in one of two things. They end in cutting ethics to fit evolution, which means immorality and madness; or they end in cutting evolution to fit ethics, which means unscientific balderdash. Many of our men of science prefer (I am glad to say) the balderdash to the immorality.

But if they really want the struggle for life to produce their polished and refined types of virtue, they must adopt Mr. Maeterlinck's method. They must make art or truth an evasive and flying thing for fat old gentlemen to run after. They must reverse the modern crusade for making education easy; they must make it difficult. So far from distributing spelling-books among millions of reluctant children, they should stick one spelling-book on top of a greasy pole or a monkey-tree, to be reached only by some child who was eccentric enough to want it. The entrance to the National Gallery should be a hole fifty feet up in the wall, only to be reached by a desperate climber. The meetings of the Ethical Society should be held in the heart of a dense forest, full of wild beasts. Then, perhaps, they might really produce their ethical Superman, refined, exalted, intellectually beautiful: and a very unpleasant fellow I should imagine he would be.

September 25, 1909

Finding the North Pole

The finding of the North Pole is a really suitable subject for a column such as this, because it cannot possibly matter a rap to any reasonable human being whether it has been discovered or not. It is a safe and soothing subject; there is no heat about the North Pole. Certainly people have killed themselves trying to find the North Pole; but that does not make the matter particularly serious; they have killed themselves trying to find a fox. A fox is a much more solemn and sacred affair than the Pole; it is alive, and runs about, while the Pole (I think) keeps still; but I am not a scientist. What the people in question were really hunting was neither the Pole nor the fox, but fun; a philosophical abstraction. I do not sneer at Polar explorers; I admire them as I do all romantic lunatics. But it is really funny to hear men of science gibe at those superstitions which hold sacred the words of a prophet or the blood of a martyr, and then talk quite seriously about killing whole shiploads of human beings in order to find an object which isn't there when you get to it, and which is already in the maps in the only place where it could ever be useful.

If it be true that Dr. Cook[1] and his two Eskimos have found the place, there is something very gratifying in the thing having been so silently and simply done. Everyone was saying that the North Pole would be discovered in an aeroplane—one felt inclined to say a motor-car. The people in motor-cars (steadily relapsing into barbarism) have already assumed the costume and appearance of exceptionally ugly Laplanders. They already wear furs and snow-goggles, and look as if they were shuffling along to spear a walrus. There should be splendid running and no stop-watches on some of the immense ice-plains; and if the friction melted the ice and the motoring section of the upper classes disappeared with a shriek, I daresay we should get on somehow. But I am led astray by these sweet and alluring images. I was remarking on the plainness of Dr. Cook's performance and apparatus. So far from doing it in a flying-ship, he did not even do it in a ship. Two legs, which most of us possess; two dogs, which are easily procurable; and two Eskimos (which form no part of my present equipment, but which, no doubt, one can find in plenty if one knows where to look) were the six instruments of his success. I feel almost inclined to discover the North Pole myself, on the principle that what man has done, man may do. But I fear there is a logical gap in that maxim; it does not allow for the idea of initiation. One cannot go on finding out something too many times, or one gets found out oneself. With a sigh, I take off my snow-shoes and countermand the order for Eskimos. We were considering the quiet and almost casual way in which Dr. Cook walked in, as if at an open door. I wonder if it has ever been done by anybody else—by somebody, perhaps, who was unable to appreciate what he had done? If three men and two dogs can find the pole on their fourteen feet, the Pole

[1] Frederick Albert Cook (1865–1940), an American physician and Arctic explorer who claimed to have reached the North Pole in 1908. His rival, Robert E. Peary, claimed that Cook was a liar and the exploit only a fraud; their argument became the matter of a highly sensational court trial which ended in Cook's claim being rejected.

may have been found in the Stone Age. It is hard to see why any sufficiently obstinate Icelandic captain or North American Indian should not have discovered the Pole without knowing it. But, of course, in this case knowing it is everything; the Pole is by no means an exciting place unless you know it is the Pole. It is no good to do it without knowing it. The best way of all would be to know you had done it without doing it; but that, alas! is impossible.

It is odd to notice in this age of machines how often the machines fail and the old methods succeed. It may be observed, for instance, in the art of murdering kings and politicians—which, however, reprehensible, is much more practical a branch of industry than finding the North Pole. Doubtless many Russian or Irish conspirators considered, like the anarchist in Stevenson's romance, that "the star of dynamite had risen for the oppressed"; but it has proved a wandering and occasionally a falling star. Relatively to the hellish energy in such explosives, the number of successful anarchist outrages effected with them has been singularly small. Nearly all the great recent assassinations have been effected with dagger or pistol at close quarters, as they might have been effected against Elizabeth or Oliver Cromwell. Lincoln, Garfield, Carnot, McKinley, Elizabeth of Austria, Lord Frederick Cavendish, Sir Curzon Wyllie were all murdered in the simple and old-fashioned style.

I hasten to assure the members of the Geographical Society that I do not class together morally the act of aiming at the North Pole with a compass and aiming at a fellow-creature with a gun. But they are both desperate acts requiring a good or an evil courage, and it is interesting to note in both cases how far an elaborate equipment hinders or helps. The truth is, I fancy, that in every enterprise the apparatus is perfected at the expense of some swiftness or simplicity. Science invents conveniences by design and inconveniences by accident. When we take our luggage about with us, we say we are taking our necessaries; but the Romans were at least as wise when they called them "impedimenta." If a Ceylon pearl-diver, naked and holding his breath, had to wrestle on the ocean floor with a scientific diver in full uniform of iron and plate-glass, I am not at all sure that the naked diver might not get the best of it. However this may be, I am sure there can be no doubt about the issue if an aeroplane (like Jacob) had to wrestle with an angel.

It is this that covers with considerable difficulty the comparison between the happiness of humanity in different ages or different lands. Macaulay and the old optimistic Whigs were quite satisfied with saying that the meanest artisan now has conveniences that were unknown to kings. But they forgot that very often the modern conveniences only mean things made to meet modern inconveniences. An artisan can go to a scientific steam-laundry and have his linen collar restarched; if you call that convenience. But if Gurth the Swineherd had been made to wear a starched collar he would have fallen on his knees and implored his lord to lift the burden and give him his brass collar back again. A refined gentleman of Queen Anne's reign could have the luxury of being shaved with scented soap. But a gentleman of Queen Elizabeth's reign could have the greater luxury of growing a beard.

Those who praise mere civilisation (or the morbid modern form of it) are always pointing out the desolate state of various rude societies. They say, "The Zulus have no good eye-glasses." They do not remember that the Zulus have good eyes instead. They cry aloud, "The Ojibways fell on their knees with wonder and terror on first beholding a button-hook." They do not add that the Ojibways were thrown into agonies on first trying to wear buttoned boots. They say "Over the vast, drear expanse of the Arabian desert not a bootblack is to be seen"; they do not add that the Arabs are much too sensible to want their boots blacked. It may be questioned whether the increase of medical advertisements mean the increase of health. It is a disputable matter whether the number of London hoardings devoted to soap means that the English are a clean nation or that they are a dirty one.

October 2, 1909

The Indian Nationalist Movement

Matthew Arnold, among much that was arid and arbitrary, said at least two very sound and useful things: first, that we, the modern English, are much too prone to worship "machinery"— that is, the means rather than the end; and secondly, that we ought to cultivate to a great extent the habit of letting our thoughts "play round" a subject. This page of this paper seems to be an admirable and specially appointed place for playing round. Nevertheless, if you allow your mind to play round anything that is worshipped as machinery, you will probably get into trouble. I have myself, for instance, been sternly rebuked of late for saying that what I wanted was not votes, but democracy. People spoke as if this were some sort of awful apostasy from the Liberal position; whereas, it is a humble remark of exactly the same sort as saying that I want, not the Brighton express, but Brighton; not the Calais boat, but Calais; not a Polar Expedition, but the North Pole. The test of a democracy is not whether the people vote, but whether the people rule. The essence of a democracy is that the national tone and spirit of the typical citizen is apparent and striking in the actions of the State, that France is governed in a French way, or Germany in a German way, or Spain in a Spanish way. Votes may be the most convenient way of achieving this effect; but votes are quite vain if they do not achieve it. And sometimes they do not. I venture to say that the average Frenchman was much more behind the conscription of Napoleon I. than the average Englishman was behind that mass of anti-civic nonsense, the Children Bill.[1] The art of politics is not managing a machine, but managing a personality. Parliament

[1] A multifaceted bill presented by Herbert Samuel in February 1908 and debated throughout the year. Among some of the topics it covered were the prevention of cruelty to children, baby farming, sales of cigarettes to juveniles, separate courts and prisons for juveniles and parental responsibility for crimes com-

is called "it," but England is called "she." Yet the extent to which this sense of national or local colour has been lost is really amazing. A man in a train told me the other day that some Model Settlement or Garden City or some such thing that he lived in "had the real life of an old English village." When I asked him about the inn, he told me that they had voted for having a teetotal inn. He seemed to have no sense of how he had painted out the whole picture with one sweep of the brush. It is as if he had said, "How charming is an old English village at evening, when the Muezzin is calling from the shining pinnacle of the Mosque!"

It is this lack of atmosphere that always embarrasses me when my friends come and tell me about the movement of Indian Nationalism. I do not doubt for a moment that the young idealists who ask for Indian independence are very fine fellows; most young idealists are fine fellows. I do not doubt for an instant that many of our Imperial officials are stupid and oppressive; most Imperial officials are stupid and oppressive. But when I am confronted with the actual papers and statements of the Indian Nationalists I feel much more dubious, and, to tell the truth, a little bored. The principal weakness of Indian Nationalism seems to be that it is not very Indian and not very national. It is all about Herbert Spencer and Heaven knows what. What is the good of the Indian national spirit if it cannot protect its people from Herbert Spencer? I am not fond of the philosophy of Buddhism; but it is not so shallow as Spencer's philosophy; it has real ideas of its own. One of the papers, I understand, is called the *Indian Sociologist*. What are the young men of India doing that they allow such an animal as a sociologist to pollute their ancient villages and poison their kindly homes?

When all is said, there is a national distinction between a people asking for its own ancient life and a people asking for things that

---

mitted by juveniles. A key clause provided for "the right of entry under the authority of the Secretary of State into the homes of destitute children . . . to prevent cruelty and neglect".

have been wholly invented by somebody else. There is a difference between a conquered people demanding its own institutions and the same people demanding the institutions of the
conqueror. Suppose an Indian said: "I heartily wish India had
always been free from white men and all their works. Every
system has its sins: and we prefer our own. There would have
been dynastic wars; but I prefer dying in battle to dying in
hospital. There would have been despotism; but I prefer one
king whom I hardly ever see to a hundred kings regulating my
diet and my children. There would have been pestilence; but I
would sooner die of the plague than die of toil and vexation in
order to avoid the plague. There would have been religious
differences dangerous to public peace; but I think religion more
important than peace. Life is very short; a man must live somehow and die somewhere; the amount of bodily comfort a peasant
gets under your best Republic is not so much more than mine.
If you do not like our sort of spiritual comfort, we never asked
you to. Go, and leave us with it." Suppose an Indian said that,
I should call him an Indian Nationalist, or, at least, an authentic
Indian, and I think it would be very hard to answer him. But
the Indian Nationalists whose works I have read simply say with
ever-increasing excitability, "Give me a ballot-box. Provide me
with a Ministerial dispatch-box. Hand me over the Lord Chancellor's wig. I have a natural right to be Prime Minister. I have
a heaven-born claim to introduce a Budget. My soul is starved
if I am excluded from the Editorship of the *Daily Mail*," or
words to that effect.

Now this, I think, is not so difficult to answer. The most
sympathetic person is tempted to cry plaintively, "But, hang it
all, my excellent Oriental (may your shadow never grow less),
we invented all these things. If they are so very good as you
make out, you owe it to us that you have ever heard of them.
If they are indeed natural rights, you would never even have
thought of your natural rights but for us. If voting is so very
absolute and divine (which I am inclined rather to doubt myself),
then certainly we have some of the authority that belongs to the

founders of a true religion, the bringers of salvation." When the Hindu takes this very haughty tone and demands a vote on the spot as a sacred necessity of man, I can only express my feelings by supposing the situation reversed. It seems to me very much as if I were to go into Tibet and find the Grand Lama or some great spiritual authority, and were to demand to be treated as a Mahatma or something of that kind. The Grand Lama would very reasonably reply: "Our religion is either true or false; it is either worth having or not worth having. If you know better than we do, you do not want our religion. But if you do want our religion, please remember that it is our religion; we discovered it, we studied it, and we know whether a man is a Mahatma or not. If you want one of our peculiar privileges, you must accept our peculiar discipline and pass our peculiar standards, to get it."

Perhaps you think I am opposing Indian Nationalism. That is just where you make a mistake; I am letting my mind play round the subject. This is especially desirable when we are dealing with the deep conflict between two complete civilisations. Nor do I deny the existence of natural rights. The right of a people to express itself, to be itself in arts and action, seems to me a genuine right. If there is such a thing as India, it has a right to be Indian. But Herbert Spencer is not Indian; "Sociology" is not Indian; all this pedantic clatter about culture and science is not Indian. I often wish it were not English either. But this is our first abstract difficulty, that we cannot feel certain that the Indian Nationalist is national.

October 9, 1909

Science: Pro and Con

It is queer that, while some of the most poetic of the scientific prophecies of our fathers are being fulfilled before our eyes, there should be about all the fulfilments an element of the fantastic, which in one case at least verges on the farcical. That men should fly is as legendary and wonderful as that pigs should fly; but the flying-machines have shapes which are almost as absurd as the shape of a flying pig. It is the same with the North Pole, which in my youth used to be a serious subject: it was associated with great sea-heroes and the heroic age of science; with Tennyson's tribute to Franklin[1] in Westminster Abbey. At this moment the North Pole is as grotesque as the Greasy Pole. It is being fought for, with frantic gesticulations, by comic Americans. Heaven forbid that I should make even the most casual or amateur attempt to decide between the claimants.

In America, I fancy, it is thought virile and patriotic to send State messages in a sort of slang; to announce to the slightly puzzled nations that your opponent is "offering them a gold brick"—whatever that is. I find it hard to connect it with my own merely local and traditional notions of a naval officer. I find it difficult to imagine an English Captain discovering a Cape and telegraphing to his Admiral "What 'O, she bumps!" But in this there is no matter of principle, but merely of national habit. Nevertheless, the quarrel itself and the slanging, self-advertising style in which it is conducted fall so far below the old Polar idealism that the actual discovery of the Pole seems not so much a climax as an anti-climax. As to which of them has really done it, I have no opinion, nor even any preference. Cook did it in the presence of two Eskimos, Peary in the presence of one Eskimo; but if they had done it in the presence of a million Eskimos such

[1] Sir John Franklin (1786–1847), an Arctic explorer who was commemorated in Westminster Abbey in 1875.

people could give no evidence as to whether it was the North Pole. It is as if Babbage had proved his calculating-machine to the satisfaction of a tribe of Hottentots, or Newton had demonstrated the Calculi without any refutation from the infant-school. In fact, the noise of the discussion seems a singular contrast to the stillness and secrecy of the discovery. Both these distinguished Americans seem to have gone on tiptoe, as it were—more as if they wanted to hide the North Pole than to find it.

But my only business here is to remark on the slight element of bathos in this and some other achievements. It is as if some sublime *Argo* had suddenly turned turtle. It is as if the one step from the *Fram*[2] to the North Pole was the step from the sublime to the ridiculous. If ever there was a man who, on all artistic principles, ought to have found the North Pole, it was Nansen. He was tall enough to be the North Pole—to be left there as a gigantic trophy and a beacon to ships. But it seems as if something rules human affairs which prefers (as the children do) to have a harlequinade after the most exquisite fairy play—something that likes King Arthur to turn into a Pantaloon and Sir Lancelot into a policeman. I think it is wholesome; it keeps us from seriousness, which is idolatry.

Moreover, there is one more improtant respect in which this sudden fantasticality in the scientific principles may be of a certain use. For what we have suffered from in the modern world is not in any sense physical knowledge itself, but simply a stupid mistake about what physical knowledge is and what it can do. It is quite as obvious that physical knowledge may make a man comfortable as it is that it cannot make a man happy. It is as certain that there are such things as drugs as that there are no such things as love-potions. Physical science is a thing on the outskirts of human life; adventurous, exciting, and essentially fanciful. It has nothing to do with the centre of human life at

[2] The ship first used by the Arctic explorer Nansen to penetrate into the polar regions in 1893; it was used again in 1910–1911 by Amundsen on the Antarctic expedition that led to the discovery of the South Pole.

all. Telephones, flying-ships, radium, the North Pole are not in the ultimate sense good, but neither are they bad. Physical science is always one of two things; it is either a tool or a toy. At its highest and noblest, of course, it is a toy. A toy is a thing of far greater philosophical grandeur than a tool; for the very simple reason that a toy is valued for itself and a tool only for something else. A tool is a means, a toy is an end. You use a hammer to make a doll's house; if you tried to use a doll's house to make a hammer you would soon be convinced that you had selected a somewhat clumsy instrument. When we look through a field-glass at the German forces invading England we are using science as a tool. When we look through a telescope at the tremendous planets and the remote systems, we are using science as a toy. The telephone is one of the uses of the inquiry; the Solar System is one of its gaieties or levities. When science tells me that there is a house in Ealing that I can communicate with, I am interested; when science says there is a star in Sirius I cannot communicate with, I am amused. But in neither case can science be anything else except a tool or a toy. It can never be the man using the tool. It can never be the child playing with the toy. It can never, in short, be the thing that has natural authority over toy and tool. For the child has the kingdom of heaven, and the man has the kingdom of the earth.

The only evil that science has ever attempted in our time has been that of dictating not only what should be known, but the spirit in which it should be regarded. It does not in the least matter whether we look at a lamp-post or a tree as long as we look at it in a certain spirit. It does not in the least matter whether we talk through a telephone or through a hole in the wall so long as we talk sense. But we must not ask the lamp-post in what spirit it ought to be regarded. If we do, we shall find it as deaf as a post. We must not ask the telephone what we are to say to it. If we do, we shall find the young ladies at the exchange somewhat sharply insensible to the pathos of our position. Science must not impose any philosophy, any more than the telephone must tell us what to say. If we are going on a great and just adventure, it will be all the more glorious to go on a flying-ship. But we must not stop in the middle of the adventure to ask the flying-ship what a just adventure is. If we are rushing to get married, it may be thrilling to rush in a motor-car; but we do not ask the motor-car whom we shall marry. Generally speaking, we hardly even ask the chauffeur. That quite elementary and commonplace principle suffices for all the relations of physical science with mankind. A man does not ask his horse where he shall go: neither shall he ask his horseless carriage: neither shall he ask the driver of his horseless carriage: neither shall he ask the inventor of his horseless carriage. Science is a splendid thing; if you tell it where to go to.

On this principle a reasonable man will be quite as strongly opposed to Ruskin and the antiquaries and aesthetes as he is to Mr. Carnegie and the mere idolatry of a civilisation of iron and steel. A railway is not a disgusting thing, any more than a road-way or a waterway; it is the railway-director who is disgusting. On the other hand, an old building as such is neither ugly nor beautiful; but the old gentlemen who potter all over it are almost always ugly. Whenever a man puts on spectacles to see a statue, he is making himself unbeautiful in order to see beauty. And whenever a man assumes "culture" in order to admire antiquity, he is becoming all that is crude and vulgar in order to study what is ancient and sublime. A boy looks at a steam-engine with much more notion of its meaning than an art-critic looks at a cathedral. For all the ancient things truly exist only to teach us to be young. The quaintest carved font exists only that we may be born again, and be babyish. The most venerable altar only exists that we may be married again and go on another hon-eymoon. It is a very good thing, by the way, to be frequently married again—always, of course, to the same person.

But my meaning is here that the mere Ruskin attack on the rails and wheels of science is just as unspiritual as the mere idolatry of rails and wheels. Ruskin was a materialist—because he hated some materials. There is nothing wrong about steel rods and iron wheels so long as the steel does not blind the eyes, so long as the iron does not enter into the soul. There is nothing wrong about the body travelling on rails so long as the mind does not travel in ruts. Toddie, in the American tale about children, always said, "Wants to see wheels go wound"; and always insisted on his uncle showing him the inside of his watch; with the result, if I remember right, that the dust blew into the works. There is no earthly or heavenly objection to a man saying of trains and motors: "Want to see wheels go wound," so long as he is as innocent as Toddie. There is no objection to scientists splitting open the world like the uncle's watch; in order to look at the works of it so long as those scientists feel like children. The only objection to opening the world like a watch is an entirely extraneous one, as in the story. It is that a nameless something comes in from outside, something that is not young and not heroic; something that is dry and blinding and barren, like the east wind, blows in at every aperture. Dust blows into the works of the world, an arid and choking dust; the dust of death.

October 16, 1909

Adjectives, Nouns, and the Truth

In various poor parts of London there are excellent institutions called "Guilds of Play," in which poor children (somewhat pathetically) sing the songs or dance the dances which were natural to their fathers when England was comparatively free. Here luckless but lively gutter-snipes, who have never seen anything but chimney-pots, sing old English songs which take for granted the greenwood and the meadow. Nay, the child sings songs in praise of the legendary London, which was paved with gold, in the very entrails of the real London, that is paved with mire. I once took a Stockbroker, who is a friend of mine, to enjoy this excruciating and poetic irony. We sat on a platform all by ourselves, and in front of us danced a large number of little girls in pointed caps of pink or white cotton, little girls from the London slums, many of them pretty and nearly all of them graceful. My friend the Stockbroker was much impressed. He had never met the English poor (that is, the English people) before in his life. He did not know that the English poor are polite to excess, and contain many middle-class and aristocratic traditions, being descended from all sorts of people who have been too honourable to get on in the world. We meet refinement among the poor about five times as often as we meet vulgarity among the rich; and, when we remember how often we meet that, the calculation becomes maddening in its immensity, like the calculations of astronomy. The Stockbroker, I say, was touched by the instinctive elegance of all the little girls in front of him, and expressed it in the explosive remark that by George! they danced very well. "Yes," I said, "they dance better than we should, you and I. You would not look so pretty in a pink cap. I should not caper and twirl upon my toe with the same agility. Oh, my friend, it is we who need to be taught. The true hope of modern society is not expressed when one Stockbroker sits on a platform looking at a row of dancing schoolgirls. The true hope will only begin when one schoolgirl sits on a platform looking at a row of dancing Stockbrokers. It is not enough that I enjoy seeing a child jumping about; I always did. The real Renaissance will only come when the child sees me jumping about, which I never did. "Come," I cried to my friend the Stockbroker, "come, let us begin the divine dance of the future! Let all these children come up on to the platform and watch us, while you and I whirl round the room in a symbolic waltz, representing in every fantastic gesture of arm or leg the relations between literature and finance." My friend the Stockbroker answered: "I think it would save time if you stated with some clearness what you mean." "Very well," I said, with similar severity and shortness, "what I mean is that we ought to go to school again." He answered nothing; so I rather think that what I said was true. It is at least certain that in a large number of our discussions we are only working our way, somewhat wearily, back to mother-wit and the elementary things. Modern scepticism, for instance, is simply a reaction, a turning back. The modern sceptic starts from the twenty-fifth proposition of Euclid and hacks his way back to the axioms. The whole modern adventure is to break one's way past forests and mountain ranges till one finds the way back to the infant-school. As soon as a man feels that he has got anywhere near the end, he begins to know that he must go back to the beginning. A man passes all the most terrible truths before he finds the truisms.

Take such a case as English grammar. Did any boy or girl in their five senses ever bother about English grammar. It seemed so obvious that one could always say what one meant without knowing the parts of speech; and therefore we have most of us forgotten them. Well, we shall have to learn them again; they have become necessary. Some of the most enormous and idiotic developments of our modern thought and speech arise simply from not knowing the parts of speech and principles of language, which we once knew when we were children. The answer to most modern sophistries can be found in Smith's Latin Grammar or Brown's English Grammar. In the present political and religious crises, I read my old Greek Grammar with the utmost excitement, understanding it for the first time. For most fundamental falsehoods are errors in language as well as in philosophy. Most statements that are unreasonable are really ungrammatical.

For instance, most of the modern nonsense may be summed up as the victory of the adjective over the noun. When I was a boy I was told that the adjective "qualified the noun"; I had not the faintest notion of what it meant; but I have now. However gigantic or overpowering is the adjective, it cannot alter the nature of the noun to which it is applied. If I say (as I do most heartily say), "I like big boots," I do not mean that I like boots as big as Brixton villas. They would not be boots at all. I must mean something like "Boots as big as boots can be," or "Boots much bigger than any that I have as yet obtained." The adjective qualifies the noun; but it cannot abolish the noun. I want big boots; but it is boots I want, not bigness.

Now I only ask that the modern reader will run his eye through any modern magazine or book or newspaper, apply that principle simply and systematically, and see what remains. He will find in a vast number of cases that the adjective is ornate or exquisite to the point of artificiality; but that the word it is applied to is entirely forgotten. Thus, when they say, "Give us a broad religion," it is reasonable enough, since one religion is really broader than another. But every religion is a religion; that is, it ties a man to something. A faith can be free up to the exact point where it is unfaithful. Or, again, there are politicians who call themselves "independent" politicians; and who boast that they are not attached to any party. They are not; but they would very much like the party to be attached to them. They have some theory or proposal or other; they cannot be any broader than that theory or proposal. The truth is that if a man wishes to remain in perfect mental breadth and freedom, he had better not think at all. Thinking is a narrowing process. It leads to what people call dogma. A man who thinks hard about any subject for several years is in horrible danger of discovering the truth about it. This process is called becoming "sectarian," also "hardening in later life"; it can also be described as "giving up to party what was meant for mankind." It is a terrible thing when a man really finds that his mind was given him to use, and not to play with; or, in other words, that the gods gave him a great ugly mouth with which to answer questions, and not merely to ask them. The crocodile finds it easy enough to open his mouth and wait for a black man or an explorer. It is in knowing the exact moment at which to shut it that the really fastidious and dexterous crocodile shows his training. In the same way the modern man fancies he has reached supreme culture because he opens his intellect. But the supreme culture (in the forcible modern phrase) is to know when to shut your head. There is one odd

aspect of the man with this sort of open mind—a man whom
one imagines with an open mouth. It is that being thus gaping
and helpless, he is really brutal and oppressive. He tyrannises;
he forces on all other men his own insolent indecision. He forbids
his followers to come to any conclusion till he has done so. He
will allow no one else to find the truth, as Peary will allow no
one else to find the Pole. He is the worst tyrant that the world
has seen; he is the persecuting sceptic. He is the man who has
held up the whole world now for over a hundred years. I thought
of one or two examples, but there is no space to mention them.
Perhaps it is just as well.

October 23, 1909
The Proper Emphasis in Morality

Those great professors of evolution and ethical science, at whose
feet I have so meekly sat all my life, have generally said two
things about the morals of nations and tribes. First they said that
all creeds were the same, because they were the Message of Man.
Second, they said that all creeds were different, because they
were the Accidents of Evolution. It was a little difficult to follow;
but, as far as I could make out, all religions were the same, and
therefore religion did not matter. But all moralities were different, and therefore morality must be preserved. Being a trifle
confused by all this, I was driven back upon forming some kind
of conclusion or compromise of my own about how the mass
of mankind feel on cutting throats or picking pockets or poisoning beer. My theory is no more than a conjecture; I do not
insist on it; but, such as it is, I think I can state my theory more
clearly than most of my scientific teachers managed to state
theirs.

It seems to me that the mass of men do agree on the mass of morality, but differ disastrously about the proportions of it. In other words, all men admit the Ten Commandments, but they differ horribly about which is the first Commandment and which is the tenth. The difference between men is not in what merits they confess, but in what merits they emphasise. All the nations of the earth are troubled about many things; they only fight about what is the one thing needful. The spoilt son of some Chicago millionaire who puffs smoke in his father's face for fun will not, in so many words, deny the rightness of the commandment, "Honour thy father and thy mother." He will only think it a small and somewhat laughable matter; while he will be quite solemn about the command, "Thou shalt do no murder"—all the more because he must feel that he is the kind of person whom one murders. On the other hand, a Chinaman, who thinks little of his own life or anyone else's, who will kill me for a penny or himself for twopence, would not in so many words deny the doctrine "Thou shalt do no murder." He would merely feel that a murder was a pleasant human weakness. He could say of murdering, as Mr. Michael Finsbury said of lunching, "It's a thing that might happen to anybody." But about the commandment "Honour thy father and thy mother" that Chinaman would be adamant. The Chinaman may be a trifle careless, not to say untidy, about life in this or that missionary or ambassador, but he pays honour to the fountain of life. He will throw away his own life for twopence, but he will pay diamonds to dignify those ancestors who have given him the very life that he throws away. Yet the Yankee and the Chinaman do not differ on morality, but only on the scale of morals. Nay, they do not differ in theory, but only in practice. The American does not approve of impudence; he merely indulges in it. Meanwhile he avoids by instinct the cruelties of China. The Chinaman does not admire murder; he merely does it. Meanwhile he avoids by instinct the vulgarities of America. Men do not differ much about what things they will call evils; they differ enormously about what evils they will call excusable. The sins are substantially the same all over the earth. What men fight each other about is the question of which are the venial and which the mortal sins.

This simple distinction will save us from many mad conclusions to which we are driven by popular and valuable writers. To judge by Macaulay and Kingsley, and many hearty and humane men of genius, one would fancy that all Italians were totally indifferent to truth, all Spaniards calmly contemptuous of mercy, all Irishmen free from the faintest feeling against murder, all Frenchmen unacquainted even with the sensation of reverence. All this is nonsense. Spaniards, Frenchmen, Italians, Irishmen, have all held for centuries a morality in which cruelty, untruthfulness, murder, and blasphemy were all admittedly wrong. All that differed was the emphasis; the emphasis on what was *very* wrong. If this plain point had been recalled we should not have had all these endless and objectless arguments about the Church, the State, and the School Board; about Denominational Education and Undenominational Education and Secular Education and all the rest of it. Of course it is absurd to say that English children in Church schools or Secular schools, in Catholic or Protestant schools, will learn a totally different morality. High Churchmen will not be taught to poison Low Churchmen; Low Churchmen will not be taught to eat High Churchmen. Should assassination or cannibalism be touched on in either place they will certainly be reproved. The thing that remains, the thing that makes the difference, is exactly that one thing that can never be conveyed by a reporter, that can scarcely even be imitated by a ventriloquist—emphasis. We do not mind what is said; we want to know what is shouted. Nay, we do not want to know what is said, but rather what is not said: what receives the savage emphasis of silence.

But if anyone doubts that modern men have moralities *practically* very different, he has only to read the papers. I have recently seen two reports of speeches made at the Y.M.C.A. to little boys assembled at that respectable institution. The Y.M.C.A. sounds sufficiently harmless; the speakers and promoters of the meetings were, doubtless, good men, gravely conscious of their responsibilities to the young. Yet I speak soberly when I say that (tested by my own personal morality) the whole thing was rather more immoral than Fagin's school for thieves. It was intended to teach the boys business habits. One address was given by the author of "Get On or Get Out," and was to that ennobling effect. The young were warned against excessive modesty; he told each boy to thrust himself forward as much as possible. The other address consisted of sentences like "Always know something that the other boy doesn't know." The orators of the Y.M.C.A. are Christians, and I hope I am also; yet I suppose it would puzzle them if I said (as I certainly do say) that I would rather my children were brought up to worship Bacchus and Apollo than brought up in the moral atmosphere of the above business-like maxims. To cringe to your employer and steal a march on your comrades, to become hard and impudent at the very age that should be generous and shy, to add the coldness of maturity to the crudity of childhood, to cease to be a boy without becoming a man, to be a sort of monkey plus spiritual pride . . . to get on! That is the finished product, the prize boy of these philanthropists of the Young Men's Christian Association. And to me he seems neither Young nor a Man nor a Christian, nor fit to be associated with. Yet, believe me, the moral difference is only a matter of proportion and degree. The author of "Get On or Get Out" would not say in so many words, if pressed, that modesty is not a beautiful thing. He would only say that something must be sacrificed in the rush of the commercial system, and modesty, being a mere filagree ornament, must be sacrificed first. But we who think modesty the very youth and poetry of all other qualities, *we* say that the whole commercial system must be destroyed if it obstructs modesty. The Y.M.C.A. would not deny that humility is a virtue. It is because there are some people who think it *the* virtue that the row begins.

I hasten to say that I do not attribute to the Y.M.C.A. as a whole, a very large and amiable body, any participation in these pieces of pert individualistic philosophy. But we are not talking of what an institution lays down, but of what it permits and makes possible. A dancing Dervish is possible among Moslems, though most respectable Moslems would have the strongest objection to being dancing Dervishes. A dancing Dervish at Dr. Clifford's chapel would not merely be discouraged; he would be prevented. Tortures can exist in Russia, though most Russians loathe them; they could not exist in Battersea. And it is only in certain moral atmospheres that the monstrous Boy who Gets On can even get himself born on earth.

October 30, 1909

Objections to Spiritualism

I am, I believe, one of the few Englishmen who really love and respect Americans; I love that old-world simplicity which makes their minds like ancient crystals. If any shadow cast upon these pages has seemed to fall for a moment between America and myself, it is the fault of neither. It is all Commander Peary's fault. That irritating mariner has succeeded in losing his title to popularity before proving his title to fame. He may or may not have found the North Pole; but it is certain that he has lost all the rest of the planet. But America really has some great qualities, which one can afford to acknowledge now that the modern world has abandoned the absurd pretence that she holds the future of humanity. One of the really fine American elements is this: that, being a democracy, America mentions really interesting things. Things that happen anywhere, in China or Rome or Berlin, are not suppressed because they are bad taste, but printed because they are good copy. Thus (from one point of view) America sometimes seems really more a part of Europe than England.

For instance (I offer a casual challenge), how many of you know that Lombroso has become a Spiritualist? Perhaps the question ought to be divided into two parts. First of all, how many of you know that Lombroso ever became anything, even a new-born babe? How many have heard of Lombroso? Leaving that awful question, it is enough to say that Lombroso did become a new-born babe, and shortly after that a Scientific Materialist; at least, I should think his Materialist philosophy must have been invented at an immature age. But, second, how many of you know that, having been a great Materialist, Professor Lombroso has become a Spiritualist? I read one of Lombroso's books when I was young and strong; and remember that he said something about our iridescent veils and what he could do to them with scissors. He now believes in some most remarkable things which I find set forth very clearly and picturesquely in a popular American periodical—*Hampton's Magazine*. He believes, as do many distinguished men of science, in Eusapia the medium. He believes that a peculiar mystical vapour blows from a particular portion of her head. On other occasions the vapour blows exclusively from her left leg. The wound in Eusapia's head "was caused in early girlhood by a blow of a stewpan or by a fall. Sometimes Eusapia says the one, sometimes the other." What is this lawless and unreasonable emotion within me that makes me hope that it was by a blow of a stewpan?

But I trust no Spiritualists will suppose for a moment that I am merely making game of Eusapia; pulling her leg, as people say. I should not venture to pull her leg, especially her left leg, for fear that monstrous clouds might be emitted to overwhelm me. Moreover, I have no sympathy whatever with the common boisterous sceptic. The sceptics only denounce Spiritualism because they do not believe in it. I only denounce Spiritualism because I do believe in it. I think that there is something there to find, and that most of these investigations find the wrong end of it. This wrong approach is more perilous in the case of exalted actualities than in the case of conveniences or trifles. It is awkward to get hold of the sow by the wrong ear; but it is positively dangerous to get hold of the angel by the wrong wing. Very broadly, the real objection to Spiritualism is that it calls entirely upon unknown gods—that is, upon any spirits that may be strolling about. There is something inevitably vulgar about this universal invitation in things of the soul. Spiritualism is to religion exactly what a Matrimonial Agency is to love. These Spiritualists do not worship gods; they advertise for gods. They lay themselves open to evil as did Mrs. Bardell (in Serjeant Buzfuz's speech), when she put up an innocent invitation to single gentlemen. But (as Serjeant Buzfuz said) the serpent is on the watch. We all know what does happen only too often to such silly women as advertise in matrimonial papers for a single gentleman. They get someone who is hardly ever a gentleman and is often not even single. In the same way, I fear, the Spiritualists often open their doors to very disreputable deities. They entertain angels unawares—fallen angels. Like the people in the Matrimonial Agency, their appeal is too broad to procure the best; exactly because the nets they fling are wide, the fish they catch are small. But I do not deny the facts of Spiritualism. I do not deny the existence of Matrimonial Agencies. I wish I could.

But, apart from this feeling of mine that Spiritualism is dangerous, the article in *Hampton's Magazine* is really most arresting in the matter of whether it is genuine. Here we have a European man of science with a solid reputation, saying definitely (as another, with a similar reputation, has often said, Sir William Crookes)[1] that things have happened under his eyes such as the mass of mankind promptly and plainly call miracles. I will not engage in a verbal controversy with the sceptic, because long experience has taught me that the sceptic's ultimate scepticism is about the use of his own words and the reliability of his own

[1] Sir William Crookes (1832–1919), a famous chemist and president of the Chemical Society and of the Royal Society. He became interested in spiritualism, the possibilities of mental telepathy and clairvoyance; as an active member of the Society for Psychical Research, he was connected in the popular mind at least with belief in spiritualism.

intelligence. The sceptic at a séance is generally doomed hence-forward, not so much to explaining how the medium must have been a deceiver, as to explaining how he himself might easily have been a dupe. But I think he does himself an injustice in attributing this enormous gullibility to himself. I will still trust his word, though he can no longer trust his eyes.

I think the opinion of an average honest man is unimpeachable about what happened—not, mind you, about the explanation of what happened. The ordinary sceptical attempts to upset such simple and solid testimony are really more fantastic and elaborate than the wildest assertions of the Spiritualists. Some, for instance, complain that certain conditions, of darkness, silence, or what not, have been found to favour these phenomena. In fact, they object that ghosts always come by night. They might as well object that bats only come by night. I bet there are at this moment in the Hotel Cecil as many people who have seen a ghost as people who have really had a tête-à-tête with a bat. Shooting stars, I am told, are generally seen at night; and that explains why many people have never seen them. If you ask me why ghosts and devils are denied, while bats and shooting stars are reluctantly conceded, I can only answer that it is the not inter-esting and by no means undignified thing which we have to call Bigotry. Every time I have met a bat (I have never seen one) he has simply flapped me in the face and fled, which, perhaps, is considered humorous in bat circles. It would not be difficult for a sceptic to argue that the flap might have been a leaf blown in my face or a corner of my own cloak flapping, or one of my enormous and luxuriant whiskers fluttering on the midnight breeze. The more brilliant scientists would not stop at that. They would be capable of saying that I had hit myself in the face. They would appeal to the well-known physio-psychic fact that an absent-minded journalist, when walking along a lane at eve-ning, will often (by a nervous trick) hit himself in the left eye with the right foot. I have no space to give the authorities for this detail. But, in spite of them, I believe that bats exist; I also believe that the spirits of the séance exist. But I think that, like the bats, the spirits are ugly things of darkness; and when they slap me on one cheek I do not turn the other.

November 6, 1909

Distortions in the Press

Lord Rosebery, I think, once offered the paradoxical suggestion that newspapers should consist of news. He proposed to exclude all comment, moral, political, and (I hope) financial. It may be doubted whether the journals under his Lordship's review would be disarmed by so simple a reform. Newspapers have been known before now to indulge in methods even more direct than comment. The comment at the worst can only be fallacious; the news can be false. Or even if it is not false, it may be so selected as to give a totally false picture of the place or topic under dispute. Selection is the fine art of falsity. Tennyson put it very feebly and inadequately when he said that the blackest of lies is the lie that is half a truth. The blackest of lies is the lie that is entirely a truth. Once give me the right to pick out anything and I shall not need to invent anything. If in my History of the World, published some centuries hence, I am allowed to mark the nineteenth century only by the names of Mr. Whitaker Wright[1] and Jack the Ripper, I will promise to add no further comment. If I am free to report this planet to the Man in the Moon as being inhabited by scorpions and South African millionaires, I will

[1] Whitaker Wright, a company promoter and financier whose schemes had a huge collapse in 1900, was brought to trial twice, the second time in 1904 for possible tampering with the company records. He was sentenced to seven years imprisonment, but on the day of sentencing, he went into a room adjoining the courtroom and killed himself by swallowing cyanide.

undertake to leave the facts to speak for themselves. I will undertake to create a false impression solely by facts. I shall not ask
to say what I choose, so long as I can choose what I choose. So
long as I am not asked to tell the truth, I will cheerfully undertake
not to tell any lies.

That, one innocently supposed, was the arrangement we had
all accepted. The newspapers do not need to offer any view of
the facts; for the facts themselves are as artistic and one-sided as
any view of them could be. The most perfect comment would
spoil a story that had already been picked out with the perfection
of an epigram. "The foreign news" of one of the great go-ahead
dailies is itself a comment on the complexity of Europe; and
why should we need a comment on a comment? I, for one, had
grown quite used to the established modern usage: strictly partisan information unvulgarised by any partisan rhetoric. But of
late I have begun to see a new method developing, a method
which is surely worthy of notice if only because it raises again
Lord Rosebery's question in a somewhat strange form.

The new method of journalism is to offer so many comments
or, at least, secondary circumstances that there is actually no
room left for the original facts. Lord Rosebery wished to have
the story without the moral. We seem likely now to have the
moral without the story: at any rate, to have the moral effects
without the story. A pebble is thrown into the sea, and lost to
sight for ever; we only behold the concentric ripples widening
for ever through all the waters of the world. The English or
American Press will be suddenly seized with a storm of indignation about something; new phases of that indignation will flash
forth hour after hour; but the really difficult thing will be to
discover the plain outline of the original affair. Most of my
readers must, I think, have observed instances of this overwhelming wave of irrelevance. Some brokers at Amsterdam (let
us say) throw furniture at an auctioneer. We do not hear of the
event, however, even in so plain and meagre a form as that. We
see a paragraph headed "Anti-Auctioneer Movement in Holland," and then after that, in smaller letters, "Strong Protest in

Chicago." Then it becomes a feature of the newspaper for several days under an established title, such as "The Dutch Persecution" or "The Cry of the Auctioneers." Under this heading are arranged all sorts of things in little separate paragraphs; an attempt to interview the Chinese Ambassador on the subject; Mr. Carnegie's strong opinion that furniture thrown at the head will probably hurt; the Pope's pronouncement on the ethics of auctioneering; a letter signed "Indignant Briton" demanding that all brokers (or all Dutchmen) should be turned out of England; a proposal by some energetic idiot to open a subscription for somebody; and, finally, a series of soothing assurances telling us that the affair is not likely seriously to disturb the Bank Rate, the King's health, the North Sea whale-fisheries, or the General Election. Through all this forest of inconsequent facts I wander, trying in vain to find the ultimate and cogent facts upon which to form my opinion. I want to know what the auctioneer did, why they threw furniture at him, what defence they offer for having done so, whether he threw any furniture first, and, in short, all the things I should want to know if I were a juryman and were properly trying the case. But these are exactly the facts that I can never find in the newspapers. Anecdotes of the auctioneer's childhood, parallel instances of the tyranny of brokers in the Dark Ages, passionate pronouncements by novelists and Nonconformist ministers that we must go in and win; but not the story. This curious method has for some time marked our attitude in the case of those foreign crimes or tyrannies against which we English are so heroically ready to rebel. I remember that the accounts of the second trial of Dreyfus were so encumbered with anecdotes and European opinion and gossip generally that they had no room for any intelligible account of the evidence at all. The report of the trial itself was something that no human being could make head or tail of; questions without any answer, answers not provoked by any question, sudden and violent changes of the subject, prolonged and feverish pursuit of persons who had never been heard of before; abrupt announcements by public men referring to disclosures that had not been disclosed—

it was like reading the law reports in a nightmare. The story of
the Pannizardi telegram,[2] for instance, was told in such a way
as to make no sort of sense at all; it was only long afterwards
that I pieced the true facts together, with some remarkable results
to myself. We are perpetually in danger of the same mistake in
all our modern English indignations about Russia, about Spain,
about the Congo. It is only too probable that there is much
wrong; but I want to hear the wrong, not to hear about it. As
it is, it is almost always on some utterly extraneous and impertinent point of creed, social type, or historical analogy that our
protestors insist. I will give but one example. I did not see the
unfortunate Ferrer[3] tried; but I can easily imagine that this trial
may have been hasty and unjust. I remember what our own
courts-martial[4] were in Africa, in face of a far less formidable
rebellion.

Now, if Ferrer was unfairly tried, his judges should be
denounced, though he were the filthiest brigand or pickpocket
in Spain. But the indignant journalists do not say, "In such and
such respects Ferrer was unfairly tried." They tell me instead
that he was a great educationist. That is what I mean by intro-
ducing irrelevant moralities instead of the story. Why should
not a great educationist be shot like anybody else; why should
he not deserve shooting like anybody else? I know more than
one educationist whom I should like to have a pot at. Great
educationists before now have been oppressors and profligates,

[2] One incident in the Dreyfus case was the sending of a telegram by a Major
Pannizardi in November 1894; although the telegram claimed nothing about
Dreyfus' guilt, and indeed Pannizardi did not know Dreyfus, nevertheless, a
combination of poor decoding of the document and prejudice in the courtroom
led to the telegram's being used as an additional piece of evidence against Dreyfus.

[3] A theoretical anarchist who was accused and convicted as one of the chief
instigators of anti-government riots in Barcelona in July of 1909. He was executed
the following October.

[4] Possibly a reference to the "Breaker" Morant case, in which two Australian
officers were executed for the killing of twelve Boer prisoners; their defense was
that "as a reprisal, shooting prisoners was now accepted practice".

cruel torturers, or vile corruptors of youth. I do not say that Ferrer was not a just and honourable man; I do not know anything about it, thanks to the newspapers. He is not the first just and honourable man that has been executed by other just and honourable men in times of armed rebellion. I am only concerned to protest against the intellectual method which transfers the public feeling from the injustice of his sentence to the excellence of his profession or his hobby. Plenty of poor people have been killed in the Spanish riots, and I confess I am not comfortable about this English journalistic habit, which feels the blow of the tyrant not as a blow against humanity, but only as a blow against education and eminence.

November 13, 1909

Newspaper Truths and Advertising

There was a time, for all I know, when this page of this periodical was occupied by facts. If so, I ask the oldest readers to remember their youth and imagine that I am curtly narrating the following incidents as having happened lately in London.

Last Wednesday, the *Spectator* published a soothing and well-balanced article called "Our English Weather." The weather, it seems, is temperate; so was the article. On the whole, however, it maintained that the English climate was mild and required little artificial help for any Londoner inheriting the Viking Blood. As a result of this, the head of a famous firm selling asbestos stoves withdrew all its advertisements from the *Spectator*, saying that it grieved his logical mind that artificial warmth should be called needful in one part of the paper and needless in another.

In the *Clarion*, which is probably the most solidly popular and prosperous of Socialist papers, a hearty old leveller uttered the opinion: "Dirt often means Work; and there are better men among the Great Unwashed than among the Great Unworking." Blink's Soap, which had previously advertised in the paper, withdrew its advertisements, after making the editor the fair offer that he should cease to be a Socialist.

In the *Art Journal* the President of the Royal Academy wrote to the following effect: "Whatever other disadvantages it may have entailed, there can be little doubt that the early Greek practice of going without clothes in early youth and on ceremonial occasions did much to perfect that exquisite knowledge of the poise and changes of the body which have made the art of Hellas immortal." Several West-End tailors immediately withdrew their advertisements.

The *English Review*, which pays special attention to poetry, included lately a poem by Mr. W. B. Yeats, beginning with the two lines—

> Let there be nought for the night, Kil Cronach,
> Between my head and the good grey rain.

The advertisers of Parkinson's Patent Umbrella entered into a long and painful correspondence with the proprietors of the magazine, which ended in the disappearance of their old and familiar advertisement.

The *Westminster Gazette*, criticising the lighter drama in the ordinary course of its journalistic duty, remarked that one particular play, produced by Mr. George Edwardes, had not a very good libretto. Mr. George Edwardes was suddenly torn and racked with a degrading sense of inconsistency. He could not bear the *Westminster Gazette* to be so disconnected in its ideas. Somebody else said his play was bad in the very same paper in which he, with a more detached judgment, said it was good. He withdrew his advertisement from the paper.

Now among those six utterly and ravingly nonsensical anecdotes, one actually happened. But, upon my honour, I do not think that a rational person, unread in the English papers, could tell me which. The whole proposition belongs, not to topsy-turvydom (for topsy-turvydom is logical), but to some sphere inconceivable to the ordinary human intellect. We all knew that there were advertisements in papers; and some of us, when exhausted by the articles, have got much amusement out of them. But it never crossed the brain of any man in his five wits that the articles had to square with the advertisements. We never supposed that the prose articles by biologists and physicians were to be modelled on those sombre paragraphs which begin with a young man feeling worn and nervous in Glasgow and end with Tompkinson's Tonic. We did not suppose that the poetry of a paper existed permanently, as it were, under the eye of the fluent poet of Bungay's Saving Salts. Yet this is the claim that has quite seriously been made; it has been made (for I rend the veil otherwise impenetrable) by Mr. George Edwardes against the *Westminster Gazette*. Mr. George Edwardes, being (in the ordinary sense) sane, does in cold blood declare that the text of a paper must be altered to suit its advertisements. To hear that is like hearing the crack of Doom. On occasions like this one has a sense as of the universe being in travail. Something seems ready to burst. I rather think it must be laughter.

Yet in this case there is hope as well as despair. Indeed, there is hope because there is despair; it is when the invalid has the courage to despair of his right hand (or left leg) that there begins to be hope for his whole body. There is something about the cool nature of Mr. George Edwardes's suggestion which may serve to bring all journalism to its senses. If we are really to write up to the advertisements, I think it would pay us better to write the advertisements. If I am to be controlled by Smith's Soap I think I may as well be paid by Smith's Soap: Smith has probably much more money than any honest newspapers. Of course Mr. Edwardes and his friends do not say in so many words that they object to all criticism. They always say (the phrases are charmingly settled and stereotyped) that they do not object to fair criticism. I have met hundreds of men who said that they would not object to a fair criticism, but I never met one man who admitted that he had received one. But Mr.

Edwardes disposes finally of his own case in this respect by saying that the *Westminster Gazette* criticism was obviously inspired by malice and spite. Now this is a smashing test; this is *always* the thing that people say when they have literally nothing else to say. If a critic tells a particular lie, that particular lie can be pointed out. If he misses a specific point, that point can be explained. If he is really wrong in this or that, it will be on this or that that the insulted person will eagerly pounce. But "malice and spite" are vague words which will never be used except when there is really nothing to pounce on. If a man says that I am a dwarf, I can invite him to measure me. If he says I am a cannibal, I can invite him to dinner. If he says I am a coward, I can hit him. If he says I am a miser, I can give him half-a-sovereign. But if he says I am fat and lazy (which is true), the best I can answer is that he speaks out of malice and spite. Whenever we see that phrase, we may be almost certain that somebody has told the truth about somebody else.

Therefore, as I say, there is hope in the very hugeness of the wrong. For it may be observed in history that most tyrannies have fallen, not by an ultimate act of rebellion, but by a final and indefensible declaration of despotism. Man, because he is the image of God, would rather have even the practice of wrong than the theory of it. He would rather endure tyranny than admit tyranny. Therefore most of the rebellions against oppression have been made, not at the moment when the oppressor first began to oppress, but only at the moment when the oppressor first declared himself as such. It was when Gesler put his own hat on top of a pole to be worshipped that William Tell arose. Probably Gesler had put a number of other people's heads on poles, without in any way attracting Tell from drinking ale or practising archery in his back garden. Caesar was assassinated because he was trying to be a king, not because he had already become an autocrat. What smashed the Stuarts was their divine right, not any of their human wrong. It is always the *claim* that maddens men, much more than the acts. There is never any real revolt against any human abuse, until it has made its open and monstrous claim upon humanity. It is due to Mr. Edwardes to say that he has been brave enough to make the first full and precise claim for the complete subordination of art to money. Now that the despot has declared himself (and even tried to be crowned at Westminster), we may look to men for the revolt.

November 20, 1909

Politicians and Their Constitutions

One genuine point of resemblance between the voice of the people and the voice of Heaven is that they are both very often rather difficult to understand. Honestly, I think the priests were nearer to Heaven than the politicians are to England. The common curate may at least be trying to be like the divine ideal, whereas I am sure that the statesman is not even trying to be like his cabman. Yet this is what representative government implies, or ought to imply. It ought to mean men striving to express the mystery of democracy, as priesthoods try to express the mystery of deity. If a man has been elected by a million voters, he ought to walk at once powerfully and doubtfully, as if he were a million men. An elegant young barrister ought to stride towards Westminster, saying to himself, with sincere conviction, "I am five thousand farmers in the West of Yorkshire." If the thought makes him walk a little more heavily and with a slight slouch, so much the better. He is all the more a representative. If on arriving at St. Stephen's, he could contrive to stare all round with an ox-like stoop and speak with a thick Yorkshire accent—that would really be representative government. Perhaps, after all, this is the real reason of that bovine stupidity which can be seen in some celebrated statesmen. Their husky voices and hazy statements are meant to suggest the mur-

mur of an invisible multitude; their extraordinary way of walking is an imitation of a badly managed procession. If a man
represents two men, it is obvious that he ought to walk like a
quadruped. When he represents a hundred, it is not surprising
that he walks like a centipede.

This theory, however (which has cost me three minutes' earnest thought), must, I fear, be abandoned. I am afraid it must
be frankly confessed that representatives do not represent; that
politicians do not resemble the respectable working-classes in
anything—except their highly respectable objection to work.
Now if we agree that the elected representatives of the nation,
who do at least fight for votes and are formally elected, are not
very real representatives of the English, the case is even clearer
with those who largely govern the modern State without having
gone through any ritual of election at all. No; I do not mean the
King or the House of Lords. I mean the critics: the men who
have found their way to almost pontifical thrones, but who have
never faced a single crowd to speak to it; who have not even the
courage of a common Cabinet Minister. I mean those writers
who pronounce upon pictures or on the dràma from some fixed
place in some magazine or newspaper. In fact, I mean people
like me. But at least I can say that I have addressed meetings of
real people from a real cart, and lost numerous votes to the
Liberal candidate. My friend Mr. Bernard Shaw even wanted
me to stand as his colleague for the County Council. I often
please myself with the thought of how the audience would have
roared with laughter whenever we appeared on the platform side
by side, like the Two Macs at the music-hall. I think I would
really have accepted the candidature if I could have been quite
certain of being defeated. But life is full of unforeseen disasters:
I might even have got in, and a nice mess I should have been in
then. Let us return, however, to the critics. Now the peculiar
point about the critics is this—that they are not, as far as one
can see, bad representatives, but literally not representatives at
all. Some Members of Parliament are almost exaggerations of
some national type. Mr. Chaplin is not only a squire, but is

almost a stage squire. Mr. Will Crooks is as good as a character
in Dickens. Other politicians, again, approximate to, though
they fall short of, the spirit of their constituents. Considered as
a City Alderman, Mr. Balfour leaves something to be desired
in fatness and redness, but he is entirely satisfactory as regards
slowness. Mr. Winston Churchill, if he is in some sense a hereditary ruler, is at least a hereditary demagogue. But the art critics
and the dramatic critics seem to be a totally distinct race; I can
trace in them no resemblance to the human outline. They are
separated by a great chasm of "culture" and fastidiousness from
the people for whom they write. They foresee the amusements
of the public, not as wine-tasters oversee wine-drinking, or horse-
doctors inspect horses—that is, by right of knowing more than
most people about something which most people know. Rather
they oversee them as teetotalers count the public-houses, or as
a giraffe, with lifted head, might oversee a fish-market. This
division and disgust is a dangerous attitude, even when it is a
right attitude; for there is in all arrogance the beginning of ignorance. If you merely oversee a thing you are very apt to overlook
it. Obviously the right condition for a healthy community is
that the people and the critics should have the same basic joy in
beautiful or comic things; but that the people should not know
why they feel the joy, while the critics should tell them. Sir
Philip Sidney's nurse may have liked "Chevy Chase" quite as
much as Sir Philip Sidney; but she would never have said of it
that it was like the sound of a trumpet. A sailor from Piraeus
may have wept at a Greek tragedy as much as Aristotle; but he
probably did not explain (between his sobs) that he was undergoing the καθαρσις, or purification of the emotions by pity and
terror. This is the sensible state of things with regard to critics;
they are the analysts of pleasure. As men they should laugh or
cry at a theatre; and then afterwards, as critics, defend themselves
for having done so. They should justify to the public its own
feelings in the act of justifying their own. But in modern England
one thing is very clear: that something has gone wrong with
this natural relation of the critics to the commonwealth. The

writers in question never attempt to explain why humanity likes this or that; generally they get no further than explaining why they do not like it themselves. Either something is very wrong with our public or something is very wrong with our critics. Perhaps both.

It is chiefly in theatrical critics, of course, that one sees this. In a theatre one can hear the people, the pack in full cry. But no one bursts into a loud yell before a picture in the New Gallery, and we do not see cheering mobs round a bookstall. And nothing is more startling than the contrast between the positive unanimity of the people and the strange isolation and perplexity of the critics. I saw a play the other day which was received by the whole audience from stalls to gallery with an earthquake of applause and assent; it was "The Servant in the House," by Mr. Rann Kennedy, at the Adelphi. Personally, I think it deserved its triumph; but that has nothing to do with what I am urging here. Of course, the critics were not bound to praise it merely because it was popular; but their case was much more singular than that. The point is that from reading the criticisms of two or three of the leading dramatic critics (who have a slightly pedantic objection to the democratic morality of the play) no one could possibly have conceived, first, why it was so popular, and secondly, why on earth it should be popular. Now a critic, even if he differs from the human criticism, ought to be able to explain it. That is his business. But the dramatic critics, even those like Mr. Max Beerbohm, whom I both like and admire, have altogether surrendered the attempt to lead the human march. They merely walk in the other direction. It is not the nature of Man but the nature of Max that is expressed. The critics are like wine-tasters who should really prefer claret sour; they are like horse-doctors who should have an aesthetic preference for lame horses. They differ from their clients not only about the means, but about the most ultimate aim.

November 27, 1909

Ghosts and World Affairs

Mr. Stead's statement about his spiritual interview with Mr. Gladstone has brought certain modern discussions to a head— the flippant will say to a swelled head. I will not pretend that Mr. Stead's activity has been without an element of unintentional humour. But if Mr. Stead is absurd, he is not even half so absurd as the newspapers and speakers that have attacked him. Perhaps Mr. Stead does not know much about ghosts; that is why he is so fond of them. But those who have assailed and derided Mr. Stead manifestly know nothing at all about them. Everybody seems to be arguing as if only one of two things could be true— (1) that Mr. Gladstone spoke to Mr. Stead from heaven; (2) that Mr. Stead has worked a common fraud. I cannot say which of these two suggestions strikes me as the more preposterous and improbable. It seems equally incredible that Stead should tell an ordinary lie to me and that Gladstone should tell an extraordinary truth to Stead. Mr. Stead is a quite sincere man, but his criticism is another matter. I would always believe what he says, but I should never think of believing what he believes.

Mr. Stead and the other spiritualists, then, are generally truthful men. But let us for the moment leave truth and narrow ourselves to fact. Apart from the intentions or the impressions, what, so far as we can follow them, are the occurrences? Well, I will take the liberty of dogmatising about the situation as it stands. There is no doubt whatever, for any fair and free human mind which has studied the experiment, that it is possible to obtain messages and explanations which come, I do not say from a spiritual source, but certainly from an unknown source. Jones and Brown can sit down with a planchette, and it will write things which may be written by their common sub-consciousness, or by the ghost of Queen Elizabeth, or by the Devil, but which are not, in the plain English sense, written either by Jones or Brown. This is quite certain. All the three causes I have mentioned are seriously and strictly mystical causes. I know distinctly less about my own sub-consciousness than I know about the Devil; and I am, in comparison, quite an intimate friend of Queen Elizabeth. At least I know there was such a lady; and my social intercourse with the "subliminal self" does not yet permit me even to ask him if he exists. The brute fact is that certain communications do come to entirely honest people through planchette, through table-rapping, through automatic writing, through professional mediums. The communications may be dishonest, but the people are not. In truth, the communications may be dishonest because they are genuine. They may be genuine messages from hell, the home of dishonesty. But a man is not dishonest because he receives them, because he believes them, or because he believes them to have come from heaven.

The extraordinary thing is, not that Mr. Stead has had a message from the mighty dead, but that Mr. Stead has believed it. Messages from the mighty dead are easy enough to get. When I was a boy I used to play with a planchette as carelessly as I played with a cricket-bat; I have never operated through a medium, but I suppose that the doubts and the certainties are much the same. If it had ever occurred to me to believe the things that the planchette wrote down I should be a raving maniac by this time. Gladstone pronouncing on the Budget would have been a very mild interlude in our old orgies of supernatural interviewing. Moses was perfectly ready to provide us with ten new commandments; Cromwell would be converted to Catholicism as soon as look at you. There was one story in particular about a secret marriage of one of my aunts to Cardinal Manning, which I am very glad did not find its way to Mr. Stead and the serious newspapers. One day, I remember, "Planchette," without the faintest justification, advised an acquaintance of mine to get a divorce. When we remonstrated, the oracle inscribed on the paper a long, illegible word beginning with O R R. Now, there is no word in English beginning O R R. We insisted on greater lucidity; and eventually the long word turned out like this—" 'Orrible revelations in 'igh life." Suppose Mr. Stead had encountered this august spirit and taken its communication seriously! I abandoned planchette as a toy, because even as a toy I found it left behind a strange and stale flavour of ignominy, as of a man who had been drunk the night before; and this smelt a little of evil. But I never dreamed at any time of believing in any of the Virgils, Newtons, and Isaiahs who used to come and give us information. I trust them no more than the monologues in a mad-house. It happens that most of my literary admirers live in asylums. Every day or two I receive a warm and flattering letter beginning "Hanwell. Friday morning. Dear Sir,—I am in full intellectual agreement with your admirable," etc., or "Colney Hatch. Tuesday. Sir,—We are evidently kindred spirits," or words to that effect. I am grateful to these gentleman, but if one of them remarked incidentally that he was Mr. Gladstone, I should not be surprised into belief. My attitude would be the same in the case of Spiritualist pretensions. I do not believe a person who is obviously quite mad because he is also quite dead. Moreover, there is another principle which will be found a practical tool in such proceedings as this. The principle may be generally defined somewhat in this way. While it is a first forcible objection to any story that it is intrinsically improbable, it is, moreover, a second and further objection that it is superficially probable. The first shows that it *was* invented, the second shows that it *would be* invented. Suppose, for instance, that somebody came to me with some spiritual theory say, that Mr. Bernard Shaw is Satan. Now, I know Mr. Bernard Shaw to be a very kind and simple man; and that is a reason for doubting that he is Satan. But I also know that many people who do not know him think he is cynical and fiendish. Therefore I not only see the error, but I see where the error came from. I can not only say: "You did not get this impression from Shaw's character"; but I can say: "You did get it from Shaw's caricatures."

Or take the instance of another opinion, which is (though the reader may scarcely believe it) actually held. I have occasionally had a pot-shot in this paper at the theory that Bacon wrote

Shakespeare. But that theory itself is solid commonsense compared with some of the other theories that Baconians swallow
along with it. One of these is that Bacon was the son of Queen
Elizabeth. Now, this is rank nonsense, not because it is bizarre
or recherché, but, on the contrary, because it is vulgar and
obvious. Really, of course, Elizabeth is the last woman in England to have been Bacon's mother. But, vulgarly and superficially, she is the first person to be thought of as Bacon's mother—
that is, unless we are so poor-spirited as to suggest the claim of
Lady Bacon.

Now, the objection to believing that Mr. Gladstone's soul is
brooding over the Budget is the same as the objection to these
vulgar theorists who tried to find some celebrated person in a
ruff to be Bacon's mother and could think only of Queen Elizabeth. Most people only knew Gladstone in connection with
politics, and therefore spiritualism makes him talk about politics.
But when one thinks how enormous and awful is the soul of a
man, with what a load of love and sin and gigantic secrecy it
goes through the gate of death, it is overwhelmingly unlikely
that when we see that spirit again we shall see it worrying about
its profession or place in the newspapers. Every public figure is
like a little islet that is only the last peak of a submerged mountain. It is unspeakably improbable that the ghost of Newton
would talk about astronomy or the ghost of Nelson about the
Navy or the ghost of Gladstone about the Budget. I would only
believe in these ghosts if they spoke to me in strange and unde-
cipherable tongues about things that I have never known.

December 4, 1909

Honesty in Vegetarianism

A friend has sent me a sort of guide or prospectus of the food
eaten by vegetarians, or, to speak more strictly, I believe, by
fruitarians. It has given me more solid pleasure than any book

of poetry or philosophy I have read for years. Not that I want
to eat the fruitarian foods; Heaven forbid. A man may be interested in the ingenuity and picturesqueness of a scheme of advertisement without having the desperate design of sampling any
of the wares. Suppose I had lived in Renaissance Italy, I might
have received some pleasant little pamphlet such as this, adver-
tising "Borgia Biscuits; the best for Bishops"; or, "Try Lucrezia,
the Latest Soporific; Invariably Ends an Illness"; or, "Pope Alexander's Painless Chianti: the late Cardinal Colonna writes 'Since
then I have used no other.' "

In such a case I should order tons of the entertaining prospectus, but none of the food. I feel almost an equal degree of
fastidiousness about the Fruit Foods, some of which sound to
me as ominous as Borgia Biscuits. I think the drinks are the
worst. After the menu of a breakfast resembling a rather restrained
dessert are these stern words: "One cup Brunak." One, and no
more. I should think so. Falling down in convulsions would
seem the least that could happen to a man after having drunk
anything with a name like that. Then there is "Stomike Coffee";
it gives one a pain to hear of it. Then, after some jolly dinner
of sliced protose and cardoons will come the command "glass
of Mostelle." What would happen if a man took two glasses? Is
it so heady and Bacchanalian a drink that a glass and a half would
strike any man senseless? And what are Manhu Foods? They
sound a bit cannibalistic to me. On the whole, however, I think
that the most fearful item, fearful in its very quietude and simplicity, is the frequently recurring item, "Wallace's Bread and
butter." I do not know Wallace; doubtless he is a brilliant, a
sinister, a cunning and audacious man. But what can he do to
bread and butter?

Then, of course, there is the larger and more philosophic riddle
of why the vegetarians, or fruitarians, try to make their dishes
sound, or even seem, like meat dishes? Why do they talk nonsense about nut-cutlets or tomato toad-in-the-hole? Why do they
make nutton rhyme to mutton, and nutter rhyme to butter? It
seems a futile poetical exercise. It cannot be supposed to take

anyone in. We meat-eaters might as well pretend that cutlets grow on trees. We might as well talk about picking sausages in the hedgerows, or growing fish-cakes in our own garden. But while it is not deceptive, it is degrading. It is beneath the dignity of men who (though a trifle mad) are manifestly sincere believers in their cause, that they should elaborately mimic the shapes and titles of the system which they seek to dethrone. We expect Food Reformers to be prigs; but they need not be snobs too. If they really think it wrong to eat meat, if they honestly consider it a kind of cannibalism, why should they introduce reminders of the revolting habit they have renounced? When South Sea Islanders are reclaimed from cannibalism, I never heard that their food was dressed so as to look like a missionary. I never heard that the dishes were called "Smith Sauté" or "Brown à la Maître d'Hôtel." Moreover, these disguises are artistically very inappropriate to the cause in question. There is poetry in nearly everything, even in a fruit diet. But the poetry depends wholly on simplicity; there is a certain human and traditional beauty about the idea of a man living on wild fruits in a wood or on rich fruits in a garden; but not about a man eating mashed and mis-named fruit along with a cup of Brunak. These fruitarian gourmets and epicures take away from a fruit diet the one real attraction that it has ever had for human imagination—its directness, its coolness and cleanliness, its scent of Eden. I will eat nuts with any man—or with any monkey. But they must be nuts—not nutton, or nutter, or nusco, or nutrogen, or nuttolene, or nuttose, or nutarian Cashew.

The true compromise lies somewhere here. Some people, I believe, adopt the compromise about drink of being teetotalers between meals. Well, I am a vegetarian between meals. From breakfast to lunch not a leg of mutton crosses my lips. During all that time I am an earnest and active nutarian, munching away and laying up stores of health. It is this careless habit of eating a turkey or a salmon at odd times during the day that does so much harm. Only four times a day I will eat, like a man; for the rest I will browse happily, like all the beasts of the field.

These, at least, are the only terms, I fear, on which I can entertain the idea of being a fruitarian at all. If this reasonable treaty is refused by vegetarian fanatics, I must close my new fruitarian primer with a sigh. But, in any case, if I am to be misled with a taste of such innocence as is not for man, I will have it ancient and undiluted, the good old Arcadia of the shepherds and shepherdesses, with water in every fountain and fruit on every tree. I will not have the fountains of Arcadia running with Brunak, nor the trees of Arcadia growing nothing but McDoddie's Evaporated Vegetables. I will not have the land of shepherds invaded by insane doctors with their accursed digestive coffees and non-alcoholic wines. No, no; even in illusions there is all the difference between health and disease. Arcadia is an illusion of this earth; but it is a clear illusion. We cannot have natural food, because we human beings cannot have anything natural; only the supernatural is left for us. The apple is eaten; the fear is on all flesh; by the sweat of our brow shall we eat bread until we return to the dust. But not Wallace's bread, if you please, nor even his butter; nor do I think the tale of Eden would have ended better if the apple had been in the form of Apple Tea Essence— except in so far that it might have been less attractive. Food that is frigid without even being simple, a society that keeps well by always treating itself as ill—this is something beyond the burden of Adam, and not to be borne. I won't stand that, as the little boys say—no, not for nuts.

December 11, 1909

Political Invective in England

We often congratulate ourselves on the good-humour with which our politicians offer and accept attacks; but I sometimes fear that this is mainly due to an equally good-humoured understanding that the attacks shall not really touch the spot. It is difficult to say exactly what principle governs political invective in England. On the one hand, the most stately nobleman will talk stark Billingsgate;[1] on the other hand, the most plunging Revolutionists display, at certain moments, a sudden reticence. As far as I can make out, the principle is this: that you can say anything about a man so long as it is not true. You can accuse a man of the most blackguardly extravagance, as long as you are sure he is a miser. You can call a politician a peace-loving coward if you have real private information that he is a pirate on the high seas. The very phrase reminds me of a case in point, which really occurred the other day. Some landlord or other, speaking against the Budget, actually described the existing English Cabinet as "a ragged crew of piratical tatterdemalions." Seldom have I rolled in such mental luxury as after I read those words. There rose before my mental eye the enormous and smiling image of Mr. Haldane. I saw Mr. Asquith and Mr. Sydney Buxton quite plain, as I had seen them last . . . at a dinner. Never, surely, were tatterdemalions so utterly piratical. Pistols were stuck in every belt, cutlasses hitched to every ragged trouser; the toast of "Blood and Plunder!" drunk in rum . . . but my vision has unduly overwhelmed me, and I wake with a start, as from a dream. In sober truth, all recent English politics has owed its success to this grand principle of misdirected extravagance. We forbid truth; but we do not forbid violence. A charge may be quite wild as long as it is wildly inapplicable.

This can be seen clearly by looking through the old Conservative comic papers and controversial posters against the late Mr. Gladstone. He was a very conservative kind of man, and therefore there were no limits to denouncing him—as a demagogue. The very things about him that were most mild and traditional were made symbols of fantasy and anarchism. For

[1] This was the site for many centuries of a fish-market where the porters were known for their foul and abusive language; thus, to talk Billingsgate means to use foul and abusive language or to scold in a vulgar fashion.

instance, being by temper conservative, he happened to wear rather old-fashioned collars, such as he had worn when a Tory. These collars were expanded in pictures into a wild eccentricity, till people fancied that Gladstone, in his madness, had invented the collars. Or again, he pursued for pleasure the very ancient and blameless branch of woodcraft which consists in cutting timber. At once it was suggested that there was something madly destructive in this, as though he blew up trees with a bomb. Though his axe was an old and innocent as Homer, it was always somehow suggested that his axe was as crude and crimson as the axe of the guillotine. But he was quite safe, because he was being attacked for the wrong reason. They denounced him as a crazy innovator, and his answers were easy: if they had attacked him as a pedantic Tory, the problem might have been less easy to settle. I could give many further instances of this in the case of living English politicans. They would let me repeat freely all the frantic lies that are told about them. But if I began, however faintly, to say what I thought true about them, they would all bring libel actions in a body. There is only one articulate English person I can think of who will not bring a libel action against me however much I provoke him, and that is myself. It happens, indeed, that I have flourished and fattened on this habit of the critics of never fixing on a man's real faults. A little while ago I was asked to give evidence before the Committee on the Censorship, and, being of a meek and law-abiding nature, I did so. Whereupon a weekly paper of excellent standing (I think it was the *Outlook*) cheerily accused me of having shoved myself in with sheer impudence, and given my evidence by main force. "It does not appear that Mr. Chesterton was invited," it said; "he invited himself." How on earth it could "appear" that I was invited, unless a reward had been offered for me with blasts of a trumpet from the steps of the Royal Exchange, I do not know. The letter of invitation was sent to me, strangely enough; not to the *Outlook*.

The writer, not having the slightest evidence to go on, must have gone on some general view of my character. I must be supposed to be the kind of man who would walk into a committee-room labelled "Private" and give evidence which nobody wanted on something which I did not understand. Now, apart from the disgusting vices required, I do not possess the virtues necessary for such a practical joke. I am thoroughly English in my lack of moral courage. In the few physical dangers that have held me up, I can at least say that I did not collapse. But my moral awe of Authority is quite flattening. I could no more tell ten other men lawfully appointed that they ought to have my testimony than I could take the King's cigar out of his mouth or smash the Venus of Milo in the Louvre. Yet you see that an enemy, willing to wound, imagines that if he accuses me of this monstrous and almost heroic vulgarity, he will have hit me on the raw; whereas I am as indifferent to that charge as Don Quixote could be to a charge of corpulence. If he had said that I was very nervous when giving evidence, it would have been much more humiliating—and quite true. The egotism of this example is, I beg leave to state, involuntary. As I said before, if I gave the case of anybody else's attackable side, I should be stopped. "Le culte de moi" has increased in modern English literature largely because himself is the only person a man is allowed to attack without going to prison. In old days men managed by hook or crook to publish Scandals of the Court or Horrible Revelations of High Life. But now a man must publish his own scandals for want of any other; he must find the horrible revelations inside his own head. This is called "sincere artistry."

No doubt it is, generally speaking, normal and inevitable that we should be accused of the wrong things; when one is accused of the right things, one so often gets hanged. It is not for you or me to complain of the kind accident whereby our enemies never look for the skeleton in the cupboard, but employ themselves healthily in digging up the back garden. You, the reader, can afford to smile at those charges of forgery and financial fraud which are so regularly brought against you by all your acquaintances. So long as they say nothing about arsenic, or what happened that dark November in the New Cut, you are all right.

I also . . . but I think I will not tell you at the mention of which crime out of fifty-seven I can scarcely repress a start. Souls are always secrets; but I think modern England carries secrecy far beyond the spiritual need for it. We do not merely supress private things, but public things too; indeed; we suppress public things especially. A considerable English county, let us say, is governed by Lord Valancourt of Normantowers. I do not expect to know his soul, which is for Providence; but I think I might be allowed to know his name, which is Schmidt. Dear old ladies, with an utter ignorance of England which is charmingly English, used to express an alarm lest journalism would too much penetrate private life. They need have no fear. Life that is worth calling life is always private, not to say somewhat unintelligible. There is always something odd and impudent about a man's claim on a title-page to write another man's "life." Life, I say, is always private; but biography is public, and it might be as well to have it true.

December 18, 1909

Worship of the Future

A little while ago I happened to review in a daily paper a pre-posterous advertisement called "The Declaration of Futurism." It described the various ways in which a gentleman named Ma-rinetti and his friends were going to exalt the future and trample on the past. To quote a much more vigorous writer than Mr. Marinetti (I mean Mr. W. W. Jacobs): "Silly ways they was, most of 'em; and the sillier they was the more old Sam seemed to like 'em." In the same way, the sillier they were, the more Mr. Marinetti seemed to like them. One way was to destroy museums and everything in them; which sounds to me very long and laborious. To reduce, let us say, a granite figure of Memnon to a fine powder would take more time and trouble than making another one, with the latest improvements. Another way (as the books on conjuring say) was to encourage motor-cars to go anywhere and do anything. Mr. Marinetti wished, so to speak, to hurl the automobiles against the immovables, such as St. Peter's, the Pyramids, or the Parthenon. I suggest that Mr. Marinetti—who has obviously a sweeping and somewhat Oriental imagination—arrange a great allegorical conflict on these lines. Let us have in the arena of the desert (a literal arena) a great tournament between the Past and the Future. Let Mr. Marinetti get into his motor-car ten miles off, crowd on full speed, and charge a Pyramid. Then we shall see which wins.

In the article to which I allude, I limited myself wholly to pointing out what I conceived to be the fundamental fallacy in the whole of this worship of the Future—a fallacy by no means confined to Mr. Marinetti and his mad friends in their motors. There is one quite simple objection to the Future as an ideal. The objection is that the Future does not exist. The Future is non-existent; therefore the Future is dead. It is "le Néant," as Danton said. The Past is existent, and therefore the Past is alive. He who lives in past affairs lives in vivid and varied affairs, in turbulent, disputatious, and democratic affairs. He who lives in the future lives in a featureless blank; he lives in impersonality; he lives in Nirvana. The past is democratic, because it is a people. The future is despotic, because it is a caprice. Each man is alone in his prediction, just as each man is alone in a dream. If I turn my face to the past I immediately find myself in the presence of Phidippides, who could outrace me; of Coeur-de-Lion, who could knock me down; of Erasmus, who could greatly improve my Latin; of Newton, who could explain very clearly things that I could not understand; of Robin Hood, who could beat me in a game of archery; or of William Shakespeare, who might possibly be my superior in a game of *bouts-rimés*. But when I turn my face to the future, then everybody bows down to me; then everybody prostrates himself; because there is nobody there but myself.

As I wish to get on to the sequel of the story, I will only pause a moment to indicate the application of my principles to Mr. Marinetti and his motor-car. The application, indeed, is plain— Mr. Marinetti utters a contradiction in terms when he says that he likes motor-cars but dislikes museums. If men do not study previous science, they certainly will invent no further science. The poet's motor-car has been built up by the most elaborate and even meticulous study of the past. Sculpture or music might conceivably spring up spontaneously; but if there is one thing of all others that depends on the past it is mechanical science. Motor-cars are probably invented by people who pass half their lives in museums. It is at least evident that the Italian writer has chosen a most unfortunate example to show his independence of his fathers that begat him. If he were going to be a naked savage, he would at least have only life to thank them for. But if he is going to be a luxurious modern motorist in a fur coat and goggles, why then he must go down on his knees and thank every man who ever lived, from the first barbarian who stripped off the furry skin of a beast to the last optician who invented a system of lenses. When Mr. Marinetti has invented a really modern motor-car, a car that does not include the ancient institution of wheels, or allow for the old-world posture of sitting, I shall be very much interested to hear of that car. But I will not go in the car, even if he asks me.

Well, I wrote my article attacking the Futurists, and the result is that they send me a present of three nice thick books; a trifle insane, perhaps, but very readable, and presumably well meant. Perhaps if I go on writing against the Futurists I shall get a whole library of Futurism. One of the things I cannot make out about Mr. Marinetti is whether he is a French author or an Italian author. One of these three books is in Italian, so I cannot read it. Two of them are in French, so I can read them; and, as far as is reasonably possible, I do read them. They are rather rum.

I admit that it is unfair to translate poetry literally, but, allowing for that, I think the reader will admit that a poem that ends like this has something about it decidedly odder than any foreign idiom. I translate quite fairly the last eight lines of a rather clever poem called, "La Folie des Maisonnettes."

> The Sunset crushed all the village
> Under its powerful and bloody knees.
> Then, rearing again its majestic trunk,
> With one beautiful and insolent gesture,
> Flung gold upon the corpses
> And passed away towards the mountains with great strides
> To bite—there, where they trembled—the pure lips
> Of the stars.

Now it is only fair to Mr. Marinetti to say that there is a definite amount of good poetry scattered through his crazy pages; even in the lines I have quoted there is the good phrase about the scornful sunset flinging gold on the dead cities. I cannot say that I have ever seen a sunset kneeling on my house and crushing it with bloody knees; nor did I ever see a sunset that seemed at all likely to bite the pure lips of the stars, at any early opportunity. But I have seen an effect as of powdered gold flung fitfully upon level and sepulchral streets at evening; and I give the devil his due. I grant Mr. Marinetti his scattered gold. With a beautiful and insolent gesture I fling this concession on Mr. Marinetti's corpse; and I pass on with great strides to bite the pure lips of some other subject.

But indeed the important subject is quite other; since it concerns not these Futurists merely, but many much more prosperous and much less amusing people, who commit this primary moral error of turning from the present and past, which are full of facts, to the future, which is void even of abstract truth. The real moral of the matter is this: that decadence, in its fullest sense of failure and impotence, is now to be found among those who live in the future, not in those who live in the past. We still associate decadence vaguely with archaeology, and doubtless there is justification for the idea. I have met distinguished historians and antiquaries, in talking with whom one instinctively remembered that demoniacs always lived among the tombs. But looking backward is not the only form of weakness. Looking forward is, in all our actual experience, a form of weakness too. The Futurist does not really invade the future like a conqueror; he only flies to the future as a fugitive flies to sanctuary. In the street of Bye-and-Bye, said Henley, stands the Hostelry of Never. And indeed this is truer than he meant. The love of the untried is truly the love of Nothing: Futurism is very near to Nihilism. The street of Bye-and-Bye, in which Mr. Marinetti has his publishing offices, is in a part of the human city by no means remarkable either for deserving success or obtaining it. In every practical matter you and I have known, Futurism has been a learned name for failure. The street of Bye-and-Bye is at the corner of Queer Street.

But above and beyond any such external weakness, the worship of the future is weak. It is, indeed, something weaker even than weakness. For weakness has at least always been understood as filled and excused by passion, which is itself strong. There is passion in the past. Men have even been said to fall in love with ancient statues or with queens who died long ago. But there is no passion in the future—only airless vacuums of scientific Utopia and inevitable economics. There is nothing in the future, except pedants. Therefore, I am sorry to see those who might have been poets becoming pedants.

December 25, 1909

The Failure of the Aesthetes

The word "aesthete" has come to mean something more (or less) than its exact meaning: a man whose pleasures are principally in artistic feeling. A pleasure in "Pickwick" is an artistic pleasure; but a person reading "Pickwick" outside an ale-house would scarcely be jeered at by passing rustics as an aesthete. Admiration for the Life Guards is aesthetic; but it is not as an aesthete that the housemaid is commonly rebuked by her mistress. In popular connotation it has come to mean two distinctive things. First, it means a certain type or tint of beauty—the somewhat mixed, melancholy, and tentative; the aesthete means the mild man who matches a russet waistcoat with olive trousers, rather than the man (perhaps the equally lovely man) who matches a golden waistcoat with crimson trousers. Second, it has come to mean the arrangement of effects rather than the primary creation of them. The aesthete of ordinary tradition aims at harmony rather than beauty; beauty is a fact, and harmony only a relation between facts. If his hair does not match the mauve sunset against which he is standing, he hurriedly dyes his hair another shade of mauve. If his wife does not go with the wallpaper, he gets a curtain or a divorce. Such is the symbolic figure of the aesthete both in satiric and sympathetic literature; and he does actually exist even in the real world. I have met him often and gone through his picture galleries and reviewed his books of poetry.

I have just been turning over a heap of children's Christmas books. Most of the fairy-tales are still told or retold; most of the decorative illustrations are still designed and executed, by the old original aesthete, the man before mentioned with the mauve hair and the decorative divorce. It is a great mistake to suppose that he has vanished, that he was killed by "Patience"[1] or driven out by the Decadents in frock-coats. He is still there, and dominating a great deal of art and literature, especially, as I have said, the art of literature intended for children. "Patience" only popularised him; the Decadents only brought him up to date. The world of art and culture still lies under his two main laws or

---

[1] A Gilbert and Sullivan opera first produced in 1881 which ridicules the affectations and absurdities of the aesthetic movement spearheaded by Oscar Wilde.

principles: that the highest art is something lean and doubtful; and that faultless combination is the great occupation for an educated man. First, the grey mare is the better horse, more beautiful than the golden horses of the sun. Second, the grey mare must not be yoked with any fierier creature, but only with the pale horse of death.

Now here comes in the extraordinary fact about aesthetes. It has sunk slowly and deeply into my soul in the course of turning over the piles of Christmas publications. The extraordinary fact is that aesthetes do not really understand even their own business of harmony and appropriateness. They make marvellous misfits; they mass together totally inconsistent atmospheres and imagery. They make disgraceful *mésalliances* between authors and artists. For example, critics of the wild and weary school have filled columns with congratulations touching Aubrey Beardsley's illustrations to the "Morte d'Arthur." Now, in truth, the man who got Aubrey Beardsley to illustrate the "Morte d'Arthur" might just as well have got Burne-Jones to illustrate "Martin Chuzzlewit." Nay, much better, for Burne-Jones's art was at least a kind of half-mocking echo of mediaeval beauty, which was one of the moods of Christendom; while the Chaucerian jollity of Dickens was another mood of Christendom, and even a mood of the Middle Ages. But the spirit in Beardsley's art was utterly alien and heathen: a yellow, Oriental devil. To attach it to a rugged Christian tale of love, war, and God, such as the "Morte d'Arthur," is like illustrating a Christmas carol with pictures of Chinese tortures. I heartily concede that, looked at from a certain artistic angle, the wild designs of Beardsley have their fear and fascination and are creepy as well as crazy. There is a certain aching moment under the gas of cities when all faces look like masks. Beardsley immortalised that moment with quite mystical precision. There is a black mood of civilisation when everything seems thin and fictitious, when all the houses seem cut out of cardboard and all the women made out of wire. Beardsley could call up that mood out of Tartarus as if with a magic spell. I do not say that this ironic artificiality should never be touched in art, though I think it should always be touched slightly and even with scorn; and I most certainly agree that it could not be touched better than by Beardsley, for all his little idiot-faces and roaming irrational lines. But it is indeed extraordinary that anyone, even a publisher (to say nothing of a whole chorus of critics), should think that this clever inventor of frilled monkeys and periwigged imps was specially suited to trace in their gigantic outlines the valour, the lust, and the remorse of Lancelot.

But, indeed, the difference is a deeper one and divides much modern work from the old. It is not merely that Beardsley's pallid and quivering figures are unsuited to depict the heavy men in war-harness who buffet against each other in the great grey forest of Malory. Certainly one mildly expects Sir Lancelot to have something resembling a pair of legs, things with muscles in them and some supposititious bones; one does not expect him to have two long wavering reeds instead of legs. But the weakness is integral in modern art of the Beardsley sort; and the point is not without its interest. It may be said that in Malory's time good art was cut in marble and bad art was cut in wood; but both were solid, especially the bad art. Both were in three dimensions; you could walk round them, like a statue. Nowadays even good art is often cut in cardboard. That is to say, even good art is only good when seen from a certain exact standpoint. Shift your point of view ever so little and the edges of the cardboard show. I have just been cutting out figures for a toy theatre for Christmas, and I know all about cardboard.

I have heard people protest against the profanity of burlesque Hamlets and burlesque Macbeths. But, indeed, this is the strength of Macbeth, that he can be burlesqued. Murder is a serious matter. You may make fifty glorious jokes over the corpse of Duncan, and you must still come back to the fact that a dead Duncan in your private house is a serious matter. You can walk round the corpse; it is not made of cardboard. You can make Macbeth comic—and you still leave him tragic. You can burlesque a play of Shakespeare: but you cannot burlesque a play of Maeterlinck. For this reason, that the play of Maeterlinck is itself a mad burlesque, the moment you look at it from any point of view but Maeterlinck's. In the pure Maeterlinck mood the gaping infantile questions, the dreary chorus-like answers, the cowed innocence, the random and thwarted action, are true pictures of a certain agnostic view of life. Once shift your sympathy by an inch, and "Pelleas and Melisande" becomes a roaring farce like "Charley's Aunt." So it is with Malory and Aubrey Beardsley. There is a mental attitude in which we do see people as they are in Beardsley: white waxen faces, false smiles, feeble bodies. But we always see people as they are in Malory: monotonous in their love of war and women, men with the ways and thoughts of men. If I had to illustrate the tales of Malory I should like to hack my human figures out of timber. That is what makes it so strange that they should be illustrated by a man who always tried to make his pictures thinner than the thinnest paper. Therefore (as I say) I have this great complaint against the aesthetes; that they do not even know their own business. They do not feel atmospheres and harmonies. They do not feel parallels and sympathies between art and art. They only make brutal forced marriages between fashion and fashion. If Green Bindings are "up" and the Brontës are "up," then it is Green Bindings for Brontës. That is the substantial result of aesthetic publishing. I had intended to quote quite a large number of instances from the pile of Christmas books before me: to point out how again and again, and everywhere, in every sort of artistic toy-book or illustrated fairy-tale, the aesthete who wrote the book could not have chosen his illustrator, and the aesthete who illustrated could not even have read the book. But these, if described, must be described at some later time.

1910

January 1, 1910

Christmas and the Progressive Movement

I have before me the handsome and even formidable Christmas
Number of a paper which is kindly sent to me every week, called
the *Christian Commonwealth*, described on the front page as "the
Organ of the Progressive Movement in Religion and Social Ethics." I have never been able to make out what the Progressive
Movement is, except that it is rather like a policeman who always
tells people to "move on," without telling them where to go.
But I will never deny that the Christmas Number of the Organ
of the Progressive Movement is full of very interesting things.
Only, despite a considerable parade of the printed word "Christmas," they seem to me exceedingly un-Christmassy things. On
one page is a defence of Christian Science, on another a review
on Eugenics, on another a number of interesting articles about
Table-Rapping and Mediums, on another a diatribe by an energetic Suffragette, on another an excellent article by Mr. Edward
Carpenter[1] on Pagan Sun Worship; and last, but not least, a page
specially dedicated to my old friends the Food Reformers.

Now I may be old-fashioned, but to me the above list of things
does not absolutely reek of a rollicking Christmas. I do not
positively smell mince-pies when I think of Mrs. Eddy and Mr.
Podmore,[2] of Sir Francis Galton,[3] or even Mr. Edward Carpenter. I do not think that if all those four persons had suddenly sat

---

[1] Edward Carpenter (1844–1929), a friend of Walt Whitman who wrote on a
variety of matters, including homosexual love, civilization and art. His 1920
book *Pagan and Christian Creeds: Their Origin and Meaning* hints at his interest in
the matters Chesterton is speaking of.

[2] Frank P. Podmore (1856–1910), a contemporary writer interested in Spiritualism, thought transference and mesmerism. His writings include *Apparitions
and Thought Transference* (1894), *Modern Spiritualism* (1902) and *Mesmerism and
Christian Science* (1909).

[3] Sir Francis Galton (1822–1911), a scientist whose works on eugenics Chesterton deplored.

down to dinner with Bob Cratchit on Christmas Day they would have thrown themselves into the dinner (or thrown the dinner into them) with the right gradation of gaiety. And this is another and better example of the curious truth I urged last week—I mean the practical failure of modern cultured people to realise those very qualities of mood and spirit about which they talk so much. Christmas is at least a mood; and they cannot express that mood. The Christmas dinner for Food Reformers (as given in this periodical) runs as follows: Mock Goose; Mock Fowl; Nut Sausages; Mock Fish Cutlets; Chestnut Savoury; and a Christmas Pudding to be made with nut-suet and with "preparations such as Vegeton, Marmite, Carnos, etc., which are sold by all Health Food Stores." It would be harsh to suggest that Mock Goose and Mock Fish Cutlets are very appropriate dishes for the Mock Christmas. Yet there is seriously a truth in this, which may be more mildly expressed. For these "broad-minded" people are always telling us that belief is not confined in certain forms, but is a certain spirit. To which I answer, "Very well, trot out the spirit; give me a little of it in a liqueur-glass. If religion is only a matter of taste, call the waiter, and let me taste my religion. I shall know whether it tastes right or not." And then the New Theologians bring me something which is made in the shape of a goose and tastes of half-baked beans.

Hitherto the human race has supposed that Christmas consisted of certain facts and fixed principles. It has also supposed that Christmas pudding consisted of certain definable and traditional materials. The progressive person comes by, saying gaily, "Why confine your soaring soul within the mere formularies of currants, suet, and eggs? Take anything, anything that this varied Cosmos has evolved. Every brick in the street is a potential pudding. Poisons are but a blundering search after pudding. Make your universal Christmas pudding out of materials as universal as the spirit of Christmas. Make it of glue, soot, potato-peelings, blacking, hog's-wash, rags, bones, rubbish, Spiritual Healers, Hygienic Marriages, Eastern Pessimism, flying teacups, Prussian Atheists, and Nut Sausages—and your Christmas pudding will be Larger, Broader, and More Mystic." To which I reply, "All right, so long as it tastes like Christmas pudding." But it doesn't. I do not know or dogmatise about the potentialities of hygiene or hog's-wash; but I do know the taste of Christmas pudding—and of Christmas.

This is just what I have maintained about the imaginative anarchy of such aesthetes as Aubrey Beardsley. As long as the artist will be judged by anatomy and proportion, the critic will be bound to call some of his figures fine, if others futile. But suppose he says, "By pulling a man's legs out longer and longer like macaroni, by sticking his eyes in his blank face like currants, I do not mean to represent anatomy and proportion; I only mean to express the inner spirit of Arthurian Romance": then our answer is easy. "*That*, at any rate," we say, "you certainly have not expressed at all." A Beardsley figure as Arthur's body is only impossible. It is unthinkable as his soul. Even the anatomy of such illustrations is more correct than their psychology. So it is with these vague reformers of sentiments such as that of the winter feast of Christendom. They are always explaining that the spirit is more than the letter, that the body is less than the soul.

There is one very vile habit that the pedants have, and that is explaining to a man why he does a thing which the man himself can explain quite well—and quite differently. If I go down on all-fours to find sixpence, it annoys me to be told by a passing biologist that I am really doing it because my remote ancestors were quadrupeds. I concede that he knows all about biology, or even a great deal about my ancestors; but I know he is wrong, because he does not know about the sixpence. If I climb a tree after a stray cat, I am unconvinced when a stray anthropologist tells me that I am doing it because I am essentially arboreal and barbaric. I happen to know why I am doing it; and I know it is because I am amiable and somewhat over-civilised. Scientists will talk to a man on general guess-work about things that they know no more about than about his pocket-money or his pet cat. Religion is one of them, and all the festivals and formalities that are rooted in religion. Thus a man will tell me that in keeping Christmas I am not keeping a Christian feast, but a pagan feast. This is exactly as if he told me that I was not feeling furiously angry, but only a little sad. I know how I am feeling all right; and why I am feeling it. I know this is the case of cats, sixpences, anger, and Christmas Day. When a learned man tells me that on the 25th of December I am really astronomically worshipping the sun, I answer that I am not. I am practising a particular personal religion, the pleasures of which (right or wrong) are not in the least astronomical. If he says that the cult of Christmas and the cult of Apollo are the same, I answer that they are utterly different; and I ought to know for I have held both of them. I believed in Apollo when I was quite little; and I believe in Christmas now that I am very, very big.

Let us not take with such smooth surrender these tenth-truths at tenth hand, such as the phrase that Christmas is pagan in origin. Let us note exactly how much it really means. It amounts, so far as our knowledge goes, solely to this—that primitive Scandinavians did hold a feast in mid-winter. What the dickens else could primitive Scandinavians do, especially in winter? That they put on the largest log in winter: do the professors expect such simple pagans to put on the largest log in summer? It amounts to this, again—that many tribes have either worshipped the sun or (more probably) compared some god or hero to the sun. Just so many a poet has compared his lady to the sun—without by any means intending that she was a Solar Myth. Thus, by talking a great deal about the solar solstice, it can be maintained that Christmas is a sort of sun-worship; to all of which the simple answer is that it feels quite different. If people profess to feel "the spirit" behind symbols, the first thing I expect of them is that they shall feel how opposite are the adoration of the sun and the following of the star.

The Alleged Decline of Christmas

That the celebration of Christmas Day is fading is an illusion. It is an illusion of a natural and even necessary kind; for it arises from a recurrent situation in human psychology, like the eternally recurrent astonishment of middle-aged people at very young people falling in love. The Christmas pudding is still quite as big as it was when I was a baby; it is only that I in my turn have taken on the contours of a yet larger Christmas pudding. But the illusion does not merely arise from such trivialities as time and space; it is also a noble illusion, rooted in something heroic in the spirit of man. For man must always think of his beloved thing as in some kind of danger, besieged by all its enemies and on the point of breaking down. And one of the commonest forms in which this chivalrous peril is pictured is in that of extreme old age and an air of final eclipse, as in the prayer of Priam or the Passing of Arthur. This hearty and honourable sentiment is quite as common among reformers and levellers as among the most sentimental Tories. Gladstone spent his last years at the head of a Cabinet of Radicals attempting a very radical change; but his popularity was expressed in the title of the Grand Old Man. Even while he stood for an innovation, he almost boasted of being an anachronism. Walt Whitman, a genuinely great man, attempted to free himself from the past almost to the point of madness and indecency. He sought to live in a sort of shapeless and barbaric present. That his poetry might be utterly original, he threw over rhyme—and, some would say, reason too. And yet when he wished to express (in a fine poem) the ideal for which he fought, he was forced to strike this same note of antiquity and pathos. He called it "The Old Cause," as if he were a Jacobite.

There are, indeed, some who note the alleged decline of Yule without any of this sadness, but rather with philosophical delight. There are some who would be quite festive on Christmas Day

if they found nobody observing it. Not only are there Scrooge
and his like, there are also the free Hedonists and the Neo-Pagans
and the worshippers of an emancipated pleasure. Of the two
kinds of anti-Christmas person, I personally prefer Scrooge; he
had more sense of humour. But however that may be, there are
plenty of people nowadays who will attack Christmas, not because
it is an indulgence, but because it is a definite and specially timed
indulgence. They object to it, so to speak, not because it is a
feast, but because it is not more of a movable feast. Such critics
suggest that happiness should always be permitted to spring up
spontaneously; and should not be artificially concentrated in any
time or place. They are sad when they see a stout and elderly
uncle obliged to run round the room on all fours, making such
noises as he conceives to be natural to a bear. But they object
to this (they carefully explain) only because the uncle is under a
sort of social coercion; they do not object in the abstract to
lightness or extravagance in uncles. Let humanity, they say, wait
till happiness alights on it momentarily and naturally like a butterfly. Leave the City uncle walking down Cheapside about his
own business; and wait until natural instinct leads him out of
sheer happiness to go down on all fours and make noises like a
bear. Do not oblige grey-haired bankers and politicians to pull
crackers and wear coloured caps on one ritual occasion. Rather
leave it till the exquisite instant comes to them accidentally. Let
the banker suddenly be heard pulling crackers in the inner office
at half-past eleven on a May morning. Let the statesman, in the
middle of a peroration on Tariff Reform, take a coloured cap
from his tail-coat pocket and put it on in the pure excitement
of the moment.

Such is the plausible and even attractive scheme which the
emancipated Hedonists would substitute for such feasts as
Christmas. But their scheme rests (like many other modern
schemes) upon a curious primary mistake about human nature.
It is very doubtful if, left entirely to himself and his club acquaintances, the City uncle would play bears from year's end to year's
end; yet it does not by any means follow that he does not enjoy

the atmosphere of childishness and fantasticality when once he has been forced into it. The very phrase we use when we say that a child "makes us laugh" contains the idea of a certain coercion. The man who can dance all by himself, like a lonely fairy, is as rare as the man who can learn all by himself, like a Scotchman on the make. Most men need institutions to make them distinguish themselves; and they also need institutions to make them enjoy themselves. For, paradoxical as it sounds, men shrink from enjoyment; they make one automatic step backwards from the brink of hilarity; because they know that it means the loss of dignity and a certain furious self-effacement. It is to get over this first reluctance of every reveller that men have created also coercive festivals such as Christmas Day.

The truth at the back of almost every human institution, from a marriage to a tea-party, is the fact that people must be tied by the leg even to do justice to themselves. In such matters coercion is a sort of encouragement; and anarchy (or what these people call liberty) is really oppressive, because its atmosphere discourages everybody. If we all drifted in the air like utterly detached bubbles, if no one knew how long anyone else would be within an inch or a yard of him, the practical result would be that nobody would have the courage to begin a conversation with anybody else. It is so embarrassing to begin a sentence in a friendly whisper and have to howl the last part of it because the other person is floating away into the free and formless ether. People must be tied together in order to talk; for twenty minutes at a dance or for forty years in a marriage; for an hour at a dinner or for three hours at a Christmas dinner. But if anything is to be got out of the relation, it must be a secure one, so far as it goes; and this is true of all pleasure and of all toil. The anarchist says that a man should never speak till he feels inclined; but this would only mean that the modest man would never speak. He must be "brought out"; by force, if necessary. The anarchist says that a man should not feast except of his own accord: that would mean, at any rate, that women would never feast. They must be made to. The anarchist says that no man should work unless he wishes to. At that rate no healthy man would ever work at all; for I hope every healthy man can think of occupations much more entertaining. The anarchic philosophy fails utterly because it ignores this psychological fact of the initial reluctance to do even desirable things. If there are two godlike and glorious things in the world they are an English breakfast and a sea-bath. Yet I have never known any brave and honourable man who denied that he detested getting out of bed and plunging into cold water. The forms and rites of Christmas Day are meant merely to give the last push to people who are afraid to be festive. Father Christmas exists to haul us out of bed and make us partake of meals too beautiful to be called breakfasts. He exists to fling us out of the bathing-machine into the heady happiness of the sea.

January 15, 1910

Education and Ethics

Many eminent men who have been quite rational about other things have been quite mad about education. This is really a very odd thing; because education is the one point on which it is essential to be reasonable and even moderate. It is much more necessary to be sane about education than about the Empire or the Budget or the Lords or the Menace of Germany or the Menace of Socialism. And that for a very plain reason. Men do not go mad by mobs, but by individuals; and education is the one thing in which the individual has direct and despotic power. If I have a fad about taxation, I can only vote for it. But if I have a fad about education, I can pass it unanimously—and apply it to Tommy. This does not occur in any other cases of political opinion: no other public theory can be thus privately applied. You may want to fire off guns at the Germans, like a distinguished Socialist of my acquaintance. But Nature does not give you one individual German to be fired at with a pocket pistol all day. Nature may give you one individual child to be fired at with a pocket theory all day. I may wander pensively at evening among the woods and slopes of Buckinghamshire, tenderly dreaming of what I would like to do to the Peers. But nobody gives me a Peer, bound hand and foot, for me to do what I like with. Nature does give numberless people infants bound hand and foot for them to do what they like with. All Englishmen may deal with all Peers; but that is a different thing from every Englishman dealing with every Peer. Therefore I say that if there is one thing that a man ought to be careful and even cautious about, it is education. And yet it is certainly true that about education some of the wisest men have been not only hazy, but crazy. Rousseau was right about humanity, because he was really thoughtful about humanity. But he was literally childish about childhood. Herbert Spencer, in his moral system taken as a whole, was prim and prosaic to the point of Methodism. But in his scheme for the nursery he was audacious to the point of literal insanity. He wanted the poor miserable infants to learn by "experience" and by the punishments of Nature. If a child falls into the fire and is reduced to a delicate, feathery ash, Spencer suggests (very truly) that he won't do it again. Nor anything else.

Now this introduction, though familiar and obvious, is necessary, because two of the greatest literary men now alive in Europe have just written about the moral views to be inculcated into children; one much more obviously, picturesquely, and at much greater length, but both in such a manner as to bring them, in clear popular versions, before the British public. Count Tolstoy has permitted the publication, in the *Nation* Literary Supplement lately, of a lucid account of how he would teach children morality. And Maurice Maeterlinck has, in his more symbolic manner, treated the same subject in "The Blue Bird," the great infantile allegory now being acted in London. Both these men are great, both in earnest, both, it seems to me, mad, and both wrong. Tolstoy writes with a diamond on crystal; his clearness is really sublime. Nobody, friend or foe, can have the slightest doubt about what he means; and that is the purest triumph of literature. I hate his philosophy myself: but I almost love him for making it so hateful. This clarity creates an atmosphere of courage. It is said in some proverb that those who live in glass houses must not throw stones. But those who live in diamond houses may throw stones; especially if the stones are diamonds too. Tolstoy's house and his missiles are really made of diamond—that is, of adamant. They are hard, luminous, and dogmatic—that is, intelligent. But all this only serves to show up more clearly the maniacal nonsense (no milder phrase will convey it) which Tolstoy talks about education. For what he says is briefly this: Every child must be told that he has a soul and a body, and that all evil comes from obeying his body and all good from obeying his soul. The child is to keep a little notebook, apparently, and recall at the end of the day the occasions on which he has wickedly obeyed his body, and those on which he has wisely obeyed his soul. It is further to be explained to him that in our souls we are all naturally loving and united (a lie) and that it is our animal bodies that delight to bark and bite, for 'tis their nature to. To say that the body begets evil and the soul good is to say that the Publican is worse than the Pharisee; and if that is not un-Christian, what is? A great fuss was made when, some time ago, Tolstoy was turned out of the Russian Church. I don't know why he was turned out of the Russian Church; but I suppose it was because his form of morality was not liked.

But I have no wish to introduce the highest truths about ethics, but only the plainest facts about babies. Can anything be conceived more practically ridiculous than the Tolstoy scheme, if we take it in conjunction with any of the staring problems of the playground and the nursery? I take one problem which must have met most people who have ever seen children for one whole day—I mean the problem of getting them to go to bed. Any child worth calling a child, at the end of an exciting party, wants to sit up for ever. And he would sit up for ever but for the wise

the other is his body. As for his soul, God bless it, his soul would
certainly stop awake till it went mad. Parents actually have to
protect the child's body from the flaming and destructive assaults
of the child's soul. Half the bother of the nursery is that the
children must obey their parents even in order to obey their
bodies. Human creatures with immortal souls have to be forced
to be physical. The real translation of the ἄνθρωπος φύσει
πολιτικός[1] is "Man is naturally unnatural." Children often
gravely neglect their bodies, and they often grossly over-culti-
vate their souls. What advice could be more mad to say to any
innocent heir of Adam than the broad statement than he must
distrust everything that goes into his body, but trust everything
that comes into his head? It is quite true, of course, that children
do sometimes sin corporeally—as in the matter of jam; but I
would much rather have a child whose body told him to steal
jam than one whose soul told him to imitate Tolstoy.

And now, in such space as remains, let me turn to the other
modern educationalist. Maeterlinck is much more humane than
Tolstoy, and his ideas of spiritual education are more suave,
more subtle, but not less false. The most dramatic moment in
the play of "The Blue Bird" is also the most unchildlike, the
most glaringly unfitted for children. The little hero and heroine
have come to the Kingdom of the Dead—full of darkness and
putrescence and potential spectres, very powerfully suggested.
The boy hesitates whether to turn the jewel, which will reveal
to him all the spirits present; the girl, in terror of the ghosts,
implores him not to. He buries his face, he turns the jewel; and
the whole scene alters to a startling sweetness of sunshine and
summer flowers. She asks in bewilderment, "Where are the
dead?" He answers "There are no dead," and the curtain falls.
A very fine artistic climax—and a lie; and not the kind of lie that
children tell or that children understand. Really, it will not do.
Children, as was remarked by an authority whom I prefer to
Tolstoy and Maeterlinck, are typical of the kingdom of Heaven;

---

[1] This may be translated as "Man is by nature a political animal" (Aristotle).

Tolstoy and Maeterlinck, are typical of the kingdom of Heaven; and especially in this, that they know the difference between falsehood and truth, even when they tell the falsehood. If people do go cold on a bed, do cease to speak and walk, are put in a box and buried in the ground, it is quite useless to tell children that there are no dead. Tell them the dogma of immortality, if you are so lucky as to believe in it. Leave the thing alone, if you are not. There are plenty of other things to talk to children about—toffee or pirates, or Western Australia or the weather. But do not believe for a moment that you can feed them on phrases which contradict facts.

For it is in this respect that the modern intellectualist falls, in the most marked manner, far below the intellect of mediaevalism or antiquity. The most orthodox doctors have always maintained that faith is something superior to reason but not contrary to it. But Maeterlinck's faith is something contrary to reason, but not superior to it. He merely denies what he cannot destroy. The modern sceptic makes a claim upon credulity more wild and sentimental than was ever made either by the meekest or the maddest theologian. He does not merely ask us to believe in the invisible; he asks us to disbelieve in the visible. There is much in the modern world to assist his tendency; Maeterlinck may go perpetually swifter and smoother in his modern motor car through throngs of modern, timid, and evasive men. But there will be a frightful clash and collision when first he runs into a child.

January 22, 1910

Political Interruptions

We hear a great deal just now about political interruptions which cause laughter, but I heard one the other day which might well cause tears. The circumstances are not specially relevant. Let it

hall filled in the strange way that is so common in such cases. I mean that the audience consisted of some elderly people right up in the front, who were prominent but silent, and some very undeveloped people right at the back, who were noisy but shy. Between these two there was a great gulf fixed, and one's voice echoed desolately across it. I happened to be expressing an opinion on the truth of which I need not linger, but an opinion to which I am firmly wedded, that the military and naval strength of Germany is much exaggerated. I think the people who see the Kaiser as omnipotent are like the people who saw the Emperor of the French as omnipotent just before 1870. It is not a prediction, but a tradition. Their heads are really full of the last war, not of the next: like the cautious and sensible Irishman in the story, they are prophesying what has happened already. Moreover, I am old enough to remember that, through all the early days of Imperialism and Mr. Kipling, it was Russia that was always represented as this ruthless giant, clad in steel and striding ever nearer and nearer. It seems as if a ruthless giant somewhere must be absolutely necessary to their scheme of the universe. Then other things happened, and our journalists had suddenly to leave off railing at Russia for being strong, and begin railing at Russia for being weak. That is exactly what they had done some fifteen years before about the strength and the weakness of Napoleon III. But I do not desire to dwell on this opinion, true or false, but to lead up to the strange and touching interruption which on this occasion it called forth. When I had remarked that Frenchmen and Germans of my acquaintance, as well as Englishmen specially well informed, took a much more moderate view of the matter, there came from the back of the hall a shrill, boyish voice, uttering these remarkable words: "Yer don't read yer papers."

I could have fallen on his neck and wept. Such innocence as that has something tragic and sublime about it. It had never crossed his mind, you see, even for one wild moment, that a man might read his papers and not implicitly believe them. No suspicion had ever dawned on his mind that there was a slight party bias delicately discernible in the *Evening News* or the *Star*; that there was a slight note of eagerness, almost amounting to exaggeration, in the *Daily Mail*. For him every printed word was not only a solemn fact, but was the supreme form of truth, beyond which there was no appeal. And he could only suppose that some defect in my eyesight, or in my education, prevented me from learning the great truths which the posters of the *Daily Mail* had to tell. My mother had not taught me to read, or I had spent all my halfpennies in chocolate cigars; and so I was shut out from those feasts of infallible information of which the gates stood so wide for him. The growth of this singular spirit is somewhat distressing, especially in country districts. For if there is one fine and rich quality which we do expect in a rustic, it is suspiciousness. I am distressed by this spread of simple faith. I am sure that no yokel ever believed in the ghost as these yokels believe in the newspaper. I am sure no peasants in the Middle Ages gave such smooth and swift and automatic credence to any tales of fairies or legends of saints as these honest lads do to the vast cosmopolitan crazes and partisan travesties of the halfpenny Press. There was always a dim element of irony and doubt mixed with popular poetry and popular religion. But journalism demands blind and prostrate faith. And journalism seems to get it.

One of the worst features of this vast illusion consists in this: that, newspapers lying thick as leaves everywhere, so many people grow accustomed to certain images or occurrences in newspapers long before they happen to have seen them in real life. It is obvious that when a fire, a murder, or an interrupted wedding occurs, very few can immediately see it, while millions immediately read about it. But the result is that millions have a conventional picture in their minds which is as different as possible from the real picture, but which nevertheless colours their sentiments and even deflects their philosophy. What notion, let us say, has the average Englishman of what really happens when there is "A Scene in the House," "A Welsh Revival Meeting," "A Freak Dinner," "A Skirmish with the Mad Mullah"? I will take one example from the same fragment of my own experience. All through the present political crisis and all other political crises, I have read in the papers a vast amount about meetings being broken up by "an organised opposition." The words suggest to me what I have no doubt they also suggest to the millions of people who read them. They suggest a cunning strategist who has planted blocks and groups of his boldest and most effective men in various parts of a hostile meeting to open a campaign of question and repartee which shall culminate in the moral defeat of the platform. That is what I always read into the words "organised opposition." This is what really happens. About twenty minutes after the speakers have begun to address a small and sympathetic assembly, chiefly consisting of their friends with their wives and children, the door at the end of the hall abruptly opens and about fifteen boys walk in in a line as stiffly as if they were made of wood. They sit down as far away as possible from the people whom they propose to defy; and no entreaties or taunts will induce them to come an inch nearer. They say abruptly at intervals—"Good old Joe!" or whoever may be their favourite statesman. If the man on the platform says that bread ought to be cheap, they say—"What about Chinese Labour?" If he is discussing the Navy, they say—"What about the Big Loaf?"[1] In moments of special animation they say—"Who are you?" a very sensible question. Towards the end of the proceedings they get up all at once and all go out together, still looking like wood and making a sort of wooden clatter with their feet. It was only after this dark manoeuvre that it dawned on me that the stiff pantomime that I had just been watching really was this cunning, elaborate, and diabolically diplomatic thing called "an organised opposition."

In such cases surely newspaper phraseology misleads. One does not talk about the mechanism of a poker. One does not talk about the organisation of a row of pokers. In the incident

---

[1] Big loaf and little loaf were political catch-phrases that were used by the Liberals during the fiscal controversy which took place around the year 1906.

I describe there was no sort of art, and even no sort of deception. Nobody pretended for a moment that these boys were voters, or that they had come to listen, or that they had come separately or by accident. The thing was perfectly defensible on the assumption that politics is a game; but even in that sense one could not call it a game of skill. The only point, however, that I wish to make here is that round such common newspaper phrases as "an organised opposition" there clings a connotation of drama, tactics, and intellectual excitement which entirely disappears when one sees the real thing—the little boys in their adorable simplicity stumping in and stumping out again.

Of course, one could give hundreds of other instances. When the newspapers describe "A Scene in the House," one gets an impression of green benches broken up, hats smashed, and the Speaker's wig all crooked on his head. A friend of mine was in the House while one of these "scenes" was going on. Happening at the moment to be thinking about a sonnet or some such thing, he did not know there had been a scene till he read it in the paper next morning. This is where the modern imaginative world called journalism differs from the old imaginative world of peasants and children. In fairy tales the objects were mostly familiar; it was only the power that was mystical. A peasant had never seen a bean-stalk grow up into the sky; but he had seen a bean-stalk and he had seen the sky. A child had never seen a cat in boots; but he had seen boots and a cat. The trouble with the new world of fancy is that it consists so much of vast things of which plain people can form no picture: financial hoards, scientific machinery, colossal navies, enormous emigrations— images so huge that they do not stir the imagination, but crush it.

January 29, 1910
Modern Moral Creeds

I once incautiously wrote in this column an article about some absurd mountebanks called Futurists, especially in connection with a periodical of theirs called "Poesia." The result of this rash act is that "Poesia" is bound upon my back for the rest of my life. An enormous parcel reached me this morning, which proved to be the second number, with more about the necessity for strength, daring, and "a scorn of woman." It is a handsome volume, about the size of a moderate Gladstone bag, full of poetry in all sorts of languages; and I am prepared to sell it to anybody for the sum of 1-1/4d. if he will come and take it away himself. The wild, free, soaring Futurists profess, of course, a contempt for Christianity and the creed of forgiveness; they assure us earnestly—nay, eagerly, that they themselves are awfully ruthless and cold. But it seems to me that excessive forgiveness is their special weakness. They are altogether too gentle and too meek. I write two columns to point out, in the ordinary course of duty, that their philosophy is rubbish; and all they do is to keep on sending me Christmas presents. This is the asceticism of pardon: it is giving the cloak to the thief and turning the cheek to the smiter. I express my dislike of the cut of Mr. Marinetti's coat, and he gives me his cloak also. The cheeks of the Futurists are formally smitten; and they only give me more of their cheek.

My subject, however, is not the Futurists, but something else for which they happen to afford a tiny text. The principal feature (or, at least, the most intelligible one) in this number of "Poesia" is a prose rhapsody, with the title or *motif*, "Tuons le clair de lune!" The first instinct of a Cockney, of course, is to translate this, "Let us shoot the moon." Many a free, wild, soaring poet has done that before now; indeed, I think it must have been a poet who invented that dark and delicate metaphor. As a matter of fact, I suppose, the poet who invented that phrase was that same great poet who made the proverbs, the ballads, and the fairy-tales; in collections of verse he is called Anon; and in great hours of history he is called the People. Certainly it would be hard to find an effect more distinctly and exquisitely literary than that which covers the midnight flitting of a bankrupt with this fantastic excuse of some astronomical form of sport. The phrase "shooting the moon" contains everything in the situation; its furtive daring; its nocturnal vigilance, its improbable explanations. To this is added the silver touch of poetry, in that notion of hunting Diana the Huntress. If therefore I could hope that Mr. Marinetti wrote in English slang as well as in French and Italian, I could warmly sympathise with his project. "Tuons le clair de lune" may with advantage mean "Let us shoot the moon." It might also with advantage mean "Let us have no more moonshine"—that is, let us have no more Futurism. But I fear it does not mean any of these sensible things. And it is just what I think it does mean that affords a sort of avenue of introduction to much more important things and much more important people. So far as I can understand the rather silly and self-conscious theorising of these people, they probably mean by "killing the moonlight" what they mean by all their effeminate nonsense about the scorn of woman; they mean, I suppose, that they wish to eliminate those more dreamy affections which very superficial people will always call sentimental. And it is about this foolish modern fancy of making war upon a mood that I wish to get rid of some of my more disagreeable feelings.

For the last fifty years or so everybody has been saying that a moral code or a religious creed or a system of commandments and vetoes, can so terribly narrow the mind. When I say everybody, of course I mean everybody except the overwhelming majority; that is simply the modern philosophical use of the term. It is sometimes put in the form, "Everybody who counts"; and modern philosophers refuse to go by counting heads, because they will not even admit that average human beings have heads to be counted. However that may be, the multitudinous teachers of the time have all asserted and reasserted this statement, that moral creeds and codes, especially when they are negative, make men's minds narrow. This view involves a great mistake, which we are beginning very slowly to see.

Suppose I am a moral prophet standing upon a mountain and giving from graven tablets new and terrible commandments to the tribes of men. Suppose, let us say, I tell them, "Never murder a black-haired stockbroker who is short-sighted." This sounds very hard at first; very stern, grim, and definite. But in truth it is a declaration of freedom as well as a declaration of restraint. In the very act of forbidding the murder of dark, short-sighted stockbrokers I imply a complete emancipation for the murderers of other stockbrokers or other men. Blonde, blue-eyed stockbrokers may be butchered without an instant's hesitation; long-sighted or normal-sighted stockbrokers may be massacred till their corpses strew the ground like autumn leaves. As for people who are not stockbrokers, words absolutely fail me to express the orgie of innocent carnage to which they can be made to contribute. In this particular instance, perhaps, I am taking a *recherché* or (as Stevenson would say) a recondite pleasure; for the massacre of financiers is one of the many popular sports which, since the Middle Ages, have fallen into an unfortunate neglect.

But the principle is equally clear with regard to our own more passive indulgences. If your moral code merely says, "Do not drink Green Chartreuse," it stands to reason that you can drink Madeira or methylated spirit if you want to. If your tribal scriptures tell you that you must not bet on donkey-races, then they tell you that you may bet on the races of yachts, horses, hippopotamuses, and performing fleas. Every negative scheme of veto is a positive scheme of liberty. The more a moral system looks like a line of black negations, the more probable it is that the people under such a system enjoyed an expanse of freedom and of joy.

But the "advanced" people are always trying to introduce what they call positive morality, which really means positive slavery. Instead of saying that I must not think of So-and-So, but may think of anything else, they say that I may think of the sublime and daring So-and-So, and must not think of anything else. They destroy the large liberality of the old negative code. They make a new and dreadful narrowness—the narrowness of taste. It is not now enough that I do not do what my neighbour dislikes: I must like what my neighbour likes. I must be Celtic and prefer dreams to facts, or I must be Dionysian and prefer facts to decency, or I must be Futurist and prefer fancies to facts and dreams. The old morality forbade me to "shoot the moon": it was a cruel sport: the bullet aimed at that luminary so often rebounded and hit the landlady. But the new morality forbids me, not to shoot the moon, but even to enjoy the moonlight. Pessimists destroy the sun, Futurists destroy the moon; the modern man may only follow one mad star. The freedom of true morality is finely expressed in the Eden story, which shows how Man was free to eat all the fruits in the garden except one. But if the Book of Genesis had been written by modern idealists, there would have been only one exquisite, artistic, hygienic fruit that Adam was allowed to eat.

February 5, 1910

The Ignorance of the People

We are all living in a much more extraordinary country than we know. That is the one quite valuable effect of a General Election on the mind. If we saw a primly dressed old spinster with a Prayer Book, we should be at least interested to learn that she believed in cannibalism. If we watched a quiet little clerk trotting up to his office, it would arrest our attention to be told that he thought he was the rightful Pope of Rome. But, believe me, England is packed with people quite as prosaic who believe things quite as demoniac or gigantesque. And the real and eternal fun of a election is that these people express themselves. They write letters. They ask questions. A man begins actually to understand that England is Elfland.

If I say that there is something quite eerie and elfish about the ignorance of people, I must hasten to add two important explanations. First, I do not mean ignorance in any disputable or imaginative sense; in any sense which can conceivably be a difference of opinion. Personally I think Haeckel[1] (let us say) an extravagantly ignorant man; to anybody who knows Christian history, his remarks about Christian history are enough to make an ox laugh. Personally I think Lord Milner[2] an ignorant man, specially ignorant about England, of course, but pretty fairly ignorant about everything except journalism. But these are opinions, or rather, convictions. I do not profess that they are patent facts. Christianity and England are things not so very easy to understand. But I am talking about ignorance of indubitable fact—such ignorance as I should show if I said that Dickens wrote "Vanity Fair" or that Shropshire was an island.

Now, the amount of this sort of definite black-and-white ignorance is something almost past belief. For example, a nice old vicar in Hampshire was severely rebuked the other day by the *Daily News*, though he had done nothing worse than believe everything that was said in the *Daily Mail*. But oddly enough, the *Daily News* did not remark at all on the one really extraordinary thing in this very ordinary old gentleman's remarks. He described Lloyd George as a little solicitor and McKenna as a little schoolmaster simply because he had seen these descriptions in his daily paper that morning. But after that the dear old gentleman added an indignant phrase of his own: "Winston Churchill, a newspaper reporter." I am sure he added it in entire

---

[1] Ernst Heinrich Haeckel (1834–1919) was a German biologist whose book *The Riddle of the Universe* (1899) was an ill-conceived attempt to transport Darwinian biology to a philosophical and theological explanation of the universe.

[2] Sir Alfred Milner (1854–1925), a British statesman who earned Chesterton's contempt as a governor of the Cape Colony, governor of the Transvaal and Orange River and high commissioner for South Africa during the Boer War period.

Churchill, a newspaper reporter." I am sure he added it in entire
good faith. I am sure he really thought that Mr. Winston Churchill had raised himself from rough beginnings in the gutters of
Grub Street. He probably thought there was no more connection
between Winston Churchill and Randolph Churchill than between
Will Crooks and Sir William Crookes. The fact that Mr. Winston
Churchill is a hereditary statesman, the child of one of the most
exalted and opulent of the great aristocratic houses, is a fact which
might be urged in Mr. Churchill's favour or against him. It
might be used to show that he is a born ruler and fighter; or it
might be used to show that he is a corrupt and luxurious *poseur*.
But it is a fact; as it is a fact that there is a cross on St. Paul's.
But of this fact, merely as a fact, this good country clergyman
was simply and blankly ignorant. This is the kind of innocence
and credulity that really reveals itself on every side during a
General Election. The other day a lady, hearing I was a Liberal,
asked me if I really thought it would be better for the Germans
to rule us. Supposing this to be legitimate party satire, I answered
in similar vein. I said that a good many Germans do rule us
already: and get coronets for doing it. The simple words she
said in reply stunned me like clubs of stone. I found she thought
that Mr. Asquith did, literally and openly, recommend that the
Kaiser should be made King of England. She thought that was
his public programme. Her only doubt was whether this well-
known Liberal scheme was really quite wise. I repeat, we are
rediscovering Fairyland.

But the second truth to be added to any description of public
ignorance is much more sharp and arresting. The truth is this—
that this ignorance is not separately, nor even specially, characteristic of the poorer classes. On the contrary, it is rather
curiously common and continuous in the educated classes. It is
found among vicars, even more than among vagrants. It marks
ladies even more than landladies. It would be harder to find a
cabman (round Westminster anyhow) who does not know that
Winston Churchill is an aristocrat; it would be easier to find five
of these country clergymen who do not know it. It would be

like myself really wanted to be ruled by Germans; it would be easier to prove it to fifteen fastidious gentlewomen of small private means. The small gentry aim especially at being protected; and they are protected, even from the most glaring truths. But over and above this, there is in what are called the educated classes a vast amount of what can be called accidental ignorance; the ignorance of London people about the country, of country people about the latest urban developments, of good party men about the arguments in the opposition newspapers, of strong sectaries about the tenets of other religions. Stirred up all together, they make a rich and savoury mass of misunderstanding into which it is a delight to plunge.

The truth is that there are no educated classes; simply because there is no such thing as education. There is this kind of education and that kind of education, and therefore there are this and that styles of educated men. A man may have lectured about horses before the Royal Society, and yet he may not find that he knows all about horses on Derby Day—nay, he may be able to dissect a horse without being any the more able to ride him. A young politician may know a great deal about economics, and still not know much about economy. And the mistakes made by bishops, bankers, or biologists are just as much due to their ignorance as the mistakes of a child about the alphabet or a savage about the moon. Each one of us is ludicrously ignorant of something; most of us of most things. The whole difference between a conceited man and a modest one is concerned only with how far he is conscious of those hundred professions in which he would be a failure, of those hundred examinations which he could not pass. I do not mind Roberts knowing he is the best billiard-player, and even rearing his head to the stars on that account. But I like him to remember (to say over to himself, as a sort of litany) that he may be the worst trombone-player in the world, that he may be, and probably is, a poor darner of socks, a third-rate naval architect, a bad mimic, a disappointing tight-rope dancer, an unsatisfactory Latin commentator, and quite a failure in the tilting-yard. It may be difficult to keep all these potential failures of oneself before one's imagination at once. But it is worth trying, being full of gigantesque humility.

One way to do it would be to confer degrees of special ignorance like the present degrees of special knowledge. A man might have letters after his name stating the things he knew particularly little about. D.D., instead of meaning Doctor of Divinity, might mean Deficient in Divinity. F.R.S., instead of standing for Fellow of the Royal Society, might stand for the words Fellow Rotten at Science. It would be very sweetening and salutary for all of us if we had to put on all our visiting-cards or local directories some statement of our more startling forms of ignorance. But I, for one, should have such a magnificently long string of letters after my name that it would be really inconvenient.

February 12, 1910

The Decay of Controversy

Many people are presumably under the impression that a great deal of controversy has been going on in England during the last few weeks. Those people are wrong. During the last few weeks England has been singularly free from controversy of any real kind. And this curious latter-day decay of true controversy is so marked as to call for some outlines of inquiry or cure. The essential qualities or conditions of any genuine controversy may be rapidly stated—perhaps more rapidly if we take an imaginary instance by way of a working model.

Take any little homely incident we might hear of any day; suppose we find a governess hanged on a palm-tree in Kew Gardens. By the inherent principles of the British Constitution, it becomes necessary to discover whether this crime was committed by Mr. Balfour or Mr. Asquith. For to admit any other sources of serious evil in our community would gravely endan-

mitted by Mr. Balfour or Mr. Asquith. For to admit any other sources of serious evil in our community would gravely endanger the balance of our political machine. Well, in this or any other discussion, the essentials of controversy are these. First: Agreement on Fundamental Tests. Thus, both disputants must agree that it is decidedly wrong to hang governesses on palm-trees. Second: Different Theories of the Facts. There must be a distinct and plausible tale of how Mr. Balfour dragged the governess into the artificial hot-house to prove to her the advantages of Protection. It must be quite distinct from the other logical and ingenious narrative describing how Mr. Asquith lured her among the palms that she might see a beautiful example of foreign imports. Third: Knowledge by a Common Audience of All Developments. It will not do if a document denouncing Mr. Asquith is washed up inside a bottle to form the isolated pleasure of some South Sea Islanders. It will not do if the proofs of Mr. Balfour's guilt are kept entirely for the private but uproarious pleasure of Mr. Asquith's family. Fourth and last: Ultimate Simplicity of Problem. The arbiters must be examining whether Mr. Asquith hanged a governess, not whether he hedged a bet, or wore a bad hat, or persecuted a religion, or shot a fox. They must be inquiring whether Mr. Balfour did that particular bad thing, not whether he has ever been doing any particularly good thing. Those, I say, are the essentials of a general controversy: admitted first principles, clear and different accounts of the case; knowledge by everybody judging of everything that occurs; and one plain question to answer.

Now, oddly enough, none of these conditions really exists in an English Election. Indeed, the first two ideas are strangely reversed; each is stuck absurdly into the place of the other. The combatants do not agree about ultimate attitudes and then disagree about the particular proposals and methods. On the contrary, they often differ about the final test, and they constantly agree about the superficial catch-word. A good controversy might arise, for instance, between two men, each having the same ideal of the poor made happy, or of the poor independent, but honestly differing about whether some special thing, Socialism or Old-Age Pensions, would have that effect. That is what party war ought to be. But party war is exactly the opposite. It is not a fight between two men with the same view of the poor about whether Old-Age Pensions would fulfil that view. It is a fight between two men with totally opposite views of the poor, who both say they are in favour of Old-Age Pensions. It is actually about the ultimate that they differ; it is truly and literally about the immediate proposals that they often agree. When all is said, I fancy, one side does stand dimly but genuinely for democracy; the other side does stand for the deliberate maintenance of a governing class. But both sides (according to themselves) stand for cheaper bread, larger pensions, more employment, a strong navy, and European peace. Our practical situation comes to this; that our two parties have different principles, but the same posters. If the party system proceeds as at present, I should strongly recommend both sides to avoid the unnecessary expense of separate publishing departments. Why should there not be a Central British Bureau for the production of placards and pictures applicable to any side of any question? A triumphant Britannia, a justly indignant John Bull, a starving mother and child, and a leering German Jew are all quite equally useful to Liberals and Conservatives. Our differences are not like the branching of some mighty and noble tree which is united in the stem but separates as it grows. Our differences can only be compared to a combat between two cuttlefish who should get their tentacles inextricably interlaced: so each creature would remain separate, and yet at the point of battle it would be impossible to tell which was which. Along the dust and smoke of the actual line of battle there is nothing but a blinding and confusing identity. All those who are really fighting each other are merely imitating each other. The private view may remain the same, but the public proposal tends more and more to be a mere riot of plagiarism. Our politics will soon consist of men who all propose the same thing—only for different reasons.

As it is about the first two controversial essentials, so it is

then they raised fortifications, to defend their difference; then they lived behind the fortifications and met only those whom they had no need to fight. First people argued with other people and made newspapers to print their arguments; then they hid behind their own newspapers and read only their own arguments. The result has been that true controversy has become almost impossible, because the judge who hears the counsel for the prosecution is not the same as he who hears the counsel for the defence.

It is useless for a man to argue in the papers of his own party: he is merely refuting some argument of which his readers have never heard. It is useless for him to argue in the opposition papers, for the simple reason that he will not be allowed to. Therefore huge patches of England become more and more solid and separate. Choleric old uncles used to object to Home Rule because it would "bring back the Heptarchy." Lord bless you, dear old souls, you live in the Heptarchy. There is no political unity about England at all. And if you want to know why Ireland, weak and poor as she is, is so often able to dictate English policy, I will tell you: it is exactly because Ireland is more nearly united than any other nation in Europe.

And as for the last point, that of the plain question, is there any doubt about that? If so, I will only ask two questions. What has this Election been about? And when the Lords, with that high civilising wisdom of which Lord Curzon speaks, appealed to the country, on what did they appeal?

February 19, 1910

Man in the Cosmos

It is difficult in these days to escape from the topic of politics even by deliberately talking about something else. For there are a considerable number of people who will at once attribute any disaster, from the weather to the Brighton railway smash, to the particular politicians whom they dislike. A Tariff Reformer of my acquaintance said genially that he was sure Mr. John Burns set fire to Arding and Hobbs' at Clapham Junction, so that he might cut a fine figure in Battersea. The discovery of the North Pole (that other disaster) might, perhaps, be traced to Mr. Taft, though this could only be argued by supposing the Pole in the position which a wit attributed to America itself: "It had often been discovered before; but it was always hushed up." As for the floods in Paris, they may be presumed to be the work of that admirable poet, M. Rostand, whose play of "Chantecler" we have all been waiting for so long. If M. Rostand went to the moon, like his own hero, it is possible that he might do something to the tides; but even from that point of vantage I cannot see how he can have had anything to do with the comet.[1] The comet, at any rate, has dropped in entirely by accident; the comet is not an election dodge, and has nothing to do with the necessity of saving England by voting for Snooks. Let us talk about the comet.

Keep your seats; do not give way to panic. Have no fear that I am going to moralise about the smallness of man's petty struggles in the presence of the colossal starry scheme. I have no intention of drawing a moral about those

> Who shriek and sweat in pigmy wars
> Before the stony face of Time,
> And looked at by the silent stars.[2]

---

[1] Halley's comet was visible in 1910, and increasingly from January to May.
[2] See *Literary Squabbles*, ii.

I refrain, from the simple reason that to do this is not to moralise, but to immoralise—or, to use the more lucid word, to demoralise. The moral of the paltriness of mankind is an immoral moral. Tennyson was quite wrong in this, and "the petty fools of rhyme" were quite right. People do not look very wise, perhaps, when they shriek and sweat; but they would look a deal sillier if they all held their tongues and did nothing merely because the stars were silent. If the morning stars never sang together, we can only congratulate ourselves on having inaugurated choir-practice; and if the sons of God did not shout for joy, the sons of men may just as well do so. And as for the stony face of Time, one guileless journalist, at least, will undertake to shriek and sweat in its presence with considerable nonchalance. Time is a category to be controlled and kept in its place; and the true philosophy is not so much to take Time by the forelock as to take him by the nose. The true philosophy, in short, is to kill time and so create eternity—if only for ten minutes.

No; that argument about man looking mean and trivial in the face of the physical universe has never terrified me at all, because it is a merely sentimental argument, and not a rational one in any sense or degree. I might be physically terrified of a man fifty feet high if I saw him walking about my garden, but even in my terror I should have no reason for supposing that he was vitally more important than I am, or higher in the scale of being, or nearer to God, or nearer to whatever is the truth. The sentiment of the overpowering cosmos is a babyish and hysterical sentiment, though a very human and natural one. But if we are seriously debating whether man is the moral centre of this world, then he is no more morally dwarfed by the fact that his is not the largest star than by the fact that he is not the largest mammal. Unless it can be maintained *a priori* that Providence must put the largest soul in the largest body, and must make the physical and moral centre the same, "the vertigo of the infinite" has no more spiritual value than the vertigo of a ladder or the vertigo of a balloon.

Man is no more overshadowed and outdone by the tail of a

comet than by the tail of a peacock or the tail of a monkey. All three tails may be called superiorities; but can hardly without a stretch of language be called moral superiorities. Comparatively early in his historical career man realised, and faced with some stoicism, the melancholy fact that he was without a tail. He has all the isolation of the tail-less fox in the fable; but he does not share that quadruped's irritating and pedantic desire for uniformity. He is willing to leave to the other things in nature their strange adornments and fantastic superiorities. He has been known to dock the tails of dogs, but seldom those of peacocks; and docking the tail of a comet has always appeared to him a barren and even doubtful adventure. He allows all the creatures of heaven and earth to wave at him like taunting fans or plumes their furred or feathered or flaming appendages. But he retains an inward conviction that there is in his very defect a certain indefinable dignity; and that (as a flippant man would say) it was when his tail ended that his story began.

It is not that moral, then, that should be drawn from our transition from the topic of politics to the topic of astronomy. No; it is a vulgar thing to be intimidated into voting for Snooks merely because Snooks is rich. It is, if possible, a more vulgar thing to be intimidated into reverencing a comet merely because the comet is large. So far as that goes, the heavens are no more noble than a *Daily Mail* poster; the message of the Harmsworths[3] is printed in very large letters; the message of the stars is written in very large bonfires. But there is a message of the stars that is really worthy and imaginative; and it is this, doubtless, that the great men of science have meant when they used a language of cosmic contrast and irony which their duller and more cowardly followers have twisted into a contempt for man.

The true splendour of such things as the comet is felt at once by a child; yet it is not easy to define for any mature person. It

[3] Alfred Charles William Harmsworth (1865–1922), a journalist and newspaper proprietor who, in 1908, was the chief proprietor of the *Times*. He was created a baronet in 1903.

is a pleasure somewhat analogous to that of military glory—that is, it is full of energy, yet, in one sense, confessedly empty; it is tall, and thrilling like a trumpet, and yet, in a sense, confessedly secondary. So much of the force of Nature that we see is fruitful; and there are some who can only respect and enjoy it when it is fruitful. There are some who love only orchards and vines and corn; there are some who hate the moon as a thing half-witted, and loathe the sea as a lifeless load of coldness and division. Nature for them is the good wind that turns the windmill, the good river that turns the watermill. But some—the majority, I think, at least in the North—love to hear the barren winds blow at night and see the wasted water shoot into the objectless abyss. It is not the solemnity, but rather the high levity, of the universe. It is (in the grave use of idle words) tremendous sport. You do not think a comet a comic thing, perhaps? You still think it better than Man because it stretches very far? Well, there is no room for more argument. A French Marshal took a book down for Napoleon, saying, "Je suis plus grand." "Vous êtes plus long," said the Emperor.

February 26, 1910
Jekyll and Hyde

There are many books which we think we have read when we have not. There are, at least, many that we think we remember when we do not. An original picture, perhaps, was imprinted upon the brain, but it has changed with our own changing minds. We only remember our remembrance. There is many a man who thinks he can clearly recall the works of Swift or of Goldsmith; but, indeed, he himself is the principal author of the "Gulliver's Travels" or "The Vicar of Wakefield" which he recalls. Macaulay, with his close reading and miraculous memory, was quite certain that the Blatant Beast was killed at the end of "The Faery Queene"; but it was not. A brilliant and scholarly friend of mine quoted a stanza as one in which not one word could safely be altered—and quoted it wrong. Hundreds of highly educated people are quite fixed in false versions touching facts that they could easily verify. The editor of a Church newspaper (in rebuking Radicals) asseverated again and again, after contradiction and challenge, that the Catechism commands a child "to do his duty in that state of life to which it has pleased God to call him." Of course, the Catechism says no such thing; but the editor was so certain that he would not even open his prayer-book to see. Hundreds of people are sure that Milton wrote "To-morrow to fresh fields and pastures new." Hundreds of people are sure that Jesuits preached that the end justifies the means; many of them are sure that they have seen some Jesuit's statement to that effect; but they have not.

But it is a stranger thing still that memory can thus trick us about the main artistic effect of really fine books. Until about a year ago I believed that I had a vivid recollection of "Robinson Crusoe." So, indeed, I had, of certain images of the wreck and island; above all, of the admirable fact that Crusoe had two swords instead of one. That is one of the touches of the true Defoe; the very inspired poetry of the accidental and the rough-and-tumble; the very romance of the unromantic. But I found I had completely forgotten the really sublime introduction to the tale, which gives it all its spiritual dignity—the narrative of Crusoe's impiety; his two escapes from shipwreck and opportunities for repentance; and, finally, the falling upon him of this strange judgment: food, security, silence—a judgment stranger than death.

With this case in mind, I am in no position to exult over my fellow-critics when they prove that they have not read properly the books that, as it happens, I have read properly. But I have been somewhat singularly impressed with the most cultivated and authoritative criticisms of the dramatic version of "Jekyll and Hyde," in so far as they refer to Stevenson's original romance. Of the play I cannot speak, but with the romance I am very well acquainted, which is more than can be said of those who have lightly and gracefully criticised it on the present occasion. Most of them said that Stevenson was a charming artist, but no philosopher; that his inadequacy as a thinker was well represented in the tale of "Jekyll and Hyde," which they proceeded to describe with the wildest inaccuracy of detail and a complete oblivion of the design. One idea, above all, has established itself firmly in their minds, and I daresay in many other people's. They think that in Stevenson's tale Jekyll is the good self and Hyde the bad self; or, in other words, that the protagonist is wholly good when he is Jekyll and wholly bad when he is Hyde.

Now, if Hamlet had killed his uncle in the first act, if Othello had appeared as a *mari complaisant*, it could not have upset the whole point of Shakespeare's story more than this upsets the whole point of Stevenson's story. Stevenson's story has nothing to do with pathological pedantries about "dual personality." That was mere machinery; and as he himself seems to have thought, even unfortunate machinery. The business of the powders I think he himself thought clumsy; but he had to make the tale a modern novel and work the transformations by medicine, unless he was prepared to tell it as a primeval fairy-tale and make them by magic. But he did not care a jot about either compared with the mystical idea in the transformation itself; and that had nothing to do with powders or dual personalities, but only with heaven and hell—like "Robinson Crusoe."

Stevenson goes out of his way to emphasise the fact that Jekyll, as Jekyll, was by no means perfect, but was rather a morally damaged piece of goods. He had "a sly cast," in spite of his handsome presence; he was nervous and secretive, though not ill-natured. Jekyll is not the good man: Jekyll is the ordinary mixed, moderately humane man, whose character has begun to suffer from some evil drug or passion. Now, that which is thus sucking and draining him is the habit of being Hyde; and it is here that the fine moral of Stevenson comes in, a moral as superior as it is opposite to that popularly put into his mouth. So far from preaching that man can be successfully divided into two men, good and evil, he specifically preached that man cannot be so divided, even by monstrosity and miracle; that, even in the extravagant case of Jekyll, the good is still dragged down by the mere existence of the bad. The moral of "Dr. Jekyll and Mr. Hyde" is not that man can be cut in two; it is that man cannot be cut in two.

Hyde is the innocence of evil. He stands for the truth (attested by a hundred tales of hypocrites and secret sins) that there is in evil, though not in good, this power of self-isolation, this hardening of the whole exterior, so that a man becomes blind to moral beauties or deaf to pathetic appeals. A man in pursuit of some immoral mania does attain an abominable simplicity of soul; he does act from one motive alone. Therefore he does become like Hyde, or like that blood-curdling figure in Grimm's fairy-tales, "a little man made of iron." But the whole of Stevenson's point would have been lost if Jekyll had exhibited the same horrible homogeneity. Precisely because Jekyll, with all his faults, possesses goodness, he possesses also the consciousness of sin, humility. He knows all about Hyde, as angels know about devils. And Stevenson specially points out that this contrast between the blind swiftness of evil and the almost bewildered omniscience of good is not a peculiarity of this strange case, but is true of the permanent problem of your conscience and mine. If I get drunk I shall forget dignity; but if I keep sober I may still desire drink. Virtue has the heavy burden of knowledge; sin has often something of the levity of sinlessness. One of the dramatic critics who dealt with the Jekyll and Hyde drama was particularly lofty in his superiority to Stevenson, and said he was not an author to be taken seriously. He also (I need hardly say) seemed to separate the central figure into unmixed good and evil, thereby missing the whole idea of the story. He added that if Stevenson had been a Thinker (or words to that effect) he would have seen that a purely good or purely bad person would be idiotic and could not act. I should like very meekly to ask this great metaphysician (if this should meet his eye) *why* a purely good or purely bad person could not act? There are kind motives and cruel motives. Why should not a being act always on kind motives or always on cruel motives? It seems to me the most urgent point in modern ethics and religion.

This is all, perhaps, a little too sombre; but the truth is, these critics have attacked the one topic on which I am learned. I will trifle with history and theology, because, though my interest is great, my knowledge of them is highly superficial. But on novel-reading I am exact to pedantry. Touching the plots of sensational romances, I am a Porson[1] or a Bentley,[2] and I will crush them with the cartloads of my erudition.

March 5, 1910

The Idea in the Theatre

I do not see why I should not, if I choose, devote this page to the dramatic criticism of dramas that I have not seen; last week I felt it necessary to break out concerning the play "Jekyll and Hyde," and this week there is really nothing to talk about but "Chantecler." Perhaps this artless principle might become a fixed feature of journalistic art. There might be in every paper two criticisms of any current play. "What It Is, By One Who Has

[1] Richard Porson (1759–1808), a Greek scholar who edited four plays of Euripides. He was recognized as one of the leading scholars in interpreting ancient Greek literature.

[2] Edmund Clerihew Bentley (1875–1956), a writer, joined the *Daily News* in 1901 and later the *Daily Telegraph* in 1912. He invented "Clerihew" verse form which was first published in his work *Biography for Beginners* which was illustrated by G. K. Chesterton. Bentley is remembered for two highly individual achievements: he added a new word to the language (Clerihew) and he wrote what was described as the best detective story of the century.

Seen It," 'What It Ought To Be, By One Who Has Not Seen It." Thus the admitted need for a classical standard might be satisfied. Thus we might see side by side the disembodied ideal and the embodied fact. Anyhow, I am not going to Paris simply to write an article; it is bad enough to get on to a boat at Dover; it is worse to get on to another boat when you arrive at Paris. I will criticise "Chantecler" by the light of the excellent photographs in this paper, by the light (or darkness) of the dramatic critics; and, above all, by my long study and long admiration of the great genius of Rostand.

Rostand seems to me to be not only a very great man, but what is more important, a very great symbol. He is the flower in our age of the infinite energy of France; and the nature of French energy is well expressed in the quarrel between him and the thin-blooded intellectuals who affect to despise him. Now the best French spirit is substantially this: that logic is a living and creative thing, that it bears children. It is not true to say of deduction that it is dry and thin; its results are gigantic and generously astonishing. The French Revolution began with the most abstract maxims; it ended in the most glowing martyrdoms and the most fascinating and pardonable crimes. The French take one small idea and do a very strange thing to it. They do something that none of the intellectuals ever dream of doing to any idea out of their million ideas. They believe it. And believing it, they fulfil it. If men are equal in theory, they shall be equal in practice. And they are—when the French make the experiment. Now this is exhibited in a small but startling way in this play of "Chantecler."

I speak first of the mere theatrical arrangement and scheme of the play. Rostand noticed one tiny unquestionable fact about men and birds. He knew that no other creature on this planet can be even remotely compared to man in the matter of what man has done. He is inevitably Christian enough to perceive that beavers build dams, but they do not build bridges, still less suspension-bridges. Ants build ant-hills, but they do not build ant-cathedrals or ant-statues or ant-Nelson Columns. He also knew (if he is the man whose works I have enjoyed) that the animals nearest to man in soul are not those that are most like him in civilisation. It is the horse that has given his name to chivalry, not the beaver. The attempt of some romantic cavalier to ride upon a beaver would be (to say the least of it) as dubious as the proposal that a horse should build a dam. Man loves the lonely animal, not the civilised and gregarious animal. You pat a dog; you do not pat a rat. Nor do you pat an ant—you do not even try. If an ant were as big as an omnibus, it would certainly be easier to pat him; but even then I doubt if you would. All these alleged parallels between human society and beehives or beaver-dams are really quite objectless, though very provocative. Well, through all this welter of wild biological comparison M. Rostand has seen, with the strange, abstract good sense of the Frenchman, that there is one connection between man and the other animals that could be put to theatrical effect. It is at once a trivial and a tremendous example of how France sees through all tangles the only practical thing—the idea.

Our brilliant actors, such as Sir Herbert Tree or Mr. H. B. Irving, are always anxious to enact new and fantastic roles. They will take pleasure in performing the part of a bestial diabolist like Hyde or a simple Christian like Colonel Newcome; but I am sure that they would not restrict their imitations to mere humanity. A fine actor might find pleasure in exactly catching the quick elegance of a cat or the pathetic rigidity of a dog. A good actor might not only ape the aristocrat; he might ape the ape. But about all imitations of animals (though they do really open an avenue of artistic invention and fact) our chief actors and actresses may conceivably be cold. It is not merely because Sir Herbert Tree might not wish to exhibit himself as a monkey catching fleas—a part that he would perform with all his huge genius for the grotesque. After all, he does not mind acting Bottom and wearing a donkey's head. Many characters he has acted—Svengali, and the great Russian official—were morally lower than the monkey, or even the flea. No; the objection is a practical objection. If Sir Herbert Tree acted an insect, Sir Herbert Tree must have six legs. If Sir Herbert Tree acted a beaver, Sir Herbert Tree must have four legs. Now, it is not easy to get an actor-manager to go about on all fours, even when he has the comic genius of Sir Herbert Tree.

With leading actresses, I am told, the project would be even more difficult. Of course, there is the other way, which was invented in the old pantomimes. There they made one quadruped out of two bipeds; one comic actor was the front of the elephant and another comic actor the tail. The humbler actor behind obviously had the fun of the occasion. For whenever he jumped in the air the whole elephant appeared to be standing on its head. Whereas, whenever the front man jumped into the air the elephant seemed merely to be rearing nobly, like a rampant lion on a shield. Therefore, I think this quadrupedal arrangement would be unworkable with regard to the present position of the actor-manager. I fear that if (let us say) Sir Herbert Tree and Mr. Lewis Waller[1] were at two ends of the same animal, that animal would be of a singularly jumpy sort.

Therefore the idea of enacting quadrupeds must be dismissed, along with the even more attractive idea of enacting beetles. And so, in our slow English manner, by a process of exhaustion, we come within sight of that simple fact which the Frenchman saw suddenly in a flash. There is in the world another race, remote from humanity, that has two legs. They are birds; let us write a play about them. You cannot dress up Sir Herbert Tree as an elephant, although an elephant is the nearest of all the animals to the image of God. You can dress him up as a cock—in fact (when "Chantecler" is translated) you probably will. That is what I mean by the practical talent of the French. Through all the tangle of integuments, bones, glands, the mammalia, the vertebrae, etc., the Frenchman sees clearly the one fact: he sees two legs standing like solid and sombre pillars in the desert. I

[1] Really William Waller Lewis (1860–1915), an English actor-manager famous for his roles in romantic parts and in Shakespearean drama; he was long connected with the Lyric Theatre.

had meant to say so many other things about "Chantecler," but I discover that I have nearly filled my space; I discover it with public regret and profound internal relief. It is enough to say that this direct perception of the enormous developments of one simple idea is the peculiar genius of France. We in England had sophists like Bolingbroke and Burke—and so only produced more sophists, like Disraeli and Kipling. They had one small copybook truth—and so produced a Revolution.

March 12, 1910

Historical Scepticism

There are people in this world who really hate the heroic. Granted that there is an extravagance always tending to overrate human achievements, there is an extravagance of triviality also, tending to underrate achievement, to take pleasure in a change from the poetic to the prosaic. That is why realistic novels are sometimes as interesting as romantic novels. It is simply because realistic novels are quite as arbitrary and fantastic as romantic novels. In the romance the hero is always jumping and perpetually falls on his feet. In the realistic story the hero is always plodding and perpetually falls on his nose. But in ordinary life it is unusual either to alight on a distant crag or to fall flat over a too proximate door-scraper. The romancer collects every instance of a beautiful triumph; the realist selects every case of an ugly cropper; but the bias of the realist is as extreme and as unscrupulous as that of the wildest romantic fabulist. If you throw enough mud, some of it will stick, especially to that unfortunate creature Man, who was originally made of mud. A realistic novel is written by stringing together all the tag-ends of human life—all the trains we miss, all the omnibuses we run after without catching, all the appointments that miscarry and all the invitations that are declined; all the wasted half-hours at Clapham Junction, and all the infant prodigies that grow up into stupid men; all the rainy days and all the broken engagements; all the Might-Have-Beens and all the Hardly Weres. Realism is the art of connecting everything that is in its nature disconnected. But to do this properly a man must be a great artist and rather a good liar.

There are, then, partisans of the prosaic. They are not in the least facing life as it is; life as it is, is almost too splendid—nay, too beautiful, to be faced. No man shall see life and live. They are making a special and personal selection, just as the aesthete or the optimist is making a special and personal selection. They nose about for the meannesses of mankind. They hunt for mortal humiliation. We know that they have this prosaic pugnacity in matters of fiction. But it is an interesting fact that they have it also about history. In history itself there is a school which may be called anti-romantic; and it is perpetually occupied in trying to explain away the many romances that have really happened.

When I was a boy I was told that General Wolfe before the assault on Quebec had recited the great lines of Gray about glory and the grave, and declared he would rather have written them than take Quebec. The story is a fine one, full of the eighteenth-century feeling of stoicism and heathen happiness before death, of the kinship of arts and arms, and of the soldier's splendid contempt for mere soldiering. When I was a man I was told to put away this childish legend, and I put it away. It had been disproved. Wolfe had never said anything of the sort. And now, with a great jump, I read in *T.P.'s Weekly* that the thing is substantially true after all.

Now, I will take this story of General Wolfe and Gray's "Elegy" as a working instance of the way that the historical sceptics do the trick. They will discredit a story for which there is excellent evidence on the ground of certain omissions or discrepancies in that evidence. But they never make the least reference to whether these are of the kind that occur in true stories or of the kind that occur in false. Some slips are obviously the slips of a liar; other confusions arise in honest narration, and in honest narration alone. Some blunders prove falsehood; other blunders prove truth. Let us take this Quebec story and go into it a little.

The sceptics, it seems, begin by making the story manifestly ridiculous in order to deny it. "Is it likely," they say, "that General Wolfe would have quoted Gray while he was leading his troops in deadly silence to surprise the French?" Why, of course not; and nobody I ever heard of—certainly not I myself in my infancy—ever imagined that Wolfe talked about literature within earshot of the enemy; or selected the occasion of a steep and silent ascent to recite the whole of Gray's "Elegy." Picture the soldiers crawling and clambering through the darkness, hardly daring to pant too loud; and imagine the General putting his mouth to the ear of a midshipman and shouting in a hoarse whisper—

> The curfew tolls the knell of parting day,
>   The lowing herd winds slowly o'er the lea,
> The ploughman homeward plods his weary way,
>   And leaves the world to darkness and to me.
>
> Now fades the glimmering landscape on
>   the sight—

and all the rest of the verses. Of course Wolfe said it, if he ever said it at all, on some occasion previous to the actual assault—at some distance of time and place at which it was possible for people to speak out loud. Do the critics think that during the whole Canadian campaign the English soldiers conversed by talking on their fingers?

Well, the popular story is that some time before the assault, perhaps on the previous day, Wolfe recited a good part of the "Elegy" (chiefly the part about "the paths of glory" and "the grave") to a midshipman named Robinson. But, apparently, the only person who can be referred to was a Scotchman named Robison: which, of course, is a perfect example of the mistakes that only the truthful can make. Any ignorant Englishman, seeing the Scotch name Robison, might think it was merely a misprint for Robinson. As it does not matter a rap to the story whether his name was Robinson or Rehoboam, of course men would tell the tale in its familiar form. If there is in Westmoreland a person whose name is spelt Smiph, he must not complain if he is turned into Smith in stories in which he is a secondary figure. If there is in North Cornwall a fine old family of Jomes, it will probably become Jones for the purposes of popular narrative. Those are things which are modified, not in order to complicate a fraud, but in order to simplify the truth. And it is the whole case against the pedantic opponents of the romantic element in history that they do not seem able to distinguish between this instinctive omission of the irrelevant, which is simply the art of telling stories, and that introduction of ingenious and over-elaborate detail which is the whole art of telling lies. If popular traditions change, it is rather by dropping things out than by putting things in. The story grows simpler through the ages, not more complex.

Then the massive sceptical mind moves on to the next great difficulty in the story. Not only is it the awful truth that the midshipman Robinson was really Robison, but he was not really a midshipman. "Robison was rated as a midshipman in accordance with the usual convention that gives every gentleman employed on a ship of war an official rank, as he was afterwards rated as a colonel when Profesor of Mathematics in the C Cadet Corps at St. Petersburg." Now, these are very interesting facts, but the insistence on them seems again to betray a singular ignorance of the way in which an honest man tells a true story. A man says, "Wolfe said to a midshipman." He does not say, "Wolfe said to a person rated as a midshipman in accordance with the usual convention that gives to every gentleman employed on a ship of war an official rank, as he was afterwards rated as a colonel when Professor of Mathematics in the C Cadet Corps at St. Petersburg." I can quite imagine Mrs. Nickleby telling the story in that way, but nobody else.

It does not affect the story in the slightest degree whether Mr. Robison was a midshipman, or a music-master, or a boot-black, or an Ethiopian king, or a person rated as a midshipman in accordance with the usual convention which gives, etc. But it does affect the story that we should get to the story with some reasonable speed, and hear what was said by Wolfe, the only person in whom we are interested at all. Therefore, of course, the popular narrator said "midshipman," simply because one can say "midshipman" quicker than one can say "Jack Robinson"—or "Jack Robison."

March 19, 1910

English Criticism of Rostand

I hear that an attack is being made by some of the French critics upon "Chantecler" and the Rostand reputation generally—an attack taking the form of a charge of "mere rhetoric" and a protest against extravagant and even insolent puns. That some such hostile impression might exist in England I could well understand. To begin with the simplest reason, the little I have happened to see in the way of English translation of Rostand has been laughably inadequate. I even remember seeing a version of "Cyrano de Bergerac" in which the last line of the Ballade of the Duel was translated quite literally. As everybody knows, each verse of that impromptu poem ends with the line "A la fin de l'envoi je touche"—that is, "I hit you at the end of the *envoi*," or last verse. Obviously, it should be roughly rendered "I hit you when the ballad ends" or "And at the ballad's end the blow," or anything of that kind. In this learned translation, Cyrano was made to say at the end of every stanza, "And at the envoy's end I touch." Not a person in ten in an English theatre would know that "touch" is a French technical term for a hit in fencing. Not one person in twenty would know that the *envoi* is the ritual last verse of an old French ballade. If therefore Cyrano said "At the envoy's end I touch," it is impossible to conceive what an English crowd would think he meant. I can only suppose they would associate it with tickling the nose of an ambassador.

But, of course, this verbal mistranslation is only the emblem of a much deeper sort of misunderstanding. It is no disgrace to an intelligent Englishman of a certain type that he cannot care for Rostand's military brilliancy; just as it would be no disgrace to a classically minded Frenchman that he could see nothing beautiful in the tangled forest of Browning. There is an English temper to which the violence of French satire seems merely vulgar, while the rigidity of French rhetoric seems merely stiff and thin. Such a type of Englishman would be annoyed both ways by a Rostand drama. The nose of Cyrano de Bergerac seems to him as gross as the nose of Ally Sloper.[1] The rhetoric of Cyrano de Bergerac seems to him as artificial as that of Bombastes Furioso.[2] The two spiritual roots of difference lie in two French qualities which the English scarcely possess at all: first the power of feeling that hatred is something holy; and second the power, not merely of laughing at oneself, but of laughing unmercifully. Our English idea of a hero is built upon the sailor, the accessible and open-hearted fellow, who kills everybody with the kindest feelings. Our hero is Nelson or Harry V.—I mean the genial and magnanimous Henry V. of Shakespeare, not the morbid and cruel Henry V. of history. Nelson wears his heart on his sleeve, as he wears his Orders on his coat. Shakespeare's King Henry broods over his beloved subjects, and seeks to give them (in a splendid line) "a little touch of Harry in the night." But Cyrano, though he fills the stage, is by no means a universal gentleman. Cyrano, though he lives and dies for love, is by no means, in the general sense, a loving or a lovable character. It is his vice, he says, to wish everybody to hate him. He compares

---

[1] A rowdy hero appearing in a popular comic strip at the time, "Ally Sloper's Weekly Newspaper".

[2] A person who talks big or in an extremely pretentious manner. This word is taken from the hero of the same name who appears in a burlesque opera by William Barnes Rhodes (1813). It is a parody of *Orlando Furioso*.

love to the loose Vandyck collars that are coming into fashion, and hatred to the stiff Elizabethan ruff which he still retains; it is uncomfortable, but it holds a man's head up: "La Haine est un carcan, mais c'est une auréole."[3] To be a bitter and exact critic of society, to lash the age, to demand that acting, writing, fencing should reach a severe standard, to wage a lonely war on stupidity—this is a French idea: it is the idea of Rostand's Cyrano, just as it is the idea of Molière's Misanthrope. It is hard for an Englishman (at least, it is hard for me) heartily to like this idealistic cruelty. It is hard for us to imagine scorn as something fruitful and even festive: to behold that bitter tree bearing lovely blossoms and delightful fruit. It is hard for us to realise a pageant of blazing wit and romantic activity all produced by such stiff anger as has produced an anchorite or a suicide. It is as if all the gay Athenian comedies had been written by Timon of Athens. But though this sentiment of sacred hate is not easy to us, that is no reason why we should not do justice to it. And France may fairly claim that such philanthropy has been founded by the Misanthrope.

The other un-English quality is best represented in "Chantecler" itself. The Englishman can laugh at himself, but the Frenchman can sneer at himself, can laugh at himself till himself gets quite cross. It was very French to parade the fierce satiric poet Cyrano, the very romance of unpopularity, defying human society and taunting death. It was very French to devote a whole tragedy (as in "L'Aiglon") to the mere memory of Napoleon, the mere size of his shadow. It had the same heroic impossibility as that great Spanish legend in which two knights led out the corpse of the Cid on horseback and all the armies of the Moors fled before it. But it was most French of all, after exhibiting these towering heroes, suddenly to exhibit them again as cluck-

---

[3] This quote is from Rostand's *Cyrano de Bergerac*, act II, scene viii. It may be translated as, "Hatred is a yoke, but it is also a halo." Cyrano's meaning is that while one may suffer from the contempt of the mass of men, their hatred may also be a kind of glory or justification.

ing fowls in a farmyard and a cock crowing on a dunghill. First, Cyrano's "panache," his high, unbroken feather, brushes the stars; next, it is only the feather of a chicken waddling about a yard. First, Napoleon's trumpet is like the trumpet of the Resurrection, calling to the quick and the dead; next, it is only cock-a-doodle-do from the ragged hero of a hundred cock-fights.

Precisely because Rostand, a romantic and patriotic Frenchman, laughs at the omnipotence of the Gallic cock, many foreigners are enabled to laugh at it who by no means laugh at equally foolish things of their own. The phrase, for instance, that the sun never sets on the British Empire, is quite as intrinsically ludicrous as the idea that the sun cannot rise without the Gallic cock. That measureless, unthinkable furnace which flings its remoter firelight over such star-dust as our earth, and many like it, is not much more insulted by one idea than by the other. There is mockery in the notion that those awful ancestral fires are encouraged when they hear the cock; there is surely equal mockery in the suggestion that they are discouraged if they do not see the Union Jack. But the difference is that no patriotic English poet will write a romantic drama to point out the cosmic comicality of supposing that the distant and fiery star needs, for its comfort, a little touch of John Bull in the night. But it is French satire that always scores off French heroism; it is the same nation in the two moods; sometimes, as in Rostand's case, it is even the same individual. France has claimed, not without reason, to be the Roman Eagle; she has claimed the eagle and earned it. But she has always gone back of herself to the admission that she is not the eagle, but the cock.

I had intended in this article to deal with the French criticisms of Rostand, and I find I have dealt only with the English. Making the sun rise when you choose seems to me but a faint expression of the difficulty of making a newspaper article go where you want it to. Upon the two specific points of rhetoric and punning I have only space for admonitions which may sound the more sincere for being necessarily brief. The first is this: when people talk about "mere rhetoric" as if it were something artificial, ask them why there always has been rhetoric at very real moments of politics, why there has always been rhetoric when there were bullets and blood. And when people complain of puns, ask why the age of Shakespeare was the age of punning, and also why our one piercing poem of poverty, our one *unbearable* poem, "The Song of the Shirt,"[4] is full of verbal quips.

March 26, 1910
Socialistic Morality

It is a great pity that our headlong and hurried Press is always half a century behind the times. The reason is in no way recondite; it is behind the times because it is hurried and headlong. That which is forced to be rapid is specially likely to be trite. If you have five minutes to write a sentence on a slate, doubtless a man of your talents will produce a polished and yet audacious epigram, exquisite in literary form, and startling in its intellectual stimulus. But if you have five seconds to write it in, you will probably begin to write "Honesty is the best policy." If even at the shortest notice (say, after the entremets[1]) you are told that you have to respond to the toast of Decayed Pawnbrokers, you will no doubt begin your speech with some thunderbolt of wit which will call down Homeric laughter and secure historic immortality. But if you are jerked to your feet quite abruptly over the port, you will be conscious of a wild notion of beginning, "Unaccustomed as I am to public speaking." Upon this very simple fact of human nature—that bustle always means banality—the whole gigantic modern Press, the palladium of our

[4] A poem by Thomas Hood (1799–1845).
[1] The sweet dish served between the cheese and the fruit at a French meal.

liberties, is built. Leader-writers write the flattest Liberalism or
Toryism to feed the impatient printing-machines, just as private
persons scribble their dullest and most conventional notes to
catch the post. But the principle extends to the theories as well
as the expression of them. The things which the newspapers call
startling are things that the real people in the world have long
ceased to be startled at. To journalists Darwin is still a novelty,
while to biologists he is an antiquity, and even a rather damaged
antiquity. In the newspapers it is considered startling that aristocrats should talk Socialism. In Society it would be considered
rather startling if they didn't. In the somewhat over-emancipated
social sphere which the aristocrats adorn, scores of lords and
ladies talk Socialism; and certainly nobody is shocked at it. In
fact, the aristocracy has many natural motives for encouraging
the Socialistic morality. That is one reason why I rather distrust
the Socialistic morality.

Turning over a popular sheet a moment ago, I noticed an odd
example of this sort of antiquated astonishment. It was a report
of Mr. Bernard Shaw's recent address to the Eugenic Education
Society, and it was headed "Daring Suggestions for Improving
the Human Race." Now, this is unjust to Mr. Shaw in a double
sense. The things under discussion were not daring suggestions,
nor did Mr. Shaw (to do him justice) suggest them. The suggestions which the journalist describes as daring are simply the
old, battered, dunderheaded fads about the possibility of evolv-
ing a human race like a racehorse. This is one of the most ancient
follies of this earth; fantastic men of genius like Plato and Mr.
Shaw have sometimes talked about it, but always in joke; and
on this occasion Mr. Shaw did not defend it, even jocularly. Mr.
Shaw likes his jokes a little fresher than that. When we turn from
the headline to the report, we find that the lecturer was chiefly
occupied in clearing these cartloads of Eugenical rubbish out of
the path of common-sense. The proposal to produce the best
human beings scientifically is one that is open to an interminable
list of objections, of which the first (and perhaps not the least
important) is that it cannot be done.

Mr. Shaw himself admitted that, if asked to superintend the marriages of a whole nation, he might feel puzzled and shy; and, if Mr. Shaw felt shy, there are no words for what other people would feel. If I see a man setting up on an enormous scale and at considerable expense to human feelings a factory or gigantic machine, I feel myself fully justified in urging the two facts: first, that the man does not even know what article he wishes to produce; and, second, that even if he wanted an article very much, he has no notion of how to produce it. Someone defined metaphysics as looking in a dark room for a black hat that isn't there. This is unfair, for metaphysics is merely common sense. It is only metaphysics that tells a man not to look for a hat that isn't there. But (to judge by the Eugenists) the science of Sociology really does mean waiting in a wild place for something that won't happen.

Eugenics is not merely a sham science, it is a dead science; a great deal more dead than astrology. To extract the Superman by forced marriages is not merely a mad notion, but a dead notion; a great deal more dead than the notion of extracting evidence by red-hot pincers. One after another all men with active minds, from the old Greek philosophers to Mr. Shaw and Mr. Wells, have thought of the notion, looked at the notion, and, in consequence, chucked the notion. So far as this part of his address was concerned, Mr. Shaw was, if not slaying the slain, at least clearing away the corpses. He merely brushed away such wreck and debris of the Eugenical idea as may have remained after Mr. Wells's unanswerable onslaught on it in "Mankind in the Making." The only daring suggestion for the improvement of the human race that Eugenics suggests to us is that the world would be a jollier place if there were fewer quacks in it.

But in another part of his address, it would appear, Mr. Bernard Shaw did become merely modern, and in consequence nonsensical. I do not refer to his large and hearty offer to make "an entire abolition of property and marriage, as we understand it." The revolutionist is bound to begin by saying that he will prove that, even if he ends up (as he did) by substantially proving the opposite. The Eastern king must preface all his announcements by saying that he is the preserver of the sun and moon. The Western sociologist must preface all his announcements by saying that he is the destroyer of the sun and moon. Property and marriage (the sun and moon of any sane society) are really quite as safe with Mr. Shaw as they would be safe without the Akond of Swât. The real part of the address which irritates the virility of reason is that concerned with the punishment of crime. Mr. Shaw maintained (quite truly) that having committed a murder does not make a man a murderer—that is, does not make him a prospective and perpetual assassin. This he put in his own lively and legitimate manner by saying that we should allow a murderer two or three murders, as we allow a dog one or two bites. After that (apparently) we should shoot him without trial, like a mad dog.

In any case, Mr. Shaw suggested, punishment is futile. Now, there is a very simple answer to this; by the parallel Mr. Shaw himself chooses. Personally, I fear that the same decadence which treats men as dogs in argument will treat them like dogs in practice. But let that pass. If I am to be compared to a dog, why should I not be compared to a sane dog? One cannot punish a mad dog; but one does punish a sane dog, because he is sane. He has a will, and is capable of considering the consequences of his choice. The Shaw argument seems to be that we should not punish because a healthy man may sin. But it is exactly because a healthy man may sin that we do punish. We use the argument of consequences precisely because a good man may stab—or may not stab. The obedient dog may bite—that is, he may refrain from biting. Punishment exists to influence his open mind. If he must bite, he must be shot. But the Shaw sociology can only be maintained by saying that our whole human pack consists of mad dogs. In that case we must all be shot—I am not sure by whom.

April 2, 1910

English Ideas about the French

There is no more strange and even amusing modern figure than the Foreign Correspondent of an English paper; I mean the man permanently placed at Paris or Rome or Constantinople, and sending a thin, continuous stream of information to London. The importance of this individual rests on our favourite fallacy about the authority of the "Man on the Spot." Mrs. Micawber was of opinion that her husband would succeed in the Medway Coal Trade if he would come down and "see the Medway." Many of our politicians and pressmen are of a similar order of practicality: they feel that a man must take a just view of the problem of the Rhine Provinces if he has *seen* the Rhine. Yet surely a little elementary common sense might teach anybody that to be on the spot very often means to be in the very centre of all that is disputable and partisan. I have known Englishmen who returned from a round of hospitalities in France or Russia, in which they had lived exclusively with one set, heard only one class of opinions, and who reported those opinions dispassionately as the solid certainties of travel and experience. What should we in England think if a German spent a week or two with us, and then wrote in a German paper "The Budget is an admirable achievement; I discussed it with Mr. Lloyd-George, himself an English politician. Tariff Reform is making great strides, according to the *Morning Post*, an English paper of great accuracy. Free Trade is essential to the Empire; I have heard them say so in Manchester and at the celebrated Cobden Club"? Yet many Englishmen dogmatise quite as insanely at second-hand about the complex quarrels and counter-assertions of foreign political parties. Many highly educated tourists, many foreign correspondents, report things to England of which the only upshot is that the Catholics are in a bad way, according to the Protestants; that the Republicans are highly unsatisfactory in the opinion of the

Royalists—in short, that we cannot trust the Montagu Government if we may believe the *Capulet Gazette*.

To this fatuous state of affairs I frankly prefer the old hazy prejudice against the whole of a foreign nation. It is surely more reasonable to shrink from an entire race because you know nothing about it. It is surely less reasonable passionately to support a party because you know nothing about it. Moreover, in the old cloudy prejudice there was often some general colour of truth. The Englishman felt that the French were cynical and over-civilised; the Frenchman felt that the English were snobbish and subservient to one class. The English believed the French were frog-eaters; the French might have answered by saying that the English were toad-eaters. These charges, coarse and vague as they were, had some general origin and significance in fact. But the Man on the Spot is almost always wrong, for he hears only the most intemperate and fantastic accusations from one side, and that without understanding the local and traditional senses of the words, the allowance to be made for atmosphere, the proportion of ritual, or the personal equation of anger. If a Frenchman heard the speech of the noble Lord who said that Mr. Asquith's Government was "a ragged crew of piratical tatterdemalions" the Frenchman might quite possibly go away with the impression that the noble Lord meant what he said; whereas it is doubtful if he even attached any meaning to his words. Partisan atmosphere differs; and each must be understood by itself. But the Man on the Spot sees everything spotty: for him all the mud that is thrown sticks. Sometimes his one-sidedness is astoundingly naïve. In an excellent daily paper which sides with the French Government against the French Church (a quite tenable position), I see a statement from Paris to the effect that certain grave defalcations have been discovered in Governmental business—that some of the funds diverted from the congregations to various public objects have largely disappeared; but the Government is energetically investigating the matter, while (in a sort of contemptuous parenthesis) some Nationalist and Catholic newspapers are trying "to make capital out of it." To my simple mind it does not seem very extraordinary that the Catholics should try to make capital out of it, as they have lost capital over it. The simple human story of the thing seems something like this: that the Government took away money from convents to give to museums (or some such things); the convents lost it, and the museums never got it. It went to brighten the lives of one or two prosperous private gentlemen. That the people from whom the money had originally been taken should call attention to this fact does not strike me as outside the normal limits of calculable human nature. If we wished to test the thing in our own country, we should imagine something like this. Suppose Mr. Balfour confiscated all the Nonconformist chapels on the ground that they were seditious and anti-patriotic, or on the ground that the Free Churches, by denouncing war, weakened us in the face of Germany, or that by their Salvationist methods they spread hysteria. Then suppose it was discovered that every one of the chapels so seized by the State had been turned into a picturesque villa for Mr. Balfour himself, who thus came into the possession of some two thousand private houses, with the City Temple as his town residence and *pied-à-terre* for the season. Suppose this state of things, and it is surely not inconceivable that the dispossessed Dr. Clifford and Dr. Horton might go so far as to "make capital" out of the discovery. I for one should not blame them for that ingenious and Jesuitical course of action.

But such an imaginary Franco-English comparison may have quite the wrong effect if it confirms us in our fancy that such corruption is peculiar to foreigners. France is the land of revolution because it is the land of revelation; its history is a perpetual apocalypse, the breaking of seals, the opening of vials, the rending asunder of heavens; that which is said in the inner chamber shall be proclaimed on the housetops. France is the land of revelation; England is the land of mystery. The point is not so much that one is honest or the other dishonest; it is that one believes that things are cured by publicity, and the other that things are best cured in private. The English have a multitude of proverbs to that effect. The English say, "Dirty linen should be washed

at home." The French answer, "No; not when it is stolen linen."
The motto of English aristocracy is "Let sleeping dogs lie"; if
they decline to sleep it calls them the hell-hounds of anarchy.
The motto of democracy is "Most said, soonest mended; let us
tell everybody and be done with it." The spirit of French government is that of a detective. The spirit of English government
is rather that of a diplomatist. It is not, as I say, a mere question
of moral honour. There are (I am told) honest diplomatists; and
it is quite certain, after the perusal of some police news, that
there are dishonest detectives. But the vital pride and dignity of
a detective is that he reveals secrets; that of a diplomatist, that
he keeps them. When we see scandals exploding in France, let
us remember that the whole French machine is meant to explode
them; while our best statesmen always seek to reform an abuse
without admitting it.

In fact, these frauds in French politics prove the honesty of
France rather than the dishonesty of France. They are the kind
of crimes that occur when men are so keen on principles as to
be too little respecters of persons. When Moslems are really
fighting Hindoos, you will find that the flag of the Prophet
protects Moslem brigands; you will find that the temple of Brahma
protects Hindoo forgers. So long as a man is on the right side,
he may be the wrong sort. Thus some of the real criminals of
the Dreyfus case were protected because they were anti-Jew.
Thus the swindlers of the liquidation were protected because
they were anti-Catholic. If we English wish to understand the
thing, we have one domain in which we can see it—Ireland.
One man, an agent of our Government, committed crimes, per-
jured himself to fix them on innocent men, sent them to jails,
where one of them died—and walks the world unpunished at
this instant. Can you match that story in Europe? The simple
explanation is that wherever there is a fight the fanatics protect
the knaves.

April 9, 1910

Stories Spoilt by Great Authors

Under the title "Good Stories Spoilt by Great Authors," a considerable essay might be written. In fact, it shall be written. It shall be written now. The mere fact that some fable has passed through a master mind does not imply by any means that it must have been improved. Eminent men have misappropriated public stories, as they have misappropriated public stores. It is always supposed (apparently) that anyone who borrows from the original brotherhood of men is not bound to pay back. It is supposed that if Shakespeare took the legend of Lear, or Goethe the legend of Faust, or Wagner the legend of Tannhäuser, they must have been very right, and the legends ought to be grateful to them. My own impression is that they were sometimes very wrong, and that the legends might sue them for slander. Briefly, it is always assumed that the poem that somebody made is vastly superior to the ballad that everybody made. For my part I take the other view. I prefer the gossip of the many to the scandal of the few. I distrust the narrow individualism of the artist, trusting rather the natural communism of the craftsmen. I think there is one thing more important than the man of genius—and that is the genius of man.

Let me promptly, in a parenthetical paragraph, confess that I cannot get Shakespeare into this theory of mine. As far as I can see, Shakespeare made all his stories better; and as far as I can see, he could hardly have made them worse. He seems to have specialised in making good plays out of bad novels. If Shakespeare were alive now I suppose he would make a sweet springtime comedy out of an anecdote in a sporting paper. I suppose he would make a starry and awful tragedy out of one of the penny novelettes. But as Shakespeare does not support my argument I propose to leave him out of my article.

In the instance of Milton, however, I think my case can be stoutly maintained; only that Milton's story being Scriptural is not perhaps so safe to dogmatise about. In one sense Milton spoiled Eden as much as the snake did. He made a magnificent poem, and yet he missed the poetical point. For in "Paradise Lost" (if I remember right) Milton substitutes for the primal appetite for a strange fruit an elaborate psychological and sentimental motive. He makes Adam eat the fruit deliberately, "not deceived," with the object of sharing Eve's misfortune. In other words, he makes all human wickedness originate in an act of essential goodness, or, at the worst, of very excusable romanticism. Now all our meannesses did not begin in magnanimity; if we are cads and blackguards (as we are) it is not because our first ancestor behaved like a husband and a gentleman. The story, as it stands in the Bible, is infinitely more sublime and delicate. There all evil is traced to that ultimate unreasoning insolence which will not accept even the kindest conditions; that profoundly inartistic anarchy that objects to a limit as such. It is not indicated that the fruit was of attractive hue or taste: its attraction was that it was forbidden. In Eden there was a maximum of liberty and a minimum of veto; but some veto is essential even to the enjoyment of liberty. The finest thing about a free meadow is the hedge at the end of it. The moment the hedge is abolished it is no longer a meadow, but a waste, as Eden was after its one limitation was lost. This Bible idea that all sins and sorrows spring from a certain fever of pride, which cannot enjoy unless it controls, is a much deeper and more piercing truth than Milton's mere suggestion that a gentleman got entangled by his chivalry to a lady. Genesis, with sounder common-sense, makes Adam after the Fall lose his chivalry in a rather marked and startling manner.

The same theory of deterioration might be urged in the case of Goethe and the Faust legend. I do not speak, of course, of the poetry in detail, which is above any criticism. I speak of the outline of Goethe's "Faust"—or rather, of the outline of the first part; the second part has no outline, like Mr. Mantalini's Countesses. Now the actual story of Faust, Mephistopheles, and Margaret seems to me infinitely less exalted and beautiful than the old story of Faust, Mephistopheles, and Helen. I had the pleasure of seeing in Yorkshire the old wooden puppet play of "Faustus" that has since been performed in London; and the Yorkshire dolls were much more living than some of the London actors. The marionettes were trying to express themselves as men; there were times, alas! when eminent actors tried to express themselves as marionettes; but that is not the true objection. The true objection is this: that, in the mediaeval play, Faust is damned for doing a great sin: swearing loyalty to eternal evil that he may possess Helen of Troy, the supreme bodily beauty. The old Faust is damned for doing a great sin; but the new Faust is saved for doing a small sin—a mean sin. Goethe's Faust is not intoxicated and swept away by the intolerable sweetness of some supernatural lady. Goethe's Faust, so soon as he is made a young man, promptly and really becomes a young rascal. He gets at once into a local intrigue—I will not say into a local entanglement because (as in most similar cases) only the woman is entangled. But surely there is something of the bad side of Germany, there is something of the vulgar sentimentalist, in this hotch-potch of seduction and salvation! The man ruins the woman; the woman, therefore, saves the man; and that is the moral, *die ewige Weiblichkeit*. Somebody who has had the pleasure shall be purified because somebody else has had the pain; and so his cruelty shall finally be the same as kindness. Personally, I prefer the puppet play: where Faust is finally torn by black devils and dragged down to hell. I find it less depressing.

Again, the same principle, as far as I can make out, marks Wagner's version of "Tannhäuser"—or rather, his perversion of "Tannhäuser." This great legend of the early Middle Ages, plainly and properly told, is one of the most tremendous things in human history or fable. Tannhäuser, a great knight, committed a terrible transcendental sin, that cut him off from all the fellowship of sinners. He became the lover of Venus herself, the incarnation of pagan sensuality. Coming out of those evil caverns to the sun, he strayed to Rome and asked the Pope if such as he could repent and be saved. The Pope answered, in substance, that there are limits to everything. A man so cut off from Christian sanity (he said) could no more repent than the Pope's stick cut from a tree could grow leaves again. Tannhäuser went away in despair, and descended again into the caverns of eternal death, only, after he had gone, the Pope looked at his stick one fine morning and saw that it was sprouting leaves. To me that tale is one terrific crash of Agnosticism and Catholicism. Wagner, I believe, made Tannhäuser return repentant for the second time. If that is not spoiling a story, I do not know what is.

Lastly (to take a much smaller case), I have noticed all over Europe discussions about the morals of the play of "Salome," which Wilde could not get acted in English and afterwards rewrote in French. I do not see anything very practically immoral about the play, though much that is morbid and turgid. What strikes me most about Wilde's "Salome" is that it is startlingly inartistic. It spoils the whole point of a particularly artistic incident. The brilliant bitterness of the old Bible story consists in the complete innocence and indifference of the dancing girl. A subtle despot was plotting a statesmanlike clemency; a secretive Queen was plotting savage vengeance. A dancer (a mere child, I always fancied) was the daughter of the vengeful Queen and danced before the diplomatic despot. In riotous relaxation he asked the little girl to name any present she liked. Bewildered with such fairy-tale benevolence, the girl ran to ask her mother what she should choose; the patient and pitiless Queen saw her chance, and asked for the death of her enemy. In place of this strong, ironic tale of a butterfly used as a hornet, "Salome" has some sickly and vulgar business of the dancer being in love with the Prophet. I am not sure about its being bad morality; for its morality is its effect on mankind. But I know it is bad art; for its art is its effect on me.

April 16, 1910

Truth and Slander

There is one thing in English politics and society that is becoming perfectly intolerable. It is this: that one is not allowed to tread on anybody's toe, even by accident. Deliberate malice or deliberate, righteous indignation are quite another matter; they go along with deliberate respect. Some men cross Europe to kiss the Pope's toe, and I would willingly cross America to tread on Mr. Rockefeller's toe. But there is a certain amount of treading, of trampling on tiny vanities or indirect interests, which is simply unavoidable in the course of any inquiry into anything or any progress towards anywhere. It is impossible (a biologist tells me) to walk down any road without crushing millions of very small bodies. It is impossible (my publishers tell me) to follow any train of thought without crushing a certain number of very small souls. So soon as any modern man tries to tell what seems to him the truth about any complication, and quite accidentally, merely in the course of his remarks, happens to urge the ill-effects of some type or trade or sect, in an instant all is in an uproar, as if he had deliberately gone out of his way to deal a poisoned stab. He has insulted stockbrokers, he has slandered Supralapsarians, he has affronted the men of North Wiltshire, he has questioned the honour of Albinos—and all because of some remark he made about some quite particular aspect of some quite doubtful question. I repeat that it is getting intolerable.

Here is a case that occurred only the other day. A witness before the Divorce Commission (perhaps the first political Inquiry for decades that has had anything whatever to do with the English people) said, among a great many more or less tentative suggestions, and in answer to a great many delicate questions, that he had known cases of tallymen from drapery shops making unjustifiable advances to poor women and offering to remit their payments. I have no notion how far what he said was true; but that is all he said. It was not even the Commission saying it; it was not a Judge saying it. It was simply one witness saying he had heard of a draper doing that which is wrong, just as he might have said that he had known a surveyor commit bigamy, or seen a cabman pick a pocket. But as soon as this was said it was found necessary (and made possible) for a formidable and impressive Representative of All the Drapers to give evidence before the Commission; to hurl back, I suppose, the insult to the whole profession; to declare, I imagine, the general chivalry and Galahad-like qualities of drapers' travellers as a class—in short, to permit the draper to wash his foul spot off his drapery.

Now I think this is getting a little unreasonable. The essence of its unreason can be uttered by recurring to our phrases about the intentional and the incidental wrong. I am writing this article, for instance, in a gentleman's house in Yorkshire, a house which happens to be situated at the top of a steep hill, which some (less elegant and active than myself) might call a stiff climb. Now suppose this gentleman, growing slightly bored with my brilliant society, were to kick me out of the house to-morrow, and suppose I, in revenge, were to go and tell everybody that his house was on an inaccessible crag—I think I should be doing wrong. Or even suppose that I, knowing that he wished to sell his house, were to go about talking to all the probable buyers and emphasising the steep ascent, describing with rich and poetic word-painting the fatigues and despairs of that pilgrimage—even then, though I said nothing but truth, I should be uttering a malicious slander. I should be a spiritual liar because my motive would be spiteful and false. But if it were my ordinary, scientific duty to make a relief map of the physical geography of Yorkshire, then it would be my duty to mark the slope up to my friend's house as a very abrupt slope; and I submit that he would have no cause of quarrel with me even if a possible buyer did shrink in terror from the miniature reproduction of that precipice. As it is with anyone asked by the State to make a physical map, so surely it should be with such persons as are asked by the State to make a moral map. A Bishop, as we all know, means an overseer, which is much the same as a map-maker. Perhaps some of our

English Bishops (who are among the most modern and advanced persons now in England) might suitably be provided with aeroplanes. Perhaps it was some such idea that induced the Irvingites[1] (I think) to call their Bishops angels. In any case, all this is a tribute to the truth, the very important truth, that a man must be very much in the air before he knows anything of the earth. Of all real rulers or teachers is asked a sort of bird's-eye view; they are expected to see the landscape as a whole. Any discernible object such as the Eiffel Tower, the Pyramids, or the Tower of Babel, they are expected to notice and remark. The Bishops of the early Church did notice these things; which perhaps explains why so many of them were killed. But certainly it is the business of everyone bearing official testimony, whether temporary or permanent, to remark the irregularity of the landscape or the inequality of the law. He must not mind the fact that every individual valley wishes to be exalted, or that every individual hill has a great objection to being brought low.

The distinction between the two kinds of testimony is therefore sufficiently clear. If I am a waiter at a restaurant and get the sack (as I probably should), it would be malicious in me to denounce that particular proprietor or talk of the gluttony and intemperance of that particular restaurant. But if, years afterwards, I were asked to give my general recollections as a waiter, it would be most unfair to reproach me because those general impressions were accidentally to the disadvantage of the house that had given me the sack. Anybody existing in the mere daylight of common-sense can see the distinction between the two cases. And yet that distinction is so commonly and constantly ignored that liberty of speech has almost vanished from England.

For a long period past it has been a public joke that our Parliamentary Inquiries and our Special Commissions come to nothing. In a million paragraphs, in a thousand caricatures, it has been suggested that to put a Commission on a thing is to put a

---

[1] Members of a religious sect founded by Edward Irving (1792–1834), a minister of the Church of Scotland.

tombstone on it. Much of this is, no doubt, due to elements of spiritual unreality and hypocrisy in our whole system which are at once too vast and too delicate for treatment here; in other words, they would involve the two things that modern journalism is afraid of—religion and surnames. But I do believe that much of the futility of these public inquiries is due to this pervading idea that one may happen to insult a whole class or make enemies of a whole profession. It is not enough that in some cases, I suppose, these attestations in social inquiries are privileged, like the attestations in criminal inquiries. The witness does not fear criminal arrest, but social and atmospheric inconvenience. He is restrained at the last moment from telling the full and frightful truth about governesses, not from fear of the police, but from fear of the governess. And there is just this subtle plausibility in the case: that, in a criminal inquiry, we are asking whether one particular governess gave something poisonous to some particular children; whereas, in a Royal Commission on Education, we are asking whether any governess gave anything whatever to any children. And this is bound to be in some sense a more delicate, or even a more damaging, inquiry. In consequence, therefore, there is a meeting of half a million governesses in Hyde Park, brandishing flags and cudgels and roaring for blood. But really, as I said before, it is unreasonable; a man ought to be permitted to give his good-tempered and reasonable impression of whether drapers go wrong in this way or governesses in that without being lynched for a sort of impersonal libel.

Of course, there is only one cure for it: the cure for nearly everything that is wrong in this country. I mean the wild and alien suggestion that there is a thing called a Citizen; that a draper is interested in the honour of England, and not merely in the honour of drapers; that a tallyman is (among other things) a man; and a governess, *inter alia*, a woman. But that we shall not admit for a very long time.

April 23, 1910

The Life and Death of Institutions

I wonder when modern people will begin to perceive the plain fact that Evolution (at this word you will please bow your head twenty-seven times or go through some other sacerdotal rite) that Evolution, I say, however fascinating or even inspiring as a picture of the facts of the past, is totally useless as a moral code for the future. A great scientific theory has a dignity of its own. There is no reason why it should also profess to be a piece of ethical or social advice. Nor, I think, do people try to make new moralities out of any of the other great scientific generalisations. I have never heard the Law of Gravity adduced as a reason for knocking people down. I have never known the Circulation of the Blood offered as an excuse for bloodshed. I never knew running away from your wife called Centrifugal Force; or tearing her hair out described as Capillary Attraction. But the ancient theory of a slow variation of species, the theory of which Lamarck, Darwin, Haeckel and others have given diverse and disputed versions, this one scientific scheme of facts the idealists and moralists seem quite unable to leave alone. They are always trying to twist out of it crude and fanciful theories of right and wrong. They are still at it, though Huxley, the greatest of the Darwinians, told them long ago that Evolution and Ethics were two totally different things, and that the less evolutionary their ethics were the better. They still go blandly boring on, saying that a man's mind must grow and develop in the same sense in which all Nature has grown and developed. They might as well say that a man's head must go round and round, just as the Solar System goes round and round. Some of their heads do.

But the practical impotence and futility of the thing can be quite plainly and shortly shown. People are, let us say, endeavouring to abolish some institution, an ancient institution, or a deep-rooted institution—which, by the way, are two very different things. No; I will not say the House of Lords—I will say the Inter-Imperial Corporation of Old Clothes Men at Camberwell. The principle is the same, and sometimes even the people are very similar. But I do not here desire to discuss the merits either of the House of Lords or the Old Clothes Men's Corporation. I only wish to point out how the Evolution argument breaks down utterly in every practical case, and is useless either for attack or defence. For what happens in most modern discussions of the sort is something like this: The opponent of the Corporation rises to his feet and says, "The old order changes, yielding place to the new; and however necessary the Old Clothes Men may have been in barbaric times when man was less fastidious about wearing someone else's trousers, he is now a meaningless survival. The practice of one person wearing six superimposed hats may have been useful in the ages of ignorance to strike terror into savage outlaws; but our enlarged intelligence has realised that the mere unadorned countenance of the merchant is far more mysterious and awe-inspiring. Old Clothes Men belong to the childhood of the world and must pass like other beautiful dreams. We have come to maturity. For a season it is well that the babe should be guarded in the cradle; but the time comes when he must arise in the strength of his youth, for his motor-car is waiting at the door. For a season it is well that the egg should be hard and unbroken; but broken it must be in due season, that the sublime form of a chicken may emerge. So must man now break that of his kindly protecting shell of Old Clothes. The hour is come. The sands are run out. The dawn is risen. The cup is full. The Old Clothes Man has done his work, and the flamboyant figure of the New Clothes Man irradiates an astonished earth."

Then the reformer sits down, amid loud Progressive cheers. Then the defender of the Corporation rises, amid loud Conservative cheers; and he says something like this: "It may be that the old order changes, but it is our view that it should change in a slow, a constitutional, an evolutionary manner. Some day, perhaps, other people's trousers may appear to man as repulsive as does the scanty clothing of our painted forefathers to us. When you have altered human nature, perhaps it will be possible to establish the Utopian principle of 'one man one hat.' But until men have reached that point, we hold that a many-hatted aristocracy is a safeguard of order; we say that that solemn tiara protects the slow mind of man. As long as humanity is childish, as at present, we need such artificial coverings. We have not yet come to maturity. Some day, perhaps, man, made godlike, shall climb into the motor-car that throbs at his door; but for many centuries yet he must be a babe guarded in the cradle. Some day, perhaps, we may see the beloved and beautiful Egg of the Constitution give forth the flaming Chicken of Perfect Freedom—(cheers)—but for many centuries we must patiently and piously stare at the egg. The hour has not come; the time is not yet. The dawn will rise in heaven's good time; the sands will run out we know not when. But, till they do, I for one will champion that Old Clothes Man who has been the protector of the poor; and, while one rag is still flying of the banner of the Old Pair of Trousers, I will never desert it." (Prolonged cheers.)

That is an accurate and, I trust, inoffensive summary of nearly every modern argument I have heard about any alleged reform. And you see that the argument is quite inane. You see it is inane because, according to the theory of slow change, you can never prove at any given moment that any given institution has grown old, or has not grown old. The reformer says the institution was once living, but is now dead. The Conservative says it may be some day, but is still living. Neither of them can prove his case, for the very simple reason that there is no roughly fixed lifetime for an institution, as there is for an animal. If a lady assures us that her lap-dog is ninety-seven (and if we believe her) then we have no hesitation in addressing such a quadruped as "old man." On the other hand, if an elephant or a crocodile gives up the ghost at the tender age of two, we feel it appropriate to observe that those whom the gods love die young. There is an average age for dogs and elephants; but there is no average age for churches, or nations, or clubs, or sects, or corporations. There are churches that are more vigorous after nearly two thousand

518

years than many of their rivals after a month. There are nations that are always dying and never dead. On the other hand, there are sects that die very young (perhaps because the gods loved them), and I have known clubs which were certainly born tired. There being no fixed biological birth and death for institutions, these biological parallels about youth and maturity and old age are all useless and utterly at sea. You see (I hope) the drivelling pointlessness of all that argument about the egg. The real point is so simple. The right time for a chicken to come out of the egg is the time when it does come out of the egg. We only know it is the right time because it happens. But do we really mean, in human affairs, that the right time for a convict to come out of Portland is whenever he *does* come out, having brained three warders? Is the right time for the child to come out of the cradle any time when he happens to fall out? If any egg breaks (to release the chicken), the time has come for it to be broken. Do these people mean that, whenever any law is broken, it ought to have been broken? That doctrine would lead to sheer passive acceptance and cowardly inaction. But they do not mean that; they do not mean anything very much; for their wits have been addled like an egg by Evolution. I implore my fellow-countrymen, when they are discussing an institution, to discuss, like men, whether it is a good or a bad institution, whether it fulfils this or that public purpose, and not to ask dismally whether the time has yet come, or hopefully whether the time has not come. What time, in the name of eternity?

April 30, 1910

Bigotry of the Rationalists

The French are at present engaged in one of those really interesting arguments which are so rare in politics—an argument as to whether one can be impartial about history. It is a good example of their national habit of refreshing fundamentalism. There are two kinds of revolutionists, as of most things—a good kind and a bad. The bad revolutionists destroy conventions by appealing to fads—fashions that are newer than conventions. The good do it by appealing to facts that are older than conventions. In this country we have all grown heartily sick of the discussion about sectarian and unsectarian education; and I hasten to assure my rapidly disappearing audience that I am not now going to discuss it. I have been in the thick of it before now, and could never make much sense of either the Radical Puritan or the Tory Anglican position. As far as I can make out, the unsectarian schools do teach the religion of the sects, while the sectarian, or Church schools, don't teach the religion of the church. That was my cloudy experience, and it has left me a little confused. But these cheery Frenchmen have passed their twilight territory and come to something much more lucid and amusing. They are discussing, not whether religion can be unsectarian, but whether anything can be unsectarian. I do not mean they would deny that one can teach some things without bias. I suppose one can teach any exact science without a bias—except astronomy; I imagine one can teach any game without a bias—except bowls. But these disputants do raise the whole question of whether what is commonly called culture—history, citizenship, literature, and the great languages—can be taught without a philosophy being either implied or assumed. The argument began, of course, in connection with an alleged bias against religion in the State text-books; but it has developed into an equally animated allegation of a general bias against nationalism, chivalry, and the military virtues. The Nationalists say it is the business of the State to teach its children patriotism, and it teaches them anti-patriotism.

Now, without pronouncing on the French problem, which must necessarily be very hard for a foreigner to understand, I think we may all say that we must admit there is some truth in this. It is not only true that Rationalists might in their writings on indifferent subjects introduce such a bias against the religious or romantic point of view; but I think it indubitable that Rationalists do. They do not do it meanly or treacherously. They are so bigoted that they do it unconsciously. There is no person so narrow as the person who is sure that he is broad; indeed, being quite *sure* that one is broad is itself a form of narrowness. It shows that one has a very narrow ideal of breadth. But, moreover, there is an element involved in the Rationalist position which makes this unintentional bigotry peculiarly natural. A man who is in a house may think it a very large house. He may think it a much larger house than it is. But he knows it is a house, because of its shape and appearance; because there are doors and windows—therefore there is a world outside. In the same way, a man inside a church may think it the true church. He may think it a very broad and free church. But he knows it is a church, because it is shaped like one; therefore he knows that there are things beyond and outside the church. But suppose a man lived in a house of mirrors so craftily constructed that he really thought he was alone on an open plain. Suppose a man lived in a church painted inside so splendidly with sky and cloud that he thought he was in the open air under the dome of heaven. He would be in the same position as the typical Rationalist. Instead of being conscious that he stands in a large church, he is simply unconscious that he stands in a small universe.

There are two or three principal ways in which this blameless bigotry may appear. One is the instinctive association in the mind of the writer between certain practical methods and certain ultimate merits. Thus a man will often use wealth as identical with prosperity, and then use prosperity as identical with happiness. Then he will talk of the decayed and dismal condition of Italy as compared with the rapturous felicity of Bolton and Ancoats. In short, he will show how Puritanism or Rationalism have brought about the *prosperity* of Lancashire. But he honestly does not notice that it is only the prosperity of the prosperous. And even they have a muggier sort of prosperity than most of the children of Adam would endure. Or, again, such a man will identify health with cleanliness, merely because cleanliness is one of the minor contributions to health. It never occurs to him, even for one wild instant, to compare a consumptive Countess with an athletic dustman. I have seen speeches by solemn Bishops and pompous schoolmasters which even identified physical cleanliness with ethical purity: they declared (in an ardour of self-admiration) that the English public schoolman is clean both inside and out. As if everybody did not know that, in the British Empire as much as in the Roman Empire, the dandies and the profligates take rather more baths than anybody else.

But my point here is only to defend the Rationalist historian from the charge of mere conspiracy and hypocrisy, which his fiery French enemies fling against him. He does not cunningly omit the obvious case for religion or patriotism; he has really never heard it. Writers like Buckle, Lecky, and even Hallam were not unfair; they were simply bigoted. They never really reflected that people can be happy without riches or rich without money. The modern Rationalist historian has never really reflected that one can be healthy without baths, or that one can bathe without bath-rooms.

Another unconscious trick of the kind is the abuse of the *post hoc, ergo propter hoc*. Certain events are connected together, while others, in the same historical relation, are not connected together. Thus, people will say, "Elizabeth threw off the yoke of Pope and Spaniard, and then Shakespeare wrote 'Romeo and Juliet.' " As a matter of fact, you might just as well say, "Charles II. returned amid loyal rejoicings, and then John Milton went and wrote 'Paradise Lost.' " The Puritan literature had begun long before Charles II. returned; so had the Renaissance literature, with its Italian love-tales, begun long before the Reformation or the Armada. The Reformation did occur soon after the Renaissance; but that it was not (to say the least of it) the same thing can be simply inferred from the fact that the countries where the Renaissance most markedly occurred were commonly the countries where the Reformation didn't. Indeed, I think that the most human, generous, and comprehending consideration of Puritanism would be to regard it as a revolt against the Renaissance rather than a revolt against the Middle Ages. It was an outbreak of the barbaric mysticism of the North against the classical clarity of the South. Bunyan was a rebel against Shakespeare much more than Shakespeare was a rebel against Chaucer. It is easy to fancy Chaucer and Shakespeare sitting down at the same tavern-table; but if Bunyan had sat down with them I think one of them would have been embarrassed. Perhaps all three.

Scores of cases could be given on other sides of other quarrels. Thus if a historian says, "The French Revolution ended in the despotism of Napoleon, and the return of the Bourbons," he speaks quite truly; but he speaks quite unjustly. The order is correct; but the use of the word *ended* begs the question. It would be equally true to say "The French Revolution ended in the Reform Bill, the liberation of Italy, and the beginnings of justice to Ireland." Perhaps it would be even truer to say "The French Revolution did not end at all."

May 7, 1910

The Fallacy of Precedent and Progress

When one is convinced that a certain fallacy is poisoning all public life, it is best, I think, to wait till it is uttered by someone whom one really admires, and then express one's admiration in the form of furious abuse. The error of which I speak is one that I have heard a million times from the most motley and variegated sorts of people; but the other day I saw it uttered by one of the few men of unmistakable genius and bold and honourable spirit now giving life to our literature. I mean that fine writer Mr. John Galsworthy, and I address especially to him the following bitter complaint. The fallacy I wish to impugn might be roughly described as the fallacy of Precedent and Progress. It consists in always unintelligently quoting the most recent change as an argument for the next change. By this process, Radicalism gets much more into a rut than Conservatism. The people who say they are pursuing progress are really only obeying precedent. By this system a Conservative means a man who must stop where his grandfather stopped; and a Progressive means a man who may only walk where his grandfather told him to. My own temperament is such that I would rather stand still without knowing where I was than walk on without knowing why I was doing it; the former is not so tiring.

The practical way the fallacy works is this. Take, for the sake of argument, the clause recently introduced by the Lords into the Children's Act, by which no child is allowed into any inn or hostelry. I will not stop to argue about this; it is enough to say it was founded on the great primary temperance principle that everything about public-houses should be settled by the people who have never been inside them. It thus involved the absurd notion, common to Peers, Puritans, and other professional politicians, that a public-house is a peculiarly secret sort of private house, where awful things occur of which no whisper can reach the street. These people talk about a tavern as if it were some sort of sacred enclosure, within which devils were worshipped, and from which the profane vulgar were kept out. It never seems to occur to them that a public-house is very like a public street, because it is public. If an inn-parlour is quiet and kindly, it is because the village outside is quite and kindly. If a public bar is squalid and noisy, it is because the street outside is squalid and noisy. If some of the famous first-class restaurants are vulgar and vicious, it is because the rich society of motorists and millionaires is itself vulgar and vicious. It has nothing to do with passing the portals of licensed premises. If a child hears foul language standing inside the Blue Pig, he will certainly hear it also waiting outside the Blue Pig. But I am here concerned not with the origins of such a measure, but with its possible effects. Now, suppose some politician were to get up and propose that children should be kept out of bookshops, because of the unquestionable fact that some modern books are immoral. If anyone protested that such a fad invaded freedom, the reformer would immediately say, "Ah, yes, all those arguments were used about children and public-houses, and yet that great reform was passed with enthusiasm by all branches of the Legislature." Then a man would rise and say, "I think it disgusting that children should be allowed in butchers' shops, to see the blood and bones of slaughtered animals. Ah, yes, you may call me a faddist; but were not the promoters of the Children's Bill and the Children's Bookshop Bill also called faddists?" And when the Progressives have passed that also according to precedent, a yet wilder figure will rise and demand that children should be kept out of the streets, because of the depressing sights that they will see there. "Call me mad!" he will cry, "as you called the promoters of the Bookshop Bill and the Butchers' Bill; I am proud of my unpopularity, for so persecuted you the prophets that were before me." And at last children will be comfortably locked up in the coal-cellar for good and fed through a grating, without it having once occurred to anyone to ask whether the precedent was a wise precedent, or even whether it really applied. It has never once struck anyone that false prophets are stoned as well as true ones, and that although men have sometimes hated their best friends, a democratic reformer ought to have some other credential besides the hatred of democracy.

In a recent issue of the *Nation* Mr. John Galsworthy wrote a graceful and humane article, called "Gentles, Let Us Rest," to the general effect that we should grant Female Suffrage, if only for peace and quietness. I am not discussing Female Suffrage here; it is sufficient to say that I know many much stronger arguments for it than this. But in the course of his argument Mr. Galsworthy went on to say, what so many other people have said before: that perhaps the majority of women do not want the vote; but, after all, the majority of agricultural labourers may not have wanted the vote either. Now, I say at once, and without hesitation, that if the majority of agricultural labourers really and seriously did not want the vote it was a very undemocratic thing to give it them. What should the unhappy creatures be allowed to decide if they are not to decide that? How can there be a set of people quite fit to settle Home Rule for Ireland, and yet quite unfit to settle whether they shall settle it? Why on earth does Mr. Galsworthy wish to keep up the farce of democracy at all if the majority of ordinary people are always wrong, even about what is their business and what isn't? Why on earth should he extend the franchise because he distrusts the masses? If there is at any given moment a definite group of advanced and educated persons who know the people's interests better than the people, why does not Mr. Galsworthy take the obvious course and let that group rule the people? Why does he not turn the Suffragettes into an aristocracy, instead of a sham democracy? Why does he not give Miss Pankhurst a coronet instead of a vote? If she is to force votes on a majority that dislikes votes, she may just as well be an aristocrat, for she is already an anti-democrat.

Of course, as a matter of fact, there is a fallacy in the precedent. Nobody alleges that agricultural labourers thought there was something unmanly about mixing in politics. The female opponents of Female Suffrage do maintain, rightly or wrongly, that there is something unwomanly about mixing in politics. Among the men it was, at worst, a negative ignorance: they did not ask for a vote as they did not ask for a telephone: they did not know what it was or what it would do. But in the women it is a positive conviction, correct or otherwise; they do not ask for a vote, because they do know what it is, but think it inconsistent with certain definite traditions, or, if you prefer it, prejudices. Millions of ordinary women do associate voting with a cold, coarse, arrogant kind of woman, with a necktie and a new morality. This impression may be unfair; but it is positive. But no men associate voting with a mean, cowardly, or effiminate kind of man, with a flowing tie or a false aestheticism. Any male indifference to a vote must be negative, not positive; the man must be either very ignorant and know nothing about a vote, or very wise and know too much about it.

Before I forget it, I am asked to correct a remark I made on a small point of fact. I was under the impression that Oscar Wilde wrote "Salome" first in English; I am assured by a friend of his that he wrote it first in French. The point affects no discussion; but it is as well to have it right.

May 14, 1910

The Racial Question and Politics

That able and ironic journalist who writes the paragraphs called "Table Talk" in the *Daily News* has got into a discussion with some of those wild theorists who think that everything can be explained by "race." They are amazing people. There is nobody to beat them at the great scientific art of first laying down a rule too absurd for anyone to believe and then softening it with exceptions too bewildering for anyone to follow. I remember one man who was a champion of this school. He was an Australian; I forget his name, but I remember his theory; which was that Europe was divided into dark-haired people and fair-haired people, and that all the good had come from the fair-haired people and all the bad from the dark-haired people. Also all the fair-haired people lived in the north of Europe and loved light, liberty, justice, and civilisation; while, on the other hand, all the dark-haired people lived in the south of Europe, and were very fond of darkness, misery, oppression, superstition, and failure. No doubt the doctrine would considerably simplify our social and political relations if it could only be established; but in this latter formality there were hitches, as even the ardent theorist himself began to perceive. For instance, he was a democrat and admired the French Revolution; but certainly that effort had been largely made by dark-haired men, often by very dark-haired men, like the southern French contingent who (as Mr. Belloc writes) "came north and destroyed the monarchy." This brought the theorist to a pause, but it did not baffle him. After a few minutes' reflection, he cried, with great cunning, "Ah, that was a fair-haired spirit working in the dark-haired people." It was then mildly pointed out to him that not only had the dark-haired people fought for the Revolution, but the fair-haired people had fought against it; the Germans and the Scandinavians had rallied to royalty and aristocracy. "And there you are again!" retorted the logician triumphantly. "You see, that was the temporary manifestation in a fair-haired people of a dark-hair philosophy." I have often wished I were that man. He must have found the making and defending of theories very easy and jolly work.

My Australian friend has vanished from my existence for ever, but he seems to have left a very good substitute and representative in Mr. Joseph Banister, of Hampstead, the gentleman who has raised the racial question in the *Daily News*. Mr. Banister briefly and lucidly explains that Socialism is only the uprising of the base and slavish pre-Aryan tribes, who live in low places like Edinburgh and Dublin, against the brave and beautiful Aryan people who live in high places—like Hampstead. The people at present in possession of most of the property, the Rothschilds, the Ecksteins, and the rest, owe their purity and chivalry chiefly to the fact of their Aryan origin (so, at least, I understand Mr. Banister's argument), while, on the other hand, if a man is very poor, you may comfort him by telling him that he is also pre-Aryan. The following startling description of a Labour Member will possess interest, not to say entertainment, for those who happen to know any Labour Members—

The leaders of the various socialistic, pro-foreign, and anti-national movements in England are generally of Scotch, Welsh, or Irish origin; they usually possess the low stature, low foreheads, black hair, high cheek-bones, thick lips, dark complexions, and beady eyes of the pre-Keltic races; and their speeches and writings are characterised by the shallowness, frothiness, ignorance, conceit, boastfulness, abusiveness, untruthfulness, exaggerations and unfairness which distinguish the utterances of the people of non-Aryan origin.

Now, if anyone were mildly to point out to Mr. Banister that this exuberant description does not quite fit the facts, I am sure he would betake himself at once to the simple but ingenious logic of my friend who found the fair-haired notions in the dark-haired heads. If you ventured to remark, for instance, that Mr. Shackleton is scarcely "of low stature," he would say that this was the Aryan vastness swelling out a non-Aryan (Mr. Shackleton) to its own enormous outline. If you were to remark that Mr. Ramsay Macdonald, so far from having a low forehead and all the other apish attributes, is a quite unusually handsome man, Mr. Banister would cry out, "Ah, yes; that is the not uncommon case of Aryan good looks grafted, as it were, upon an essentially ugly pre-Aryan person." If you suggested that Mr. Henderson is quite the reverse of dark, Mr. Banister would say that he is a pre-Aryan accidentally bleached like an Albino. If you were to urge further that he is quite the reverse of short, it would be answered that he is a pre-Aryan pulled out, like a telescope. If you said that you had examined Mr. Keir Hardie in vain, looking for his beady eyes; that you had made a disappointing journey to Mr. Snowden's house, on purpose to see his thick lips; and that you had stared quite hard at Mr. Will Crooks without being able to detect anything alarmingly pre-Aryan about his cheek-bones—if you urged all this, the answer would be the same wild and smiling absurdity—*exceptis excipiendis*:[1] if the facts do not fit into the theory, then the facts are exceptions, and there is an end of them. The exceptions prove the rule, and prove it all the more if the world contains nothing but exceptions to it, and hardly any examples at all.

If Mr. Banister be supposed to refer to other groups, if by his "anti-national" party he means the Nationalist Party (it sounds like his paradox), we should again have to go patiently and

---

[1] This may be translated as, "excepting the exceptions".

ploddingly to work, pointing out to him that the facts did not fit anywhere: that Daniel O'Connell was not short; that Mr. T. P. O'Connor is not dark; that Mr. Stephen Gwynne's eyes are not in the least beady, nor Mr. Dillon's lips thick—and so on, until Mr. Banister had transferred his crazy theory to some other mixed and ordinary group of men. Never once would it flash across the Aryan mind on the heights of Hampstead that all such race theories are rubbish; that political, religious, and commercial groups of men come together because they agree about politics, religion, or commerce; and that there is no group which does not contain, within the range of local possibility, all shapes of skull and all shades of complexion. There is no negro on the front Conservative bench; and there is none in the Irish Party. There is no Eskimo in Mr. Asquith's Government; nor is there in the Socialist Party of Great Britain. But within limits geographically probable there is every sort of person on both sides and in all sections.

The objection to this appeal to prehistoric "race" is much sharper and more final even than the objection that its facts are mostly fancies and its deductions fallacies. The objection to the race theory is that it is not wanted. It is explaining something that explains itself. It is, indeed, ludicrous to suppose that, in the chaos of falling Rome, men carefully sorted themselves out according to the shapes of their skulls: they had precious little interest in skulls except to smash them. But the point is that we know more or less how they did sort themselves out, and why. Any man who is a Christian knows why the Christian Celts fought with the heathen Teutons; also why the Christian Teutons fought with the heathen Teutons afterwards. We do not need to know about the skulls; we know about the brains. That general resistance to the barbarians, which extends from the half-historic Arthur to the wholly historic Alfred, obviously was not a racial war; for the two kings were of different races. But we not only know what it wasn't, we know what it was. It was a religious war, and the religion it saved survives still. Just so it is idle to say that men become Socialists because they are short and dark

and thick-lipped. I *know* why men become Socialists, for I have
been one myself.

May 21, 1910

Jokes and Good Sense

I introduce myself on this page every week with all the feelings
of the stage villain when he exclaims, "At last I am alone." I
can soliloquise as if in a desert; not even the superhuman patience
of the Comic Man in the overhearing of soliloquies could hold
out against my soliloquies. No one will expect to find me flat-
tened between the first two pages of an illustrated magazine.
Everybody reads a magazine; but nobody I ever heard of reads
the first page of a magazine. A magazine is a thing one opens
anywhere but at the beginning. So I am safe—safer than in the
darkest forest or the most desolate mountain-peak. I am alone.
Here I give my short and scornful laugh. Profiting by this luxury
of a monologue without an audience, I propose to be indecently
egotistical and utter a soul-rendering personal complaint. If I am
not entirely a villain, neither am I solely or unmixedly a comic
man. I have occasionally in my life made jokes, and I have also
occasionally been serious. And this, I had always understood,
was the not unusual practice of my fellow-creatures. But I have
discovered that this explanation is not considered sufficient in
my case; I am always supposed to be engaged with some tortuous
or topsy-turvy intention. When I state the dull truth about anything, it is said to be a showy paradox; when I lighten or brighten
it with any common jest, it is supposed to be my solid and
absurd opinion. If I ask a rational question of an opponent, it is
considered a wild frivolity. But if I make an ordinary idle pun,
it is gravely explained to me that my analogy is rather a verbal

parallelism than a philosophic example of the operations of a common law. Thus I was in controversy lately with some writers on a certain journal who maintain that such a doctrine as that of miracles (let us say) is not a truth, but the symbol of a truth. I merely asked them, "What is the truth of which it is a symbol?" You would think that was a courteous, relevant, and reasonable question. The answer of the journal was to cast up its eyes and clasp its hands, and ask distractedly how it could be expected to argue with such a wild, elusive, ever-changing, fantastical, and irresponsible jester as myself. On the other hand, I casually summed up the distinction between the supernatural and the unreasonable by the phrase that one might believe that a Beanstalk grew up to the sky without having any doubts about how many beans make five. For this a writer, intelligible and presumably human, actually rebuked me, gravely asking me whether I believed in the Beanstalk! When I make common jokes they are regarded as highly uncommon opinions. When I state solid opinions, they are regarded as giddy jokes. But no matter. A time will come.

Two quite amusing cases of it occurred only the other day. It happened that I had to make an after-dinner speech in response to some remarks which had turned on the topic of water, in what connection I cannot recall; perhaps it was geography and water-sheds, or perhaps it was municipal politics and water-works; or perhaps pathology and water on the brain; or perhaps temperance reformers who (according to some) have water on the brain after another fashion. Anyhow, I had to say something; so I explained that, in my opinion, water was a medicine. It should be taken in small quantities in very extreme cases; as when one is going to faint. I denounced the harshness and inhumanity of those who would forbid the use of water altogether; I would not even go so far as to say that water should only be procurable by a doctor's prescription at a chemist's. Sudden domestic crises might arise, extraordinary circumstances under which the sternest moralist must excuse water-drinking. But on habitual water-drinking I frowned with unmistakable sternness, pointing out how many fine young men had begun by persuading themselves that they must do as other fellows did; and who are now incurable teetotalers themselves.

Now in all this nonsense there is just this grain of fact, that it is very wise to drink water when you feel faint, and often not so wise to drink wine or spirits. That is truth enough to form the basis of a mock theory. But afterwards an earnest idealist actually came and argued with me about it; gravely pointing out that water does not contain a quality which it seems is called "alcohol"; pointedly urging that water, if filtered, distilled, and analysed every hour or so in a strictly scientific style, would generally be found to be free from deadly poison. This wonderful man really thought, in his wonderful mind, that I had meant every word I said.

Now for the other side of my sad case. Not only did this man think me serious when I was joking, but he also thought me joking when I was serious. In attempting to explain away and soften a little the severity of my war upon water, I fell into talk with him about the temperance problem generally. And I said (as I always do whenever I get the chance) that the objection to most temperance legislation is simply that it is religious persecution. That is to say, it is the imposition upon a whole people, by force, of a morality that is not the morality of that whole people; that is not the morality of half the people; that is simply a special morality sincerely held by a group of governing, active, and influential persons. It is not self-evident that beer is bad; it is not the general opinion of mankind that beer is bad: it is one honest and logical opinion held by one public-spirited and powerful group. To enforce such an opinion by the police is persecution. I also said: "The one vile piece of oppression and injustice that makes my blood boil more than all the other tyrants and torturers of the earth is the recent practice of taking away the old Christmas beer from the old people in workhouses." Now, in saying this, I am not only serious, but savage: I feel inclined to burn something, or shoot somebody, rather than that such inhuman humbug should endure. Nothing proves more sharply that our modern humanitarianism is a rut of words, a routine of associations, than the fact that, while we profess to be furious at the cruelties done to childhood, we are not even faintly stirred by the cruelties done to old age. Once picture an old man as plainly as you picture a child, and you will see at once that a poker-blow on the head is often less to a child than the sudden removal of a custom and a comfort from an old man. Brutality to children is hellish, and one cannot get lower than hell; but, if there are any dark shades in infamy, we might at least say that the young are young, that they often forget wrongs; that they generally survive them; that if they do, they inherit our splendid mortal life. But that those who are close to that unthinkable tragedy which is before us all, whose powers and pleasures are narrowing of their own nature, who cling to custom as to the cord of sanity, that these poor old people should have their few days blasted and revolutionised whenever a professor gets a bee in his bonnet—this seems to me the last dregs of impudence and impiety. I am serious about this, if being murderous is being serious. Well, when my idealistic friend heard me say this about beer in workhouses, he burst into a perfect yell of hilarity and delight; cachinnation caught him again and again, and between his happy shrieks he managed to say, "Oh, that's very good . . . you always are so paradoxical . . . how these funny ideas come into your head I don't know . . . oh, that's very good indeed!" And the earnest idealist went away shaking with laughter, and left the paradoxical jester shaking with rage.

But a time will come. In fact, between ourselves (if such bosh goes on much longer), I really think it will.

May 28, 1910

The Death of Edward VII

Death has struck the ancient English Monarchy at the very moment when that Monarchy was about to re-enter history. For the first time, certainly for a hundred years—probably for three hundred—the personality of the King of England profoundly mattered to English politics; at that moment the personality has been changed. In our whole present public crisis the appeal was to the Monarchy: the Monarchy was actually reviving while the Monarch was dying. To any patriotic man this fact must be even more impressive than the disappearance of a great and popular personality. We may be of those who, like Lord Rosebery[1] and others, feel the present crisis quickening towards political chaos; who feel the ship of State to be flying faster and faster down a flood; and who hear from far in front the faint but ceaseless thunder of the rapids of revolution. We may be of that other and much sadder school (with whose sincerity I, for one, have sometimes been bitterly haunted) which thinks that England is drifting, not on to the breakers, but into a backwater: that we have before us not seething democracy, but stagnant oligarchy; that the English ship of State is not heading for the storms of the French or the Irish Channel, but only for the dead aquarium and open tanks of Venice. But, whatever be the order of our hope or fear, we can all feel that England is in a crisis, and that England is taking a turn. We all know that the King mattered mightily to the turn that it took; and we all know that the King is dead. These are the things that make men feel that fierce coincidence which is almost superstition.

Superstition, indeed, might have much to say touching this national tragedy, if people took superstition quite seriously. But

---

[1] Archibald Philip Primrose Rosebery (1847–1929), an English statesman and author whose adherence to Gladstonian liberalism led him to speak in defense of imperial ideas and reformation of the House of Lords.

it is the whole mistake to suppose that people do take it seriously. Superstitions are a sort of sombre fairy-tales that we tell to ourselves in order to express, by random and realistic images, the mystery of the strange laws of life. We know so little when a man will die that it may well be sitting thirteenth at a table that kills him. Superstitions really are what the Modernists say that dogmas are: mere symbols of a much deeper matter, of a fundamental and fantastic agnosticism about the causes of things. Thus, in our present public bereavement, anyone seriously anxious to prove that "the heavens themselves blaze forth the deaths of Princes" could say with unanswerable truth that we were lit this year by the same monstrous meteor[2] that is said to have hung over the fall of Caesar and the last fight of Harold. Thus, again, those attached to mediaeval popular fancies may point out that this year Good Friday fell on Lady Day,[3] as it did when the Black Plague was eating the nation; or in that darker war with Joan of Arc, in which our England was disgraced both in defeat and victory. But there are very few of such seriously superstitious persons. Healthy humanity uses such signs and omens as a decoration of the tragedy after it has happened. Caesar was right to disregard Halley's Comet; it had no importance until Caesar had been killed. Rationalists, who merely deride such traditions, fail by not feeling the full mass of inarticulate human emotion behind them. On the very night that King Edward died, it happened that the present writer experienced some of those trivialities that can bring about one's head all the terrors of the universe. The shocking news was just loose in London, but it had not touched the country where I was, when a London editor attempted to tell me the truth by telephone. But all the telephones in England were throbbing and thundering

[2] Halley's Comet, which appeared in 1066, the year of the Conquest, when Harold was defeated at Hastings; it also appeared in 1910, the year of Edward VII's death. However, the dating is wrong for its appearance in the year of Caesar's fall, 44 B.C. since it is recorded in 87 B.C. and 12 B.C.

[3] March 25, the day that commemorates the Annuciation of the Virgin Mary.

with the news; it was impossible to clear the line; and it was impossible to hear the message. Again and again I heard stifled accents saying something momentous and unintelligible; it might have been the landing of the Germans or the end of the world. With the snatches of this strangled voice in my ears I went into the garden, and found, by another such mystical coincidence, that it was a night of startling and blazing stars—stars so fierce and close that they seemed crowding round the roof and tree-tops. White-hot and speechless, they seemed striving to speak, like that voice that had been drowned amid the drumming wires. I know not if any reader has ever had a vigil with the same unreasoning sense of a frustrated apocalypse. But if he has, he will know one of the immortal moods out of which legends rise, and he will not wonder that men have joined the notion of a comet with the death of a King.

But besides this historic stroke, this fall of a national monument, there is also the loss of a personality. Over and above this dark and half-superstitious suggestion that the fate of our country has turned a corner and entered a new epoch, there is the pathetic value of the human epoch that has just closed. The starting-point for all study of King Edward is the fact of his unquestionable and positive popularity. I say positive, because most modern popularity is negative; it is no more than toleration. Many an English landlord is described as popular among his tenants, when the phrase only means that no tenant hates him quite enough to be hanged for putting a bullet in him. Or, again, in milder cases, a man will be called a popular administrator because his rule, being substantially successful, is substantially undisturbed; some system works fairly well and the head of the system is not hated, for he is hardly felt. Quite different was the practical popularity of Edward VII. It was a strictly personal image and enthusiasm. The French, with their talent for picking the right word, put it best when they described King Edward as a kind of universal uncle. His popularity in poor families was so frank as to be undignified; he was really spoken of by tinkers and tailors as if he were some gay and prosperous member of their own family.

There was a picture of him upon the popular retina infinitely brighter and brisker than there is either of Mr. Asquith or Mr. Balfour. There was something in him that appealed to those strange and silent crowds that are invisible because they are enormous. In connection with him the few voices that really sound popular sound also singularly loyal. Since his death was declared there have already been many written and spoken eulogies; one that sounded indubitably sincere was that uttered by Mr. Will Crooks.

If you dig deep enough into any ancient ceremony, you will find the traces of that noble truism called democracy, which is not the latest but the earliest of human ideas. Just as in the very oldest part of an English church you will unearth the level bricks of the Romans, so in the very oldest part of every royal or feudal form you will unearth the level laws of the Republic. In that complex and loaded rite of Coronation which King Edward underwent, and his successor must soon undergo, there is a distinct trace of the ancient idea of a King being elected like a President. The Archbishop shows the King to the assembled people, and asks if he is accepted or refused. Edward VII., like other modern Kings, went through a ritual election by an unreal mob. But if it had been a real election by a real mob—he would still have been elected. That is the really important point for democrats.

The largeness of the praise of King Edward in the popular legend was fundamentally due to this, that he was a leader in whom other men could see themselves. The Tory squires that follow Mr. Balfour are not at all like Mr. Balfour; the Radicals who shout behind Mr. Asquith are not at all like Mr. Asquith. It is in their pleasures, perhaps, more than anything else, that such men are divided. Squires as a class do not care about metaphysics, which is Mr. Balfour's hobby. Genuine Radicals as a class do not care about legality, which is Mr. Asquith's hobby. But the King's interest in sport, good living, and Continental travel was exactly of the kind that every clerk or commercial traveller could feel in himself on a smaller scale and in a more thwarted manner. Now, it emphatically will not do to dismiss this popular sympathy in pleasure as the mere servile or vulgar adoration of a race of snobs. To begin with, mere worldly rank could not and did not achieve such popularity for Ernest Duke of Cumberland or Alfred Duke of Edinburgh or even for the Prince Consort; and to go on with mere angry words like snobbishness is an evasion of the democratic test. I fancy the key of the question is this: that, in an age of prigs and dehumanised humanitarians, King Edward stood to the whole people as the emblem of this ultimate idea—that however extraordinary a man may be by office, influence, or talent, we have a right to ask that the extraordinary man should be also an ordinary man. He was more representative than representative government: he was the whole theme of Walt Whitman—the average man enthroned.

His reputation for a humane normality had one aspect in which he was a model to philanthropists. Innumerable tales were told of his kindness or courtesy, ranging from the endowment of a children's hospital to the offer of a cigar, from the fact that he pensioned a match-seller to the mere fact that he took off his hat. But all these tales took the popular fancy all the more because he himself was the kind of man to share the pleasures he distributed. His offer of a cigar was the more appreciated because he offered himself a cigar as well. His taking off his hat was the more valued because he himself was by no means indifferent to decent salutations or discourteous slights. Philanthropists too frequently forget that pity is quite a different thing from sympathy; for sympathy means suffering with others, and not merely being sorry that they suffer. If the strong brotherhood of men is to abide, if they are not to break up into groups alarmingly like different species, we must keep this community of tastes in giver and receiver. We must not only share our bread, but share our hunger.

King Edward was a man of the world and a diplomatist; but there was nothing of the aristocrat about him. He had a just sense of the dignity of his position; but it was very much such a sense as a middle-class elective magistrate might have had, a

Lord Mayor or the President of a Republic. It was even in a sense formal, and the essence of aristocracy is informality. It is no violation of the political impartiality of the Crown to say that he was, in training and tone of mind, liberal. The one or two points on which he permitted himself a partisan attitude were things that he regarded as commonsense emancipations from mere custom, such as the Deceased Wife's Sister Bill. Both in strength and weakness he was international; and it is undoubtedly largely due to him that we have generally dropped the fashion of systematically and doggedly misunderstanding the great civilisation of France. But the first and last thought is the same: that there are millions in England who have hardly heard of the Prime Minister, and never heard of Lord Lansdowne, to whom King Edward was a picture of paternal patriotism; and in the dark days that lie before us it is, perhaps, just those millions who may begin to move.

June 4, 1910

The Character of King Edward

The calamity of the King's removal was unofficially acknowledged almost before it was officially acknowledged. The people were prompter in mourning than the officers of State in bidding them mourn; and even one who doubted whether the King deserved his popularity would be forced to admit that he had it. The national mourning—taken as a whole, of course—is all the more universal for being irregular, all the more unanimous for being scrappy or even intermittent. Armies of retainers clad in complete black, endless processions of solemn robes and sable plumes, could not be a quarter so impressive as the cheap black band of a man in corduroys, or the cheap black hat of a girl in pink and magenta. The part is greater than the whole. Nevertheless, the formal side of funeral customs, as is right and natural, is already engaging attention. Sir William Richmond, always prominent in any question of the relation of art to public life, has already sketched out a scheme of mortuary decoration so conceived as to avoid the inhuman monotony of black. He would have a sombre, but still rich, scheme of colour, of Tyrian purple, dim bronze and gold. Both artistically and symbolically, there is much that is sound in the conception. Mere black might seem a more fitting dress for devils than for Christian mourners, except that the mourning dress of devils would (I suppose) be blue. There is something almost atheistic about such starless and hueless grief; it seems not akin to distress, but to despair. Indeed, Sir William Richmond, consciously or unconsciously, is in this matter following an ecclesiastical tradition. The world mourns in black, but the Church mourns in violet—one of the many instances of the fact that the Church is a much more cheerful thing than the world. Nor is the difference an idle accident: it really corresponds to chasms of spiritual separation. Black is dark with absence of colour; violet is dark with density and combination of colour: it is at once as blue as midnight and as crimson as blood. And there is a similar distinction between the two views of death, between the two types of tragedy. There is the tragedy that is founded on the worthlessness of life; and there is the deeper tragedy that is founded on the worth of it. The one sort of sadness says that life is so short that it can hardly matter; the other that life is so short that it will matter for ever.

But though in this, as in many other matters, it is religion alone that retains any tradition of a freer and more humane popular taste, it may well be doubted whether in the present instance the existing popular taste should not be substantially gratified, or, at least, undisturbed. King Edward was not the kind of man in whose honour we should do even beautiful things that are in any sense eccentric. His sympathies in all such matters were very general sympathies: he stood to millions of people as the very incarnation of common-sense, social adaptability, tact, and a rational conventionality. His people delighted in the million snapshots of him in shooting-dress at a shooting-box, or in racing-clothes at a race-meeting, in morning-dress in the morning or in evening-dress in the evening, because all these were symbols of a certain sensible sociability and readiness for everything with which they loved to credit him. For it must always be remembered in this connection that masculine costume is different at root from feminine costume—different in its whole essence and aim. It is not merely a question of the man dressing in dull colours or the woman in bright: it is a question of the object. A Life Guardsman has very splendid clothes; an artistic lady in Bedford Park may have very dingy clothes. But the point is that the Life Guard only puts on his bright clothes so as to be like other Life Guards. But the Bedford Park lady always seeks to have some special, delicate, and exquisite shade of dinginess different from the dinginess of other Bedford Park ladies. Though gleaming with scarlet and steel, the Life Guard is really invisible. Though physically, no doubt, of terrific courage, he is morally cowardly, like nearly all males. Like the insects that are as green as the leaves or the jackals that are as red as the desert, a man generally seeks to be unseen by taking the colour of his surroundings, even if it be a brilliant colour. A female dress is a dress; a male dress is a uniform. Men dress smartly so as not to be noticed; but all women dress to be noticed—gross and vulgar women to be grossly and vulgarly noticed, wise and modest women to be wisely and modestly noticed.

Now, of this soul in masculine "good form," this slight but genuine element of a manly modesty in conventions, the public made King Edward a typical and appropriate representative. They liked to think of him appearing as a soldier among soldiers, a sailor among sailors, a Freemason at his Lodge, or a Peer among his Peers. For this reason they even tolerated the comic idea of his being a Prussian Colonel when he was in Prussia; and they took a positive pleasure in the idea of his being a Parisian boulevardier when he was in Paris. Since he was thus a public symbol of the more generous and fraternal uses of conventionality, we may be well content with a conventional scheme of mourning; especially when in this case, as in not a few other cases, the conventional merely means the democratic. King Edward's popularity was such a very popular kind of popularity that it would be rather more appropriate to make his funeral vulgar than to make it aesthetic. It is true that legend connects his name with two or three attempts to modify the ungainliness and gloom of our modern male costume; but he hardly insisted on any of them, and none of them was of a kind specially to satisfy Sir William Richmond. The aesthetes might perhaps smile on the notion of knee-breeches: but I fear that brass buttons on evening coats would seem to them an aggravation of their wrong. Even where King Edward was an innovator, he was an innovator along popular and well-recognised lines; a man who would have liked a funeral to be funereal, as he would have liked a ball to be gay. We need not, therefore, feel it so very inappropriate even if in the last resort the celebrations are in the most humdrum or even jog-trot style, if they satisfy the heart of the public, though not the eye of the artist.

And yet again, in connection with those aspects of the late King which may be and are approved on more serious and states-manlike grounds (as, for instance, his international attitude towards peace), this value of a working convention can still be found. It is easy to say airily, in an ethical text-book or a debating-club resolution, that Spaniards should love Chinamen, or that Highlanders should suddenly embrace Hindus. But, as men are in daily life, such brotherhood is corrupted and confused, though never actually contradicted. It is the fundamental fact that we are all men; but there are circumstances that permit us to feel it keenly, and other circumstances that almost prevent us from feeling it at all. It is here that convention (which only means a coming together) makes smooth the path of primal sympathy; and by getting people, if only for an hour, to act alike, begins to make them feel alike. I have said much against aristocracy in this column, and shall continue to do so till I am sacked; but I will never deny that aristocracy has certain queer advantages, not very often mentioned. One of them is that which affects European diplomacy: that a gentleman is the same all over Europe, while a peasant, or even a merchant, may be very different. A Dutch gentleman and an Irish gentleman stand on a special and level platform; a Dutch peasant and an Irish peasant are divided by all dynastic and divine wars. Of course, this means that a peasant is superior to a gentleman—more genuine, more historic, more national: but that, surely, is obvious. Nevertheless, for cosmopolitan purposes, such as diplomacy, a gentleman may be used—with caution. And the reason that has made aristocrats effective as diplomatists is the same that made King Edward effective: the existence of a convention or convenient form that is understood everywhere and makes action and utterance easy for everyone. Language itself is only an enormous ceremony. King Edward completely understood that nameless Volapuk or Esperanto on which modern Europe practically reposes. He never put himself in a position that Europe could possibly misunderstand, as the Kaiser did by his theocratic outbursts, even if they were logical; or the Tsar by his sweeping repressions, even if they were provoked. Partly a German, by blood, partly a Frenchman, by preference, intermarried with all the thrones of Europe and quite conscious of their very various perplexities, he had the right to be called a great citizen of Europe. There are only two things that can bind men together; a convention and a creed. King Edward was the last, the most popular, and probably the most triumphant example of Europe combining with success upon a large and genial convention. Tact and habit and humanity had in him their final exponent in all the Courts, reviews, racecourses, and hotels of Christendom. If these are not enough, if it is not found sufficient for Europe to have a healthy convention, then Europe must once more have a creed. The coming of the creed will be a terrible business.

June 11, 1910

The Collapse of the Victorian Compromise

The hot weather, which has been almost coincident with the new reign, might serve, perhaps, as another omen, if I were one who liked omens—or liked hot weather. Unfortunately, I am one of those heretics who tend (during a strong summer) to the somewhat hasty opinion of certain early Christians, that Apollo is a devil. Or if he be a beneficent deity, he is one of a highly searching and even ruthless sort; a flaming fact, picking out and emphasising all other facts; making the world far too realistic. The chief gift of hot weather to me is the somewhat unpopular benefit called a conviction of sin. All the rest of the year I am untidy, lazy, awkward, and futile. But in hot weather I *feel* untidy, lazy, awkward, and futile. Sitting in a garden-chair in a fresh breeze under a brisk grey and silver sky, I feel a frightfully strenuous fellow: sitting on the same garden-chair in strong sunshine, it begins slowly to dawn on me that I am doing nothing. In neither case, of course, do I get out of the chair. But I resent that noontide glare of photographic detail by the ruthless light of which I can quite clearly see myself sitting in the chair. I prefer a more grey and gracious haze, something more in the Celtic-twilight style, through which I can only faintly trace my own contours, vast but vague in the dusk and distance.

And in this way, oddly enough, I think the turn of the year's weather may be found a sort of omen, after all; for the change from the England that is behind us to that more equivocal and mysterious England that is in front of us is not unlike the change from the cool laziness with which I am contented to the hot laziness of which I am ashamed. It is the whole difference between being asleep, and waking up to feel sleepy. The sun of truth is risen; the facts of the world are staring at us with a somewhat sinister clearness; but the Englishman, I fear, has not yet got out of his garden-chair. For that epoch which may vaguely be called Victorian—though it began before Queen Victoria's accession and continued after her death—was very like the subtle relaxation of a suitable and comfortable climate. It was the time of a curious sort of protected freedom, in which the Englishman managed to feel universal without really looking at anything that he greatly disliked. It was the time, for example, when the novel changed from the liberties of Fielding and Sterne to the limits of Thackeray and George Eliot; and yet both Thackeray and George Eliot are obviously priding themselves on a liberal and unlimited view of life. Fiction gave up its universal scope to achieve a universal appeal. French novels were written for adults, and confined to adults. English novels were thrown open to schoolgirls—and cut down for them. In Paris the baby was forbidden to read the man's literature; in London the man was often compelled to read the baby's. Both conditions can be described as liberty.

But without turning the accident of a new reign into too stiff a symbol, there are many indications that the Victorian compromise has broken down. To touch but lightly on the case mentioned above, the ethics of fiction, it is pretty plain that new licence is being claimed, and that of the least healthy sort. A school of novelists, chiefly female, pour on the market tales in which there is not one indecent word and not one decent sentiment. Now these sophists have all the advantage that belongs to those who break an understanding while their opponents keep it. It is poisonous to a people that they should hear half-truths if they must not hear the whole truth. The whole truth is generally the ally of virtue; a half-truth is always the ally of some vice. I personally should prefer that decent people should reply with the whole truth; I would rather refute these writers than repress them. But it is highly probable that we shall do either one or the other; and in either case we violate the balance of the Victorian tradition. If we repress them, we violate Victorian liberty. If we refute them, we violate Victorian decorum.

But this collapse of the compromise affects numberless other things besides novels—for instance, newspapers. In the Victorian atmosphere a newspaper was a vague, popular voice tempered to a respectful tone. The rich men who owned the journals were moderate because they were rich, but they were positive because they were men; they shared the passions and prejudices of the mass of their readers. For instance, the English Press was incredibly childish in its misunderstanding about foreign politics; it tried to measure everything with a London umbrella, to cover everything under a London top-hat. It tried to talk about the French Revolution without having even understood that it was a Revolution, let alone a French one. They lectured the Roman Church without attempting to understand either the Christian word "Church" or the pagan word "Roman." But though in these matters the Victorian papers were wrong, they were still representative. They did not understand foreign nations, but they did understand their own nation. Ideas about Ireland quite as idiotic as those of the leader-writer on the *Times* possessed the minds of all the compositors who printed the paper. Russia was quite as wildly misunderstood in public-houses even as she was in Parliament; and about the real dogmas of the French Republic the servants in the servants' hall were really almost as ignorant as their masters and mistresses upstairs. These blunders were national blunders; the newspapers only had them because everybody made them. They were only enormous mirrors or reflectors which flashed over the world the local flame or beacon of England; but the flame was local and quite genuine. Therefore under that Victorian compromise the big wealthy newspapers might very well be left as they were. They were rich enough to be a tyranny; but, thank God, they were stupid enough to be a mere mob. They did not misrepresent England, though they misrepresented everything else to the last flaming fringe of the solar system.

But just as we have lived to see the rise of a cold and lewd sort of novel, so we have lived to see the rise of a cold and lawless and quite cynical kind of journalism. It does not share the national prejudices, but only exploits them. Nay, more, it does not accept prejudices; it actually manufactures them. In short, the Press has ceased to be roughly representative, and become almost solely oppressive. The newspaper proprietors now possess England almost entirely because they are typical rich men, and not because they are typical men who happen to be rich. Of course, I know it is not easy to distinguish to a shade between representation and oppression; that is why all oppressors have managed to succeed. If the chief and the clan agree, it is not always simple to decide whether the chief is agreeing with the clan or the clan agreeing with the chief. I only think that in modern England the clan is nowhere.

This puts the newspaper in the same equally poised and perilous position as the novel; it may be attacked from either side. If we have a democratic outburst, the newspaper office may be wrecked by the mob. If we have a despotic reaction the newspaper office may be shut up by the police. But in no case will it have so cosy and respectable a time as it has had during the age of newspapers, the great Victorian epoch. And this, indeed, raises the strongest case of all—the political case; though with this it would scarcely be discreet to deal fully just now. It will suffice to say that nearly everyone is now discussing the political future with a disproportion amounting to folly, for this simple reason: that they will talk of the Socialist Party in the modern House of Commons as if it were the revolutionary party. In the vivid and virile sense, no parties are revolutionary; the Labour Party is no more likely to take to pikes than the Primrose League. In every other sense, all the parties are revolutionary. Imperialism is as wild a revolt against Balfour as is Socialism against Asquith; they have all broken up the Victorian compromise.

June 18, 1910

The Coming Triumph of Socialism

I recently protested in this place against that trick of amateur science which consists in learnedly explaining something which explains itself; it was in connection with some weird reason for the rise of Socialism. I am not a Socialist; but I know the reason for the rise of Socialism well enough. It arises from the recondite circumstance that an extraordinary number of people have not got enough to eat; and that a perfectly plausible scheme has been propounded for remedying this revolting state of affairs. But there is another element also which is tending just now to the triumph of Socialism; and non-Socialists ought to realise it clearly before it is too late. The fact is this—that the State or the Municipality are now so constantly left as the only champions of the very things that Socialism is said to threaten—local liberties, old associations, and personal rights.

An excellent instance is the fantastic fight in Kensington, round Edwardes Square and Earl's Court Terrace. I do not mean that I think this battle, picturesque as it is, will convulse the country with civil war. If ever there is a revolution in London the mob will scarcely be content with unscrewing a bolt or bar, or with taking a company-promoter's gate to pieces. The mob is more likely to take the company-promoter to pieces; or, at least, to invent some guillotine-like tool for unscrewing his head. In the glad old days when there were riots in London, a cry of 'prentices would resound "Clubs! Clubs!" I do not think they would have been content with the inspiring shout, "Screw-drivers! Screw-drivers!" The quite sensible and spirited people in Edwardes Square are not raising an extra-legal riot: they are testing the state of the law; therefore, very properly, they keep within the law. Somewhat wilder scenes would ensue if London ever remembered the dagger blazoned on her shield: and it would need some heavy firing to set the Thames on fire.

But the real lesson of the romance of Edwardes Square is in the false position of our propertied class in this country. Certain literary traditions still lingering everywhere have falsified for most of us the whole notion of the English aristocracy. The noble novels of Scott were influenced by ancient Scottish gentility, and especially by the utterly different patriarchal kingdoms of the Highlands. The clever and crazy novels of Ouida described something utterly different from English ladies and gentlemen;

presumably Turkish Sultans and Sultanas. Many entertaining historical novels (such as the brisk French tales of the Baroness Orczy) go back to the French noblesse before the Terror, again a very different class; and even about the French nobles our novelists are generally wrong—making them old-world arrogant feudalists; whereas they were often very much up to date, and rather Republican. But out of all these false analogies put together the average reader has somehow realised a picture of the perfect nobleman, his blood as old as a Highlander's, his manners as formal as a French abbé's, and his whole life as loaded with ancient splendours and beautiful sleepy ritual as any Eastern King's. Hundreds of novels, hundreds of plays, hundreds of Royal Academy pictures have repeated the image of the proud, but ruined Peer, stately and sensitive, seeing the relics of ancestral beauty sold up by blatant tradesmen or invaded by vandal mobs. In the presence of this legend it needs a certain leap of sincerity to face the actual fact. The actual fact is that with us aristocracy is not only mercantile, but mercantile in a quite vulgar and ugly way. It is mercantile not even in the style of Tyre or Venice, but in the style of Glasgow and Birmingham. And the drab deformity, the inhuman hideousness, of these modern cities is not the creation of democracy; it is the creation of aristocracy. It is the work of those great plutocratic combinations through which most of the aristocracy arranges and employs its wealth. It is actually the nobs, and not the snobs, who vulgarise the landscape.

It is not the shabby bill-poster, pasting up the crude advertisements of some sauce or pill, who himself originates or desires the ugliness. He himself would just as soon paste up the Cartoons of Raphael. If he is not merely indifferent he might have a mild preference for pasting up the Declarations of a Revolution and Reign of Terror. Anyhow, he is an instrument: the person who wants the street defaced by an advertisement of the sauce is the person who owns the sauce, or the person who owns most shares in the sauce. The person who owns most shares in the sauce is very probably in the House of Peers. He is, perhaps, voting in that Chamber that the Embankment shall not be defaced by electric-cars (which are often comparatively beautiful) at the very moment when hundreds of his vassals are making half the walls of London hideous with shrieking proclamations of his wares. It is not the railway-porter who makes England ugly with railways or railway-stations—in so far as these things are ugly. The railway-porter would just as soon be steering a gondola. In fact, there is a dreamy look in the eye of the average railway-porter which leads me to think that his true place would be in that visionary city of the sea. If the hordes of average human beings work in ugly factories, serve in ugly shops, drive ugly vehicles, or use ugly tools, it is not they that have invented and distributed these ugly things: it is the people who have riches and refinement; it is the very people who have the noble horses and the splendid parks. The grocer's assistant sells ugly tins of gum or jam, or what not; but the man who originally sold them is possibly a lord and almost certainly a landlord. A hackney coach may be an ungainly structure, but the man who drives it very often has a coronet on his cab, and, if he were so commanded, would have a coronet on his head. In this sense it is quite true that our mercantile aristocracy has "made our England what she is"— and a very nasty sight it has made of it.

The Battle of Edwardes Square is a beautiful instance. Edwardes Square is an exquisite example of everything which (in books, pictures, and magazines) aristocrats are supposed to defend. It is a pool of old-fashioned peace and beauty, a little inland lake of that ancient and largely lost gentility which was at least artistic as well as artificial, which was at least gentle as well as merely gentlemanly. That stilted yet sincerely delicate atmosphere of old Kensington which Miss Thackeray[1] has caught in her novel as lightly as in a lyric, that almost eighteenth-century elegance which her great father loved to linger on, does really in some

---

[1] Anne Isabella Thackeray, later Lady Ritchie (1837–1919), daughter of the novelist William M. Thackeray and herself a talented editor, biographer and novelist. The work referred to here is the novel *Old Kensington* (1873).

faint manner possess the place. I have known more than one golden evening in that square when in my inmost soul I was not quite so certain that Queen Anne is dead.

Now it happened that this island of tradition actually belonged to a nobleman, a nobleman who bore the very title of the place—an excellent nobleman, I have no doubt: I know nothing whatever against him. But he by no means played the part that would have been his in any hearty and healthy novelette. Students of popular art and literature can conceive how splendidly the nobleman of romance would have stood stretching his ancestral sword over this sacred soil, guarding its ancient beauty from vulgarians and innovators. The nobleman of actual fact simply sold the place—not, as he might have done in Ireland, to the people who lived there; but, as is usually done in modern England, to a company, to a ring of remote financiers, not one of whom, perhaps, had ever seen the place. These financiers (having no taste in pools of old-world silence) propose to use the place to store motor-cars. The inhabitants, who like their square, object; and the only thing that stands up for them is the Borough Council.

Now, unless such things can be stopped, Socialism must almost certainly come. In a fight between public powers and private owners, our sympathy might be with the private owners. But this is not such a fight. This is a fight between the municipality and the company, two mere institutions, equally public, equally cold, equally anonymous, equally lacking in the least sentiment of private property. If small genuine properties are not renewed, the world will certainly become Socialist, preferring the corporation that is just as well as cold.

June 25, 1910

Modern Woman's Views on Divorce

I have just picked up a little book that is not only brightly and suggestively written, but is somewhat unique, in this sense—that it enunciates the modern and advanced view of Woman in such language as a sane person can stand. It is written by Miss Florence Farr, is called "Modern Woman; her Intentions," and is published by Mr. Frank Palmer. This style of book I confess to commonly finding foolish and vain. The New Woman's monologue wearies, not because it is unwomanly, but because it is inhuman. It exhibits the most exhausting of combinations: the union of fanaticism of speech with frigidity of soul—the things that made Robespierre seem a monster. The worst example I remember was one trumpeted in a Review: a lady doctor, who has ever afterwards haunted me as a sort of nightmare of spiritual imbecility. I forget her exact words, but they were to the effect that sex and motherhood should be treated neither with ribaldry nor reverence: "It is too serious a subject for ribaldry, and I myself cannot understand reverence towards anything that is physical." There, in a few words, is the whole twisted and tortured priggishness which poisons the present age. The person who cannot laugh at sex ought to be kicked; and the person who cannot reverence pain ought to be killed. Until that lady doctor gets a little ribaldry and a little reverence into her soul, she has no right to have any opinion at all about the affairs of humanity. I remember there was another lady, trumpeted in the same Review, a French lady who broke off her engagement with the excellent gentleman to whom she was attached on the ground that affection interrupted the flow of her thoughts. It was a thin sort of flow in any case, to judge by the samples; and no doubt it was easily interrupted.

The author of "Modern Woman" is bitten a little by the mad dog of modernity, the habit of dwelling disproportionally on the abnormal and the diseased; but she writes rationally and

humorously, like a human being; she sees that there are two
sides to the case; and she even puts in a fruitful suggestion that,
with its subconsciousness and its virtues of the vegetable, the
new psychology may turn up on the side of the old womanhood.
One may say indeed that in such a book as this our amateur
philosophising of to-day is seen at its fairest; and even at its
fairest it exhibits certain qualities of bewilderment and disproportion which are somewhat curious to note.

I think the oddest thing about the advanced people is that,
while they are always talking of things as problems, they have
hardly any notion of what a real problem is. A real problem
only occurs when there are admittedly disadvantages in all courses
that can be pursued. If it is discovered just before a fashionable
wedding that the Bishop is locked up in the coal-cellar, that is
not a problem. It is obvious to anyone but an extreme anti-
clerical or practical joker that the Bishop must be let out of the
coal-cellar. But suppose the Bishop has been locked up in the
wine-cellar, and from the obscure noises, sounds as of song and
dance, etc., it is guessed that he has indiscreetly tested the vin-
tages round him; then indeed we may properly say that there
has arisen a *problem*; for upon the one hand, it is awkward to
keep the wedding waiting, while, upon the other, any hasty
opening of the door might mean an episcopal rush and scenes
of the most unforeseen description.

An incident like this (which must constantly happen in our
gay and varied social life) is a true problem because there are in
it incompatible advantages. Now if woman is simply the domestic slave that many of these writers represent, if man has bound
her by brute force, if he has simply knocked her down and sat
on her—then there is no problem about the matter. She has been
locked in the kitchen, like the Bishop in the coal-cellar; and they
both of them ought to be let out. If there is any problem of sex,
it must be because the case is not so simple as that; because there
is something to be said for the man as well as for the woman;
and because there are evils in unlocking the kitchen door, in
addition to the obvious good of it. Now, I will take two instances

from Miss Farr's own book of problems that are really problems, and which she entirely misses because she will not admit that they are problematical.

The writer asks the substantial question squarely enough: "Is indissoluble marriage good for mankind?" and she answers it squarely enough: "For the great mass of mankind, yes." To those like myself, who move in the old-world dream of Democracy, that admission ends the whole question. There may be exceptional people who would be happier without Civil Government; sensitive souls who really feel unwell when they see a policeman. But we have surely the right to impose the State on everybody if it suits nearly everybody; and if so, we have the right to impose the Family on everybody if it suits nearly everybody. But the queer and cogent point is this: that Miss Farr does not see the real difficulty about allowing exceptions—the real difficulty that has made most legislators reluctant to allow them. I do not say there should be no exceptions, but I do say that the author has not seen the painful problem of permitting any.

The difficulty is simply this: that if it comes to claiming exceptional treatment, the very people who will claim it will be those who least deserve it. The people who are quite convinced they are superior are the very inferior people; the men who really think themselves extraordinary are the most ordinary rotters on earth. If you say, "Nobody must steal the Crown of England," then probably it will not be stolen. After that, probably the next best thing would be to say, "Anybody may steal the Crown of England," for then the Crown might find its way to some honest and modest fellow. But if you say, "Those who feel themselves to have Wild and Wondrous Souls, and they only, may steal the Crown of England," then you may be sure there will be a rush for it of all the rag, tag, and bobtail of the universe, all the quack doctors, all the sham artists, all the demireps and drunken egotists, all the nationless adventurers and criminal monomaniacs of the world.

So, if you say that marriage is for common people, but divorce for free and noble spirits, all the weak and selfish people will dash for the divorce; while the few free and noble spirits you wish to help will very probably (because they are free and noble) go on wrestling with the marriage. For it is one of the marks of real dignity of character not to wish to separate oneself from the honour and tragedy of the whole tribe. All men are ordinary men; the extraordinary men are those who know it.

There is another equally curious case of unconsciousness of the true crux and contradiction in this ethical difficulty; but if I deal with it, it must be on another occasion. I must make my articles fit into a page, as these sages must try to make their systems fit into a world.

July 2, 1910

The Bonds of Love

I pointed out last week that our makers of ultramodern moralities (and immoralities) do not really grasp how problematical a problem is. They are not specially the people who see the difficulties of modern life; rather, they are the people who do not see the difficulties. These innovators make life insanely simple; making freedom or knowledge a universal pill. I remarked it in connection with a clever book by Miss Florence Farr, and took as an instance the proposition (which she seemed to support) that marriage is good for the common herd, but can be advantageously violated by special "experimenters" and pioneers. Now, the weakness of this position is that it takes no account of the problem of the disease of pride. It is easy enough to say that weaker souls had better be guarded, but that we must give freedom to Georges Sand or make exceptions for George Eliot. The practical puzzle is this: that it is precisely the weakest sort of lady novelist who thinks she is Georges Sand; it is precisely the silliest woman who is sure she is George Eliot. It is the small soul that is sure it is an exception; the large soul is only too proud to be the rule. To advertise for exceptional people is to collect all the sulks and sick fancies and futile ambitions of the earth. The good artist is he who can be understood; it is the bad artist who is always "misunderstood." In short, the great man is a man; it is always the tenth-rate man who is the Superman.

But in Miss Farr's entertaining pages there was another instance of the same thing which I had no space to mention last week. The writer disposes of the difficult question of vows and bonds in love by leaving out altogether the one extraordinary fact of experience on which the whole matter turns. She again solves the problem by assuming that it is not a problem. Concerning oaths of fidelity, etc., she writes: "We cannot trust ourselves to make a real love-knot unless money or custom forces us to 'bear and forbear.' There is always the lurking fear that we shall not be able to keep faith unless we swear upon the Book. This is, of course, not true of young lovers. Every first love is born free of tradition; indeed, not only is first love innocent and valiant, but it sweeps aside all the wise laws it has been taught, and burns away experience in its own light. The revelation is so extraordinary, so unlike anything told by the poets, so absorbing, that it is impossible to believe that the feeling can die out."

Now this is exactly as if some old naturalist settled the bat's place in nature by saying boldly, "Bats do not fly." It is as if he solved the problem of whales by bluntly declaring that whales live on land. There is a problem of vows, as of bats and whales. What Miss Farr says about it is quite lucid and explanatory; it simply happens to be flatly untrue. It is not the fact that young lovers have no desire to swear on the Book. They are always at it. It is not the fact that every young love is born free of traditions about binding and promising, about bonds and signatures and seals. On the contrary, lovers wallow in the wildest pedantry and precision about these matters. They do the craziest things to make their love legal and irrevocable. They tattoo each other with promises; they cut into rocks and oaks with their names

and vows; they bury ridiculous things in ridiculous places to be
a witness against them; they bind each other with rings, and
inscribe each other in Bibles; if they are raving lunatics (which
is not untenable), they are mad solely on this idea of binding
and on nothing else. It is quite true that the tradition of their
fathers and mothers is in favour of fidelity; but it is emphatically
not true that the lovers merely follow it; they invent it anew. It
is quite true that the lovers feel their love eternal, and independent
of oaths; but it is emphatically not true that they do not desire
to take the oaths. They have a ravening thirst to take as many
oaths as possible. Now this is the paradox; this is the whole
problem. It is not true, as Miss Farr would have it, that young
people feel free of vows, being confident of constancy; while
old people invent vows, having lost that confidence. That would
be much too simple; if that were so there would be no problem
at all. The startling but quite solid fact is that young people are
especially fierce in making fetters and final ties at the very moment
when they think them unnecessary. The time when they want
the vow is exactly the time when they do not need it. That is
worth thinking about.

Nearly all the fundamental facts of mankind are to be found
in its fables. And there is a singularly sane truth in all the old
stories of the monsters—such as centaurs, mermaids, sphinxes,
and the rest. It will be noted that in each of these the humanity,
though imperfect in its extent, is perfect in its quality. The mermaid is half a lady and half a fish; but there is nothing fishy
about the lady. A centaur is half a gentleman and half a horse.
But there is nothing horsey about the gentleman. The centaur
is a manly sort of man—up to a certain point. The mermaid is
a womanly woman—so far as she goes. The human parts of the
monsters are handsome, like heroes, or lovely, like nymphs;
their bestial appendages do not affect the full perfection of their
humanity—what there is of it. There is nothing humanly wrong
with the centaur, except that he rides a horse without a head.
There is nothing humanly wrong with the mermaid; Hood put
a good comic motto to his picture of a mermaid: "All's well that

THE ILLUSTRATED LONDON NEWS

ends well." It is, perhaps, quite true; it all depends which end.
Those old wild images included a crucial truth. Man is a monster.
And he is all the more a monster because one part of him is
perfect. It is not true, as the evolutionists say, that man moves
perpetually up a slope from imperfection to perfection, changing
ceaselessly, so as to be suitable. The immortal part of a man and
the deadly part are jarringly distinct and have always been. And
the best proof of this is in such a case as we have, considered—
the case of the oaths of love.

A man's soul is as full of voices as a forest; there are ten
thousand tongues there like all the tongues of the trees: fancies,
follies, memories, madnesses, mysterious fears, and more mysterious hopes. All the settlement and sane government of life
consists in coming to the conclusion that some of those voices
have authority and others not. You may have an impulse to fight
your enemy or an impulse to run away from him; a reason to
serve your country or a reason to betray it; a good idea for
making sweets or a better idea for poisoning them. The only
test I know by which to judge one argument or inspiration from
another is ultimately this: that all the noble necessities of man
talk the language of eternity. When man is doing the three or
four things that he was sent on this earth to do, then he speaks
like one who shall live for ever. A man dying for his country
does not talk as if local preferences could change. Leonidas does
not say, "In my present mood, I prefer Sparta to Persia." William
Tell does not remark, "The Swiss civilisation, so far as I can yet
see, is superior to the Austrian." When men are making commonwealths, they talk in terms of the absolute, and so they do
when they are making (however unconsciously) those smaller
commonwealths which are called families. There are in life certain immortal moments, moments that have authority. Lovers
are right to tattoo each other's skins and cut each other's names
about the world; they do belong to each other in a more awful
sense than they know.

July 9, 1910

The Dangers of Modern Compromise

There is an atmosphere of compromise everywhere at the present instant, and of what always goes with compromise—secrecy. Everybody is beckoning to everybody else, and taking everybody else apart for a few minutes' conversation. The silence round the funeral of the late King is not a stately silence of bowed figures or bared heads: it is rather that maddening silence in which one sees groups of people arguing and gesticulating without hearing a word that they say. I confess that I dislike these hurried business bargains made in the churchyard: I am willing that debate should cease if it gives place to contemplation; but I do not like debate to cease when it only gives place to intrigue. I prefer even the mere cry of a maniac—such as the cry that the Cabinet killed the King. It is quite comically plain, of course, that, even if Mr. Asquith is an assassin as gory as Kidd, or as venomous as Borgia, the very last person he would have wanted to murder was the late King. I can imagine many other political corpses cheerfully strewn along Mr. Asquith's sanguinary path before he came to contriving the one death that has upset half his plans. But even mere screams of idiotcy like that are more soothing to my own particular civic soul than this busy and bustling silence. Carlyle and other sages have doubtless preached that it is chiefly in silence that something is done. But my own experience is rather that it is chiefly in silence that somebody is done; and the somebody who is done is generally the average British taxpayer.

I will confess to such quixotry as to feel generally that compromise is a little compromising. The whole tone and tint of our public and private diplomacy seems to me somewhat blurring to honour. All "settlements" smell rather of money—like marriage settlements. All "arrangements" tend a little to be, like Mr. Whistler's pictures, arrangements in mud and gold. But I do not press this extreme idealism upon politicians. I know that most politicians are engaged in trying to imitate the other politicians, which cannot be considered as a school of virtue. Moreover, I am not so fanatically theoretic that I cannot see that there is something in the change of affairs when they come to be handled and employed. Certainly there is one sort of shining idealism that is like the sheen on new, stiff, and sticky furniture. If the furniture is any good at all (which is frequently not the case) it will be better when it has been a little used and mellowed. Many an armchair have I mellowed in my time; leaning backwards in it until the obstinate back gives way, with a comfortable crash; grinding its sturdy legs firmly into the floor till the needless and inconvenient castors are wrenched off and roll happily away. This mere softening of the crudity of a piece of furniture by practice and experiment may, no doubt, be an advantage; and only the other day, when I had just mellowed a large sofa, and the servants were picking up the pieces, they were compelled to admit that I had taken away altogether that unhomely, shiny look as of something just come from a shop which had previously offended the eye. But while I am willing to give to any piece of furniture another and a bolder shape merely by sitting on it, there are limits to this disruptive process. There comes a point in the life of every chair when its owner should emphatically make up his mind whether he wishes to use the chair for a chair or to use the chair for firewood. Both courses are practical; nay, both are poetical. It may be even that the chair is more lovely when crowned with an aureole of ardent flames than when merely surmounted by a somewhat shapeless journalist. But a compromise between those two courses is emphatically to be discouraged. I strongly object to sitting on the most comfortable chair if three legs of it are being used for support, while one leg is being used for firewood. I do not agree with those constitutional evolutionists who think it enough to say that new things will approach us partially and with prudence. I am not satisfied when the Socialist says that Socialism will only come slowly. I am not comforted when the Protectionist says that Protection will be introduced with great tact and care. If the fourth leg of my chair is burning, I would rather be shrivelled at a quick fire than roasted at a slow one.

This state of compromise is at once dull and dangerous—like a fog in the Channel. There are no battles, but only accidents, and one ship runs into another without having even the fun of ramming her. A compromise upon Female Suffrage is being brought before the House of Commons—a compromise which, like most other compromises, cunningly contrives to include all that is dubious or menacing in the measure, while leaving out all that is enthusiastic and humane. It gives more power to the women who have too much political power already; it gives none to the women who alone can really need political power. If (on the one hand) it is unwomanly to crowd to polls and Parliaments, this Bill does that wrong to womanhood. If (on the other hand) it is unmanly to leave women voteless in slums and factories, this Bill leaves them there. If I were a Suffragist on generous and democratic lines, as many of them are, nothing would induce me to support so oppressive a compromise. I would as soon have been an Abolitionist and agreed that no niggers should be free except the niggers who were already nigger-drivers.

The same evil compromise hovers over party politics; but I shall have little space to deal with that, to my own regret and possibly to the Editor's relief. I am not preternaturally impressed by the fact that Mr. Asquith, Mr. Balfour, and Mr. Lloyd George are all to meet in an unreported Conference; for I know they have been meeting in unreported conferences about twice a week for the last five years. To suppose that statesmen, any two of whom can at any moment of their Parlimentary existence say anything they like to each other, by the simple operation of getting into a hansom cab or sitting down in a quiet part of the Terrace, will have anything astonishing to say to each other at a conference, affects me as slightly simple-minded. Even if they were practically of different social classes it would be easy enough to have twenty or thirty conferences; there would be no difficulty about private conversations between the Duke of Norfolk and

Mr. Keir Hardie if they wanted to have them. But as these
Cabinet Ministers belong practically to the same class, and dine
with each other constantly, the question is not so much whether
they should have a private conference, as whether they have ever
had anything else. If they left off having private conferences it
might perhaps be a beneficent reform; but I do not urge it. What
is really new and perilous, if one may say so, is the publicity of
the privacy. As long as these contracts and compromises are
made behind the back of the citizen, he is not responsible. But
if he turns his back on them, he is responsible. It is one thing
when statesmen get behind doors in order to discuss. It is another
when they slam the doors in the face of the public in order to
discuss. This process is not to be put to the account of any of
the living statesmen engaged in it; it has been going on for a
long time, and they are perhaps in some ways almost as much
its victims as we. The truth remains that the British Government
has, in a sense, been hunted from hiding-place to hiding-place;
and has always invented new places in which to hide. The Parliaments met, professing to represent the people; but they were
careful not to admit the people. When at last their debates had
to be reported, they transferred their final debates to the Cabinet,
and these were not reported. Now, fleeing from the blaze of
journalism and the blare of rumour, they seem to be inventing
another secret organ; and I know more than one democrat who
finds it too secret to be satisfying.

July 16, 1910

The Man Next Door

The other day I went to see the Irish Plays, recently acted by
real Irishmen—peasants and poor folk—under the inspiration of
Lady Gregory and Mr. W. B. Yeats. Over and above the excel-

lence of the acting and the abstract merit of the plays (both of
which were considerable), there emerged the strange and ironic
interest which has been the source of so much fun and sin and
sorrow—the interest of the Irishman in England. Since we have
sinned by creating the Stage Irishman, it is fitting enough that
we should all be rebuked by Irishmen on the stage. We have all
seen some obvious Englishman performing a Paddy. It was,
perhaps, a just punishment to see an obvious Paddy performing
the comic and contemptible part of an English gentleman. I have
now seen both, and I can lay my hand on my heart (though my
knowledge of physiology is shaky about its position) and declare
that the Irish English gentleman was an even more abject and
crawling figure than the English Irish servant. The Comic Irishman in the English plays was at least given credit for a kind of
chaotic courage. The Comic Englishman in the Irish plays was
represented not only as a fool, but as a nervous fool; a fussy and
spasmodic prig, who could not be loved either for strength or
weakness. But all this only illustrates the fundamental fact that
both the national views are wrong; both the versions are perversions. The rollicking Irishman and the priggish Englishman
are alike the mere myths generated by a misunderstanding. It
would be rather nearer the truth if we spoke of the rollicking
Englishman and the priggish Irishman. But even that would be
wrong too.

Unless people are near in soul they had better not be near in
neighbourhood. The Bible tells us to love our neighbours, and
also to love our enemies; probably because they are generally
the same people. And there is a real human reason for this. You
think of a remote man merely as a man; that is, you think of
him in the right way. Suppose I say to you suddenly—"Oblige
me by brooding on the soul of the man who lives at 351, High
Street, Islington." Perhaps (now I come to think of it) you *are*
the man who lives at 351, High Street, Islington; for this journal
has a wide circulation. In that case substitute some other unknown
address and pursue the intellectual sport. Now you will probably
be broadly right about the man in Islington whom you have

never seen or heard of, because you will begin at the right end—
the human end. The man in Islington is at least a man. The soul
of the man in Islington is certainly a soul. He also has been
bewildered and broadened by youth; he also has been tortured
and intoxicated by love; he also is sublimely doubtful about
death. You can think about the soul of that nameless man who
is a mere number in Islington High Street. But you do not think
about the soul of your next-door neighbour. He is not a man;
he is an environment. He is the barking of a dog; he is the noise
of a pianola; he is a dispute about a party wall; he is drains that
are worse than yours, or roses that are better than yours. Now,
all these are the wrong ends of a man; and a man, like many
other things in this world, such as a cat-o'-nine-tails, has a large
number of wrong ends, and only one right one. These adjuncts
are all tails, so to speak. A dog is a sort of curly tail to a man;
a substitute for that which man so tragically lost at an early stage
of evolution. And though I would rather myself go about trailing
a dog behind me than tugging a pianola or towing a rose-garden,
yet this is a matter of taste, and they are all alike appendages or
things dependent upon man. But besides his twenty tails, every
man really has a head, a centre of identity, a soul. And the head
of a man is even harder to find than the head of a Skye terrier,
for man has nine hundred and ninety-nine wrong ends instead
of one. It is no question of getting hold of the sow by the right
ear; it is a question of getting hold of the hedgehog by the right
quill, of the bird by the right feather, of the forest by the right
leaf. If we have never known the forest we shall know at least
that it is a forest, a thing grown grandly out of the earth; we
shall realise the roots toiling in the terrestrial darkness, the trunks
reared in the sylvan twilight.

But to find the forest is to find the fringe of the forest. To
approach it from without is to see its mere accidental outline
ragged against the sky. It is to come close enough to be superficial. The remote man, therefore, may stand for manhood; for
the glory of birth or the dignity of death. But it is difficult to
get Mr. Brown next door (with whom you have quarrelled about

the creepers) to stand for these things in any satisfactorily symbolic attitude. You do not feel the glory of his birth; you are
more likely to hint heatedly at its ingloriousness. You do not,
on purple and silver evenings, dwell on the dignity and quietude
of his death; you think of it, if at all, rather as sudden. And the
same is true of historical separation and proximity. I look forward to the same death as a Chinaman; barring one or two
Chinese tortures, perhaps. I look back to the same babyhood as
an ancient Phoenician; unless, indeed, it were one of that special
Confirmation class of Sunday School babies who were passed
through the fire to Moloch. But these distant or antique terrors
seem merely tied on to the life: they are not part of its texture.
Babylonian mothers (however they yielded to etiquette) probably loved their children; and Chinamen unquestionably reverenced their dead. It is far different when two peoples are close
enough to each other to mistake all the acts and gestures of
everyday life. It is far different when the Baptist baker in Islington thinks of Irish infancy, passed amid Popish priests and impossible fairies. It is far different when the tramp from Tipperary
thinks of Irish death, coming often in dying hamlets, in distant
colonies, in English prisons or on English gibbets. There childhood and death have lost all their reconciling qualities; the very
details of them do not unite, but divide. Hence England and
Ireland see the facts of each other without guessing the meaning
of the facts. For instance, we may see the fact that an Irish
housewife is careless. But we fancy falsely that this is because
she is scatterbrained; whereas it is, on the contrary, because she
is concentrated—on religion, or conspiracy, or tea. You may
call her inefficient, but you certainly must not call her weak. In
the same way, the Irish see the fact that the Englishman is unso-
ciable; they do not see the reason, which is that he is romantic.

This seems to me the real value of such striking national sketches
as those by Lady Gregory and Mr. Synge, which I saw last week.
Here is a case where mere accidental realism, the thing written
on the spot, the "slice of life," may, for once in a way, do some
good. All the signals, all the flags, all the declaratory externals

of Ireland we are almost certain to mistake. If the Irishman speaks to us, we are sure to misunderstand him. But if we hear the Irishman talking to himself, it may begin to dawn on us that he is a man.

July 23, 1910

Bourgeois Culture in Rural England

The following paragraph from a daily paper of the first class tells one, as such paragraphs often do, rather less than one would like to know about something that may be rather interesting—

> Godalming, Sunday Night.—The Hambledon (Surrey) Rural District Council has decided to apply to the Home Secretary for the abolition of the Haslemere Charter Fair, which dates from the reign of Queen Elizabeth. "Great difficulty is experienced," the Council state, "if the stallholders are obstreperous, and the police are unable to deal with them efficiently owing to the fact that, as long as the Charter is in force, the men are able to set up their stalls in the streets of the town. This they have frequently threatened to do when pressure has been brought to bear on them."

The situation, it will be observed, is not very lucidly stated. The stallholders, whoever they are, are obstreperous, whatever that is. And in their last and most abandoned frenzies of obstreperosity (or obstreperositude) they are in the habit of threatening that they will set up their stalls in the streets of the town, instead of setting them up in the parish church, or in their own back bedrooms, or in some remote wilderness far from the foot of man or wherever the stall-holders do set them up. But though the story is not told very clearly, it seems sufficiently plain that it is a quarrel between Modern England and Merry England; between the new and fussy middle-class which makes Fabians and officials, and all that is left of the ancient populace of the countryside. For my part, I cannot conceive what is the fun of having the fair without the fun of the fair. What is the good of a civic occasion if it does not block up the thoroughfare? What is the use of stalls if they are not in the streets? What is the cosmic purpose of cheap-jacks if they are not obstreperous? What should a local fair be if it is not coarse, noisy, and inconvenient? People seem to have lost all local patriotism.

They have indeed lost many such things, by this strange imposition of bourgeois culture and fastidiousness on the relics of healthier ages. A country vicar arbitrarily destroyed two of those wonderful Miserere wood-carvings which tell us the whole tale of the Middle Ages, on the ground that they were coarse, or (as the Hambledon Rural District Council would express it) obstreperous. The reverend gentleman deliberately desecrated his own church and defrauded his own country, merely because his ancestors, who believed in Christianity, believed also in life and in looking at all sides of life. With this case before us, there seems no limit to the principle adopted by the Hambledon Rural District Council.

It may be said that mediaeval cathedrals are obstreperous. They are really a sort of riot and revelry in building; a battle of graven angels, a dance of graven devils. Perhaps this speechless struggle in stone may give a sense of uproar, and jar on nerves that need to be soothed with the smooth lawns and recurrent villas of Suburbia. Besides, the cathedrals are often actually set up in the streets of the town—like the stalls at the fair. So we must not be surprised if we find the police trying "to deal efficiently" with the obstreperous Cathedral of Durham; or a Dean industriously demolishing Westminster Abbey for kicking up such a row near the riverside. Some of those mouldering men on the old carvings are more alive and emancipated than the crowds that pass underneath them. And if you destroy a feast

that links us with Elizabeth because it is festive, surely you may
destoy a building that links us with Rufus because it is big. If
you may smash a Tudor antiquity for taking up time, surely
you may smash a Norman antiquity for taking up space.

This row is Surrey really arises, I suppose, from the fact that
Surrey is the debateable land between London and England. It
is not a county, but a border; it is there that South London meets
and makes war with Sussex. Hence, in these Surrey towns and
villages are driven desperately against each other two quite excellent types of men, the very thought of whose meeting is a mental
despair. Both contain the queerest talents and the kindliest virtues; both have done much for England; both are capable, if
sympathetically comprehended, of being the pleasantest com-
panions in the world; both, as becomes honest men, are deeply
discontented with our modern civilisation. And yet there is not
one word that one can say which the other will not certainly
mistake; there is not one virtue that either can exhibit which the
other will not revile as a vice; they will both offend each other
by their beauties and depress each other with their delights. These
two classes, roughly, are the cultivated clerks, touched with
Puritanism, Socialism, or art, and the old English agricultural
labourers. There never were two sets of people more unfit to
understand each other than the yokel and the clerk. And all over
two or three counties round London yokels and clerks are mixed
and jostled together; often sown alternately, like peas and beans
in a field. Perhaps one might say like tares and wheat in a field,
for the only quite obvious solution is to wait till the harvest and
bind the tares into bundles and burn them. But I have not affirmed
which are the tares.

The cultured clerk and the rustic are each the other inside out
and upside down. The rustic is externally stiff with conventions.
A ponderous politeness marks all his words and gestures; he
recites ritual phrases about beer and the weather; he expects
people to keep their places, gentlemen to be gentlemen, parsons
to be parsons, ladies to smile, and poachers to poach. But under
all this load of literalism and an ancient mode of life his inmost

mind has often the queerest kind of independence. Sudden turns of his speech will have quite a cruel candour. He will utter improprieties or a brutal cynicism with a venerable innocence which is quite exasperating. He does not really take himself seriously; for Christianity is sunk somewhere out of sight in his soul. He will openly exhibit himself as the village drunkard or even the village idiot; he will tell old tales of fights in which he was beaten, of dreams or bets that did not come true. His soul sings like one little ribald bird in an ivy-covered castle of custom.

Abruptly opposite is the case of the high-minded clerk, the man of the artistic middle-class. He comes into the country with the absurd idea that one can be unconventional in the country; which is the most conventional place on earth. He will walk about the country lanes in sandals; or he will be a vegetarian and deal with the greengrocer but not the butcher. All this seems to the conventional rustic simply stark madness, without any ideal or excuse, as if the man had put gloves on his feet or eaten mustard without beef. On the other hand, while the clerk is clad freely and wildly in jaeger and sandals, his inmost soul is not free and wild. His artistic dress seems so disreputable in the country that the finches might drop dead off the hedgerows and the cattle in the fields go mad at the sight of it. But while his appearance is thus disreputable, his soul is secretly respectable. He is all the more a Puritan for being an aesthete. He would never utter an impropriety, or even a cynicism; he takes himself with entire seriousness; his conscience never has a holiday; his eccentricities are not outbreaks of his temperament, but deductions from his principles; he is never so dull as when he is mad. These two strange inversions confront each other on the Surrey hills; the aesthete, quaint outside and conventional inside; the gaffer, quaint inside and conventional outside. Whatever the issue of the fight is, I hope it will not abolish the Haslemere Charter Fair.

July 30, 1910

Sightseers and Ordinary Men

It would be really interesting to know exactly why an intelligent person—by which I mean a person with any sort of intelligence— can and does dislike sight-seeing. Why does the idea of a char- à-banc full of tourists going to see the birthplace of Nelson or the death-scene of Simon de Montfort strike a strange chill to the soul? I can tell quite easily what this dim aversion to tourists and their antiquities does not arise from—at least, in my case. Whatever my other vices (and they are, of course, of a lurid cast), I can lay my hand on my heart and say that it does not arise from a paltry contempt for the antiquities, nor yet from the still more paltry contempt for the tourists. If there is one thing more dwarfish and pitiful than irreverence for the past, it is irreverence for the present, for the passionate and many-col- oured procession of life, which includes the char-à-banc among its many chariots and triumphal cars. I know nothing so vulgar as that contempt for vulgarity which sneers at the clerks on a Bank Holiday or the Cockneys on Margate sands. The man who notices nothing about the clerk except his Cockney accent would have noticed nothing about Simon de Montfort except his French accent. The man who jeers at Jones for having dropped an "h" might have jeered at Nelson for having dropped an arm. Scorn springs easily to the essentially vulgar-minded; and it is as easy to gibe at Montfort as a foreigner or at Nelson as a cripple, as to gibe at the struggling speech and the maimed bodies of the mass of our comic and tragic race. If I shrink faintly from this affair of tourists and tombs, it is certainly not because I am so profane as to think lightly either of the tombs or the tourists. I reverence those great men who had the courage to die; I reverence also these little men who have the courage to live.

Even if this be conceded, another suggestion may be made. It may be said that antiquities and commonplace crowds are indeed good things, like violets and geraniums; but they do not go together. A billycock is a beautiful object (it may be eagerly urged), but it is not in the same style of architecture as Ely Cathedral; it is a dome, a small rococo dome in the Renaissance manner, and does not go with the pointed arches that assault heaven like spears. A char-à-banc is lovely (it may be said) if placed upon a pedestal and worshipped for its own sweet sake; but it does not harmonise with the curve and outline of the old three-decker on which Nelson died; its beauty is quite of another sort. Therefore (we will suppose our sage to argue) antiquity and democracy should be kept separate, as inconsistent things. Things may be inconsistent in time and space which are by no means inconsistent in essential value and idea.

This explanation is plausible; but I do not find it adequate. The first objection is that the same smell of bathos haunts the soul in the case of all deliberate and elaborate visits to "beauty spots," even by persons of the most elegant position or the most protected privacy. Specially visiting the Coliseum by moonlight always struck me as being as vulgar as visiting it by limelight. One millionaire standing on the top of Mont Blanc, one millionaire standing in the desert by the Sphinx, one millionaire standing in the middle of Stonehenge, is just as comic as one millionaire is anywhere else; and that is saying a good deal. On the other hand, if the billycock had come privately and naturally into Ely Cathedral, no enthusiast for Gothic harmony would think of objecting to the billycock—so long, of course, as it was not worn on the head. But there is indeed a much deeper objection to this theory of the two incompatible excellences of antiquity and popularity. For the truth is that it has been almost entirely the antiquities that have normally interested the populace; and it has been almost entirely the populace who have systematically preserved the antiquities. The Oldest Inhabitant has always been a clodhopper; I have never heard of his being a gentleman. It is the peasants who preserve all traditions of the sites of battles or the building of churches. It is they who remember, so far as anyone remembers, the glimpses of fairies or the graver wonders of saints. In the classes above them the supernatural has been slain by the supercilious. That is a true and tremendous text in Scripture which says that "where there is no vision the people perish." But it is equally true in practice that where there is no people the visions perish.

The idea must be abandoned, then, that this feeling of faint dislike towards popular sightseeing is due to any inherent incompatibility between the idea of special shrines and trophies and the idea of large masses of ordinary men. On the contrary, these two elements of sanctity and democracy have been specially connected and allied throughout history. The shrines and trophies were often put up by ordinary men. They were always put up for ordinary men. To whatever things the fastidious modern artist may choose to apply his theory of specialist judgment, and an aristocracy of taste, he must necessarily find it difficult really to apply it to such historic and monumental art. Obviously, a public building is meant to impress the public. The most aristocratic tomb is a democratic tomb, because it exists to be seen; the only aristocratic thing is the decaying corpse, not the undecaying marble; and if the man wanted to be thoroughly aristocratic, he should be buried in his own back-garden. The chapel of the most narrow and exclusive sect is universal outside, even if it is limited inside; its walls and windows confront all points of the compass and all quarters of the cosmos. It may be small as a dwelling-place, but it is universal as a monument; if its sectarians had really wished to be private they should have met in a private house. Whenever and wherever we erect a national or municipal hall, pillar, or statue we are speaking to the crowd like a demagogue.

The statue of every statesman offers itself for election as much as the statesman himself. Every epitaph on a church slab is put up for the mob as much as a placard in a General Election. And if we follow this track of reflection we shall, I think, really find why it is that modern sight-seeing jars on something in us, something that is not a caddish contempt for graves nor an equally caddish contempt for cads. For, after all, there is many a churchyard which consists mostly of dead cads; but that does not make it less sacred or less sad.

The real explanation, I fancy, is this: that these cathedrals and columns of triumph were meant, not for people more cultured and self-conscious than modern tourists, but for people much rougher and more casual. Those leaps as of live stone like frozen fountains, were so placed and poised as to catch the eye of ordinary inconsiderate men going about their daily business; and when they are so seen they are never forgotten. The true way of reviving the magic of our great minsters and historic sepulchres is not the one which Ruskin was always recommending. It is not to be more careful of historic buildings. Nay, it is rather to be more careless of them. Buy a bicycle in Maidstone to visit an aunt in Dover, and you will see Canterbury Cathedral as it was built to be seen. Go through London only as the shortest way between Croydon and Hampstead, and the Nelson Column will (for the first time in your life) remind you of Nelson. You will appreciate Hereford Cathedral if you have come for cider, not if you have come for architecture. You will really see the Place Vendôme if you have come on business, not if you have come for art. For it was for the simple and laborious generations of men, practical, troubled about many things, that our fathers reared these portents. There is, indeed, another element, not unimportant: the fact that people have gone to cathedrals to pray. But in discussing modern artistic cathedral-lovers, we need not consider this.

August 6, 1910

The Custom of Gradual Change

It is proverbial, of course, that England is politically attached to that process which some call proceeding step by step, and others call taking two bites of a cherry. We may indeed question the universal truth of this description. Englishmen, after all, have done one or two violent and definite things. King Charles the First's head, I regret to say, was not sawn off slowly, but struck off sharply, with what the curate in "The Private Secretary" called a good hard knock. The English aristocrats of the Revolution did not nibble at James II. like a cherry; they dropped him like a hot potato. Neither did they nibble at William of Orange like a cherry; rather, they swallowed him—like a pill. The massacre of Wexford and the slaughter after Culloden left nothing to be desired as far as thoroughness is concerned. The late Cecil Rhodes was an Evolutionist in a foggy sort of way; but the Jameson Raid was not at all evolutionary. And whenever there has been the smallest chance of tyrannising over anybody in Ireland the English Parliament has displayed a bounding swiftness and dazzling rapidity of action which confounded and rebuked those who had sneered at its slowness in all other matters. But though we may have shown some slight haste in the meaner matters of fear or avarice, we can honestly claim that we have shown a responsible and judicial slowness in the higher department of human good.

It may also be doubted whether this custom of gradual change is quite so practical as some have represented it. The disadvantage of going step by step is that when you have made one stop you are often forcibly prevented from making the next, as any philosopher may discover who tries to go step by step through somebody else's cornfield. The philosopher had much better make one wild leap and land in the middle of the corn. No one ever really knows how long an experiment will be allowed to last; no one really knows how much sustained public force there is behind any trend of reform, or when it may suddenly give out. It is all very well to talk of revolution as a leap in the dark; but every step of reform is a step in the dark, and I would as soon leap over the edge of Shakespeare's Cliff as step over it. The result (at the bottom) would be much the same. And we do constantly find in English history that calamity has overtaken these partial proposals before they achieved their final object.

Many who abolished public executions believed that this would lead to the abolition of all executions. But I think there can be no doubt that it has led rather to their perpetuation, on the principle that what the journalistic eye does not see the humanitarian heart does not grieve over. A political compromise is like two children tugging at a cracker till it comes in two in the middle. One child gets one half, but the other half flies further away. In short, the situation is a paradoxical one, which can only be conveyed in such forms of speech as are mysteriously called Irish. The real objection to taking two bites of a cherry is that you only get one bite.

That is the real difficulty of the few democrats who are in favour of Female Suffrage. Mr. Shackleton's Bill, recently discussed in the House of Commons, was, of course, a perfect example of our cautious and compromising kind of legislation. It makes a man smile to remember how all the old ladies who appear to conduct the Jingo and anti-Socialist newspapers set up screams of terror at the sight of the Labour Members, as the Marats and Couthons of a new Terror. The old ladies may rest in peace. Many other people are indeed becoming bored with the half-hearted fictions of Parliament. Mr. Balfour may let off an intelligent observation which in that atmosphere sounds as startling as a pistol-shot. Mr. Asquith may, and almost certainly does, welcome the horseplay of the Suffragettes as some sort of relief to the suffocating tedium of party politics. But so long as there is one Labour Member left in the House, the old flag of the British Constitution will still be flying. So long as the Labour Party remains, there will be at least one solid block of slow, reverent, and strictly Conservative compromise. There they stand, a wall of able, honest, successful, and profoundly respectable men, a permanent barrier against the anger of idealists, the wild free-thought of Bishops, the fantasticality of aristocrats, and the fighting dogmas of the Catholic Irish. The Labour Members seem to be the only people left who believe in the party system. Neither the Liberals nor Conservatives believe in themselves; but the Labour Party believes in both of them. And Mr. Shackleton rose full of all the old English constitutional idea of obtaining perfection piecemeal, standing for the principle that half a loaf is better than no bread. As a personal taste in bakery, I think it depends which half. In a fairy-tale of my childhood, a wicked stepmother sought to persuade a good princess to share an apple with her, on the seemingly plausible principle that half an apple is better than no fruitarian diet. But the princess rapidly discovered the principle to which I refer—that it rather depends which half—for the half she got was full of deadly poison.

Supposing (for the sake of argument, for I cannot conceive it to be very likely) that Mr. Shackleton's Bill does obtain further facilities and passes the House of Commons; and supposing (again for the sake of argument, though this is immeasurably more likely) that it passes the House of Lords, it will then be regarded by all such simple Suffragists as have any democracy in them as the beginning of Suffrage legislation. I am almost certain it will be the end of Suffrage legislation. The vague mass of mildly idealistic men and women who have supported the movement in order to see something happen will fall away, having seen something happen. The very prominent and wealthy women will be quieted and will silently strengthen their position, as all their class has done for the last four hundred years. And the working-women will remain like the working-men—full of faith, hope, charity towards a race of politicians very much lower than themselves.

The essence of the position, therefore, amounts to this. If you are on the side of woman against man, or (in other words) if you are a criminal lunatic, you should welcome Mr. Shackleton's Bill because some women get something which some men dislike their having. If you hold a more decent opinion, that, upon the whole, the tyranny of the world is that of male over female rather than that of rich over poor, then you may welcome Mr. Shackleton's Bill as a sort of symbol. If you think (as many do, both rich and poor) that England is on the whole better governed by rich men than by Englishmen, then you should take Mr. Shackleton's Bill into your arms like a new-born babe and cherish and strengthen it above all things. But if, by any wild chance, you originally became a Suffragist because you believed in the ultimate rule of the people, then you ought to stamp it down into the mire.

August 13, 1910

Varieties of Murder

Somebody remarks in a newspaper that there is an epidemic of murders. It is an instance of the morbid modern fondness for words that express fatality. I should not regard myself as any more likely to murder the station-master at Beaconsfield because there were an increasing number of crimes in South Bucks. I do not expect it any more than I expect to commit bigamy through smelling a bigamist's tulips, or bribery through borrowing a politician's umbrella. I am sure I could safely use a Levantine usurer's soap, if he has any; I am sure that if I rubbed against a pick-pocket in a crowd I should take nothing from him, whatever he might take from me. In short, "an epidemic of murder" is as silly and slavish a phrase as "a plague of priggishness" or "a pestilence of equivocation"; we might as well speak of superciliousness raging in all the hospitals of Swansea, or of whole populations struck down raving with stinginess. In ninety-nine cases out of a hundred there must be a moral reason for an immoral act. Murder is a private matter—at least, until it is committed. But the eager use of such devastating scientific terms is but a part of our evasion of responsibility and our dark adoration of fate. In politics, where a man ought to be specially free and firm in judgment, we are specially pestered with these dreams of doom, these dead analogies from dust and ocean, earthquake and eclipse. If sixty rational and respectable citizens choose to vote Tory, it is called the Flowing Tide. If the sixty rational citizens decide to vote Radical, it is called the Swing of the Pendulum. One witty candidate, menaced with the flowing tide by his opponent, pasted up a notice: "Vote for Smith and Dam the Flowing Tide." Similarly, I should say with decision, "Vote for whom you choose and hang the pendulum."

That a number of murders might be due to some legal inefficiency or loosening of the discipline of a nation is more plausible. I know more than one intelligent person who thinks that the police at present have no time to seize assassins because they are so busy seizing boys' cigarettes, arresting little girls for drinking lemonade in hotels, seeing that Tommy does not lick his coloured chalks in the nursery, seeing that the baby is put to bed at the right hour, and all such constabulary labours and perils. I have not the text of the Children's Bill by me, but my list will be roughly correct. Nevertheless, I cannot think that our constabulary throws itself into the problems of the nursery with quite such all-forgetting enthusiasm as Mr. Herbert Samuel doubtless intended it to do. Those long conversations which can sometimes be observed in progress between policemen and nurses may be wholly concerned with educational and psychological points of difficulty; but these conversations are the only form of nursery interest that I have ever seen the constable display. His interest in the children is, to say the least of it, indirect; and I am quite sure that any healthy-minded policeman would be happier holding a murderer than holding a baby. Therefore, I think this other theory that the political intellect has turned from the subject of murder to the more absorbing subject of education must also be given up.

But the true and clinching consideration which proves that crimes can be part of no mere drift or doom is the abrupt, individual, and sometimes quite inconceivable oddities that occur in them. All the murders are alike in so far that they ultimately murder; that violent death is their upshot. But in their origin and idea they are as different as any two or three eccentricities can be; as different as a man shooting giraffes from a man col-

lecting tram-tickets, as different as a vegetarian in a restaurant
from a saint in a cave. For here indeed is one of the most obvious
of the four or five fallacies upon which the towering fabric of
popular science is reared. I mean the application of modes of
reckoning proper to uniform facts to facts that are in their nature
miscellaneous. Or, in other words, counting things together
because they are alike in their effect, as if they were alike in their
cause. If we are dealing with hailstones (let us say) it is reasonably
adequate simply to count the hailstones—if you can; I am told
it is difficult. But if it can be said by a scientist with his hand
on his heart that only three hailstones (or more probably, three
and a half) have fallen at Bournemouth since the year 1066, then
we shall not be far wrong in calling Bournemouth a safe place
from hail. But if instead of asking how many hailstones have
fallen we ask how many stones have fallen, then the case is quite
different. Hailstones not only all go to the same place; they also
all come from the same place. It always hails for the same reason,
whatever it is. If each individual hailstone has a motive it is
probably a tribal motive.

But if it were reported on equally good authority that only
three and a half stones had fallen in Bournemouth, the generalisation would involve a fallacy, for there need be no real similarity in the cases. The first stone might be thrown by an invalid
into the sea; the second stone might be thrown by a healthy boy
through a window; the third might be hurled with murderous
intent by a mad politician interested in the extension of the
franchise. As for the half stone left over, I suppose that would
be thrown by a moderate politician, on our old principle that
half a stone is better than no slaughter; it might be called the
Conciliation Stone. But the point is this: that the invalid, the
schoolboy, and the fanatic have not enough in common to constitute any general rule at all about the falling or non-falling of
stones. They all play with pebbles for various reasons and at
different times. The schoolboy (being without sin) will probably
cast the first stone, in the course of some early-morning ramble;
the invalid is more likely to be inspired to fling one feeble pebble

in the splendour of the setting sun; while the political idealist may very probably wait till darkness, because his deeds are evil. But even this matter of time is very vague; statesmen, seas, and windows are cockshies at all times of the day and night. There might be these petrobolous types, or there might be none of them, or there might be many other types. Bournemouth might proudly entertain a gentleman who dropped rocks on his own feet by way of penance, or a gentleman who dropped them on other people's heads out of misanthropy; or a gentleman who habitually, when he went for a walk, dropped pebbles in a trail behind him, like Hansel and Gretel, for fear he should lose his way. All these ordinary human varieties would enrich and complicate the question of the falling stones; and merely to count the number of stones that had fallen in one year would be almost useless, since we should have no guide or law to explain the outbursts and cessations of stones. In short, wherever we have a problem of few cases and various causes, it is very hard to make anything of it. Now, murders are peculiarly a matter of few cases and various causes. So very few of us ever get murdered at all, even when we deserve it, that there are no data sufficient for a synthesis. And then, even if we *are* murdered, remember what a large number of reasons there might be for murdering us. Even as you read this article six persons are perhaps plotting your end; and all for entirely different, yet quite convincing reasons.

August 20, 1910

The Accuracy of Science

A somewhat squalid police mystery, which is still pending, has been chiefly remarked as an illustration of the extraordinary strides of science in wireless telegraphy. Certainly it is not unnatural that most modern people should desire to discuss electricity rather than crime. It is instinctive to dwell on those airy matters of science in which we have progressed so much rather than on those solid matters of morals in which it is highly doubtful if we have progressed at all. It is pleasanter to reflect on the mind of man bridging the starry abysses and dissecting the atoms of the ultimate, rather than to remember that the heart of man is still mysterious and barbaric, deceitful above all things, and desperately wicked. And the wonders of wireless telegraphy are indeed most fascinating and inspiring to anyone who takes the right view of physical science—which is to regard it as a fairy tale, always beautiful, and sometimes true, but never, in the supreme sense, important. There is something high and lurid in the thought of those human whispers meeting like secret winds in the monstrous solitudes of the sea. There is something elfin and poetic in the idea of human words, shot into the distance like arrows, and hanging poised and waiting like birds. Few of the fairy tales of science, indeed, have provided anything so vast and so fantastic as this covering of the sea with a net-work of unseen legends; building invisible post-offices and unsubstantial pillar-boxes in the void.

But there is one aspect of this almost eerie exactitude of science that claims more consideration. It cannot be disputed that our age has been and is still marked by an advance in this ruthless and rigid accuracy, this sharp and polished dexterity of the sciences and the machines. Whether a man detests the tendency, as Ruskin did, or accepts it, as Whitman did, or simply thinks it slight and secondary, and of little direct effect on happiness (as most ordinary people think, including the present writer), there can be no rational dispute about the existence of the practical science, about its strength, or about its precision. This being so, a grave difficulty follows. We are now confronted with the colossal and really terrifying responsibility of doing things that we can really do. As long as people only dreamed of flying or tried to bridge the sea, they were as innocent as any other fancies of the intellect; but dreams that come true are very dreadful things.

The dreamer always feels, with subconscious horror, that he has had something to do with it. And when we embark on anything, the real risk is not defeat: the real risk is victory. To a deep and delicate conscience, it is comparatively little to feel responsible for a thing's failure. The really terrible thing is to feel responsible for its success.

Here is a hard case with our legal and ethical methods. Savage tools and methods may be both clumsy and cruel, but they are all the less cruel for being clumsy. The barbarian may have no notions beyond those of fire and sword; but his sword will be of wood or flint, and if he gets fire (as I was told in youth) by rubbing two sticks together, he must rub a long time. Mud walls do not a prison make, nor bamboo bars a cage; and even the minds most innocent and quiet among the Hottentot criminal class must often have conceived simple modes of escape from such detention. From time to time in my youth members of my present trade—simple, unaffected journalists—used to turn up with the information that they had just been tortured by savages. I salute them with all reverence: to be tortured, even by savages, must be distinctly unpleasant. But I would much rather be tortured by savages than tortured by civilised men. The thumb-screw and the boot, in rude hands, would alarm me less than a much simpler apparatus (say a stair-rod, seven hairpins, and a pot of glue) in the hands of one whose eyes shone with the light of science. I should always have a notion that the savages would make a mess of the boot and thumbscrew business somehow. I should always vaguely expect that the thumbscrew would not fit, being made for a chimpanzee sort of thumb; I should always fancy they would get the boot on the wrong leg. But science has always shown a capacity, and even an alacrity, in the creation of cruel and destructive things. It stands to reason that a person who knows enough about the body to help it, knows enough about it to hurt it; and it would be a delicate question to decide whether science has turned out more pills or more cannon-balls. The rationalists of the Renaissance were almost as rapid in invent-ing poisons as the rationalists of the nineteenth century were in inventing medicines; and some say that the effect of both is much the same. An excellent example of a scientist is the respectable Doctor Guillotin. He happened to live at a time when it was highly necessary to kill people quickly, and therefore he invented a machine for killing people quickly. But if he had lived in some other age—say, under Nero or in the morbid period just after the Reformation—he would probably have invented a machine for killing people slowly. And he would probably have invented a good machine. And he would probably be much admired by many modern people who worship the means of civilisation instead of the end. There are many ladies and gentlemen I know who would seriously approve of the rack if it were kept quite clean and worked by electricity.

But in a cruder society, this perfection of machinery is inconceivable. Savagery has many vices and some virtues; but it has, above all, the great virtue of inefficiency. No constitution can be quite so mad in practice as it is on paper, and no father of his people is quite so tyrannical as he would like to be. We cannot condemn the kings and jailers of certain rough systems for the very reason that those systems are so rough; so rough as to be scarcely systems at all. The jailer escapes—because the prisoner escapes. Therefore in any wild and insecure society, we can contemplate without intolerable horror a possibility that should always be present to us. I mean the possibility that we may be making all the bad men jailers and all the good men convicts. I mean, in short, the idea that our moral system may be so highly disputable that it may actually segregate the worst types in society and the best types in revolt against society. This is always a dreadful possibility; but so long as the jailer and the prisoner struggle almost on equal terms, we may be well content that their moral systems should be dubiously balanced also. But if we make the prisoner really a prisoner; if we put him quite helplessly in the hands of his jailers for ever; if we band all nations against him; if we shut all ports before his passage; if steel traps stand open for him everywhere and secret voices betray him in the wilderness of the sea—then surely it is certain that we ought to have a proportionally fixed and infallible moral certainty that we are doing the right thing with him. Instead of losing its dogmas, the modern world is bound to bind its dogmas tighter. It must be more certain that it is right, not less certain. Its dogmas must be as definite as the verdict and as hard as the handcuffs, as logical as an extradition treaty and as universal as wireless telegraphy.

Now here is the whole trouble. Unluckily, it is not true, it is quite the reverse of the truth, that as our science grows more accurate our morality grows more defined. It is not true (as it ought to be) that as our method grows more unfailing our creed grows more infallible. It is, in fact, exactly the other way. Actually, it is just now, when the police are most perfect as an organisation, that people feel them most imperfect as an idea. Precisely now, when the prisoner cannot possibly get out of prison, we are most deeply doubting whether he ought ever to have been in prison. Now that nothing can keep his head out of the noose, we are most profoundly sceptical about whether anything should put his head in it. In the days when men really believed in the rope, the rope often broke. Now that numbers of people are intrinsically sceptical about it, it is twisted out of cords of iron. Thus a deep chasm has been cleft between public and private life, which may yet be found to constitute a real lesion and malady in our commonwealth. Wonderful wireless telegraphy may some day whisper in mid-ocean the name of a murderer at the very moment when no large-hearted private citizen would whisper it to his next-door neighbour.

There are two escapes from this dilemma. One is to re-establish a barbaric chaos, with broken prisons and derided laws. The other is to re-establish a clear morality. I rather fancy the latter course will be found the better in the long run.

August 27, 1910

Little England and Big Empire

Somebody recently ventured to say somewhere that a Scotchman was not, perhaps, in all respects exactly the same as an Englishman. Upon which the *Times* and the *Spectator* both said together, with the loud promptitude and precision of a couple of alarum clocks, "Do you want the Heptarchy?" As I am used to these papers waking up suddenly from time to time and saying this, it did not surprise me; and I could supply without reading the rest all the triumphant contrast drawn by the learned writers between our united and glorious British Empire and the well-known details of a Heptarchic existence. The answer to the question seems to me simple and crude. "I never tried the Heptarchy. It was before my time. But I have tried our united and glorious British Empire; and I know it is chaotic, hysterical, immoral, inconsequent, incompetent, and very badly governed. And its weaknesses and perils are not such as any mere governmental unity can either control or cure. Merely uniting people under one flag or one police does not strengthen them if their lives are all disruptive and incompatible, if their economics have gone rotten or their morals gone mad. It does not safeguard a district that all its soldiers wear the same kind of clothes if half its population wears hardly any kind of clothes; nor is the word Union (to which I bow my head seven times) by any means so uplifting and patriotic when it means for most people the workhouse. The large modern State does not secure genuine unity at all. Many of the large States are simply large anarchies—America, for instance. The United States are essentially disunited States. No doubt some of our British patriots would like to swamp us in the American civilisation, offering the Anglo-American throne to Mr. Roosevelt. But I am by no means certain that Theodore,

King of the Anglo-Saxons, would be so much better a ruler than Alfred, King of the West Saxons.

When I think of King Theodore I confess I think the Heptarchy a sane and practical alternative. I know how King Theodore would rule his huge and duplex Empire: by newspaper interviews, Masonic banquets, and a general moral show of everybody minding everybody else's business. I know how he would explain England to America and America to England, and explain them both wrong. I know how the Baptist ministers in Plymouth would settle the negro problem in Florida; I know how the Baptist ministers in Boston would settle the wayside inns of Kent. Endless denunciations of distant vices, endless defiance of distant dangers; endless exploiting of people who know nothing by people who know too much; endless entanglements between the worst indecency of rabbles and the worst secrecy of oligarchs; the poor rioting for what they do not know, and the rich scheming for what they dare not say; all the facts fourth-hand and all the principles fourth-rate—these, palpable and visible before us, are the actual fruits of Union, of the large, highly organised modern State. And, above all, this evil is branded on the brow of it, that each group or neighbourhood has too much power outside its borders and too little inside. Norwood can interfere with Natal, but it cannot govern Norwood. Surrey can insult Servian tyrants; but it must submit to Surrey tyrants. Lewisham cannot be a law to itself; it can only manage to be a sort of mild anarchy to the Tsar. Brighton may slightly disorder Spanish affairs; but it cannot order its own. The Londoner is a slave in London by the same political process that makes him a tyrant in Cork.

Now I fancy that under that hearty and typical Little Englander, King Alfred the Great, Wessex was practically governed very much more after the manner of Wessex men. Alfred the Great may be called the splendid and supreme Little Englander; for he was deliberately content with something even littler than England. Of all those qualities in Alfred which are so rootedly and refreshingly English, none was more English than his in-

stinctive opposition to Imperialism. When the course of events
and the example of other conquerors should naturally have led
him to press his frontiers further and further, and attempt an
utter expulsion of Danes, he dwelt contentedly within moderate
dominions, to which he never added but in self-defence. And I
am quite sure that it was because his kingdom was a small one
that it came to be called a golden kingdom and his reign a golden
reign. Not only was Alfred the Great a Little Englander, but it
was exactly because the England was little that the Alfred was
great.

Therefore I venture to say, with great seriousness, that when
people talk about the horrors of bringing back the Heptarchy,
they should be politely asked how much they or anybody else
know about the Heptarchy—whether we do not know too little
about the Heptarchy and rather too much about the Union?
Alfred, of course, lived after the Heptarchic time and in a British
Empire not quite as big as a modern small nationality. The
founders of the house of Wessex had doubtless extended their
domains; Alfred only defended them. But it is perfectly typical
of the ancient wholesome instincts of mankind that the man who
has been loved for a thousand years is not the man who took,
but the man who defended; not the conqueror, but the man who
was nearly conquered. Egbert, perhaps, was an Imperialist; that
is why he is not called Egbert the Great. In those ceremonial
eulogies upon Alfred which are now from time to time pro-
nounced by persons of another religion, and sometimes of another
race, it has become customary to represent him as the founder
of the Navy League and the Imperial Liberal Council. They try
to make out that his wretched, reasonable little fleet against the
pirates was the foundation of the British Navy. But it is not in
this way that the historic cult of Alfred can be understood. The
cult of Alfred is, and has always been steadily for ten centuries,
a popular cult. As with all really great men, the legends are more
appropriate than the facts. School-children and servants are still
as pleased with the idea of his singing in disguise in the Danish
camp as with the idea of a royal Duke dressed as a nigger min-

strel. They still like the idea of the King minding cakes, as they would like the idea of the Pope toasting muffins. All the facts remembered about Alfred (it should be noted) are little physical facts—that he carried a note-book in his bosom, that he learnt as a boy out of a bright-coloured book; that he made clocks of candles. For a thousand years a million people have known these things, who cared nothing for the translation of Boethius or the Treaty of Wedmore[1]—or the Pact of Chippenham, as a distinguished historian irritates me by calling it. Now, Alfred had other lessons for the savages and heathen anarchists with whom he fought. To them he might well stand for peace and for translations from the Latin. But his lesson for us is the lesson of simplicity and actuality. His message to us is a message of cakes and candles, of things plain like the spelling-book and personal like the note-book. For what is wrong with our civilisation can be said in one word—unreality. We are in no danger either from the vices or the virtues of vikings; we are in danger of forgetting all facts, good and bad, in a haze of high-minded phraseology. And if the people of Wessex (which still exists) want to survive these dark ages as they survived the dark ages of old, they must ask definitely for what they want, for the Wessex cakes and Wessex candles and Wessex alphabet, and certainly not accept the word "Heptarchy" as an answer.

September 3, 1910

King and Emperor in England

We few poor Radicals who alone reverence the past, or seem to have any relish of the royal chronicles of England, have lately been confronted with a proposal calculated to make us take to

---

[1] The peace treaty following Alfred the Great's victory over the Danes in 878; he forced Gurthrun the Dane to become a Christian and divide England with him, Alfred obtaining the south, including London.

our beds, to laugh at leisure, or die in peace. For indeed the thing passes all language, and is fit only for death or laughter.

It has actually been proposed in an English paper that the King of England should consent to be called Emperor of the British. The primary answer is obvious. Why not Sultan of the British? Why not Kaiser of the British, or Pope of the British? Why not Tsar? Why not Shah? Why not Grand Lama of Great Britain? Why not Doge of the British Empire? Why not Stadtholder of the United States of Britain? Why not Mogul of the Three Kingdoms? Why not Mikado of the Isles? Why should there be a Dey of Tripoli, and no Dey of Turnham Green? Why should Tartary have had a Cham, while Tonbridge has no trace of a Cham? Why should we hear (with helpless envy) of there having once been an Akond of Swât, when it is vain to hope for any Akond of Surbiton? I know not how to comfort my fellow-countrymen for the loss of all these sumptuous and soaring titles, except by reminding them (however sad it may seem) that they are a great people, with a history of their own. We do not call our ruler an Emperor for the same reason that we do not call him a Brother of the Sun and Moon: because it is our national tradition to call him something else. Brother of the Sun and Moon is a much vaster and grander title than either Emperor or King; and if you want something grander still, I am sure I could invent it. Uncle of the Universe would be good, or Cousin of the Cosmos. These are greater titles than King of England—in mythology. But not in history.

At this rate all the old Republicans will have to make a guard of honour round the English throne. If the Imperialists do not understand how great a thing is a King of England, we do. Any greedy and nameless adventurer who could master a few tribes or steal a few provinces in dim Asia or barbaric Central Europe could call himself an Emperor. But even to call yourself King of England was a great business; still more to be one. To be a King like Edward I., or even like Edward III., is to look down as from a pinnacle upon all the chance brigands and freedmen and compromising courtiers who have managed to "wear the purple" in the anarchies of East and West. To call a British King, wearing the crown of Arthur and Alfred, by the foolish foreign name suggested, is to me almost madly laughable: I would as soon call England by the improved name of Heligoland.

Moreover, Emperor is not a higher grade than King. Really the two things are on different ladders; they are in different scales and categories, like a Knight-Banneret[1] and an R.A.;[2] or like an Arch-Druid and a Colonel of Volunteers. But in strict truth, to make the King an Emperor is to degrade the King to the rank of Commander-in-Chief. Lord Roberts[3] and Lord Kitchener[4] are Emperors. The General in Command of the Roman Army, who was called the Imperator, became (very gradually and only to a slight degree even officially) the tie and symbol of that practical unity which the Roman Republic had made throughout the known world. It was a unity resting on military qualities, and therefore the military head of the State, rather than the religious or the legal, became the emblem and sacrament of its sway. But almost up to the last the Imperator was supposed to be an official, and not (in the full religious and romantic sense) a King. The really patriotic peoples, like France and England, had Kings—when they did not have Republics. Emperors were always left for the unpatriotic peoples—collisions and confusions of tribes who seemed incapable of spontaneous unity. Whenever some soldier of fortune managed by brute force to make some welter of Goths

[1] In feudalism, the title given to nobles who, because of their distinguished service in the field, had the right to lead their vassals to battle under their own banner.

[2] Rear Admiral.

[3] Frederick Sleigh Roberts (1832–1914), a field marshal, commander-in-chief in India (1885–1893), commander-in-chief in Ireland (1895–1899), appointed to supreme command in South Africa at the end of 1899. He at once increased the number of mounted troups, remodelled transport with the help of Lord Kitchener and decided to invade Free State.

[4] Horatio Herbert Kitchener (1850–1916), a field marshal whose early career was spent in Egypt and the Sudan; in 1899 he became Lord Robert's chief of staff in South Africa.

and Huns and Iberians behave itself for a month, he felt that he was reviving the Roman Empire; and, with rational truth and very proper modesty, he called himself by the inferior title of "Emperor." He was only an Imperator, a Colonel reading the Riot Act, a soldier forcing peace upon a miscellaneous Europe. So it is with those unhappy men (perhaps the unhappiest of all modern men) who have to rule the inchoate, the mixed, the non-national parts of Christendom—Austria, Germany, and Russia. *They*, of course, call themselves by the old rude military term, Caesar, Kaiser, Tsar—in short, Field-Marshal. There is no nation for them to embody and to be. There is still nothing but a whirlpool of tribes and the tradition of the Roman arms. But a King like St. Louis, a King like King Edward, was a very different business. Royalty was the noblest of all ideals—next to Republicanism. Nay, one may go further: royalty was the most Republican of all ideas, next to Republicanism.

Next after mankind, the most human thing is a man. The old vivid nations said that if all men could not rule, one man should rule; but not some men—not a picked cabal of the wealthy, the cultured, and the cold-bloodedly impudent. The mediaeval monarchy in the patriotic peoples (England, France, Spain, Scotland) took this one man and made him part and organ of the people: they offered him as flesh upon an altar; they made him sacramental. If it was to some extent idolatry, one may say in its defence that it was also human sacrifice. For the darkest and grandest, even if the bloodiest, of all mysteries is that where there is blood shed on the altar, but the idol and the victim are the same.

A King means a Nation: an Empire means the absence of a Nation. The ruler of Austria-Hungary has to be an Emperor; what else can he be? There is no solid and fighting people that sees in him their mere instrument and certain flag. He cannot be a father to one people; he is forced to be a grandfather to a great many. The French never called themselves an Empire until that brief interval when they really were an Empire—that is, when a military man was temporarily trying to rule a European chaos. The English never called themselves an Empire at all. That seems to me the grandest of all the grand facts of our history. Our cognisance has always been the lion and not the eagle. Nor are these two heraldic animals a mere irrelevant fancy. Admittedly, they are both noble and dominant creatures. But the imperial eagle, who is the smaller, sees vaster landscapes from on high. The lion is larger, but he walks in his own ground.

When Disraeli offered to Queen Victoria the title of Empress of India the thing was perilous, but perfectly reasonable. Queen Victoria was Empress of India, because India is not (or, at least, was not then) a nation. She did stand towards the tumultuous races and tossing creeds of that continent as the Roman Emperors stood to the dim tribes and dynasties of Germania and Gaul. In plain common-sense, I think, a settled Government has a right to hold down rebellious nations, at least until somebody is ready to inform it which nation is rebelling. But it is really High Treason to say that the English Crown is as insecure in England as it is in India; and it is only the insecure crown that is called an Imperial Crown. Disraeli's innovation was, of course, bound to bring certain perversions and impossibilities in its train: he himself had a nation, but it was not the English nation, nor, indeed, any nation with a territory and a flag. He had it, however, and was very honourably proud of it. In fact, he was one of those fortunate people who are actually named after their own nation; I cannot at the moment think of any other example— except the estimable Mr. England[5] (who was a pirate) and M. Anatole France; and he, I fancy, has really quite a different name. But if the great Jew who led the English Tories understood patriotism (as I do not doubt that he did) it must have been a decidedly special and peculiar kind of patriotism; and it necessarily laid him open to this mistake about the relative positions of the terms Emperor and King. To him no doubt Emperor seemed obviously a higher title; just as Brother of the Sun and

[5] Jasper Seager, a pirate who went by the name "Edward England" "on account of his country". He was one of Blackbeard's mentors.

Moon would have seemed to him a higher title than Second Cousin of the Evening Star. Among Orientals all such titles are towering and hyperbolical; and the only possible question is which title towers the highest and which tells the largest lie. But of kingship as it has been felt among Christian men he had no notion, and small blame to him. He did not understand the domestic, popular, and priestly quality in the thing; the idea expressed in the odd old phrase of being the breath of his people's nostrils; the mystical life pumped through the lungs and framework of the State. You cannot have a King or a Republic until you have a People; both are creative and collective things. A Monarchy turns a million men into one man who can be seen. A Republic turns a million men into one woman who cannot be seen. Both require faith and a power of fashioning a fixed thing and fighting for it. But an Empire merely makes an authority from nowhere attempting to master an anarchy from everywhere. And if ever we call our King an Emperor, we shall be publicly admitting that we are only a chaos, and have no country of our own.

September 10, 1910

The Intrusions of Officialdom

Whether one is a Socialist or not, one may well admit that Socialism (like most schemes propounded by people not startlingly above or below mankind) promises some advantages and involves some risks. The strictest Socialist will agree that one pays something for Socialism, just as the firmest Churchman will agree that one pays something to keep up the Church; just as the Navy League would agree that we pay something, and even a great deal, to keep up the Navy. So much for self-evident truisms, of which I am very fond.

Now comes a very queer thing. It is happening everywhere, and is, in the most amazing way, unnoticed. Suppose we all paid tithes with the utmost rigour, and not one stone of a church, not the faintest vestige of an ecclesiastical building, could be found in the length and breadth of England, I think we should open our eyes. Suppose we were crushed by colossal taxation for the Navy, while at the same time there was not the tiniest British boat anywhere on all the seas of the world, I think there are discontented spirits among us who would remark upon the fact. Yet this is actually the situation with regard to Socialism. To Socialism, as to any other bargain, there is a good side and a bad side. The good side we may or may not get ultimately and enjoy; but the bad side we have got already. It is useless for the few remaining followers of Herbert Spencer to discuss whether the English, in entering Socialism, will sell themselves into slavery. They are already in the slavery: but they have not sold themselves into it. For they have not got any money for it, nor even the promise of any. It is vain for Individualist orators to adjure the people not to lose their birthright for a mess of pottage. Their birthright is lost; it is the mess of pottage that cannot be found. It is almost the only kind of mess that we have not managed to produce.

That this startling state of affairs is strictly true I will prove from any poor street in any town you like to name. It is not the question whether Socialism will do us harm. Socialism has already done us nearly all the harm it could do. It is only the good that it is prevented from doing. We have permitted it to fulfil all the threats and gloomy prophecies of its foes; we have only forbidden it to fulfil any one of the kindlier promises of its friends. Obviously, the advantage of Socialism would be that, if the State were supreme everywhere, it could see that everybody had enough money and comfort. Equally obviously the disadvantage of Socialism would be that if the State were supreme everywhere, it might easily become a tyrant, as it has been again and again.

To pack the whole matter as solidly as possible, officials could certainly go round and feed the whole people with bread. But it has often been found that in practice they feed the people with insults.

The incredible state of our country just now can be put in one sentence. The officials are already going round distributing the insults; they are not yet distributing even the promise of the bread. If you doubt my meaning or my statement, I advise you to knock at one front door after another all the way down a poor street and ask. You will not ask as the official asks, because you are a gentleman. But you will soon discover that the official has been there before you; and you will learn generally what happens. The son of a widow, a needlewoman, let us say, is sent by a strict law to a special school. It is there discovered that he cannot see the blackboard very plainly. A doctor descends upon the widow, and tells her to take her son to some remote hospital to be examined. She does so (being the meek and broken subject of an already Socialistic State) and most probably she finds she cannot be attended to. She has to travel to the remote hospital again, and perhaps again, spending sums on trams and trains which correspond to a £5 note for you and me. Eventually her son's eyes are examined. That happy youth is told that he ought to have a particular pair of spectacles, one glass slightly differing from the other; the exact amount of convexity in the lens or of astigmatism in the eyes is stated on a scientific document; and there is an end of the matter. There, I repeat heavily and literally, is the entire end of the matter. The poor woman has got everything out of the Government in the way of command and coercion that she could possibly get under the most despotic system. Her child has been forcibly taken from her, forcibly sent to school, forcibly sent to strain his eyes, forcibly overhauled about his eyes, trailed ceaselessly on a tram, hurled ceaselessly into a hospital. In short, he has got everything that is absolute out of the Government—except the spectacles. He has the rapture of regarding a precise definition on paper of the sort of glasses he ought to have; glasses that his mother is no more capable of buying than she is of buying champagne or diamond shirt-links. If she wants the simplest medical apparatus she must fall back upon one of the most elaborate and fantastic of all the forms of individual charity. The schoolmaster and the doctor have already taken away the woman's liberty of action as much as if she were a slave. The only thing they have not given her is the means of carrying out their commands. In short, the official and semi-official inquisitors who perpetually pass up and down our poor streets are Socialists with none of the advantages of Socialism; they actually excuse themselves for giving the largest orders with the fact that they do not give the smallest fragment of the money. Upon them has descended at last that taunt of almost incredible tyranny stored up for some ten thousand years; here, at last, we have again the rulers who really command men to make bricks without straw.

I have taken this one case of medical examination among the poor because it happened to come my way; but the thing is being done everywhere, in every shape, and in every department. Officials come round and leave little cards about the hygienic way in which to give children food. They leave the cards: they do not leave the food. Lady scientists come round with bright little essays about milk; they do not come round with the milk. Poor children are told in laundry classes to pass a garment through three waters, but nobody gives them so much as one water. Children are told in cookery classes to pass the viand from a saucepan to a stew-pan; but nobody offers to lend them even the saucepan. If there is any notion extant of an individual citizen's rights in his own house and human family, if there abides any legend of the human chanticleer crowing in his own farm-yard—that song has already ceased. Government has already made the ordinary man pipe another tune: only Government has not paid the piper. The officials have already *gained* the right to order the poor man about like dirt. Only they have not yet earned the right. They have not even attempted to earn it, by making him one halfpenny less poor.

It is said that Britain was once called the Island of Saints, and

I think its inhabitants must really be marked by a saintly meekness and a saintly unworldliness. The Jingo poets describe us always as a masculine and masterful people, striding across territory and subduing tribes to our will. But I can only explain the actual facts on the theory that the English are a tender and almost timorous people, who alone of all men will submit to the last and wildest pests of the tyrant. The abject populace in the decline of Rome had to be pacified with bread and circuses. But the modern English populace can actually be pacified with circulars instead of circuses. With circulars—and no bread.

Whether we call this thing that seems to be coming on us by the name of Socialism or the more disputable name of slavery, one thing about it appears to be quite clear. If we are going to subject the poor to the sterner side of Socialism first, we must let them see the more comfortable side of Socialism some time soon. Or (to put the matter the other way) since we are already ruling them like slaves, we must at least begin to think about feeding them like slaves. Kicks and carrots, it is said, are the two ways with a donkey: and I am far from denying that the English democracy is a donkey. But I certainly think it hard that he should now be having all the officials kicks without the faintest suggestion of the official carrots. Of my own opinion I do not speak. My own opinion is that it is the educated people who want ordering about, if anybody wants it. I confine myself to the urgent clinching of this truism. We might conceivably leave the poor free to die like the flies in winter. The idea is horrible and heathen; but, after all, most modern thinkers are heathen, and a good many of their are horrible. The rigid line of logic still remains. If we imprison folk we must feed them. If we may send the menu to them, they may send the bill to us.

September 17, 1910

The Philosophy of William James

No one who met the late Professor William James even for a moment will fail to find some note of mourning for him of a personal as well as a public kind. He was full of those particular fine qualities that most people do actually find in Americans, though most people are surprised to find them. He was full of enthusiasm, of generous appreciation, of spirituality and simplicity. There are no men less prone than Americans to a mere materialism; indeed, their fault is quite the other way. In so far as America has really worshipped money, it has not been because money is tangible. Rather it has been because money is intangible; and Americans cultivate it always in its least tangible form— in the form of shares, trusts, promises, implicit understandings, and illegal powers. They worship the invisible strength of money; they adore it as a sort of airy magic; no men on the earth think less of the actual pleasures that it stands for. The Yankee millionaire likes adding more noughts on to a figure in his private books; it is a spiritual pride with him. Nothing can make him see that, in adding noughts, he is truly and indeed adding nothings. Thus, even when the American is avaricious, the American is not greedy. And when he is the reverse of avaricious, when he is, like Professor James, naturally magnanimous and idealistic, he is capable of being the most childishly unworldly and even saintly of all the white men of this world. William James was really a turning-point in the history of our time, and he had all that sincerity and intellectual innocence that is needed in such a pivot. For a turning-point, like any other point, must be simple and indivisible.

Like Bernard Shaw and others among the intelligences of our unrestful age, William James will probably be counted valuable rather for a revolution in the mode of teaching than for any of the actual things he taught. Of course, he himself cared more for his dogmas than for his art of exposition, because he was a capable and healthy man. One cannot teach a truth clearly if one is actually thinking about the teaching and not about the truth. There, as elsewhere, the pure theory of art for art's sake must be abandoned; it is only because Rembrandt really tried to embody the old woman that the old woman has managed to embody Rembrandt. But whatever they were for James himself, James's doctrines are scarcely of so much value to the world as his spirited and satisfying style and temper. What Mr. Bernard Shaw did for the discussion of economics and politics Professor James did for the discussion of psychology and metaphysics. He forced them to join the undignified dance of common-sense; he insisted that the philosopher should have modesty enough to make a fool of himself, like the rest of mankind. Everyone is some sort of psychologist, since everyone has some sort of psychology. Just as real religion concerns everyone born with a heart, so real philosophy concerns everyone born with a head. According to Professor James, psychology was a kind of surgery in which each man must be content to be both the operator and the patient; every man must dig up his own soul like his own garden. But it was above all in his eyes a solid study. Economics is not really the study of tables and statistics which are more remote than money; it is the study of bread, which is more actual than money. So in the highest philosophy only the actual is important, and a truth is more of a fact than a phenomenon.

This practical plea of James for popularising philosophy is his finest achievement. It is always supposed that metaphysics must be full of technical and elaborate terms. Some would even argue that the word metaphysics itself is not one to be used playfully in the nearest pot-house. But, for all that, the ultimate study of thought and of the mind ought to be the simplest of all studies; not, I mean, simple in its task, but perfectly simple in its language. If we say something of universal scope we can obviously say it as easily of a plain or comic thing as of any other thing. Technical terms belong to the study of special physical facts— birds or beasts, or stars or stones, or weather. If somebody (with a turn for original observations) remarks that one swallow does not make a summer, that is a matter depending on special study of such seasons and birds. There are some seventeen swallows in the neighbourhood of my house, and some gloomy persons are of opinion that seventeen swallows have not succeeded in making a summer.

But merely the truth, whatever it is, is one only applicable to the particular bird and season. It could throw no light, for example, upon the fascinating problem of whether one Polar bear would make a winter. Natural History must be unnatural to the extent of using scientific and almost secret terms. So if the scientists choose to call the swallow *hirundo vulgaris*[1] (or whatever they do call it) and if they choose to call making a summer "aestivation," I think they are cheeky, but within their rights. But I object to their using this mysterious language when they are not talking about whether one swallow makes a summer, but only about whether one swallow makes two swallows. Abstract truths like logic and mathematics can obviously be illustrated as well by common examples as by abstruse ones. And I object to the man who gives the Latin name for the most recently discovered bean-plant when he is only engaged in proving how many beans make five. If two sides of a triangle are always greater than the third side (and all this I steadfastly believe) it can be proved from three-cornered hats or three-cornered tarts. I object to that fastidious mathematician who refuses to prove it except from the two secret triangles of the pentacle.

When full allowance has been made for his healthy and human reversal of the tone and methods of philosophy, it will appear even more regrettable that the actual system (or denial of system) with which Professor James later associated his name, was of the insufficient sort that it was. It was his glory that he popularised philosophy. It was his destruction that he popularised his own philosophy. "Pragmatism is bosh," said a man of unphilosophic training but good general brains to me the other day. Professor James appealed to the ordinary man; and the ordinary

---

[1] The more frequently used term is *hirundo rusticae*.

man condemned him. But let us remember that while this exhibits the rightness of the condemnation, it also exhibits the rightness of the appeal. Pragmatism *is* bosh; but the best test of this is the test of the great Pragmatist himself; the appeal to the nature and reason of the ordinary man. Pragmatism substantially means that the sun being useful is the same thing as the sun being there. The ordinary man in London in this present romantic summer would immediately reply that there is a considerable difference between the two ideas; that the sun is frequently not there when he would be particularly useful. The ordinary man in Arabia would probably add that he is often there when he is quite the reverse of useful. And it is not sufficient for the Pragmatist to reply that these are cheap and illiterate answers: they are. But the whole point of Pragmatism (at least, of Professor James's Pragmatism, of Pragmatism at its best) is that it asks how ordinary people do actually use and feel ideas. Now ordinary people do actually feel the notion of truth and the notion of utility as utterly separate. The highest official figure[2] of modern Europe happens to be a man of peasant origin; and his view of Pragmatism (other issues apart) would be echoed by all the peasants of the earth.

September 24, 1910
History and the Theatre

It is reported that at the sumptuous performance of "Henry VIII." now proceeding under the management of Sir Herbert Tree, the urns and goblets of the banquet are specially wrought

---

[2] Probably Pope Pius X, who was born of humble parents in Rieti, Italy.

in real and solid silver and in the style of the 16th century. This bombastic literalism is at least very much the fashion in our modern theatricals. Mr. Vincent Crummles[1] considered it a splendid piece of thoroughness on the part of an actor that he should black himself all over to perform Othello. But Mr. Crummles's ideal falls far short of the theoretic thoroughness of Sir Herbert Tree; who would consider blacking oneself all over as comparatively a mere sham, compromise, and veneer. Sir Herbert Tree would, I suppose, send for a real negro to act Othello; and perhaps for a real Jew to act Shylock—though that, in the present condition of the English stage, might possibly be easier. The strict principle of the silver goblets might be a little more arduous and unpleasant if applied, let us say, to "The Arabian Nights," if the manager of His Majesty's Theatre presented "Aladdin," and had to produce not one real negro but a hundred real negroes, carrying a hundred baskets of gigantic and genuine jewels. In the presence of this proposal even Sir Herbert might fall back on a simpler philosophy of the drama. For the principle in itself admits of no limit. If once it be allowed that what looks like silver behind the footlights is better also for really being silver, there seems no reason why the wildest developments should not ensue. The priests in "Henry VIII." might be specially ordained in the green-room before they come on. Nay, if it comes to that, the head of Buckingham might really be cut off; as in the glad old days lamented by Swinburne, before the coming of an emasculate mysticism removed real death from the arena. We might re-establish the goriness as well as the gorgeousness of the amphitheatre. If real wine-cups, why not real wine? If real wine, why not real blood?

Nor is this an illegitimate or irrelevant deduction. This and a hundred other fantasies might follow if once we admit the first principle that we need to realise on the stage not merely the beauty of silver, but the value of silver. Shakespeare's famous phrase that art should hold the mirror up to nature is always

[1] See January 16, 1909, footnote 1.

taken as wholly realistic; but it is really idealistic and symbolic—at least, compared with the realism of His Majesty's. Art is a mirror not because it is the same as the object, but because it is different. A mirror selects as much as art selects; it gives the light of flames, but not their heat; the colour of flowers, but not their fragrance; the faces of women, but not their voices; the proportions of stockbrokers, but not their solidity. A mirror is a vision of things, not a working model of them. And the silver seen in a mirror is not for sale.

But the results of the thing in practice are worse than its wildest results in theory. This Arabian extravagance in the furniture and decoration of a play has one very practical disadvantage—that it narrows the number of experiments, confines them to a small and wealthy class, and makes those which are made exceptional, erratic, and unrepresentative of any general dramatic activity. One or two insanely expensive works prove nothing about the general state of art in a country. To take the parallel of a performance somewhat less dignified, perhaps, than Sir Herbert Tree's, there has lately been in America an exhibition not unanalogous to a conflict in the arena, and one for which a real negro actually was procured by the management. The negro happened to beat the white man, and both before and after this event people went about wildly talking of "the White Man's champion" and "the representative of the Black Race." All black men were supposed to have triumphed over all white men in a sort of mysterious Armageddon because one specialist met another specialist and tapped his claret or punched him in the bread-basket.

Now the fact is, of course, that these two prize-fighters were so specially picked and trained—the business of producing such men is so elaborate, artificial, and expensive—that the result proves nothing whatever about the general condition of white men or black. If you go in for heroes or monsters it is obvious that they may be born anywhere. If you took the two tallest men on earth, one might be born in Corea and the other in Camberwell, but this would not make Camberwell a land of giants inheriting the blood of Anak. If you took the two thinnest men in the world, one might be a Parisian and the other a Red Indian. And if you take the two most scientifically developed pugilists, it is not surprising that one of them should happen to be white and the other black. Experiments of so special and profuse a kind have the character of monstrosities, like black tulips or blue roses. It is absurd to make them representative of races and causes that they do not represent. You might as well say that the Bearded Lady at a fair represents the masculine advance of modern woman; or that all Europe was shaking under the banded armies of Asia, because of the co-operation of the Siamese Twins.

So the plutocratic tendency of such performances as "Henry VIII." is to prevent rather than to embody any movement of historical or theatrical imagination. If the standard of expenditure is set so high by custom, the number of competitors must necessarily be small, and will probably be of a restricted and unsatisfactory type. Instead of English history and English literature being as cheap as silver paper, they will be as dear as silver plate. The national culture, instead of being spread out everywhere like gold leaf, will be hardened into a few costly lumps of gold—and kept in very few pockets. The modern world is full of things that are theoretically open and popular, but practically private and even corrupt. In theory any tinker can be chosen to speak for his fellow-citizens among the English Commons. In practice he may have to spend a thousand pounds on getting elected—a sum which many tinkers do not happen to have to spare. In theory it ought to be possible for any moderately successful actor with a sincere and interesting conception of Wolsey to put that conception on the stage. In practice it looks as if he would have to ask himself, not whether he was as clever as Wolsey, but whether he was as rich. He has to reflect, not whether he can enter into Wolsey's soul, but whether he can pay Wolsey's servants, purchase Wolsey's plate, and own Wolsey's palaces.

Now people with Wolsey's money and people with Wolsey's mind are both rare; and even with him the mind came before the money. The chance of their being combined a second time is manifestly small and decreasing. The result will obviously be that thousands and millions may be spent on a theatrical misfit, and inappropriate and unconvincing impersonation; and all the time there may be a man outside who could have put on a red dressing-gown and made us feel in the presence of the most terrible of the Tudor statesmen. The modern method is to sell Shakespeare for thirty pieces of silver.

October 1, 1910

Patriotism and National Self-Criticism

The right and proper thing, of course, is that every good patriot should stop at home and curse his own country. So long as that is being done everywhere, we may be sure that things are fairly happy, and being kept up to a reasonably high standard. So long as we are discontented separately we may be well content as a whole. Each man is cultivating his garden; and you cannot cultivate a garden without digging it up or without stamping it down. And these gardens of the children of men are so strange and so different that each man is probably alone in knowing even which are the flowers and which the weeds. But so long as grunts, snorts, curses, and cries of despair come over every garden wall we may be pretty certain that things are all right, that the flowers will arise in splendour and the wilderness blossom like the rose. So long as good Americans go on railing at their anarchy and graft, so long as good Englishmen curse our snobbery and squirearchy, so long as there are Germans to murmur at officialism and Scotchmen to make game of theology, so long as Irishmen insist that they are conquered, and Frenchmen are quite sure they are betrayed—so long as this genial and encouraging groan goes up from all Europe, so long we may feel certain that Christendom is going forward with her mighty cohorts triumphant on her eternal way.

But this wholesome habit of grumbling by one's own fireside has been crossed by customs considerably more perilous and responsible. The commonest trick, of course, is to lash one's self into a kind of cold and abstract rage about somebody else's business that one very imperfectly understands, to demand of heaven and the High Court of Parliament how long the poor women of Japan are to black their teeth or the police of Russia to black their newspapers, without in the least knowing how it feels to a Jap or a Russian, or whether the thing, in its own environment, seems as natural as blacking one's boots or as comic as blacking one's face. Nevertheless, these criticisms of foreign countries, although commonly wild and impertinent, are not the worst forms of international interference, and may sometimes even do good. The Russian censor's ink may not be so black as it is painted; still, the general tendency of such officials is towards obscurantism and oppression, and a foreign protest, even if ignorant, may work on the side of the internal freedom of that country. Again, if it be wrong to look a gift horse in the mouth, it is yet more ill-mannered so to examine an Oriental lady who has dressed and painted herself, not for your taste, but for that of Oriental gentlemen. Still, it would be safe to hazard that Oriental ladies are, on the whole, too much controlled by the conventions of the harem rather than too little; so that there again it may be argued that criticism from outside may encourage reform within. I am no admirer of the popular preacher or idealistic publicist on a platform who rises to a whirlwind of seraphic scorn and self-satisfaction because he himself (as it happens) has never cut up an Armenian with a scimitar or boiled a missionary in a pot. But if there is a Turk somewhere who cuts up Armenians in a light, absent-minded kind of way, not seeing any harm in it, I think he might be told that it is "not done." If there are any cannibals who conduct their cuisine in ignorance of the fact that there is a feeling against it in more fastidious tribes, then I think they should be told of this foreign disapproval. And I can imagine that even if the European critic made mistakes (as no doubt he would) about the details of anthropophagy, the criticism might still convey the required rebuke from outside. Even if the critic described as baked a bishop whom every child remembered vividly as boiled, even if he referred to curates when they were not in season, I still think that the sincere horror of the European's tone might shake the Cannibal Islanders in this, their mere insularity of taste.

But another kind of international criticism has arisen which is more mischievous than the most ignorant of these denunciations. And that is the habit not of wildly and ignorantly blaming, but wildly and ignorantly praising, another nation. This, I say, is worse: because it hinders the real patriots of that nation in their attempt to cure its real abuses. No one but a patriot can know the worst about his people. No one but an American citizen can understand the real incubus of Mr. Rockefeller: a gigantesque nightmare. We can catch glimpses of the vision, but it must always be different from our own. No one but an Englishman, again, can understand how helpless and how omnipotent are the English aristocrats: how the English aristocrats have lost faith in everything, even in aristocracy: and how yet they fill all the seats and avenues, a crowd that cannot be cleared by the police. No one but a Frenchman has any right to rebuke French brutality: the other nations are not brutal (or virile) enough to understand it. No one but a German has any business to balance the beautiful dreaminess against the practical obedience of his people, or to guess which will win.

And this reminds me that I have before me a flaring instance of the ill-luck of such international admirations. It is a document that takes no account of such obviously perplexing elements as French brutality and German dreaminess; it proceeds on the simple principle of French badness and German goodness. Frenchmen, it says, are feminine. They have a horror of severe methods, which is doubtless why they have to be rebuked for crowding round the guillotine. They are hysterical, which must be the reason of the steady toil and greed and wealth of their peasants. Germans, on the other hand, are masculine. Germans are simple: this can be noted in the German artistic books and book-covers, in the hundred Aubrey Beardsleys to our one that sprawl on every German decorative page. Germans are silent, like the Kaiser.

I am sorry that I have no larger space left to deal with this outburst, an article called "The Psychology of the Conqueror," by an Englishwoman in Germany. It reminds me of "Ouida"[1] at her worst and the penny novelettes at their best. The English-woman prostrates herself before the beautiful big boots of the Prussian soldier in a riot of sentimentalism. Like other female writers on the Viking Breed, she gets a little mixed. She says she has noticed a trait which may be called the psychology of the conqueror; which is as if I said that I had noticed a cabbage which was the Botany of the Brussels Sprout. She also calls it the knowledge of the power of force—a very recondite discovery like that of the potency of the energy of the might of violence. Also her perfect German is praised in a somewhat confused manner, being first described as a strenuous conqueror, and then as a very meek dog on a chain who is much too frightened to bark too loudly or to frolic too blithely. The Government, it seems, fills all Germans with awe; and there are (so far as I understand the argument) no robberies or swindles of any sort in Germany. The one most firmly embedded in my memory

---

[1] The pseudonym of Maria Louise de la Ramée (1839–1908), a prolific writer of romantic novels of high society. She was an unconventional and eccentric character.

[2] In 1906, there occurred an incident which amused the world. An ordinary jailbird named William Voigt dressed himself in a Prussian military uniform bought in a second-hand shop; he commanded several soldiers to follow him, and marched them into Koepenick to arrest several government officials; he then got everybody on a train to Berlin, where he presented his prisoners to even higher functionaries, who only very gradually uncovered his real identity. He was tried and went to jail for a brief time, but he had proved, as even the Germans admitted, that in Germany "they will all lie on their bellies before a uniform."

was the swindle of the bogus Captain Koepenick.[2] That certainly illustrated German submissiveness, but scarcely, I think, German efficiency.

Evidently, however, it has not crossed the lady's mind that Prussian discipline may, perhaps, arise not from the fierceness of the people, but rather from their tameness. As a matter of fact, the Germans have not conquered very much in history as a whole. About fifty years ago they beat the French, and about fifty years before that the French very soundly beat them. We are simply blinded by one accident of chronology if we let the Prussians' capturing Paris make us forget that the Parisians have captured at some time nearly every town in Europe. If we set history as a whole, there is no more doubt that the French people are the more military than there is that the German people are the more musical. But if you ask why it is worth while to answer such pro-Teuton servilities, the truth is exactly here: Germany is a great and splendid nation; there are millions of sensible German patriots grappling with the sins and follies which are part of her problem. And just when they are doing their best, this insane idolatry from the foreigner comes in, upsets all the German wise men, and comes to the rescue of the German fool.

October 8, 1910

History and Inspiration

We most of us suffer much from having learnt all our lessons in history from those little abridged history-books in use in most public and private schools. These lessons are insufficient—especially when you don't learn them. The latter was indeed my own case; and the little history I know I have picked up since by rambling about in authentic books and countrysides. But the bald summaries of the small history-books still master and, in many cases, mislead us. The root of the difficulty is this: that there are two quite distinct purposes of history; the superior purpose, which is its use for children; and the secondary or inferior purpose, which is its use for historians. The highest and noblest thing that history can be is a good story. Then it appeals to the heroic heart of all generations, the eternal infancy of mankind. Such a story as that of William Tell could literally be told of any epoch; no barbarian implements could be too rude, no scientific instruments could be too elaborate for the pride and terror of the tale. It might be told of the first flint-headed arrow or the last model machine-gun; the point of it is the same: it is as eternal as tyranny and fatherhood. Now, wherever there is this function of the fine story in history we tell it to children only because it is a fine story. David and the cup of water, Regulus and the *atque sciebat*,[1] Jeanne d'Arc kissing the cross of spear-wood, or Nelson shot with all his stars—these stir in every child the ancient heart of his race; and that is all that they need do. Changes of costume and local colour are nothing: it did not matter that in the illustrated Bibles of our youth David was dressed rather like Regulus, in a Roman cuirass and sandals, any more than it mattered that in the illuminated Bibles of the Middle Ages he was dressed rather like Jeanne d'Arc, in a hood or a visored helmet. It will not matter to future ages if the pictures represent Jeanne d'Arc cremated in an asbestos stove or Nelson dying in a top-hat. For the childish and eternal use of history, the history will still be heroic.

But the historians have quite a different business. It is their affair, not merely to remember that humanity has been wise and great, but to understand the special ways in which it has been

[1] A reference to the story told in Horace (*Ode*, Book III). Regulus was a Roman general captured by the Carthaginians in the Punic Wars; under free passage—that is, with the understanding that he would return—he was sent to Rome to plead for a peace treaty; instead, he urged the Senate to carry on the war until Carthage was utterly destroyed. As a man of honor, he then returned to Carthage: "atque sciebat quae barbarus tortor pararet. . ." ("Full well he knew what the barbarian torturer was making ready for him. . . .")

weak and foolish. Historians have to explain the horrible mystery of how fashions were ever fashionable. They have to analyse that statuesque instinct of the South that moulds the Roman cuirass to the muscles of the human torso, or that element of symbolic extravagance in the later Middle Ages which let loose a menagerie upon breast and casque and shield. They have to explain, as best they can, how anyone ever came to have a top-hat, how anyone ever endured an asbestos stove.

Now the mere tales of the heroes are a part of religious education; they are meant to teach us that we have souls. But the inquiries of the historians into the eccentricities of every epoch are merely a part of political education; they are meant to teach us to avoid certain perils or solve certain problems in the complexity of practical affairs. It is the first duty of a boy to admire the glory of Trafalgar. It is the first duty of a grown man to question its utility. It is one question whether it was a good thing as an episode in the struggle between Pitt and the French Revolution. It is quite another matter that it was certainly a good thing in that immortal struggle between the son of man and all the unclean spirits of sloth and cowardice and despair. For the wisdom of man alters with every age; his prudence has to fit perpetually shifting shapes of inconvenience or dilemma. But his folly is immortal: a fire stolen from heaven.

Now, the little histories that we learnt as children were partly meant simply as inspiring stories. They largely consisted of tales like Alfred and the cakes or Eleanor and the poisoned wound. They ought to have entirely consisted of them. Little children ought to learn nothing but legends; they are the beginnings of all sound morals and manners. I would not be severe on the point: I would not exclude a story solely because it was true. But the essential on which I should insist would be, not that the tale must be true, but that the tale must be fine.

The attempts in the little school-histories to introduce older and subtler elements, to talk of the atmosphere of Puritanism or the evolution of our Constitution, is quite irrelevant and vain. It is impossible to convey to a barely breeched imp who does not yet know his own community, the exquisite divergence between it and some other community. What is the good of talking about the constitution carefully balanced on three estates to a creature only quite recently balanced on two legs? What is the sense of explaining the Puritan shade of morality to a creature who is still learning with difficulty that there is any morality at all? We may put on one side the possibility that some of us may think the Puritan atmosphere an unpleasant one or the constitution a trifle ricketty on its three legs. The general truth remains that we should teach, to the young, men's enduring truths, and let the learned amuse themselves with their passing errors.

It is often said nowadays that in great crises and moral revolutions we need one strong man to decide; but it seems to me that that is exactly when we do not need him. We do not need a great man for a revolution, for a true revolution is a time when all men are great. Where despotism really is successful is in very small matters. Everyone must have noticed how essential a despot is to arranging the things in which everyone is doubtful, because everyone is indifferent: the boats in a water picnic or the seats at a dinner-party. Here the man who knows his own mind is really wanted, for no one else ever thinks his own mind worth knowing. No one knows where to go to precisely, because no one cares where he goes. It is for trivialities that the great tyrant is meant.

But when the depths are stirred in a society, and all men's souls grow taller in a transfiguring anger or desire, then I am by no means so certain that the great man has been a benefit even when he has appeared. I am sure that Cromwell and Napoleon managed the mere pikes and bayonets, boots and knapsacks better than most other people could have managed them. But I am by no means sure that Napoleon gave a better turn to the whole French Revolution. I am by no means so sure that Cromwell has really improved the religion of England.

As it is in politics with the specially potent man, so it is in history with the specially learned. We do not need the learned man to teach us the important things. We all know the important

things, though we all violate and neglect them. Gigantic industry, abysmal knowledge, are needed for the discovery of the tiny
things—the things that seem hardly worth the trouble. Generally
speaking, the ordinary man should be content with the terrible
secret that men are men—which is another way of saying that
they are brothers. He had better think of Caesar as a man and
not as a Roman, for he will probably think of a Roman as a
statue and not as a man. He had better think of Coeur-de-Lion
as a man and not as a Crusader or he will think of him as a stage
Crusader. For every man knows the inmost core of every other
man. It is the trappings and externals erected for an age and a
fashion that are forgotten and unknown. It is all the curtains that
are curtained, all the masks that are masked, all the disguises
that are now disguised in dust and featureless decay. But though
we cannot reach the outside of history, we all start from the
inside. Some day, if I ransack whole libraries, I may know the
outermost aspects of King Stephen, and almost see him in his
habit as he lived; but the inmost I know already. The symbols
are mouldered and the manner of the oath forgotten; the secret
society may even be dissolved; but we all know the secret.

October 15, 1910

Rebellion and Dogma in France

There is, I have been told, in the middle of the territory of Italy
a small republic which is as independent as Monaco. And the
joke of it is, apparently, that this small republic is still at war
with Austria, not having been among the Italian States that ultimately made a treaty with that Empire. Austria, however, remains
calm. It is not much use to be at war with Austria if you cannot
get at Austria; and this bellicose commonwealth is surrounded

on all sides with neutral territory, which it must not cross. Rutland, for all I know, may be burning with a desire to invade Russia; but it cannot do so without the permission of larger and more fainthearted counties all round it. I wonder whether this Italian republic preserves its militant attitude, whether the ordinary citizens walk about the streets armed to the teeth, whether bugles are blown or tocsins sounded at all available opportunities, while all around that self-isolated citadel spread the peaceful plains of modern Italy. I only know this, that if there were, indeed, such an armed city state in the midst of vast neutrality and quiet, it would bear a remarkable resemblance to the permanent condition of one of the great nations of Europe. What that little republic is in the solid bulk of Italy, that is France in the solid bulk of Europe. Other nations are at peace with France; but France is never at peace.

With this key two days in Paris will yield truth and entertainment; without it twenty years will leave an Englishman utterly at sea about the meaning of everything. He will be equally bewildered by French liberty and by French tyranny: unless he understands that they are the kinds of liberty and tyranny that occur at a crisis. Now Government will seem to strike as harshly as in Russia; now lawlessness will seem to rise as unrebuked as in Callao; and all the time everything is being discussed with radiant lucidity and rigid logic, as if it were a matter of mathematics. For in a revolution all men become theorists; because custom has broken down. There can never be a rebellion against dogma; for a return to dogma must always follow the destruction of routine.

Take, for the sake of argument, a few actual occurrences; and imagine them happening in England. Suppose I walked down Piccadilly whistling "Charlie is my darling" (a musical feat of which I am quite incapable), and suppose a friend tapped me on the shoulder and told me that I might really get into trouble with the police if I thus threatened Buckingham Palace with the claymores and tartans of the Highland hills. Yet something very nearly the same happened to a friend of mine only the other day in a French provincial town. He walked down a quiet street singing to himself an old Breton ballad called "Monsieur de Charette," of which the quaint words and the tune had taken his fancy. To him it was a mere matter of archaeology, like a Norse saga or a Provençal song; but his companion seriously warned him that trouble—not serious trouble, but tiresome suspicion and questioning at least—might follow him by official influence if he sang this musty old rhyme. For, as it dates from the war in La Vendée, it is often used as a Royalist signal or appeal. My friend felt as if he were convicted of treasonably helping Simon de Montfort for quoting "The Blind Beggar of Bethnal Green." But in France the Barons' War is still going on. In mere date the Stuarts did not disappear so very long before the Bourbons; there is not so vast difference in time between 1745 and 1793. The vast difference is in the temper of the two nations: that the return of the Stuarts is as legendary as the return of King Arthur; but the return of the Bourbons is as practical as passion can make it; as practical as the return of Protection in English politics. In one sense, of course, we may possibly doubt whether either Bourbons or Protection are very practical. But they are on the *tapis*; they are present to the public mind; and people can get the jumps about them. In other words, the psychology of Frenchmen is the psychology of civil war.

That will serve for an instance of the order that we should call tyranny. Take, with the same hypothetical change, an instance of the freedom that we might call licence. Suppose you went to Clacton-on-Sea (merely for the sake of argument, I assure you), and saw written up on an enormous placard, "Help for Biffins! Victim of the Vengeance of the Emperor of Clacton!" Knowing, with your clear-headed grip of the British Constitution, that there is no Emperor of Clacton, you would permit yourself a smile of indifference and suppose it was a practical joke or the poster of a pantomime. But in a bright, Cockney little seaside place on the Norman coast I found the walls aflame with posters denouncing the Mayor under the dreadful title of "Emperor," demanding if France was a Republic or no, and calling on everybody to rally round a particular commercial traveller, "Victime de la Vengeance de l'Empereur." To judge by these placards, the Mayor of this little watering-place must be one of the most remarkable men in Europe—a combination of Napoleon and Nero, Cromwell and Machiavelli. I also gather, from some remarks at the end of the proclamation, that he is by profession a brigand. This also would cause no little stir of interest in Clacton-on-Sea.

Now it is easy for us (who have such grossly contrary vices) to laugh at the French repression and the French licence as equally fantastic and exaggerative. It is easy to sneer at the French Government for being afraid of a Breton ballad, or at the French populace for pillorying a wild provincial Mayor. We do not sufficiently notice that our two sneers contradict each other. If French officials are frivolous in their repression, then French people are not frivolous in rising against that repression. If the people are unreasonable in their revolt against rulers, then the rulers are not unreasonable in anticipating and fearing such a revolt. The British Philistine really cannot have it both ways: he cannot pretend at once that foreign Governments are without excuse when they oppress, and also that foreign mobs are without excuse when they rise against oppression. But the real explanation is that in France the people and the Government, whenever they are opposed, deal stroke and counterstroke exactly as they do in a literal revolution. And the French speciality is this: that France does thus tend to divide itself into two active portions, like the two parties in a French duel. In England each group of convinced persons is attacking a huge unconvinced mass called the Public. A procession of Ritualists, with crosses and banners, passes down the street, tries to convert the Public, and probably fails. A procession of Mr. Kensit's Protestants, with Bibles and banners, passes down the same street and tries to convert the same Public: the Protestants are far more ritualistic than the Ritualists, and they fail even more completely. Nobody actually touches the solid block of English public opinion at all. But in France Mr. Kensit and the Ritualist curate would meet face to face in the street, and perhaps deluge it with blood; at any rate, no cloud of common indifference and doubt would come in between them. It would appear from history that this has always been so. The Massacre of St. Bartholomew was simply an ordinary Parisian riot, in which the Catholic populace killed the unpopular Protestant minority for being unpatriotic, just as in the French Revolution the same populace killed the aristocrats for being unpatriotic. The perpetrators were unscrupulous, but they were certainly enthusiastic; the nation was really divided into two religious armies. But, at the same time, in England we have exactly the modern phenomenon. We find rowdy minorities with religions vainly attacking a respectable majority with no religion. The Public stolidly supported Mary against Protestant rebels and Elizabeth against Catholic rebels. It was somewhere about that dreadful time that we began to have Respectability for a religion.

To all this there is only one important moral. Whatever else is fair, it is outrageously unfair to represent any party in France as if it were gratuitously attacking an inoffensive thing. There is no such thing in France as an inoffensive thing. The good things are, if anything, more offensive than the bad; I use the word offensive in its strict Latin sense. It is ridiculous, for instance, in the quarrel between the Republic and the Church, to talk as if the Republic were merely a colourless official Government. There are men in the Government as much vowed to root out Christianity from Western Europe as the Pope is vowed to maintain it. In this great nation everyone is logical, and therefore no one is impartial. We cannot judge it like a stolid and settled Government. We must wait for the end of the French Revolution: and that is a nuisance, for it will never end.

October 22, 1910

The Payment of Politicians

There is a nursery jingle existing, I believe, in many forms and describing the chief types or trades; the version of my own childhood ran: "Tinker, tailor, soldier, sailor, gentleman, apothecary, ploughboy, thief." It is not to be offered as a strictly exhaustive summary of the *quidquid agunt homines*,[1] omitting as it does all mention of astrologers, ostrich-farmers, organists, professional monstrosities, and other happy walks of life, nor is it, indeed, strictly logical in its categories, some of which may be supposed to overlap. Thus, a man might be a sailor and a thief, like Blackbeard or Captain Kidd; or a gentleman and an apothecary, like the father of Arthur Pendennis; or a gentleman and a tailor, like the Great Mell; or a gentleman and a thief, like many of the founders of our noble families. Even tinkers are only human, and have been known to disregard what Mr. Belloc calls the essentially mystical idea of property. Or, again, it has often happened that a tailor and a gentleman have finally parted company, mutually attributing to each other the last profession on the list. The ploughboy has been known to become a soldier, beating his ploughshare into a sword. It is said by some moralists that a man in any of these trades can be a gentleman, and there is no doubt at all that in any of them he can be a thief.

This crossed and confused calculation is very prevalent in more serious social things. We are divided horizontally into classes, vertically into parties and religions, transversely into tempera-

---

[1] The passage reads:

Quidquid agunt homines, votum, timor, ira, voluptas,
  Gaudia, discursus, nostri farrag libelli est.

  (All that men do—their wishes, fear, and rage,
  Pleasure, joy, bustle, crowd my motley page.)

This passage from Juvenal *Satire I* was the motto for the first forty numbers of the *Tatler* in 1709.

ments and incalculable types; and in this complexity we often have collisions in practice which cannot properly exist in reason: a war of Hebraists against humpbacks or a dispute between French Royalists and men with red hair. Sometimes these inconsequent quarrels sound like fantastic football matches, "Pantheists v. Brewers" or "Dukes v. Early Christians." For these are not an atom more illogical and absurd than many of the antitheses employed in practical politics. Thus "Unionist against Free Trader," which I saw the other day, is quite as senseless as "Baconian against Teetotaller"; it is quite as unmeaning as "Vivisectionist against Pre-Raphaelite." The terms refer to totally different points of difference. Or, again, "The alternative between Tariff Reform and Socialism" (which I also saw the other day) is as inane as the alternative between Bigamy and Sunday Closing, or the alternative between the Atomic Theory and the Channel Tunnel. There is not the slightest reason in rational philosophy why any Protectionist should not be a Socialist, or any Socialist a Protectionist. Some of the most eminent Socialists, like Mr. Blatchford, are Protectionists. Some of the most eminent Protectionists, like Lord Milner, are practically Socialists. And the worst example of this tangle of types and trades can, perhaps, be found in this problem of the Labour Members and their official payment which has split all our politics across.

Now, rationally speaking, it is obvious that an elective assembly ought to be elected on one principle or another, by areas or by trades or by creeds, but not by all of them mixed up. The representation should go by tinker, tailor, soldier, sailor, etc., or by Middlesex, Sussex, Essex, Wessex, etc.; but the House should not exhibit the absurd complication of a quarrel between a town and a trade, a duel between a profession and a valley. This difficulty really does inhere in those who call themselves Labour Members instead of calling themselves Socialists. A Duke may be a Socialist—in fact, he generally is. But a Duke cannot call himself a Labour Member without a certain element of charades at Christmas clinging about him in the action. Owing to economic inequality, Parliament is too prevalently genteel, just as the local magistracy is too prevalently genteel. But the modern world, instead of abolishing the gentility, has added to it a sort of shabby gentility; it has balanced one class narrowness with another class narrowness. Leaving untouched the mass of M.P.s who must be capitalists, it has merely added a few M.P.s who must be proletarians. Leaving four-fifths of the magistrates chosen because they are landlords, it merely adds two or three magistrates chosen because they are labourers—an equally ridiculous reason. The only two successive reasons that should make anyone a magistrate or a member are, first, that he is a man; and, second, that he is a suitable man. But the principle accepted at present is something like this: that because an aristocracy of dentists have gained too much power in the State we must instantly balance them with a new aristocracy of hairdressers. Only a few faint voices would join mine in suggesting that we might balance it by a democracy of men. Everyone argues and explains about the relations between the Liberal Party and the Labour Party. No one points out the evident truth that there can be no relations between a Liberal Party and a Labour Party; any more than there can be an argument between agnostics and auctioneers. There cannot be either antagonism or agreement between the fact that ten men have worked with their hands and the fact that ten other men have come to certain conclusions with their heads. They might actually be the same ten men. As a fact, most Labour men are Liberals; and many Liberals undergo labour. I am a Liberal, and I am undergoing labour of the most laborious description at this moment.

On just and public grounds, therefore, the self-evident remedy is payment of members. Do not pay a member because he is a millionaire; do not pay a member because he is a dustman. Pay a member because he is a member; because he has a particular work to do for Society. Do not reward him privily and meanly, as you do the tinker or the tailor, merely because he tinks or tails. Reward him publicly and chivalrously—as you reward the soldier or the sailor—because he serves the State. Probably, even after the change, the House will still largely include and collect aristocrats, for aristocrats have no conscientious objection to receiving public money, even in the smallest sums. But anyone who fancies that the money will be the main motive, either of the aristocrats or of the democrats, who are paid out of the public purse, does not know either the age he lives in or the country he belongs to, or democracy or aristocracy or any actual thing.

It is utterly childish to say that if we pay members the money-making politician will get in. The money-making politician has got in. It is the man who only wants his daily bread who cannot get in. For two hundred a year, for bread and beer and a bare lodging, you could get the services of an earnest, public-spirited, and honourably ambitious man. But you can get for nothing the services of a man basely ambitious and already precariously rich. For he is used to lending money on a risk; to buying an election this year in order to have a financial influence next year: he can borrow enough to make him a member on the chance of paying it back if he is a Minister. It is useless to discuss whether the adventurer will enter Parliament: the adventurer has entered it. That is, the financial adventurer has entered it—entered it with extraordinary ease under the existing financial arrangements. It is exactly the better sort of adventurer—the intellectual and sincere adventurer, the man who has ideas which he will not sell—who is kept out. The patriot would be content with mere pocket-money if he could get it. It is the pickpocket, the man who wants other people's pocket-money, who is always ready to pay a trifle to get into a crowd of rich people.

October 29, 1910

Respecting Other Peoples' Opinions

What precisely do people mean when they talk about "respecting other people's opinions"? I do not mean that they mean nothing; I really want to know what they mean. I understand respecting the other people; I understand what it means when it says in the Bible, "Honour all men." For men have certain capacities or functions which are noble in themselves, and cannot be wholly abdicated. Just as there is some importance attaching to Nero merely as an Emperor, so there is some importance attaching to Nero merely as a man. So I can imagine a Christian man, alone with one of our eminent financiers, perceiving traces of the human form in the financier and respecting that form, even in a moment of excitement. Or, again, we might hit a millionaire, or even kill him; but we must not chain him up in a kennel. It would insult mankind. I might vote for an eminent banker's execution, or even assist in his assassination; but I would not put him between the shafts of my hansom-cab, not only because the toil of pulling me would be excessive for the most agile banker, but far more because I should then be insulting him as a man and not as a tyrant or a usurer. I should be insulting myself as well as him. Thus I can understand any idea of toleration affecting the persons of men; I can more or less vaguely comprehend the statement that we should not burn anybody, not even a Theosophist, or that we should not disfranchise anybody, not even a Thug. But I cannot see how thoughts, as such, can have any of this human sanctity about them, or why I should respect an idea which I think a nasty idea merely because it has got into somebody's head. I think myself quite sufficiently humane if I resist the temptation to break his head open to find it.

In turning over an old pile of miscellaneous newspapers, I came upon two paragraphs which I should like to lay before those who hold this language. The first paragraph is itself an excellent summary of the language; the second may be called a corollary or case for application. The first paragraph ran thus—

> The Liberal movement in religion will specially insist that all religions are to be respected, that any form of honest belief or unbelief should be treated with reverence.

That sums up the conventional attitude quite neatly. The second paragraph was this—

A sad event has just been reported from the Solomon Islands, two Presbyterian ministers having been attacked, killed, and eaten. There has, it seems, been a revival of old religious customs throughout the Solomon group.

The incident is tragic, and my own controversial purpose is quite serious; but it is practically impossible not to smile faintly at this startling but quite exact use of the word "religion." There is certainly a horrible humour in the idea of the Solomon Islanders growing frivolous and sceptical and neglecting the quiet cannibalism of the dear old home. But just as they were thoughtlessly eating beef and mutton like heathens, a religious revival swept the islands. A sort of Oxford Movement, a wave of deeper Churchmanship (as they say at the Church Congress) passed through that community, and they went back to all the pious domesticities of their fathers. Doubtless the godly old folks received their repentant children; I will not say that they killed the fatted calf for them; but it cannot be doubted that the upholders of the old system were perfectly serious and convinced in thinking the revival a good one. It cannot be doubted that they respected their cannibal religion. But do we respect it? Or if we say we do respect it, what, precisely, do we mean by respect?

The answer now generally given is precisely the one I would contradict. We do not (at least, I do not) respect any sect, church, or group because of its sincerity. Sincerity merely means actuality. It only means that a man's opinion undoubtedly is his opinion. But if a man's opinion is that he ought to burn dogs alive, I do not respect him because he really feels like that; on the contrary, I should respect him more if I could believe that it was an elegant affectation. If a man holds that swindling everybody successfully is a mark of the Superman, I do not respect him any more because he holds it firmly; I should much prefer that he should hold it lightly. I do not think the more of a devil-worshipper because he truly loves devilry; nor the more of the torturing Nero because (like all second-rate artists) he takes his art seriously. Matthew Arnold used to talk a great deal about the "high seriousness" of the good poets. He ought to have taken more notice of the low seriousness which is the special mark of bad poets, of bad philosophers, and even of bad men. It is precisely when a man takes his casual human vice with this low seriousness that it masters him and drives him mad. He becomes at once pompous and furtive, and commonly ends in the evil pride of some perversion.

The true doctrine surely is this—that we respect the creeds held by others because there is some good in them, not because they are creeds and are held. In other words, an honest man must always respect other religions, because they contain parts of his religion—that is, of his largest vision of truth. I will respect Confucians for reverencing the aged, because my religion also includes reverence for the aged. I will respect Buddhists for being kind to animals, because my morality also involves being kind to animals. I will respect Mohammedans for admitting a general human justice, for I admit it also. But I will not admire Chinese tortures because they are performed with ardour; nor enjoy Hindoo pessimism because it is sincere, and therefore hopeless, pessimism; nor respect the Turk for despising women merely because he despises them very heartily. Thus we perpetually come back to that sharp and shining point which the modern world is perpetually trying to avoid. We must have a creed, even in order to be comprehensive. We must have a religion, even in order to respect other religions. Even if our whole desire is to admire the good in other worships, we must still worship something—or we shall not know what to admire.

Through all my own dreams, especially waking dreams, there run and caper and collide only four characters, who seem to sum up the four ultimate types of our existence. These four figures are: St. George and the Dragon, and the Princess offered to the Dragon, and the Princess's father, who was (if I remember right) the King of Egypt. You have everything in those figures: active virtue destroying evil; passive virtue enduring evil; ignorance or convention permitting evil; and Evil. In these four figures also can be found the real and sane limits of toleration. I admire St. George for being sincere in his wish to save the Princess's life, because it is an entirely good and healthy wish. I am ready to admire the Princess's wish to be eaten by the Dragon as part of her religious duties; for the Princess is generous, if a little perverse. I am even ready to admire the sincerity of the silly old potentate of Egypt who gave up his daughter to a dragon because it had always been done in his set. But there is a limit, the ultimate limit of the universe, and I refuse to admire the dragon because he regarded the Princess with a sincere enthusiasm, and honestly believed that she would do him good.

November 5, 1910

Faith Healing and Medicine

I have read recently, within a short period of each other, two books that stand in an odd relation, and illustrate the two ways of dealing with the same truth. The first was Mrs. Eddy's "Science and Health," and the other a very interesting collection of medical and ecclesiastical opinion called "Medicine and the Church." It is edited by Mr. Geoffrey Rhodes, and published by Kegan Paul. Of the first work, the Christian Science Bible, my recollections are somewhat wild and whirling. My most vivid impression is of one appalling passage to the effect that the continued perusal of this book through the crisis of an illness had always been followed by recovery. The idea of reading any book "through the crisis of an illness" is rather alarming. But I incline to agree that anyone who could read "Science and Health" through the crisis of an illness must be made of an adamant which no malady could dissolve. Nevertheless, it is a mistake to oppose Christian Science on the impossibility or even the improbability of its cures. There is always this tendency for normal men to attack abnormalities on the wrong ground; their arguments are as wrong as their antagonism is right. Thus the only sensible argument against Female Suffrage is that, with her social and domestic powers, woman is as strong as man. But silly people will attack Female Suffrage on the ground that she is weaker than man. Or again, the only sensible argument against Socialism is that every man ought to have private property. But the wretched Anti-Socialists will give themselves away by trying to maintain that only a few people ought to have property, and even that only in the shape of monstrous American trusts. In the same way, there is great danger that the modern world may give battle to Mrs. Eddy upon the wrong *terrain*, and give her the opportunity (or rather, her more clear-headed lieutenants) of claiming some popular success. There is such a thing as spiritual healing. No one has ever doubted it except one dingy generation of materialists in chimney-pot hats. If we seem to stand with the materialists, and Mrs. Eddy seems to stand for the healing, she will have a chance of success. A man whose toothache has left off will think with gratitude of the healer, and with some indifference of the scientist explaining the difference between functional and organic toothaches. I will grant what Mrs. Eddy does to people's bodies. It is what she does to their souls that I object to.

Mrs. Eddy summarises the substance of her creed in the characteristic sentence: "But in order to enter into the kingdom, the anchor of Hope must be cast beyond the veil of matter into the Shekinah into which Jesus has passed before us." Now personally I should prefer to sow the anchor of Hope in the furrows of primeval earth; or to fill the anchor to the brim with the wine of human passion; or to urge the anchor of hope to a gallop with the spurs of moral energy; or simply to pluck the anchor, petal by petal, or spell it out letter by letter. But whatever slightly entangled metaphor we take to express our meaning; the essential difference between Mrs. Eddy's creed and mine is that she anchors in the air, while I put an anchor where the groping race of men have generally put it, in the ground. And this very fact, that we have always thought of hope under so rooted and realistic a figure, is a good working example of how the popular religious sense of mankind has always flowed in the opposite direction to Christian Science. It has flowed from spirit to flesh, and not from flesh to spirit. Hope has not been thought of as something light and fanciful, but as something wrought in iron and fixed in rock.

In short, the first and last blunder of Christian Science is that it is a religion claiming to be purely spiritual. Now, being purely spiritual is opposed to the very essence of religion. All religions, high and low, true and false, have always had one enemy, which is the purely spiritual. Faith-healing has existed from the beginning of the world; but faith-healing without a material act or sacrament—never. It may be the ancient priest, curing with holy water, or the modern doctor curing with coloured water. In either case you cannot do without the water. It may be the upper religion with its bread and wine, or the under religion with its eye of newt and toe of frog: in both cases what is essential is the right materials. Savages may invoke their demons over the dying, but they do something else as well. To do them justice, they dance round the dying, or yell, or do something with their bodies. The Quakers (I mean the really admirable, old-fashioned Quakers) were far more ritualistic than any Ritualists. The only difference between a Ritualist curate and a Quaker was that the Quaker wore his queer vestments all the time. The Peculiar People do without doctors; but they do not do without oil. They are not so peculiar as all that.

The book which Mr. Geoffrey Rhodes has edited is just what was wanted for the fixing of these facts of flesh and spirit. When I was a boy, people used to talk about something which they called the quarrel between religion and science. It would be very tedious to recount the quarrel now: the rough upshot of it was something like this: that some traditions too old to be traced came in vague conflict with some theories much too new to be tested. Many things three thousand years old had forgotten their reason for existing; many things a few years old had not yet discovered theirs. To this day this remains roughly true of all the relations between science and religion. The truths of religion are unprovable; the facts of science are unproved.

It really looks just now as if a reconcilition would be made between religion and science, a reconciliation well embodied in Mr. Rhodes's work. I will not any longer dispute the divine mission of Mrs. Eddy. I think she was supernaturally sent on earth to reconcile all the parsons and all the doctors in a healthy hatred of herself. Here *is* the reconciliation of science and religion; you will find it in "Medicine and the Church." In this interesting book all the clerics become as medical as they can, and all the doctors become as clerical as they can, with the one honourable object of keeping out the healer. The chaplain sits on one side of the bed and the physician on the other, while the healer hovers around, baffled and furious. And they do well; for there really is a great link between them. It is the link of the union of flesh and spirit, which the heresy of the healer blasphemes. The priest may have taken his spirit with a little flesh, or the doctor his flesh with a little spirit; but the union was essential to both. With the religious there might be much prayer and a little oil; with the scientific there might be much oil (castor oil) and precious little prayer. But no religion disowned sacraments and no doctors disowned sympathy. And they are right to combine together against the great and horrible heresy—the horrible heresy that there can be such a thing as a purely spiritual religion.

November 12, 1910

English Pride and Reality

There is one little trick which I most sincerely wish my countrymen would kindly drop. I do not in the least mind their asserting their own virtues to other people; I can even applaud it. But I wish they would leave off explaining their own virtues to themselves. I wish they would leave off saying things like this: "Probably the most powerful agent in making Englishmen universally moral and home-loving has been the weathercock on the parish church," or what not. I wish they would not say, "Nothing has more powerfully contributed to make our Courts of Justice the model of the world than the habit of carrying blue bags"—or whatever it may be. I wish they would not say, "The success of Englishmen in governing the lower peoples (such as the Irish) has probably been due to the manly, honest, truthful shape of our cricket-bat," etc., etc., etc. National vanity seems to me rather a fine thing. Indeed, all vanity (I speak under the correction of the ages) seems to me rather a fine thing. Vanity is a desire for praise; even the gods have it, and it exists in heaven. Vanity means thinking somebody's praise important, more important than yourself. But pride (which does not exist in heaven, but at quite an opposite address) is thinking yourself more important than anything that can praise or blame you. And I dislike this English mode of oblique self-flattery, because it is not national vanity, but national pride. I applaud the sentiment contained in the verse—

> Two skinny Frenchmen,
> One Portugee,
> One jolly Englishman
> Lick 'em all three.

This is heroic, because it is a challenge. It refers to the future: it offers to meet the attenuated foreigners under definite conditions. But I do not like the verse when it is translated into prose. Then it always reads: "It is not at first sight easy to explain the numerous instances in which one Englishman has fought in the prize-ring with a Portuguese pugilist and two French ones. In each case his victory has probably been due to the superior physical and moral training in our," etc.

It is quite right that the Neapolitans should have a proverb, "See Naples and then die." That is healthy local vanity. But it is not right that the Neapolitans should write anything like this: "Much medical speculation has exhausted itself on the problem of the numerous deaths that follow a visit to Naples. We are of opinion that the unhappy visitors have in all cases been unable to sustain the spectacle of that singular beauty and splendour which," etc. It is quite natural that people living in the small, ancient, and slightly smelly town of Musselborough should repeat the rhetorical rhyme—

> Musselborough was a borough
> When Edinburgh was nane;
> Musselborough will be a borough
> When Edinburgh's gane.

That stirs my soul like a trumpet. But I should certainly draw the line somewhere. I should draw the line if I saw in a local paper—let us say, the *Musselborough Mollusk*—any such words as these: "The curious survival of the town of Musselborough some centuries after the total disappearance of the city of Edinburgh, is a fact that has puzzled many historians. The reason probably is that Musselborough, being more deeply rooted in the past, was also more fully stored for the events of the future; and this survival after the destruction of Edinburgh is probably"—and so on.

In all such cases I would venture (as they say in Parliament and other frivolous debating clubs) to move the original question. Does an Englishman frequently fight with two Frenchmen and one Portugee? Do many tourists die immediately after seeing Naples? Is Edinburgh, as a point of geographical detail, now destroyed? And (along the same disquieting line of inquiry), "Are Englishmen more moral than other men?" "Are English Courts of Justice the model of the world?" And "Have Englishmen been specially successful in governing lower races—such as the Irish?" Let us, first of all, make quite sure that we are better than everybody else before we explain our own superiority with a reverent astonishment. I noticed this very oddly exemplified in a recent controversy, which does not, as regards its subject-matter, concern us here. It is enough to say that the writer in question believes himself to be a free thinker—and he never was more mistaken in his life. He was attacking a recent criminal trial that has taken place in one of the Southern States of Europe; and he could not rid himself of the fixed notion that every trial ought to take place in a London police-court. He started with the assumption that the English is the ideal legal system. It did not seem to occur to him that it is not very easy to find the ideal legal system. Police methods would only be perfect if men were perfect. And if men were perfect, there would be no police methods at all.

At first I could not understand such a man as the writer in question taking it totally for granted that all foreign trials were to be judged on an English model. I should have thought that a man who could stretch his mind to understand Norwegian dramatists or Russian novelists might have managed to stretch his mind to understand a system of law that is almost universal in the one civilised continent of the world. But a few days afterwards I happened to be at a City dinner, and heard one of our most distinguished Judges make an excellent speech. And there, sure enough, the sentence came again, "And the cause of our high reputation in this matter, the reason of the great success of our English courts, is to be found in our sound old English custom"—of wearing a three-tailed wig, or what not? When a great lawyer himself is bamboozled by the law, it is not wonderful that a good, innocent, provincial, and groping Agnostic should be taken in by it too.

In the *Morning Post* only this morning I see a solemn leading article blaming a politician for attacking an editor. Seeing that editors have no other purpose on this planet except to attack politicians, I cannot very clearly see where the wickedness comes in. Is an editor a soldier, or is he only a spy? The *Morning Post* speaks of the "courage" of the *Spectator*. Really, with the kindest will in the world, I do not think it requires much "courage" to maintain any of the opinions of the *Spectator*. But, according to the *Morning Post*, it must be positively cowardly; for it is free to attack statesmen because they have no right of reply. But the sentence that really caught my eye was one ending, "the good tradition which has done much to keep English political life at a high level." Has it been kept at a high level? I wonder.

November 19, 1910

The Age of Antiquities

Some time ago I received from the Wessex Press at Taunton a book much too learned to be reviewed—by which I do not mean (as is often the case) much too learned to be read. It is highly interesting, with all its erudition; and it concerns a subject to which I am attracted in an entirely amateurish manner—I mean the wars of King Alfred in the West Country. It is by Mr. William Greswell, and is called "The Story of the Battle of Edington," sometimes called Ethandune, or Ethandun, or Hedington: the crowning victory of Alfred, which really cleared South England of the heathens. No one knows for certain where the battle was fought, and I cannot imagine a more fascinating study than that of this obscure and yet enormous conflict. It settled our religion almost before the beginning of our history; and there is no intelligible history without a religion. It was like a Battle of Armageddon at the beginning, instead of the end, of the world. That shadowy battle which brought back Christianity is a kind of pendant to the shadowy battle of Arthur in Lyonesse by which, it is said, we lost it. But liking and learning are two very different things; and I could not review Mr. Greswell's book merely by my interest in Ethandune any more than I could criticise the last book on astronomy, though I may stare at the stars; or the latest text-book on numismatics, though I have often been gratified and relieved at the sight of a coin.

The trouble with these specialist works about the holes and corners of history is that they are almost secrets. The only man who could have criticised the book has been employed to write it. We talk of people who live by taking in each other's washing; but the eminent archaeologists of Europe must surely live by taking in each other's monographs! It is sufficient to say that Mr. Greswell is strongly of opinion that the battle was fought in Somersetshire, quite near to Alfred's old lair in Athelney; and I have some sentimental sympathy with Somersetshire being thus honoured, for certainly it was the Somerset men who stood by Alfred in the worst time, and presumably turned the tide by their loyalty. The only point of fact on which I might make a minute note concerns the passage in which Mr. Greswell argues from the place of surrender. If, he says, the fight occurred in Wiltshire, why was the treaty at Wedmore and not at Chippenham? If I remember aright, Mr. Oman,[1] in his book on England before the Conquest, maintains that the surrender and treaty *were* made at the Wiltshire town, and not at Wedmore at all. He even calls the Treaty of Wedmore the Pact of Chippenham, which is a very desperate and ruthless thing to do. Whether or no he is right to maintain this, I am, of course, quite unfitted to discuss. But if he is right, it would get over this one objection of Mr. Greswell, the Somerset champion. I use the last phrase for the sake of brevity; I fear it sounds rather pugilistic. But if people will start quarrels between sporting English counties about battles long ago the pugilistic atmosphere is difficult to avoid. I only say that nothing will induce me to interpose my person between Greswell, the Somerset Bruiser, and Oman, the Wiltshire Pet.

But there is one matter, much more general and entertaining, which this book incidentally suggests. That is a great modern mistake about antiquity. Mr. Greswell says that the celebrated White Horse in Wiltshire cannot be ancient, far less prehistoric.

[1] Sir Charles W. C. Oman (1860–1946), author of *England before the Conquest* (1910).

"For in the first place it is stated by Francis Wise, in his 'Further Observations upon the White Horse,' that the animal had been carved within the memory of people then living. It was certainly 'new-modelled' in 1778 by Mr. Gee, a surveyor, and another restoration took place in 1853." Now, obviously, if the White Horse has survived from old times, it must have been "new-modelled" by millions of men besides Mr. Gee, the surveyor; and "another restoration" must have taken place about every twenty years in the darker ages. What led Mr. Gee to take such an interest in White Horses I do not know; perhaps it was merely the coincidence of his name. But it is quite clear that a pattern cleared in the chalk can only be kept up from age to age if successive generations have some interest in it, whether of nomenclature, nationality, or religion. All continuity must be a series of restorations. And all restorations must invariably be revolutions. Nevertheless, the really interesting person is Francis Wise. I fear I have not the faintest notion who he was: I can only hope that he showed the same ardour in fulfilling his surname as was so bright an ornament in the character of Mr. Gee. Francis Wise declares that the White Horse was carved within the memory of people then living. Presumably, the people had told him so. The interesting question is whether this is final evidence of its recent character or is not. I think it is not.

When Mr. Oldbuck, the Antiquary in Scott, proves that a mound is one of the entrenchments of Agricola, Edie, the beggar, blows his theory to pieces by saying that he remembers when the mound was made. The intelligent reader always immediately assumes that the Antiquary is utterly wrong and the beggar entirely right. I will not say that the reader does any injustice to the learning and research of Jonathan Oldbuck. But I do say that he does a grave injustice to the invention and sense of humour of Edie Ochiltree. It would at least take the Antiquary two or three months to make up the theory that the Romans had made the mound; but it would not have taken the beggar two or three seconds to make up the lie that he had seen it made. And for his motive, his motive was sufficient and admirable. To score one of the biggest scores in all fact or fiction. To be the hero in one of the best scenes in all British romance.

First, therefore, I eliminate some of those who saw the White Horse carved, who "minded the biggin' o't." They can be explained by that ordinary vanity, gossip and slightly malicious humour, which makes the peasant permanently the most human of humanity. But there is something yet clearer and more controversial. It can be plainly shown, I think, that unconsciously, by a flowing and historic process, men tend to say that things are recent when they are really very ancient. Tradition is not a dry and dusty and antiquated affair. Tradition is as vital and dramatic as treason, which is the same word. The silent passing of a scrap of history from father to son is as personal and passionate as the silent passing of a scrap of paper from traitor to spy. And there is the same tendency to refer everything to the last authority. The tradition, as a matter of fact, has come down through numberless generations; but each person remembers it by the person who had it last. He does not think of it as a thing connected with his first forefathers; but as a thing connected with his father. Hence the tendency (in drink, quarrel, or old age) is to refer everything to the generation just before. And so it is really true that old traditions often declare for new monuments. It is now continually assumed that old men and old legends will describe things as too old. This is not so. Old men and old legends often describe things as much too new.

Once, when I had just visited Stonehenge, I went into a little inn on the borders of the great plain, where I saw a quaint map of the place many centuries old. This chart stated, without one quiver of hesitation, that the stones had been set up to commemorate the victory of Aurelius, the British King, over the Saxons. There was no doubt about Stonehenge in those days. There is plenty of doubt now; but there is no doubt at all that it is much older than that. Tradition had simply connected the standing stones with a Christian triumph. And if ever we defeat the German navy no doubt people will some day say that Stonehenge stands in commemoration of it.

November 26, 1910

Revolutions in South America

In a monstrously amusing work,[1] recently published by Dr.
Horton and the Rev. Joseph Hocking, the authors remark, in
their unfailing humorous style, that the South American Republics are remarkable for their stagnation. There is also, of course,
the secondary and unspoken inference that they are very weak
and cowardly. As far as I can make out, they show their stagnation by always having rebellions; and they show their cowardice by constantly getting killed. This view, this old and
innocent English view of the South American Commonwealths,
is already fading away. The South American Republics are now
doing the one thing that is really reverenced by the modern
religious spirit—they are getting rich. But, according to the old
denunciation of them, their crimes could be roughly divided
under three heads: they were citizens of a small State, like the
great Athenians and the great Florentines; they were poor, like
the early Christians; and they were very fond of fighting in the
street, like all great citizens of great nations, from the greatest
days of ancient Rome to the greatest days of Modern France.
The northern part of America is tranquil (but for a nigger roasted
here and there), but it is tranquil not because there is no tyranny,
but because there is no rebellion. It is possible that many good
Presidents have been shamefully shot in South American Republics. But it is equally obvious that many eminent financiers have
been shamefully and indefensibly left unshot in the North American Republic. In small democracies, it may be that suspicion
rises too swiftly, that scandal is too riotous and reckless, as it is
in any free village. We may admit that there may be too much
mistrust in Nicaragua. But few will deny that there is too much

---

[1] Dr. Robert F. Horton and Joseph Hocking were prolific anti-Catholics. The
book mentioned here was probably *Shall Rome Reconquer England?* (1910).

Trust in New York. According to the ordinary human, healthy, heathen, common sense of things, the case of North America is infinitely more awful: streets full of men dead is not so frightful a vision as one of the millionaires mildly alive. Doubtless the South Americans must be asked in judgment for the lives of the men they have slaughtered; and even the North Americans will have a good many black and red men to answer for. But when the North Americans are asked about the men they have not slaughtered, I wonder what excuse they will have to offer.

It is interesting, and even refreshing, to observe that modern Europe seems to be following South America rather than North America. We have simple and rapid revolution in Portugal as in Peru. We do not have dreary, doubtful, and corrupt evolution, as in New York or Philadelphia. The difference between the two types of civilisation is really quite simple. Among the Latin peoples the principles remain roughly the same, while the system perpetually alters. Among Anglo-Saxon peoples the system remains the same, while the principles constantly alter, and sometimes do not exist. I hasten to add that there are no such people as Latins, and no such people as Anglo-Saxons. Delicately considered, I think, it does not affect the argument. There is a society that tolerates Mr. Rockefeller when he is maniacally rich; there is another society that might have shot him even when he was moderately poor. He might have been made a Peer in England. He might have been made a corpse in Ireland. That is the fundamental difference of the two societies; and no argument about details can ever alter it. These bursts of revolt in the Southern countries are explained in various ways by various Englishmen, by their own very provincial English prejudices. English Protestants say that these calamities fall on the Latins because they are Catholic. English Tories say that these calamities fall on them because they are Republicans. For my part, my principal doubt is whether these calamities are calamities. It seems to me that the South of Europe has preserved the one quite precious thing—revolution made easy. The revolution may be right or wrong. On many essential points I think the recent revolutions wrong. But right or wrong they can be achieved; as they can in South America.

Now it is a hideous and depressing fact that in all the Protestant countries of the North, revolution has become impossible. You cannot (apparently) rebel against the landed aristocracy of England or the military machine of Prussia. English aristocracy and Prussian bureaucracy both govern by a sort of spell or charm; my patriotism leads me to add that the Prussian spell is the spell of fear; the English is partly the spell of love. Englishmen love a gentleman; Prussians only dread an official.

But whatever it is, the spell is hypnotic and complete. Revolutions do not come to a natural and swift completion, as they do in South Europe and South America. All riots in England and in Germany peter out; as did the recent riot in Berlin; as did the much milder manifestation in Trafalgar Square. Protestantism has really this permanent boast: that the tyrannies established by Protestantism endure. The English landed aristocracy (created by the pillage of the monasteries) has endured. The Prussian despotism (created by the war against Catholicism) has endured. If a strong State means a State in which revolutions cannot happen, then England and Prussia are strong States. But if there is a place where a revolution cannot occur, I am still inclined to go back to my old question. I am inclined to ask whether it is because there are no men so bad as to be oppressors, or whether (perhaps) it is because there are no men so good as to be mutineers.

When I read of a revolution such as that of Portugal, I sigh and say to myself, "O that I lived in some such stagnant country!" I wish it were possible to give such prompt and natural effect to any public wish, even if it were a bad wish. For if you can knock down a good system and set up a bad one (as, in one sense, they are certainly doing in Portugal), the converse is also true. When the people find out that it is a bad system, they can knock that down too, and put back the good system. The whole self-adaptation and flexibility of the State permits of such returns.

But we in England cannot, apparently, undo any of our mistakes; not even any of those enormous and now obvious mistakes which we made in the sixteenth century. So, on the whole, I am for following the fashion of the South American Republics. I am for having a revolution (a mild revolution) about once every six months. But I am afraid we shall not succeed in having one; because some strange doctrine against such things sits upon us like a nightmare.

We have the main fact established. Apparently Southern nations revolt, and Northern nations do not. The only problem is: what is the reason? Is it because there are no real tyrannies in Glasgow and Chicago? Or is it because there are no real liberties there? Is it because the yokel in the Essex flats has reached the highest stature and fullest fruition of humanity? Is it because the clerk in Cheapside has all his heart's desire? Or is it because (as I sometimes fancy) they have been so stunted in their stature and so starved in their desire that they cannot remember their rights, and so cannot resent their wrongs? Are we really above riots—or below them?

In this connection the incident in Portugal may be counted a striking one. The English newspapers as a whole, of course, could not give any human being the faintest notion of what it was all about. The ancient cynic said that speaking exists to conceal the thoughts. That was a suggestive paradox. But there is no paradox in saying that printing exists to conceal the facts. That is a now tiresome truism. In one English paper, however, I did really read an intelligent account of what the Portuguese disliked and what they rebelled against. In this journal it was gravely and convincingly explained that the Portuguese had rebelled against a thing called "The Rotation." This infamous system (it appears) consisted in one party coming into power for a time, getting State payments with the tacit permission of the other party. This is indeed an awful condition. Let us hope England will never come to it.

December 3, 1910

The Delusions of Kipling

That genuine Anglo-Indian magician, Mr. Rudyard Kipling, was brought up in a land of spells and trances, of glaring and tropical illusions. He has been called a realist; and this is true in one sense, but entirely untrue in the other. If realism means an astonishing genius for making things seem real, Mr. Kipling is, or has been, a great realist. If it means caring a button whether things are real or not, he never has been and never could be. The East is in him; the glamour of that self-deception that floats thinly on a sea of despair. Vividness has nothing to do with truth; in fact, truth often tends to look a little misty and atmospheric. It is the lies that glow and glare and impose themselves. Very few things are so vivid as a vivid dream. The reason is obvious: we can take waking things lightly, but the nightmare on the chest is always heavy. A man walking about in the daylight can shut his eyes to many things, and wink at the rest. But this is the whole horror of a man being asleep: that he cannot shut his eyes; something has got inside the brain and is burning it. There is this thing in all Mr. Kipling's most brilliant stories—for instance, "The End of the Passage." There is this thing also in the whole civilisation and philosophy of the East, with its soundless curses and silent invitations. It is all grave and graphic, because it is all fundamentally false. A mesmerist deceiving a man glares at him with prominent and compelling eyeballs; but a man telling the truth has careless eyes. This is the whole difference between those red-hot and relentless visions of Asia which Mr. Kipling understands so well, and that cool and somewhat cloudy common-sense of Europe which he has scarcely every comprehended. A mirage looks more solid in the desert than a man's native town looks in England.

But nowhere is Mr. Kipling so deluded by all this vivid unreality as in his strange view of England. In India it was natural enough. He saw the English officer exactly as some prostrated

Hindoo sees him. He saw him as the conquering Raj, brother
of the sun and moon, bestriding the universe, whose shadow
shall never grow less. But though we admit that Mr. Kipling
has lived in this country only for intervals in his wandering life,
it is still quite extraordinary how utterly he has missed the point
of it. Nothing but Indian magic, which he has described so
exquisitely, can explain the detail and clarity of his illusion. For
he talks of England exactly as if it were some place he had visited
in a vivid dream (like those splendid sprawling maps in his own
fine story of "The Brushwood Boy"); but his account has no
relation whatever to England as it is—no more than the "Arabian
Nights" has to the Egyptian Question, no more than Irish Bulls
have to do with Irish cattle-breeding.

In a recent utterance Mr. Kipling set himself to defend the
hereditary principle in English politics, especially in the case of
the House of Peers. There is a vast deal to be said for the House
of Peers; there is far more (a monstrous amount) to be said in
favour of the hereditary principle. The real argument for the
hereditary principle is that it is in one sense democratic. It is the
exaggeration and extravagance of a common human feeling.
Every son looks back to his father; every father looks forward
to his son. There is also a great deal (though far less) to be said
for the existing House of Lords. The real argument for the House
of Lords is that it is in one sense democratic. It consists of a
huge number of entirely ordinary and accidental men. Any of
these dull men might, perhaps, have been respectable enough to
be summoned on a jury; none of them, perhaps, would have
been so ambitious or wicked as to be elected for the House of
Commons. If I defended the Peers, it would always be the Peers
who do not attend. The stupid Peers are a genuine English gentry: I would trust them with many things. The clever Peers are
mostly mere adventurers: I would not trust them with a postage-
stamp. Still, there is this tenable case for the Lords, this case that
could be maintained in a sensible and civilised style. Mr. Kipling,
therefore, says something else.

Mr. Kipling falls back on the one argument that we all know

to be untrue. He argues that in our society the best people come to the top. He calls them "the picked men." One is naturally inclined to ask, "Who picks them?" In cold fact, they either pick themselves or are picked by even baser men who have passed in front of them. In a plutocracy it is always a case of picking—and stealing. But in the Kipling philosophy it is a case of gradual selection of the best. He solemnly assumes that the picked man will be the best man; he solemnly explains that the best man will probably bring up his sons in the best atmosphere. And he solemnly adds, with an elephantine credulity too colossal to be measured, that if the man is not fit he will fall out of the race.

Now everybody alive knows that this is all nonsense. Everybody knows that, morally speaking, all our modern struggle might be called the survival of the unfittest. The men who get to the top are not "picked men." They are not picked by God, which is merit. They are not picked by man, which is democracy. As every rational man of the world knows, they are picked by vanity and vainglory—by one vulgar fellow helping another vulgar fellow to a peerage, in the hope that he may get one himself. As a fact, in all English departments, the worst men are on top. I am sure most Jews in Petticoat Lane are nicer than most Jews in Park Lane. Among many other minor virtues, the Jews in Petticoat Lane are Jews. They profess and practise their religion: which is a fine thing. Our trades in this country are not, in fact, working so as to bring the best foremost. It is not the holiest and most highminded greengrocer who gets the peerage: it is precisely the poorest-spirited and most crawling specimen in all that excellent trade. And so one comes back to the vital error of Mr. Kipling. Brought up in an outlying province of the Empire, he was naturally provincial. He caught the echo of an evolutionary movement going on in England: and he drew the wrong deduction from it, as many Evolutionists did.

He fell headlong into the first great folly of Evolution. He thought that victory goes to the brave. Now, on bare Evolution, nothing is more evident than that victory often goes to the cowardly. The soldier who runs away is a bad soldier, for men profess a special human honour. But the hare who runs away is a good hare; and the better he runs the more of a hare he is. The politician who changes his coat is a bad politician. But the chameleon who changes his coat is a good chameleon; it is the only earthly way (as far as I know) of being a good chameleon. So long as Mr. Kipling keeps his poor little provincial faith in animal evolution, so long he will find "the picked men" are the worst possible men that could be picked.

In Nature (as it appears on the surface) timidity is as successful as tyranny. In politics (in so far as they follow Nature) slaves are as powerful as oppressors. Nature fires under the white flag. The whole object of Nature is to hide herself; she cowers and craves to be invisible. She tells her terrible lions to tone in with the tame hues of the desert; she bids her snowland bears be as innocently white as the snow. In the same craven spirit, Evolution makes Lords so small that they disappear under a row of coronets, as under a row of extinguishers. In the same craven spirit, Evolution produces M.P.'s so green that they become invisible on the green benches to which they cling. All this is, indeed, evolutionary—that is, anarchic. But it is not the triumph of the brave; it is the wild triumph of the timid. The men at the top of the tree in England are the cowards who would climb a tree anywhere. They are at the top of the tree because they dare not trust themselves anywhere else. On sound evolutionary principles indeed, birds of a feather flock together. And when flocking with white birds, the white feather is the best one to fly.

December 10, 1910

The Four Classes of England

The tendency of mankind to split up everything into three is hard to explain rationally. It is either false and a piece of superstition; or it is true and a part of religion. In either case it cannot be adequately explained on ordinary human judgment or average human experience. Three is really a very uncommon number in nature. The dual principle runs through nature as a whole; it is almost as if our earth and heaven had been made by the Heavenly Twins. There is no beast with three horns, no bird with three wings; no fish with three fins and no more. No monster has three eyes, except in fairy tales; no cat has three tails, except in logic. Sages have proved the world to be flat and round and oblate and oval; but none (as far as I know) have yet proved it to be triangular. Indeed, the triangle is one of the rarest shapes, not merely in the primal patterns of the cosmos, but even in the multifarious details of man's civilisation. There are three-cornered hats, certainly, and three-cornered tarts; but even taken together they scarcely provide the whole equipment of civilisation. Three-cornered tarts might be monotonous as a diet; as three-cornered hats would certainly be inadequate as a costume. The tripod was certainly important in pagan antiquity; but I cannot help thinking that its modern representative, the three-legged stool, has rather come down in the world. Evolution and the Struggle for Life (if I may mention such holy things in so light a connection) seem to have gone rather against the tripod; and even the three-legged stool is not so common as it was. Victory has gone to the quadrupeds of furniture: to the huge, ruthless sofas, the rampant and swaggering armchairs. It seems clear, therefore, that there is nothing in common human necessities, just as there is nothing in the structure and system of the physical world, to impregnate man with his curious taste for the number three. Yet he shows it in everything from the Three Brothers in the fairy-tale to the Three Estates of the realm; in everything from the Three Dimensions to the Three Bears. If the thing has a reason, it must be a reason beyond reason. It must be mystical; it may be theological.

And yet, queerly enough, no men have used this triune trick of speech more innocently and absolutely than the Rationalists. Comte, for instance, divided all human history into three stages. It is a long time since I have read him, but I think they were something like the Mythological, the Metaphysical, and the Positive. According to him, that is, man began by saying the sun was a god; he went on to say that heat was a principle; he ended his career on this earth by having nothing at all to say except that he felt devilish hot. Well, that theory need not detain us. We are well past the Positive stage now, and are (please heaven!) rapidly returning to the Mythological. But there is another case of this queer affection of the free-thinker for the purely mystical three. It is, I think, a much more dangerous case, because Comte was dealing with those wide reaches of time about which the most learned must be ignorant; whereas this was a criticism by a highly cultivated man upon the concrete facts of our particular society.

The dogma against which I protest is that of Matthew Arnold when he divided all England into Barbarians, Philistines, and Populace; or, in other words, into the aristocracy, the middle classes, and the labourers. This false triad existed before his time; but it has been enormously emphasised by his example. Everybody writes, legislates, votes, and, to some extent, acts on the assumption that we have to deal with three kinds of Englishmen, which are supposed to correspond roughly to the landlord, the employer, and the labourer. The first is haughty, elegant, and idle; the second is serious, business-like, and exacting; the third is represented as a democratic idealist or a drunken rough, according to which side he votes. Upper class, middle class, lower class—these are supposed to be the main divisions and social mistakes of England. I believe the division to be gravely false, and I believe it to be gravely dangerous.

At the present crisis (or collapse) of English politics it is vividly necessary that people should understand two facts—two facts that are always left out in our journalistic generalisations about the three classes. The first fact is that there is an aristocracy above the aristocracy; the second fact is that there is a democracy below the democracy. I hasten to add that I use the words "above" and "below" merely in reference to social domination; in a moral sense I often suspect that the people at the bottom are the best;

and I am quite certain that the people at the top can be the worst. But the people at the very top are quite distinct from mere aristocrats, and the people quite at the bottom are not of the kind that call themselves democrats.

England is really divided, not into three, but into four classes. There are, of course, innumerable shades of difference and even of transition; but these four compartments, and not the old three compartments, really contain the actuality of England. I should divide our society into its four parts, roughly, as follows—

(I.) The Governing Class. This is a quite small and extremely wealthy clique, nearly all intermarried by this time; but not by any means all of the same social type or tribal origin. It has been built up on the framework of the old English nobility. But it does not contain all aristocrats or even all nobles; certainly it does not consist exclusively of noblemen, or even of gentlemen. Some of the greatest English gentlemen belong to it; also some of those who cannot be said to belong to that class. The realities that bind it together are two; first, an immense amount of money, which permits a particular and very luxurious kind of life; second, a taste or hobby or ideal of governing other people. The manners of this top class are extremely frank and cynical, and what the main body of England would call vulgar. Its women are often charming, but are exactly like charming actresses. Its men are blasé and contempuous about the party politics which they conduct, but they are full of a strange curiosity and mental thirst about everybody's business but their own: they love to talk to a newspaper writer about newspapers, or a moneylender about money (I mean, other people's money), or to a Japanese about Japan, or to a cannibal about cannibalism. It is, psychologically speaking, I think, the same thing as the mood of the little boys who say on rainy afternoons, "What shall we do now?"

(II.) The second class I will call the Ladies and Gentlemen. They include thousands of aristocrats with small or moderate means; relatives of Dukes, who get their living as curates, or as colonels, or as Socialist agitators. They also include the profes-

sionals, the more dignified merchants, the arts, the main bulk
of the middle class. They seldom meet a Lord; they never drop
an "h"; they have dress clothes, but do not wear them regularly.
Many of them have really ancient blood. But they are not in the
Political Ring; they are not in the Governing Class. This is sufficiently proved by the fact that they all believe in it. The lower
aristocracy shudders at Mr. Lloyd George. The higher aristocracy dines with him.

(III.) The third class are those whom one may call (in anger)
the Clerks, but whom one should also call (in admiration) the
Citizens. They are the self-respecting, self-supporting men in
black coats and bowlers who fill most political and religious
meetings. From them come the Labour Members, and nearly
all the very idealistic social forces of the day. Their reading can
be exact, while their accent is Cockney. They make the lower
part of the middle class and the upper part of the working class.
They are very refined.

(IV.) The fourth class is the People of England, innumerable
millions of cabmen, navvies, dustmen, and crossing-sweepers.
They are not at all refined: and if ever they begin to talk there
will be fun.

December 17, 1910

Objections to the Party System

In this place, and at this time, it would be very wrong to take
the brutal, tactless, and provocative course of attacking either of
the great English Parties. But most English people will agree
with me when I adopt the tactful, delicate, and modest course
of attacking them both. If you denounce either Party you rally
reluctant supporters to the other one. But if you denounce and

despise both Parties, you can count on a hearty welcome from both of them.

The eminent Fabian who writes under the name of "Hubert," in the *Manchester Sunday Chronicle*, has written an open letter to Mr. Belloc on his public refusal to obey the Party Whips. By the way, the very word Whip conveys the whole truth of Mr. Belloc's case. A whip has only two meanings—it means mere torture, or it means mere sport. To the credit of modern English politics, I admit that it means mere sport. Our Party leaders crack the whip; they do not lay on the lash. But the cracking of the whip is quite sufficient for the kind of animals they have to herd. Men tell more truth by their metaphors than by their statements. And the mere fact that Party discipline is called "obeying the Whip" ought to show any free man what Mr. Belloc means.

Those who object intelligently to the Party System do not do so on the absurd ground that there ought to be no parties. Corporate action is a human need; every man may think for himself, but in no conceivable state can every man act for himself. If there is an intellectual war there must be intellectual armies; if there are intellectual armies there must be intellectual discipline. Mr. Belloc and the anti-Party school would readily admit that. They do not object that it is a disciplined fight; they object that it is a sham fight. They maintain that by occupying the stage with two stage armies, you actually prevent its being a platform for real corporate conflicts. So far, at least, their case is surely plausible. It is certain that if we make a fantastic or arbitrary line of division across the nation, we must necessarily prevent impor- tant disputes, because our arbitrary division will jumble up friends and enemies. Those who agree will find themselves on opposite sides; those who disagree, on the same side. If we made the main business a war of tall men against short men, then Reform of the Peers could not be discussed, because Lord Rosebery and Mr. Lloyd George are both short. The present Government could not be discussed, because Mr. Balfour and Mr. Haldane are both tall. If we made it dark men against fair men, Socialism

could not be discussed, because Mr. Shackleton is dark, while
Mr. Henderson is fair; Ireland could not be discussed, because
Mr. Stephen Gwynn is fair, while Mr. Hugh Law is dark.

Now it is maintained by the opponents of the System that
this is much like the actual state of politics; that the issues on
which men are now divided and disciplined are (like stature or
complexion) relatively irrational and accidental compared with
the deeper issues, which would split the parties across. This is
certainly plausible. It is tenable that the existence of God is more
interesting than party politics; but if it were discussed, it would
divide both camps into Theists and Atheists. It is tenable that
Woman is a more important thing than a General Election; yet
on that question there was a free fight along each of the front
benches. Even Catholicism and Protestantism (some have ventured to hint) bulk rather larger in human history than either
the Primrose League or the National Liberal Club. Yet the strict
English Puritans sit side by side with the fiercest Irish Catholics,
and the English aristocratic Catholics sit side by side with the
fiercest Irish Protestants. On nearly all points of living practice,
on all the necessary dogmas of daily life, on personal liberty, on
parental authority, on the laws of sex and the nature of patriotism, Conservative would fight Conservative and Liberal would
fight Liberal. Only, they are prevented from fighting—by the
Party System.

Now "Hubert," in his letter to Mr. Belloc, tries to get over
this. He tries to represent that the party division is not arbitrary,
but essential; and in order to maintain it he falls back on that
good old Victorian phrase "temperament," which has before
now darkened many a heroism and diminished many a treason.
He suggests that there are some people temperamentally progressive and some temperamentally conservative. Well, he is
wrong. There is, indeed, the thing which he calls temperament,
and I call temper. It does colour one's common life; the sky and
landscape alter it; also it alters the sky and landscape. But temper
is not the key of the universe; temper is not truth. A good-
tempered man is not a saint; nor is a bad-tempered man nec-

essarily a sinner. We all see truth as a light through very various windows; the question is, which of us wish to pull down the blinds? "Hubert" suggests that the comic opera was really correct is saying that every little boy or girl is born a little Liberal or else a little Conservative. I merely answer that if he means what he says, he is a Calvinist of the lowest type. By the old Calvinism, a babe was predestined to perdition: by the new and more calamitous creed, a babe is predestined to be a Unionist or a Radical.

But the popular writer in the *Sunday Chronicle* is wrong on two pressing points. The first is slight, but significant; the second is very large indeed. First, it is not true that our Party system corresponds to a clash of instinct and psychological colour. Lord Crewe is no more an innovator by temperament than Mr. Bonar Law, if so much. Mr. Austen Chamberlain is no more a conservator by temperament than Sir Edward Grey, if so much. Mr. Joseph Chamberlain left the Liberal benches to sit on the Unionist benches; Mr. Winston Churchill left the Unionist benches to sit on the Liberal. Their temperaments (which are rather unmistakable) are said to have remained the same.

But there is one much bigger blunder in this theory of reform versus conservation. It is simply this—that, rightly or wrongly, the modern Tory Party is not a conservative party. Our modern Conservatives do not profess to conserve. The historic tradition of John Bull in the nineteenth century was a tradition of Free Trade, of a small standing Army, of serious Protestant morals, of the worship of personal liberty. Any foreigner, from St. Petersburg to Dieppe, seeing that unmistakable image, would say—"That is England." Now, I do not think that our young Tories are wrong in attacking this John Bull if they think him a fallacy; on the contrary, I think them right. But when they propose to substitute Prussian Protection for his Free Trade, French Conscription for his small Army, Imperialism for his Insularism, Paganism for his Protestantism—then all pretence that they are preserving an old England explodes and disappears. The Imperialists are as much in revolt as the Socialists. Conservatives and Liberals are alike innovators, only they are both rather timid and tiresome in their style of innovation.

Therefore this last defence erected against Mr. Belloc's attack collapses entirely. It is already admitted (apparently) that the Parties do not represent two clear philosophies. The able writer on the *Sunday Chronicle* suggests that they may correspond to two types of human nature. But it is not so. There is no madness of novelty that may not be found among Tories; there is no sleep of custom that may not be found among Radicals. The thing is as unnatural to the instincts as it is to the intellect.

December 24, 1910

The Autocracy of the New Creeds

The death of Mrs. Eddy is a more important historical event than the General Election, in the noise of which it may pass unnoticed. So far, indeed, the expression is inadequate. Anybody's death is more important than any General Election. But though both Mrs. Eddy and the last Parliament embodied chiefly the restlessness and fugitive quality in our time, the advantage is with the prophetess as against the politicians. We know, at least, what Mrs. Eddy did; but if anyone knows what the last Parliament did, he is keeping it to himself.

But there is a more curious point of contrast. Our chief trouble at present is that words and things do not fit each other. We are in a net of old names and phrases, and phrases that are most thin and worn and senile are exactly the phrases of novelty—words like "progress" and "reform." The new realities, the fresh and growing facts of society, have no adequate titles. And it is a very dangerous thing to let a thing grow up unchristened. At present there is far too wide a contrast between public and private life; between what is said in the newspaper and what is said at the breakfast-table; between what is said in an after-dinner speech and what is merely said after dinner. The most obvious passing instance is the Election itself. Every newspaper is bound to tell you that the Election is a heroic crisis and crusade; but every newspaper man will tell you in hearty terms, that it is a nuisance and a devastating bore.

But there are numberless instances on all sides. If a modern writer or speaker has to denounce Socialism, for instance, he says, "The raving Atheist with his red tie and his red flag will be repudiated by every moderately decent citizen." If he has to praise Socialism, he says, "Become a Socialist and a hero. You will be cursed and cast out from among men; you must find comfort in the grass of the roadside and the vision of a higher humanity." And all this time there is not a soul of us moving in educated society who does not know dozens and dozens of curates and undergraduates, and clerks and young architects, who are all Socialists, being soberly attracted to it as a neat and scientific system. Or, again, when he has to attack Socialism he will glorify Individualism, talk of the competition of personalities, of the value of character, of men carving their way, and so on. Yet all the time he must know quite well that our present commerce is as impersonal as it can possibly be; that it has long been solely a struggle between vast companies and corporations, that it is now ceasing even to be a struggle, and is becoming an alliance between them. Few people are so anonymous as the capitalists; few so featureless and shadowy as the captains of industry. When you bank with Blenkinsop and Pottle, you do not see the unforgotten features of Blenkinsop start forth from among the shades of memory; you do not hear the deep, vibrating voice of Pottle sounding along the wires of the world. You are much more likely to discover that one is dead and the other never lived; and the business is managed by a young man named Pidge. And here is the real danger of Socialism, if you count it a danger, as I do. It is too impersonal; it proclaims that no one shall be human lest anyone should be inhuman. The rising generation in the respectable class is becoming increasingly Socialist, precisely because that class is so respectable; because it is so used to vast departments and deputy managers and the whole experience of being kicked about by something too large to be kicked back. But I digress. My instances were intended only to show how our public phraseology conceals the biggest facts of to-day—the huge impersonality of capital, the hugh respectability of Socialists. But Mrs. Eddy offers a more arresting example. She shows how, while all the million modern pens can be heard noisily scribbling about democracy, all the silent modern souls profoundly believe in despotism. Religion is the last reality of man; and the modern despotism has come out in the modern religions. If there was one thing reiterated and re-echoed in all our papers, pamphlets, and books, it was that the coming religion must be a "free religion." Whatever else it was (people said), it must avoid the old mistake of rule and regimentation, of dogmas launched from an international centre, of authority sitting on a central throne. No pope must control the preacher—no council, even; it was doubtful whether any church or congregation had the right. All the idealistic journalism of the nineteenth century, the journalism of such men as Mr. Stead or Mr. Massingham, repeated, like a chime of bells, that the new creed must be the creed of souls set free.

And all the time the new creeds were growing up. The one or two genuine religious movements of the nineteenth century had come out of the soul of the nineteenth century; and they were despotic from top to bottom. General Booth had based a big theological revival on the pure notion of military obedience. In title and practice he was far more papal than a pope. A pope is supreme, like a judge; he says the last word. But the General was supreme—like a general. He said the first word, which was also the last; he initiated all the activities, gave orders for all the enthusiasms. The idealistic Liberal journalists like Mr. Stead fell headlong into the trap of this tremendous autocracy, still faintly shrieking that the Church of the future must be free. It might

THE ILLUSTRATED LONDON NEWS

be said of this great modern crusade that its military organisation was an accident. It is one of the glories of Mrs. Eddy to have proved that it was not an accident.

For after General Booth's success in England, the next striking incident in Protestant history was Mrs. Eddy's success in America. Christian Science also grew up in a world deafened with discussions about free churches and unfettered faith. Christian Science also grew up as despotic as Kehama,[1] and much more despotic than Hildebrand.[2] The tyrannies of popes, real and legendary, make a long list in certain controversial works. But can anyone tell me of any pope who forbade anything to be said in any of his churches except quotations from a work written by himself? Can anyone tell me of a pope who forbade his bulls to be translated, lest they should be mistranslated? Religion is the sub-consciousness of an age. Our age has been superficially chattering about change and freedom. But sub-consciously it has believed far too much in barbaric and superstitious authority; it has worshipped strong men, it has asked for protection in everything: this can be seen in its two most genuine expressions—its novels and its new creeds. The great free, progressive modern intellect, through all the abysses of its being, has asked to be kicked. General Booth and Mrs. Eddy have kicked it; and serve it right.

I do not agree with the moderns either in the extreme anarchy of their theory or in the extreme autocracy of their practice. I even have the feeling that if they had a few more dogmas they might have a few less decrees. I merely point out that what we say when we are criticising churches is startlingly different from what we do when we are making churches; and that this illustrates the failure of our phraseology. We are struggling and

[1] See Robert Southey's *The Curse of Kehama*, a story of an Indian rajah who obtains supernatural power.

[2] Pope Saint Gregory VI; under Leo IX, he created a reform program aimed at correcting the corruption of the Church. As Pope, he was crucial in the campaign against clerical simony and lay investiture.

entangled in a fallen language, like men in the folds of a fallen tent.

December 31, 1910

The Character of Tolstoy

A little time ago a paragraph appeared in the newspapers stating that Professor Haeckel of Jena had left the Lutheran Church. Considering that the Professor has been driven through life by a dreary thirst for the destruction of all religion, it seemed a rather odd paragraph—like a headline which should announce "Mr. Keir Hardie Resigns from the Carlton Club," or "Dr. Clifford Quits the Church of Rome," or "Mr. Blatchford Throws up his Bishopric." I do not know what it meant, nor do I very profoundly care. Haeckel is nearly as dead as Luther. The two great collapses of the Prussian spirit have both happened at Jena: the first was the failure of an army; the second the failure of a book.

The whole incident, indeed, had rather the air of a parody on the discussions about a much greater man—about Tolstoy and his separation from the Russian Orthodox Church. For about Tolstoy also the problem was not so much why he was turned out of the Church as why he was ever allowed to belong to it. Tolstoy was a very great man; and if he had been a very small man, he would still have had a right to hold his opinions. I have a right to hold a low opinion of Disraeli and his manner; it is a right which I exercise. But I do not think I have a right to belong to the Primrose League while proclaiming that opinion. Leader-writers on the Yellow Press have a right to hold the opinion that all Socialists are profligates, or the equally rational opinion that all Socialists have tails. But they do not expect to belong to the

Social Democratic Party, or the Fabian Society, or the *Clarion* Fellowship while enunciating these views. It is true, of course, that many of them may reconcile these things by what is now called a Higher Synthesis. A Higher Synthesis (generally speaking) means writing different opinions only under different names.

Tolstoy was a logical man; and I do not remember that he ever complained of the severance between himself and orthodoxy. I hope he did not, for the credit of his logic. He had no more right to be a Russian Catholic than Mr. Kensit has to be a Roman Cardinal—or a Roman Cardinal has to be a Secretary of the Protestant Alliance. Let us resist this deliquescence of the brain. Men found institutions to further certain ideas; the enemies of those ideas have no place in those institutions: an honourable man ought to feel a traitor and an eavesdropper in a church with which he disagrees. And so have felt all the highly honourable men in my experience, from Dr. Stopford Brooke to Mr. Lloyd Thomas, with his Free Catholic Church. The Upstanding Glassites[1] (a Scotch sect, I believe) may or may not know what the Bible means; but they have an indubitable right to know what they mean. And no Glassite can feel really and satisfactorily Upstanding if he gets the benefits and the bounteous sacraments of Glassism (or Glassity) while preaching something other than that which he knows the Glassites mean. This decency, which you or I would observe towards the tiniest sect or the squalidest little club, may (I think) lawfully be extended even to those faiths that have covered empires and seen the ending of ages.

The question has recurred in an odd way of late even in England; and, again, in connection with Tolstoy. A discussion has arisen about certain school libraries (in the popular schools, I believe) which have excluded some of Tolstoy's little tales. This seems to me to raise the question in its most real, and therefore

---

[1] The original name of a sect begun in Scotland by John Glass, who held, among other things, that there was no need for a national church. They were also called "Sandemanians" after Robert Sandeman, Glass' son-in-law, who took over leadership after Glass' death.

its most interesting, form. Children must hear nothing but the vital truth, so far as we can give it them. I say the vital truth: it is found mostly in fairy-tales, in my opinion. Another opinion may find it in good realistic tales (as in those of Miss Alcott): another (for all I know) may find it in that Unnatural thing called Natural History. But we all feel that children should hear the truth and nothing else: the lies they will invent for themselves.

Now, suppose that you had nine children, and that you knew Tolstoy. How would you positively act in so vital a relation? I can only say how I should act. If Tolstoy had been my friend, I should have boasted everywhere, and boasted with justice, of the intimacy of so original and intense a mind—a man of genius who must have stimulated even when he provoked. If I could have pointed him out to my nine children from their nursery window as he went marching by, with his plain peasant's blouse and his proud aristocrat's head, I would have made him as popular with them as the postman or the lamplighter. I could have reverenced him as an eccentric father or respected him as an eccentric uncle; I might even have followed him as a party leader or been glad to see him canonised as a saint. But if he had come within twenty miles as a tutor to my children, I would have chased him off the land. I would have let loose a dog. I would have fired off a cannon; anything rather than that children should be taught by Tolstoy. I would have provoked civil war (from which my English temperament is profoundly averse) rather than allow one helpless, top-heavy little infant to learn Tolstoy instead of learning truth.

Tolstoy was a good man who taught thoroughly bad morals. Human history has been full of these men; in fact, they are responsible for a great bulk of the calamities of human history. The Roman Stoics were good men, but when they taught that each man must be sufficient to himself, they taught a false morality, which did infinite harm. The English and Scotch Puritans were good men (some of them), but when they preached that art must be kept entirely out of religion they preached a false morality, which has done infinite harm. Mr. Smiles, the industrial optimist who wrote "Self-Help" (I wonder whether he invented the name "Smiles"), was, I daresay, a good man; but when he preached that the way to help God was to help yourself (to money, as a rule), he preached a false morality, which is doing harm to this day. And Tolstoy was a good man, though he was a typical aristocrat; and lessons can really be drawn for all of us from his sincerity, his self-control, his consistency in mental pursuit. But the last fact is still that he preached a false morality. He did preach, and preach explicitly, courageously, and with a quite honourable clearness, that if you see a man flogging a woman to death you must not hit him. I would much sooner let a leper come near a little boy than a man who preached such a thing.

The educational authority that refused to circulate Tolstoy among children was quite right, and, in any case, was quite within its rights. If a certain number of honest Tolstoyans have a certain number of honest little boys, let them teach their own little boys that it is always wrong to fight. They will find it hard, by thunder!—as Stevenson's pirates say. But a national school has no more right to allow Tolstoy to teach the national children that resistance is wrong, than it has to allow Mahomet to teach them that polygamy is right. Tolstoy was a great man; Mahomet was a greater; but the education of young children does not consist in telling them the various and contradictory opinions of great men. I could quote opinions of great men in favour of hideous cruelty, howling anarchy, vicious insanity, and blank surrender. It consists, as I said before, in telling them, so far as is possible, what we conceive to be the truth: the fundamental verities of life. It is not of necessity unreasonable to keep out of the nursery authors much more valuable than Tolstoy will ever be. Our educationists would probably shudder at keeping Shakespeare from children. Yet would not anyone keep Rabelais from children? Nevertheless, there are no two things more certain than that Rabelais in France and Shakespeare in England are the two real literary giants of the Renascence, and that Rabelais is slightly the more morally healthy of the two.

Let us clear ourselves of this suffocating modern superstition about eminent individuals. Great names do not necessarily mean great intellects; and certainly great intellects do not mean great souls. Tolstoy had a right, like anybody else, to hold that nations were bad, or that armies and force were wicked, or that parental control was a wrong thing. But, if Tolstoy had a right to disagree with humanity, surely humanity has a right to disagree with Tolstoy! And it does disagree with Tolstoy. The very names of its institutions prove it. National schools must object to Tolstoy when he objects to nations. Educators must object to Tolstoy if he maintained that children should not be controlled. Let human beings find Tolstoy at the end of their lives if they like. It is monstrous that they should find him there at the beginning.

INDEX OF PROPER NAMES

11/20/09; 12/29/09; 1/1/10; 1/8/10; 2/5/10; 3/12/10; 4/2/10.

Dillon, John. 3/14/08; 5/14/10.

Disraeli, Benjamin. 1/25/08; 3/5/10; 12/31/10.

Douglas, Sir James. 5/9/08.

Dreyfus, Alfred. 12/5/08; 7/17/09.

DuMaurier, Major. 3/20/09.

Dundee, John G. of Claverhouse, Viscount. 4/10/09.

Earle, Ferdinand. 9/19/08.

Eddy, Mary Baker. 1/18/08; 1/9/09; 7/31/09; 8/14/09; 1/1/10; 11/5/10; 12/24/10.

Edward I, King. 9/3/10.

Edward III, King. 9/3/10.

Edward VII, King. 8/7/09; 5/28/10; 6/4/10.

Egbert, King. 8/27/10.

Eldon, John Scott, 1st Earl of. 3/27/09.

Elen, Gus. 7/10/09.

Eliot, George. 5/1/09; 7/2/10.

Elizabeth I, Queen. 4/11/08; 3/27/09; 9/25/09; 11/27/09; 4/30/10; 7/23/10.

England, Mr. 9/3/10.

Erasmus. 12/18/09.

Euclid. 6/27/08.

Euripides. 10/31/08.

Faith, Saint. 2/8/08.

Farr, Florence. 6/25/10; 7/2/10.

Flammarion, Camille. 2/20/09.

Forel, August Henri. 12/12/08; 1/9/09.

France, Anatole. 3/28/08; 9/3/10.

Francis, Saint. 6/27/08; 9/12/08; 4/17/09.

Franklin, Sir John. 10/9/09.

Frederick the Great. 12/26/08; 3/20/09.

Galsworthy, John. 5/7/10.

Galton, Sir Francis. 1/1/10.

Garrick, David. 7/16/09.

George III, King. 1/16/09.

George, Lloyd. 12/26/08; 2/5/10; 4/2/10; 7/9/10; 12/17/10.

Gilbert, William S. 5/1/09.

Gissing, George. 7/24/09.

Gladstone, Herbert. 8/22/08; 1/30/09; 7/24/09.

Gladstone, William E. 1/25/08; 10/17/08; 11/27/09; 12/11/09; 1/8/10.

Godiva, Lady. 7/18/08; 8/8/08.

Goethe, Johann Wolfgang von. 6/13/08; 4/9/10.

Goldsmith, Oliver. 2/26/10.

Gray, Thomas. 3/12/10.

Green, John Richard. 8/7/09.

Greenwood, G. G. 3/27/09.

Gregory, Lady. 7/16/10.

Greswell, William. 11/19/10.

Grey, Sir Edward. 12/17/10.

Grove, Lady. 1/25/08.

Guillotin, Dr. Joseph Ignace. 8/20/10.

Gwynne, Stephen. 5/14/10; 12/17/10.

Haeckel, Ernst Heinrich. 10/31/08; 1/23/09; 4/23/10; 12/31/10.

Haldane, Richard Burdon, Viscount. 10/17/08; 12/11/09; 12/17/10.

Hallam, Henry. 4/30/10.

The text of this book has been set in Bembo by the Indiana University Print Services. Printed on Warren's Olde Style paper by Thomson Shore, Dexter, Michigan. Bound in Kennet cloth by John H. Dekker & Sons. Cover and jacket design by Darlene Lawless.